The Advice and Consent of the Senate

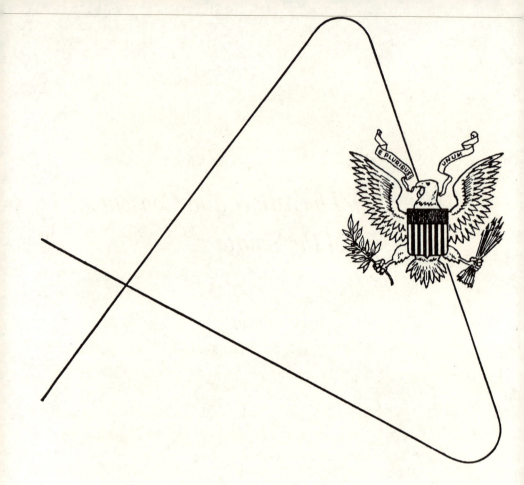

The Advice

A STUDY OF THE CONFIRMATION OF APPOINTMENTS

JOSEPH P. HARRIS

and Consent of the Senate

BY THE UNITED STATES SENATE

GREENWOOD PRESS, PUBLISHERS
NEW YORK   1968

First Greenwood reprinting, 1968

LIBRARY OF CONGRESS catalogue card number: 68-23294

Printed in the United States of America

To
POLLY

PREFACE

       Senatorial confirmation of appointments by the President is essentially an American practice, virtually unknown in other major countries of the world, except countries in Central and South America which have patterned their constitutions after ours. In this country it exists not only in the national government but in the states and cities, where it has been copied from the federal Constitution. The actual operation in state and city governments, however, is quite different from that in the national government.

    The requirement that the appointment of officers of the United States by the President shall be subject to the approval of the Senate is one of the important powers of that body and is a basic part of the division of powers between the President and the Congress. Heretofore this function of the Senate has been neglected by most political scientists; no definitive study has been made of its history, operation, and effects. A number of writers on government have criticized senatorial confirmation of appointments, particularly appointments to minor positions, on the ground that it serves to perpetuate patronage appointments; but no serious proposal has ever been made to alter this provision of the Constitution. Many sensational controversies have arisen between the Senate and the President over appointments, and it may be questioned whether the Senate's participation in the appointing power has in its actual operation borne out the confident expectations of the framers of the Constitution that it would serve as a salutary check on the President and provide a safeguard against unfit appointments.

    I was led to undertake the study because of the series of bills and riders which were introduced in Congress practically every year from 1935 to 1945 to extend senatorial confirmation to many subordinate administrative positions. Several of these proposals were enacted into law, and most of them passed the Senate without opposition. They constituted one of the greatest threats to the federal civil service within recent years. Happily, similar bills have not been pushed in Congress lately, and the trend has been in the opposite direction. The issue, however, is a perennial one; it arose again in 1952 in the consideration of President Truman's reorganization plans, and it may be expected to recur in the future.

The purpose of this study is to trace the history of the confirmation of appointments by the Senate from the framing of the Constitution to the present and to analyze the practical operation and effects of the practice. In recent controversies over the roles of the President and the Senate with regard to appointments the constitutional issues have loomed large; for this reason special attention has been given to the debates over the appointing power in the Constitutional Convention of 1787 and to contemporary discussions of this section of the Constitution. What was the purpose of the framers of the Constitution in requiring the approval of the Senate to appointments? And has the actual experience conformed to the intentions of the founding fathers? What have been the practical operations and effects of senatorial confirmation? Has it provided a salutary safeguard against unwise and unfit appointments and the possibility of abuse of the appointing power if that power were vested in the President alone? Has it resulted in higher or in lower standards of qualifications of persons appointed as officers of the federal government? What effect has it had on patronage appointments? What are the various relationships between the President and the Senate in their joint exercise of the appointing power? What faults or weaknesses exist in the system, and what reforms or improvements should be made?

The central issue to which this study is directed is which officers should be appointed by the President and confirmed by the Senate and which should be appointed otherwise. The decision is an important one, for the method of appointment of subordinate officers vitally affects the administration of the government and the federal civil service. For certain classes of officers the requirement of senatorial confirmation of appointments has worked reasonably well and has provided, as the framers of the Constitution intended, a salutary safeguard against unfit appointments; for other classes it has worked badly, resulting in the perpetuation of partisan and patronage appointments to positions which belong in the career civil service; for still others, senatorial confirmation has become for the most part an empty formality of little practical significance. Three official commissions that surveyed the organization and administration of the federal government within the last forty years each made the identical recommendation that subordinate administrative officers in the executive departments and agencies be appointed by the responsible executive officers, normally from the civil service, instead of being appointed by the

President and the Senate. No action was taken to carry out these recommendations, however, until 1952, when President Truman, after a series of sensational scandals unearthed by congressional investigations of the internal revenue service, submitted to Congress four reorganization plans to place postmasters, collectors of internal revenue and customs, and marshals under the career civil service. Only one of the plans, that relating to collectors of internal revenue, went into effect; the others were rejected by the Senate.

A second major problem with which this study is concerned is the policies, procedures, and practices of the Senate in passing upon presidential nominations. These practices vary widely for different types of officers, and they have changed with the years. What tests does the Senate apply in passing on nominations? For what reasons have nominees been rejected? In which appointments should the President be permitted wide latitude of choice and his nominations be approved unless the nominee is definitely disqualified or unsuitable? For which offices should the Senate consider the President's nominations with care and reject nominees not only because of their disqualifications for the office but because their views are not agreeable to a majority of the Senate? Have the methods and procedures used by the Senate for inquiring into the qualifications of candidates been suitable? If not, in what ways should they be altered? Has the Senate secured adequate information to enable it intelligently to pass upon the nominations that come before it? Has the requirement of senatorial confirmation caused able men to decline federal appointment? Is the custom of "senatorial courtesy"—under which the Senate will reject a nomination because of the objections of a senator from the state in which the office is situated, or from the state in which the nominee resides—justified? What have been the effects of the custom?

These are some of the principal questions which this study attempts to answer. It is assumed that senatorial confirmation of appointments of the principal officers of the government is a basic part of the Constitution and is unlikely ever to be amended or repealed. The Senate will undoubtedly never consent to give up this important function, which is a part of the division of powers between the President and the Congress. But though the Constitution will in all probability remain unchanged, the classes of officers appointed by the President and confirmed by the Senate may change, and the practices of the Senate in passing upon appointments are also subject to modification.

I wish to express my gratitude to the University of California and the Committee on Public Administration of the Social Science Research Council for financial assistance that has greatly aided me in the conduct of the study. A large part of the study was made while I was on sabbatical leave of absence from the University in 1949 and 1950; during this period and the two following years I also received a special grant from the Institute of Social Sciences of the University of California. I am greatly indebted to many persons: members of

Congress, federal officials, members of the Washington press, and others with whom I have discussed specific cases and the general practices and effects of senatorial confirmation. The editors of the American Political Science Review *and the* Political Science Quarterly *have kindly consented to the publication in this volume, in slightly revised form, of two articles which appeared earlier in these journals. Especial thanks are due the following persons who have read parts of the manuscript and whose criticisms and comments have been most helpful: Messrs. Louis Brownlow and Don K. Price, Professor Leonard D. White, and my colleagues, Professors Peter H. Odegard, Charles Aikin, Leslie Lipson, and Dwight C. Waldo.*

I have been greatly aided by the able research assistance of Dr. Felix Nigro, Patricia Howse, and Edith Carper, who participated in the study at different periods; but I take sole responsibility for the findings and conclusions and for any errors in fact or in judgment that it may contain.

JOSEPH P. HARRIS

Berkeley, California
May 15, 1953

CONTENTS

[xi

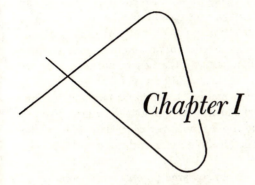

Chapter I

INTRODUCTION

It has been doubted whether this executive function [confirmation of appointments] *of the Senate is now a valuable part of the Constitution. It was designed to prevent the President from making himself a tyrant by filling the great offices with his accomplices or tools. That danger has passed away, if it ever existed; and Congress has other means of muzzling an ambitious chief magistrate. The more fully responsibility for appointments can be concentrated upon him, and the fewer secret influences to which he is exposed, the better will his appointments be.* James Bryce.[1]

Unfettered presidential discretion would be more plausible if the United States had a real Cabinet—if, in other words, there were some collective responsibility, and if decisions were not taken by an executive unadvised except by politicians, who are outside of the government and whose interventions are not advertised. This is a consideration that should not be lost sight of: executive responsibility for appointments in Great Britain and executive responsibility for appointments in the United States are quite different. The one is collective, the other individual; the one can be enforced, the other cannot. There may be, therefore, grave dangers in a presidential appointing power unchecked by the Senate. Lindsay Rogers.[2]

IN THE NINETEEN years from 1933 through 1951 the President submitted a total of 339,316 nominations to the Senate, an average of 17,858 annually.[3] At the end of the period, however, the number submitted each year was approximately four and one-half times as large as at the beginning. President Hoover submitted 30,224 nominations during his term of office, or an average of 7,556 annually; President Truman in a corresponding period submitted 139,634 nominations, or an average of 34,908 annually. In 1949, the highest year, 55,311 nominations were received by the Senate. An analysis of the huge numbers of nominations sent annually to the Senate indicates that the great bulk of them—actually 99 per cent—are appointments and promotions of officers of the armed services, postmasters of the first three classes, and career employees of the Foreign Service, Coast Guard, Public Health Service, and the Coast and Geodetic Survey. Nominations in these services are rarely considered individually by the Senate but as a rule are routinely passed en bloc; hence the confirmation process for these offices has become for the most part an empty formality. Of the 26,284 nominations submitted in 1951, those of officers of the armed services totaled 23,421, or 90 per cent; postmasters, 1,177, or slightly more than 4 per cent; and those of the Coast Guard, Foreign Service, Public Health Service, and Coast and Geodetic Survey, 1,364, or 5 per cent.

Senatorial confirmation of these extremely large numbers of appointments in the military and civilian career services is of minor importance. In 1951 no nomination in these groups was rejected and none was withdrawn, though 16 had not been acted on when the Senate adjourned. Senatorial confirmation of appointments to the very much smaller number of other civilian positions is of real significance, however; these appointments numbered only 237 in 1951, or less than 1 per cent of the total. Although this number may appear small in comparison with the much larger number of nominations of officers of the armed services, actually it is very large when consideration is given to the character and importance of the offices included in the group and to the time required of the President and the Senate to consider individually the qualifications and suitability of the persons nominated. It is unlikely that the framers of the Constitution envisaged that as many as 237 nominations would ever be passed on by the Senate at a single session.

It is with nominations of the top political officers of the government, and the chief military officers, totaling 1,321, over which the President and the Senate have frequently struggled, that this study is concerned. These officers provide the leadership, exercise general direction and control, and set the tone of the government. For the most part, they are the policy-determining officers of the government, although in the group are included many subordinate officers and employees who do not determine policies but work under the direction and control of administrative superiors.

The several major classes of civilian officers included within this group, with statistics, are given in the table on the facing page.

The Senate follows somewhat different practices and customs in its consideration of nominations within each of these classes; the President is accorded wide latitude in the selection of members of his Cabinet, but nominations to other offices are scrutinized with varying degrees of care, and nominations to offices situated within the individual states come within the special rule of "courtesy."

Senatorial confirmation of appointments is a subject which has heretofore received little attention, though it is recognized as one of the important powers of the Senate.⁴ In recent years it has attracted wide public attention because of numerous bills and riders passed by the Senate to extend the requirement of confirmation to large numbers of subordinate administrative positions. These proposals, several of which were enacted into law, were widely regarded as one of the greatest threats to the civil service in recent years. One of the first measures of this type to be adopted was a rider to the 1935 appropriation for work relief, which required that federal directors of relief in each state must

MAJOR CLASSES OF CIVILIAN OFFICERS SUBJECT TO CONFIRMATION

	Positions	Nominations Sent to Senate, 1951
Secretaries and other officers of executive departments	287	30
Boards, commissions, and heads of independent agencies	198	59
Judges	336	27
Diplomats	69	25
Representatives on international bodies and conferences	57	19
Field officers (attorneys, marshals, collectors, etc.)	326	71
Miscellaneous	48	6
	1,321	237

be appointed by the President and confirmed by the Senate. As a result, the administration of the federal work relief program, which had previously been remarkably free from politics and patronage appointments, soon became highly political in a number of states. Because the Social Security Board turned down an applicant for a job sponsored by the chairman of the Senate Committee on Appropriations in 1936, the angered senator retaliated the following year by attaching to the appropriation for the board a rider requiring retroactive confirmation of all employees of the board who were receiving salaries of $5,000 or more annually and who had been appointed outside the civil service. All the employees were subsequently approved by the Senate, but the board hastened to place these positions under civil service to avoid what it regarded as a serious threat to its administration.

Similar provisions applicable to positions in the United States Housing Authority were adopted in 1937; to positions in the Antitrust Division of the Justice Department and certain positions in the Commerce Department, in 1939; in the Selective Service Administration, in 1940; and in the War Manpower Commission and the Army Specialist Corps, in 1942. Several sweeping measures of this type failed of adoption. In 1938, 1943, and 1944 the Senate passed measures or appropriation riders requiring senatorial confirmation of all employees throughout the government who received salaries variously specified from $4,000 to $5,000 and above. These measures were vigorously opposed by the National Civil Service Reform League, the League of Women Voters, and other organizations interested in advancement of the civil service, and were denounced in the press, as well as on the floor of the Senate.

The leading sponsor of legislation to extend the requirement of senatorial confirmation has been Senator Kenneth McKellar of Tennessee, who introduced bills and riders to appropriation measures with such provisions every year from 1937 through 1945. The principal concern of the Tennessee senator was to extend the requirement of senatorial confirmation to the appointment of employees in higher grades of the Tennessee Valley Authority, which would have enabled him to dictate appointments in all grades of that organization. In spite of the fact that the TVA Act specifically required that all appointments be on the basis of merit and prohibited political influence, McKellar had carried on a running battle with the TVA to secure the appointments in the agency. His attempts to require senatorial confirmation of the higher administrative employees of the TVA were strenuously opposed by its friends, who recognized that the result would be to introduce patronage appointments and to discredit its administration. When one of the bills of this type was before the Senate in 1938, Senator Norris declared that it would place TVA "right in the lap of the politicians" and make it a political "jack pot."

The movement in the Senate to extend the requirement of senatorial confirmation to the higher grades of administrative employees was due in large part to the fact that patronage appointments, which had been available in unpredecented numbers to members of Congress in the first term of the Franklin Roosevelt administration, had become scarce. Appointments to positions in the emergency agencies established in Roosevelt's first term, which were regarded as temporary, were exempted from the civil service. In these years the offices of Democratic members of Congress became recruiting centers for the exempted agencies, and regular procedures were set up whereby office seekers were required to secure the endorsement of the state and local party organizations. Many members of Congress posted notices that only those with such endorsements need apply for jobs.

In 1937, at the end of Roosevelt's first term, the large number of jobs in new and emergency programs which had been available for political appointment had been filled. Several new programs that were regarded as permanent activities, such as social security, were placed under civil service, though the Social Security Board was authorized to appoint attorneys and experts outside civil service. And the officers in charge of programs exempted from the civil service increasingly insisted on giving appointments only to qualified persons and therefore resisted congressional pressures for patronage. It was under these circumstances that sentiment in the Senate began to favor extension of senatorial confirmation to all employees receiving specified salaries. Except for certain local officers, such as postmasters, collectors of customs and internal revenue, attorneys, and marshals, senatorial confirmation had never been required for administrative employees; consequently the proposed measures were a departure from the previous practice.

President Roosevelt moved in 1937 to cover into the civil service the large number of employees who had previously been exempted, recommending in his message to Congress transmitting the report of his Committee on Administrative Management that the civil service be extended "upward, outward, and downward." He endorsed the recommendation of the committee that only policy-determining officials should be politically appointed, that is, appointed by the President, by and with the advice and consent of the Senate. This recommendation, however, received little support in Congress. The bill introduced by Senator Robinson, the Democratic leader, instead of authorizing the inclusion under the civil service of all positions that were not policy determining, provided for the extension of senatorial confirmation to many subordinate positions. When the Ramspeck-O'Mahoney Act placing postmasters of the first three classes under civil service was passed in 1938, the Senate insisted on retaining senatorial confirmation of postmaster appointments.

In recent years there has been an increased tendency for the Senate to specify that officers created by new legislation shall be appointed by the President and confirmed by the Senate. Although for a hundred years it had been the practice of the President alone to appoint persons to represent this country in international bodies and conferences, one of the reservations of the Senate to the Charter of the League of Nations in 1919 was that all appointments of representatives to the League or to any of its commissions or committees must be approved by the Senate. After the treaty was defeated, the Senate subsequently inserted similar provisions in the separate peace treaties with the Central Powers. In 1945 the Senate similarly specified that our representatives to the Assembly, the Security Council, and other major bodies of the United Nations must be approved by the Senate.* Another example of the same tendency is the provision in the Reorganization Acts of 1945 and 1949 which required that the heads and assistant heads of any new agencies created by the President through reorganization plans should be appointed by the President, by and with the advice and consent of the Senate, unless such positions are placed under civil service. In recent years, legislation passed by Congress creating new agencies and commissions, including advisory bodies, has usually specified that the officers in charge shall be appointed by the President and confirmed by the Senate. The requirement of senatorial confirmation of appointments to advisory bodies appears to be a departure from the previous practice.[5]

* See chap. xvi, below.

The requirement that appointments by the executive shall be subject to the approval of the upper house of the legislature is an institution peculiar to our country. The appointments of the colonial governors were usually subject to the "advice and consent" of the governor's council, whose members, however, were appointed by the governor. This arrangement was continued in the original state constitutions of a number of states, but the governor's council was selected by the legislature rather than the governor, and in several states the appointing power was given to the legislature rather than to the governor.[6] The appointment of judges, for example, was vested in the legislatures of seven states under their new constitutions, and in four states the nominations were made by the governor and had to be approved by a branch of the legislature.[7] The struggle that had occurred in the colonies between the popular assembly and the colonial governor was fresh in the minds of the framers of the new state constitutions, with the result that the governor's powers were reduced and those of the legislature were increased. The governor's appointing power was generally curtailed, and his selections were subject to the "advice and consent" usually of a council chosen by the legislature.[8]

The experience of the states that entrusted the appointment of officers to the legislature itself appears to have been unsatisfactory. The evils of legislative appointment of public officers were well known to members of the Constitutional Convention of 1787, who frequently referred to the intrigue, caballing, and irresponsibility which had marked the selection of officers by the state legislatures. A majority of the Convention members were determined to avoid these excesses in the federal government, and several urged that the appointing power be vested in the President alone. Several members proposed the establishment of a council of appointments similar to that in New York State, which consisted of the governor and other members elected by the legislature; but this plan was rejected. Such a system was severely criticized by Hamilton in *The Federalist* (No. 77). "While an unbounded field for cabal and intrigue lies open," he said, "all idea of responsibility is lost." The council was abolished in the New York constitution of 1821 after it had become thoroughly discredited.[9] The strong influence of the federal Constitution led many states subsequently to amend their constitutions and to adopt similar provisions concerning appointments.

The practice of senatorial confirmation of appointments by the state legislatures, however, has been quite different from that in the federal government. It is quite unusual for a nomination of the governor to be rejected by the state senate; in some states this has not occurred for years. The nominations of the governor are usually contested only when there is strong disagreement between the governor and a majority of the state senate. Since appointments by the governor for the most part are limited to state-wide offices, there is no custom of "senatorial courtesy" in the states. In some states the governor is empowered to make certain local appointments, usually to fill vacancies, which are made while the senate is not in session and do not require its approval. The governor usually consults members of the legislature, as well as other prominent members of the party, before making such appointments.

Owing to the fact that most state legislatures meet less frequently than Congress and remain in session for only a limited time, the state governors are in a stronger position than the President in the exercise of the appointing power. Since many of the state offices become vacant when the senate is not in session, far greater use is made of recess appointments, and when the senate comes later to pass on the nomination, there is a strong presumption in favor of the nominee. There has also been less disposition on the part of the state senates to inject politics into the consideration of the governor's appointments in an attempt to embarrass the administration.[10]

Legislative confirmation of appointments is also widely used in this country in municipal governments and other governmental units. The mayor's appointments of department heads under the mayor-council form of government are often subject to the approval of the council. In cities with the weak mayor-council form of government, the council appoints the principal city officials. Since about 1900, however, there has been a tendency to vest the appointing power in the mayor, thereby creating what is often referred to as the strong mayor-council form of government. In the city-manager form of government, which has enjoyed a steady and continuing growth, the manager is given the exclusive power to appoint the heads of the city departments and the principal city officers. It is regarded as essential for the manager to have this power if he is to be held responsible for the city administration. The results obtained under the older forms of city government in which the appointing power is divided between the mayor and the council have generally been unsatisfactory. Political appointments are the rule, and the level of competence of such appointees has not been high. Able and experienced managers, before accepting an appointment as city manager, ordinarily insist on an understanding with the council that they will be free of any pressure in the selection or removal of the department heads under them.[11]

Senatorial confirmation of appointments is virtually unknown in other countries, except those that have patterned their constitutions on ours. The principal officers of the British government, for example, are selected by the prime minister and his cabinet and are nominally appointed by the Crown. Their appointments are not passed upon by Parliament. This is also true in other countries of the British Commonwealth and those on the continent of Europe. Only in the several countries of Central and South America that have used our Constitution as a model are executive appointments confirmed by the legislative body, and in these countries the executive domination of the legislature has usually turned the requirement into a formality.

Writers on government have generally been critical of the requirement of senatorial confirmation. In his famous essay on "Representative Government," John Stuart Mill many years ago expressed the view, which had been earlier advanced by some members of the federal Constitutional Convention, that a legislative body should not participate in the appointing power. Wrote Mill:

> There is no act which more imperatively requires to be performed under a strong sense of individual responsibility than the nomination to employments. . . . Besides, the qualifications which fit special individuals for special duties can only be recognized by those who know the individuals, or who make it their business to examine and judge of persons from what they have done, or from the evidence of those who are in a position to judge. . . . Numerous bodies never regard special qualifications at all. Unless a man is fit for the gallows, he is thought to be about as fit as other people for almost anything for which he can offer himself as a candidate. When appointments made by a public body are not decided, as they almost always are, by party connections or private jobbing, a man is appointed either because he has a reputation, often quite undeserved, for *general* ability, or frequently for no better reason that that he is personally popular.[12]

Visitors to this country who have studied and written about the American government have usually been critical of senatorial confirmation, regarding it as a basic defect in the Constitution. In his classic study, *The American Commonwealth,* Lord Bryce wrote that the confirming power which the framers of the Constitution had granted to the Senate was probably intended as nothing more than a check upon the President's appointing power, to safeguard against the appointment of unfit persons, but in practice the Senate had assumed the right to reject a nominee to any office except the President's Cabinet "on any ground which it pleased, as for example, if it disapproved his political affiliation, or wished to spite the President." Consequently, he stated, it had become a "political factor of the highest moment." Through the custom of "senatorial courtesy," members of the Senate had "enslaved" the President as regards appointments, and had secured for themselves "a mass of patronage by means of which they could reward their partisans, control the federal civil servants of their state, and build up a faction devoted to their interest." Although successive Presidents have "chafed under the yoke," Bryce stated, they have usually found it prudent to yield to the demands of the senators.[13]

Other British political scientists have written in a similar vein. Professor Brogan urged that senatorial confirmation should be abandoned, "not because it is in itself of great importance, but as a means of weakening the spoils system." Harold Laski assumed that the Senate would never consent to giving up its power to pass upon judicial appointments and suggested instead methods whereby its action would become a mere formality; and Professor Finer stated that the power of the Senate over appointments, designed to prevent the

Presidency from degenerating into an autocracy, had "developed into a simple engine of Senatorial rapacity, very expensive to the nation."[14]

American writers have been hardly less critical of senatorial confirmation, particularly of the custom of senatorial courtesy. Woodrow Wilson wrote that it was in dealing with nominations that the most friction arose between the President and "his overlord, the Senate," and that the abuses of the "consultative privileges of the Senate" appeared to some as the "ugliest deformity in our politics," "the weakest and the most tried and strained joint of our federal system."[15] One of the severest American critics of senatorial confirmation was Professor Henry J. Ford, who condemned as "sheer usurpation" the claims of senators to the right to dictate federal appointments in their states.

It is not enough [wrote Ford] to expose and denounce such a perversion of constitutional authority as "the courtesy of the Senate"; the principle that should animate popular agitation is that any participation whatever in appointments to office is an evil ... At the time the Constitution was adopted the people were assured that the "advice and consent" clause did not confer any power of choice on the Senators, but was simply a check upon possible abuse of power. The early commentators, Kent and Story, both expounded the clause in this way. But the practical effect has been to disorder and corrupt our whole system of government by destroying the constitutional function of Congress as an organ of control. Representative bodies perform the function only when they have no say as to who shall fill the offices.[16]

Dorman B. Eaton and William Dudley Foulke, both leaders of the civil service reform movement, were equally vehement in their denunciation of congressional patronage, which they attributed in large part to senatorial confirmation.[17] Professor Haynes in his able study of the Senate treated at length the history and practice of the Senate in passing upon nominations but attempted no over-all evaluation of the requirement. On the whole, however, his treatment was critical, particularly of senatorial pressures for patronage and the custom of "courtesy." Commenting on the recent contests of nominations to the Supreme Court (those of Hughes, Stone, and Parker), he stated:

It may prove a more difficult task in the future for the President to find strong men and able jurists, of the caliber of those who have built up the Supreme Court's prestige, who will allow their names to be placed in nomination, if they must first be subjected to an inquisition in committee hearings as to their past records, pertinent or not ... and then must have their nomination made the subject of bitter debate on the floor of the Senate, where racial, sectional, and political considerations may bulk so big that the questions of the nominee's character and fitness are half forgotten.[18]

In his briefer but incisive study of the Senate, Professor Rogers made a qualified defense of senatorial confirmation, pointing out that if the President enjoyed the appointing power alone, he would be able to use it to build up a personal political machine to assure his renomination or that of another of his choosing, as Republican Presidents have done in the South, where they have had a free hand.* Robert Luce, a distinguished member of Congress and a painstaking student of the legislative process, also criticized senatorial confirmation, which he witnesed from the other end of the Capitol. Criticizing the fights which the "radicals" in the Senate had made against the appointment of conservatives to the bench, he maintained that if this should become the established practice, "there may well be doubts as to whether the fathers did wisely in giving the Senate any part at all in the excutive function of choosing men to determine what is the law and men to carry the law into effect." He condemned the practice under which senators demand the right to dictate appointments because of their power of "advice." "There is every reason why the Executive should consult," he wrote, "none why he should obey."[19]

W. F. Willoughby, another critic of senatorial confirmation, wrote: "There is almost nothing to be said in favor of this system either from the standpoint of principle or of the manner in which it has worked in practice." He maintained that unless the President has the selection of the principal officers he cannot be held responsible for the faithful execution of the law and the efficient administration of the government. "To share this power with another agency," Willoughby contended, "means a diffusion of responsibility which is always to be avoided unless there are overwhelming reasons for so doing." Instead of confining itself to approving the officers enumerated in the Constitution and other "superior" officers, the Senate, he stated, had "taken to itself the duty of selecting in the first instance those who shall be appointed to a large class of important positions.... The practice is thus an integral part of the 'spoils system' which has established itself so strongly upon the country."[20]

A defense of senatorial confirmation has been made by Professor Charles Hyneman, who regards the requirement as a safeguard against undesirable appointments and an essential part of our democratic institutions. He maintains that it was the intention of the framers of the Constitution to give the Senate "full participation in the political process of choosing men for public office," or else they would have worded the Constitution to indicate that the Senate could only approve or reject.[21] Somewhat inconsistently, however, he concedes that the President should have the "major influence" in the selection of the highest officials in his administration, contending, as Hamilton did in 1787, that the requirement of senatorial confirmation does not hamper his choice, since the Senate can only approve or disapprove his nominations and cannot dictate his appointments.† Most writers today are agreed that Hamilton was in error and that, apart from Cabinet officers and certain others, the Senate exerts considerable influence in the selection of persons for appointment. Hyne-

* See quotation at the beginning of this chapter.
† Hamilton's statement in *The Federalist* (No. 66) is quoted in chap. ii, below.

man concedes that the senators of the President's party, through the custom of senatorial courtesy, dictate appointments of federal officers in their own states, but maintains that these positions "are not crucial to the President's administrative program." President Truman in 1951 discovered to the contrary that collectors of internal revenue could become quite crucial to the success of his administration.

Four major arguments are advanced by Professor Hyneman in defense of senatorial confirmation: First, since the President must be advised by someone, "Where could he turn for advice in which he could place greater confidence? The Senators come from different parts of the country. They know, or know about, the leading men of the nation. They are acquainted with the President's plans ... [and] they enjoy the confidence of the people."[22] This argument was advanced in the Constitutional Convention in 1787 by members who favored appointment in the legislative body, and has been recently voiced in support of legislative proposals to extend senatorial confirmation to large numbers of subordinate positions.* Second, it enables the Senate to pass upon "policy-determining" officials. Professor Hyneman contends that there are many officials below the level of bureau chief who make important policy determinations, and that appointments of these officials should therefore be confirmed by the Senate; he also takes the extraordinary position that "their determinations of policy ought not to be subject to review and reversal by superior administrative officials."[23] Third, it permits the Senate to weed out "undesirables." Hyneman advances the argument that a few prominent officials "who make fools of themselves" can greatly embarrass the political party in office, and for this reason Congress has been unwilling to "trust the screening entirely to administrative officials." He contends, moreover, that even "the most lowly employee can bring the federal service into disrepute," hinting that senatorial confirmation should be required for many lower-grade positions.[24] Implicit in this argument is the assumption that the screening by the Senate has been effective in weeding out "undesirables"—an assumption which needs to be tested. It may be noted that the officials and employees who have discredited the federal service have usually been political appointees, often persons who owed their appointments to individual senators.

The final argument advanced by Professor Hyneman in defense of senatorial confirmation is "the desirability of congressional patronage." He maintains that a certain amount of patronage for members of Congress is needed to finance party activity, and that it affords them a degree of independence of state and local party machines. Coming from a political scientist, this argument is highly unusual, although it probably reflects accurately the sentiments of many members of the Senate. Members of the House have been among the strongest critics of senatorial confirmation. The patronage which they have

---

* See chap. xix, below.

secured has generally been limited to postmasterships. In recent years the House has successfully blocked most of the attempts to extend the requirement of senatorial confirmation to large numbers of employees.*

Senatorial confirmation has been frequently defended by members of the Senate, particularly during debates over recent proposals to extend the requirement to minor offices and positions. Among the most significant statements in its defense were those made by Senator Thomas of Utah in connection with the controversy over the appointment of Judge Roberts in 1939, the statements made by Senator Johnson of Colorado in the debate over a McKellar rider in 1938, and those made by Senator Douglas of Illinois in his contest with the President over the two Illinois judgeships in 1951.† The leading critics in the Senate have been Senator Norris of Nebraska, who was a consistent and vigorous advocate of the merit system, and Senator Hatch of New Mexico, who led the fight on the McKellar bill in 1943.‡

Members of the Senate defending senatorial confirmation have usually contended that the phrase "advice and consent" means more than a mere vote of approval or disapproval of the President's nominations and requires the President to consult with individual senators before making a nomination to an office in their state, or before nominating a citizen of their state to a national office. Former President Taft, after he left the White House, wrote:

Any discussion of the subject is lacking which does not make some reference to the solemn argument of solemn senators in the effort to enlarge the meaning of the words "advice and consent of the Senate"... The usual contention is that these words require that the President, before making a nomination, consult the Senate. ... Such a construction leads ... to the conclusion that a Republican President ... must consult Republican Senators from a state before making an appointment in that state, although no constitutional or statutory obligation is upon him in respect to Democratic Senators.[25]

The major arguments advanced in favor of senatorial confirmation and in defense of the custom under which senators of the President's party are permitted to select the federal officers in their own states, are as follows:

1. The system provides a salutary safeguard against unfit appointments. This was one of the main reasons the framers of the Constitution had for adopting the final compromise which required the President to obtain the advice and consent of the Senate to appointments.

2. It limits and controls the exercise of the appointing power by the President and avoids the dangers of vesting excessive powers in the hands of one man.

3. The President cannot know personally the qualifications of the numerous officers whom he appoints and must take the advice of others. The senators, who come from the several states, are informed about the person under con-

* See chap. xix, below.
† These statements are quoted in chaps. xiii and xvii, below.
‡ See chap xix, below.

sideration; hence they are the logical as well as the constitutional advisers of the President.

4. Article II, section 2, of the Constitution, which provides that officers shall be appointed by the President "by and with the advice and consent of the Senate," requires him to consult the Senate, which shares the appointing power. The framers of the Constitution intended that the Senate should exercise an important role in the appointing power and that its function should not be merely nominal or perfunctory.

5. The people of each state hold their senators responsible for federal appointments within the state; consequently the senators exercise diligence and care in selecting persons for such appointments.

6. The requirement of Senate confirmation causes executive officers to exercise care in selecting persons for appointment, knowing that their choices will have to stand the inspection of the Senate. It affords the Senate an opportunity to inquire into departmental appointing practices and to ascertain whether the officers to be appointed are really needed.

7. The power of the Senate to pass upon appointments is a safeguard against the encroachment of the federal government on the rights of the states, particularly the smaller states, and affords the people of each community a voice in the selection of local federal officers.

8. Although senatorial confirmation has undoubtedly resulted in some instances in political appointments, this is a part of the democratic process, and it is preferable that political patronage be subject to control by the Senate than to be left to the unfettered discretion of the President. The appointments of officers in the armed services, by far the largest group confirmed by the Senate, are not influenced by partisan or political considerations.

Those who have opposed the extension of senatorial confirmation to subordinate positions and have criticized the custom of "senatorial courtesy" maintain that the President should appoint and the Senate should confirm only the heads of executive departments, members of commissions and agencies, judges, diplomats, and a small number of the most important subordinate officers who exercise "policy-determining" functions. These positions, which may be regarded as political—though not necessarily partisan—in character, must be at the disposal of the administration in order that it may be held responsible for the policies and the operations of the government. Ambassadors, ministers, and judges are required by the Constitution to be confirmed by the Senate. All other positions, it is contended, should be filled by the officers in charge of the department or agency, and, with few exceptions, should be placed under the civil service.

The principal arguments advanced by those who hold that presidential appointment and senatorial confirmation should thus be limited to the principal officers of the government are as follows:

1. The exercise of the appointing power is essentially an executive function; in passing upon the nominations of the President the Senate is performing an executive function which has been vested in it by the Constitution. Although this control is appropriate for the principal, policy-determining officers of the government, it should not be extended to subordinate offices and positions. Executive officers cannot be held responsible for the proper administration of agencies under their direction unless they are permitted to choose their principal assistants.

2. The most essential element in the wise exercise of the appointing power is the establishment of definite responsibility. The Senate, being a numerous body, cannot be held responsible for appointments; under the power of confirmation, especially when extended to lower positions, its members are able to exert a determining influence without responsibility.

3. In any organization, the higher administrative positions can be filled satisfactorily only by persons who have had the necessary training and experience and possess special qualifications, and as a rule only those in charge can judge which persons are adequately qualified. In addition, the executives who are responsible for any activity have a strong incentive to appoint only qualified persons to such positions; persons who are not responsible for results are likely to be influenced by other considerations.

4. The provision in the Constitution for appointment by the President, by and with the advice and consent of the Senate, applies only to officers; it does not apply to employees. It was the intention of the framers of the Constitution that only the principal officers of the government would be appointed in this manner. Congress is specifically authorized to provide otherwise for the appointment of "inferior" officers.

5. The Senate, like all legislative bodies, is subject to favoritism, logrolling, and manipulation in its actions on appointments. Its action on the President's nominations are often based on partisan considerations rather than on the qualifications of nominees.

6. Senatorial confirmation has perpetuated patronage appointments to many positions which ought to be placed in the career civil service. As a result, these positions have usually been filled by unqualified political appointees, recommended by the senators or the party organization, and qualified and experienced civil service employees have thus been deprived of the opportunity of advancement.

7. Effective working relations in any administrative organization can be achieved only when those in subordinate positions are clearly and directly responsible to their superiors and have undivided loyalties. Such relations are impossible when subordinates owe their appointment and, as often happens, their retention and advancement as well, to political sponsors.

8. The President and the Senate are unable to give individual attention to

the thousands of appointments which each year require their approval; thus their action, for all except a few important officers, has become an empty and undesirable formality.

It is assumed in this study that senatorial confirmation of the principal officers of the government is a basic part of our constitutional system and an important element in the division of powers between the President and the Congress. The issue, then, is not whether senatorial confirmation should be retained, but rather to which offices it should apply. Senatorial confirmation of appointments has worked reasonably well for certain types of officers and has provided the kind of protection against bad appointments which the framers of the Constitution anticipated. For many others, however, it has become to a large extent an empty formality, and for certain offices it has served to perpetuate patronage appointments where nonpolitical, career appointments should be the rule. In recent years the issue whether it should be required for subordinate administrative positions has frequently arisen, and in all probability it will continue to arise.

The Constitution enumerates only a few officers for whom presidential appointment and Senate confirmation are required; these include ambassadors, ministers and consuls, and judges of the Supreme Court. It also provides, however, that "officers of the United States" whose offices are established by law shall be appointed in this manner, and it authorizes the Congress to provide for the appointment of "inferior" officers by the President alone, by department heads, or by the courts.

Who are "officers of the United States"? What is the meaning of "inferior" officers? The debates of the Constitutional Convention throw little light on the subject, for the section providing for the appointment of "inferior" officers was adopted toward the close of its sessions and was subjected to little debate and discussion. The question is one on which the courts have not passed. No case has ever been taken to the Supreme Court to test the authority of Congress to require Senate approval of appointments, and it is unlikely that such a case will come before the Court. When the question has arisen collaterally, the Court has avoided ruling on the subject by holding that persons appointed by the President and confirmed by the Senate are "officers of the United States," and that those appointed otherwise are "inferior" officers.[26] Although the federal courts have frequently interpreted the term "officer" as used in various federal statutes, these decisions do not indicate a uniform usage and, in any event, do not apply to the term as used in this section of the Constitution. The decision concerning which officers should be appointed by the President and confirmed by the Senate is essentially political in character and has appropriately been left to legislative rather than judicial determination.

Through statutory provisions Congress has required senatorial confirmation of the appointment of approximately 125,000 positions. This vast extension of the requirement to many minor positions far down the administrative or military hierarchy is not required by the Constitution, though it is possible under it. Congress might have followed a different course, making Senate approval a requirement for only the principal officers of the government and placing all other positions under the career service. It is significant that such a policy has been recommended by three national commissions which surveyed the organization and administration of the federal government in recent years. The first commission to make this recommendation was the Commission on Economy and Efficiency appointed by President Taft, which made its report and recommendation in 1912, when the number of officers appointed by the President and confirmed by the Senate was approximately 10,000. The same recommendation was made by the President's Committee on Administrative Management in 1937, but by this time the number subject to senatorial confirmation had risen to about 40,000. And by 1949, when the Hoover Commission made a similar recommendation, the number of positions subject to senatorial confirmation had risen to well above 100,000. This tremendous expansion of the number of positions subject to senatorial confirmation has in large part been due to the growth of military establishments, the increase in numbers of postmasters of the first three classes, and the increase in the number of persons in the commissioned civilian services.

In order to determine the proper scope of senatorial confirmation, it is necessary to ascertain what its practical operation has been and what effects it has had on the offices to which it has applied. The history of the relationships and conflicts between the President and the Senate over appointments, which is traced in the following chapters, is essential to an understanding of the problem. These chapters review not only the significant contested nominations but also the practice in uncontested cases, which is of even greater importance. Since much of the current discussion concerning senatorial confirmation of appointments turns on constitutional issues, it is important also to inquire what was the purpose and intention of the framers of the Constitution concerning the exercise of the appointing power. This is done in the following chapter, which reviews the debates of the Constitutional Convention of 1787 and other significant discussions and writings of the time. Somewhat more than half of this study is given over to a historical account of senatorial confirmation and the relations between the President and the Senate in appointments. Contests since 1929, when the Senate opened its doors during its consideration of nominations, are given more space than earlier ones. Several notable recent contests, particularly those over the nominations of Brandeis (1916), Warren (1925), Parker (1930), Roberts (1939), Lilienthal (1947), and Olds (1949) are reviewed at length. The latter half of the volume contains an account of the custom of "senatorial courtesy," the procedure of the Senate in passing on nominations, and finally, an analysis and appraisal of the effects of senatorial confirmation of each of the major classes of officers for which it is required.

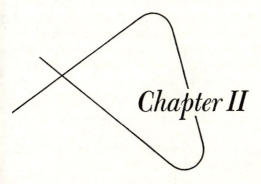

Chapter II

DEBATES ON THE
APPOINTING POWER IN THE
CONSTITUTIONAL CONVENTION

No new appointments would be suffered as heretofore in Pennsylvania unless it be referred to the Executive; so that all the profitable ones will be at his disposal. The first man put at the helm will be a good one. Nobody knows what sort may come afterwards. The Executive will always be increasing, here as elsewhere, till it end in Monarchy. Benjamin Franklin in the federal Constitutional Convention of 1787.[1]

According to the plan as it now stands, the President will not be a man of the people as he ought to be, but a Minion of the Senate. He cannot even appoint a tide waiter without the Senate.... With all these powers, and the President in their interest, they will depress the other branch of the Legislature, and aggrandize themselves in proportion.... He objected to the mode of appointing, as blending a branch of the Legislature with the Executive. Good laws are of no effect without a good Executive; and there can be no good Executive without a responsible appointment of officers to execute. Responsibility is in a manner destroyed by such an agency of the Senate. James Wilson in the federal Constitutional Convention of 1787.[2]

THE METHOD of appointing the principal officers of the government was the subject of frequent debate in the federal Constitutional Convention of 1787, and the provision finally adopted—that "The President ... shall nominate, and by and with the Advice and Consent of the Senate, shall appoint ..."—was the result of a compromise between two widely different points of view.[3] One group, consisting of Roger Sherman and Oliver Ellsworth of Connecticut, Elbridge Gerry of Massachusetts, Benjamin Franklin of Pennsylvania, Gunning Bedford of Delaware, George Mason of Virginia, and John Rutledge of South Carolina were afraid of granting the appointing power to the executive on the ground that it would lead toward monarchy, and believed that the power would be more safely entrusted to the upper branch of the legislature. They maintained that a single person could not be as adequately informed about the persons to be appointed as the members of the Senate. Mason voiced the opinion of this group at the session of June 4:

The Executive may refuse its assent to necessary measures, till new appointments shall be referred to him. . . . We are, Mr. Chairman, going very far in this business. We are not indeed constituting a British Government, but a more dangerous monarchy, an elective one. . . . The people will never consent. . . . He could never agree to give up all of the rights of the people to a single magistrate.[4]

Another group, including Gouverneur Morris and James Wilson of Pennsylvania, Nathaniel Gorham of Massachusetts, Alexander Hamilton of New York, and James Madison of Virginia, favored the creation of a strong executive, who they believed would be better qualified and more responsible in making appointments than a numerous body. They were not afraid of the threat of monarchy or despotic power exercised by a single executive, and frequently referred to the unsatisfactory practice which prevailed in the state legislatures, where appointments were usually marked by intrigues, deals, and machinations. This group favored granting an independent appointing power to the President; but in the end they agreed to the compromise by which the President was given the power to nominate, and the approval of the Senate was required before an appointment could be made. They believed that the power to nominate was substantially equivalent to the power to appoint. "Every advantage to be expected from the power of appointment," wrote Alexander Hamilton in *The Federalist*, "would, in substance, be derived from the power of *nomination*. . . . There can, in this view, be no difference between nominating and appointing."[5] The history of the exercise of the appointing power by the President has disproved Hamilton's contention; the power to nominate is not the same as the power to appoint, and the role of the Senate in giving its advice and consent has not been limited to a passive review of the qualifications of the persons nominated by the President, as Hamilton expected it would be.

Early in its deliberations the Convention reached a decision that the executive should have the power to appoint all officers not otherwise provided for—an appointing power, it should be noted, independent of the legislative body. This provision was agreed to on June 1, without debate and apparently with little opposition.[6] All states except Connecticut, which divided on the issue, voted for it. In view of the limited appointing power then exercised by the governors of the several states, this broad grant of an independent appointing power to the President was truly remarkable. No state constitution granted to the governor an independent appointing power. In several states the governor had little or no appointing power; in those states in which he exercised a limited appointing power, it was always with the advice and consent either of a council appointed by the legislature, or by the legislature itself.[7] Only in Massachusetts, Maryland, New Hampshire, and Pennsylvania were judges appointed by the governor, and in three of these states he shared the appointing power with a council.[8]

The granting of an independent appointing power to the President was in keeping with the policy of establishing a strong national government and providing for energy and responsibility in its administration. This policy, espoused principally by Wilson, Gouverneur Morris, Hamilton, and Madison, came to prevail, though not without vigorous opposition from the more timid delegates who feared that the executive would abuse his powers and use them to perpetuate himself in office.[9] The issue of a strong executive arose early in the Convention over the question whether a single or plural executive should be established. Edmund Randolph proposed an executive of three persons, in order to represent the major geographical divisions of the country. This proposal was opposed by James Wilson of Pennsylvania, who favored "a single magistrate, as giving most energy, dispatch, and responsibility to the office." Those who advocated a strong executive, independent of the legislative body, finally prevailed, but only after a strenuous debate near the end of the Convention.[10] In defense of the provisions of the Constitution concerning the executive, Hamilton later declared that "energy in the Executive is a leading character in the definition of good government."[11]

The decision of the Convention granting the executive an independent appointing power for all officers "not otherwise provided for" was modified on June 13, when a motion offered by Madison was adopted that judges should be appointed by the second branch of the legislature. This division of the appointing power between the President and the Senate, each to appoint certain types of officers, remained in effect until the closing days of the Convention; the compromise was finally reached whereby the President was given the power to nominate all principal officers, including judges, but the advice and consent of the Senate was required before an appointment could be made. The resolution granting an independent appointing power to the executive, having been made, was not subsequently challenged; but the resolution authorizing the Senate to appoint judges was contested and vigorously debated whenever it came before the Convention. James Wilson, Gouverneur Morris, and Nathaniel Gorham were among those who strongly opposed vesting an appointing power in the legislative body, pointing to the bad practices which obtained in the several states. Their motions that judges should be appointed by the executive, however, were defeated whenever they came to a vote. Twice the Convention rejected proposals that the executive should appoint judges subject to the concurrence of the upper house, the provision finally adopted for all principal officers.

In the end, those who opposed the appointment of judges by the Senate gained their point, but the group who feared that the executive would abuse the appointing power also won a victory when concurrence of the Senate was made a requirement for all principal appointments. Those who favored a strong executive and wished to avoid the political machinations of legislative bodies in the exercise of an appointing power believed that they had won; but subsequent history indicates that, on the whole, victory rested with the other side.

The Virginia Plan proposed at the outset of the Convention provided that "a National Executive be instituted; ... and that besides a general authority to execute the National laws, it ought to enjoy the Executive rights vested in Congress by the Confederation."[12] The question arose of the exact meaning of the phrase "Executive powers." James Wilson stated that he conceived of executive powers as "those of executing the laws, and appointing officers not appertaining to and appointed by the Legislature."[13] James Madison moved to specify the meaning more precisely by substituting the words: "with power to carry into effect the national laws, to appoint to offices in cases not otherwise provided for ..."[14] After brief discussion, the motion was adopted. In the course of the discussion, Madison stated that he did not know that the words "to appoint to offices" were absolutely necessary, since this power was perhaps included under the power to execute the laws, but he thought they might "serve to prevent doubts and misconstructions."

The Virginia Plan provided that the national judiciary should be chosen by the legislature. When this resolution came before the Convention for discussion on June 5, James Wilson led the opposition, stating: "Experience shewed the impropriety of such appointments by numerous bodies. Intrigue, partiality, and concealment were the necessary consequences. A principal reason for unity in the Executive was the officers might be appointed by a single responsible person."[15]

John Rutledge of South Carolina was "by no means disposed to grant so great a power to any single person. The people will think that we are leaning too much toward Monarchy." Madison was not satisfied with placing the power to appoint judges either in the legislature or in the executive, and moved to lay the matter over to be decided after further reflection. The motion carried. In opposing the appointment of judges by the legislature, he pointed out that "beside the danger of intrigue and partiality, many of the members were not judges of the requisite qualifications. The Legislative talents, which were very different from those of a Judge, commonly recommended men to the favor of Legislative Assemblies." Despite these observations, Madison was not convinced that judges should be appointed by the executive and was "rather inclined to give it to the Senatorial branch, as numerous eno' to be confided in—as not so numerous as to be governed by the motives of the other branch; and as being sufficiently stable and independent to follow their deliberate judgments."[16] Madison later changed his position and advocated the appointment of judges by the executive.

Alexander Hamilton suggested that judges should be "appointed or nominated by the Executive to the Senate, which should have the right of rejecting or approving."[17] This was the first time that the method of appointment finally adopted was suggested during the Convention. Hamilton's suggestion apparently attracted no further discussion or comment at this time, and when it was later proposed by Gorham and Madison, it failed to win the approval of the Convention, though it was finally accepted in the closing days. It is significant that Hamilton, a leading advocate of a strong executive, was the first member to propose this method of appointment. The power which he proposed that the Senate should exercise was that of *"rejecting or approving";* his wording clearly indicated that he did not contemplate that the Senate should participate in the nominating power.

The committee of the whole reported on June 13 that members of the Supreme Court should be appointed by the second chamber, and members of the inferior courts by the national legislature.[18] Two days later, William Paterson presented the New Jersey Plan, which provided for the appointment of judges by the executive, who, however, was to be elected by the legislative body. On June 18, Alexander Hamilton presented his plan, which provided that the executive should appoint the heads of the departments of finance, war, and foreign affairs, and should nominate all other officers, subject to approbation or rejection by the Senate.[19] The Pinckney plan, however, vested the appointing power in the Congress.[20]

The next debate on the appointing power occurred on July 18, when a resolution was introduced "that a national judiciary be established to consist of one supreme tribunal the judges of which [shall] be appointed by the second branch of the National Legislature."[21] In opening the debate Nathaniel Gorham said that appointment by the second branch would be preferable to appointment by the entire legislature, but he thought even that branch too numerous "and too little personally responsible, to ensure a good choice." He proposed instead that judges be appointed by the executive, with the advice and consent of the second branch, a method which he said had been used in Massachusetts for 140 years.

James Wilson moved that appointments should be made by the executive, stating that if his motion did not prevail, he would support the plan proposed by Gorham. Luther Martin advocated appointment by the second branch of the legislature, which "being from all the states it would be best informed of characters and most capable of making a fit choice." Roger Sherman maintained that there would be better security for proper choice in the Senate than in the executive. "It would," said he, "be composed of men nearly equal to the Executive, and would of course have more wisdom. They would bring into their deliberations a more diffusive knowledge of characters. It would be less easy for candidates to intrigue with them, than with the Executive Magistrate." George Mason saw "insuperable objections" to appointment by the executive, who because of his residence for a period of years at the seat of the government would be unduly influenced to make appointments from that state. This contention was disputed by Gorham, who said:

As the Executive will be responsible, in point of character at least, for a judicious and faithful discharge of his trust, he will be careful to look through all of the States for proper characters. The Senators will be as likely to form their attachments at the seat of Government where they reside as the Executive. If they cannot get the man of the particular State to which they may respectively belong, they will be indifferent to the rest. Public bodies feel no personal responsibility, and give full play to intrigue and cabal.[22]

Edmund Randolph contended that responsibility in the Senate might be secured by requiring the votes to be entered on the journal, and Bedford stated that the executive would have to rely on information from others, and therefore the talk of "responsibility of the Executive . . . was chimerical." Wilson's motion lost by a vote of two to six. The motion by Gorham for nomination and appointment of judges by the executive, by and with the advice and consent of the Senate, failed of adoption by a tie vote. Madison then moved that they be appointed by the President, subject to a disapproval of the Senate by a two-thirds vote, but action on the motion was postponed.

When Madison's motion was before the Convention three days later, July 21, the subject whether judges of the Supreme Court should be appointed by the executive or by the Senate was again debated. In defense of his motion, Madison stated "that it secured the responsibility of the Executive who would in general be more capable and likely to select fit characters than the legislature, or even the second branch of it, who might hide their selfish motives under the number concerned in the appointment."[23]

Charles Pinckney maintained that the "executive will possess neither the requisite knowledge of characters, nor confidence of the people for so high a trust." This position was supported by Ellsworth, who declared that the executive "will be more open to caresses and intrigues than the Senate" and asserted that nomination would be virtually equivalent to appointment. Randolph favored appointment by the executive, stressing that his responsibility would ensure fit appointments, whereas appointments by legislative bodies have generally resulted from cabals, personal regard, and other considerations unrelated to qualifications.

Gouverneur Morris restated his position in support of appointment by the executive, stating that he would be better informed about candidates than the Senate since the administration would cover the entire country. If the executive could be trusted with the command of the army, Morris maintained, he could be trusted with making appointments. Elbridge Gerry said that he could not conceive that the executive could be as well informed of character throughout the Union as the Senate, and Mason regarded the appointment by the executive as "a dangerous prerogative." Madison's motion, modified to require only a simple majority of the Senate to disapprove a nomination, was lost, three to six, and the provision for the appointment of judges of the Supreme Court by the Senate was retained.

The draft reported by the Committee on Detail on August 6 provided for the appointment of ambassadors, as well as judges of the Supreme Court, by the Senate, and the appointment of the treasurer by both houses of the legislature. This latter provision was the subject of debate on August 17, when Reed of Delaware moved to leave the appointment of the treasurer to the President. "The Legislature," he maintained, "was an improper body for appointments. Those of the State legislatures were a proof of it. The Executive being responsible would make a good choice."[24] Mason opposed the motion on the ground that the legislature, representing the people, ought to appoint the keepers of the public moneys. The motion was lost, but on September 14, the final day of consideration of the text of the Constitution, a motion by Rutledge was adopted to strike out the section and let the treasurer be appointed in the same manner as other officers.[25] This was opposed by Sherman on the ground that "as the two Houses appropriate money it is best for them to appoint the officer who is to keep it." Gorham and King contended that the people were "accustomed and attached" to the appointment of the treasurer by the legislature, and would not be in favor of another manner of appointment. Pinckney supported the motion, pointing out that in South Carolina, where the treasurer was appointed by the legislature, "bad appointments are made and the Legislature will not listen to the faults of their own officer."

When the section providing for the appointments of ambassadors and of judges of the Supreme Court by the Senate was taken up on August 23, it was again opposed by Gouverneur Morris and James Wilson, and consideration of it was put over. On the following day, the provision that the President "shall appoint officers in all cases not otherwise provided for by this Constitution" was taken up. Sherman objected that many officers, such as general officers in the army in time of peace, should not be appointed by the President, and moved to add the words "or by law," which would have permitted Congress to reduce the appointing power of the President. It is significant that the motion lost, only Connecticut voting in favor of it. Dickinson moved to amend the section to permit Congress to delegate the appointing power to state legislatures or executives, but his motion received so little support that it lost without a count of the states.[26] So the matter stood until the Special Committee on Postponed Matters made its report on Sepember 4, in which it was provided that "the President shall nominate, and by and with the advice and consent of the Senate, shall appoint Ambassadors, and other public Ministers, Judges of the Supreme Court, and all other Officers of the U. S., whose appointments are not otherwise herein provided for."[27] When this provision was debated by the Convention on September 6 and 7, it was strongly opposed by Wilson and others on the ground that it placed too much power in the Senate.*

Gouverneur Morris, who had previously advocated appointment by the executive, now supported the plan. "As the President was to nominate," said he, "there would be responsibility, and as the Senate was to concur, there would be security. As the Congress now make appointments there is no responsibility."[28] Charles Pinckney, who had previously favored appointment of judges of the Supreme Court by the upper house, now spoke briefly against giving the Senate the power to confirm any presidential appointments except those of ambassadors. Although the compromise provision which gave both the President and the Senate a share in the appointing power had previously been rejected twice by the Convention and again was the subject of a lively debate, it was finally adopted with an amendment to authorize the President to make recess appointments.

At various times during the Convention, proposals were made to create an executive council to advise the President. Although the powers of such a council were never defined in the Convention debates, presumably one of its functions would have been to advise on appointments. Its leading advocates were Mason, Sherman, Ellsworth, Franklin, and Dickinson. A draft reported by a special committee on August 22 provided for a privy council to the President, consisting of the President of the Senate, the Speaker of the House, the Chief Justice, and the heads of the departments;[29] but the proposal was subsequently rejected by the Committee on Postponed Matters on the ground that it would enable the President "by persuading his Council to concur in his wrong measures to acquire protection for them."[30] In opposing the creation of an executive council, King advanced the argument that it would not be necessary for the Senate to be in constant session, for it was not meant "that all the minute officers were to be appointed by the Senate or any original source, but by the higher officers in the department to which they belong."[31] This statement, which was not controverted, is significant because it indicated that the framers of the Constitution intended that only the principal officers of the government would be appointed by the President and confirmed by the Senate.

George Mason declared that "in rejecting a Council to the President we were about to try an experiment on which the most despotic Governments had

* See the quotation from Wilson at the beginning of this chapter.

never ventured," and Benjamin Franklin contended: "We seem too much to fear cabals in appointments by a number, and to have too much confidence in those of single persons...A Council would not only be a check on a bad President but a relief to a good one."[32]

In view of the common practice in the state governments of providing the governor with such a council, it is noteworthy that the proposal was rejected. The omission of an executive council was one of the principal grounds on which Mason and some others were later to oppose the adoption of the Constitution.

On September 15, the next to the last day of the Convention, Gouverneur Morris moved to add the clause: "but Congress may by law vest the appointment of such inferior officers as they think proper in the President alone, in the Courts of law, or in the heads of Departments." The motion was seconded by Sherman, and though it lost on the first ballot, when it was put a second time it was agreed to without opposition. Madison doubted the necessity for the provision, and pointed out that some officers below the heads of departments ought to have the power to appoint lesser officers.

Debates in the State Constitutional Conventions

The provisions dealing with the appointing power attracted relatively little attention in the several state conventions called to consider the ratification of the proposed federal Constitution. George Mason declared before the Virginia convention that the absence of an executive council was a "fatal defect," and that the "improper power of the Senate in the appointment of public officers" resulted in "dangerously blending the Executive and Legislative powers."[33] Oliver Ellsworth, writing under the pseudonym "A Landholder," replied to the arguments of Mason for an executive council, asserting that the states which had used them had found them "useless, and complain of them as a dead weight." He defended the securing of information from department heads as being trustworthy and responsible.[34]

Luther Martin, a delegate to the federal Convention from Maryland, stated in a speech to the legislature of Maryland that there had been considerable opposition to the provision concerning the appointing power on the ground that it makes the President "king, in everything but name," for he would have "a formidable host, devoted to his interest, and ready to support his ambitious views."[35] In several other states, however, the opposite objection was voiced: that the Constitution deprived the President of an independent appointing power which he ought to enjoy as chief executive, and made him dependent on the Senate. The "blending" of legislative and executive powers was decried as contrary to the principle of separation of powers, and it was feared that the Senate would become all powerful and would wield its power along what John Adams called "aristocratical" lines. In his "Letters of a Federal Farmer,"

Richard Henry Lee maintained that "the President is connected with or tied to the Senate; he may always act with the Senate, but he can never effectually counteract its views. The President can appoint no officer, civil or military, who shall not be agreeable to the Senate."[36]

The same position was stated in the North Carolina convention by Samuel Spencer: "The President may nominate, but they [the Senate] have a negative on his nomination, till he has exhausted the number of those he wishes to be appointed. He will be obliged, finally, to acquiesce in the appointment of those whom the Senate shall nominate, or else no appointment will take place."[37] James Iredell replied that "the Senate has no other influence but a restraint on improper appointments."[38]

William R. Davie, a delegate to the federal Constitutional Convention from North Carolina, stated that the provision in the Constitution requiring confirmation of appointments by the Senate had been adopted as a compromise between the large and the small states. "The small states," he said, "would not agree that the House of Representatives should have a voice in the appointment to offices; the extreme jealousy of all the states would not give it to the President alone."[39] The same point was made by Roger Sherman and Oliver Ellsworth in their report to the governor of Connecticut on the Constitution: "The equal representation of the States in the Senate and the voice of that branch in the appointment to offices will secure the rights of the lesser as well as the greater states."[40] But this would appear to be an afterargument in defense of the Constitution rather than a consideration which importantly influenced the delegates to the Convention. Although the smaller states generally supported measures strengthening the Senate, the debates do not reveal that the provisions concerning the appointing power as finally agreed upon were the result of a compromise between the large and the small states; it was rather a compromise between those who believed in and those who feared a strong executive. In each group there were some delegates from large states and some from small states.[41]

In Pennsylvania the Constitution was opposed on the ground that it placed too much power in the hand of the Senate, and gave the Senate an opportunity to make the President its tool. James Wilson led the defense, stating that although the section in question was not his "favorite part of the Constitution," he maintained that in the confirmation of appointments "the Senate stands controlled. If it is that monster which it is said to be, it can only show its teeth; it is unable to bite and devour ... With regard to appointment of officers, the President must nominate before they can vote." He denied that the President would become the tool of the Senate, stating that it could do nothing without him. "Clearly, sir, he [the President] holds the helm, and the vessel can proceed in neither one way nor another without his concurrence."[42]

Hamilton on the Appointing Power

The leading defense as well as the most thorough exposition of the provisions in the Constitution concerning the appointing power was written by Alexander Hamilton in *The Federalist.*[43] Commenting on the appointing power, Hamilton wrote (in No. 66):

It will be the office of the President to NOMINATE, and with the advice and consent of the Senate to APPOINT. There will, of course, be no exertion of CHOICE on the part of the Senate. They may defeat one choice of the Executive and oblige him to make another; but they cannot themselves CHOOSE—they can only ratify or reject the choice of the President. They might even entertain a preference to some other person, at the very moment they were assenting to the one proposed, because there might be no positive ground of opposition to him; and they could not be sure, if they withheld their assent, that the subsequent nomination would fall upon their own favorite, or upon any other person in their estimation more meritorious than the one rejected. Thus it could hardly happen that the majority of the Senate would feel any other complacency toward the object of an appointment than such as the appearances of merit might inspire, and the proofs of the want of it destroy.

History has proved Hamilton to be in error. Even in Washington's administration the Senate declined to approve the appointment of one Benjamin Fishbourn to be the naval officer of Savannah, not because he lacked the necessary qualifications, but because the two Georgia senators had another candidate. And the following day Washington yielded and sent to the Senate the nomination of the candidate who was the choice of the Georgia senators.* Nominations to federal offices situated within a state have long since come to be looked upon as the perquisite of the senators of that state, provided the senators are of the same party as the President, and recently it has been contended by members of the Senate that the Constitution requires the President not only to consult individual senators before making nominations, but also to accept their recommendations.†

Concerning the method provided for appointment of federal officers, Hamilton declared that "It is not easy to conceive a plan better calculated than this to promote a judicious choice of men for filling the offices of the Union," and he sagely remarked that "on this point must essentially depend the character of its administration."[44] Strongly defending the selection of officers by a single executive officer, he maintained:

...one man of discernment is better fitted to analyze and estimate the peculiar qualities adapted to particular offices, than a body of men of equal or perhaps even superior discernment. The sole and undivided responsibility of one man will naturally beget a livelier sense of duty and a more exact regard to reputation. He will on this account feel himself under stronger obligations, and more interested to

---

* See below, chap. iii, for an account of this case.
† See chap. xiii, below.

investigate with care the qualities requisite to the station to be filled, and to prefer with impartiality the persons who may have the fairest pretensions to them. He will have fewer personal attachments to gratify than a body of men.[45]

Hamilton went on to point out the inherent weaknesses of legislative bodies in making appointments to public offices.

In every exercise of the power of appointing to offices by an assembly of men we must expect to see a full display of all the private and party likings and dislikes, partialities and antipathies, attachments and animosities, which are felt by those who compose the assembly. . . . The intrinsic merit of the candidate will be too often out of sight. . . . The coalition will commonly turn upon some interested equivalent: "Give us the man we wish for this office, and you shall have the one you wish for that." This will be the usual condition of the bargain. And it will rarely happen that the advancement of the public service will be the primary object either of the party victories or of party negotiations.[46]

He maintained that there was in reality no essential difference between the power to nominate and the power to appoint, and expressed the belief that the requirement of Senate approval would be a salutary check on the President, which "would have a powerful, though, in general, a silent operation. It would be an excellent check upon a spirit of favoritism of the President, and would tend greatly to prevent the appointment of unfit characters from state prejudice, from family connection, from personal attachment, or from a view to popularity."[47]

Hamilton ridiculed the argument that the President would be able to use the power of nomination to corrupt or seduce a majority of the Senate. He likewise decried the proposal for a council of appointments such as that used in his own state of New York, declaring that it led to intrigue and cabal and defeated any real sense of responsibility.

A more cogent defense of the provisions in the Constitution governing appointments has never been written. It is readily apparent, however, that Hamilton oversimplified the problem and was in error in assuming that the individual members of the Senate would not exert influence on the President in making nominations. He did not foresee the influence which political parties were soon to exert on appointments, the practices which soon developed to make the power to nominate virtually a formality for certain types of federal offices, or the prominent role which members of the Senate were soon to play in dictating nominations in their own states.

John Adams on the Power of Appointment

Although favoring the Constitution as a whole, John Adams was perhaps the most vigorous critic of the provisions concerning appointments. A staunch advocate of the executive power, Adams believed that the President alone should have the power of appointment. It is of significance to compare the ideas of Hamilton, the most able defender of the constitutional provisions governing appointments, with those of John Adams, the most able critic. Writing to Jefferson from London in 1787, Adams stated:

You are apprehensive of monarchy, I of aristocracy. I would, therefore, have given more power to the president, and less to the senate. The nomination and appointment to all offices I would have given to the President, assisted only by a privy council of his own creation; but not a vote or voice would I have given the Senate or any senator unless he were of the privy council. Faction and distraction are the sure and certain consequences of giving to a senate a vote on the distribution of offices.[48]

In the autumn of 1789 John Adams wrote to Roger Sherman vigorously criticizing the appointment provisions of the Constitution and predicting that political parties would quickly arise and that partisan considerations would dominate the actions of the Senate in passing upon nominations of the President. He foresaw the use of appointments as political spoils and that individual senators would exert pressure to secure patronage for personal advantage. The major points of his criticism of the requirement of senatorial confirmation of appointments were as follows:

1. It lessens the responsibility of the Executive. . . . The blame of an injudicious, weak or wicked appointment, is shared so much between him and the Senate that his part will be too small.

2. It turns the minds and attention of the people to the Senate, a branch of the legislature, in executive matters. It interests another branch of the legislature in the management of the executive.

3. It has a natural tendency to excite ambition in the senate. . . . A senator of great influence will naturally be ambitious and desirous of increasing his influence. Will he not be under a temptation to use his influence with the President as well as his brother Senators, to appoint persons to office in the several states who will exert themselves in elections . . . to increase his interests and promote his views? In this point of view, I am very apprehensive that this defect in our constitution will have an unhappy tendency to introduce corruption of the grossest kinds, both of ambition and avarice, into all our elections, and this will be the worst of poisons to our constitution.

4. The negative on appointments will involve the Senate in "reproach, obloquy, and suspicion, without doing any good." If they do not use it, they will be censured and ridiculed for their servility; if they do use it, they will incur the resentment of the Executive and also of disappointed candidates.

5. We shall soon have political parties which will "strive and intrigue to use every appointment to increase their power and factious divisions will prevail on every nomination."

6. The Senate does not have the necessary time to consider appointments, and the business of government will be infinitely delayed.

7. Confirmation by the Senate "will weaken the hands of the Executive.... Officers of the Government, instead of having a single eye and undivided attachment to the Executive branch, as they ought to have, consistent with law and the constitution, will be constantly tempted to be factious with their factious patrons in the Senate. The President's own officers, in a thousand instances, will oppose his just and constitutional exertions, and screen themselves under the wings of their patrons in the Senate."

8. Confirmation by the Senate will not enhance public confidence; the people will be suspicious and jealous of the factious schemes in the Senate to influence the President in his appointments.[49]

In defense of confirmation of appointments by the Senate, Roger Sherman replied to Adams:

It appears to me the senate is the most important branch in the government.... The Executive magistrate is to execute the laws. The Senate, being a branch of the legislature, will naturally incline to have them duly executed, and, therefore, will advise to such appointments as will best attain that end. From the knowledge of the people in the several states, they can give the best information as to who are qualified for office; and though they will, as you justly observe, in some degree lessen his responsibility, yet their advice may enable him to make such judicious appointments, as to render responsibility less necessary.[50]

Debate on the Removal Power in the First Congress

One of the major constitutional issues to come before the first session of Congress had to do with the power of the President to remove public officers. A resolution introduced in the House of Representatives by James Madison on May 19, 1789, looking to the establishment of a Department of Foreign Affairs, provided that the head of the department should be appointed by the President, by and with the advice and consent of the Senate, and should be "removable by the President."[51] After a brief debate the resolution carried by a "considerable majority" and was referred to a committee for the preparation of a bill.[52] When the committee made its report several days later, the provision fixing the method of appointment was objected to as being superfluous, since the Constitution provided that the President should make such appointments, and it was dropped from the bill without debate. The provision that the head of the Department of Foreign Affairs should be "removable by the President" was objected to by Representative Benson on the ground that it appeared to be a legislative grant of authority to the President, whereas this power was a part of the executive power granted to him by the Constitution. After a debate, this provision also was dropped, and there was substituted the phrase "when the principal officer of the department is removed by the President," which was an acknowledgment of the constitutional power of the President to remove officers whom he appoints. The bill as amended finally carried by a vote of 29 to 22[53] after one of the most notable debates in the history of Congress, which lasted five days. The voluminous debate over the issue of the removal power of the President indicated that the First Congress was fully aware of the constitutional implications of its decision. A number of its members who had been delegates to the Convention of 1787 spoke in detail about the reasons which had influenced the framers of the Constitution. Although the removal power lies outside the scope of the present study, this historic debate is of interest because it frequently touched upon the appointing power, and in some respects it indicates even better than the brief reports of the Convention of 1787 the prevailing ideas about the respective roles of the President and the Senate in the exercise of the appointing power.

Four interpretations of the Constitution were advanced in the debates: first, that the power of removal was inherently a part of the executive power and rested in the President alone; second, that it rested with the President and the Senate jointly, being incident to the appointing power; third, that the only method of removal was by impeachment; and fourth, that the power was not fixed by the Constitution, and therefore was left to the Congress to decide.[54] James Madison led the debate in support of the position that the power of removal belonged exclusively to the President as a part of the executive power. Throughout the debate, Madison stressed the principle of executive responsibility as a cardinal feature of the Constitution, saying: "It is evidently the intention of the Constitution that the first magistrate should be responsible for the executive department; so far, therefore, as we do not make officers who are to aid him in the duties of that department responsible to him, he is not responsible to the country."[55]

The opposing point of view, advanced by Alexander White of Virginia, Elbridge Gerry of Massachusetts, and others, was that the power of removal is incident to the power of appointment, and as such was granted by the Constitution to the President and the Senate jointly. Gerry denied that the appointing power was inherently an executive function, pointing out that in many states it was exercised by the legislature instead of by the governor. William Smith of South Carolina took the extreme position that the only method of removal was that of impeachment; in this he received little support.

Fisher Ames maintained that the executive power was vested in the President, and that the heads of departments and other officers were his assistants and therefore must be directly responsible to him. "The Constitution places all executive power in the hands of the President; and could he personally execute all the laws there would be no occasion for establishing auxiliaries; but the circumscribed powers of human nature in one man demands the aid of others."[56]

In a notable passage, Madison contended that the appointment of officers was inherently an executive function, and that under the basic constitutional principle of separation of powers, the Senate should have nothing to do with the selection of officers. Although he admitted that the Constitution granted to the Senate a share in the appointing power, he said that he had never regarded the provision as one of the most meritorious parts of the Constitution, and contended that this power of the Senate should not be extended beyond the precise limits fixed by the Constitution.

The Legislature creates the office, defines its powers, limits its duration, and annexes a compensation. This done, the legislative power ceases. They ought to have nothing to do with designating a man to fill the office. That I conceive to be of an executive nature. Although it be qualified in the Constitution, I would not extend or strain that qualification beyond the limits precisely fixed for it. We ought always to consider the Constitution with an eye to the principles on which it was founded. In this point of view, we shall readily conclude that if the Legislature determines the powers, the honors, and emoluments of an office, we would be insecure if they were to designate the officer also.[57]

Fisher Ames asserted that the exercise of the removal power by the Senate "would be subversive of the great principles of the constitution, and destructive of liberty, because it tends to intermingle executive and legislative powers in one body of men." He declared that the Senate would be certain to abuse the power, to intrigue with subordinate officers, and to retain persons who ought to be removed, and thus share in the executive power.[58] Abraham Baldwin of Georgia, a member of the Convention of 1787, stated that "the mingling of the powers of the President and Senate was strongly opposed in the convention.... Some gentlemen opposed it to the last; and finally, it was the principle ground on which they refused to give it their signature and assent."[59]

Throughout the debates, those who favored the removal power of the President pointed out that he could not be held responsible unless he were able to select his subordinates and were permitted to discharge those in whom he no longer had confidence. "I contend," declared John Lawrence, "that every President should have those men about him in whom he can place the most confidence, provided the Senate approve his choice."[60]

The necessity for the President to have the power of removal was cogently stated by Madison:

Vest this power in the Senate jointly with the President, and you abolish at once the great principle of unity and responsibility in the executive department, which was intended for the security of liberty and the public good. If the President should possess alone the power of removal from office, those who are employed in the execution of the law will be in their proper situation, and the chain of dependence will be preserved; the lowest officers, the middle grade, and the highest, will depend, as they ought, on the President, and the President on the community.[61]

The debate in the Senate on the removal power of the President unfortunately was not reported, for at that time the Senate sat behind closed doors.

There is available only the one-sided account of Senator William Maclay, who led the opposition to giving the President the power of removal, contending that the "depriving power should be the same as the appointing power."[62] He argued that to subject public officers to any form of removal other than by impeachment would result in their "abject servility," and men of independent spirit would not accept office. He regarded the granting of the removal power to the President as dangerous and warned that the virtues of the first President "would depart with him, but the power which you give him will remain." Maclay objected in particular to the provision which authorized the appointment of the chief clerk (who, he declared, would really do the work of the department) by the head of the department. "This," he said, "is a direct stroke at the power of the Senate." The vote in the Senate resulted in a tie, and Vice-President Adams cast the deciding vote in favor of the bill.

What, then, did the framers of the Constitution intend in regard to the exercise of the appointing power? What did they envisage as the role the President would play? The Senate? Although the federal Convention early in the course of its deliberations agreed that (1) the President should appoint the principal officers not otherwise provided for in the Constitution, and (2) the Senate should appoint judges of the Supreme Court, this division of the appointing power was finally rejected, and a compromise was reached under which both the President and the Senate shared in the appointment of the principal officers of the government. The debates revealed two opposite points of view: one group of men feared the abuse of the appointing power by the executive and favored appointments by the legislative body; another group of more resolute men, eager to establish a strong national government with a vigorous administration, favored the granting of the power of appointment to the President. The compromise finally agreed to was regarded by the advocates of a strong executive as a victory, for they believed that there was no essential difference between the power to appoint and the power to nominate. In view of the limited appointing power enjoyed by the governors of the states at the time, it is significant that the Convention early decided to give the executive an independent power to appoint officers not otherwise provided for. It is equally significant that this decision, having been reached, was not thereafter challenged in the debates, whereas the decision to give the appointment of judges of the Supreme Court to the Senate was attacked whenever it came before the Convention.

The exact meaning of the words *nominate* and *advice and consent* contained in the section relating to appointments was not discussed in the brief debate which took place on the provision in the closing days of the Convention. The wording of the section—"The President ... shall nominate, and by and with the advice and consent of the Senate, shall appoint ..."—indicates that the power to nominate was given exclusively to the President. It was frequently stated in the Convention debates that since the President would nominate, the responsibility for good appointments would be his. The phrase "advice and consent" was used in the Convention as synonymous with such terms as "approval," "approbation," and "concurrence," and it was held that this provision gave the Senate a "negative" on appointments by the President. The debates in the Convention do not support the thesis since advanced that the framers of the Constitution intended that the President should secure the *advice*—that is, the recommendations—of the Senate or of individual members, before making a nomination. To the contrary, Hamilton argued that since the Senate could only approve or disapprove the President's choices, there would be no tendency for its members to press their own candidates on the President. Madison maintained that for the legislature, which creates an office, to designate the person to fill it would be highly improper and contrary to the basic Constitutional principle of the separation of powers.

The debates in the Constitutional Convention were concerned wholly with the appointment of the principal officers of the government, it being assumed that minor officials would be appointed by other executive officers. The section as finally adopted enumerated several classes of officers thus to be appointed—ambassadors, public ministers and consuls, and judges of the Supreme Court—and provided that Congress could by law vest the appointment of *inferior* officers in other hands.

In the debates over the adoption of the Constitution little criticism was voiced that too much power was given to the President over appointments; the major criticism was of the opposite tenor: that the President should have been given the power to make appointments with no requirement of Senate concurrence. Hamilton and other defenders of the proposed Constitution, however, maintained that there was little difference between the power to appoint and the power to nominate, which rested with the President alone. They defended the provision requiring Senate approval for nominations of principal officers as a salutary check on the President and a safeguard against bad appointments.

The defenders of the proposed Constitution contended that the Senate would act on appointments solely with regard to the fitness of the persons nominated and would approve nominations if the nominees were qualified and reject nominations of unfit persons. Only John Adams, who was not a member of the Convention, foresaw clearly the future rise of political parties and that partisan considerations rather than the fitness of nominees would often be the controlling consideration of the Senate in passing on nominations. Much of the debate accordingly dealt with issues of the past, particularly the danger that the President would use the appointing power to establish a monarchy, and proved to be somewhat irrelevant to the issues of the future.

Throughout the debates the need for definite responsibility in the appointment of public officers was constantly stressed. Those who favored nomination or appointment by the executive maintained that he would be responsible, but that in a legislative assembly there would be no responsibility. This group contended that the President could be held responsible for the execution of the laws only if he was permitted to select his principal assistants. Those of the opposing view held that talk of responsibility was "chimerical" and that "energy in government" might lead to despotism. Those favoring executive responsibility were in the majority.

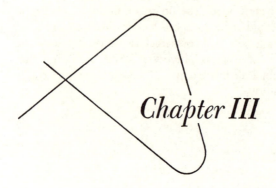

Chapter III

EARLY HISTORY OF
SENATORIAL CONFIRMATION OF
APPOINTMENTS: 1789–1828

The applications are made chiefly through members of Congress. These, oftentimes to get rid of them; oftener still perhaps, for local and electioneering purposes, and to please and gratify their party, more than from any real merit in the applicant, are handed in, backed by a solicitude to succeed, in order to strengthen their interest. Washington to the Secretary of War, Oct. 21, 1798.[1]

Nomination to office is an executive function. To give it to the legislature as we do, is a violation of the principle of separation of powers. It swerves the members from correctness, by temptations to intrigue for office themselves, and to a corrupt barter for votes; and destroys responsibility by dividing it among a multitude. By leaving nomination in its proper place, among executive functions, the principle of the distribution of powers is preserved, and responsibility weighs with its heaviest force on a single head. Thomas Jefferson to Samuel Kercheval, 1816.[2]

Washington and the Senate

No PRESIDENT exercised greater care than Washington in selecting persons for federal office; he consulted widely and maintained exceptionally high standards for public office.[3] John Adams wrote to a friend concerning Washington's practice in making appointments: "No man, I believe, has influence with the President. He seeks information from all quarters, and judges more independently than any man I ever knew. It is of so much importance to the public that he should preserve this superiority, that

[36

I hope I shall never see the time when any man will have influence with him beyond the powers of reason and argument."⁴ The first President faced the task of establishing the new government in public esteem, and consequently gave particular attention to the loyalty of his appointees to the new Constitution and to their standing in their own communities. Washington wrote to Edward Rutledge on May 5, 1789: "I anticipate that one of the most difficult and delicate parts of the duty of my office will be that which relates to nominations for appointments."⁵

Washington insisted that he alone was responsible for the persons whom he nominated, and though he consulted members of Congress and others about appointments, he rebuffed any attempt at dictation. When James Monroe, then a member of the Senate from Virginia, wrote to Washington in 1794 advising against the appointment of Alexander Hamilton as special envoy extraordinary to negotiate a treaty with Great Britain, Washington sharply reminded him that the President alone was responsible for nominations and invited him to submit in writing any information that would disqualify Hamilton.⁶

Washington utilized members of his Cabinet to make investigations and to consult with the state delegations of both houses of Congress concerning appointments. He turned to Hamilton more than to other members of the Cabinet for assistance, partly because of his confidence in the judgment and dis-cretion of Hamilton, but also because more than half of all appointments were in the Treasury Department. Party lines had not yet been fixed, and partisan considerations were not important, though Washington insisted that his ap-pointees be loyal to the new government. On one occasion he stated that he would not knowingly appoint any person to any office of consequence "whose political tenets are adverse to the measures which the *general* government are pursuing; for this, in my opinion, would be a sort of political suicide."⁷

On another occasion an intimate friend applied for a lucrative position, which everyone expected he would receive. A political enemy applied for the same position, and though his application was regarded by friends of the Presi-dent as presumptuous, he got the nomination. To a friend who remonstrated with him about the nomination, Washington replied:

My friend I receive with cordial welcome; he is welcome to my house and welcome to my heart, but, with all his good qualities, he is not a man of business. His op-ponent is, with all his politics so hostile to me, a man of business; my private feelings have nothing to do with the case. I am not George Washington, but President of the United States. As George Washington, I would do this man any kindness in my power; as President of the United States I can do nothing.⁸

The first nomination sent to the Senate was that of William Short, on June 15, 1789, to take charge of American affairs in France in the absence of Jefferson, who had been granted permission to return home for several months. "For this purpose," stated Washington in his message to the Senate, "I nominate William Short, Esq., and request your advice on the propriety of appointing him. I have directed the Secretary of Foreign Affairs to lay before the Senate, at such time as you think proper to assign, papers which will acquaint you with his character."[9] At the Senate's request, Secretary Jay in person submitted the papers on the following day, and Short was confirmed. Washington's later nominations were submitted with less formality and were not accompanied by an offer to submit information, nor was it ordinarily requested.

The question of the procedure which the Senate should follow in giving its advice and consent to a nomination arose when the nomination of William Short came before it. One group favored a viva voce vote. William Maclay advocated a secret ballot in order to avoid administration pressure on the members; but his colleague from Pennsylvania, Robert Morris, opposed a secret ballot, saying that it was beneath the dignity of the Senate, which, in passing upon nominations, ought to be "open, bold, and unawed by any consideration whatever." Maclay gives the following account of his defense of the use of a secret ballot:

...Every Senator when voting openly would feel inconvenience from two quarters, or at least he was subjected to it. I would not say, in European language, that there would be court favor and court resentment, but there would be about the President a kind of sunshine that people in general would be well pleased to enjoy the warmth of. Openly voting against the nominations of the President would be the sure mode of losing this sunshine. This was applicable to all Senators in all cases. But there was more. A Senator, like another man, would have the interests of his friends to promote. The cause of a son or brother might be lodged in his hands. Will such a one, in such a case, wish openly to oppose the President's judgment?[10]

Vice-President Adams, according to Maclay, "rose in the chair and delivered his opinion how the business ought to be done. He read the Constitution, argued, and concluded: 'I would rise in the chair, and put the question individually to the Senators: Do you advise and consent that Mr. Short be appointed *chargé d'affaires* at the court of France, do you and do you?' "[11] Daniel Carroll spoke for the viva voce method, stating that the ballot was productive of caballing and bargaining for votes. This was controverted by Maclay, who maintained that a secret ballot was the antidote against caballing, for men made bargains for certainties. Ellsworth opposed balloting, saying that it "suited bashful men best, but was the worst way for bad and unprincipled men." Maclay's motion for vote by ballot was adopted by a vote of 11 to 7, much to the annoyance of the Vice-President. Adams, according to Maclay, proceeded to raise all sorts of petty and technical questions, and an hour and a quarter of the "most idle discourse imaginable" followed.

On August 5, 1789, a motion was introduced in the Senate: "That it is the opinion of the Senate, that their advice and consent to the appointment of officers should be given in the presence of the President." A committee was appointed to consult the President concerning the "mode of communication proper to be pursued between him and the Senate in the formation of treaties, and making appointments to office." After Washington met with the committee on August 8, 1789, he recorded in his diary the "sentiments" which he had expressed on the subject.

With respect to nominations. My present ideas are that as they point to a single object unconnected in its nature with any other object, they best be made by written messages. In this case, the Acts of the President, and the Acts of the Senate will stand on clear, distinct, and responsible ground. Independent of this consideration, it could be no pleasing thing I conceive, for the President, on the one hand to be present and hear the propriety of his nominations questioned; nor for the Senate on the other hand to be under the smallest restraint from his presence from the fullest and freest inquiry into the Character of the Person nominated. The President in a situation like this would be reduced to one of two things: either to be a silent witness of the decision by ballot, if there are objections to the nomination; or in justification thereof (if he should think it right) to support it by argument. Neither of which might be agreeable; and the latter improper; for as the President has a right to nominate without assigning his reasons, so has the Senate a right to dissent without giving theirs.[12]

The special committee followed the wishes of the President, and on its recommendation the Senate reversed its previous decision and provided for a viva voce vote on nominations submitted in writing by the President.[13] All Presidents have followed the precedent established by Washington of submitting nominations in writing,[14] and if a vote is taken, it is viva voce, although it should be noted that until 1929 appointments were considered in closed executive session and the votes were not made public.

Another question which early arose in the consideration of appointments of ministers to foreign countries was whether the Senate could pass upon the advisability of establishing the ministry and the grade, as well as the person nominated. When Washington nominated ministers to Paris, London, and The Hague in December, 1791, the nominations were held up several weeks while the Senate debated a resolution opposing the establishment of "ministers plenipotentiary to reside permanently at foreign courts." Finally the appointments were confirmed, by a close vote, because of the special need for representatives at the particular courts. Washington asked Jefferson for an opinion concerning whether in diplomatic appointments, it was within the jurisdiction of the Senate to pass upon the grade of the office as well as upon the person nominated. Jefferson replied that the process of appointment of foreign ministers involved five distinct steps for determinations: (1) the destination, (2) the grade, (3) the nomination of the person, (4) the appointment, and (5) the commission. Steps three and five were specifically granted to the President by the Constitution; the Senate participated only in step four, that of appointment. Jefferson reasoned that since the President was given the exclusive function of nomination, the earlier act of determination of rank was also his, since it was even farther removed from the process of appointment, the only step in which the Senate shared.[15] Washington also conferred with Madison, then a member of the House, concerning the subject, and on April 27, 1790, recorded in his diary that Madison's opinion coincided with that of Jefferson and Jay, namely, that the powers of the Senate extended "no farther than to an approbation or disapprobation of the person nominated by the President, all the rest being Executive and vested in the President by the Constitution."[16]

Another problem that soon arose was how senators could become informed on the qualifications of persons who had been nominated. William Maclay recorded in his journal on June 3, 1790:

The nominations for the officers of the army had come in yesterday and were taken up this day. I had made some objections a few days ago to giving my advice and consent to the appointment of men of whom I knew nothing. Izard got on to the same subject and bounced a good deal. However, the thing was got over by members rising and giving an account of the officers appointed from the different states, and all were agreed to.[17]

This method of relying on the information and judgment of the senators from the state in which the office was situated or the state in which the appointee resided became the established practice. When the nomination by Washington of James Iredell to be Associate Justice of the Supreme Court came before the Senate, Pierce Butler from South Carolina spoke very highly of him, but a senator from New Hampshire stated that although he had the highest regard for the opinion of the senator from South Carolina, he wanted to hear from the gentlemen from the state where Iredell resided. Whereupon Hawkins of North Carolina secured the floor and confirmed all that Senator Butler had said, and the Senate approved the nomination.[18]

The First Case of "Senatorial Courtesy"

Congress had been in session for only three months of its first term when the Senate for the first time rejected a presidential nominee and at the same time established the precedent of "senatorial courtesy." Washington nominated one Benjamin Fishbourn to the post of naval officer of the Port of Savannah, and although he apparently had excellent qualifications for the position, the Senate rejected the nomination, as a courtesy to the two senators from Georgia, who had a candidate of their own. The following day Washington withdrew the nomination of Fishbourn and yielded to the two Georgia senators by nominating the candidate they desired; but with the nomination he wrote a dignified letter to the Senate requesting that thereafter, before rejecting a nomination, it communicate with the President and secure the information which led him to make the nomination. In his message Washington stated:

Whatever may have been the reasons which induced your dissent, I am now persuaded they were such as you deemed sufficient. Permit me to submit to your consideration whether on occasions where the propriety of nominations appear questionable to you it would not be expedient to communicate that circumstance to me, and thereby avail yourselves of the information which led me to make them, and which I would with pleasure lay before you.[19]

Washington pointed to the high qualifications of his original nominee, who had had a distinguished military career, had been elected to the state assembly, had served as president of the state executive council, and had been chosen by local officials to be collector of the Port of Savannah.

Thus, in one of the first confirmation cases, the Senate acted in a manner quite different from that envisaged by Hamilton, who had maintained that there would be no exertion of choice on the part of the Senate. In this early case the senators from Georgia did exert a choice on the President, to which he eventually yielded. As a courtesy to the Georgia senators, the Senate rejected an exceptionally well qualified nominee without regard to his qualifications, so that the senators could press for the nomination of their candidate.

The Fishbourn case initiated the custom which requires the President to consult with the senators from the state in which a vacancy occurs, and to nominate a person acceptable to them; if he fails to do so, the Senate as a courtesy to these senators will reject any other nominee regardless of his qualification. The custom is usually invoked, however, only by senators of the same party as the President. It did not become firmly established in Washington's administration, for he continued to hold to the doctrine that the power of nomination belonged exclusively to the President and continued to consult widely in making his selections. Under later Presidents with less prestige, less force of character, and less determination, the rule became firmly established with respect to senators of the same political party as the President.*

Congressional Pressures for Appointments

Washington followed the practice of consulting the members of the House of Representatives as well as members of the Senate concerning appointments in their states. Indeed, Maclay complained that he gave more attention to the advice of representatives than to senators, who under the Constitution were charged with this particular function.[20] Political pressure for appointments was the rule from the very first, and it was common practice for applicants to press their claims through the members of Congress.[21] Although Washington usually followed the wishes of state delegations if they were in agreement and if their

* See chap. xiii, below, for detailed treatment of the custom of courtesy.

candidate was qualified, nevertheless he insisted on high standards and saw to it that an independent investigation was made before he appointed anyone. Some members of the Senate pressed their recommendations upon the President, though his austerity and dignity did not encourage such a course; other senators were much more diffident in asking for the appointment of their friends, and did so apologetically. Senator Cabot of Massachusetts felt called to apologize when bringing a name to the President's attention.[22] The influence of members of the Senate on appointments in Washington's administration is summarized by Fish as follows:

During the first administration the influence of the senators was simply that of men with special opportunities for information. Other prominent men sent advice, and Washington's broad acquaintance resulting in his receiving directly many requests for office, particularly from army officers. . . . The administration, moreover, like any intelligent employer of labor, refused to confine its selection to those who sought employment either directly or indirectly, but searched out able men from all over the country.[23]

Members of the Senate also exerted pressure on the President concerning nominations to offices not situated within a particular state. In 1794 Madison and Monroe called upon Washington, as a committee representing a group of members of both houses, to urge the appointment of Aaron Burr as minister to France. Washington refused, stating that he had made it an invariable rule never to appoint to a high and responsible office a man of whose integrity he was not assured, and offered to appoint either Madison or Monroe. The group in Congress caucused and refused to withdraw their support of Burr for the post. When Madison and Monroe saw Washington a second time, the President stated with some irritation that his decision was irrevocable. The caucus continued to support Burr and sent word to the President a third time that they would make no other recommendation; but the Secretary of State, to whom the message was given, refused to deliver it to the President.[24]

Another confirmation case in Washington's administration established the precedent that the Senate will consider not merely the qualifications but also the political views of the nominee. In 1795 Washington nominated John Rutledge of South Carolina to be Chief Justice of the Supreme Court to succeed John Jay, who had resigned to become governor of New York. Rutledge had been Associate Justice from 1789 to 1791, and had resigned to become chief justice of the supreme court of South Carolina. It was generally assumed that Washington would appoint one of the members of the Supreme Court as Chief Justice, and Samuel Chase, then chief justice of the general court of Maryland, was recommended to Washington by a close friend. Upon hearing of the election of Jay as governor of New York, Rutledge wrote a remarkable letter to Washington applying for the Supreme Court appointment, and

Washington immediately replied offering it to him.[25] Before receiving the appointment, Rutledge made a speech in Charleston vigorously criticizing the Jay Treaty with Great Britain, which the Senate had ratified on June 24, 1795. The treaty was the subject of a violent attack by anti-British groups and was equally strongly defended by the Federalists. When the news of Rutledge's speech was circulated, the Federalist press in the North strenuously opposed his appointment. It was rumored that Rutledge, who was advanced in years, was subject to mental derangement, and that the speech could have been made only by a person suffering from mental disorder.

Rutledge was given a recess appointment and served as Chief Justice during the recess of Congress, leaving Philadelphia to conduct circuit court. Washington sent the nomination to the Senate when it convened, but the Federalists were able to reject it by a vote of 14 to 10. Jefferson wrote to William B. Giles: "The rejection of Mr. Rutledge by the Senate is a bold thing, because they cannot pretend any objection to him but his disapprobation of the treaty. It is, of course, a declaration that they will receive none but Tories hereafter into any Department of the Government."[26]

Although the rejection of Rutledge is frequently explained on the ground of mental disorder, this was strongly denied by his friends. His rejection was due to his opposition to the Jay Treaty, which Charles Warren states had become a "touchstone of Federalism." The Senate thus established a precedent of inquiring into the political views and ideas of persons nominated for public office and of rejecting a nominee whose views do not correspond to those of the majority of the Senate.

John Adams' Difficulties over Appointments

John Adams continued the policy of appointing only qualified persons, but during his term political conformity became increasingly a test for appointments, and qualification standards were lowered. A decided trend in this direction had begun in Washington's second term. Although Washington had held that he would appoint only persons who supported the policies of the government to offices of *consequence,* Adams extended this policy to subordinate offices as well.[27] On one occasion he declared that "Washington appointed a multitude of Democrats and Jacobins of deepest dye. I have been more cautious in this respect."[28] However, he vigorously denied that he had ever adopted a rule that would bar appointment or promotion to any man because of his political creed, and maintained that in considering appointments he took into account political principles and discretion along with other qualifications. To Wolcott, Secretary of the Treasury, Adams wrote, "There is danger of proscribing, under imputations of democracy, some of the ablest, most influential, and best characters in the Union."[29] The presidential election campaign of 1796 was such a bitter partisan struggle that in parts of the country

Federalists and Republicans shunned one another on the streets, and in some places there were separate taverns and saloons for each party's followers.[30] Under this circumstance, it was not to be expected that the victorious party would appoint members of the opposite party to federal office.

Adams and his Cabinet heads continued the practice of consulting the state delegations in Congress concerning appointments in their states. During Adams' administration, however, the recommendations of members of Congress concerning appointments were no longer regarded as simply recommendations which could be accepted or rejected and could be treated in the same way as other recommendations from leading citizens. Evidence indicates that by this time it was customary to follow the recommendations from members of Congress, and thus virtually to permit congressmen to nominate federal officers within their states. When one Benjamin Adams applied for the appointment of his nephew, President Adams replied that if he appointed the nephew without "the previous recommendations from the senators and representatives from your state, the Senate would probably negative him."[31]

The Senate practice of pressing candidates on the President was strongly condemned by Senator George Cabot of Massachusetts. In a letter to Timothy Pickering in 1799, after he had left the Senate, Cabot wrote:

...the power of the Senate was in no sense *initiative or even active,* but *negative* and *censorial,* and was never to be exercised but in cases where the *persons* proposed for office were *unfit.* I have always rejected the idea of non-concurrence with a nomination merely because the nominee was less suitable for the office than thousands of others: he must be positively *unfit* for the office, and the public duty not likely to be performed by him, to justify in my mind the non-concurrence. It has always appeared to me that a departure from this principle would soon wrest from the President altogether the essence of the nominating power, *which is the power of selecting officers;* and I am fully persuaded that the disposal of offices is of all things the most dangerous to a *body* of men. The motives to provide for the friends of each other, and to feed their dependents, are so powerful, that they will always be yielded to by men who do not stand *individually* responsible to public opinion. I am persuaded that any body of men as numerous as the Senate, possessing such a power, however pure they may have been originally, will be corrupted by it, and will corrupt others.[32]

The number of civil appointments available to Adams was relatively few. Practically all federal officers enjoyed indefinite terms, and Adams made few removals.[33] Office seeking was conspicuous from the very beginning of the government, but the pressure was still light in comparison with that to which later Presidents, particularly Jefferson and Jackson, were subjected. It should be noted also that Adams did not use the power of patronage to build up a following of his own. His original Cabinet included three holdover members from Washington's administration, who earlier had formed the practice of consulting Hamilton about important matters, a practice which they continued under Adams and which eventually led to their dismissal. It was extraordinary that Hamilton, a private citizen, was more influential than the President in the distribution of offices. Years later, in 1809, Adams described his predicament in a series of letters to the Boston *Patriot:*

But I soon found myself shackled. The heads of departments were exclusive patriots. I could not name a man who was not devoted to Hamilton, without kindling a fire. The Senate was now decidedly federal. During President Washington's whole administration of eight years, his authority in the Senate was extremely weak.... I soon found that if I had not the previous consent of the heads of departments, and the approbation of Mr. Hamilton, I run the utmost risk of a dead negative in the Senate.[34]

Because of the threat of war with Great Britain in 1798 and 1799, the Provisional Army was brought up to strength, Washington was recalled as Commander in Chief, and many commissions were issued by the President. The appointment of officers was apparently made chiefly on partisan considerations, and members of Congress secured appointments for their supporters. In a letter to the Secretary of War in October, 1798, Washington complained about this pressure and the appointment of persons for "electioneering purposes."* The following March he wrote an even stronger letter, indignantly pointing out that the careful screening which he and two major generals had done had been overriden by congressional influence.

The two Major Generals and myself were called to Philadelphia in Nov. last, and there detained five weeks very inconveniently to all of us at an inclement season, in wading through volumes of applications and recommendations to Military Appointments; and I will venture to say that it was executed with as much assiduity and under as little influence of favor and prejudice, as a work of that sort (from the materials laid before us) ever was accomplished: And what has followed? Why a Member of Congress who had a friend to serve or a prejudice to endulge, could set them at naught.[35]

In 1799 Adams sent to the Senate the nomination of William Vans Murray as minister to France to negotiate a treaty. The nomination was opposed by the Federalists, who felt that no minister should be appointed until France made overtures to this country. A committee of five, headed by Sedgwick, which considered the nomination, decided to call on the President to remonstrate against the appointment. Adams at first refused to meet with the committee, insisting that it was contrary to the Constitution for a committee of the Senate to confer with the President about a nomination. He finally agreed to do so, provided the meeting was regarded as unofficial and would not constitute a precedent. Sedgwick later admitted that the proceeding was "an infraction

---

* See quotation at the beginning of this chapter.

of correct principles." In the strained meeting which followed, Adams refused to withdraw the nomination, insisting that the function of making nominations was granted exclusively to the President. He stated to the committee, however, that if the Senate rejected Murray, he would then nominate a commission of three. Sedgwick and his colleagues reported to the party caucus in the Senate the reception they had received, and it was decided to reject the nomination. In the meantime, however, Hamilton wrote to Sedgwick advising the appointment of a commission of three, and stating that the "mode must be accommodated with the President."[36] Without waiting for Murray to be rejected, Adams submitted the additional names of Chief Justice Oliver Ellsworth and Patrick Henry. All three nominations were confirmed without opposition, but since Henry was too old to serve, Governor Davis of North Carolina was named in his place.

Jefferson's Nominations

Thomas Jefferson, the accepted leader of his party, had relatively little difficulty in securing the confirmation of his nominees, though at the outset of his first term the Senate was still in the hands of the Federalists. Albert Gallatin, his choice for Secretary of the Treasury, refused to accept the appointment until it had been confirmed. Gallatin had incurred the particular opposition of the Federalists because of his criticism of the policies of Hamilton, and had been continually a thorn in the flesh of Hamilton's successors in the Treasury. Gallatin had grave doubts that his appointment would be confirmed, and Jefferson consented to hold it up until the Senate had acted on the appointments to other positions in the Cabinet. But all were confirmed. Gallatin arrived in Washington in May, 1801, and Jefferson's Cabinet was complete.[37]

Members of Congress continued to be the principal purveyors of information concerning appointments; but Jefferson, like Washington, sought and received information from other sources as well. Successful candidates for federal offices situated in the several states usually had the backing of the delegation of the state in Congress. The New York state delegation entered into an arrangement for the proposal of a slate of candidates, which Burr submitted to the President, and the slate was accepted, though with a few changes.[38]

At the end of Jefferson's second term, when his popularity and influence had declined, his last nomination—that of his close friend William Short, to be minister to Russia—was unanimously rejected by the Senate, much to Jefferson's mortification. At the request of Emperor Alexander I of Russia, Jefferson had agreed to an exchange of ministers and had dispatched Short to St. Petersburg. The rejection apparently was due to the prevailing opposition in the Senate to the establishment of diplomatic posts on a continuing basis at the courts of other countries, rather than to any personal objection to Short. Knowing that the nomination would face opposition, Jefferson delayed sending in the name of Short until the end of the session, hoping for a more favorable turn in his relations with the Senate.[39]

In 1804 John Quincy Adams, then serving in the Senate, wrote to his father that the "subject of appointments in the Senate has undergone a great revolution since you presided here." He criticized the partisan manner in which the Senate passed upon nominations, the failure to inquire into the qualifications of nominees, and the practice of members to eulogize nominees from their own states, regardless of the nominees' qualifications.[40]

Jefferson's ideas concerning the respective roles of the President and the Senate in appointments were strikingly similar to those of Hamilton and Adams. Writing to Gallatin, his Secretary of the Treasury, in 1803, Jefferson warned him to be very careful about showing letters of recommendation "even to our friends":

Recommendations when honestly written should detail the bad as well as the good qualities of the person recommended. That gentlemen may do freely if they know their letter is to be confined to the president or the head of a department. But if communicated further it may bring on them troublesome quarrels. In Gl. Washington's time he resisted every effort to bring forth his recommendations.[41]

This advice indicates that Jefferson's department heads were accustomed to obtaining recommendations for appointments from sources other than members of Congress, and that they placed considerable reliance upon such advice. Jefferson, in a letter to Madison, stated his conception of the purpose and the scope of the review of nominations by the Senate:

I have always considered the controul of the Senate as meant to prevent any bias or favoritism in the President toward his own relations, his own religion, toward particular states, etc., and perhaps to keep very obnoxious persons out of office of the first grade. But in all subordinate cases I have ever thought that the selection made by the President ought to inspire a general confidence that it has been made on due inquiry and investigations of the character, and that the Senate should interpose their negative only in those particular cases where something happens to be within their knowledge, against the character of the person and unfitting him for the appointment.[42]

Several years after Jefferson had left the White House he wrote to Madison concerning some criticisms of postmaster appointments, which then were made by the Postmaster General and hence were not subject to senatorial confirmation: "The true remedy for putting those appointments in a wholesome state would be a law vesting them in the President, but without intervention of the Senate. That intervention would make the matter worse. Every senator would expect to dispose of all post offices in his vicinage or perhaps the state."[43]

Senate Dictation of Madison's Appointments

If Jefferson was relatively free of difficulties with the Senate in securing the confirmation of his appointments, James Madison was in trouble from the start of his administration, and his leadership was greatly weakened by the dictation he had to submit to from the Senate. He desired to appoint Albert Gallatin, the strongest member of Jefferson's Cabinet, as his Secretary of State, elevating him from the post of Secretary of the Treasury. Gallatin had incurred the bitter enmity of two members of the Senate—Michael Leib of Pennsylvania and Warren Giles of Virginia—who actively opposed his confirmation. They were able to enlist the support of a third senator, Samuel Smith of Maryland, whose brother, Robert Smith, was Secretary of the Navy, and the three warned Madison that the appointment of Gallatin could not be confirmed. This trio schemed to have Robert Smith appointed as Secretary of State. As a compromise, it was proposed that Smith should be appointed Secretary of the Treasury, which post Gallatin would vacate to become Secretary of State. Madison acquiesced in this arrangement, and Senator Smith was agreeable to it, but Gallatin, hearing of it, "dryly remarked that he could not undertake to carry both departments at once, and requested Mr. Madison to leave him where he was."[44]

Madison finally capitulated and nominated Robert Smith as Secretary of State, though he had little confidence in his ability, leaving Gallatin in the Treasury. John Quincy Adams later wrote that the result was "to place in the Department of State, at a most critical period of foreign affairs, and against the will of the President, a person incompetent, to the exclusion of a man eminently qualified," and even stated that the War of 1812 probably would never have occurred had Gallatin been appointed. "A little cluster of senators," wrote Adams, "by caballing in secret session [had placed] a sleepy Palinurus at the helm in the fury of the tempest."[45]

Madison may have been correct in his assumption that this small clique of senators could block the confirmation of Gallatin, but he paid dearly for yielding to their dictation.[46] He did not get along with his Secretary of State and later dismissed him from the Cabinet. Madison's experience indicates the wisdom of the custom that has since developed of according the President a free hand in the selection of his Cabinet.

Because of the key role which Russia was likely to play in the European conflict, Madison determined to send a minister to St. Petersburg, and nominated John Quincy Adams on March 6, 1809, two days after his own inauguration. Although Adams was unusually well qualified and had served a term in the Senate, from Massachusetts, he was rejected by a vote of 17 to 15 on the following day. Adams had broken with the Federalists over the embargo issue and had not yet been accepted by the Republicans. Madison persisted, sending his name in a second time, and Adams was confirmed in June of that year.[47]

In 1813 Madison accepted an offer from the Emperor of Russia to act as mediator between England and the United States, and appointed Albert Gallatin and James Bayard as envoys extraordinary to join with John Quincy Adams at St. Petersburg to negotiate a treaty of peace. Gallatin was given leave of absence from his office as Secretary of the Treasury and left for Europe. After preliminary negotiations for the treaty had been successfully completed, Gallatin received word from America that the Senate had rejected his nomination. In spite of the fact that the Senate had previously confirmed the appointments of Jay and Ellsworth as members of similar missions while each was serving as Chief Justice, the enemies of Gallatin in the Senate were able to secure the adoption of a resolution that the duties of an envoy extraordinary were incompatible with those of the Secretary of the Treasury.[48] This eventuality was not unforeseen by Gallatin when he accepted the mission. After several months Madison appointed another in his place as Secretary of the Treasury and renominated Gallatin as a member of the mission. The nomination was promptly confirmed. His enemies in the Senate thus achieved their objective of removing him from the office of Secretary of the Treasury.

Gallatin's appointment as an envoy to negotiate a peace treaty with Great Britain precipitated a controversy between the President and the Senate over the propriety of the President's consulting with a committee of the Senate about a nomination. The special committee to which the nomination was referred called on the President, but he declined to discuss the nomination, on the ground that the committee had not been specifically authorized by the Senate to meet with the President. When this was reported to the Senate, the nomination of Jonathan Russell as minister to Sweden was pending. The Senate countered by adopting a resolution that it was inexpedient to send a minister to Sweden at that time, and appointed a committee with specific instructions to confer with the President concerning the nomination and to report thereon.[49] Two days later the Senate adopted the resolution mentioned above, declaring that the duties of the Secretary of the Treasury and those of an envoy to a foreign power were incompatible, and created a special committee to confer with the President concerning this nomination.

These actions brought to a head the issue of the propriety of the President's conferring officially with a committee of the Senate concerning pending nominations. Madison determined to put an end to the practice, which he regarded as an invasion of the President's exclusive function of nominating, and sent a special message to the Senate in which he said:

... the Executive and Senate in the cases of appointments to office, and of treaties, are to be considered as independent and co-ordinate with each other. If they agree, the appointments or treaties are made. If the Senate disagree, they fail. If the Senate wish information previous to their final decision, the practice ... has been, either to request the Executive to furnish it, or to refer the subject to a committee of their body, to communicate, either formally or informally, with the head of the proper department. The appointment of a committee of the Senate to confer immediately with the Executive himself, appears to lose sight of the co-ordinate relation between the Executive and the Senate, which the constitution has established, and which ought therefore to be maintained.[50]

Madison argued that even as it would be improper for one house of Congress to appoint a committee to confer with the entire body of the other house, similarly it would be improper for the President to confer with a committee of either house; but he went on to offer to supply cheerfully information in his possession when this was consistent with the Constitution and established practice.

In spite of this message, the special committee appointed to confer with the President called on him; but Madison gave them a chilly reception and declined to discuss the nomination of Gallatin. Senator Rufus King, a member of the committee, wrote a long tract defending the Senate, stating that Washington had not thought it beneath his dignity to meet with a committee of the Senate, and that Presidents always met with a joint committee of the two houses at the beginning and end of each session. He declared that the use of committees was the most feasible method whereby the President could consult and advise with the Senate, for the Senate now had so many members that he could not confer with the entire body.[51] Senator Henry Cabot Lodge, however, later expressed approval of the position taken by Madison.[52]

Another appointment of Madison's rejected by the Senate was that of Alexander Wollcott, a prominent Republican leader of Connecticut, to be a member of the Supreme Court. Upon the death of Justice Cushing, Madison first selected Levi Lincoln of Massachusetts, who had been Attorney General under Jefferson. When Lincoln declined on the grounds of age and defective eyesight, Madison surprised the country by appointing Wollcott, who had been a collector of customs in Connecticut for many years. Because of his vigorous enforcement of the embargo acts, Wollcott had become unpopular with the Federalists, and his appointment was violently opposed by the press on the ground that he lacked the requisite legal ability and experience. Lincoln wrote to Madison expressing his indignation at the attack upon Wollcott and praising him as a man of "larger mind, greater perception, and discriminating powers"; concerning his legal qualifications, however, he could only say that with industrious application to professional studies Wollcott would soon equal his colleagues on the bench. Wollcott was rejected by a vote of 9 to 24.[53]

Growth of the Spoils System

In the period 1800 to 1828, patronage appointments, which had become customary in New York, Massachusetts, Pennsylvania, and other states, became a common practice in the federal government. More and more, the members of the Senate insisted upon the control of federal appointments within their own states. This is well illustrated by the correspondence between Senator Ninian Edwards of Illinois and President Monroe and between Edwards and members of Monroe's Cabinet. In December, 1820, Edwards wrote to the President opposing the appointment of a candidate of the other Illinois senator and insisting that he (Edwards) be given his share of the federal patronage within the state.[54] Secretary of the Treasury Crawford agreed to Edwards' demand for an equal division of appointments, but after consulting President Monroe, Crawford wrote to the senator that the President could not agree, for it would involve "a transfer of the right of nomination, vested by the Constitution in the President, to the Senators of the State." President Monroe showed the correspondence to William Wirt, his Attorney General, a lifelong friend and former teacher of Senator Edwards, and asked him to talk to Edwards about the matter. Wirt, being unable to see the senator before leaving town, wrote him a letter on January 15, 1821, stating:

He [Monroe] thought you did not view the subject of nominations in the correct light. . . . He thinks it wrong that a President of the United States should permit himself to be influenced by considerations of local parties in a State, and that he should nominate with reference to the local effect on the respective Senators in their States. For my own part, I should consider it a species of bribery—it would be paying them for their support, not indeed in money, but in local power and influence.[55]

The Four Years Law

In 1820, the Four Years Act, which limited the terms of collectors of customs, district attorneys, and many other federal officers to four years, was passed. This law permitted the administration to make new appointments upon the expiration of terms of office without the necessity of removing the incumbents. The bill, which was attributed to Secretary of the Treasury Crawford, was advocated on the ground that it would provide a regular accounting by officers entrusted with the custody of government funds. There had been several cases involving shortages in accounts of officers upon their death or retirement. Concerning the act, John Quincy Adams'wrote:

The Senate was conciliated by the permanent increase of their power, which was the principal ultimate effect of the Act, and every Senator was flattered by the power conferred upon him of multiplying chances to provide for his friends and dependents. . . . The result of the Act has been to increase the power of patronage exercised by the President, and still more that of the Senate and of every individual Senator.[56]

Adams charged that the real objective of the act was to promote the candidacy of Crawford for President, a charge later discounted by Professor Fish.[57] Concerning the act, Jefferson wrote:

This is a sample of the effects we may expect from the late mischievous law vacating every four years nearly all the executive offices of the government. It saps the constitutional and salutary functions of the President, and introduces a principle of intrigue and corruption, which will soon leaven the mass, not only of Senators but of citizens. It is more baneful than the attempt which failed in the beginning of the government to make all officers irremovable, but with the consent of the Senate. This places, every four years, all appointments under their power and obliges them to act on every nomination. It will keep in constant excitement all the hungry cormorants for office, render them, as well as those in place, sycophants to their senators, engage these in eternal intrigue to turn one out and put in another, in cabals to swap work, and make of them what all executive directories become, sinks of corruption and faction.[58]

Monroe and John Quincy Adams refused to utilize the law as a means of introducing the principle of rotation in office, though urged to do so by members of the Senate and others. The Senate, anxious for new appointments, refused to act on a number of reappointments made by President Monroe at the end of his term, ostensibly on the ground that their terms had not yet expired; but John Quincy Adams renominated all of them and later declared:

Efforts have been made by some of the senators to obtain different nominations, and to introduce a principle of change or rotation in office at the expiration of these commissions, which would make the government a perpetual and unintermitting scramble for office. ... A more pernicious expedient could scarcely have been devised. ... I determined to renominate every person against whom there was no complaint which would have warranted his removal.[59]

Concerning the appointments of John Quincy Adams, Carl Russell Fish has written that no President ever received greater blame by his contemporaries or greater praise by posterity. It was not until the start of Jackson's administration in 1829 that the pernicious effects of the Four Years Act began to be felt.

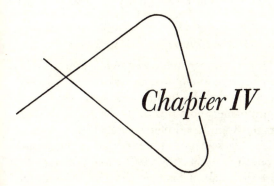

Chapter IV

BATTLES BETWEEN
ANDREW JACKSON AND THE
SENATE OVER APPOINTMENTS

I cannot consent to place before the Senate the name of anyone who is not prepared with firmness and honesty to discharge the duties of a public director in the manner they were fulfilled by those whom the Senate has refused to confirm. If for perform- ing a duty lawfully required of them by the Executive, they are to be punished by the subsequent rejection of the Senate, it would not only be useless but cruel to place men of character and honor in that situation, even if such men could be found to accept it. Message of Andrew Jackson to the Senate renominating the directors of the United States Bank, 1834.[1]

No OTHER PRESIDENT ever had as many contests with the Senate over appointments as Andrew Jackson, a former member of the Senate, and no other President ever came off so well. Jackson threw down the gauntlet to the Senate when ten nominations were rejected in the first session of his administration, and eventually all but four were confirmed. Within a year after the Senate had rejected one of his strongest supporters, Isaac Hill, editor of the *New Hampshire Patriot,* Jackson appointed Senator Woodbury from that state to his Cabinet so that the New Hampshire legislature could elect Hill to the Senate. The man whom the Senate rejected for a minor post in the Treasury soon came to serve as a member of that body. No doubt Jackson also found great satisfaction in the triumph accorded Van Buren on his return to this country after his rejection by the Senate as minister to Great Britain, and in his election, within a few months, as Vice-President, to preside over the

[53

Senate. Roger Taney, twice rejected by the Senate, was subsequently confirmed as Chief Justice of the Supreme Court and ranks among the greatest Chief Justices in the history of the country.

Rejection of the Editors

Before Congress convened in December, 1829, there was a great outcry in the Whig press against the policy of "proscription" which Jackson had adopted at the insistence of his supporters and the proadministration press. According to Marquis James, 121 of the 319 names submitted to the Senate at the first session of Jackson's administration were to fill offices vacated by removals.[2] It is significant that few of Jackson's nominations were rejected by the Senate. "Were it not for the outdoor popularity of the President," wrote Webster, ". . . we would have negatived more than half of his nominations."[3] Among the first nominations submitted by the President were the names of a number of editors who had supported him during the campaign, several of whom had urged Jackson to "kick out the damned rascals" and put in his friends. Included in the group were Major Henry Lee, brother of Robert E. Lee, James B. Gardner, Moses Dawson, Mordecai M. Noah, Amos Kendall, and Isaac Hill. The opposition to the "batch of editors" appears to have been led by Tyler, with the active support of Tazewell of Virginia, who was smarting under his failure to be appointed Secretary of State.[4] Several of the editors were among Jackson's closest advisers. Their appointments, which were regarded as a direct reward for services, were particularly offensive to the Senate. The appointment of Major Henry Lee as consul general to Algiers was rejected by a unanimous vote, on the charge that his morals were not impeccable, but the real reason was his active assistance to Jackson in the campaign. Isaac Hill was rejected ostensibly because his publishing firm had "defamed" Mrs. John Quincy Adams by publishing a book in which she was described as an English woman with little sympathy for American institutions. "The real reason for his rejection," says Bowers, "was that he had incurred the bitter enmity of the opposition by his telling paragraphs during the campaign."[5] A year later, when the President dissolved his Cabinet over the celebrated Eaton affair, he offered the post of Secretary of the Navy to Senator Levi Woodbury of New Hampshire, and thus paved the way for the election of Hill to the Senate.

Mordecai Noah, editor of the New York *National Advocate,* a Jew who had had a notable public career in addition to being an author and editor, was rejected, according to Bowers, "with much hilarity." Amos Kendall, a former Clay supporter and editor of the *Kentucky Argus,* the ablest of the group of editors, was offensive both to Clay and to Adams' supporters because of his support of Jackson. Appointed during a recess of the Senate as fourth auditor of the Treasury, Kendall had already demonstrated his abilities as an administrator.[7] The vote on his confirmation was a tie, and Vice-President Calhoun cast the deciding vote in his favor. Jackson resubmitted the name of Mordecai Noah, and this appointment also was confirmed by the vote of Calhoun.

The Rejection of Martin Van Buren

Early in 1831, after the Eaton affair had torn the Cabinet hopelessly apart, Martin Van Buren devised a plan to enable the President to reorganize his Cabinet.[8] The plan, which was reluctantly agreed to by Jackson, called for Van Buren to resign and his resignation to be followed by that of Major Eaton; this would pave the way for the President to call for the resignation of three members of his Cabinet who had been appointed on the recommendation of Calhoun. This being accomplished, Jackson proceeded to select a Cabinet that even the Whigs conceded was able. Van Buren's act was rewarded by a recess appointment to the Court of St. James's, a post which had fallen vacant.

Before the Senate met in December, 1831, Messrs. Calhoun, Clay, and Webster, all active candidates for the presidency, who regarded Van Buren as their most likely opponent, had made their plans for his rejection by the Senate. Calhoun and his followers were bitterly opposed to Van Buren, to whom they attributed the breach that had occurred between Calhoun and Jackson. Clay, an announced candidate for the presidency, was looking for an issue on which to oppose Jackson. Although the President submitted Van Buren's nomination when Congress convened in December, the debate was postponed until January 24 and 25 to afford the opponents of Van Buren time to lay their plans and prepare speeches which they believed would end his political career. When the vote came, after a long debate, a tie was contrived in order to give Calhoun the satisfaction of casting the deciding vote, though the opposition had several votes to spare. "It will kill him, sir, kill him dead. He will never kick, sir, never kick," gloated Calhoun after casting his vote; but within a few months Van Buren returned home a martyr in triumph and was promptly nominated and elected Vice-President, to preside over the body that had so recently rejected him.[9]

The debate, as was customary in confirmation cases, took place in closed executive session. When it was over, the opponents of Van Buren pushed through a motion to publish the debate, mistakenly believing that the speeches of Webster, Clay, and the others would ruin his political career. Van Buren was violently attacked for the instructions which as Secretary of State he had given to McLane, our minister to England, concerning negotiations for the reopening of trade with the British West Indies. The previous administration had attempted unsuccessfully to conclude a treaty permitting the resumption of trade between the United States and these British possessions, but Great Britain had rejected the demand that goods from the United States be admitted on the same terms as those from British colonies in this hemisphere.

The letter of instructions directed McLane to inform the British that there had been a change in administration and that this country was prepared to negotiate the resumption of trade relations with the British West Indies on the same terms extended to other countries. Although the letter had been submitted to the Senate with the treaty and had at the time attracted no unfavorable comment, it was now used as the pretext for a violent attack on Van Buren by his opponents. "I am against him, because he has humbled us in the eyes of foreign nations," declared Holmes of Maine. "He has surrendered the rights of this country to Great Britain, to sustain his party. It is the first time this country was ever thus disgraced; and I would it should be the last."[10] Chambers of Maryland denounced the instructions to McLane, saying: "To an individual who has thus outraged the character properly belonging to a great and high-minded nation of freemen, who has prostrated its dignity, and brought disgrace and dishonour upon its diplomatic reputation, I can never advise the President to confide the preservation of its respect abroad." Daniel Webster with his usual eloquence denounced the instructions as unpatriotic, unworthy, and un-American.

The pervading topic [said Webster], through the whole, is not American rights, not American interests, not American defense, but denunciation of past pretensions of our own country, reflections on the past Administration, and exultation, and a loud claim of merit, for the Administration now in power. Sir, I would forgive mistakes; I would pardon the want of information; I would pardon almost anything, where I saw true patriotism and sound American feeling: but I cannot forgive the sacrifice of this feeling to mere Party.[11]

Henry Clay declared that there had been no need for a recess appointment and criticized the administration for not waiting to secure Senate approval before sending a minister to London. He criticized the McLane instructions as being supinely yielding to the British, saying:

On our side, according to Mr. Van Buren, all was wrong, on the British side all was right. We brought forward nothing but claims and pretensions; the British Government asserted on the other hand a clear and incontestible right.... Sir, was this becoming language from one independent nation to another? Was it proper in the mouth of an American minister? Was it in conformity with the high, unsullied, and dignified character of our previous diplomacy? Was it not, on the contrary, the language of an humble vassal to a proud and haughty lord? Was it not prostrating and degrading the American Eagle before the British Lion?[12]

Clay also charged Van Buren with the introduction of proscription in the federal government. "It is a detestable system," said Clay, "drawn from the worst periods of the Roman republic, and if it were to be perpetuated—if the offices, honors, and dignities of the people were to be put up in a scramble, and to be decided by the results of every presidential election—our government and institutions, becoming intolerable, would finally end in despotism as inexorable as that at Constantinople." Marcy of New York pointed out that the spoils system had existed long before Van Buren came to public office. Besides, said Marcy, Clay himself had engaged in what he now denounced when practiced by others, and predicted that "if he shall come into power, he will take care of his friends, and if he does, I shall not complain; nor shall I be in the least surprised if he imitates the example which he now so emphatically denounces."[13]

Senator Hayne based his opposition on the ground that Van Buren, bent on advancing himself at the expense of all who stood in his way, had been responsible for alienating Jackson from his "faithful and true friends" and for breaking up his Cabinet "so unfortunate for the President and so disreputable for the country." Van Buren, maintained Hayne, had used his office for personal advantage and his conduct had not been consistent with the dignity of his station.

During the debate, Thomas Hart Benton of Missouri, a supporter of the administration, sat silent. Later he recorded his impressions of the proceedings: "Oh politics, how much bamboozling is practiced in thy name!"[14] The rejection of Van Buren he regarded as the result of a plot by Calhoun, Clay, and Webster to destroy Van Buren's chances for the presidency. He considered the charges against Van Buren unfounded and was not impressed by the oratory of the opposition.[15] Benton foresaw that the rejection of Van Buren would make rather than break him, and told Gabriel Moore of Alabama, who sat next to him in the Senate chamber, "You have broken a minister and elected a Vice President.... The people would see nothing in it but a combination of rivals against a competitor and would pull them all down, and set him up." When the news of Van Buren's rejection was brought to the President during a dinner party, he sprang from his chair and exclaimed: "By the Eternal! I'll smash them!"[16]

In London, Van Buren was congratulated by Lord Auckland, who said to him, "In all my experience I have seldom known the career of a young man in your position crowned with marked success who had not been made, in the course of it, the subject of some such outrage."[17] In America, according to Marquis James, "Billy Carroll of Tennessee furnished tidings from the West where Van Buren had never been strong: 'Two men know him now to one that knew him sixty days ago.'"[18] Van Buren returned home in triumph and was nominated and elected Vice-President within a few months.

The Rejection of the Bank Directors

At the beginning of the 1833-34 session of Congress, Jackson nominated five persons, including four incumbents, to be the government representatives on the board of directors of the Bank of the United States.[19] At the direction of the President, the four incumbent members of the board had submitted a report to him in which they criticized the practices of the Bank and advised that the government deposits be withdrawn. They charged that Nicholas Biddle ran the Bank as he wished, the board exercising no real control, that Bank funds were being used to purchase support in Congress and the press, and that Biddle had denied them information about the operations of the Bank. The reappointment of the incumbents was strenuously opposed by the Bank and its followers. "They are unfit to be there," Biddle wrote Webster, who was retained by the Bank to look after its interests in the Senate, "unfit to associate with the other members."[20]

On the advice of Henry Clay, Biddle had attempted at the previous session to secure a renewal of the Bank charter well ahead of its expiration. Congress enacted the desired legislation but was unable to pass it over the veto of the President. When the nominations of the directors came before the Senate in 1833, Senator Kane moved to recommit them to the Finance Committee with instructions to inquire into the fitness of the nominees and the truth of their charges against the Bank. The motion was rejected by 27 to 20, the usual Bank versus anti-Bank vote. A second motion to recommit the nominations, limiting the investigation to the qualifications of the nominees, was defeated by the same majority. A separate vote was then taken on the nominees, and the four incumbents were rejected by a vote of 24 to 20.

Concerning their rejection, Benton wrote that there had been no complaint against the nominees except by the Bank, and that was "limited to their conduct in giving information of transactions in the bank to President Jackson at his written request. Their characters and fitness were above question.... It was evident then that they had been rejected for the report which they made to the President; and this brought up the question, whether it was right to punish them for that act."[21] When informed of their rejection by the Senate, Jackson promptly renominated all four and sent a message to the Senate sharply challenging its action. Pointing out that the nominations had been confirmed at the preceding session, he declared that the nominees were eminently qualified and that they had been rejected solely because of the two reports they had made to the President, both of which had been transmitted to the Senate.

The truth of the facts stated in these reports [wrote Jackson] is not, I presume, questioned by anyone. The high character and standing of the citizens by whom they were made prevent any doubt on the subject. Indeed, the statements have not been denied by the President of the Bank, and the other directors. On the contrary, they have insisted that they were authorized to use the money of the bank in the manner stated in the two reports, and have not denied the charges there made against the corporation are substantially true.[22]

Jackson closed his message by stating that he was unwilling to nominate to the position of Bank director any person who was not prepared to discharge the duties of the office in the manner in which they had been discharged by the directors whose renomination the Senate had rejected.*

The renominations were referred to the Committee on Finance, of which Tyler was chairman, and again it recommended against confirmation. The report of the committee criticized the President for resubmitting the names of persons who had been rejected, and questioned the constitutionality of this action. It also attacked the President for presuming to discuss the reasons of the Senate for its rejection of the nominees. It must be presumed, stated the report, that the Senate acts on its views of public policy. In the meantime the four rejected directors became busy on their own behalf and submitted a memorial to the Senate defending their action in reporting to the President, at his request, practices which they regarded as illegal or improper. "All of their representations," wrote Benton, "were in vain." The Senate again rejected the Bank directors, and maintained "the seal of secrecy inviolate" on the real reason for their rejection, which Benton declared was "the reporting of the misconduct of the bank."[23]

The Rejection of Roger B. Taney

On June 23, 1834, in the final week of the session of Congress, Jackson sent to the Senate the nomination of Roger B. Taney to be Secretary of the Treasury. On the following day Taney was rejected by a vote of 28 to 18—the first Cabinet appointment ever defeated by the Senate.[24] The rejection was not unexpected. Although Taney had been given a recess appointment nine months earlier, Jackson anticipated that the nomination would be rejected, and delayed sending it to the Senate until the last week of its session.†

Taney was rejected because of his withdrawal of federal funds from the Bank of the United States on the specific direction of the President. His predecessor, William J. Duane, had refused to carry out the President's instruction and had been dismissed. Jackson then appointed Taney, his Attorney General, as Secretary of the Treasury. The withdrawal of federal funds from the Bank a few months before its charter was due to expire aroused a storm of protest throughout the country, and it was the subject of a three months' debate in the Senate after Congress convened.

The rejection of Taney was foreshadowed by the earlier rejection of the nomination of Andrew Stevenson, Speaker of the House of Representatives, to be minister to London. As an administration man Stevenson was credited with being responsible for the defeat in the House of the resolution passed by the Senate condemning the withdrawal of federal funds from the Bank, and his nomination was strongly opposed by Bank senators. Biddle wrote to

---

* See quotation at the beginning of this chapter.

† The threat of rejection prevented Madison in 1809 from nominating Gallatin to be Secretary of State. See chap. iii, above.

Webster that Stevenson's defeat would be "the greatest moral and political lesson which the slaves of the Executive could receive."[25] The Bank supporters recognized that if Stevenson's appointment was confirmed it would be difficult to defeat Taney. Stevenson was accused of being subservient to Jackson in order to get the London post, which had been vacant since the rejection of Van Buren two years earlier. This was disputed by administration supporters, nevertheless he was rejected according to plan.

Roger Taney was appointed Attorney General by President Jackson in 1831 after the dissolution of his first Cabinet over the celebrated Eaton affair. Although a leading member of the Maryland bar and recently elected attorney general of Maryland, he was relatively unknown outside his own state. As Attorney General he became a strong opponent of the Bank when he observed its corruption of members of Congress and the press. In December, 1831, when the President conferred with the Cabinet about his message to Congress on the State of the Union, Taney took exception to the rather neutral statement concerning the Bank that Secretary of the Treasury McLane had inserted at the behest of Nicholas Biddle.[26] When it later became apparent that Congress would pass an act renewing the charter, Taney urged Jackson to veto the bill in unmistakable terms, and left a suggested draft of a veto message. When this policy was announced by the President to his Cabinet, Taney being absent, not a single member was in favor of an unequivocal veto.[27] After Amos Kendall had prepared a first draft of the veto message, Jackson sent for Taney, and Taney spent several days at the White House revising and rewriting the message, which was to become a notable campaign document in the presidential election of 1832. It reiterated the charges of misuse of funds and other abuses by the Bank, reviewed the legal and economic arguments against renewing the charter, and declared that the issue was between powerful wealth, represented by the Bank, and the common man.[28] Biddle called the message a "manifesto of anarchy" and, mistaking its effect, had thirty thousand copies printed and distributed in the belief that it would help the campaign of Clay.[29]

After his second inauguration, in March, 1833, Jackson called upon members of his Cabinet for advice in regard to the policy he should follow with respect to the Bank. He asked them whether they thought it would be better to withdraw federal deposits from the Bank; to renew the charter with modifications; to replace the old Bank by a new one; or to deposit federal funds in state banks. Only the replies of Taney and McLane were significant. Taney strongly opposed rechartering the Bank, or setting up a new one, and advocated withdrawing federal deposits and placing them in selected state institutions. McLane also opposed rechartering the Bank but strongly advised against withdrawal of federal deposits until a successor bank could be established. For several months the President was undecided. Van Buren, now Vice-President and heir apparent, cautioned against withdrawal. Taney urged withdrawal before Congress convened, believing that it would be impossible afterward and that the Bank, with federal deposits at its disposal, would be able to defeat the President in the forthcoming fight in Congress. Evidence had been uncovered of "loans" and retainers that Biddle had made to members of Congress, and of his use of Bank funds to buy the support of newspaper editors and others of influence. In the meantime McLane was elevated to the position of Secretary of State, replacing Livingston, who was appointed minister to France. William J. Duane, a Philadelphia lawyer and McLane's nominee, whose appointment had been decided upon before the issue of withdrawal of deposits arose, was appointed Secretary of the Treasury.

It soon became apparent that Duane, who strongly opposed the withdrawal of federal deposits, might refuse to remove them even on the direction of the President. Jackson discussed with Taney the possibility that, to carry out this policy, it would be necessary to appoint him Secretary of the Treasury. Taney questioned his own qualifications, but in September, 1833, wrote to the President, who was vacationing at Rip Raps, Virginia, strongly urging withdrawal and stating that he would accept the appointment as Secretary of the Treasury if that became necessary. Taney's letter powerfully appealed to the fighting instincts of Jackson and quickly brought him to a decision. Pointing out that a bitter fight would ensue if the federal deposits were withdrawn, Taney stated that no other President would ever have the courage to fight Nicholas Biddle and the Bank, or would have the ability to overthrow them. Taney warned the President that he might lose the fight, and stated that if he should now decide not to match forces with the Bank, he (Taney) would understand. Jackson cut short his vacation and returned to Washington at once to announce to his Cabinet his decision to discontinue federal deposits in the Bank by October 1. Duane refused to carry out the President's instructions and maintained that withdrawal of the deposits would be unconstitutional. Jackson advised him that the opinion of the Attorney General "being our legal adviser ... ought to govern the heads of departments as it did the President."[30] Duane continued his refusal and declined to resign, whereupon he was dismissed and Taney was appointed in his place.

With the assistance of Amos Kendall, Taney proceeded immediately to put Jackson's instructions into effect. No further federal deposits were placed in the Bank, and state banks were selected to receive them. Biddle struck back by calling in loans and curtailing credit throughout the country, thus hoping to coerce Congress into reversing the action of the President and rechartering the Bank. His actions brought on a widespread financial crisis, and loud protests were made to the President and Congress, but within a few months it became apparent that the panic was of Biddle's making. "Go see Nicholas Biddle," said Jackson to protesting delegations who urged him to restore the deposits in order to relieve the growing panic throughout the country. Biddle overplayed his hand, and prominent bankers threatened to expose the fact that he had brought on the panic. Within a few months he was forced to reverse his policy and again extend credit, and the panic quickly ended.

After Congress convened, a three months' debate took place in the Senate, and finally a resolution condemning the withdrawal of federal deposits from the Bank as illegal and calling for their restoration was adopted but failed to pass the House. The prospect for the passage of an act to recharter the Bank over the veto of the President was dim, but there was still hope. The rejection of Taney was regarded by Biddle and the friends of the Bank as essential in its fight for a new charter. Bank senators eagerly awaited his nomination, confident of its rejection; Jackson did not accommodate them, however, but waited until the end of the session to send it in. Without waiting for the nomination to be made, Congressmen in both houses made attacks on Taney. He was charged with being the pliant tool of the President, with defying the law and the resolutions adopted by Congress, and with bringing on the panic by his illegal act. His friends, however, came to his defense, pointing out that instead of being a "pliant tool," he had been the leading advocate of withdrawal before the President had made up his mind. The vote on the nomination was taken in a closed session, as was customary, apparently with little debate and with no formal charges. The vote followed the customary line-up on Bank issues. The two senators from Taney's own state of Maryland voted against confirmation, and at least four opposing senators voted against resolutions adopted by the legislatures of their states.[31] It was reported that six of the senators who voted against Taney indicated that they would be willing to vote for him for any other federal office. Jackson wrote to Edward Livingston, "Nicholas Biddle now rules the Senate, as a showman does his puppets."[32]

Taney returned to his home in Maryland, and dinners were given in his honor at Baltimore and at Frederick. He continued to advise the administration as a private citizen. When he undertook to resume his law practice in Baltimore he found that many of his old friends in banking circles had now turned against him. When a vacancy occurred on the Supreme Court in the following January (1835) in the circuit which included Maryland, President Jackson nominated Taney. At that time, members of the Court were assigned to conduct circuit court and customarily were appointed from one of the states included within the circuit.

A storm of protest against the nomination was raised by the Whigs, who regarded it as a reward to Taney for his "servility," and as an "effrontery" on the part of the President. "Their wrath," Charles Warren states, "was unbounded, their denunciations of the nominee were violent in the extreme, and they thrust aside all consideration of his pre-eminent professional qualifications, in their desire to punish him for his acts as an executive official."[33] His legal qualifications were attested to by the fact that Chief Justice Marshall favored confirmation of his nomination. A New York paper said: "Is it to be supposed that the same Senate who had deservedly rejected him will now approve his nomination as an expounder of the Constitution? The idea is ridiculous." Another paper said: "We hope that the senate will not only apply the veto to the pretensions of this man, but that it will pass a decided resolution to oppose the elevation of any man who is not perfectly sound in regard to the fundamental principles of the Constitution as expounded by Daniel Webster."[34]

It was evident that the vote on Taney would be close. His opponents brought forward a plan for redistricting the judicial circuits which would have placed Maryland in the circuit of a sitting justice and thus would have made Taney ineligible. This plan, which was favored by Webster, passed the Senate but was defeated in the House, where Jackson's friends argued that the bill was intended "to destroy one of the worthy citizens of Maryland."[35]

Taney's nomination was taken up by the Senate on the last day of its session, after the clock had been stopped at midnight, on a motion made by Webster for indefinite postponement. Several senators who had promised to support the appointment voted for the motion, and it carried by 24 to 21. President Jackson, who was in the President's room at the Capitol to receive last-minute messages, on hearing the news "replied that it was past twelve o'clock and he would receive no more messages from the damned scoundrels."[36]

In December of the same year (1835) there were two vacancies on the Supreme Court, those of Chief Justice and an Associate Justice. Jackson sent in the nomination of Taney to take the place of Chief Justice Marshall, who had died that year, and that of Philip P. Barbour to be Associate Justice. Both nominations were opposed by the Whigs, particularly that of Taney. A New York paper declared that he is "unworthy of public confidence, a supple, cringing tool of power," and a leading Whig paper exclaimed that the nomination of Taney as the "Judicial High Priest of the Nation" after his rejection by the Senate "for a trust far less critical and important on account of his partisan servility" was an insult to the Senate and "the most dangerous blow which has been given our Constitution and law.... If Mr. Taney be now confirmed, all will be lost." Webster wrote about the appointment: "Judge Story thinks the Supreme Court is *gone,* and I think so too."[37] The resignation of Tyler of Virginia and the election in his place of a Jackson man placed the Democrats in control of the Senate, and the nomination of Taney was confirmed on March 15, 1836, by a vote of 29 to 15. Calhoun, Clay, and Webster held out to the last against Taney. "There is hardly an opprobrious epithet which, as he told me himself afterwards, Clay failed to use against the nomination," said Reverdy Johnson in a speech in Congress in 1864 after the death of Taney.[38] Four or five years later, Clay, according to Reverdy Johnson's account, called upon Chief Justice Taney to tell him that after following closely his record on the Court, he was "satisfied now that no man in the United States could have been selected, more abundantly able to wear the ermine which Chief Justice Marshall honored."

On receiving the news of his confirmation as Chief Justice in March, 1835, Taney, who had twice been rejected by the Senate, wrote to Jackson expressing his deep gratitude.

There are indeed circumstances with my appointment which render it even more gratifying than it would have been in ordinary times. In the first place, I owe this honor to you, to whom I had rather owe it than any other man in the world, and I esteem it higher because it is a token of your confidence in me. In the second place, I have been confirmed by the strength of my own friends, and go into office not by the leave, but in spite of the opposition of the men who have so long and so persever-ingly sought to destroy me, and I am glad to feel that I do not owe my confirmation to any forebearance on their part."[39]

The outcome of his fight with the Senate over appointments was entirely to Jackson's satisfaction. The nomination of Barbour to the Supreme Court was also confirmed, as was the nomination of Amos Kendall to be Postmaster General, which had been held up for more than a year. Two days before his second term came to an end in 1837, Jackson wrote to a friend that he was looking forward with deep satisfaction to "the glorious scene of Mr. Van Buren, once rejected by the Senate, sworn into office by Chief Justice Taney, who also [had been] rejected by the factious Senate."[40]

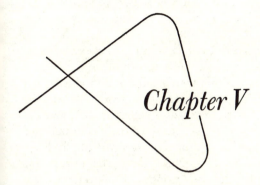

Chapter V

EFFORTS OF THE SENATE
TO CONTROL APPOINTMENTS

My office was crowded up to the hour of twelve o'clock with visitors, and I was greatly annoyed by the importunities of office-seekers. It is most disgusting to be compelled to spend hour after hour almost every day in hearing the applications for office made by loafers who congregate in Washington, and by members of Congress in their behalf, and yet I am compelled to submit to it or offend or insult the applicants and their friends. The people of the United States have no idea of the extent to which the President's time, which ought to be devoted to more important matters, is occupied by the voracious and often unprincipled persons who seek office. President Polk, April 6, 1846.[1]

When I came into public life in 1869, the Senate claimed almost entire control of the Executive function of appointment to office. Every Senator, with hardly an exception, seemed to fancy that the national officers in his State were to be a band of political henchmen devoted to his personal fortunes. What was called "the courtesy of the Senate" was depended upon to enable a Senator to dictate to the executive all appointments and removals in his territory. Senator George F. Hoar.[2]

DURING the forty years from the beginning of Van Buren's term in 1837 until the end of Grant's administration in 1877 the spoils system was at its height. All Presidents in this period spent much of their time interviewing office seekers and members of Congress soliciting appointments for their followers. Congressional patronage, however, was not limited to offices that were subject to senatorial confirmation; fourth-class postmasters, for example, whose nominations did not require confirmation were appointed on the recommendation of members of Congress. The custom of permitting senators of the same party as the President to select the persons to be appointed to federal offices in their states had become firmly established, enforced by the custom of the Senate to reject a nominee to such an office if any member objected to his appointment.

During this period the Senate reached out for control over executive appointments to a degree unequaled either before or since. President Tyler found himself early in his term without any substantial following in either party in the Senate, and many of his nominations, including four to his Cabinet, were rejected because senators of both parties wished to embarrass him and discredit his administration. Practically all Presidents in the period encountered difficulties in securing Senate approval of their nominations, particularly Tyler, Polk, Fillmore, Johnson, and Grant. Lincoln followed the practice of accepting the lists of nominees prepared by the state delegations in Congress, yet maintained sufficient control to utilize the patronage as a means of holding the Republican party together to carry out his program.[3]

Under Johnson's administration the Senate virtually took over the function of making executive appointments: it passed a law denying the President the removal power, and approved only those nominations to which its members had previously agreed. Grant weakly gave way to the patronage demands of members of the Senate, but even he had a number of contests over nominations and twice withdrew his nominations for Chief Justice of the Supreme Court. At the end of his term the Senate was in virtual control of executive appointments, but the excesses of the spoils system led to strong criticisms of congressional patronage and a widespread demand for civil service reform.

The Rejection of Tyler's Nominations

The administration of President Tyler was notable for the number of presidential nominations rejected by the Senate. In the last two years of Tyler's term the Senate rejected four nominations to his Cabinet,[4] four nominations to the Supreme Court,[5] and nominations of persons as ministers to France and Brazil, as well as nominations to many minor posts. Only one nomination to the Cabinet had been rejected before that time,* and with the single exception of the rejection of Henry Stanbery as Attorney General in 1867 (in the bitter aftermath of the impeachment proceedings against President Johnson), no other nomination to the Cabinet was again rejected until 1925—eighty years later.

Soon after his elevation to the Presidency on the death of William Henry Harrison, Tyler broke with the Whig leaders in Congress and found himself a President without a party. Repudiated by the Whigs, he had not been accepted back by the Democratic party, which he had left to accept the Whig

---

* Madison was prevented from nominating Gallatin as Secretary of State in 1809 because of the opposition of three members of the Senate. See chap. iii, above.

nomination for Vice-President. Toward the end of his term he attempted to use the appointing power to build up a following in the ranks of the Democratic party, hoping to secure its nomination for President in 1844, and he even put out feelers to Van Buren, whom he regarded as his leading opponent, to ascertain if he would accept a nomination to the Supreme Court; but all to no avail.[6] Since members of both parties were anxious to embarrass him, the Senate rejected his nominees without giving much attention to their qualifications. As the end of Tyler's term approached, the Whigs blocked his nominations to the Supreme Court in the expectation that the vacancies would be filled by Clay, their candidate for President in 1844. After Polk was elected, Warren states, "there was no longer the slightest excuse for a failure to confirm Tyler's appointees,"[7] but his nominations continued to lie on the table.

On March 3, 1843, the last day of the session, the Senate, by a vote of 27 to 19, rejected the nomination of Caleb Cushing as Secretary of the Treasury to replace Walter Forward, a Whig, who had resigned. President Tyler, who, according to custom, was in a room adjoining the Senate chamber to receive last-minute messages from Congress, promptly sent a message to the Senate renominating Cushing. Tyler, it will be recalled, had been the chairman of the special committee of the Senate which criticized Jackson for his renomination of the Bank directors.* The Senate promptly rejected Cushing the second time, by a vote of 29 to 9. When Tyler learned of this action he angrily wrote out a message nominating him for the third time, omitting his first name: "I nominate Cushing as Secretary of the Treasury, in the place of Forward, resigned." A third time the Senate rejected him, with only two members voting in favor of the confirmation. On the same night, Henry A. Wise was three times nominated as minister to France and was rejected each time. Thomas H. Benton in his *Thirty Years' View* wrote that "Nominations and rejections flew backwards and forwards as in a game of shuttlecock—the same nomination in several instances being rejected ... within the same hour."[8]

At the following session, the Senate rejected David Henshaw, who had been given a recess appointment as Secretary of the Navy. He received only eight favorable votes, and James M. Porter, appointed during the recess as Secretary of War, received only three. None of the appointments was rejected because of lack of qualifications of the nominee; the rejections were due to the bitter hostility of the Whigs toward Tyler.

The first Tyler nominee to the Supreme Court to be rejected was John C. Spencer of New York, who Warren states was a "lawyer of great talent." Originally a Whig who had opposed Tyler, he later accepted the appointment as Secretary of War and subsequently as Secretary of the Treasury. A contemporary later wrote that Spencer had administered the office of Secretary of the Treasury "with an ability, assiduity, integrity and faithfulness seldom

* See chap. iv, above.

equalled since the days of Hamilton," and stated that he was "a man of great abilities, industry, and endurance, curt manners, and an irascible temper."[9] But the Whigs were furious at him for accepting appointments from Tyler, and regarded him as a traitor to the party. Henry Clay, whom Spencer had opposed as presidential candidate, wrote to Crittenden that "if Spencer be confirmed he will have run a short career of more profligate conduct and good luck than any man I recollect." He was rejected in the Senate on January 31, 1844, by a vote of 26 to 21. Although "the rejection was thus placed on high moral grounds," wrote Warren, "the fact was that it was due solely to Whig politics."[10]

Tyler's other nominations to the Supreme Court were of lawyers of outstanding ability and reputation. In 1844 he nominated Judge Edward King, a distinguished lawyer of Philadelphia, and Reuben H. Walworth, chancellor of the state of New York. Both nominations were placed on the table without action, when the Senate adjourned in June, and they remained tabled for nearly a year. Walworth, though unquestionably of the highest legal ability, was opposed by the Whigs, who urged that the position be left vacant until after the 1844 election. "Better the bench be vacant for a year," editorialized a Whig paper, "than filled for half a century by corrupt or feeble men, or partisans committed in advance to particular beliefs."[11]

Shortly before the end of his term, in 1845, Tyler made a final attempt to fill the two vacancies on the Supreme Court, withdrawing the nominations of King and Walworth and submitting in their stead the names of John Meredith Read of Philadelphia and Samuel Nelson, chief justice of the New York supreme court. Nelson's qualifications were so outstanding that his nomination was confirmed at once, but the Senate adjourned without acting on the nomination of Read. There was considerable difference of opinion about the qualifications of Read, a former United States district attorney. James Buchanan wrote that "there are few lawyers, if any, in Philadelphia his superior, a man of firmness, energy and industry. . . . He holds a ready and powerful political pen and is a gentleman of the strictest honour and integrity." His nomination was praised by the Democratic press; but Richard Peters, a prominent Whig, wrote to Judge McLean that Read was "as suited for a judge as I am for an admiral."[12]

Conflicts between the President and the Senate, 1845–1861

In the administrations of Presidents Polk, Fillmore, and Buchanan, five nominations to the Supreme Court were rejected, all for partisan reasons. Four of the five were made in the last year of the term of the President, after the party in power had lost control of the Senate. These rejections indicate the strong partisanship of the time.

When Polk became President, the position on the Court from the circuit which included Pennsylvania still remained vacant. The rivalries in Pennsylvania politics made the position a difficult one to fill. On the recommendation of the Vice-President, Polk nominated George W. Woodward, a judge of an inferior Pennsylvania court. Warren states that Woodward was a man of "high talents and sterling ability, but without any extended reputation and somewhat radical in his views." Secretary of State James Buchanan, who was from Pennsylvania, urged the appointment of John M. Read, whose nomination by Tyler had earlier failed of confirmation. Polk decided against the appointment of Read, a former Federalist, believing that he could not be "relied on in his constitutional opinions." In his diary on December 24, 1845, he observed that all Federalists who had been appointed to the Supreme Court had after securing the life appointment soon become "broadly Federal and latitudinarian in all their decisions involving questions of Constitutional power," and resolved to appoint an original Democrat and a strict constructionist.[13] Buchanan bitterly protested because his choice had not been named and the President had nominated a man from Pennsylvania to the Supreme Court without consulting him.

The nomination of Woodward was rejected by a vote of 20 to 29, Senator Cameron from Pennsylvania and five other Democrats joining with the Whigs to vote against it. It was reported to Polk that Cameron had explained the action of the six Democratic senators, saying that "the only way to treat an ugly negro who was unruly, was to give him a d——d drubbing at the start, and he would learn to behave himself." Polk wrote in his diary on February 11, 1846, after Cameron had called on him: "I then told him that the public understood that there was a Democratic majority of six in the Senate, and that the effect of rejecting my principal nominations at the commencement of my administration ... was calculated to weaken my administration, and destroy or impair my power and influence in carrying out the measures of my administration."[14]

Polk also suffered other rejections of his nominations by the Senate, which he interpreted as attempts to embarrass his administration for political reasons. "I learned tonight," he wrote on April 21, 1846, "that the Senate by the votes of Mr. Calhoun and his wing of the Democratic party united with the whole Whig party had rejected the nomination of Dr. Amos Nourse as collector at Bath in Maine. This is, in addition to other evidence, a pretty clear indication that Mr. Calhoun intends to oppose my administration. ... He is playing a game to make himself President. ..."[15] In the same session, when Polk was notified that his nomination of Henry Horn to be collector at Philadelphia had been rejected by the Senate, he wrote concerning the Democratic senators who had voted with the Whigs against the nomination: "They now vote against my nominations, as I suppose out of spite. The sooner such party men go into the ranks of the Whig party the better."[16]

Polk repeatedly records his disgust at the constant stream of office seekers and members of Congress seeking appointments for their constituents. "The passion for office among members of Congress is very great, if not absolutely disreputable, and greatly embarrasses the operation of the government. They create offices by their own votes and then seek to fill them themselves."[17] On January 7, 1847, he complained:

Members of Congress and men of high station sign papers of recommendation either from interested personal motives or without meaning what they say, and thus the President is often imposed on, and induced to make bad appointments. When he does so the whole responsibility falls on himself, while those who have signed the papers of recommendation and misled him, take special care never to avow the agency they have had in the matter, or to assume any part of the responsibility.[18]

Polk cited a remarkable instance, which he stated was an illustration of many others: The person appointed as surveyor of the Port of St. Louis was rejected because of the opposition of the senator from that state who had originally recommended him. When the senator called to urge the appointment of another, he explained the rejection by saying that the man previously appointed was without character and wholly unqualified. When Polk showed the senator his own letter of recommendation, he replied: "Well, we are obliged to recommend our constituents when they apply to us."

Of the nominations to the Supreme Court made by President Fillmore, three were rejected. In 1852 he nominated Edward A. Bradford, a leading lawyer of Louisiana, but the Senate failed to act upon the nomination before it adjourned. Fillmore's next choice was George E. Badger, a senator from North Carolina, who had been Secretary of the Navy under Harrison and Tyler. Warren writes of him: "He was an able and eloquent lawyer, well fitted for the position, and a strongly conservative Whig."[19] Although the Senate, under the rule of senatorial courtesy, would ordinarily be expected to approve an appointment of one of its own members, the strongly Democratic Senate rejected the nomination of Badger. One ground for the rejection was that he was not a resident of one of the states included in the circuit in which the vacancy occurred, but the real reason for the action of the Senate appears to have been the fact that the nominee was a Whig and was opposed by the Democratic press of the South. On February 11, 1853, by a vote of 26 to 25, the Senate postponed consideration of the nomination until March 4, when the term of Congress ended. "This is one of those purely party operations which the country will not sustain," said the New York *Times*. "There was no possible objection ... except that he is a Whig."[20]

Fillmore tried once more to fill the position before his term expired. Taking into account the opposition to Badger on the ground that he did not reside in the circuit, he offered the nomination to Judah P. Benjamin, who had just been elected to the Senate from Louisiana. When Benjamin declined the nomination, Fillmore sent in the name of Benjamin's law partner, William C. Micou, on February 24, 1853. At this late date in the session, the strongly Democratic Senate refused to confirm any Whig nominee, and took no action.

One month before the end of his term, President Buchanan nominated Jeremiah S. Black of Pennsylvania, his Secretary of State, to fill a vacancy that had occurred in the Supreme Court. Black had previously served for three years as Attorney General of the United States in Buchanan's administration, and earlier had been chief justice of the Pennsylvania supreme court. His nomination was bitterly opposed by Stephen A. Douglas and his followers, as well as by the antislavery press, and it was rejected on February 21 by a vote of 26 to 25.

Lincoln's Handling of Appointments

Virtually a clean sweep was made of the holders of federal offices that were subject to appointment by the President, after the Republican victory in 1860. Fish records that of the 1,639 officers appointed by the President, 1,457 removals were made, and since new appointments could not be made to federal offices in the South, it is apparent that the change was practically complete.[21] The accounts of Lincoln's early days in office all tell of the great scramble for offices. Stanton wrote that it was "terrific" and stated that Lincoln was undertaking to handle "the whole patronage small and great leaving nothing to the Chiefs of Departments."[22] Office seekers besieged the President. Joseph Medill of the Chicago *Tribune* sought the appointment of the postmasters in the Northwest, who "would work to extend our circulation," and Horace Greeley of the New York *Tribune* pressed for postmaster appointments for the same reason.[23]

The maneuvers by which the Iowa delegation in Congress secured the appointment of Samuel Freeman Miller, a prominent Republican from that state, to the Supreme Court in 1862 illustrate the political pressures for appointments and the dominant role played by members of Congress. In order for Iowa to secure a place on the Court it was necessary for the state to be placed in a new circuit which did not have a sitting member. The Senate bill which combined Iowa with Illinois would have precluded Miller's appointment, since Lincoln was expected to appoint a person to the Court from that state. A member of the House Judiciary Committee from Iowa, James F. Wilson, stood out for a circuit composed entirely of states west of the Mississippi, and with the support of the delegations from neighboring states succeeded in creating a new circuit composed of Iowa, Minnesota, Kansas, and Missouri, which was unrepresented on the Court.

The next step was to persuade Lincoln to nominate Miller. A friend of Miller approached the President to urge his appointment; but Lincoln, never having heard of this Miller, confused him with a former Congressman from Iowa by that name. When Governor Kirkwood and Senator Harlan of Iowa called on the President in behalf of Miller, Lincoln reached for his pen and inquired whom they wished to be appointed and for what place. Harlan replied that they wanted Miller appointed to the Supreme Court, whereupon Lincoln replaced the pen and put aside the paper, stating: "Well, that is a very important position, and I will have to give it some serious consideration. I had supposed you wanted me to make someone a Brigadier General for you."[24]

Lincoln was criticized for giving so much of his time at the beginning of his term to patronage appointments, but he faced an extremely difficult situation in attempting to hold the Union and his own party together. As a practical politician he followed the rule of expediency and made patronage appointments in conformity with the prevailing American tradition, recognizing as fairly as possible the claims of the various leaders and groups who had aided in his election. "He made no attempt to obtain the men best fitted to perform the functions of the various offices," wrote Fish, "except in the case of the very highest; for minor places he did not insist that a man be fit." And he did not forget his own friends and relatives, appointing them to places "which might profit them and not harm the country."[25] But when the interest of the country was at stake, Lincoln did not hesitate to use patronage to secure support of his legislative policies.[26] He permitted members of the Senate to name the persons to be appointed to federal offices in their states, except the minor offices, particularly postmasterships; following custom, he permitted members of the House to name the postmasters. Carman and Luthin conclude their scholarly study of *Lincoln and the Patronage* with the following evaluation:

> His wise use of the patronage in holding the party together was a necessary antecedent to the formulation of any statesmanlike policy concerning the nation.... But to witness how, as a politician, he utilized the patronage in holding together diverse conflicting factions in common purposes—the preservation of the Union, the success of his administration, and the rewarding of the party faithful—is only to enhance the greatness of Lincoln.[27]

Andrew Johnson's Fight with the Senate over Appointments

Andrew Johnson, a former member of the Senate from Tennessee, fully understood the power that the Senate held over the President in regard to appointments. In 1861 he had opposed secession by the southern states, believing that senators from the South should remain in the Senate, where they would be able to oppose the new President. "We have the power," he declared, "even to reject the appointment of the Cabinet officers of the incoming President.... So far as appointing even a minister abroad is concerned, the incoming Administration will have no power without our consent, if we remain here.... [it]

has not even the power to appoint a postmaster whose salary exceeds $1,000 a year, without consultation with, and the acquiescence of, the Senate of the United States."[28] Little did Johnson foresee that within seven years, as President, he would be engaged in a bitter struggle with the Senate over appointments.

The conflict that took place between Johnson and Congress, led by Charles Sumner, Thaddeus Stevens, and the unspeakable Benjamin Butler, over the reconstruction policy need not be recounted here. As an aftermath of the fight, Congress, over the President's veto, passed the famous Tenure of Office Act of 1867, an act designed to curb the use of the appointing power of the President. In 1863 a bill which provided that the Comptroller could be removed only by and with the advice and consent of the Senate[29] was passed and was signed by Lincoln. Carl Russell Fish notes that even during Lincoln's term the jealousy of Congress of the growing presidential power had led to provisions prohibiting the payment of the salaries to recess appointees in certain classes until their appointments had been confirmed by the Senate, and requiring the President to submit reasons for the removal of consular clerks.[30] His power of removing officers in the military and naval service had been curtailed by an act which prohibited dismissal "except upon and in pursuance of the sentence of a court martial."[31]

When the fight between the President and the radical leaders of Congress occurred, Johnson proceeded to remove officeholders who had been appointed at the request of his congressional opponents, and to appoint his own followers. Many proposals were made in Congress to curb his removal powers. The Tenure of Office bill passed the Senate with the provision that every civil officer appointed by and with the advice and consent of the Senate, except members of the Cabinet, should hold office until a successor had been appointed in like manner and had qualified. An amendment was offered by Sumner to require senatorial confirmation of all appointments of officers with salaries of $1,000 or more, but it failed to pass. In the House the bill was amended to apply to Cabinet officers, and as finally adopted provided that members of the Cabinet should hold office for the term of the President who appointed them and one month thereafter, subject to removal by and with the advice and consent of the Senate.[32]

The Tenure of Office bill was vetoed by the President in an able message which denied the constitutionality of the restriction of the removal power of the executive, but was promptly passed over his veto by a large majority in both houses, and became law. The already strained relations between the President and Secretary of War Stanton rapidly became worse, and in August, 1867, the President suspended Stanton from office, appointing General Grant to take his place. When Congress convened in December, both houses promptly passed resolutions denying the power of the President to remove a Cabinet officer without the advice and consent of the Senate. General Grant, despite his promise to hold fast until the constitutional issue could be tested in court, gave up the office and turned the keys over to the Adjutant General. That officer surrendered them to Stanton, and Stanton once more took possession. The President had no better luck with his appointment of General Thomas. On the order of Stanton, Thomas was arrested, but he failed to sue for a writ of habeas corpus so that the law could be tested before the Supreme Court. Impeachment proceedings were brought by the House against the President, the principal ground being that he had acted illegally in removing Stanton.[33]

Henry Stanbery, Attorney General under Johnson, resigned in order to serve as counsel to the President in the impeachment proceedings of 1868, along with William M. Evarts and George William Curtis. After the trial, Johnson nominated Stanbery again to be Attorney General, but the Senate, smarting under the acquittal of Johnson, rejected him. This action of the Senate was described by Gideon Wells as "a factious and partisan exhibition of Senators which all good men must regret to witness."[34]

This was the second rejection of Stanbery at the hands of the Senate. When he was nominated to the Supreme Court in 1866 by Johnson, the Senate passed a bill, introduced by Lyman Trumbull of Illinois, to reduce the number of Associate Justices of the Supreme Court to seven. In the House the question was asked whether the bill "abolished the judge whose appointment the President sent to the Senate the other day?" To this Wilson of Iowa replied that this was its effect as well as its purpose. The bill became law, and it was unnecessary for the Senate to act on the nomination.[35]

Rejection by the Senate of Grant's Nominees

In 1869 Congress passed a judiciary act increasing the number of members of the Supreme Court to nine and providing for a new class of circuit judgeships, one for each of the nine circuits. In selecting the persons to be appointed to these nine circuit judgeships, President Grant usually followed the recommendations of his Attorney General, Ebenezer Rockwood Hoar of Massachusetts, and made excellent appointments. The Attorney General, determined that only able men who would honor the bench should be appointed, quickly incurred the displeasure of members of the Senate, since nearly every member had his own candidate. The recommendations of the Attorney General prevailed over those of the senators in all except two cases, and in one of these the President was forced to withdraw the nomination because of the disapproval of the bar and public protest.[36] The high standards set by Hoar for these appointments, and particularly the unfavorable reports he made on candidates sponsored by the senators, aroused their strong hostility. To members of the Senate he was plain-spoken concerning nominees whom he regarded as unfit. "Such a man in such a place," wrote his biographers, "was intolerable to politicians with friends to reward and influence to maintain."[37] When Senator Chandler introduced a resolution calling for more information concerning certain nominations, Hoar curtly refused to supply the information, stating that he was responsible to the President and that the Senate should make its request to him.

In the autumn of 1869 President Grant nominated Hoar to a vacancy on the Supreme Court. The selection was attributed not only to the high regard which the President had for his Attorney General but also to the fact that the friction between Hoar and members of the Senate had reduced his usefulness as Attorney General. His nomination was commended on all sides by the public and the press; the *Nation* called the choice an "admirable one" and indicated that it would elevate the Supreme Court in the public eye. "His distinguished abilities are conceded and his elevation to the Supreme Bench is received with profound satisfaction by all," wrote the New York *Times*. "One of the best that could have been made," stated *Harper's Weekly,* which referred to his "vigorous independence, soundness of judgment, masculine good sense and legal learning."[38] In the Senate, however, the nomination met with strong opposition. The opponents wanted an immediate vote, but the matter was postponed. President Lowell of Harvard wrote to Hoar: "Don't let your nomination be withdrawn. Let the responsibility lie with the knaves who hate you for your impregnability, and haven't the courage to say so. Give 'em the additional pang of being obliged to vote. It is all an honor to you."[39]

Charles Francis Adams, Jr., wrote to Hoar congratulating him "and the country on the action of the Senate on Wednesday ... a great mission has been forced upon you: nothing less than to return the Senate of the United States to its proper function in the system of government."[40] When the vote was taken on February 3, 1873, Hoar was defeated by a vote of 33 to 24. "What could you expect," exclaimed Senator Cameron, "for a man who has snubbed seventy senators!"[41]

When Chief Justice Chase died in 1873, President Grant offered the position to his close personal and political friend, Senator Conkling of New York, but Conkling declined the appointment. The President then nominated his Attorney General, George H. Williams, a former member of the Senate and territorial governor of Oregon. The nomination surprised both the bar and the country, and eventually led to much criticism. The *American Law Review,* in January, 1874, temperately stated that Williams, in his various high offices, "has acquitted himself in such a manner as neither to invite distinguished praise, nor, except in the Pacific Railroad case, to provoke much adverse criticism. ... While it would be idle to deny that the nomination was a disappointment to all who hoped that the seat of Marshall might be filled by a fitting successor," yet it was a relief that a worse selection had not been made.[42] The press generally was critical of the nomination, the *Independent* stating that "the general feeling of the public is that the President should have done better, with such names as Evarts, Cushing, Curtis, Hoar—to say nothing of the present members of the Supreme Court."[43] The Springfield *Republican* declared that "the nomination surprised and disgusted every lawyer in the United States who has the honor of his profession at heart. It fell like a blow upon every respectable member of the Federal Judiciary."[44]

As public sentiment against the nomination mounted, Williams declared that he had been viciously slandered, and his friends demanded confirmation as a vindication. Senator Conkling considered introducing a bill to abolish the office of Chief Justice as a presidential appointment and to provide that it should be filled by selection of the Associate Justices from among their numbers. The New York Bar Association passed a resolution stating that the nominee was "wanting in those qualifications of intellect, experience, and reputation which are indispensable to uphold the dignity of the highest National Court." At Williams' request President Grant withdrew the nomination on January 8, 1874.

The next selection by Grant for the position of Chief Justice was Caleb Cushing, a former Attorney General, who had also been a judge of the supreme court of Massachusetts. Warren states that he was preëminently qualified for the position and that as a "profound jurist, he probably excelled either Marshall or Taney or Chase."[45] He was a personal friend of Grant, and his appointment appears to have been dictated by a desire of Grant to reward him for his services as counsel in an international arbitration case. Cushing's previous friendship with Johnson and Tyler and the fact that he had been successively a Whig, a Tyler man, a Democrat, and finally a Republican did not commend his appointment to the Senate, which had rejected him as Secretary of the Treasury in Tyler's administration. Because of his great legal attainments and reputation, the selection was commented on favorably by the press, and had his nomination been acted on at once there is little doubt but that his appointment would have been confirmed.

The nomination was criticized by the Radical Republican press, which called him a "pro-slavery Democrat." The fact that he was seventy-four years of age was commented on unfavorably. Before the Senate acted on the nomination there came to light a letter which provided a ready excuse for his rejection. In 1861 Cushing had written a letter to Jefferson Davis, President of the Confederate States, introducing a young man who was returning to Texas. This was a simple, friendly act, and in no way implied any lack of loyalty to the Union cause, but it was termed an "astounding development" and led to an outcry against Cushing by the Radical Republicans. Grant withdrew Cushing's name within less than a week after he had submitted it.

The abuses of patronage and the spoils system in the administration of Grant led to a widespread demand for civil service reform. Patronage appointments, however, were to a large extent controlled by members of Congress rather than by the President and his department heads; and as a consequence the majority in both houses opposed civil service reform. In response to public pressure, Congress enacted a civil service law in 1871 which authorized the President to establish examinations as an entrance requirement for certain classes of employees, but it failed to appropriate any funds for the purpose. Grant appointed a distinguished commission headed by George William Curtis, but two years later the members of the commission resigned in protest over some notorious appointments by the President, and the first effort at civil service reform came to an untimely end.[46]

An illuminating account of appointment and confirmation practices of the time is given by George F. Boutwell, Secretary of the Treasury under Grant and subsequently a member of the Senate from Massachusetts:

One of my last acts as Secretary was to advise the President to nominate a Mr. Hitchcock for collector of the port of San Diego, California. Mr. Hitchcock was a lawyer by profession, a graduate of Harvard and a man of good standing in San Diego. Mr. Houghton, the member [of Congress] for the San Diego district, recommended a man who was a saloon keeper and a Democrat in politics, but he had supported Houghton in the canvass. Houghton's request was supported by Senator Sargent. . . . The President appointed Hitchcock and one of the first questions of interest to me [in the Senate] was the action of the Senate upon the nomination of Hitchcock, which I supported.

Sargent appealed to what was known as the courtesy of the Senate, a rule or custom which required the Senators of the same party to follow the lead of the Senators in the matter of nominations from their respective states. To this rule I objected. I refused to recognize it, and said I would never appeal to the "courtesy" of the Senate in any matter concerning the State of Massachusetts. Hitchcock was rejected. The President nominated Houghton's candidate.[47]

General Benjamin F. Butler, a member of the House who was thoroughly detested in the Senate, prevailed upon President Grant to nominate William A. Simmons for collector of the Port of Boston. The nomination raised a storm of protest from the leading businessmen of that city. It was referred to the Committee on Commerce, of which Boutwell was chairman, and the committee voted unfavorably on the nomination. Butler came to Senator Boutwell and threatened to spend half a million dollars to defeat him if he blocked the appointment. In spite of the threat, Boutwell refused to appeal to the "courtesy" of the Senate but opposed the nomination on the ground that the nomination was repugnant to a majority of the Republican party. In opposing the nomination, Senator Sumner of Massachusetts appealed to the courtesy of the Senate, but by that time he had wandered so far from his party that the appeal carried no weight and Simmons was confirmed. Senator George F. Hoar from Massachusetts later recorded in his autobiography that this appointment, which was unpopular with the Republicans of Massachusetts, cost Grant the support of the delegation from that state and the renomination for a third term.[48]

By the end of Grant's administration the Senate had achieved a definite hegemony; the policies of the government were being directed by a few of its powerful leaders, to whom Grant weakly yielded. Senators like Conkling, Sumner, Cameron, Sherman, and Edmunds, wrote Senator Hoar, would have been personally offended if the President had sent them a private message concerning their position on pending legislation. "If they visited the White House, it was to give, not to receive advice. . . . Each of these stars kept his own orbit and shone in his own sphere, within which he tolerated no intrusion from the President or from anybody else."[49] Professor Burgess later stated that the ascendency of Congress over the President was breaking down the constitutional system of checks and balances and turning the government into a parliamentary system, in which the Senate exercised the major control. Members of Congress of the same party as the President dictated federal appointments in their states; the role of the President was thus being rapidly transformed into a perfunctory function of forwarding their nominations to the Senate.[50]

Chapter VI

REASSERTION BY THE
PRESIDENT OF HIS
RIGHT TO NOMINATE

This question of senatorial patronage is the salient point in the improvement of the civil service. It is the interest of the country that its business shall be well done and that the area of patronage shall be limited. But if the office-holders are to look after party politics, to make nominations, and to win party victories, they will be appointed, not for fitness to discharge the legitimate duties of their offices, but for skill in wirepulling. No Senator would diminish their number.... The appointing power may be regulated by law to the end that honesty, efficiency, and economy may be promoted, but it must not be transferred to the Senate. It must be left where the Constitution placed it. President Hayes.[1]

Let these nominations be confirmed and what has become of the "courtesy of the Senate," that beneficent principle which recognized the Senators of each state as best fitted to determine the propriety of any appointment from their state? Senator Roscoe Conkling, Dec. 12, 1877.[2]

IN THE FIRST TWO decades after the Civil War the Senate called more and more for information about nominations and removals. "These are the outward signs," stated Carl Russell Fish, "of the inward political growth of a new power of the Senate—the attempt of the senators by combinations to make the President the mere clerk to transmit to the Senate as a constitutional body, nominations handed to him by the individual senators."[3] This usurpation by the Senate of the power of nomination was strongly combated by Hayes, Garfield, and Cleveland, who reasserted the position taken by Washington and other early Presidents that the power to nominate was vested exclusively in the chief executive. The ascendancy of the Senate in the years immediately following the Civil War was measured to some extent by the number of contests and rejections of the President's nominations. In spite of the fact that the President and a majority of the Senate were of the same political party, 58 of Grant's nominations were contested and 9 were rejected. In Hayes's term, 92 contests occurred and 51 nominations were rejected; in the four-year term of Garfield and Arthur, 44 nominations were contested and 10 were rejected. It is significant that Cleveland, who during most of his two terms of office faced a Senate controlled by the opposite party, had only 30 contests and 8 rejections of his nominations.[4] The tide had turned.

Presidents McKinley and Theodore Roosevelt had few contests with the Senate over nominations, but Roosevelt insisted on maintaining high standards for appointment and refused to accept the recommendations from senators of his party, of men who did not come up to his standard. Wilson, too, avoided squabbles with members of Congress over patronage, at the same time insisting upon reasonably high standards for appointment.

Conflict between Hayes and the Senate

When Hayes became President in 1877, the leaders of the Senate fully expected to be consulted about his selections for the Cabinet, and several had candidates of their own. Conkling, who looked upon himself as the leader of the Senate, wanted the post of Postmaster General for his trusted lieutenant, Thomas C. Platt; Cameron of Pennsylvania insisted that his son, Don Cameron, be continued as Secretary of War; and Blaine, a newcomer to the Senate, had his candidate. Friends of General Logan, who had been defeated for reëlection to the Senate, urged his appointment.[5] But Hayes had other ideas; he resolved to make his own choices and not accept the dictation of these great men of the Senate. He turned down Conkling's suggestion of Platt, and his decision not to appoint any member of the Grant Cabinet precluded the appointment of Don Cameron. Instead of accepting Blaine's candidate, Hayes turned to Hoar of Massachusetts, also a new member of the Senate, who suggested Judge Devens of that state. When his nominations were announced several days before the inauguration, they attracted wide acclaim in the press, but incurred the anger of the leaders of the Senate because their candidates had not been selected.[6]

Desiring to heal the serious breach in his own party, Hayes appointed to his Cabinet several prominent persons from the Liberal faction of the party, as well as Stalwarts. The appointment of Carl Schurz, a leading advocate of civil service reform and opponent of the Southern reconstruction policies of the Grant administration, and a former member of the Senate, was particularly obnoxious to the Stalwarts in the Senate. Conkling and Cameron were strongly opposed to the appointment of William Evarts, who had defended Johnson in his impeachment trial. He was a distinguished New York attorney but not a member of the Conkling machine. Hayes decided to appoint one person to his Cabinet from the South and contemplated the appointment of General Johnston of Confederate fame as his Secretary of War; but he was strongly advised by members of the Senate against such a choice. He then selected Senator David Key of Tennessee, to whom he offered the post of Postmaster General. This nomination was strongly opposed in the Senate because Senator Key was a Democrat.

When Hayes's nominations to his Cabinet were submitted to the Senate, they were not immediately acted upon, as was customary, but all were referred to committees. The membership of the Senate committees was yet to be determined, and no committee was organized to transact business. The decision was widely interpreted as an indication that the leaders of the Senate intended to reject some of the nominations. The action broke also the well-established tradition of the Senate to approve immediately the nomination of sitting members of the Senate. Two nominees—Key and Sherman—were members of the Senate, and Schurz was a former member.

The Republican press, which had praised highly Hayes's selections, denounced this action of the Senate; telegrams, resolutions of party meetings, and letters from prominent citizens in near-by cities poured into Washington urging immediate approval.[7] "It was all meant as an attack upon the President," declared Professor Burgess, "for exercising his own independent discretion in nominating the members of his cabinet, instead of asking Blaine, Conkling and Cameron, and some others each to nominate a member for him."[8]

The following day, the nomination of Sherman was recalled from committee and was approved; but the same courtesy was not extended to Senator Key. The public protest became so great that all committees hastily organized, met, and reported the nominations, and within three days after the nominations were submitted all were approved. At the very outset of his administration Hayes had won a notable victory over the oligarchy of the Senate.[9]

Throughout his single term President Hayes pressed for civil service reform and instituted such reforms as were possible without the enactment of legislation. In his final message to Congress on December 6, 1880, he stated:

The first step in the reform of the civil service must be a complete divorce between Congress and the Executive in the matter of appointments. The corrupting doctrine that "to the victors belong the spoils" is inseparable from congressional patronage as the established rule and practice of parties in power. It comes to be understood by applicants for office, and by the people generally, that Representatives and Senators are entitled to disburse the patronage in their respective districts and States. It is not necessary to recite at length the evils resulting from this invasion of the executive functions.[10]

In spite of the strong planks which both major parties had adopted pledging civil service reform, and in spite of the vigorous recommendations of the President, Congress took no action. After two years in the White House, Hayes wrote in his diary, "No proper legislation is to be expected as long as members of Congress are engaged in procuring offices for their constituents."[11]

At his first meeting with his Cabinet, Hayes appointed a committee to formulate rules about appointments to office, and afterward he instituted a number of important policies to curb some of the excesses of the political appointments, short of civil service legislation. He let it be known that there would be no sweeping changes in the public service, that dismissals would be made only for the good of the service and not to make room for political appointments, that departments would be given a free hand in making appointments, and that congressional recommendations would not be regarded as binding. As a result, his inauguration did not see the usual throng of office seekers pouring into Washington.[12] Throughout his term the grosser forms of patronage appointments were curbed, and Hayes wrote in his diary that "the practice of congressional appointment is for the time being largely abandoned."[13]

One of the first steps of the new administration was to investigate the notoriously political and corrupt administration of the New York customhouse. In 1877 Secretary of the Treasury Sherman appointed a special commission of three men, headed by John Jay, to make an investigation. The report of this commission exposed the corrupt and incompetent administration, which allowed many federal employees to engage actively in partisan politics.

The Jay Commission [states Eckenrode] made the interesting discovery that 200 small politicians were supported by the New York custom house without performing any public service whatever; they were Conkling's ward heelers, paid for party work with sinecures. Ignorant politicians held positions demanding technical training. The New York custom officers undervalued imports landed in New York in order to force importers to come to that place in preference to other ports. And almost every other imaginable abuse flourished. The salaries of all employees were relentlessly levied on for party purposes.[14]

President Hayes concurred in the recommendations of the Jay commission. He issued an executive order prohibiting federal employees from actively participating in partisan politics and ordered that "useless men be discharged and that salaries be no longer taxed for campaign purposes."[15] In this attempt to take the New York customhouse out of politics, Hayes and Sherman were well aware that it had been used by Senator Conkling as a pet preserve to reward his faithful followers, and that Chester Arthur, the collector, and Cornell, the naval officer, were main henchmen in the Conkling machine. Conkling launched a vitriolic attack on the President, asserting that the issue was whether the control of federal appointments should be exercised by the senators of the various states or by the President.[16]

Arthur and Cornell refused to give up their activities in the Republican organization; whereupon, in September, 1877, Hayes asked for their resignations, offering Arthur the post of consul in Paris. Both refused to resign, and in October the President sent to the Senate the names of Theodore Roosevelt (father of the President) for collector, and L. Bradford Prince for naval officer. Arthur and Cornell remained in office while this was going on. The nominations were referred to the Committee on Commerce, of which Conkling was chairman; but the committee took no action in the special session, except that Conkling called upon Sherman for a statement of the reasons for the removal of Arthur and Cornell. Before the regular session convened in December all but two of the Republican representatives from New York had joined in a petition urging the President to retain Arthur and Cornell. To this, Hayes tartly replied that when he wished the advice of congressmen he would ask for it, and resubmitted the nominations.[17] On December 9 Hayes wrote in his diary: "I am now in a contest on the question of the right of Senators to dictate or control nominations. Mr. Conkling insists that no officer shall be appointed in New York without his consent, obtained previously to the nomination."[18]

Two days later the Committee on Commerce reported unfavorably on the nominations of Roosevelt and Prince. In the executive session that followed, Conkling appealed to the courtesy of the Senate and charged that Hayes aimed at "debasing the senators and centering all power in himself." He declared that "Conkling's cause was the cause of every senator of both parties" and argued that it was an insult to the Senate for the President to replace the appointees of a senator without consulting him.[19] The rule of senatorial courtesy held. The Republican senators supported Conkling, and the nominations of Roosevelt and Prince were rejected by a vote of 31 to 25.

After Congress adjourned, the President suspended Arthur and Cornell and appointed in their places E. A. Merritt and S. W. Burt. These nominations were in the nature of promotions. Merritt had instituted many reforms as surveyor of the port since his appointment the previous year; and Burt was the chief deputy for Cornell and had actually performed the duties of the office.

When Congress convened in December, 1878, Hayes sent in the nominations of these men. Conkling and his allies held up action for two months. According to an article in *Harper's Weekly*, "the supporters of Senator Conkling burst into furious denunciation of the act as a gross insult to the Senate, and a treachery, a defiance, a stab in the back, a foul blow, an outrage, a persecution, and every other kind of infamous proceeding toward the Senator."[20] On January 15, 1879, the Senate in executive session heard a statement from John Sherman giving the reasons for the removal of Arthur and Cornell. When it was proposed to make Sherman's letter public, Conkling rose in vehement opposition and attacked Hayes bitterly.

The Committee on Commerce finally reported adversely the nominations of Merritt and Burt, the Republican members unanimously opposing the nominations and the Democrats abstaining from voting. On February 2, Hayes wrote in his diary that the results of his fight with Conkling would go far to settle the questions of the right of senators to dictate appointments and whether government offices should be manipulated for political purposes.[21] When the Senate again took up the matter, Conkling reported the action of his committee and presented the replies of Arthur and Cornell to the charges against them. Sherman asked for the opportunity to reply to their letters, and two days later the President himself sent a message to the Senate repeating the charges. On February 3, 1879, the Senate finally acted after an executive session of seven hours, in which Conkling raged that the whole purpose of the President was to build up a political machine of his own, and urged the members not to "sit tamely by and see the power of the government turned against innocent men."[22] The Senate wearied of Conkling's exhortations and, when the vote was taken, confirmed both nominations by substantial majorities.[23] Thus ended the first but not the final chapter of Senator Conkling's battle with the President over the control of federal patronage in New York.

Resignations of Senators Conkling and Platt

President Hayes was mistaken in the belief that his fight with Senator Conkling would settle the respective roles of the President and the members of the Senate concerning appointments. In 1881 Conkling invoked the rule of courtesy to block the confirmation of the appointment of Judge W. H. Robertson, whom Garfield had nominated to be collector of the New York port. Failing in this, he took the extraordinary step of resigning from the Senate, confidently expecting to be reëlected by the Stalwart-controlled state legislature and thus to be vindicated in his assertion of the right to control all federal appointments in New York. Conkling and Platt, who also resigned, were both defeated for reëlection. The career of Senator Conkling was virtually at an end, though Platt was later elected again to the Senate and became the undisputed boss of his party in New York. The resignation of the two senators made the most sensational test case of senatorial courtesy in the history of the country.[24]

At the New York Republican state convention of the preceding year Senator Conkling had forced through a resolution pledging the delegation to the nomination of Grant for a third term as President. There was a great deal of Blaine sentiment in the state, however, and the delegation refused to stay hitched. Before the convention met, Judge Robertson, a delegate from Westchester County, announced that he would vote for Blaine, and when the break came, he led part of the New York delegation to Garfield.

In an attempt to heal the breach between the Blaine and Conkling forces, the convention nominated Chester A. Arthur for Vice-President; but Conkling's support of the ticket during the campaign was unenthusiastic. After the election there was much speculation concerning who would control federal patronage in New York. The Conkling forces claimed that Garfield had agreed to give the senator from New York absolute control of all federal appointments in the state. The first contest was the election of a United States senator. On January 3 an editorial in the New York *Tribune* stated "on authority" that the President would not take any part in the contest, but added significantly:

The incoming administration will see to it that the men from New York and from the other states, who had the courage at Chicago to obey the wishes of their districts in the balloting for president and who thus finally voted for Garfield, shall not lose by it.... The administration of President Garfield is to be an administration for the whole Republican party. It will foment no quarrels ... but it will not permit its friends to be persecuted for their friendship.[25]

The editorial, which was attributed to Blaine, infuriated the Conkling men because it indicated that recognition would be given to the Independents. "What was the meaning of the article," fumed Conkling, "but that the men who had faithfully voted for Grant need expect no quarter from the administration, while the men who had basely violated their pledges by abandoning Grant for Garfield were to be rewarded for their treachery?"[26] Whitelaw Reid, editor of the New York *Tribune,* wrote to Garfield, warning him that Conkling would insist on complete control of the New York patronage.[27] Garfield determined to work out an amicable arrangement with Conkling for the distribution of New York patronage and on March 20, 1881, invited the two New York senators for a conference. Conkling demanded control of all appointments in New York and opposed the appointment of Judge Robertson to any important post in the country. "Nothing could be more preposterous or insolent," wrote Senator Hoar, "than the demand of a Senator from any state that a President, just elected, ... should ostracize his own supporters. It would have been infamous for Garfield to yield to the demand."[28]

Two days later the President sent in nine nominations that had been agreed upon at the conference, which the New York *Times* termed "a complete surrender to the dictation of Senator Conkling." The President later sent to the Senate five additional New York appointments of Independents without consulting the senators from the state. Included in this group was the name of Judge Robertson to be collector of the Port of New York, the prize political plum, which was regarded as essential to the control of the party organization. The appointment to this position of an ardent Blaine supporter who had openly defied Conkling and the Republican machine was a political bombshell and was received with astonishment in all quarters. The removal of Merritt, who had been appointed to clean up the administration, incurred the protests of civil service reformers.

The nomination infuriated Conkling, and he determined to block it in the Senate. It provided a test to determine whether the President or the senator from New York would control the New York patronage. When it appeared unlikely that the nomination could be defeated in the Senate, an effort was made to persuade the President to withdraw it or to get Judge Robertson to request that his name be withdrawn. Hearing of this, Whitelaw Reid sent a telegram to Garfield urging him to stand firm, for if he yielded, he would become a "laughing stock," and Conkling would become the President for the rest of his term.[29] The President was impressed by this advice, and told Hay when he brought the dispatch to the White House: "Robertson may be carried out of the Senate head first or feet first. I shall never withdraw him."[30] When Postmaster General James called on the President with a written protest against the nomination, signed by himself, Conkling, Platt, and Vice-President Arthur, Garfield told him that he should run the Post Office Department and not bother about appointments to the New York custom-house.

Senator Platt attempted to effect a compromise. The President, however, refused to budge from his position, and Platt was unable to get Judge Robertson to withdraw. Garfield recorded in his journal that he talked to about twenty senators concerning the appointment, probably many of whom urged him to withdraw the nomination. In a letter to a friend, Garfield stated that he had decided to avoid the error of Grant, who had surrendered all control over New York patronage to Conkling, and that of Hayes, who had erred on the other side by appointing Conkling's opponents, for the most part, thus widening the breach within the Republican party. Garfield had decided to steer a middle course, giving Conkling a generous share of appointments but also appointing Robertson, who had supported him at Chicago. If there was to be a fight over the patronage in New York, Garfield thought it better to meet the issue head on, rather than to give way to the demands of Conkling. "This brings on the contest at once," he wrote, "and will settle the question whether the President is the registering clerk of the Senate or the Executive of the United States."[31]

As early as 1871 Garfield attacked senatorial courtesy as a dangerous usurpation: "The power of confirming appointments is rapidly becoming a means by which the Senate dictates appointments. The Constitution gives to the President the initiative in appointments as it gives the House the initiative in revenue legislation."[32] On April 19, 1872, he said: "The one thing which is absolutely necessary," is that Congress "abdicate its usurped and pretended right to dictate appointments to the Chief Executive."[33]

A caucus of Republican senators unanimously voiced their disapproval of the nominations of Robertson and of the other Independent Republicans from New York, and appointed a special committee to convey to Garfield their remonstrance and warning of the disasters certain to befall the party in New York unless the nominations were withdrawn. The President, it is said, defiantly stated to this committee: "I do not propose to be dictated to. Any Republican Senator who votes against my nominations may know that he can expect no favors from the Executive. Senators who dare oppose the Executive will henceforth require letters of introduction to the White House."[34]

On May 2, 1881, the Republican senators set up a "committee of safety" to recommend the order of business, including contested nominations. This was a threat to the President that unless he withdrew the objectionable nomination he would be unable to secure the confirmation of others. Three days later, Garfield countered by withdrawing the nomination of five Conkling Stalwarts on which the Senate had not acted. Conkling tried to secure an agreement with the Democrats to vote against the confirmation of Robertson, but failed; it then appeared that Robertson would probably be confirmed. Conkling was disposed to fight it out in the committee, but Senator Platt urged a different course. "We have been so humiliated as United States Senators from the great State of New York," stated Platt, "that there is but one thing for us to do— rebuke the President by immediately turning in our resignations and then appeal to the Legislature to sustain us."[35] Hearing of this plan, Blaine prophesied, "Conkling will not saw off the limb of a tree when he is on the other end."[36] But Conkling and Platt, despairing of being able to block the approval of Robertson, did just that. Platt was ridiculed in the press for his "me too" resignation, though he later maintained that it was his original suggestion. On May 14 Conkling and Platt sent in their resignations to the Governor of New York, and four days later the Senate confirmed Robertson without a record vote.

In Albany, the Independents, hearing of the resignations, adjourned the legislature until they had time to lay their plans, and when the election of two United States senators came to a vote, the Conkling forces found that they did not command a majority. After two months Platt saw that the fight was hopeless and withdrew. The deadlock was finally broken and two other persons were elected.

The Conkling-Platt episode represents the high-water mark in the claims of senators to control the patronage within their states, a claim in so extreme a form that the President could not yield and maintain any semblance of exercising the functions of his office. Earlier presidents who yielded to similar demands found that their influence with Congress suffered as a result. Garfield determined to face the issue at the outset rather than evade it. Although the party caucus in the Senate had earlier supported the claims of Conkling, an outraged public opinion brought about a different decision.

Cleveland and the Senate

Before Congress convened in regular session in 1885 President Cleveland had made 643 suspensions of officers subject to senatorial confirmation. In the campaign of 1884 Cleveland had supported civil service reform and pledged himself to make removals only for cause. As required by law, he submitted to the Senate soon after it convened the names of the persons to whom he had given recess appointments in place of those suspended. The Republicans, who were in a majority in the Senate, criticized the large number of suspensions. Although in 1869 the Tenure of Office Act was amended and the requirement that the President inform the Senate of the reasons for any suspensions made during the recess of the Senate was dropped, the Senate committees to which these nominations were referred called upon the departments for information concerning the reasons for the suspensions. At the direction of the President the departments supplied information about the new nominees but not about suspensions, offering the explanation that to supply that information would not be in the public interest. Action on the nominations was held up until this issue between the President and the Senate could be resolved. At the end of three months, only 15 of the 643 nominations had been approved.[37]

The issue came to a head in a case involving the suspension of one George M. Duskin as district attorney in Alabama and the appointment of John D. Burnett in his stead. The Senate committee called upon the Department of Justice for all the papers and information relating not only to the nomination of Burnett but also "all papers touching on the suspension and proposed removal from office of George M. Duskin."[38] The Attorney General submitted the papers relating to the nomination of Burnett, but stated in his letter that he had received no directions from the President concerning the transmission of the papers relating to the suspension of Duskin.[39] Thereupon the Senate adopted a resolution calling upon the Attorney General to submit all papers relating to the conduct of the office concerned during the preceding year, which included the last six months of the period served by Duskin. The Attorney General replied that all papers concerning the qualifications and nomination of Burnett had already been transmitted to the Senate committee, and that it was not considered in the public interest to transmit the papers relating to the suspension of Duskin.[40]

The Senate Judiciary Committee next submitted a report to the Senate strongly criticizing both the Attorney General for his action, and the President for the large number of suspensions which he had made. The majority report declared that the issue was whether "either House of Congress [should] have access to the official papers and documents in the various public offices of the United States, created by laws enacted by themselves." The report called for the adoption of a resolution censuring the Attorney General for his refusal "under whatever influence" to send to the Senate the papers he had been directed to transmit. A second proposed resolution stated that until the requested information has been supplied "it is the duty of the Senate to refuse its advice and consent to proposed removals of officers."[41] The vote in the Judiciary Committee followed party lines. The Democratic minority filed a report challenging the position taken by the majority, stating that neither the Constitution nor existing law justified the action of the Senate in inquiring into the reasons for the suspensions.

President Cleveland sent a lengthy message to the Senate reviewing the issues of the controversy, defending the withholding of information concerning his reasons for the suspensions, and asserting the constitutional authority of the President to suspend and remove executive officers.

The demands and requests which by the score have for nearly three months been presented to different departments of the Government, whatever may have been their form, have but one complexion. They assume the right of the Senate to sit in judgment upon the exercise of my exclusive jurisdiction and executive function, for which I am solely responsible.[42]

To the contention of the majority report that the Senate was entitled to have access to the official papers and documents of any office which it had created by the enactment of laws, Cleveland stated that "these instrumentalities were created for the benefit of the people and to answer the general purposes of the Government under the constitution and the laws, and they are unencumbered by any lien in favor of either branch of Congress growing out of their construction, and unembarrassed by any obligation to the Senate as a price of their creation."[43]

Cleveland denied that the papers in question were official merely because they were kept in the departmental files.

I regard the papers and documents withheld and addressed to me or intended for my use and action purely unofficial and private, not infrequently confidential, and having reference to the performance of a duty exclusively mine. I considered them in no proper sense as upon the files of the Department, but as deposited there for my convenience, remaining still completely under my control. I suppose that if I desired to take them into custody I might do so with entire propriety, and if I saw fit to destroy them no one could complain.[44]

The Senate debated the proposed resolutions over a period of two weeks. On the second day, a Democratic member, speaking against the majority report, pointed out the significant fact—which had escaped attention by the President and the Department of Justice, that the term of Duskin had expired and therefore his suspension was no longer an issue. The resolution censuring the Attorney General was adopted by a straight party vote of 30 to 26; but party lines broke over the second resolution, which passed by a majority of only one vote.[45] Soon afterward the nomination of Burnett was approved, and thereafter the Senate never again challenged the right of the President to suspend federal officers or inquired into his reasons for doing so. A number of the other nominations were held up for a period, some even eight to ten months, but in the end almost all were confirmed.[46]

The following year, Senator Hoar introduced a bill repealing the Tenure of Office Acts of 1867 and 1869, and it passed both houses and became law. In defending his bill, Hoar contended that these acts were unconstitutional because the power of removal was lodged exclusively with the President, and he maintained that less than ten members of the Senate really objected to their repeal. The prestige of the Senate, he stated, was lowered in such encounters with the President, for the Senate had always been worsted. Civil service reform required that the responsibility be imposed on the President. The acts were finally repealed, but in the Senate only four Republican votes were cast in favor of repeal.[47]

The Senate lost prestige in this contest with the President. Public opinion responded to the vigorous message of the President defending the executive power and regarded the controversy as merely a maneuver by Republican senators to keep Republican officeholders in office until their terms expired. Thereafter few nominations made by Cleveland were rejected by the Senate.

In Cleveland's second term, his nomination of William B. Hornblower to the Supreme Court in September, 1893, was rejected upon appeal to the rule of courtesy by Senator Hill of New York. The President then sent in the name of Wheeler E. Peckham, and this nomination was also rejected because of the objection of Senator Hill. Both nominees were conceded to be lawyers of outstanding ability, but they belonged to the party faction opposed to Senator Hill. President Cleveland then countered by sending in the name of Senator Edward Douglas White of Louisiana, and under the courtesy customarily extended by the Senate to its own members, this nomination was confirmed at once. Although Senator Hill was able to block the President's choices of New York attorneys, he was unable to secure the nomination of his own choice.

Insistence of Theodore Roosevelt on Qualification Standards

President McKinley, who was a former member of Congress, had few contests with the Senate over appointments. Theodore Roosevelt also followed the policy of getting along with the members of the Senate and avoiding patronage fights over local appointments, but he insisted on suitable standards for federal officers and asserted the right of the President to nominate. A former member of the United States Civil Service Commission and a firm supporter of civil service reform, Roosevelt followed the rule that members of Congress "may ordinarily name the man but I shall name the standard and the men have got to come up to it."[48] He exercised particular care in making judicial appointments, inquiring from all sources of information until he was certain that the best available man had been chosen. On two occasions he refused to accept a nominee of Senator Platt of New York and nominated men of his own choosing over the protest of the senator. He habitually took care, however, to consult the senators and to avoid an open fight. Replying to a petulant letter from Senator Platt in 1903 complaining that the President had passed over Platt's choice for a district judgeship in New York, Roosevelt pointed to the large number of eminent lawyers who had endorsed the man he planned to nominate and stated: "It is, I trust, needless to say that I fully appreciate the right and duty of the Senate to reject or to confirm any appointment according to what its members conscientiously deem their duty to be; just as it is my business to make an appointment which I conscientiously think is a good one."

Three days later, President Roosevelt wrote to Senator Platt to advise him of his decision, which was to nominate the person he himself had selected, stating in the letter that "it was a matter of greatest regret" to him that their judgments did not agree.

In 1906 Theodore Roosevelt again turned down a recommendation of Senator Platt for a judicial appointment. This action drew a strong protest from the senator, who stated that "it ought to suffice for me to simply say that I prefer Y. to H." Furthermore, Senator Platt contended, the appointment of the President's selection would "be recognized as an affront to the Senior Senator from the State of New York." Again Roosevelt wrote to Platt, asserting the right of the President to make the final selection:

In the next place, as to the "affront" to you; I do not understand how you can make such a statement. It is my business to nominate or refuse to nominate, and yours, together with your colleagues, to confirm or refuse to confirm. Of course the common sense way is to confer together and try to come to an agreement. It is just exactly what I have been doing in this matter.... As you do not indicate any possible objection to him, save that you insist upon having some one else, I must decline to consider that there will be any affront to you involved in appointing him.

Finally, I am sorry to say I must emphatically disagree with you and disagree with your statement that it ought to suffice me to have you simply say that you prefer Y. to H.... I cannot consider such a proposition. I have not considered my own individual preference and I cannot consider yours.[49]

In 1903 there came to light a good deal of laxity and fraud in federal land offices in the state of Oregon. The President notified the Oregon senators that he would not reappoint a certain land official whose term was about to expire, and asked them to suggest a fit person. Both senators declined to select a successor, believing that they could force the President to retain the incumbent.

On August 25, 1903, the President sent identical letters to each senator, in which he stated:

I cannot permit the incumbent to retain his position because there is a deadlock about his successor. He will be removed at once. In appointing his successor, and in appointing all other officers to these places, I must keep in mind that it is I who am primarily responsible for the appointment, not the Senators. If I appoint a man who is unfit, then of course you must refuse to confirm him; and as a matter of fact, if you will give me a man of whom I can approve, I will gladly appoint him."[50]

Roosevelt stated in his letter that since the Oregon senators had not selected a successor to the incumbent, he had selected a man whom he hoped they would accept. He also advised them that the other land offices in Oregon were in a disgraceful condition and that the incumbents would be removed immediately, and invited them to submit at once the names of first-class men for their places. Subsequent investigations of land-office frauds resulted in the sending of one of the senators to the penitentiary, but not until after he had written to the President in 1905 hotly criticizing the investigations, stating that they were destroying the party in Oregon. Bishop states that in the summer of 1905 Roosevelt several times was moved to very plain speech with senators who were pressing him to make improper appointments or promotions in the Army, or were trying to shield some person in the federal service who was found guilty of misconduct. To Senator Platt, who had urged clemency for an employee, he wrote tersely on May 22, 1905: "He was heard in full and given ample opportunity to defend himself. He was thoroughly investigated, and not only was it necessary to dismiss him, but it may be necessary to indict him."[51]

Taft's Proposal to Extend the Classified Service

Like all Presidents, Taft was inundated with applications from office seekers at the start of his term. Pringle states that three-fourths of his early letters and more than one-fourth of all mail throughout his term dealt with appointments.[52] Like other Presidents, Taft found the task of handling this flood of applications exceedingly distasteful as well as time consuming. By the end of 1910 he was determined to strengthen the civil service and to extend the classified service, even if it resulted in a Republican defeat, and told his brother: "I have adopted an ironclad rule that all local officers, i.e., postmasters, collectors, appraisers, etc., shall remain in office or be reappointed and no congressman or senator can have them removed. This is going to cause some kicks, but it is going to save me a lot of trouble and will make the service much more economical.[53]

In his annual message in 1910 Taft informed Congress that he had placed all assistant postmasters under civil service and recommended that first-, second-, and third-class postmasters be given similar protection.[54] Since these classes of postmasters were subject to confirmation by the Senate, legislation would be required to place them under civil service. Taft stated in his message that he was aware that this would require a considerable concession from the Senate with respect to its quasi-executive power, but defended his recommendation on the ground that it was in the interest of good administration and efficiency and "would relieve the congressmen who are now burdened with the necessity of making recommendations of a responsibility that must be irksome and can create nothing but trouble."[55] Taft's Commission on Efficiency and Economy recommended that the federal field officers appointed by the President and confirmed by the Senate be covered into the civil service. It also urged that the subordinate positions under these officers be placed under civil service, and maintained that this would result in a considerable reduction in the number of employees. Taft repeatedly recommended the extension of the civil service in messages to Congress, stating in one that "the President and members of Congress devote to matters of patronage time which they should devote to questions of policy and administration"; but he was unable to secure the necessary legislation.[56]

After leaving the White House, Taft later wrote of the burden imposed on the President by congressmen seeking appointments for their constituents and maintained that congressional patronage "more often injures than helps the user," for an appointment makes "one ingrate and ten enemies." In a lecture on the power of appointment, at Columbia University in 1916, he advocated that the President should appoint only the heads of departments and a political undersecretary in each. "All other officers in the departments," he said, "including the Assistant Secretaries and Chiefs of Bureaus, should have permanent tenure and not change with each administration."[57]

Wilson's Handling of Appointments

"It is with nominations," wrote Woodrow Wilson in 1885, "that there is the most friction in the conduct between the President and his overlord, the Senate."[58] His own administration thirty years later was marked by a number of such conflicts, though in the main he got along with the Senate and gave way when it was necessary in order to maintain the support of members of his party. The enmity between Wilson and Senator Reed of Missouri may be attributed, at least in part, to quarrels over patronage, though the real explanation is probably that Wilson refused to accord the customary patronage to an implacable foe. The most important senatorial confirmation case in Wilson's administration was the appointment of Louis D. Brandeis to the Supreme Court.* After a bitter fight, which lasted five months, the contest was decided by a strictly partisan vote, only one Democrat—Senator Newlands of Nevada— voting against confirmation. On important nominations Wilson was able to

---

* This is treated in the next chapt'

secure the unified support of his party, and on those of lesser importance he usually withdrew the nomination if it met with substantial opposition within the party. In dealing with the Senate about appointments, Wilson, like Lincoln, kept a proper perspective and did not permit patronage disputes to come between him and the members of his party whose support he needed in his legislative program.

In the closing days of the Taft administration, the Progressives joined with the Democrats to prevent the Senate from going into executive session to confirm 1,300 nominations submitted by Taft.[59] When Wilson became President in 1913 the Democrats had been out of office for sixteen lean years, and there was more than the usual rush of office seekers for appointment. McAdoo reports that thousands of them descended on Washington expecting recognition. Up to this time the President had personally handled the distribution of patronage. McAdoo suggested to the President that he could relieve himself of this burden by turning it over to the departments, and that this would also be in conformity with good business practice. Wilson was delighted with the proposal and immediately adopted it, publicly announcing that applications should be made to the departments concerned and that he would see applicants for office only on his own invitation.[60]

When Wilson was elected President he had few political debts to pay and was able to pick his Cabinet with great care, appointing the persons he believed to be best qualified, in some instances persons with whom he was not personally acquainted. His selection of Bryan for Secretary of State, however, was determined by political considerations. Bryan had a large following in the Democratic party, whose support Wilson needed. He later embarrassed Wilson because of his untiring efforts to find offices for the large host of "deserving Democrats" whom he knew personally.[61] Another appointment dictated by political considerations was that of Albert S. Burleson, who had served eight terms in Congress. Wilson brought him into the Cabinet because of this long experience, to serve as an unannounced "liaison officer" with Congress, particularly the House. As Postmaster General he handled the requests of members of Congress for postmasterships in their districts.

When the matter of postmasterships first came up, Wilson was determined that only the best-qualified persons should be appointed and asked for the entire list of applicants and the papers relating to them. Burleson sent over to the White House a huge volume of papers relating to several score of appointments due to be made immediately. Some of the candidates had secured hundreds of letters supporting their applications.

When Burleson made his first call on Wilson, whom he knew only slightly, these papers were piled high on the President's desk. Wilson opened the conversation by stating that his administration would be progressive, and that he did not propose to consult with "stand pat" or reactionary senators and congressmen about appointments but was going to appoint honest, capable, forward-looking men. Burleson, who later related an account of the conference to Baker, stated that he "never felt more depressed in his life. I knew it meant ruination for him." He decided to put the issue squarely up to the President at once and told him:

Mr. President, if you pursue this policy, it means that your administration is going to be a failure. It means the defeat of the measures of reform that you have next to your heart. These little offices don't amount to anything. They are inconsequential. It doesn't amount to a damn who is postmaster at Paducah, Kentucky. But these little offices mean a great deal to the senators and representatives in Congress. If it goes out that the President has turned down Representative So-and-so and Senator So-and-so, it means that that member has got bitter trouble at home. If you pursue the right policy, you can make the Democratic party progressive, as Cleveland made it conservative. And you can avoid the kind of rows that Cleveland had in Congress.

. . . .

As your Postmaster General . . . I am going to make 56,000 appointments. I will see honest and capable men in every office. But I will consult with the men on the Hill. I have been here a long time, Mr. President. I know these congressmen and senators. They are mostly good men. If they are turned down, they will hate you and will not vote for anything you want. . . .[62]

At the close of the conference Wilson asked that the papers be left with him and promised to think the matter over. A week later the President yielded to Burleson's point of view and thereafter accepted his recommendations without question.

Wilson followed the usual custom of consulting senators of his party about appointments, and in the early months of his administration many accounts appeared in the press about such conferences.[63] In two respects, however, he broke with tradition, for he frequently went to the Capitol to consult with members of the Senate, Republicans as well as Democrats.[64] It may be assumed, however, that his conferences with senators of the opposite party were quite different from conferences with members of his own party, and the practice of consulting Republican senators was discontinued after two years.[65]

It was not long before differences arose between the President and members of his own party. Several early appointments proposed in New York aroused the opposition of Senator O'Gorman; in these cases the President eventually withdrew the nomination and submitted another name, though it was not invariably the choice of the senator. This conflict was due to the fact that the Democratic party in New York was divided into a Tammany and an anti-Tammany faction. Senator O'Gorman, a Tammany man, strongly objected to several nominations which had been pressed upon the President by Secretary of the Treasury McAdoo, an anti-Tammany man. The prestige and power of the New York senator were at stake, and doubtless he was under pressure from

Tammany to demand control of the patronage. O'Gorman "stood on his constitutional right to withhold his advice and consent" to any appointment in New York that did not meet his approval, and eventually others were nominated whom the Senator approved.[66]

President Wilson also had difficulties over nominations for federal offices in his own state of New Jersey. The two New Jersey senators objected in 1914 to the appointment of a district judge who was not their choice, but they decided to make no issue of it, Senator Hughes saying that "the final responsibility for selecting the judge rested with the President."[67] Later in the year, however, when the President appointed a collector of internal revenue at Camden, Senator Martine objected on the ground that his senatorial prerogative had been infringed. Senator Hughes, who had secured the appointment of the collector at Newark, supported the right of the President to appoint any good Democrat in his own state, but the Senate rejected the nomination.[68]

In December, 1914, on the objection of Senator Reed, the Senate rejected without roll call the nomination of W. N. Collins to be postmaster of Kansas City and that of Ewing C. Bland to be United States marshal for western Missouri. The senator from western Missouri was customarily accorded control over federal patronage in that part of the state. Senator Reed's motion was adopted by the Senate without a single voice being raised in behalf of the President's nominee. "What happened in the Senate today," stated the New York *Times*, "is almost unprecedented in the history of the government. Few Presidents have had the control over their party that Mr. Wilson has exercised, but no one can recall so sudden and sharp a rebuke administered to a President by a House of Congress in which his party had safe control."[69] The Judiciary Committee went even further in asserting senatorial displeasure: because the President had appointed a United States marshal in western Missouri without consulting the senator from that part of the state, it appointed a special committee to investigate the recess appointments of the President. Senators Stone of Missouri, Williams of Mississippi, and Thomas of Colorado spoke against the committee report, but none voted against its adoption.

An editorial in the New York *Times* severely criticized the President for his action:

It was not necessary for him to quarrel with Senator Reed, Senator Martine, and Senator O'Gorman over a few little offices of no interest except to the localities involved. The President may think that he is fighting for a principle, but what he is actually doing is to jeopardize his great influence and the future success of his Administration...for the sake of proving to the Senators that his understanding of a clause in the Constitution is right and theirs wrong.... Mr. William G. McAdoo and Mr. Franklin D. Roosevelt are not in themselves epoch-making characters; but if to their bad advice is to be ascribed the wreck of the first Democratic Administration since Cleveland's, they will have their own little niche in history—such as it is...[70]

Wilson also had several nominations rejected upon the objection of members of the opposite party. Senator Gronna of North Dakota was able to block the appointment of a Mr. Bloom as postmaster of Devil's Lake in that state, and when Mrs. Bloom was subsequently nominated, she was also rejected by a unanimous vote.[71] A more important nomination rejected because of the opposition of a Republican senator was that of George Rublee in 1915 to the Federal Trade Commission. Senator Gallinger, a conservative Republican from New Hampshire, blocked the appointment on the ground that it was personally offensive to him. Rublee had acted as campaign manager for the fusion candidate opposing Senator Gallinger in 1914. After the Senate failed to act on the nomination, President Wilson gave Rublee a recess appointment. When the nomination came before the Senate again in 1916, it was rejected by a vote of 42 to 36. Senator La Follette assailed Senator Gallinger for invoking the "personally obnoxious rule," stating that it was the first time since he had been in the Senate that the rule had been applied without adequate proof and against a national appointment. The senator from Wisconsin maintained that, although Rublee had opposed Senator Gallinger in politics, he had not done so in an obnoxious way but had conducted himself in a courteous manner.[72]

The rejection of Rublee was not due to a lack of qualifications for the position. Joseph E. Davies, chairman of the Federal Trade Commission, stated in a letter to Senator Hollis of New Hampshire, who led the fight for the confirmation of Rublee: "He is equipped to an exceptional degree for a character of public service that is unusual, and which the government can ill afford to lose."[73] Theodore Roosevelt commented: "I am genuinely sorry Mr. Rublee was rejected. There could have been no better man for the place. It is a real public loss he is not to serve."[74]

Several of Wilson's appointments drew forth objections because of the business connections of the appointees. Paul M. Warburg, nominated for the Federal Reserve Board, withdrew his name after his nomination had been passed over at the same time others were confirmed, because "he did not care to undergo the humiliation of a prospective attack based on his business affiliations when his name came to be considered by the Banking and Currency Committee and the Senate." Wilson urged him to reconsider; he did so, and after appearing before the Senate committee he was confirmed.[75]

Several objections were raised against John Shelton Williams, nominated to be Comptroller of the Currency and ex officio a member of the Federal Reserve Board. His connections with the National City Bank of New York and his deposit of a million dollars with the Munsey Trust Company when he was serving under a recess appointment as Comptroller of the Currency were questioned, but his appointment was confirmed.[76] A third nomination that received similar treatment was that of Thomas D. Jones, also nominated for the Federal Reserve Board: Jones was subjected to an attack because of his connection with the International Harvester Company. President Wilson wrote to the chairman of the Banking and Currency Committee that Jones "went into the board of the Harvester Company for the purpose of assisting to withdraw it from the control which had led it into the acts and practices which have brought it under the criticism of the officers of the Government, and has been very effective in that capacity. His connection with it was a public service, not a private interest, and he has won additional credit and admiration for his courage in this matter."⁷⁷ When Jones was questioned at the hearings concerning his association with the International Harvester Company, he stated that he approved of all the company's acts since he had been a member of the board in 1909, and that no differences had arisen between him and the other directors. This testimony seriously impaired his chances, and the committee reported against confirmation. A stream of letters opposing his confirmation came to members of the Senate from the Midwest. Before the nomination came to a vote, at Jones's earnest request the President withdrew his name and released the correspondence he had had with him. The President strongly criticized the adverse report of the Banking and Currency Committee, saying: "The time has come when discriminations against particular classes of men should absolutely be laid aside and discarded as unworthy of the counsels of a great people."⁷⁸

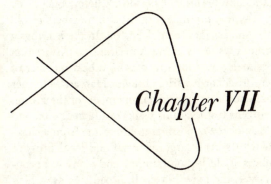

Chapter VII

THE BRANDEIS CASE

The undersigned feel under the painful duty to say to you that in their opinion, taking into view the reputation, character and professional career of Mr. Louis D. Brandeis, he is not a fit person to be a member of the Supreme Court of the United States. Memorial signed by William Howard Taft, Elihu Root, and three other former presidents of the American Bar Association.[1]

I believe that the rejection by the Senate of his nomination to the Supreme Court would be a grave misfortune for the whole legal profession, the court, all American business, and the country. President Emeritus Eliot of Harvard.[2]

EARLY in 1916, as the end of Wilson's first term approached and the presidential campaign loomed ahead, one of the most celebrated senatorial confirmation contests in history took place over the appointment of Louis D. Brandeis to the Supreme Court. Hearings were conducted by the Senate Judiciary subcommittee over a period of four months, and were twice reopened. The hearings filled two thick volumes of more than fifteen hundred printed pages, and the contest aroused public attention throughout the country. The prestige and leadership of the President were at stake. Had Brandeis been rejected, the appointment would have become an issue in the campaign and probably would have changed the result of the election. For several months the outcome was uncertain, but when the final vote came on June 1, less than a month before the Democratic national convention, the party line held and the appointment of Brandeis was confirmed.

No nominee to the Supreme Court ever faced stronger and more determined opposition. A group of leading members of the bar and prominent business-men not only entered a protest against the appointment but also engaged counsel to oppose it. Each side marshaled witnesses and vied with the other in securing the support of nationally prominent persons. The opponents led off with a petition signed by fifty-five prominent attorneys, members of old and highly respected law firms, and businessmen of Boston. In the hearings a memorial signed by seven former presidents of the American Bar Association was presented, stating that Brandeis was "not a fit person to be a member of the Supreme Court." However, President Emeritus Eliot of Harvard, a former president of the American Bar Association, prominent members of the Boston bar, and other distinguished citizens from various walks of life in Boston and elsewhere favored Brandeis. Most of the opposition to him came from a close-knit group of men identified with several large financial and legal firms of Boston. A number were members of old Boston families, and many were connected in one way or another with the New Haven Railroad, against which Brandeis had waged a long, relentless, and successful fight. An outsider, a Jew, and a skillful lawyer, who asked no quarter and gave none in his fights with some of the largest financial interests of the community, Brandeis had incurred the hostility of many members of the bar. At the time of the hearing on his nomination a Boston newspaper favorable to him ran an account showing the close interconnections of the fifty-five persons who signed a petition protesting his appointment, and calling attention to the fact that most of them belonged to a half dozen large law firms. Walter Lippmann stated in the *New Republic* that the opposition came from "the powerful but limited community which dominated the business and social life of Boston."[3]

It was not his law practice, however, which brought Brandeis their enmity, but rather his unpaid public activities in opposing the merger of the New Haven and the Boston and Maine railroads, his fight for lower gas rates and for public control of utilities, his support of minimum-wage legislation, and his war against trusts and monopolistic practices of the time. Over a period of years Brandeis had without compensation devoted a large part of his time to public causes. His practice as a corporation lawyer enabled him to observe the abuses of power by large corporations and monopolies, and he developed a philosophy opposed to bigness, irresponsible power, and some of the banking and financial practices of his day. Many influential businessmen, bankers, and leaders of the bar regarded him as an objectionable crusader, a radical, a socialist, and a person with dangerous economic ideas.[4] Although this group represented only a small segment of society, and even only a small part of the bar, it nevertheless included many of the most prominent citizens of the community. This opposition would ordinarily have been sufficient to cause the rejection of a nominee.

The New Haven Railroad, with which Brandeis waged a bitter fight, exerted a great influence throughout New England, extending to the leading banks, investment houses, law firms, and the press. In opposing its merger with the Boston and Maine, Brandeis exposed its reckless management and the fact that it was not earning the dividends it was paying and was concealing from the public the true state of affairs. Although these facts were subsequently sustained in the findings of the Interstate Commerce Commission investigation, the stockholders believed that Brandeis was responsible for the difficulties that beset the railroad and forced it to suspend dividends for more than a decade. His fights with the United Shoe Machinery Company and the insurance companies and the leading role he played in the Ballinger case won for him the bitter enmity of many influential citizens and their legal representatives.

The 1912 Campaign and After

In the presidential campaign of 1912, Brandeis, who had supported La Follette, did not follow the Progressives into the Roosevelt camp but came out and actively campaigned for Wilson. Anticipating that the trust issue might be central in the contest, Wilson sent for Brandeis early in the campaign and canvassed with him ways to win over the Progressives. Brandeis wrote a series of editorials for *Collier's* and took the stump in an extended campaign tour, speaking principally before chambers of commerce and groups interested in the trust issue.[5]

When Wilson came to select his Cabinet, he seriously considered appointing Brandeis as Attorney General. At that time an active campaign was being carried on against his appointment, by Bostonians who were identified with the New Haven Railroad and the United Shoe Machinery Company. The Boston News Bureau and *Truth*, both subsidized by the New Haven Railroad, attacked his integrity, stating that his altruism and concern over the public interest were a cloak behind which he received fat fees. James Ford Jones wrote Wilson that "men of affairs as well as lawyers, all of whom voted for you or President Taft, will regard the appointment of Mr. Brandeis as a member of your cabinet, should it be made, with profound regret."[6]

The Democratic organization in Massachusetts opposed the appointment of Brandeis to the Cabinet and even sent Wilson a photostatic copy of Brandeis' registration as a Republican. The treasurer of Wilson's campaign committee in Massachusetts, who held a private grudge against Brandeis, went to Washington to oppose the appointment.[7] Norman Hapgood, whom Wilson asked to investigate the accusations against Brandeis, reported to Wilson: "The more I study the charges against Brandeis, the more highly I think of him. I traced each to its source, and in every case it turned out to be made out of whole cloth, or, when understood, to be to the credit of Brandeis."[8] The only criticism which Hapgood could substantiate was that of lawyers who charged him with a lack of professional courtesy; this criticism Hapgood discounted. He reported to Wilson that the opposition had come mainly from "men who will oppose you anyway, as soon as the first serious struggle is on." A group of prominent Progressives in Boston, including Edward A. Filene and John H. Fahey, wired Wilson that the opposition to Brandeis had come from groups which had "sought undue privileges at the expense of our people," and called the charges which had been made against him "outrageous slanders."[9] In spite of these favorable reports, Wilson decided at the last minute to drop Brandeis from the Cabinet list and offered the post of Attorney General to James C. McReynolds, who was subsequently appointed to the Supreme Court.

Upon the death of Supreme Court Justice Lamar in January, 1916, Wilson asked Attorney General Gregory to suggest candidates for the vacancy, indicating that he wanted a man from New England. Gregory recommended Brandeis but warned the President that his nomination would be opposed and that he might have difficulty in securing the approval of the Senate.[10] Wilson apparently already had Brandeis in mind, and on January 28, without consulting any of the members of the Senate Judiciary Committee, he sent his nomination to the Senate.

Press reaction was sharply divided. The New York *Sun* declared that Brandeis was "utterly and even ridiculously unfit," and the New York *Press* termed the nomination "an insult to the members of the Supreme Court." The Boston *Transcript* regretted that the President had selected for the Supreme Court a man whom the Senate was unwilling to confirm as a member of the Cabinet, and the Boston *Herald* asserted that few of Brandeis' friends would claim that he was judicially minded. The New York *World,* however, described Brandeis as a "radical of unusual ability and character whose elevation to the Bench will be regarded by most people with emphatic approval," and the Baltimore *Sun* spoke of him as "a great force for progressive thought and action in the field of political and economic reform." The Boston *Post* said that he fully measured up to the high qualifications necessary for the position.[11]

The nomination took Congress by surprise, but it soon became apparent that it would encounter strong opposition. A newspaper poll indicated that thirty-six senators were opposed to it and many were undecided.[12] Among those who were critical of the appointment were several Democratic members of the Judiciary Committee, including Reed of Missouri, Overman of North Carolina, Hoke Smith of Georgia, Shields of Tennessee, and O'Gorman of New York, whose votes would be needed to get the nomination out of committee. Senator Overman, acting chairman of the Judiciary Committee, later said that if a vote had been taken when the nomination was received, Brandeis would have been rejected.[13]

Former President Taft said that the appointment was to him a "fearful shock . . . It is one of the deepest wounds that I have had as an American and a lover of the Constitution and a believer in progressive conservatism that such a man as Brandeis could be put on the Court. He is a muckraker, an emotionalist for his own purposes, a socialist." Taft went on bitterly to say that while Brandeis doubtless had certain high ideals, he also had much power for evil, and when he thought that his [Taft's] name had been suggested for the place, "it was to laugh."[14]

United States District Judge Charles F. Amidon wrote to Brandeis: "By your zeal for the common good you have created powerful enemies. They will do their utmost to defeat your confirmation in the Senate...You will be accused of everything, from grand larceny to a non-judicial temperament."[15]

The Hearings

The campaign for Brandeis was directed for the most part by Attorney General Gregory, who foresaw that it was imperative to hold the Democrats in line. He advised that those supporting Brandeis should carefully avoid stressing his progressive record, for this would alienate the Southern Democrats on the committee. Likewise, the impression of undue Jewish or labor support was to be avoided. Brandeis was advised to return to Boston and to keep entirely out of the fight. For a person accustomed to waging campaigns this course was difficult, but Brandeis recognized its wisdom and acted accordingly.

Knowing that many charges of unprofessional conduct would be circulated against Brandeis, Attorney General Gregory arranged for the hearings to be open to the public—an unusual procedure at the time. This move was essential to the approval of the nominee. If the hearings had been closed it would have been impossible to clear Brandeis of these charges; with open hearings, the opposing witnesses were more cautious in their statements. The hearings brought to public attention the fact that there was not sufficient factual evidence to substantiate the various accusations, or the accusations were controverted by reliable witnesses. When exposed to a searching inquiry, most of the charges and rumors of unprofessional conduct were revealed to be little more than prejudiced opinion.

George W. Anderson, federal district attorney in Boston, who had the full confidence of Gregory and Brandeis, offered his services to represent the Attorney General at the hearings, and the offer was accepted. His role was not that of counsel representing the nominee, for it was desired to avoid having the hearings take on the appearance of a trial; he acted rather as an assistant to the subcommittee by seeing to it that the evidence favorable to Brandeis was brought to its attention. Edward McClennen, a younger member of the Brandeis law firm, remained in Washington to follow the hearings and to supply any information desired by the committee. In the last days of the hearings he was on the witness stand for several days, answering the various charges that had been made against Brandeis. No one doubted that his testimony came directly from Brandeis. On the second day of the hearings, Austin G. Fox, a New York attorney, appeared to represent the fifty-five citizens who had signed a protest against the nomination. Thereafter he was permitted to select the opposing witnesses and generally to direct the opposition.

When the Judiciary subcommittee, headed by Senator Chilton of West Virginia, opened its hearings on February 9, 1916, the first opposing witness was Clifford Thorne, chairman of the Iowa State Board of Railroad Commissioners. Thorne had represented the state railroad commissions in opposing an increase in railroad freight rates in the celebrated Five Percent Case before the Interstate Commerce Commission in 1913, in which Brandeis acted as special counsel to the ICC. He testified that Brandeis had been "guilty of infidelity, breach of faith, and unprofessional conduct in connection with one of the greatest cases of this generation."[16] In this rate case the counsel for the railroads contended that their revenues were inadequate, and the attorneys representing the public contended otherwise. During the hearings, Brandeis often conferred with the attorneys representing the public, and he was regarded by Thorne as an associate on the public side. In making the closing statement of the hearings, to the astonishment and consternation of Thorne, Brandeis conceded that the net operating revenues of the railroads were "smaller than is consistent with their assured prosperity and the welfare of the community."[17] He did not concede, however, that the requested increase of rates should be granted, contending instead that economies in operation should be instituted and that rates on certain classes of freight then carried at a loss should be raised.

Whether Brandeis was guilty of unethical professional conduct, as charged by Thorne, depended on the terms of his employment by the commission. If he had been engaged to present the public case against rate increases, he should not have made so damaging a concession without consulting the counsel for the public side; if, however, he had been engaged not as an advocate of either side but rather to assist the commission in securing a well-rounded view of all pertinent facts and considerations, his statement was free of any blame. The letter of employment showed that he had been engaged on the latter terms. He had been asked to "undertake the task of seeing to it that sides and angles of the case are presented of record, without advocating any particular theory for its adoption." The letter stated further: "You will be expected to emphasize any aspect of the case which in your judgment, after examination of the whole situation, may require emphasis."[18] Other witnesses testified that Brandeis' conduct in the case was entirely proper and ethical.[19]

On February 9 one of the members of the Brandeis law firm learned that an effort was being made by Charles F. Choate, counsel for the New Haven Railroad, and others to secure some concerted remonstrance against the appointment of Brandeis to the Court. Two days later, a petition of fifty-five Bostonians, headed by President Lowell of Harvard, in opposition to the appointment was published. Their statement read in part:

"We do not believe that Mr. Brandeis has the judicial temperament and capacity which should be required in a judge of the Supreme Court. His reputation as a lawyer is such that he does not have the confidence of the people."[20]

The charges of the Boston protestants.—The first witness for the Boston group opposed to Brandeis was the notorious Clarence W. Barron, whose Boston News Bureau, subsidized by the New Haven Railroad and Charles Mellen, had conducted a vicious campaign against Brandeis over a period of years. Barron submitted a brief alleging the unprofessional conduct of Brandeis, but when he declined to divulge who had prepared it, Senator Walsh objected to its insertion in the record, as merely heresay evidence. Barron managed to place in the record an editorial in which he had asserted that the nomination of Brandeis was an "insult to New England."[21] Charles S. Mellen, former president of the New Haven Railroad, was expected to tell about the wrecking of that railroad by Brandeis, but he wired the subcommittee that he had no information except hearsay and was not opposed to the nomination of Brandeis. In view of Brandeis' long and bitter fight with Mellen, this statement was extraordinary. Earlier, Mellen had financed a series of advertisements violently attacking Brandeis as a "Railroad Wrecker."[22]

Other opposing witnesses testified that Brandeis was not straightforward, was untrustworthy, and had engaged in sharp and unethical legal practices. His ability as a lawyer all conceded. Moorfield Storey, counsel for the New Haven Railroad and a former president of the American Bar Association, stated that Brandeis' reputation "is that of an able lawyer, very energetic, ruthless in the attainment of his objects, not scrupulous in the methods he adopts, and not to be trusted."[23] Other witnesses voiced the same opinion. "A lawyer of great ability, but not straightforward," said Edward H. Hutchins, vice-president of the Boston Bar Association.[24] General Francis Peabody stated that "his reputation is that he is not always truthful, that he is untrustworthy, and that he sails under false colors."[25] Albert E. Pillsbury, a former attorney general of Massachusetts and counsel for the Boston public utilities, whom Brandeis had opposed in rate and franchise issues, went even further and accused Brandeis of "duplicity" and "double dealing" and said that he was "a man who works under cover."[26]

Most of the hearings were given over to the testimony of these and other opposing witnesses, who were asked to cite specific evidence of unethical conduct by Brandeis. They gave various examples of what they alleged was unprofessional conduct, but the evidence placed before the subcommittee failed to substantiate the charge. It is significant that the opponents of Brandeis elected to base their opposition on charges of this kind rather than state the real reason for their opposition: they regarded him as a dangerous radical. The witnesses who favored Brandeis, persons equally prominent, vehemently denied that there was any truth in these allegations. Those who were in charge of the campaign in favor of Brandeis made no mention of his extraordinary record in opposing monopolistic practices; nor did they mention his progressive views, which they recognized would not enlist the support of the conservative Democrats on the Judiciary Committee. Both sides, for different reasons, thus side-stepped the real issue.

The United Shoe Machinery Company.—The relations of Brandeis with the United Shoe Machinery Company came in for a good deal of attention.[27] Because one of his clients owned a large block of stock in the company, Brandeis served on its board of directors for a period of several years. In so doing he departed from his lifelong rule of never becoming involved in the business ventures of his clients. Not only was Brandeis an officer of the company, but his law firm acted as consulting counsel. In 1906, in the absence of the general counsel, Brandeis represented the firm in a hearing before a legislative committee, in opposition to a bill to prohibit contracts with "tying-in" clauses. Subsequently several shoe manufacturers came to Brandeis criticizing the monopolistic "tying-in" contracts of the United Shoe Machinery Company and so impressed him with the justness of their complaint that he attempted to persuade the company to revise its contracts. In this, however, he was unsuccessful. Brandeis came more and more to question the practices of the company and in 1907 decided to withdraw from the board and to discontinue to serve it as a legal consultant. He resigned on the ground of pressure of other business, without raising any issue of differences with the management.

In later years Brandeis criticized the United Shoe Machinery Company for its monopolistic practices. When the state legislature passed a law prohibiting "tying-in" contracts, the United Shoe Machinery Company got around the law by inserting a provision in its rental contracts permitting termination on thirty days' notice, which enabled it to prevent shoe manufacturers from using any equipment of a competitor. After Brandeis had severed all connections with the United company, a group of shoe manufacturers asked him to represent them in an attempt to break its monopoly contracts. This Brandeis declined to do, but he did prepare a brief on the legal issues involved. At the hearings, Winslow, president of the United Shoe Machinery Company, attacked Brandeis for criticizing practices that he had sanctioned when he was an officer of the company, and for using confidential information he had secured as counsel of the company later to oppose it. On questioning, however, Winslow was forced to withdraw these charges, and only his assertion that Brandeis had misrepresented the facts was allowed to stand.[28]

Instead of being blameworthy in this case, the conduct of Brandeis was deserving of praise. He refused to continue his connections with a company which engaged in practices he could not approve. After attempting unsuccessfully to secure changes in the company's policies, he resigned. For three years thereafter he engaged in no legal business in connection with shoe machinery manufacturing, and declined to act as counsel for a group of shoe manufacturers who desired to fight the United Shoe Machinery Company's contracts in court. The fact that he later cited the monopolistic practices of the company as an illustration of the evils of trusts was doubtless offensive to his former associates, but it was hardly unethical.

The Ballinger investigation.—Another attempt to indicate that Brandeis was not straightforward was the accusation that when he appeared before a congressional investigating committee in 1910 as the defense counsel for Louis R. Glavis, whose article exposing land frauds in the Department of the Interior had been published by *Collier's,* he did not announce that he was being employed and paid by *Collier's.* This relationship was well known to the members of the committee, the officials of the Department, and the press, and was taken for granted. Glavis at that time was only twenty-six years old and obviously was not financially able to employ expensive counsel. When the article by Glavis was accepted for publication, Norman Hapgood, the editor of *Collier's,* recognized that it would lead to a libel suit or to a congressional investigation, or possibly to both, and that *Collier's* would have to assume the responsiblity of defending itself and the author. At the conference of the editors and publishers, attended by Hapgood, Henry L. Stimson, George Wharton Pepper, and others, it was decided to engage Brandeis to represent Glavis, and the decision was reached that *Collier's* should not appear directly in the case as an interested party lest it be charged with attempting to exploit the case to its own advantage.[29]

The New England Railroad.—A similar charge was made relative to Brandeis' actions on behalf of the New York and New England Railroad. A former president of the railroad, Austin Corbin of New York, resigned in a dispute over the management and subsequently went to Judge Kelly, his attorney in New York, to have suits instituted to stop the management from paying unearned dividends and issuing bonds. Brandeis, who was engaged, brought suits in Massachusetts in the name of a Massachusetts stockholder. This was later criticized as a sharp practice, and Brandeis was later charged with having instituted the suits in the interest of the New Haven for the purpose of deliberately wrecking the New England Railroad. This was categorically denied in the hearings, by Judge Kelly and also by counsel for the New Haven.[30]

The Anti-Saloon League opposition.—Bishop Cannon appeared before the committee on behalf of the Anti-Saloon League to oppose Brandeis, who twenty-five years earlier had appeared before a committee of the Massachusetts legislature representing a brewers' association. In his statement before the legislative committee Brandeis had said that "liquor drinking is not a wrong; but excessive drinking is." Bishop Cannon objected to Brandeis because of this statement and because he had appeared as a paid lobbyist for the liquor interests.

The professional standards of Brandeis.—A number of other charges of un-professional conduct were made against Brandeis, but after they were explored by the subcommittee none was sustained. It was apparent from the testimony that most witnesses who believed that Brandeis had been unethical had little firsthand knowledge of the circumstances and situations, and, in fact, had secured their information from the scurrilous advertising campaign con-ducted by Charles S. Mellen and the New Haven Railroad against Brandeis. The powerful corporations which Brandeis had opposed had carried on a publicity campaign for years, using Barron and the subsidized Boston News Bureau as a willing tool, to destroy his reputation at the bar. That Brandeis had nevertheless retained his high reputation was indicated by the fact that for a number of years he had been selected by the board of overseers of Harvard University to visit and inspect the law school. On the committee with him were Justice Hughes of the United States Supreme Court and other judges and attorneys of great distinction. The board of overseers which selected Brandeis to serve on the committee consisted of many distinguished members of the bar of Massachusetts and neighboring states. Dean Pound stated in a letter to the subcommittee: "It cannot be that these gentlemen would have appointed him along with such colleagues to a position of such importance had they believed him deficient in professional honor or guilty of professional misconduct."[31]

The evidence indicated that Brandeis had an extraordinarily high standard of professional ethics and that his actions at times were misunderstood. Over a period of years he gave a large amount of his time to public-service activities, including legislative battles with large corporations, for which he received no compensation. When a group of stockholders of the Boston and Maine ap-proached him to assist them in fighting the merger of that railroad with the New Haven, they expected that he would charge a fee for his services. But Brandeis, seeing the great public interest involved in the case and the monopoly the merger would give the railroad over New England, would accept no compensation.[32]

For a period of twelve years Brandeis served as the unpaid counsel of the Public Franchise League of Boston in its battles with the gas company, the elevated railway, and other utilities. In the New Haven merger case, though he accepted no compensation, he paid his law firm more than $25,000 for the loss of his time. Similarly, he served as unpaid counsel in the fight with insurance companies, in defending the state minimum-wage laws of Oregon, Illinois, Ohio, and California, and in the 1910–1911 rate case before the inter-state Commerce Commission. He also was not compensated for his work as chairman of the arbitration board of the New York needle trades, which lasted from 1910 until he became a member of the Supreme Court. Nor was this all. He testified before many hearings of state legislative committees and committees of Congress on labor and corporation problems without being compensated.[33]

Throughout the hearings ran a thread of accusation that Brandeis was not as altruistic as he pretended, that behind his appearances and activities as the "people's attorney" was a concealed personal interest. It was difficult enough for some members of the subcommittee to understand his willingness to serve as counsel for the Public Franchise League without compensation; but to serve as unpaid counsel to the large stockholders of the Boston and Maine in the New Haven Railroad merger fight, to the shippers in the 1910-1911 rate case before the ICC, and to persons of wealth who were willing and able to pay for his services in other cases affecting the public interest was indeed inexplicable. E. A. Filene explained the skepticism in the minds of many, saying that if a man gave $50,000 a year to a public cause, that "would not create astonishment," but Brandeis gave his professional services, and such a gift was so uncommon it "aroused suspicions of his motives."[34]

After reviewing the charges of unprofessional conduct, Senator Walsh stated in his individual report to the Senate:

The real crime of which this man is guilty is that he has exposed the iniquities of men in high places in our financial system. He has not stood in awe of the majesty of wealth.... He has been an iconoclast. He has written and expressed views on ... movements and measures to obtain greater security, greater comfort, and better health for the industrial workers—signifying safety devices, factory inspection, sanitary provisions, reasonable hours, the abolition of child labor, all of which threaten dividends.[35]

The contest of character witnesses.—On the morning of March 14, near the end of the hearings, Austin G. Fox submitted to the Senate subcommittee a memorial signed by seven former presidents of the American Bar Association opposing the confirmation of Brandeis.* Former President Taft headed the list, which included also Elihu Root, Simeon E. Baldwin, Francis Rawle, Joseph H. Choate, Moorfield Storey, and Peter W. Meldrim.[36] The animus of several of the signers against Brandeis was easily recognized. Having in mind the Ballinger exposure, in the Taft administration, in which Brandeis played a prominent role, Walter Lippmann wrote in the *New Republic:* "One would have supposed that ex-President Taft was the last man qualified to express a judgment on Mr. Louis D. Brandeis."[37] Baldwin and Storey were actively associated with the New Haven Railroad in the merger fight, and Joseph H. Choate was an uncle of Charles F. Choate, general counsel for the New Haven.

It was initially planned by the Brandeis forces not to call any favorable witnesses but to rely instead on letters of testimonial and thus avoid the impression that Brandeis was seeking the job. But with such prominent witnesses as General Peabody, Moorfield Storey, A. S. Pillsbury, Sidney W. Winslow,

* The memorial appears at the beginning of this chapter.

and Edward Hutchins opposing, it was felt that a few favorable witnesses should testify. Sherman L. Whipple, head of a leading Boston law firm, had great effect in counteracting the testimony of opposing witnesses. Attributing to them the most honorable motives and all sincerity, he said that they had been misled by the campaign which the New Haven Railroad and the United Shoe Machinery Company had carried on to destroy the reputation of Brandeis. He also testified that they represented only a small segment of the opinion of the Boston bar, and that the great majority of the members of the bar, as well as the informed public, regarded Brandeis as a man of the highest integrity who was greatly devoted to the public interest. Newton D. Baker presented a memorial urging the confirmation of Brandeis, which had been circulated by Frances Perkins of New York. It contained the names of many prominent persons in New York and elsewhere—social workers, labor leaders, employers, publicists, economists, and others. Henry Moskowitz testified to the distinguished work which Brandeis had done as chairman of the board of arbitration of the garment industry in New York over a period of years. Other prominent witnesses appearing for Brandeis included Stephen S. Gregory of Chicago, former president of the American Bar Association, and Thomas J. Boynton, former attorney general of Massachusetts. Asa P. French, a former federal district attorney and a prominent member of the Boston bar, testified: "Among the rank and file of the Boston bar and the Massachusetts bar, so far as I know them, Mr. Brandeis has, in my experience, the reputation of being a man of integrity, a man of honor, a man who is conscientiously striving for what he believes is right."[38]

On March 15 the subcommittee adjourned its hearings, and the majority and minority reports were then prepared. The majority report was signed by Senators Chilton, Fletcher, and Walsh; the minority report by Senators Cummins and Works. So great was the interest in the case that individual reports were prepared by four of the five members of the subcommittee. Fox and his associates circulated the adverse reports throughout the country. In the meantime, a rumor was spread that Brandeis had been appointed because he had assisted Wilson in getting out of a nasty breach-of-promise suit by arranging for the purchase of alleged indiscreet letters to a Mrs. Peck. This story was later circulated in the campaign of 1916. When the yarn was brought to Brandeis' attention by a Boston minister, he replied: "No decent person should have been guilty of circulating this vile slander." He went on to say that he had first heard of the story some time after his nomination, and that it was being circulated by deliberate liars to defeat his confirmation.[39]

Weeks went by with no further action. Twice the hearings were reopened to receive additional evidence. The opponents of Brandeis circulated a rumor that Wilson did not care whether Brandeis was confirmed or not. The friends of Brandeis were impatient to get action and charged that the Republican

THE BRANDEIS CASE   [111

members were deliberately blocking a vote so as to delay confirmation until after the election, in the belief that they would then be able to defeat it. Senator Hoke Smith of Georgia, however, said that there was never a time before the final vote when a favorable vote could be secured. Senators Reed, Overman, Smith, Shields, and O'Gorman were still wavering.

Wilson's Testimonial for Brandeis

To counteract the report that the administration did not care whether or not the appointment of Brandeis was confirmed, and to spur the committee into action, George W. Anderson requested Attorney General Gregory to submit to the President a memorandum suggesting that he write a letter to the committee urging confirmation. This was done, and arrangements were made for Senator Culberson, chairman of the Judiciary Committee, to invite such a letter from the President. On May 5, President Wilson, drawing on the memorandum submitted by the Attorney General, wrote a long letter to Senator Culberson, reviewing the whole case and stating in unmistakable terms his desire to see Brandeis confirmed. He stated that the charges against him were not only unfounded but they "threw a great deal more light upon the character and motives of those with whom they originated than upon the qualifications of Mr. Brandeis." He went on to say that these charges, which had been thoroughly investigated three years earlier when he was considering the appointment of Brandeis to his Cabinet, came principally from persons who hated Brandeis because he had refused to "be serviceable to them in the promotion of their own selfish interests."

President Wilson paid the highest tribute to Brandeis when he wrote in his own words, without the aid of the Gregory memorandum, the fourth paragraph of the letter:

I perceived from the first that the charges were intrinsically incredible by anyone who had really known Mr. Brandeis. I have known him. I have tested him by seeking his advice upon some of the most difficult and perplexing public questions about which it was necessary for me to form a judgment. I have dealt with him in matters where nice questions of honor and fair play, as well as large questions of justice and the public benefit, were involved. In every matter in which I have made test of his judgment and point of view I have received from him counsel singularly enlightening, singularly clear-sighted and judicial, and, above all, full of moral stimulation. He is a friend of all just men and a lover of the right; and he knows more than how to talk about the right—he knows how to set it forward in the face of enemies. I knew from direct personal knowledge of the man what I was doing when I named him for the highest and most responsible tribunal of the Nation.[40]

On May 10 the Judiciary Committee held a short meeting to hear the letter from the President but immediately adjourned without fixing a date for the next meeting. The effect of the letter was the subject of speculation. It was reported in some newspapers that certain members of the committee resented the interference by the President, and the opinion was advanced that the letter might do more harm than good. At any event the letter put to rest the rumor that the President did not care about the outcome. Two days later the committee reopened the hearings, on the motion of Senator Sutherland, to hear further opposing testimony. The opposition secured a great deal of publicity unfavorable to Brandeis, chiefly through circulation of the minority reports. To counteract this the Brandeis supporters considered holding a mass meeting in Boston; McClennen, however, strongly advised against this on the ground that "the place will be packed with Jews and Labor men." President Emeritus Eliot of Harvard was asked whether he would be willing to act as moderator of such a meeting. He declined to do so, but wrote an unsolicited letter to Senator Culberson strongly endorsing Brandeis.* "Next to a letter from God," exclaimed McClennen to Senator La Follette, "we have got the best." The mass meeting was called off.

Personal Appeals to Doubtful Committee Members

Still the committee took no action. The adjournment of Congress was imminent, and the presidential campaign was already under way, with the national convention less than a month off. Personal appeals to the doubtful members were necessary before a favorable vote could be secured. Brandeis returned to Washington and through personal interviews won over two key members of the committee. Norman Hapgood offered to arrange a meeting between Borah and Brandeis, but Borah declined on the ground that such a meeting would be improper. One of the most influential members of the committee was Reed of Missouri, who was known to be hostile. Frank P. Walsh, editor of the Kansas City *Post,* began a campaign to influence Reed, but because of the long-standing feud between Reed and Walsh this did not have any noticeable effect. Jacob Billikopf, a prominent Jew of Kansas City, sent wires to hundreds of labor leaders in the state. These began to show results. On Sunday, May 14, Hapgood arranged an informal party at his apartment for Brandeis and invited Senators Reed and Hoke Smith, along with others. Senator Reed called, intending to stay so short a time that he left his wife in his car parked outside. Brandeis took him by the arm and together they sat down before the open fire, where for an hour, oblivious to the other guests, they discussed many subjects before the senator finally remembered that he had left his wife in the car and excused himself. Thereafter he was solidly for Brandeis.[41]

Senator Hoke Smith of Georgia, who was nursing a grievance because the President had not consulted the members of the Judiciary Committee before sending in the nomination, also attended the Hapgood party, and went away

* Quoted at the beginning of this chapter.

nollified. The President saw Shields of Tennessee, who was still doubtful, and with the aid of Gregory and Burleson, as well as Hoke Smith, brought him round. On May 20 the President attended a large celebration at Charlotte, North Carolina, in company with Senator Overman and Josephus Daniels. In his address he said: "You have every reason to be proud of your Senator, and I am glad to give him the tribute of my praises." Later Daniels reported to Wilson that Overman had been won over and would return to Washington an advocate of Brandeis.[42]

When the vote in the Judiciary Committee was finally taken, on May 24, it was 10 votes in favor of confirmation, all by Democrats, and 8 opposed, all by Republicans. The party regularity upon which the Attorney General relied had held.

When the nomination came to a vote in the Senate on June 1, the appointment of Brandeis was confirmed by a vote of 47 to 22. The three Progressives—La Follette, Norris, and Brandegee—and every Democrat except Newlands of Nevada voted for Brandeis, whereas every Republican voted against him. Seldom has there been a vote cast in the Senate that indicated so definite a partisan cleavage.

The Brandeis confirmation case is one of the most significant in the history of the Senate. It brings into sharp focus several important aspects of the process of senatorial confirmation—its strengths as well as its weaknesses. The case illustrates that a person who has played a leading role in civic and economic reform movements and has taken a definite stand on controversial public issues, particularly if he has incurred the hostility of powerful groups of society, will face strong opposition. Such a person can be confirmed only by the greatest effort, whereas a middle-of-the-road individual who has never participated in economic and social struggles or offended powerful groups is usually confirmed without opposition.

The opposition to Brandeis was due chiefly to the fact that his opponents regarded him as a dangerous radical and a crusader and hence unfit to sit on the Supreme Court, which they regarded as the bulwark of conservatism. The fact that he was a Jew and was an outsider who had become one of the outstanding members of the Boston bar doubtless was a factor in his opposition by the Boston group. Their stated reasons for opposing him, however, were entirely different—that he was not trustworthy and had been guilty of unprofessional conduct. Their charges of unprofessional conduct did not stand up under the examination of the subcommittee, though at the end, the senators who were opposed to Brandeis gave credence to practically all the charges, whereas those favoring confirmation took no stock in them. In the cases investigated by the subcommittee, it was found that the conduct of Brandeis was not only ethical and correct but indeed indicated that he had extraordinarily high professional standards.

The strategy dictated by Attorney General Gregory in the contest is highly significant. The nominee was advised to get out of town and stay out of town, and to make no statement to the press. He did not ask to appear before the committee on his own behalf, though at one time he was sorely tempted to do so. Before the final vote was taken, personal appeals by the President and members of his Cabinet were necessary to win over three wavering members of the Judiciary Committee, and a personal interview by the nominee with two others proved to be decisive. The determining factor in the contest was party alignment. Coming just before the presidential election of 1916, the vote had results that were certain to influence the outcome of the election. In a letter to Senator Owens a few days after submitting the nomination, Wilson wrote that "few things have arisen more important to the country and to the party than the matter of his confirmation."[43] If the nomination had been made in another year it is probable that it would have been rejected.

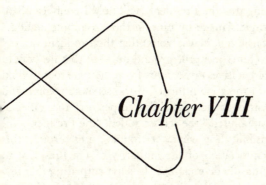

Chapter VIII

OPPOSITION BY SENATE
LIBERALS TO THE APPOINT-
MENT OF CONSERVATIVES

*The man who has never felt the pinch of hunger and who has never known what
it was to be cold, who has never been associated with those who have earned their
bread by the sweat of their faces, but who has lived in luxury, who has never wanted
for anything that money could buy, is not fit to sit in judgment in a contest between
organized wealth and those who toil. Senator Norris on the nomination of Charles
Evans Hughes to be Chief Justice of the Supreme Court.*[1]

THE REPUBLICAN presidents from 1921 to 1933 had rela-
ively few contests with the Senate over appointments. Those that did occur
were principally over the nominations of persons regarded as conservatives to
the Supreme Court or to the Cabinet. The insurgent Republicans, led by
Norris and La Follette, with the support of the Democrats, made a determined
effort to block the appointments of Hughes, Parker, and Stone to the Supreme
Court, thus serving notice on the administration that the nomination of conservatives to the Court would be opposed in the Senate. The liberal bloc was
able to bring about the rejection of the nominations of Parker to the Supreme
Court and Warren to the Cabinet. Their fight to liberalize the Supreme Court
was in a measure successful; the rejection of Parker was followed by the
appointment of Cardozo to the Court.

President Harding, whose nomination was engineered by a group of Republican senators, was elevated to the presidency precisely because he was
willing to follow their leadership. Soon after he became President, the White

House publicly announced that nominees to local offices would be selected by
the Republican senators, stating that the President "will hold Republican Senators to account for appointments made by him on their recommendation.'
In the interest of party responsibility, it was stated that the President desired
that the nominations come to him "from the ground up," but that he "would
look to the Republican Representatives or Senators from the state to give final
judgment as to the wisdom of the appointment." If the senators recommend
men "who prove to be unworthy or lack the ability to perform the duties of
the offices to which they are appointed," the release added, "the President will
place upon them the responsibility for whatever trouble arises through this
means."[2] A more explicit renunciation of the authority of the President to
nominate federal officers can hardly be imagined. It is not surprising that few
of Harding's nominees were rejected. But after three members of his Cabinet
implicated in great scandals, withdrew in disgrace and Veterans Administrator
Forbes, a Harding appointee, was convicted of fraud and sentenced to prison
members of the Senate had cause to regret that they had not subjected his
nominations to a closer scrutiny.

President Coolidge followed the usual policy of deferring to senators of his
own party with regard to federal appointments within their states, but he
maintained definitely higher standards of integrity and qualifications than his
predecessor. This was particularly true of nominations of judges, district attorneys, and marshals, which came under the supervision of Attorney General
Stone. Like Harding, Coolidge had few contests with the Senate over nominations, though a notable one occurred after his inauguration in 1925, when the
nomination of Charles Warren for Attorney General was rejected.

Soon after the inauguration of President Hoover, the White House, in
announcing the recess appointment of eleven judges, gave out the lists of their
endorsers, which was unprecedented. Hoover's selections were highly praised
by the New York *Times;* the newspaper also hailed the practice of making
public the endorsers of judicial nominees.[3] This innovation, which would
appear to have considerable merit, was not continued when the Democrats
came into power in 1933. Within a few weeks after he took office, President
Hoover announced at his press conference that he would not recognize the
Republican organization in several Southern states where there had been
patronage abuses, and that in those states the party would have to choose new
leadership before its recommendations for federal appointments would be
accepted.[4] Six months later the President released a stinging letter to the secretary of the Florida State Republican Committee rebuking the party organization in that state for attempting to dictate federal appointments and for
opposing the man whom Hoover had nominated to be district attorney in
Florida. "The appointive responsibility rests in the President," declared
Hoover, "not in any [party] organization. For seven months the Department

of Justice has investigated first one candidate and then another who were proposed by the Florida organization. The Department did not feel that they could conscientiously recommend to me any one of the names presented.... no longer shall public offices be regarded as mere political patronage, but it shall be public service."⁵

Harlan F. Stone

In opposing the appointment of Harlan F. Stone to the Supreme Court in 1925, Senate liberals made the first of their several attempts to block the appointment to the Court of persons they thought to be conservatives. Formerly dean of the Columbia University Law School and widely recognized as an able attorney and a man of the highest integrity, Stone had been appointed Attorney General by President Coolidge after Daugherty resigned under fire. The opposition to him was based mainly on the fact that his law firm had been engaged as legal counsel by the Morgan interests. In addition, Senator Walsh of Montana attempted to stir up opposition to the nomination because of a criminal action the Department of Justice had initiated against Senator Wheeler, who was charged with involvement in land frauds. The final vote on the nomination of Stone—71 for the nomination and only 6 against it—indicated that the large majority of members of the Senate took no stock in the charges against him.

In the Judiciary Committee hearings on the nomination, Senator Walsh interrogated Stone at great length concerning an action the Justice Department had instituted in the District of Columbia in the preceding year, seeking an indictment of Senator Wheeler in connection with a land-fraud case in Montana in which he had served as counsel.⁶ A special investigating committee of the Senate had absolved Senator Wheeler of any wrongful acts, and the suit against him in Montana apparently had been dropped, but on the basis of further investigation the Justice Department was attempting to secure his indictment and to bring him to trial before a federal court in the District of Columbia. Senator Walsh conducted what the Washington *Post* labeled a "gruelling examination" of Stone, "attempting to extort information from him regarding the nature of the charges" and the evidence that the Justice Department had. This was denounced by the *Post*, in a blistering editorial, as "shocking" and as "intimidation."⁷

The Judiciary Committee reported the nomination favorably, and when it came before the Senate for action on February 4, Senator Overman of North Carolina moved that it be considered in open executive session. Senator Moses, who was in the chair, ruled that the motion, being contrary to the rules of the Senate, would require a two-thirds vote in order to pass; on appeal, the ruling was sustained by a vote of 48 to 36. Senator Overman's motion then carried by a vote of 60 to 27, and the following day the Senate considered the nomination in open executive session.

On February 5 Senator Walsh obtained the floor and spoke at length in defense of his interrogation of Stone. He had little to say about Stone, for whom he professed to have the "very highest esteem," but at the end of his speech he attacked him for retaining in the Department of Justice some of the appointees of Daugherty, saying that "he has breathed the mephitic atmosphere of the Justice Department for the last year, permeated with the influence of Daugherty, whose malevolence toward Senator Wheeler was, I think, the occasion for bringing this indictment."[8]

Senator Heflin, who had earlier attacked Stone on the floor of the Senate when the nomination was still before the Judiciary Committee, spoke again, for about two hours, accusing Stone of unethical practices in a case involving the Morgan interests. Other members of the Senate who looked into these charges stated flatly that they were without foundation.

The principal speech against Stone was made by Senator Norris, who prefaced his remarks by conceding the high legal qualifications and personal integrity of the nominee. Senator Norris objected strongly to the practice which the Republican administration had followed of appointing persons identified with large corporations and great wealth to major policy-determining positions in the government. He said that, if the nomination of Stone had stood alone, he would have entered no objection, but when he considered it in the light of a number of similar appointments he felt impelled to protest. "With Morgan and Company's attorney on the Supreme Bench, with the Sugar Trust running the Attorney General's office, with the railroads themselves operating the Interstate Commerce Commission, with the greatest reactionary in the country sitting on the Federal Trade Commission, tell me—Oh, God, tell me!" he exclaimed, "where the toiling millions of honest, common people of this country are going to be protected in their rights as against big business."[9] Referring to the fact that Stone had been a member of a law firm which had served as legal counsel to the firm of J. P. Morgan, Senator Norris declared:

The man who has spent all of his life in an atmosphere of big business, of corporations, of monopolies and trusts, will be unconsciously, perhaps, and honestly, without a doubt, imbued with ideas that are a part of the man, part of the make-up of the man; and it is not necessary to charge him with the lack of ability, or with dishonesty, or with a lack of conscientiousness, in order to see that his decisions will lean in the direction of the influences and atmosphere under which he has lived and grown up. If we fill the bench and high executive offices with men who have the viewpoint of special interests, and the corporations, we will soon have put the common citizen under the yoke of monopoly, and will have put our government in the hands of trusts and corporations.[10]

Senator Borah spoke in defense of the nomination, saying that Stone was "one of the most liberally minded men who has been in the office of Attorney General for many years," and that it was with the "deepest regret" that he saw him leave the Attorney General's office where he had done "splendid work ever since he has been there." When the vote was taken, Stone was confirmed by an overwhelming majority, only six senators voting against his confirmation. His subsequent record on the Supreme Court indicated that the opposition was misplaced.

The Rejection of Charles Beecher Warren as Attorney General

Upon his inauguration in 1925 President Coolidge nominated Charles Beecher Warren, a prominent attorney and businessman of Michigan, to be Attorney General, probably with no expectation that the nomination would encounter opposition and would be rejected after a bitter fight. No nomination to the Cabinet had been rejected since 1868, when the radical majority of the Senate, smarting under its inability to impeach President Johnson, petulantly refused to confirm the nomination of Henry Stanbery. And only two other Presidents—Jackson and Tyler—had a nomination to the Cabinet rejected by the Senate, each under quite exceptional circumstances.* Because of the well-established tradition which accords the President a free hand in the selection of members of his Cabinet, President Coolidge and his advisers doubtless assumed that the appointment of Warren would be confirmed with little if any opposition.

There were other reasons why the President might have felt confident in his choice. Warren was a man of great wealth, the head of a large corporation, an attorney of high standing, a prominent member and former national committeeman of the Republican party, and formerly United States ambassador to Japan and subsequently to Mexico. The Republicans had a large majority in the Senate, though included in their ranks were several insurgents and Progressives. When the Judiciary Committee promptly reported the nomination favorably to the Senate on March 6, the Republican leaders were entirely confident of the approval of Warren.

The following day the administration forces suffered their first rebuff at the hands of the insurgents and the Democratic minority. Senator Reed of Missouri moved that the nomination be considered in open session. Senator Moses, who was presiding, ruled that this was contrary to the rules of the Senate and the motion would require a two-thirds majority for adoption. Whereupon Senator Reed appealed, and the decision of the chair was overruled by a vote of 39 to 38. The vote on Senator Reed's original motion for an open session then carried by 46 to 39 over the opposition of the administration supporters. "Despite the revolt staged today," stated the New York *Times*, "it is believed probable that Mr. Warren's nomination will be con-

* For an account of these earlier rejections of nominations to the Cabinet, see chaps. iv and v, above.

firmed by a considerable majority after the opposing senators have recorded their protests."[11] Two days later, to the astonishment of the country, the Senate rejected the nomination by a vote of 41 to 39.

The debate on the nomination was opened by Senator Walsh of Montana, who stated that "under all ordinary circumstances the nominations of the President of the United States for members of the Cabinet should be confirmed by the Senate without delay and that opposition of a political or factional character ought to be discountenanced." He went on to say that the President was charged with the execution of the laws, and "ought to be given the greatest liberty possible in the selection of those who [are] immediately under him." Nevertheless, he maintained, under the Constitution the Senate also shares in the responsibility of the selection of the principal officers of the government, and it was not intended that its approval should be perfunctory. He did not agree that presidential nominations to the Cabinet should be approved unless the nominee was morally disqualified. A person of the highest moral character, he pointed out, might be wholly unfit for office.[12]

Senator Walsh attacked the nomination on two grounds: (1) that the nominee did not have the high legal qualifications requisite to the office, and (2) that he had been identified with the Sugar Trust and hence could not be relied upon to enforce the antitrust laws. The debate centered around the second point.

Concerning Warren's legal qualifications, Senator Walsh stated flatly that he "had no reputation whatever as a lawyer," and that attachés of the Supreme Court could not recall any case in which he had appeared as counsel.[13] Little attempt was made to answer this charge before the vote was taken, so confident were the Republican leaders that they had enough votes in hand. A week later, however, before the vote was taken on Warren's renomination, Senator Pepper of Pennsylvania said that from his own knowledge of Warren over a period of twenty-five years he could state that he was one of the leading lawyers of the country. He also placed in the record telegrams from several federal and state judges of Michigan, the president and a former president of the Michigan State Bar Association, and others, which stated that Warren was a lawyer of the highest standing in his profession, a man of high integrity, and in every way qualified for office.

The primary objection of Senator Walsh to Warren was not his lack of professional qualifications but his association with the American Sugar Refining Company, referred to in the debate as the "Sugar Trust." Said Senator Walsh: "I think that he ought not to be made Attorney General not only because he is not eminent in the profession but chiefly because for years he was a representative in his State of the Sugar Trust, one of the most offensive and most oppressive trusts with which the American people have unfortunately been familiar in the present and past generation."[14]

From 1902 to 1906 Warren had been the representative of the American Sugar Refining Company in Michigan, acting not merely in a legal capacity but also as its agent. In this period he purchased the stock of a number of small refining companies, organized the Michigan Sugar Company to take over six independent concerns, and became its president. Warren continued as president of this company, which was owned in large part by the American Sugar Refining Company, until 1925, shortly before he was nominated to be Attorney General.

Senator Walsh made much of the fact that the Michigan Sugar Company was one of sixteen sugar manufacturers cited in an action recently initiated by the Federal Trade Commission, which charged that they had entered into an unlawful contract to control the marketing of sugar pulp. Referring to the fact that before he entered the Cabinet, Secretary of the Treasury Mellon had been the head of the American Aluminum Company, which had also been cited by the Federal Trade Commission for violation of the antitrust laws, Senator Walsh exclaimed: "Just imagine, the Aluminum Company of America being brought to book by Charles B. Warren for having violated the Sherman Antitrust Act!" In concluding, Walsh declared that if the nomination were confirmed Congress should repeal the Sherman Act.[15]

The administration supporters in the Senate, confident of the outcome, pressed for a vote. Senator Cummins, chairman of the Judiciary Committee, made the only statement of any length in defense of Warren. Referring to a statement of Senator Walsh before the committee, that Warren would be a fit appointment for any federal office except Attorney General, Senator Cummins maintained that the issue was narrowed to whether "a lawyer who has been faithful to one client will not be faithful to another." He pointed out that Warren's connection with the Sugar Trust had taken place twenty years earlier, and contended that there was no reason to suppose he would not be faithful to his duties as Attorney General.

Senator Cummins maintained stoutly that the President should be permitted wide latitude in choosing the members of his Cabinet. He defended Warren against the charges made because of his association with the American Sugar Refining Company from 1902 to 1906. At that time, maintained Cummins, "Mr. Warren could have had no conception that what he did was a violation of the antitrust laws." He said it was not until years later that court decisions interpreting the meaning of the Sherman Act held such actions to be conspiracies in restraint of trade.[16] At the time Warren was employed by the American Sugar Refining Company, he stated, it was regarded as a highly respectable corporation, and it was not until years later that it came to be condemned in the public mind as a vicious trust.

The most bitter and perhaps the most effective attack on Warren was made by Senator Reed of Missouri, who delivered one of his famous philippics, charging him not only with violation of the antitrust laws but with betraying his associates, with organizing a trust to cheat the sugar-beet farmers out of fair prices for their crops, and with being a representative of predatory wealth. Although Senator Walsh had conceded that Warren was a man of integrity, Senator Reed made no such concession but denounced him as a criminal and a scoundrel. He took no stock in the argument that Warren had been instrumental in changing the Sugar Trust into a legitimate business by persuading it to dispose of its stock in other sugar companies. "He wanted to save his own precious skin," Senator Reed declared; "...the conversion came to him because he feared the lash of the law upon his back and heard in the distance the clanging of a prison door."[17] He compared Warren to Albert Fall, whose criminal acts were still fresh in the minds of the senators. In an oratorical outburst, Senator Reed declared that the "march of monopoly and the continued advancement of trusts will spell disaster in the end" and that they will bring about government control and lead to socialism. He warned conservatives against enthroning great wealth in this country, stating: "Those of you who propose to stand here to-day and uphold the hands of this trust organizer, this trust promoter, this trust conspirator, thinking you are doing a service to wealth, are in the end doing it a disservice."[18]

Senator Reed saw no merit whatever in the contention that the President should be permitted to have a free hand in the selection of the members of his Cabinet; he regarded it as a vicious and wholly unsupportable doctrine. "There is no such thing as a presidential Cabinet," he said. "That is a mere name, a mere figure of speech."[19] In advocating that the Senate make a thorough scrutiny of the nominations of department heads, Senator Reed practically denied the existence of any executive power in the government. He contended that executive offices are created by Congress and are responsible to it rather than to the President. "We make the office," he declared. The fact that the President may call on the Attorney General for legal opinions, he contended, was immaterial, for every other department of the government, and Congress as well, can do so if it wishes. Senator Reed maintained that the importance of the office of Attorney General made it necessary for the Senate to consider the nomination with great care. The appointment of a man with Warren's record, he contended, a man who could "paralyze every prosecution of every trust, and grant immunity to every scoundrel who has been engaged in a conspiracy against the people of the United States," would be "so bald, so insolent, and so indefensible," as to be unparalleled. "What will the people say," he exclaimed, "as they behold the spectacle of the trusts naming the Attorney General of the United States, of the Sugar Trust presiding over the Department of Justice, and from that high place protecting the combinations of the past and the present?"[20]

The vote which followed indicated that the attacks on Warren by Senators Walsh and Reed were effectual. The unsavory record of Attorney General Daugherty, whose appointment had been confirmed by the Senate without opposition, was fresh in the minds of members, and scandals of the Harding administration were still being investigated. The vote on Warren was a tie, 40 to 40. Vice-President Dawes was at his hotel taking an afternoon nap; had he been present, Warren's appointment would have been confirmed. When the administration senators realized how close the vote would be, they made frantic efforts to get Dawes to the Senate chamber. Before the vote was announced, Senator Reed of Pennsylvania secured the floor and switched his vote, thus enabling him to move immediately for reconsideration. Senator Walsh countered with a motion to table, and the roll was called on his motion. Since a majority vote was required to table, it was thought that the motion would be lost by a tie vote, but on this vote Senator Overman of North Carolina switched and the motion carried. When the Vice-President arrived it was all over. Warren had been rejected.

The press reaction to the rejection was generally unfavorable, although the New York *World* and the Democratic papers of the South defended the action of the Senate. The majority of the press condemned the action as a partisan maneuver to embarrass the President and contended that he ought to be permitted to choose his Cabinet. The New York *Times* criticized the Democrats for combining with the insurgents, whom it dubbed "elements of arrogant self-righteousness, of malice, mischief, obstruction,"[21] and the Boston *Evening Transcript* stated that "in any clear-cut issue between the President and either branch of Congress, the people instinctively turn to the former."[22] Later, when the second debate on the confirmation of Warren took place, the New York *Times* stated in an editorial: "What will the country think of a Senate which swallows Harry Daugherty and strains at Charles Warren?"[23]

Indignant at the action of the Senate, President Coolidge, against the advice of Senate Republican leaders, determined to renominate Warren. If the President had been able to marshal public opinion on the issue, he might have succeeded in forcing the Senate to reverse itself, but characteristically he made little effort to do so. Furthermore, in the midst of the second debate, the White House ineptly issued a statement baldly announcing that if Warren was again rejected by the Senate he would be given a recess appointment. This announcement created a furor in the Senate and destroyed any chance that a renomination of Warren would be approved.

The second debate was in many respects a repetition of the first, though the proadministration members belatedly came to the defense of Warren. Significantly, the Republican leaders who had advised the President against the renomination did not participate but left the defense to new members of the Senate.

Senator Pepper of Pennsylvania made a temperate and well-reasoned speech in defense of Warren.[24] He contended that Warren's activities in acquiring the stock of Michigan sugar companies for Havemeyer and in organizing the Michigan Sugar Company were not looked upon at the time as violations of the antitrust laws. He argued that merely because Warren had once engaged in the formation of corporations which would now be regarded as illegal, it did not follow that as Attorney General he would be remiss in prosecuting such companies. He cited the example of Philander C. Knox, who as a corporation lawyer had engaged in the formation of trusts, but later as Attorney General vigorously enforced the antitrust laws. Senator Pepper contended that there was no reason to suppose that Warren, who was conceded to be a man of integrity, would not pursue the interests of the government as Attorney General as faithfully and as vigorously as he had advanced the interests of his private clients.

Senator Reed of Missouri threw a bombshell into the debate by reading a White House press release which stated that if the appointment of Warren was not confirmed by the Senate, the President would give him a recess appointment. Members of both parties were incensed by this open defiance of the Senate. Senator Reed declared: "I can not bring myself to believe that the President of the United States is so lost to a proper conception of his duty as to take a position so arbitrary, so unjustifiable, and so violative of the spirit of the Constitution."[25] Senator Walsh pointed out that although Presidents had occasionally given recess appointments to nominees who had been rejected by the Senate, no President had ever before announced publicly while the Senate was considering a nominee that he would give the nominee a recess appointment if the Senate rejected him. This announcement was regarded as a challenge of the powers of the Senate, and a motion was passed that the vote be held over until the following week.

On March 18 the Senate voted for a second time on the nomination of Warren, and rejected him by a vote of 46 to 39. A short time afterward the White House announced that Warren had declined to accept a recess appointment, and the President sent in the name of John G. Sargent, attorney general of the State of Vermont. This appointment was promptly and unanimously confirmed. Sargent, a small-town lawyer in his home state, had never been accused of being employed by large corporations, and his legal background was as spotless as it was undistinguished. His record as Attorney General under President Coolidge was not noted for enforcement of the antitrust laws.

Charles Evans Hughes

In February, 1930, Chief Justice Taft resigned from the Supreme Court because of ill-health, and on the same day President Hoover announced the nomination of Charles Evans Hughes to take his place. The appointment of

Hughes—a former member of the Supreme Court, who had resigned in 1916 to become the Republican candidate for President, a former governor of New York, and Secretary of State under Presidents Harding and Coolidge—was acclaimed by the press throughout the country. Hughes was unquestionably one of the ablest and most highly respected members of the American bar, and included among his clients many large corporations and persons of great wealth. The Judiciary Committee reported the nomination favorably, though Senator Norris, its chairman, filed a minority report. When the nomination came before the Senate, Norris and his Progressive colleagues, joined by a number of Democrats, opposed the nomination. Although the final outcome was never in doubt, one of the most notable contests in the history of the Senate over a nomination to the Supreme Court occurred.

The opposition centered its attack on Hughes chiefly for his economic views as indicated by several briefs that he had filed in cases before the Supreme Court and for his association as attorney with the largest corporations of the country. "When during the last 16 years," asked Senator Borah, "has corporate wealth had a contest with the public ... that Mr. Hughes has not appeared for organized wealth and against the public?"[26] Senator Norris stated in his minority report that Hughes had appeared before the Supreme Court fifty-four times "for corporations of untold wealth," and charged that "he looks through glasses contaminated by the influence of monopoly as it seeks to get favors by means which are denied to the common, ordinary citizen."[27] Although conceding that Hughes was one of the greatest lawyers in the country, Senator Norris stated that in his judgment other qualifications were necessary. Referring to Hughes's lucrative law practice, he declared:

He has not seen the man who suffers, the man who knows what it is to be hungry and not have the necessary money with which to buy food. His vision has extended only to that limited area which is circumscribed by yellow gold. . . . I am not willing that there should be transferred from that kind of surroundings one who shall sit at the head of the greatest judicial tribunal in the world; I am not willing to say that that kind of man, regardless of his ability, should go on the Supreme Bench.[28]

Senator Borah opened his remarks in opposing the appointment of Hughes by reviewing a recent Supreme Court decision concerning the rates of the Baltimore Street Railway Company, with which he disagreed. In this case the Court by a divided vote had held that the company was entitled to include five million dollars for the value of its franchise in its valuation, and that a return of only 6.26 per cent was confiscatory. Although Hughes had nothing whatever to do with the case in question, Senator Borah opposed his appointment to the Supreme Court on the assumption that he would have sided with the majority—an assumption based on nothing more than the fact that on occasions Hughes had acted as the attorney for public-utility companies.

Throughout the debate other senators also referred frequently to this Baltimore case, citing it as grounds for opposing the appointment of Hughes to the Court. In this they misjudged the nominee, for Chief Justice Hughes subsequently voted with a majority of the Court to reverse its earlier valuation decisions. Like Senator Norris, Borah conceded that Hughes was a distinguished American of wide reputation, high standing, and acknowledged ability, but he said: "I am only concerned with the proposition of placing upon the court as Chief Justice one whose views are known upon these vital and important questions ... views which ought [not]to be incorporated in and made a permanent part of our legal and economic system."[29]

Senator Glass opposed the confirmation of Hughes because of "his lack of sensibility" in resigning from the Supreme Court to become a candidate for President, which, he declared, shocked and "grievously distressed" the whole country.[30] The two New York senators came to the defense of Hughes, both speaking of him briefly but in the highest terms.

Realizing that every day of delay strengthened the opposition, Senator Watson, the Republican floor leader, who had sufficient votes in hand, pressed for a vote. The only speech supporting the nomination was made by Glenn of Illinois, a new member of the Senate. He reviewed the record of Hughes as a member of the Supreme Court, citing numerous cases in which Hughes had taken the side favorable to labor. He stated that Hughes had supported many labor laws and was regarded by labor itself as the "greatest friend of labor laws" ever to occupy the governor's chair at Albany.[31] Senator Glenn also pointed out that Hughes had served as counsel to the United Mine Workers of America in the celebrated Coronado Mining Company case and in another noted case. Aside from these brief references, however, no attempt was made to bring out the nominee's liberal record.

Senator La Follette declared that the issue was the "usurpation of power" by the courts. Reviewing the growing practice of the courts to declare social and economic legislation unconstitutional, he stated that "... consistent study of the record of the court during the last 40 years will demonstrate that the United States Supreme Court in case after case, involving great problems of economic and social significance to the rank and file of the people of the country, has declared laws unconstitutional because the court, or a majority of it, did not agree with the legislative purpose and the objectives sought by Congress."[32] Because of this growing tendency of the Supreme Court, Senator La Follette maintained that it was highly important to consider the economic and social philosophy of persons nominated to the Court.

The final vote on April 13 was 62 to 26 for confirmation. The Progressive Republicans, led by Norris, Borah, Nye, and La Follette, voted solidly against confirmation and were joined by about half of the small group of Democratic senators. In retrospect it would be almost universally agreed that the liberals mistook their man in opposing Hughes. His record on the Court was that of a liberal justice, who frequently sided with Justices Holmes, Brandeis, Cardozo, and Stone. The opponents did not hope to defeat the appointment of Hughes, but rather to serve notice that they would scrutinize all appointments to major policy positions and would stand ready to fight the nomination of conservatives. The case is significant because emphasis was placed, not on the ability and qualifications of the nominee, which were conceded, but rather on his economic and political philosophy. Senators Norris, Borah, and La Follette were right in insisting that this is an appropriate subject for the Senate to consider in passing upon a nominee for the Supreme Court, but they erred in the assumption that because Hughes had been an attorney for large corporations, he was necessarily committed to his clients' philosophy. It was anomalous that most of the argument against him dealt with decisions of the Supreme Court in which he had no part, on the unsupported assumption that had he been a member he would have sided with the conservative majority of the Court. The opposition served a useful purpose, though had it prevailed the country would have been deprived of the services of a Chief Justice who now ranks with Marshall and Taney.

The Rejection of John J. Parker

In the spring of 1930 the nomination of John J. Parker to the Supreme Court by President Hoover was subjected to a vigorous attack by the liberals in the Senate and throughout the country. Eventually it was rejected by a narrow vote—the first nomination to the Supreme Court to be rejected by the Senate for a period of thirty-six years.

Judge Parker was a prominent Republican of North Carolina, a former candidate of his party for governor, and formerly the national committeeman from that state. He was appointed by President Coolidge in 1925 to be a member of the fourth circuit court of appeals of the United States and was sitting as a federal judge at the time of his nomination. As a jurist he had a high reputation, which continued to grow after his rejection. In 1945 he was selected by President Truman as the alternate American member of the Nuremberg court for the trial of Nazi war leaders. Although he was opposed in 1930 by liberals and by prominent Negro leaders who thought he was prejudiced against members of their race, his record both before and after the rejection indicates that they were mistaken in their opposition. He is today widely recognized as a distinguished and liberal judge.

The final vote of 39 for to 41 against confirmation of the appointment of Parker was a notable victory for the groups that opposed him, particularly organized labor and the National Association for the Advancement of Colored People. It indicated the power of organized groups to block an appointment which they regard as objectionable. The Progressive Republicans in the Senate, led by Borah, Norris, and Johnson, who had no love for President Hoover, vigorously opposed the nomination, and most of the Democratic members joined in the opposition in an effort to embarrass the administration. The nomination was supported by the administration senators and by the press generally throughout the country, as well as by a great majority of the bar. The opposition to Judge Parker was based on three contentions: (1) that he favored "yellow-dog" contracts and was unfriendly to labor; (2) that he was opposed to Negro suffrage and participation in politics; and (3) that the appointment was dictated by political considerations.

In opening the public hearing on April 5, 1930, Senator Overman of North Carolina, chairman of the Judiciary subcommittee, placed in the record some twenty pages of endorsements of Judge Parker by prominent persons in his state—public officials, labor leaders, Negro educators—newspaper editorials, and letters from various citizens.[33] The list of endorsers was headed by Governor Max Gardner of North Carolina, who wrote that he had "the most implicit faith in his character as a man of integrity, and ability as a judge... In my opinion, Judge Parker enjoys the confidence and esteem of an overwhelming majority of the people of this state, irrespective of party affiliations. They respect him as a man, admire him as a judge, and that he would some day be elevated to the Supreme Bench had become a sort of general hope and expectancy." Referring to the "fear expressed by one group of our citizens," Governor Gardner stated that he had never known any man "whose concern for the upholding and protection of human rights" excelled that of Judge Parker.[34] This was, indeed, high praise, coming from the state governor of the opposite party.

Appearing in opposition to the appointment, President William Green of the American Federation of Labor made it clear that his organization did not question the integrity, honor, or "academic" qualifications of Judge Parker. He contended, however, that in the Red Jacket case,[35] which sustained an injunction in a yellow-dog contract case, Judge Parker had betrayed "a judicial and mental bias in favor of powerful corporations and against the masses of people." Green summed up his opposition as follows:

Labor is of the opinion that the appointment and confirmation of Judge Parker means that another injunction judge will become a member of the Supreme Court of the United States. As a result, the power of reaction will be strengthened, and the broad-minded, humane, progressive influence so courageously and patriotically exercised by the minority members of the highest judicial tribunal of the land will be weakened. There is the kernel in the nut.[36]

The opposition of organized labor to Judge Parker turned entirely on the decision of the circuit court of appeals in the Red Jacket case, which he had delivered. In this case, the court, following the decision of the Supreme Court

in the Hitchman case,[37] upheld an injunction granted by a lower court enjoin-
ing the union "from inciting, inducing, or persuading the employees of the
plaintiff to break their contract of employment," that is, to join the union.
Although Green dealt at length in his testimony before the Senate subcommittee on the evils of yellow-dog contracts, actually the legality of such contracts was not an issue in the Red Jacket case. Green contended, however, that
Judge Parker had shown by his language in that decision that he was "in entire
sympathy and accord with the legal and economic policy" of yellow-dog contracts. The passages objected to do not appear to indicate either approval or
disapproval of yellow-dog contracts but merely cite the decision of the Supreme
Court in the Hitchman case as being "conclusive on the point involved here."[38]
The attorney for the United Mine Workers in the Red Jacket case, who appeared at the hearing, stated that in his opinion Judge Parker felt that the
court was bound by the previous decision of the Supreme Court in the
Hitchman case and that the decision did not indicate that he favored the
yellow-dog contract.[39]

The other principal opposition to Judge Parker came from the National
Association for the Advancement of Colored People. Walter White, acting
secretary of the association, who appeared at the hearing, based his opposition
entirely on a statement Judge Parker had made as the Republican candidate
for governor of North Carolina in 1920. In reply to charges made by his
Democratic opponents, Judge Parker denied that the Republican party intended to enfranchise the Negro, and stated: "The participation of the Negro
in politics is a source of evil and danger to both races and is not desired by
the wise men in either race or by the Republican party of North Carolina."[40]

White declared that this statement was an "open, shameless flouting of the
fourteenth and fifteenth amendments of the Federal constitution," and that
no man who entertained such ideas "is fitted to occupy a place on the bench
of the United State Supreme Court."[41] When asked by Senator Borah if he
knew anything in the career of Judge Parker to indicate that he was unfriendly
to the Negro, White replied: "Nothing except this statement here.... Frankly
we never heard of him until he was nominated by President Hoover."[42] Judge
Parker's statement was made in reply to charges that if the Republicans were
elected they would change the state constitution to permit Negroes to vote
freely—a perennial charge used by Democrats in the South. Many prominent
Negro leaders in the South at that time took a similar position, advising members of their race to refrain from entering politics, because of the intolerant
attitude of the Southern whites.

By a vote of nine to eight the Judiciary Committee reported the nomination
adversely. The three Progressive Republicans—Norris, Borah, and Blaine—
were joined by two Republican "regulars" and four Democrats; five other
Republicans, headed by Gillette of Massachusetts, and three Democrats voted
in favor of Judge Parker.

In opening the debate, Senator Overman placed in the record a dignified letter from Judge Parker answering the charges against him. He stated that his decision in the Red Jacket case followed that of the Supreme Court in the Hitchman case, which was binding on the circuit court of appeals, and denied that he had any prejudice against Negroes. He declared that he firmly believed in the civil rights provisions of the Constitution and the right of Negroes to vote.[43] Senator Overman inserted in the record also an overwhelming array of endorsements, including a notable series of editorials from the Washington *Post,* a telegram from the president of the University of North Carolina and members of the faculty stating that they believed Judge Parker to be open-minded on all questions and a jurist of distinguished ability, letters and telegrams from the president and five former presidents of the American Bar Association and from many state and local bar associations.[44]

One of the principal opposing speeches in the Senate was made by Senator Borah, who said: "I am opposed to the confirmation of Judge Parker because I think he is committed to principles and propositions to which I am very thoroughly opposed.... He is peculiarly identified with this kind [yellow-dog] of a contract."[45] Most of his speech was devoted to a condemnation of yellow-dog contracts, but, following the line of reasoning advanced by William Green at the hearing on the nomination of Judge Parker, he attempted to show that the decision of the Supreme Court in the Hitchman case was not binding on the circuit court of appeals in the Red Jacket case. On the assumption that Judge Parker was identified with the yellow-dog contract—an assumption that was at no time substantiated—Senator Borah stated in closing his argument that "if the Senate decides that Mr. Parker should be confirmed, it is in moral effect a decision of the Senate in favor of the yellow dog contract."[46]

A good part of the debate turned on the Red Jacket case and the allegation that Judge Parker favored yellow-dog contracts. Senators Gillette, Hastings, Hebert, and others who spoke for Judge Parker maintained stoutly that in this case he had only followed the earlier decisions of the Supreme Court, which, of course, were binding on a lower court. The opposition was taken up by Senator Norris, who discussed at great length the iniquities of the yellow-dog contract, which he declared was contrary to public policy and was void. Senator Norris stated that Congress was powerless to deal with the evils of the yellow-dog contract, because it did not have the constitutional authority and could not secure that authority.

"So we are down to this one thing. When we are passing on a judge, therefore, we not only ought to know whether he is a good lawyer, not only whether he is honest—and I admit that this nominee possesses both of those qualifications—but we ought to know how he approaches these great questions of human liberty."[47]

It was frequently charged in the debate that the appointment was motivated by political considerations, that President Hoover by selecting a prominent Republican from North Carolina hoped to build up the party in the South. Although both senators from North Carolina and many other prominent Democrats in the state strongly urged the confirmation of Judge Parker, the charge that the appointment was political gained credence when Senator McKellar placed in the record a letter from First Assistant Secretary of the Interior Joseph M. Dixon to Walter H. Newton, secretary to the President, in which Dixon stated that the appointment of Judge Parker "would be a master political stroke at this time."[48]

Attorney General Mitchell stated that the President had never seen the Dixon letter and denied that the appointment was in any sense political. He said that at the request of the President he had made an inquiry of the qualifications of judges and lawyers particularly from the third, fourth, fifth, and ninth circuits, which were not represented on the Supreme Court, and recommended Judge Parker on the basis of his qualifications. Mitchell stated that Judge Parker had been endorsed by many federal and state judges; the president and five former presidents of the American Bar Association; the two senators, the governor, and former governor of his home state of North Carolina; and many prominent citizens of both political parties. The Attorney General went on to say that he had examined the decisions of Judge Parker while a member of the circuit court of appeals, numbering more than 125, and stated that "No fair-minded lawyer could read these opinions without being satisfied that Judge Parker has legal ability of the highest order, qualifying him to sit on the highest court.... A study of Judge Parker's decisions reveals him as one of the outstanding circuit judges of the country."[49] This was high praise, but it came too late to affect the outcome of the vote.

Senator Glass of Virginia stated that it would be much easier for him to vote against confirmation than for it, but that he had been unable to find any reason upon which he could conscientiously vote against the nominee. He said that he had investigated with some care the reputation of Judge Parker in the fourth circuit, and stated that he had found "the almost unanimous sentiment of the bar of Virginia, and...of the five States composing the fourth judicial circuit, to be that Judge Parker has the requisite qualifications."[50]

The final vote was 39 for and 41 against confirmation. The opposition was led by the Progressive Republicans, who were joined by Republican "regulars" from states with large Negro or labor votes and by a majority of the Democrats. Those voting for Judge Parker were mainly the Republicans who supported the administration, and a few Southern Democrats, including the senators from North Carolina and Virginia.

The defeat of Judge Parker is a notable illustration of the power of an organized interest group to block the appointment of a man they regard as unfriendly. In retrospect, it is generally agreed that both organized labor and Negroes were mistaken in their opposition and defeated a nominee who was liberal in outlook and sympathetic both to organized labor and to Negroes. The opposition of labor was based on the questionable allegation that the language of a single decision indicated that Judge Parker favored the yellow-dog contract; the Negro opposition was based on a single speech in the midst of a political campaign. Prominent Negro leaders in North Carolina came out for Judge Parker, and the state A. F. of L., before receiving instructions from Washington to take a different stand, had endorsed him. When the campaign of opposition was once started, however, labor organizations throughout the country joined in and sent letters and telegrams to members of the Senate. To both groups the defeat of Judge Parker became necessary to demonstrate their strength and influence. The day after the rejection of Judge Parker, Walter White issued a statement for the National Association for the Advancement of Colored People in which he said: "Negroes have had a striking object lesson in the efficacy of organized efforts to defend their fundamental rights."[51]

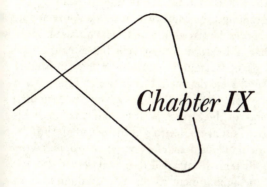

Chapter IX

OPPOSITION BY SENATE
CONSERVATIVES TO THE
APPOINTMENT OF LIBERALS

When it [the Senate] *shall have confirmed the appointment of Harry L. Hopkins it will have condoned the acts, the policies of his administration, and the atmosphere which he created; and we on this side will meet Senators on the other side and their party with that as an issue in the election of 1940.* Senator Reed of Kansas.[1]

The main issue involved in the vote which we are soon to take is whether a man can come before this Senate for approval and have that approval granted or refused on the basis of the evidence presented or whether such judgment will be influenced by politics, prejudice, racial and religious discrimination, and all the other evils which Members of the United States Senate should rise above. Senator Aiken of Vermont on the nomination of Aubrey Williams.[2]

IN HIS FIRST TERM, President Franklin D. Roosevelt had few difficulties with the Senate over nominations.* Elected to office with a large majority in 1932 in the midst of the Great Depression, he enjoyed greater popular and congressional support at the outset of his administration than any other President within recent times. The elections of 1934 and 1936 resulted in increased Democratic majorities in Congress, but disaffection within the ranks of the Democratic party appeared soon afterward. The defeat of the President's Supreme Court "packing" plan, followed by his unsuccessful

* The contests over the nominations of Hugo M. Black and Felix Frankfurter to the Supreme Court are treated in chap. xvii, below. Several other cases in this period, in which the rule of senatorial courtesy was invoked, are treated in chap. xiii.

effort in 1938 to bring about the defeat of Democratic members of Congress who had opposed his program, led to increasing difficulty in securing the adoption of his legislative program and the confirmation of his nominations. In his first term the only major presidential nomination which was strongly contested in the Senate was that of Rexford G. Tugwell; but after the 1938 election Roosevelt's nominations of outstanding liberals were consistently opposed in the Senate, and several were defeated. His choice of Hugo Black for the Supreme Court in 1937 was doubtless influenced by the fact that, since Black was a sitting member of the Senate, prompt confirmation of his nomination was virtually assured. Just as the liberals in the Senate during the Republican administration in the previous decade had vigorously opposed the appointments of conservatives to high federal office, the conservatives now turned the tables and opposed the appointment of liberals. Although in most cases they were unable to defeat the liberals, their opposition nevertheless had significant political effects.

Roosevelt also had trouble with the Senate when he attempted to cut off the patronage of Democratic senators who had opposed his legislative program. Though he was successful, in his first term, in disciplining Long of Louisiana and Holt of West Virginia, his later efforts to take federal patronage away from McCarran, the two Virginia senators, and O'Daniel were met by rebuffs in the Senate when the customary prerogative of courtesy was invoked.* The bitter animosity which arose between Roosevelt and several other Democratic senators in his second and third terms was due in part to differences over federal patronage in their states.

Rexford G. Tugwell

When the position of Under Secretary of Agriculture was created by an amendment to the appropriations act, in January, 1934, it was generally expected that the new position would be filled by Rexford G. Tugwell, then Assistant Secretary of Agriculture. And in spite of the expected opposition of the more conservative members of both parties it was generally conceded that he would be confirmed by a substantial majority. Before the nomination, Tugwell, a former professor of economics at Columbia University who belonged to President Roosevelt's "brain trust," had been named by a Mr. Wirt in his sensational charges that a group of Communists in the administration planned to take over the government. Although this accusation was generally discredited, Tugwell's opponents revived it in opposing his confirmation. At that time there were many fulminations against the "brain trust," along with increasing criticism of the Agricultural Adjustment Act, which it was Tugwell's duty to administer. When President Roosevelt on April 24, 1934, nominated

---

* These contests are covered in chap. xiii, below.

Tugwell as Under Secretary of Agriculture, the action was viewed by many as a direct reply to these critics.

It was not until June 11, as the end of the congressional session neared, that the Senate Committee on Agriculture conducted hearings on the nomination. Its failure to take any action had attracted considerable comment in the press; it was rumored that Senator Smith, chairman of the committee, was holding up the nomination because of difference with the President over patronage in South Carolina, but the senator denied this. The President was expected to intervene in behalf of his nomination, but he allowed a month and a half to go by without doing so. Finally, on June 8, Senator Robinson of Arkansas, the majority leader, moved to have the committee discharged of the nomination so that it could be voted on in the Senate. Senator Glass urged that hearings be held so that Tugwell could be questioned on a speech he made in 1931 before the American Economic Association and suggested that, instead of discharging the committee, the Senate order it to report on the nomination at a specific time. Senator Robinson agreed to this, and after a two-hour debate the motion carried.[3]

At the turbulent hearings on the nomination, conducted in an overflowing room while movie cameras were going and a radio network was broadcasting the proceedings, Senator Byrd questioned Tugwell about his speech before the American Economic Association, which had dealt with economic planning in Russia. The Virginia senator attempted to elicit from the nominee an admission that he favored economic planning for this country, which Tugwell repeatedly denied, finally saying: "There is no use in my repeating what I have said two or three times. If I haven't made it clear now, there is no use repeating it."[4]

Senator Byrd then turned the discussion to the Agricultural Adjustment Act, commenting at length on the views of the Secretary of Agriculture. Senator Norris pointed out that because the committee wasn't unanimous in agreeing with the Secretary of Agriculture was no reason "why we should consider that as one of the qualifications or disqualifications of Dr. Tugwell to be Under Secretary of Agriculture." Byrd then gave a lengthy dissertation of his views on the AAA amendments. Finally, Wheeler protested that the hearing had been turned into "a political racket" rather than an examination of the witness, a view greeted with cheers and applause by the audience. When order was restored, Senator Wheeler announced that he had "never sat in any committee meeting before where I have heard it conducted in this manner, and I object ... to this kind of procedure."[5]

Much of the remainder of the hearing consisted of exchanges of insults. Senator Murphy asserted that the whole hearing was simply an attack on the administration. Chairman Smith, in a long speech, voiced his resentment of "these dirty insinuations." After this, Wheeler suggested that they proceed with the hearing, and Senator Bone blandly wondered what all this had to do with the qualifications of Dr. Tugwell.[6] The hearing then returned to a consideration, not of Tugwell's qualifications, but of the speech he had made in 1931, with continued attempts to induce the witness to testify that he advocated the Russian system. Finally Tugwell exclaimed: "Why is it, Senator, that my word cannot be accepted...that I had no intention of advocating national planning, as I have said over and over here this morning..."[7]

Only in the last half hour of the hearing did Senators Bone and Murphy manage to interject a few questions pertaining to the witness' qualifications. The following day, Arthur Krock likened the hearing to a good comedy. He observed that in the Senate debate on the nomination "the prospects are for a good show, but the slapstick work of today was just a little too good to be duplicated." And the New York *Times* editorialized that "the cross-examination of Professor Tugwell discredited no one but his examiners." The *Times* editorial continued:

When Professor Tugwell was asked yesterday what he meant by his phrase "the anthropomorphic sequence of human existence" he tried to explain it by what the Senators thought was something still more obscure. What he should have done was to smile and say that it was a feeble attempt to describe what was going on at that moment before the Senate committee. So undignified and quarrelsome a proceeding among senators certainly deserved to be called by the most polysyllabic and awesome word that could be found in the dictionary. Never was there a better example of how not to do it.[8]

The committee voted 16 to 2 in favor of confirmation, and, as Krock had predicted, the show continued in the Senate. Senator Bailey stated that many of the witness' answers were evasive and had made an unfavorable impression on him.[9] Senator Norris accused the opposition senators of making stump speeches, during the hearing, which had no more to do with the nominee's qualifications "than the starlings roosting in the rafters of the Capitol." Senator Cutting added that "a mere suggestion from the Senator from Alabama that the proceedings be conducted in a more orderly manner was greeted with catcalls and hisses and hoots and boos from the audience."[10]

Senators Byrd, Gore, Dickinson, Clark, and Robinson of Indiana spoke against the nominee. Senator Gore claimed that Senate confirmation would mean endorsing Tugwell's philosophy that industry and the Constitution ought to be destroyed. Senator Black vehemently denied that Tugwell had ever advocated such a philosophy.[11] After a spirited debate in which Senators Norris, Neely, Bankhead, and Robinson of Arkansas also defended the nominee, Tugwell's nomination was confirmed by a vote of 53 to 24.

Ebert K. Burlew

The nomination, on December 20, 1937, of Ebert K. Burlew, a civil servant with twenty-seven years of service, to be First Assistant Secretary of Interior, touched off a senatorial investigation of the Department of the Interior that lasted a month and occupied fifteen days of hearings. Senator Pittman of Nevada, who was reported to be offended because Secretary Ickes had not always followed his wishes, conducted a one-man fight to block the appointment. At one point in the hearings, Senator Pittman complained that he had not been consulted about certain Nevada appointments.[12] Three months later the nomination was confirmed without a roll call, but only after the nominee had gone through so extended a grilling that his value to the Department as the First Assistant Secretary was seriously impaired. The case served as a warning to other top civil service employees of the hazards involved in accepting an appointment which required senatorial confirmation.[13]

The extended hearings dealt with all sorts of departmental activities, rumors, charges, investigations, certain employees who were discharged or disciplined, helium gas, and a variety of matters unrelated to Burlew and having nothing to do with his qualifications or responsibilities.[14] The embezzlement of $84,000 by a departmental employee who had set up a dummy Civilian Conservation Corps camp, which had recently come to light, was inquired into at length, though the employee concerned was being prosecuted in court at that time and Burlew had no direct responsibility in the case. Most of the twenty-seven witnesses who testified were departmental officials and employees connected in some way with the various episodes aired in the hearings. A number were special agents who had investigated these cases, and the printed hearings contain voluminous excerpts from their reports and correspondence.

Although Burlew was on the stand eleven of the fifteen days of hearings, it was not evident that there was any opposition to him personally, and only one senator—Pittman—maintained that he was not qualified. Burlew had many of the characteristics of the typical civil servant who had risen through the ranks to a top position. He was efficient, hard-working, loyal to his superiors, and had an intimate knowledge of departmental administration. Within the Department he had been criticized for a bureaucratic attitude, but this was not the basis of the opposition to him in the Senate. Also it may be noted that he was not opposed on the ground that he was a radical, or because of anything he had written; as an old civil servant he was strictly neutral on political and social issues. In this regard the case does not follow the usual pattern of the senatorial opposition to liberals nominated by Roosevelt.

The first witness to testify in the hearings was Secretary Ickes. He stated that when he first came to the Department of the Interior he was suspicious of Burlew, who had served as the personal assistant to the two preceding secretaries, and had therefore changed his status and reduced his salary. It was only after a very thorough test that he decided Burlew "possessed a value to the Department that should not be foregone" and changed his salary back to what it had been. Ickes further said that he regarded Burlew "as the most competent and best qualified member of my staff."[15] When Senator Pittman started to question Ickes about departmental investigations, Ickes pointedly replied: "I really did not know that the Interior Department was to be investigated today. I thought this was an inquiry into the qualifications and fitness of Mr. Burlew." And a little later, after Ickes asked, "Gentlemen, am I under inquiry here?" Senator Pittman dropped that line of questioning.[16] Burlew, however, had no such defense and was subjected to a grueling examination, often about departmental matters that were not his concern.

At the conclusion of extended hearings, Senator O'Mahoney stated that no evidence had been presented which reflected on Burlew's integrity or his capability. Overriding the strenuous objections of Senator Pittman, the committee reported the nomination favorably on March 2. In the Senate, Pittman renewed his attack on the nominee, alleging that Burlew had conducted a lobby to win confirmation. Finally, on April 5, after many delays, Burlew's appointment was confirmed, without a record vote. The fight waged by Senator Pittman against the nominee had served to warn Secretary Ickes that he could disregard the advice of the senator only at his peril.

Thurman W. Arnold

When the nomination of Thurman W. Arnold, a professor of law at Yale University, to be Assistant Attorney General in charge of the Antitrust Division, came before the Senate in March, 1938, Senator Borah requested that a hearing be held so that he could inquire into the views of the nominee on antitrust legislation. Senator King also wanted an investigation made because, he said, "We have too many officials with a socialist taint."[17] After the Judiciary Committee had conducted a hearing on March 11, the Senate approved the nomination on March 15 without a roll call. The case is of interest because the only issue was Arnold's treatment of antitrust legislation in his book, *The Folklore of Capitalism*.[18] In this work Arnold had stated that antitrust laws had had the opposite effect from that intended—that they had actually promoted the growth of large corporations and monopolies. Senator Borah interpreted this position as one in opposition to antitrust legislation; but in reply to questioning, Arnold stated that he was in favor of antitrust laws and favored a fair but vigorous enforcement of them. He stated, moreover, that the book was written purely as a diagnosis and did not propose any remedies. When Senator Borah suggested that the chapter on trusts should be revised to avoid a "great deal of embarrassment," Senator O'Mahoney suggested, with a touch of irony, that the witness might have written the book in a somewhat different way if he had "known that this hearing was coming."[19] The appointment of Arnold was a part of a plan to build up a strong Antitrust Division in the Department of Justice and to strengthen the enforcement of the antitrust laws, which was understood by other senators; but Senator Borah, relying on his interpretation of Arnold's writings, accused him of being an apologist for monopoly.[20] This case and that of Tugwell make it clear that a President's nominees must be prepared to defend their past writings and public utterances, which are often misinterpreted and used to oppose them. Academicians Tugwell and Arnold discovered that esotericism afforded little or no protection against senatorial attack.

Harry Hopkins

After the unsuccessful attempt of President Roosevelt in the election of 1938 to "purge" several Democratic senators who had opposed his legislative program, and after the setback the Democrats received that year, he faced increasing difficulties in securing the confirmation of his nominations, particularly of liberals. The first test case was the appointment of Harry Hopkins as Secretary of Commerce. Early in November rumors appeared in the press that Hopkins would be appointed in place of Secretary Roper, who was about to resign. A Gallup poll indicated that 66 per cent of the people questioned thought Hopkins was not qualified for the job, though 47 per cent indicated that they thought he had done a good job as Work Projects Administrator.[21] The appointment had been so widely discussed that the actual Senate hearings and subsequent debates were somewhat anticlimactic. As was anticipated, the strong tradition in favor of confirmation of Cabinet nominations, and the large majority the Democrats had in the Senate, were sufficient to assure eventual approval of the nomination.

The opposition to Hopkins centered around two charges: (1) that as Administrator of the WPA he had permitted politics to enter relief; and (2) that in the campaign of 1938, while he was head of the WPA he had made political speeches. In the final vote, the Republicans almost solidly voted against Hopkins, and they were joined by several antiadministration Democrats. In the course of the long Senate debate a number of members discussed at length the attempted "purge" of conservative members of the Democratic party, as well as allegations of politics in the WPA. The attack was essentially on the administration and the President rather than the nominee.

The contest centered on the issue of politics in the WPA while Harry Hopkins was its chief. On December 3—almost three weeks before his appointment—the New York *Times* forecast that "his selection probably would be approved eventually unless the forthcoming report of the Senate Campaign Expenditures Committee is too condemnatory of him in connection with politics in relief." When Daniel Roper resigned as Secretary of Commerce on

December 16, the opposition to Hopkins increased notably. The New York *Times* stated it was no secret that many business leaders would look upon the appointment with disfavor. On December 23, the day the appointment of Hopkins was announced by the White House, the New York *Times* reported that despite the "opposition to Mr. Hopkins arising out of complaints of the manner in which WPA funds were used in the primary and general elections," administration leaders had advised the President that his nomination of Hopkins would be confirmed by the Senate.[22] When the Sheppard committee report of its investigation of the political activities of the WPA was released, Arthur Krock declared that it was an "implicit indictment of Mr. Hopkins for—if nothing more—stubbornly defending and giving clean bills of health to the WPA when the newspapers were full of proof to the contrary. It convicts him at least of inefficiency or loyal tolerance of a bad system."[23]

Hearings by the Senate Commerce Committee began on January 11, 1939. Senator Vandenberg started the questioning of Hopkins by presenting a chart which showed that relief payments had risen during the summer and fall months preceding the 1938 election and had declined perceptibly just after it. Hopkins denied that relief payments had been increased before the election to influence its outcome, pointing out that in Michigan (Vandenberg's state) where one of the hottest campaigns was waged, the relief rolls were lowered before the election, whereas in Alabama, where the outcome had already been decided by the Democratic primary, relief payments had increased before the election—solely because unemployment in Alabama increased during that period. "In the five and one-half years I have been here," declared Hopkins, "I have done everything I could to keep petty partisan politics out of this thing." He declared that the Sheppard committee report vindicated the WPA, for in spite of the vast size of the operation, with 6,700,000 people working for it at some time, the evidence indicated that politics had been injected into relief in only a few counties.[24]

Hopkins' defense of the WPA apparently was accepted by the members of the Senate committee; they dropped this subject and turned to other matters. Hopkins might have pointed out that the politics and patronage which existed in the WPA had been due chiefly to the requirement in 1935 that made appointments of state WPA administrators subject to Senate confirmation; the politics to which the senators objected was senatorial politics. Up to that time Hopkins had administered the WPA and its predecessor, the Federal Emergency Relief Administration, with remarkable freedom from patronage and politics; but after that, the administration of the WPA in a number of states had become political, and in a few states it was marked by gross abuses, which were disclosed in the report of the Sheppard committee.[25]

Senator Vandenberg next brought up the statement attributed to Hopkins that "we shall spend and spend, tax and tax, elect and elect," which Hopkins categorically denied having made. Vandenberg then asked him if he didn't think the quotation was a good example of the New Deal's purpose to perpetuate itself. To this Hopkins replied: "I deny the whole business. I do not want to quibble either, about the exact words. I deny the whole works and the whole implication of it."[26]

Hopkins was taken to task by Chairman Bailey of North Carolina for the political speeches he had made in the primary and election campaigns of 1938. He replied that although he had made only four or five political speeches, and he did not wish to retract anything that he had said, nevertheless, "if I had it all to do over again as administrator of relief, I would not have made those political speeches."[27] When questioned about keeping subordinates in the WPA from engaging in political activities, Hopkins suggested that the Corrupt Practices Act (Hatch Act) be strengthened and that all offices be put under the civil service, except a few policy positions. He added that though he did not believe in making political appointments, he did appoint people he thought would be sympathetic to the relief works program.[28]

On January 18 the committee reported the nomination favorably to the Senate. This touched off a bitter debate that lasted several days. Senators Holt, Bailey, Bridges, Davis, and Reed of Kansas attacked Hopkins because of charges of political activities by WPA employees. Several senators who also criticized politics in the WPA under Hopkins asserted that they would vote for him because, as Senator Walsh put it, "I think we may agree that the selection of the members of his Cabinet is a peculiarly personal prerogative of the President ... and we should not withhold confirmation ... except for grave cause and unmistakable disqualification."[29]

Senators Norris, Neely, Minton, and Schwellenbach staunchly supported Hopkins. Neely commented that a more honorable, efficient, faithful public servant than Harry Hopkins had "never been subjected to senatorial investigation, dissection and disposition."[30] Schwellenbach announced that he intended to vote for the nominee without apology for anything he had ever done. "I think Harry Hopkins is an honest, capable administrator. I think he has done a marvelous job as administrator of the Works Progress Administration." He added that most of the speeches "have not been directed at Hopkins, but have been directed at the President of the United States ..."[31]

When the vote was taken, Senator Glass asked to be excused on the ground that he could not vote for Hopkins, for he did not want to give the impression that he agreed with him in any way, yet he could not vote against a presidential choice for the Cabinet. A number of other conservative Democrats, including Bailey, Burke, Byrd, Overton, and Tydings, abstained from voting. On the final vote, the nomination of Hopkins was confirmed, 58 to 27.

Frank Murphy

On December 29, 1938, the White House announced that Governor Frank Murphy had been given a recess appointment as Attorney General and would take the place of Homer Cummings, who had resigned. After Murphy's defeat for reëlection as governor of Michigan that year it had been rumored that he would be given a high federal post. Because of the criticism of him for not acting more vigorously to end the sit-down strike against General Motors the preceding year, it was expected that the attempt to secure the approval of the Senate might meet with considerable opposition. The Judiciary subcommittee, to which the nomination was referred, however, voted unanimously to recommend confirmation. At this point, Murphy, anticipating a fight on the Senate floor, requested permission to testify before the subcommittee. His request was granted; a hearing was held on January 13, 1939, at which he was the only witness.

In his testimony Murphy gave a forceful and convincing account of his handling of the sit-down strike, which was in progress when he was sworn in as governor of Michigan in 1937. Explaining something of the labor and management tension of the time, and describing the union of automobile workers as young and undisciplined, he declared that he had responded to every local request for assistance in the maintenance of law and order. The principal criticism against him was that instead of assisting the sheriff at Flint to execute a court order requiring the strikers to vacate the factory where they were engaged in a sit-down strike, he had advised postponement in order to give the contesting sides additional time to reach an agreement. Murphy explained that the order had been issued on a Friday, and he had been informed that a settlement of the strike would probably be reached before the following Monday.

I knew [Murphy said], as did the Union and the company's officials, that the literal enforcement of the writ at that moment would not only disrupt negotiations but could not be carried out without the gravest risk of property damage, riot, and even bloodshed which would leave bitterness and ill-feeling between the company and the men for years to come.... At the plants I had a large detachment of the National Guard continuously on duty prepared to preserve order and ready for any emergency.... I believe that I did my duty.... I believe that "faithful execution" by the governor of a state includes wise administration of the law and not merely its literal instantaneous application at any cost.[32]

At the end of his prepared statement, Murphy submitted letters from President Roosevelt, Newton D. Baker, and Alfred Sloan, president of General Motors, commending him for his handling of the strike. The members of the subcommittee apparently were satisfied, and asked few questions.

In the debate in the Senate on January 17, Senator Bridges said that he was against Murphy "for the same reason for which the voters of Michigan were against him—because he is a symbol in this country today of opposition to law and order." He asserted that Murphy had "the endorsement of some of the Communists of the country for the office of President of the United States,"[133] and spoke scornfully of the nomination of Murphy as a "lame duck" appointment, until Senator Minton reminded him of a few Republican "lame duck" appointees, including Chief Justices Hughes and Taft. The supposed opposition apparently dwindled away before the vote was taken, and the nomination of Murphy was confirmed by a majority of 78 to 7. Although this vote reflected the belief that the choice of Cabinet members is the President's prerogative, Murphy's unusual request for a hearing after his nomination had been approved in committee, and his explanation of the handling of the sit-down strike had made a favorable impression on many of his critics.

Thomas R. Amlie

The most severe attack on a Roosevelt nominee because of alleged radical views was directed at Thomas R. Amlie, a former Progressive congressman from Wisconsin, who was named to the Interstate Commerce Commission in 1939. Amlie had been defeated for the Progressive nomination for the United States Senate in 1938. His various writings and speeches were cited in the hearings and in the public discussion, to condemn him as a radical; but the concerted attack on him was probably in large part due to his advocacy of public ownership of the railroads. The railway interests regarded the nomination as highly inimical to them; thousands of telegrams, letters, and memorials opposing the nomination poured in on the Senate Committee on Interstate Commerce. These protests, which filled approximately a hundred pages of the printed *Hearings,* came from railway officials, traffic clubs, chambers of commerce, and other groups, as well as from individuals—chiefly persons with a financial interest in the prosperity of the railroads. Of the communications urging the confirmation, a large number were from labor unions and individuals. The persons who opposed it, who were by far more numerous, attacked the nominee for his writings and speeches and alleged radicalism; it was apparent that practically none of the objectors had any other information about him. Nearly all the testimonials urging confirmation, however, came from persons who were personally acquainted with the nominee and his record. Both houses of the Wisconsin legislature passed resolutions asking the President to withdraw the nomination on the ground that Amlie was a Communist.[34] Senator La Follette of Wisconsin said in comment: "I am not surprised at anything that Legislature would do. It will not alter my support of Amlie in the slightest degree." Whereupon the Wisconsin legislature demanded La Follette's impeachment for supporting the nominee.[35] After the protest reached a crescendo and it became apparent that the nomination could not be confirmed, Amlie requested the President to withdraw his name.

Hearings on the nomination were opened on February 6 by Senator Johnson of Colorado, chairman of the subcommittee, who stated that Congress has responsibility at least equal to that of the President to determine the qualifications of persons nominated for federal offices, especially to the Interstate Commerce Commission, because it is regarded by the courts "as the arm of Congress and not as a department of the executive branch of the government."[36] The first witness was Amlie, himself, who said he wanted to answer some of the charges against him, particularly those regarding Communism. "I am not a Communist and have never been a Communist. On the contrary, I have strongly opposed the Communist aims and program."[37] Amlie cited the numerous attacks made on him in the Communist press because of his opposition, including an accusation by the *New Masses* that he was a "red-baiter."

Amlie answered the questions of members of the committee with unusual frankness, making no attempt to evade controversial issues. Senator Johnson inquired what his political affiliation was and what party he had supported in 1932 and 1936. Amlie replied that he had been a Republican and then a Progressive, but had supported the present administration in both presidential elections. When asked if he approved of public ownership of railroads, he said that he did, adding that Commissioner Eastman also favored public ownership. When questioned concerning the effect his political and personal philosophy would have if he were confirmed as a member of the Interstate Commerce Commission, Amlie replied: "I would merely be an agent to carry out the will of Congress; and I think, perhaps, a man who has served in the Congress would feel that way more keenly than one who had not."[38]

A number of witnesses then appeared in opposition to Amlie. William D. Carroll, chairman of the Wisconsin Democratic State Central Committee, asserted that Amlie was one of the most radical men in Wisconsin and that he had had no experience to qualify him for a position on the ICC.[39] "I will venture to say that he has never signed a freight bill in his life," said Morris Fitzsimmons, a member of the Wisconsin legislature, who had introduced the memorial opposing the appointment of Amlie. Referring to Amlie's defeat for the Progressive nomination as United States senator, Fitzsimmons asserted that Amlie was even "too pink" for the Progressives.[40] Luther Walter, a co-trustee of the Chicago Great Western Railroad Company, spoke against Amlie: "The profit system has been the mainspring under which our economy has been developed. This man would destroy it."[41] When some of the senators tried to question him about his own views regarding the ICC, Walter answered, "I hate to see you try me instead of Mr. Amlie."[42] Apparently not one of the witnesses testifying against Amlie had ever known him personally.

Among those who appeared for Thomas Amlie were Representatives Kent

Keller of Illinois and Jerry Voorhis of California, both of whom had known Amlie for years; they stated that he was a competent person and that he was opposed to Communism. Mayor La Guardia sent a letter expressing his high regard for the nominee's honesty and competence. James McGill, president of an Indiana manufacturing company, Benjamin March, executive secretary of the People's Lobby, and John Bauer, a professor of economics at Cornell University, appeared for the nominee and denied emphatically that he was a Communist.

As the hearings came to an end, the New York *Times,* in editorials on successive days, opposed the nomination, stating that Amlie was not qualified by training, knowledge, experience, or temperament for the job, and "as long as we are still trying to regulate railroads under private ownership, it is clearly a liability to have commissioners who are not interested in the success of private ownership."[43] The Springfield *Republican* favored the nomination. This paper discounted the charge that Amlie was a Communist as "plain nonsense," and argued that the test which his opponents would apply for public office— "a cocksure belief in the absolute soundness and permanence of the capitalist system"—was one which was unknown to the Constitution. "Why," it inquired, "must the Interstate Commerce Commission have as members eleven men all holding the same economic views?"[44]

Early in March, informal checks in the Senate indicated that Amlie could not be approved, and it was reported that the Democratic leadership had advised the President to withdraw the nomination in the interest of peace between the White House and Congress, as well as between the government and business. On April 7 Amlie wrote to the President requesting that the nomination be withdrawn, stating that a "reactionary press and an unscrupulous political cabal" had turned the contest into a "veritable witchcraft trial." Acceding to this request, President Roosevelt in a letter to Amlie stated his regret that one as able and as devoted to the public service as he was should not be permitted to serve on the Interstate Commerce Commission.[45]

The Confirmation of Henry Wallace as Secretary of Commerce, 1945

During World War II and the years immediately preceding the entrance of the United States into the war, President Roosevelt to a large extent shelved domestic reforms and directed the energies of the administration to the acceleration of the war effort and to maintaining the unity of the country. In this period he nominated no one to whom the conservatives in the Senate might take strong exception; as a consequence he had little difficulty in securing Senate approval of his nominations. Some Democrats, however, grumbled loudly at the number of Republican businessmen appointed to prominent positions in the war agencies. The emergency agencies, for the most part, were created by executive order; hence appointments to them did not require senatorial confirmation. The unity achieved in the conduct of the war, the cessation of bitter partisanship, and the support of the foreign and war policies of the administration by conservative Democrats were factors which operated to restore harmonious relations between the President and the Senate.

As the war approached the end, a liberal group in the Democratic party strove to lead the party back to advocacy of the cause of the underprivileged, the lower-income groups, and to commit the government to a program of economic reforms. The most prominent figure in this movement was Vice-President Wallace, who was defeated for renomination in 1944 because of the bitter opposition of the conservatives within the party, particularly those from the South. Wallace personally went to the Democratic national convention at Chicago to lead the fight for his renomination, and though he lost, he greatly impressed many delegates who had been cool toward him. In spite of the fact that Roosevelt had clearly indicated—by his fainthearted praise of Wallace and his famous letters endorsing Truman and Douglas as running mates—that he wanted someone other than Wallace, after the convention Wallace threw himself into the campaign and spoke in many states where he was regarded as the leader of the liberal faction of the party.

After the election of 1944, speculation was rife that Wallace would be offered a Cabinet post as reward for his vigorous support during the campaign. The New York *Times* carried a story late in November that Wallace had been given his choice of several Cabinet posts, not, however, including that of Secretary of State, though Hull's resignation because of ill-health was expected.[46] Wallace was reported to favor the post of Secretary of Commerce, which was occupied by his bitter enemy, Jesse Jones, who had given Roosevelt only lukewarm support in 1944. On the day of his inauguration Roosevelt sent an extraordinary letter to Jones asking for his resignation. After praising Jones for his services, Roosevelt referred in the letter to the loyal support Wallace had given to the ticket during the campaign and stated: "Henry Wallace deserves almost any service which he believes he can satisfactorily perform." Stating that Wallace wanted the post of Secretary of Commerce, he asked Jones to step aside, and offered him instead a suitable ambassadorship. The letter was enormously insulting to Jesse Jones, who had long been one of the most powerful men in the country and had a strong following in Congress. The President had not even accorded him the courtesy of a personal explanation but had discharged him in a casual note.

Roosevelt's statement that Wallace, because he had loyally supported the ticket, deserved about any position he wanted and that Wallace thought he was qualified to be Secretary of Commerce was most extraordinary. Although Cabinet appointments are often made to reward political supporters, never ad any President openly defended an appointment on this ground. It might appear that the letter was simply stupid or had been hastily written with no thought that it might be made public. However, Roosevelt, the master politician, was not likely to act hastily. Jonathan Daniels records that months earlier Roosevelt had let his White House aides know that he planned to replace Jones after the election." Nor was it likely that Roosevelt was surprised at Jones's high indignation over his summary dismissal, or at his release of the letter to the press. A more plausible explanation of the letter is that Roosevelt chose this means of letting it be known that Jones was being dismissed because of his failure to support the President politically. On any other grounds the dismissal of Jones would have caused a great furor. Another explanation, though less probable, is that Roosevelt, angered at Wallace's insistence on a Cabinet appointment, had written the letter deliberately to injure his chances of confirmation.

In his reply to the President, Jones wrote: "It is difficult to reconcile [your] encomiums with your avowed purpose to replace me." He declared that he had enjoyed the confidence of Congress and the President because he had been faithful to the responsibilities entrusted to him, and that the business and financial world would find it difficult to understand why these great assets and responsibilities had been turned over to a "man inexperienced in business and finance."[48]

A bitter fight in the Senate over the nomination of Wallace was foreseen. No other member of Roosevelt's Cabinet, unless it was Hull, was held in such high respect and had such strong support on the Hill as Jones. Wallace, however, in spite of his four years as Vice-President, had made few friends among the senators. Senator George forthwith introduced a bill to take the Reconstruction Finance Corporation out of the Commerce Department and give it independent status. This bill and the nomination were both referred to the Committee on Interstate Commerce.

Hearings were held first on the George bill. The principal reason Wallace desired the post of Secretary of Commerce was that it would enable him to exercise the great lending power of the RFC to promote full employment and other economic reforms. It was precisely for this reason that the appointment was offensive to conservatives. With Commerce stripped of the RFC, the appointment would be a relatively innocuous one.

When the hearings were opened on January 24 in the spacious Senate caucus room, which was filled to overflowing, Senator George summarized the vast lending powers which had been granted to the RFC and contended that these powers ought to be exercised by an agency directly responsible to Congress, and "not hidden away in an executive office where it is immune to any reasonable examination, even by Congress itself." He did not mention Wallace, but when Senator Pepper interjected the remark that the bill was due to Wallace's nomination, Senator George replied that his motives had nothing to do with the merits of the bill.[49]

The principal witness in support of the George bill was Jesse Jones, who testified that the RFC should not be placed under the direction of a man who was "willing to jeopardize the country's future with untried ideas and idealistic schemes." Pointing to the vast powers of the RFC, he stated "We can lend anything that we think we should. Any amount, any length of time, or any rate of interest . . . to anybody that we feel is entitled to a loan." Criticizing Wallace by implication, he stated that the RFC should be run by experienced businessmen, by men who have no ideas about remaking the world, and that the power exercised by the person who directed the lending agencies was so great that it could affect the economic direction of the country.[50]

Senator Pepper came to Wallace's defense, pointing out that as Secretary of Agriculture he had been responsible for the operation of the Commodity Credit Corporation, which had lent several billions of dollars. This success, however, Jones maintained, had not been due to good management, and in reply to questioning by Pepper, he finally stated bluntly: "If you are trying to ask me if Henry Wallace is qualified for both jobs, I will say 'no.'" It was possible for one man to hold both jobs only by working enough hours, Jones said, but he did not believe there was "another fellow in the world that will do it except me."[51] Senator Bailey, chairman of the committee, interjected to prevent further questioning of Jones about the qualifications of Wallace, which he maintained was not pertinent to the pending legislation.

The following day, Henry Wallace testified to a crowded room against the George bill. Referring to the fact that his nomination was the occasion for the proposal to strip the Commerce Department of the RFC, he declared that ". . . it is not a question of my lack of experience. Rather, it is a case of not liking the experience I have."[52] The former Vice-President then testified as to his experience, citing the fact that the Department of Agriculture under his administration lent more than six billion dollars. "The real issue," he maintained, "is whether or not the powers of the Reconstruction Finance Corporation and its giant subsidiaries are to be used only to help big business or whether these powers are also to be used to help little business and to help carry out the President's commitment of 60 million jobs." He then outlined in detail the several parts of the President's economic bill of rights which he proposed to use the lending power of the RFC to advance: the right to useful and remunerative employment, to earn enough to provide adequate food, clothing, and recreation; the right of farmers to earn enough for a decent living; the right of businessmen to freedom from unfair competition and the domination of monopolies; the right of families for a decent home; the right of adequate medical care; the right of adequate protection against the fears of old age, sickness, accidents, and unemployment; and the right to a good education. If his statement was regarded by the *Nation* as "the conscience of America," it was looked upon by conservatives in Congress and out as the harbinger of socialism. At the conclusion of the hearings the committee voted 14 to 5 to recommend against confirmation, but the Senate leadership was able to postpone the vote in the Senate until after the George bill had passed both houses and become law. Without the passage of this bill, Wallace stood no chance of confirmation.

Commenting on the contest, the conservative London *Times* declared that the real issue was the New Deal, "the rights of the common man as against the privileges of money power, the same issue which divided Jefferson and Hamilton, the central political conflict that has agitated the Republic since its birth." Observing that the struggle was nearer to the realities of American political life than the recent presidential election in which the Republican candidates did not challenge the New Deal, the *Times* stated:

The Wallace-Jones debate may well come to rank in American history with the Hayne-Webster debate as pregnant with significance in the future. It involves all those mighty issues which agitate men's minds when they look forward to the world after the war—the true function of Government in a democratic state; the yearning to be rid of the scourge of unemployment; the conflict between the social conscience and the nostalgia for the old ways; the strenuous attempt to reconcile freedom and control, to prevent the one from becoming self-destructive, and the other from becoming tyrannical . . .[53]

The debate over the confirmation of Wallace continued for a number of days in a rather desultory manner, it being assumed after passage of the George bill that Wallace would be confirmed. The principal speech opposing confirmation was made by Senator Taft and consisted chiefly of a reply to an article by Walter Lippmann, who had asserted that the rejection of a Cabinet nominee by the Senate merely because it did not agree with his policies would amount to a "usurpation" of power.* Senators Wiley and Hawkes also spoke against confirmation. The strongest defense of Wallace was made by Lister Hill, who was joined by Pepper. Several senators of both parties stated that although they differed with some of the nominee's views, they would vote for confirmation in the belief that the President should be permitted to choose his own advisers. When the vote was taken the appointment of Wallace was confirmed, 56 to 32. Five Democrats—Byrd, McKellar, McCarran, O'Daniel, and Stewart—joined with 27 Republicans in voting against confirmation, and 10 Republicans and one independent voted with 45 Democrats in favor of it.

* See chap. xv, below.

The Rejection of Aubrey Williams

Another nomination which aroused strong conservative opposition in the Senate was that of Aubrey Williams, nominated to be Rural Electrification Administrator in 1945. His nomination and that of Wallace, which were before the Senate at the same time, indicated that Roosevelt did not intend to shelve permanently the New Deal social reforms. A former social worker, Deputy Administrator of the FERA and later in WPA, Williams had served as Administrator of the National Youth Administration from 1935 until it was abolished by action of Congress in 1943. Often charged with being a poor administrator, he had nevertheless made a good record as the head of the NYA. After leaving government service in 1943 he became organization director of the National Farmers' Union, which was widely regarded as a liberal or "left wing" farm organization.

Williams was known for his outspoken advocacy of the policies of the New Deal; like Hopkins he was taken to task, in the hearings on his nomination, for political speeches which he had made while administering federal relief. The most vigorous opposition to him, however, was due rather to his attitude on the race problem and his support of the Fair Employment Practices Commission, which had incurred bitter hostility in the South. As National Youth Administrator, Williams had maintained friendly relations with members of the Senate, and in the contest over his nomination a number of senators came to his defense. Others, however, particularly the Southern Democrats, whose votes he needed (Republicans could be expected to vote against the nomination on purely partisan grounds), failed to support him, because of the vocal opposition in their own states.

The nomination was also viewed with apprehension by the electric-utility interests, who feared that because of his close relations with Roosevelt, Williams would be able to secure the support of the President for an expansion of the REA program. His association with the National Farmers' Union for a brief period also cost him a number of votes in the Senate when the powerful Farm Bureau Federation and the Grange came out against him.

During the hearings in February, 1945, Williams was subjected to a probing which touched on his education, professional career, his record as head of the NYA, his beliefs, speeches, writings, and even his religion. He was constantly under attack for certain speeches, and the charge of Communistic leanings was frequently raised throughout the hearings. In defending his administration of the NYA, Williams was aided by the friendly questioning of several senators, including Ellender, Wheeler, Thomas, and Bankhead. Summarizing the accomplishment of the NYA and its contribution to the training of young men and women for war jobs, Williams testified that the Army, the Navy, the Maritime Commission, and a number of large employers had urged its continuance in 1943. It was evident that the nominee hoped that the hearings would turn primarily on his record as NYA Administrator. The question of Communism was raised early in the hearings when Senator Bankhead asked: "It has been suggested in some quarters that you are a Communist, or you are communistic in feelings and leanings. Have you ever been affiliated with any communistic association?" Williams replied in unequivocal terms: "I have never been a member of any communistic organization. I never attended a meeting. I have never knowingly employed a Communist. I have never knowingly retained a Communist."[54] Although this statement served to settle the issue for the moment, the charge was repeated and denied frequently throughout the hearings.

The attack on Williams at the hearings was led by Senator Bushfield of North Dakota, who came prepared with a dossier of Williams' former writings and speeches. Quoting brief passages from these, Bushfield called upon the nominee to explain and justify them. Typical of many such quotations Williams was asked to explain was a statement that he had made in a speech to the National Youth Congress in 1938: "You must somehow organize to get power into the hands of the workers. That is the only method by which you can ever hope to get the benefit of the great industrial machine." Admitting that he had made this statement, Williams stated that it was lifted out of context, and that in the speech he had said much more which was not quoted. Also he said that by "workers" he meant all who were gainfully employed, from the highest executive to the lowest employee.[55] One of the most damaging quotations of this sort was taken from a speech to the Workers' Alliance, an organization of the unemployed, in which Williams had said in 1938: "We've got to keep our friends in power." Williams stated that he had been much criticized for this speech and agreed that it had been a mistake.[56] Similarly, he was called on to explain a speech in which he had said in 1935 that "the only real remedy was to make society over." Williams gave a spirited reply, pointing to the millions of unemployed on relief and to the fact that many other prominent persons had spoken out against the conditions which had led to this widespread suffering. Admitting that his own thinking at that time was influenced by his responsibilities in administering relief, Willams asserted that such quotations were "preeminently unfair" when used out of context to indicate that they represented his permanent views, and professed his strong belief in the "basic structure of American life."[57] The statement which cost him the most votes in the Senate was a column which he had written for the official organ of the National Farmers' Union, attacking the "Republican–Southern Tory coalition."[58]

Utilizing the reports of the House Un-American Activities Committee, Senator Bushfield next questioned Williams about his alleged membership in or association with several Communist-front organizations. Williams vehemently denied any association with them, pointing out that the Attorney General and the Federal Bureau of Investigation had specifically cleared him of any such charges.[59] When he was asked whether he had ever addressed the American Youth Congress, he replied that he had, pointing out that Mrs. Roosevelt and the President of Vassar had also addressed the same meeting.[60]

Although many communications were received by members of the committee in opposition to Williams, and a number of protestants were invited to appear, the only opposing witness to testify was the senior senator from Tennessee, McKellar. Reading from a biographical record of Williams' experience, he inquired: "Is there a suggestion from that that Mr. Williams has ever had any experience in the kind of business that he is being called upon to look after here? ... Mr. Williams may qualify as a social-work expert, but how in the name of Heaven even Mr. Williams himself, as delightful and as ingratiating and as seductive a man as he is, could think he could successfully run the rural electrification business is something beyond me."[61] Senator McKellar interjected the religious issue into the hearing by reading a telegram from a former pastor of a church in Birmingham, Alabama, who wired that Williams had "denied the divinity of Christ after the Church had educated him for the ministry."[62] Introduction of the religious issue attracted much adverse criticism in the press and was denounced by Reinhold Niebuhr, a noted Protestant theologian, in a wire to Chairman Thomas.[63]

Before the hearings ended, Senator Lucas made a brief statement, in which he said that the testimony before the committee had been "very unfair, prejudicial, incompetent and immaterial." Because of what he had heard and read, at the outset of the hearings he had been unfavorably disposed toward Williams, Lucas said, but that after the testimony and the unfair and spurious charges he had become convinced that Williams was competent and was qualified to become Administrator of the REA. Continuing, Senator Lucas declared:

In my ten years in Congress I have never seen a witness seeking confirmation upon an important agency as this, so abused and so maligned. Ninety-eight percent of the evidence presented before this committee would not stand the test if it were offered before a court of competent jurisdiction. If you would convict this man of anything it would be that he is a humanitarian ... smear is the chief weapon being used against Mr. Williams...[64]

Senator Aiken stated that from his firsthand knowledge of Williams and the administration of the NYA, gained while he was governor of Vermont, he could testify that Williams had done an excellent job in his state and that there had been no politics in it. From this experience and in the absence of any credible evidence to the contrary, he was satisfied that Williams was well qualified to become the Administrator of the REA.[65] Toward the close of the earings Senator Bilbo questioned the nominee about his attitude on racial egregation and the FEPC, and Williams answered unequivocally that he was opposed to discrimination against any person in employment, or seeking employment, based on race. The race issue was a significant undertone of the contest. On February 16 Senator Bilbo wrote to a constituent that "We do not want this Negro-lover on this job." A group of nationally prominent persons supporting Williams replied in a paid advertisement headed: "Who will stand with Bilbo?"[66]

Although Majority Leader Barkley predicted that Williams would be approved, the opposition, consisting of a combination of Republicans and Southern Democrats, appeared to have a majority. Anticipating rejection, several Democratic senators urged Williams to have his name withdrawn, but he refused, saying that he would prefer to go down fighting. Senator Ellender, a strong supporter of Williams, told reporters, "We've got a fighting chance. If the Senate will read the printed record of the Hearings, I do not see how it can turn down Aubrey Williams. I have never seen such bias and prejudice as has confused consideration of this issue."[67]

On March 19, 1945, when the nomination was taken up, Senator Ellender made a vigorous defense of the nominee, noting that the only witness to appear against Williams was McKellar and that the other accusers had found it inexpedient to testify. When Ellender noted that only two or three Republican senators were present, Senator Lucas explained that they had agreed to reject Williams to offset the confirmation of Wallace and had made up their minds without reading the testimony. "It is not a question of ability," said Senator Lucas, "it is not a question of competency. They are out to get somebody, that is all . . . and Williams has got to be the one."[68]

After Senator Thomas had read into the record numerous telegrams from local coöperative farm groups advocating confirmation, Senator Lucas held the floor for more than two hours, praising the character, ability, and Americanism of Aubrey Williams. Few members were in attendance, however, and Senator Hatch asked for a quorum call four times in the course of the Lucas speech. Senator Willis charged that the nominee had a record of "incompetence and extravagance in Government administration" and dwelt at length on the Communist issue. In a significant passage he conceded that Williams was not a member of the Communist party but contended that nevertheless he should be rejected as a Communist because of "the company he keeps."[69]

A number of senators criticized the spurious charges which had been raised in the hearings. Senator Lucas declared that there should be a rule requiring the "observance of some propriety in connection with the handling of such cases."[70] Senator La Follette, who had known Williams when he resided in Wisconsin, asserted that the testimony against Williams would not be admitted by a justice of peace of any state, adding that "convicting individuals for their economic or political beliefs by the process of association is a very dangerous practice to be indulged in by the members of this body."[71]

Speaking for the nominee, Senator Aiken declared that it was not Aubrey Williams, but rather the Senate, that was on trial, and that if the Senate rejected him it would suffer in public esteem. "The main issue involved in the vote which we are soon to take," said Aiken, "is whether a man can come before this Senate for approval and have that approval granted or refused on the basis of the evidence presented or whether such judgment will be influenced by political prejudice, racial and religious discrimination, and all the other evils which Members of the United States Senate should rise above."[72]

Senator Taft, speaking in more moderate terms than other opponents, stated that although it was difficult to determine the qualifications needed for such a position, he had been informed by persons who knew Williams that he was wasteful and incompetent, and for this reason he would vote against him. On March 23, 1945, the nomination was rejected by a vote of 52 to 36.[73] Williams issued a statement to the press that the issue had not been his competence or whether he was a good Presbyterian, but rather his desire to place more power in the hands of the people, adding that he thought the contest had served a useful purpose but he was glad it was over.[74] The St. Louis *Post Dispatch,* in an editorial entitled "The Shame of the Senate," condemned the rejection of Williams, which it attributed to Southern reaction.[75] And the *Nation* deplored the fact that the nominations of a progressive President were left to the mercies of a "reactionary majority" in the Senate.[76]

After his rejection by the Senate, Williams, with the backing of Marshall Field, became the publisher and editor of the *Southern Farmer* and had conspicuous success. Within a few years he also built and operated a large housing project for low-income groups. Although he had been rejected by a majority of the Senate as a social worker, a theorist, and an impractical visionary, he soon became a successful businessman.

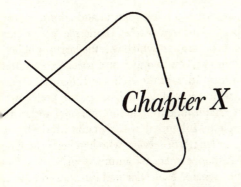

Chapter X

THE CONTESTS OVER
THE APPOINTMENTS OF
DAVID E. LILIENTHAL AND
GORDON R. CLAPP

It is very easy simply to say one is not a Communist. And, of course, if despite my record it is necessary for me to state this very affirmatively, then this is a great disappointment to me. It is very easy to talk about being against communism. It is equally important to believe those things which provide a satisfactory and effective alternative. Democracy is that satisfying affirmative alternative. David E Lilienthal.[1]

ON NOVEMBER 1, 1946, President Truman gave recess appointments to five persons to serve as members of the recently created Atomic Energy Commission: David E. Lilienthal, chairman, Dr. Robert F. Bacher, Sumner T. Pike, Lewis L. Strauss, and William W. Waymack. Because of the importance of the commission and the tense international situation, the appointments attracted wide attention and received general approval in the press. All the appointees were distinguished persons with high qualifications for membership on the commission. Each had an important contribution to make to its work, and it appeared that each was selected because of his qualifications rather than for partisan reasons. It was not expected that there would be any serious difficulty in securing Senate approval of so able a group, including conservatives as well as liberals. The only member of the group who was opposed in the Senate was David E. Lilienthal; but the bitter contest which developed over the confirmation of his appointment held up the approval of the others for several months and disrupted the work of the commission at a critical period.

David Lilienthal had a notable record as a public official and administrator. For a number of years he had been chairman of the Tennessee Valley Authority, a multipurpose government corporation which was the largest publicly owned utility enterprise in the country. As a member of a special committee he had also a leading part in the preparation of the Acheson-Lilienthal report on the control of atomic energy, which served as the basis of the policy proposed by the United States for the establishment of an international authority.

The spearhead of the opposition to Lilienthal was Senator McKellar of Tennessee, the dean of the Senate in length of service, who had been carrying on a patronage fight with the TVA management for a number of years. From 1942 to 1947, in every year but one, Senator McKellar had introduced bills or had attached riders to appropriation bills to provide that all appointments to the TVA of employees receiving $4,500 a year or more should be subject to confirmation by the Senate. These provisions would have given McKellar the whip hand over TVA. Because he was the senator from Tennessee, his approval would have been required for all major appointments. Although he did not succeed in securing the passage of these provisions, several times they passed the Senate and were stricken out in conference when the House conferees refused to agree. The fight had continued for several years, with Senator McKellar growing increasingly bitter toward Lilienthal, who as chairman of the TVA spoke in opposition to these measures.

Senator McKellar intensely resented the attacks made upon him by civic groups and the press of his own state, which had come to the defense of the TVA. As a ranking member of the Senate Appropriations Committee, McKellar had always supported the TVA requests for funds,[2] and he often claimed the credit for securing the TVA appropriations. He looked upon himself as the congressional sponsor of the TVA, and it was a source of keen disappointment to him that President Roosevelt had chosen Senator Norris to introduce the original TVA bill.

The fight which Senator McKellar conducted against the appointments of David E. Lilienthal as chairman of the Atomic Energy Commission and Gordon R. Clapp as chairman of the TVA was generally attributed to his patronage fight with the TVA. Senator McKellar had come to accept, though reluctantly, the policy of the Authority to make all appointments strictly on the basis of merit, without regard to political endorsements. This policy, which was required by the TVA Act, did not prevent the Tennessee senator from seeking appointments for his supporters and from feeling aggrieved when his candidates were not appointed. The actual break in amicable relations, however, occurred over another issue—the location of a dam to bring in additional power needed for national defense. Anticipating an increased demand for power by the aluminum industry, early in 1941 the TVA proposed the construction of two dams on the Holston River. Although the project was at first turned down by the National Defense Advisory Commission on the advice of its power expert that additional power was not needed, this decision was later reversed, and the end of 1943 was fixed as the date when the additional power would be required. With the approval of the President a deficiency appropriation was requested of Congress in the late summer of 1941, to start construction. By this time, however, it was too late to build the dams on the Holston River and meet the deadline. Consequently the TVA proposed instead the construction of Douglas Dam on the French Broad River, which could be constructed and put into operation more quickly.

At this juncture a legislative battle occurred over which dam should be built. The proposed Douglas Dam would flood an extensive farming area, including a cannery. The persons affected protested to the House and Senate Appropriations committees, and the committees turned down the requested appropriation. Disregarding the engineering advice that it was impossible to complete the dams and fill the reservoirs on the Holston River in time to meet the deadline, Senator McKellar had funds included in the deficiency appropriation for the Holston River dams.

Confronted with this situation, the TVA board took the extraordinary step of opposing an appropriation which had been handed to it on a silver platter, and in support of the President's defense program, it continued its fight for an appropriation to build Douglas Dam instead. The usual course would have been for the agency to bow to the wishes of the senator—especially to a ranking member of the powerful Appropriations Committee—and accept the dam that he wanted built in his own state. Political considerations have usually played an important, if not decisive, role in the determination of such issues. Senator McKellar regarded the TVA position as inexplicable, for he had secured an appropriation not for one dam, but for two!

President Roosevelt made a statement to the press urging the appropriation to build Douglas Dam and opposing the construction at that time of the dams on the Holston. The press in the Tennessee Valley backed the President and the TVA and attacked Senator McKellar for playing politics with national defense. When the Japanese attack on Pearl Harbor occurred shortly afterward, Congress promptly voted funds for the dams on both rivers, as defense projects. But the senior senator from Tennessee smarted under the criticisms he had received from the press of his own state, for which he held Lilienthal responsible. Senator McKellar apparently regarded the decision concerning which dam should be constructed as a political one in which the national defense requirements and the engineering advice could be overruled by partisan considerations. The TVA board showed high courage in standing by the program of the administration and the advice of its own engineering staff, refusing to accede to an obviously political decision. Its position was as unusual as it was courageous, and Senator McKellar regarded it as an enormous insult to him.

Senator McKellar subsequently opposed the reappointment of Lilienthal in 1945 to a third term on the board of the TVA, but he was able to get little support from his colleagues and did not ask for a roll-call vote. The two senators from Tennessee issued a joint statement at that time accusing Lilienthal of playing politics, and in the Senate debate McKellar declared that Lilienthal was personally and politically obnoxious to him.[3] Realizing, however, that he could not block Lilienthal's confirmation in 1945, Senator McKellar did not press his personal objection and stated that he would leave the matter up to the Senate.[4]

When the hearings opened in 1947 on Lilienthal's nomination as chairman of the Atomic Energy Commission, Senator McKellar undertook at first a singlehanded fight to block confirmation. He also carried on a similar campaign against Gordon R. Clapp, who was nominated to succeed Lilienthal as chairman of the TVA, charging both men with having Communist sympathies and retaining Communists on the staff of the TVA. His tactics were to prolong the hearings and to secure wide publicity of his charges, hoping thereby to build up opposition to the men. The nomination of Lilienthal came before the Senate section of the Joint Committee on Atomic Energy; that of Clapp was referred to the Committee on Public Works. Although not a member of either committee, Senator McKellar attended the hearings and for weeks interrogated not only the nominees but other witnesses as well, and asked the committees to subpoena numerous witnesses he thought would support his charges. Many of the same witnesses appeared at both hearings and gave similar testimony.

The fight over the confirmation of Lilienthal, however, had much wider significance than the venting of personal spite by an aged and cantankerous member of the Senate against the nominee. As McKellar hoped, he was joined in his opposition by some conservative senators of his own party and a number of leading members of the opposite party. In the course of the long-drawn-out contest the opposition shifted grounds; after the charge that Lilienthal was sympathetic to Communism had been discredited, he was attacked on the ground that he was a New Dealer. The Communism charges, however, were not abandoned. While the nomination was still before the Senate Committee, Senators Taft, Wherry, Bridges, and White issued public statements announcing their opposition. Although Senator Taft accused the nominee of being "soft" on Communism, for the most part the opposing senators attacked him for being a New Dealer, for his belief in public ownership of public utilities, for his alleged disbelief in the private enterprise system, and for the part which he had played in the preparation of the Acheson-Lilienthal report.

Senator McKellar's attack on Lilienthal was widely denounced in the press, many leading newspapers urging confirmation of his nomination. If the opposition of Senator McKellar had been more temperate and had been supported by some evidence, it might have led to the rejection of Lilienthal; instead, it was so intemperate, unjust, and unsupported by the facts that many of his colleagues became disgusted and regarded the whole proceedings as a sorry spectacle which lowered the Senate in public esteem. Senator McKellar's bitter fight against the nominee undoubtedly gained votes for him and, indeed, may have been instrumental in bringing about his confirmation.

The Hearings

The Senate section of the Joint Committee on Atomic Energy opened its hearings on January 27, 1947, and at the first two sessions questioned members of the commission and the general manager. No opposition was voiced against the other nominations, which were almost overlooked during the subsequent fight over Lilienthal's confirmation. In opening the Senate debate two months later, Senator Hickenlooper reminded his colleagues that the approval of the appointments of the entire commission and its general manager were being perilously delayed.

The issue upon which members of the committee placed greatest emphasis in their interrogation of Lilienthal was his attitude toward the Congressional Joint Committee on Atomic Energy, which had been set up as a "watchdog" of the AEC, and toward the military liaison committee which the act created. Chairman Hickenlooper inquired of Lilienthal at the outset whether his personal attitude would be that of full and complete coöperation with the joint committee of Congress and its staff. Lilienthal replied that the commission would welcome the closest contacts and relations with the congressional committee and stated that it would be a great advantage to have such a committee with which it could work.

It will be recalled that whether atomic energy should be under military or under civilian control had been the subject of long and bitter controversy, in the preceding year, when Congress considered atomic energy legislation. Although civilian control was finally adopted, it was strongly opposed by many members who favored military control. Members of the Senate committee favoring military control pressed Lilienthal for a commitment that the military liaison committee would be kept fully informed on all developments and operations, would have full access to secret records and activities, and would be permitted to attend all sessions of the commission. Senator Vandenberg declared that not a single door should be closed to the military liaison or congressional committees.[8] Lilienthal agreed to work very closely with both committees and to supply them with full information but was unwilling to agree that all commission meetings be open to the congressional and military liaison committees. He stated, however, that he felt sure the matter would be worked out to the satisfaction of all, and assured the Senate committee that there would be no disposition by the commission to withhold any essential information from the military liaison committee.[7]

This questioning by the committee revealed one of the underlying issues in the case: the struggle over whether atomic energy should be managed by a civilian or a military agency. The decision for civilian control had been made by Congress; nevertheless, those in favor of military control were reluctant to accept that decision and wanted a commission that would be sympathetic and coöperative with the military. Lilienthal was regarded as a person who would have preëminently the civilian point of view, and this accounted in part for some of the opposition to him.

The members of the Senate Committee on Atomic Energy at first appeared somewhat hostile to the nominee, but apparently were reassured by his answers. At the end of the session on January 27 the chairman informed Lilienthal that he would be asked to come back again at a time when Senator McKellar could be present to interrogate him. The hearings continued for six weeks, and in this time Lilienthal appeared six times to be interrogated by McKellar. Fifty-four witnesses appeared, most of them at McKellar's request. The contest attracted increasing public interest until it became a leading national issue, while the hearings wearily dragged on to the disgust and indignation of members of the Senate committee. After a few days Senator Vandenberg and some other members refused to take further part in the proceedings and absented themselves.[8]

Throughout the hearings, Senator McKellar attempted to link Lilienthal with Communism. On February 4, he asked the nominee if he had ever been in Russia. When Lilienthal replied that he had not, Senator McKellar inquired what was the birthplace of his parents. On being informed that it was in the vicinity of Pressburg, now a part of Czechoslovakia, Senator McKellar then asked: "As a matter of fact, Czechoslovakia is under the domination of Russia, is it not?"

Lilienthal replied that he did not know, and that his father and mother were born more than seventy years ago. "And I am sure," he said, "that you are giving them very great pain by the maltreatment that you are giving me in these hearings, Senator."[9]

Inquiring about Lilienthal's membership in the Southern Conference for Human Welfare, Senator McKellar asked: "The truth is that your sympathies are very leftist, are they not?"[10] In answering this question Lilienthal turned away from Senator McKellar and faced the whole committee. Speaking slowly and in a low voice, he delivered one of the most eloquent and stirring statements of faith in democracy ever uttered.

My convictions are not so much concerned with what I am against as what I am for—and that excludes a lot of things automatically.

Traditionally, democracy has been an affirmative doctrine rather than merely a negative one.

I believe in—and I conceive the Constitution of the United States to rest, as does religion, upon—the fundamental proposition of the integrity of the individual; and that all Government and all private institutions must be designed to promote and protect and defend the integrity and the dignity of the individual; that that is the essential meaning of the Constitution and the Bill of Rights, as it is essentially the meaning of religion.

Any forms of government, therefore, and any other institutions, which make men means rather than ends in themselves, which exalt the state or any other institutions above the importance of men, which place arbitrary power over men as a fundamental tenet of government, are contrary to this conception; and therefore I am deeply opposed to them.

The communistic philosophy, as well as the communistic form of government, falls within this category, for its fundamental tenet is quite to the contrary. The fundamental tenet of communism is that the state is an end in itself, and that therefore the powers which the state exercises over the individual are without any ethical standards to limit them. That I deeply disbelieve.[11]

When he had finished, the hushed silence of the crowded room was broken by Senator McMahon, who said: "Mr. Lilienthal, I congratulate you on that statement. In my opinion it is the creed of a very real American."

Unmoved, however, Senator McKellar continued his interrogation by asking: "Mr. Lilienthal, while you were the head of TVA, did you have any Communists in your employ? Just answer, if you can 'yes' or 'no' and then make any explanation that you can."[12]

The following day, leading newspapers throughout the country carried the statement in full. The Washington *Post* printed it in a special pamphlet for distribution, and Secretary Krug had a copy enlarged and placed on a placard at the entrance to the Department of the Interior Building.

Often in the course of the hearings, Senator McKellar alleged that certain key officials of the TVA were Communists. One of those so attacked was Herbert S. Marks, who had been appointed general counsel of the AEC. To refute this allegation, Dean Acheson, Under Secretary of State for whom Marks had served for a period as special assistant; John Lord O'Brian, an eminent lawyer and former Republican candidate for governor of New York; and Dr. John S. Dickey, president of Dartmouth College, appeared before the committee and testified that Marks was a man of the highest ideals, patriotism, and ability, and that the charges were baseless. It is remarkable that these distinguished witnesses felt called upon to appear in defense of a person who was not being considered by the committee for any position. Their testimony, however, made no impression on Senator McKellar, who continued to refer to Marks as a notorious Communist. The charges of Communism in the TVA were refuted by the testimony of former Congressman Joseph Starnes, who had been chairman of a subcommittee of the House Committee on Un-American Activities that had investigated Communism in the Knoxville area in 1940.*

Senator McKellar accused Lilienthal of continuing to receive a salary from the Commerce Clearing House of Chicago after he became a member of the Wisconsin Railroad Commission, although this was prohibited by Wisconsin state law. This accusation was also refuted by testimony at the hearing. A telegram from former Governor La Follette stated that he was fully informed about and approved the arrangement under which Lilienthal continued for a time to receive royalties from the Commerce Clearing House for editorial work he had previously performed.

Senator McKellar charged Lilienthal, as chairman of the TVA, with violation and disregard of the acts of Congress, particularly those relating to civil service, accounting, the retirement system, and flood control. Lilienthal pointed out in reply that the Tennessee Valley Act authorized and directed the TVA to establish its own personnel system and exempted it from the federal civil service system; he cited other pertinent provisions of the law concerning its relations with the General Accounting Office and its authority to carry on flood control work.

Increased Opposition

After the hearings had continued for several weeks, Senator McKellar was joined by some conservatives of both parties. On February 10, Senator Johnson of Colorado stated, while Mr. Acheson was testifying before the Senate committee, that he regarded the Acheson-Lilienthal report as "the greatest blunder in diplomacy that this country has ever made." Flushing, Acheson replied that "if there is any criticism, that criticism falls on me. I am quite willing to bear it."[13] On the same day, Senator Wherry announced that he would oppose the confirmation of Lilienthal, asserting that the post should go to a man about whom "not a shadow of a doubt" could be raised.[14] Earlier, Senator McKellar had advocated that Lilienthal should be rejected if a single senator voted against him, a proposal which Senator McMahon called "quaint," pointing out that under such a rule it was probable that no nominee would ever be confirmed.[15] Representative Eugene Cox in the House called upon President Truman to withdraw the nomination.

Within the next few days several prominent Republicans, as well as some Democratic senators, announced their opposition to Lilienthal. Senator Moore of Oklahoma issued a statement on February 12 opposing Lilienthal because

---

* The Communist charge is discussed below in the account of the contest over the confirmation of the appointment of Gordon R. Clapp.

of his "well known" advocacy of public control of hydroelectric power, saying that in view of the prospect for atomic energy as a source of power it would be a great mistake to appoint to the commission any man who held such views. "New Dealism," he declared, "and all it stands for were repudiated by the American people last November 5."[16] Senator White, the Republican majority leader, announced his opposition on the ground that Lilienthal was "temperamentally unsuited" for the position, and because of his "long hostility to legislative limitations and his dictatorial management" of the TVA.[17] Senator O'Daniel of Texas stated that he would vote against this and any other New Deal appointment. Greatly encouraged, Senator McKellar prophesied that the Senate would reject Lilienthal.

The nominee, however, was not without his defenders. Senators Hill, Sparkman, Kilgore, and McMahon—all Democrats—announced their support, as did Republican Senators Lodge and Morse. Two weeks after the hearings started it appeared that the opponents were gaining the upper hand. It was reported that only strong support by Senator Vandenberg could swing enough votes to Lilienthal to confirm his appointment.[18] The nomination was discussed in the party conferences of both parties, but no decision was announced. Rumors were widespread that pressure was being placed on the President to withdraw the nomination, and a secret meeting of the Senate committee was held on February 14. President Truman steadfastly stood by his selection, permitting himself to be quoted that the Communist charges of Senator McKellar were "absolutely unfounded."[19]

The hearings were continued in the face of mounting criticism in the press, and on March 19 Chairman Hickenlooper announced that he hoped to bring them to an end within a week. By this time the case had become top news throughout the country, and members of the Senate were receiving thousands of letters, mostly favoring Lilienthal. Many organizations adopted resolutions urging prompt confirmation of the members of the commission; frequent stories appeared in the press to the effect that the whole atomic energy program was at a standstill and would remain so until the matter was settled. Members of the commission attended Senate hearings day after day, and the staff was engaged in preparing materials for them between sessions. Because of the wrangle, the commission stopped buying uranium ore, and three hundred mines in the country were idle.[20] Organizations of atomic energy scientists actively entered the fight, supporting the President's nominees and urging prompt action by the Senate.

On February 21, Senator Taft, whose position up to this time had been in doubt, issued a statement announcing his opposition, in which he said that he regarded Lilienthal as "temperamentally unfitted to head any important executive agency in a democratic government and too 'soft' on issues connected with communism and Soviet Russia." Declaring that no senator should vote for the nominee unless "he would have been willing to appoint him," Taft stated in his release to the press that Lilienthal was "a typical power-hungry bureaucrat . . . muddled in his thinking on questions of international power," and that confirmation of his appointment would be "a real threat to our national safety."[21]

On the same day, Senator Vandenberg placed in the *Congressional Record* a letter from President Karl T. Compton of Massachusetts Institute of Technology urging the confirmation of Lilienthal. "I know of no one as well qualified and possibly available," wrote Dr. Compton. He urged prompt action by the Senate, warning that rejection would be a "very serious blow to our future progress in the atomic energy field."[22] Several days later, the committee voted eight to one for confirmation, Senator Bricker casting the only negative vote.

The Debate in the Senate

In opening the debate on March 24, 1947, Senator Hickenlooper reviewed the history of the Atomic Energy Commission and the difficulties in the transition from military to civilian administration, and stressed the great importance to the country of its work. The administration of the program, he urged, "must be above pure partisanship" and must be conducted with a vigorous and impartial conception of the basic security of the country. Pointing to the delays that had already occurred, and the loss of scientists by the project because of uncertainties, he pressed for prompt action not only on the nomination of Lilienthal but also on the nominations of the other members and the general manager, declaring that "the United States and the world cannot afford to have any further delay."[23]

Concerning the personal qualifications of Lilienthal, Senator Hickenlooper declared that he was "a man of high intelligence, great administrative ability, and vigorous devotion to the successful operation of any enterprise with which he is associated," and pointed to the long list of distinguished witnesses who had appeared on his behalf. He stated that the committee had found all the nominees to be men of experience and ability, who "have been tremendously successful in their various fields of activities."[24]

Senator Bridges challenged his colleague to state that they were the best-qualified persons in the country for the job. Senator Hickenlooper replied: "I do not think that they are necessarily the best men. I do not know . . . exactly who would be the best men in the United States." But, he stated, they are "amply able and amply capable."[25]

The appointing responsibility [said Senator Hickenlooper] is in the President. We have only an examining and confirming responsibility. . . . Our job and our obligation was to examine the appointments the President had made and sent to the Senate. We have no power to appoint. We have no power to select. We would be considered offensive if we recommended to the President whom he should appoint.

We are a legislative body and his responsibility is the appointing power. Therefore, it was our duty to see whether or not the appointees were able, whether there was anything fundamentally against them which would mitigate against the proper performance of their duty, the able performance of their duty, and we came to the conclusion that the appointees met those tests.[26]

The contention that the Senate should approve a nomination only if it found the nominee to be the best-qualified person in the country was termed 'most extraordinary" by Senator Hatch, who said such a notion was contrary to the Constitution, "which gives the President of the United States the sole right to nominate and the Senate the right to advise and consent."[27]

Senator Bridges next declared that if there was the "slightest taint" against a nominee he ought to be big enough to step down, and if he did not do so, the Senate should reject him. Senator Overton of Louisiana voiced a similar sentiment. Senator Barkley replied that if this rule had been followed, both Chief Justice Hughes and Justice Brandeis would have been rejected.

Two days later, Senator Ferguson of Michigan secured the floor and spoke in opposition to Lilienthal, charging that he had been too lenient with Communists employed by the TVA, had advocated government expansion, and was a believer in "socialist aristocracy."[28] Several days later, Senator Cain of Washington made the same contention, opposing Lilienthal for being a New Dealer and "a man whose thirst for power and authority is unquenchable."[29] Senator Bricker, the only member of the Senate committee who voted against confirmation of Lilienthal, maintained that the Atomic Energy Commission "is essentially an arm of the Congress, the legislative branch, and in our consent we have a responsibility rising almost to the level of the original appointing authority." He contended that Lilienthal was not qualified, because he had never had business experience.

Although the eight other members of the Senate committee took no stock in the charges of McKellar that the AEC had engaged employees with Communist leanings, Senator Bricker was apparently impressed, and at the close of his speech made a motion to recommit the nominations to the Senate committee for further investigation. He proposed that the FBI should be requested to investigate each nominee, and that the committee through its own staff should investigate the records of all commission employees.

Senator Knowland of California spoke in opposition to the motion but favored legislation requiring an FBI investigation in the future for these positions. He defended Lilienthal and the other nominees against the charges of Communism. "There is not one bit of evidence," said he, "that supports directly or indirectly any such theory. These men are not Communists or communist sympathizers. They are patriotic American citizens."[30] Senator Aiken stated that he could see no reason for an FBI investigation unless similar investigations were made of nominees to other high government offices, and Senator Tobey suggested that by the same reasoning every senator should be investigated.[31]

On March 31, Senator McKellar delivered an attack on Lilienthal, charging him with having appointed three Communists, whom the senator named, to high positions in the Atomic Energy Commission. Senator Knowland protested that there was no evidence in the record to prove that any of the three were Communists. But Senator McKellar was undeterred, and through a long and rambling speech continually made assertions that Lilienthal had Communists around him as his principal assistants. Senator Bridges of New Hampshire obtained the floor on April 1 to speak in opposition to the confirmation of Lilienthal, whom he accused of having the "trappy, tricky mind of a bureaucrat." "He is a typical bureaucrat," declared the senator, who "is all things to all men."[32] He attacked Lilienthal because of his unwillingness to agree in the hearings that members of the military liaison committee be permitted to attend all meetings of the commission. "Here is a man," said Senator Bridges, "who is palmed off on us as a great administrator and yet he had not thought through this most important but simple problem of military liaison."[33] No friend of the TVA, Senator Bridges accused Lilienthal of running it "like a czar," setting up trick coöperative corporations, blocking the attempt of the General Accounting Office to make "an honest audit of his books," and spending money on "propaganda and self-glorification" which he charged to "regional development and demonstration projects."[34]

Senator McMahon and Senator Smith of New Jersey warned that further delay in the confirmation of the appointments to the commission would have serious effects on its work, and read letters in this vein from Dr. Karl Compton, president of Massachusetts Institute of Technology, and Dr. J. B. Conant, president of Harvard. Senator Bridges retorted that all this was "just pure undiluted bunk." "With thousands of able men to choose from," declared Senator Byrd, "why should a selection have been made that has even a taint of some foreign 'ism' that is abhorrent to the American people?"[35]

On April 2, Senator Taft delivered one of the major speeches opposing Lilienthal. Elaborating his previous statement, he discussed his concept of the role of the Senate in passing on appointments. He deplored the practice which he said had developed for the Senate to confirm every presidential appointment unless the nominee was found to be a "thief or a criminal or was involved in a scandal." Although he conceded that the President should be free to select members of his Cabinet who were his own personal advisers, he contended that this rule should not be extended to other officers, and particularly those who exercised legislative powers. He insisted that independent commissions which exercise quasi-legislative powers are not a part of the executive branch but are responsible to Congress.[36] Concerning the Acheson-Lilienthal report

Taft declared that it was "the most naïve report that could be made by any man who has dealt with an international problem," and showed "that Mr. Lilienthal considered communism just another form of democracy."[37]

Senator McMahon hotly retorted: "Of course the Senator realizes that he, and the Communists, and the Russians and Joe Stalin have this in common: apparently none of them like the plan." When pressed by Senator McMahon as to what he would propose, Senator Taft stated that he was not prepared to offer a complete policy but that he advocated the withdrawal of our proposal to the United Nations for control of atomic energy. Despite the decision of Congress for civilian development of atomic energy, he proposed that it be returned to the military.[38]

On April 9, the final day of the debate, briefer speeches in behalf of Lilienthal were made by Senators Vandenberg, Hickenlooper, Morse, Saltonstall, Murray, Myers, Smith of New Jersey, Knowland, and Barkley; Senators Taft, Wherry, Bricker, Moore, Hawkes, Malone, Capehart, and Revercomb spoke in opposition. The speech of Senator Vandenberg, who had hitherto remained silent, attracted the greatest attention and, contrary to the rules of the Senate, was applauded by the gallery. Vandenberg declared that at the outset he was prejudiced against the appointment but had been driven by the evidence "to the belief that logic, equity, fair play, and a just regard to urgent public welfare combine to recommend Mr. Lilienthal's confirmation."

The Michigan senator ridiculed the contention that a nominee should not be confirmed if anyone opposed him, stating that to accept this notion would amount to a "surrender to 'hue and cry' regardless of truth and justice."[39] Concerning the charges that Lilienthal was sympathetic to Communism, he stated: "after weeks of testimony, I find no basis for this charge." Although he was strongly opposed to Communism, Senator Vandenberg declared he would not wish to "condemn to some sort of Siberia all persons who do not happen to subscribe to my own view as to how America ought to be run." He dismissed the argument that the military should administer the atomic energy development, saying that this issue had been decided by Congress when the legislation was enacted, and maintained that it was of the utmost importance to confirm the nominations without delay so that the work of the commission could proceed. The uncertainty in the transition from military to civilian control would not be removed, he asserted, "until the Commission is firmly in the saddle." The greatest peril facing the country was that it would not keep ahead of the rest of the world in nuclear physics, and "if we found out one thing is truer than another, it is that in peacetime we cannot drive science into laboratories with a bayonet."[40]

The fact that Lilienthal was an advocate of public ownership of utilities, said Senator Vandenberg, did not disqualify him for this position, for Congress had by unanimous vote decided that atomic energy development should be a government monopoly. To the contrary, his experience as the head of the largest public power development in this country would be a qualification for the position. Referring to the famous scientists and leading businessmen of the country who had urged the confirmation of Lilienthal, Senator Vandenberg asked significantly, "Where are the comparable witnesses against him, Senators?" In closing his statement, he declared that he had reviewed the record of the many weeks of testimony, and had found that the preponderance was in Lilienthal's favor overwhelmingly. "I have no doubt," he said, "that in the interest of the national welfare and for the sake of a square deal, Mr. Lilienthal is entitled to be confirmed."

The closing speech in behalf of Lilienthal was made by Senator Barkley, the Democratic floor leader. Speaking briefly but with great feeling, he declared that the proposition that the Senate should not confirm the nominee unless it would have appointed him was a "curious if not a spurious theory," and he challenged any member of the Senate to name any person whom the Senate could have agreed upon.[41] He decried the opposition to Lilienthal because he was a liberal or progressive, declaring that under such a test he could never have held office, and deplored the tendency to charge any man who holds "liberal, advanced, forward-looking ideals on any subject" with being soft on Communism.

The vote on Senator Bricker's motion to recommit the nominations was 38 for recommittal and 52 against it;[42] 31 Republicans and 7 Democrats voted for it; 18 Republicans and 34 Democrats voted against it. The final vote was 50 for and 31 against confirmation.[43] After three months' delay, the appointments of Lilienthal and his colleagues were confirmed, and the work of the Atomic Energy Commission could proceed.

The contest over the confirmation of David E. Lilienthal as chairman of the Atomic Energy Commission ranks as one of the most notable cases in this history of the Senate. Although it may be dismissed by some as merely an illustration of the lengths to which a single member may go in attempting to block an appointment that is personally offensive to him, the case is of much broader significance. It indicates the need for the Senate, in investigations of nominees, to adopt more effective safeguards against the airing of defamatory charges and testimony based merely upon rumor, hearsay, and gossip. The antics of Senator McKellar, who, under the courtesy extended to an aged member of long service, was permitted virtually to take over the hearings and vent his personal spleen, made the contest nation-wide news but did not enhance the prestige of the Senate. His browbeating tactics incurred the emphatic disapproval of members of the committee. The attention of the committee, and later that of the Senate itself, was for the most part directed at the unsupported charges of Senator McKellar, while the real issues were to a large degree overshadowed.

An unfortunate aspect of the hearings was the unjustifiable smearing not only of the nominee but of some persons not under consideration. It is significant that several of the most distinguished citizens in the country felt called upon to appear to testify in defense of innocent third parties. Despite this testimony, the reputations of these persons probably suffered irreparable injury. The debate in the Senate was also attended by some undesirable aspects. Although Lilienthal was widely recognized as an able administrator with a distinguished record of public service, he was called a "power hungry bureaucrat," a man with a "trappy, tricky mind," who was "all things to all men," a "czar" and a "dictator." Such epithets were not only unwarranted but were beneath the dignity of the Senate. Few, if any, persons would ever willingly go through the ordeal which Lilienthal suffered to accept public office. Although his appointment was confirmed, the price he had to pay was too high."

The overtones of the contest, as in practically all major confirmation contests, were political. The Republican party, which had recently captured control of Congress and was looking forward to the presidential election of 1948, was eager to embarrass the President whenever the occasion permitted. Nominations to major offices which require approval of the Senate afford such occasions. In the decisive vote on Senator Bricker's motion for recommital, party lines proved to be an important factor. Thirty-four Democratic senators stood by the President and voted for Lilienthal; only seven—Byrd, McCarran, McClellan, McKellar, O'Daniel, Overton, and Stewart—voted against him. The vote of the Democrats was thus approximately five to one for confirmation, and that of the Republicans was nearly two to one against it. Yet the vote in favor of Lilienthal by eighteen Republicans proved to be crucial. The influence of Senator Vandenberg and the strong speech which he made supporting the nomination tipped the scales in Lilienthal's favor. Without the widespread attention which the case attracted and the aroused public opinion, it is very probable that he would have been rejected by the Senate. For that public support Lilienthal was indebted in part to his principal opponent—the aged senator from Tennessee.

The Contest over the Appointment of Clapp

Upon the resignation of Lilienthal as chairman of the board of the Tennessee Valley Authority, in the autumn of 1946, to accept an appointment to the Atomic Energy Commission, President Truman appointed Gordon R. Clapp in his place. Clapp had been a member of the TVA staff since its beginning. Starting in a minor position in the personnel department, through merit he had risen to be director of personnel and was later promoted to become general manager of the TVA. His appointment from that position to be chairman of the board was a deserved advancement in recognition of his ability and his contribution to the development of TVA. His thorough knowledge of the administration of the Authority enabled him during the course of the hearings to explain and defend its policies and practices in a manner rarely witnessed in a confirmation hearing. His nomination was submitted to the Senate when it convened in January, 1947, and was referred to the Committee on Public Works. Already Senator McKellar of Tennessee had announced his opposition and had requested the chairman to schedule its hearings at a time when he could attend.[45]

The contest over the confirmation of Clapp, which deserves to be ranked among the leading cases in the history of the Senate, was somewhat overshadowed by the Lilienthal contest. Senator McKellar directed his campaign chiefly at Lilienthal, stating in the committee hearings and in the Senate debate that he had no personal feelings against Clapp, whom he termed a "stooge" for Lilienthal. But since he had attacked Lilienthal on the charge of tolerating Communism among TVA employees, consistency required that he bring similar charges against Clapp, whose responsibility for TVA personnel was greater than that of Lilienthal. McKellar regarded Clapp as the personal choice of Lilienthal and expected him to continue the policies which Lilienthal had stood for in the TVA.

The contest over the confirmation of Clapp differed in important details from that over the appointment of Lilienthal to the Atomic Energy Commission. The opposition to Lilienthal shifted from the charge of Communist sympathies to the assertion that he was a New Dealer. New Dealism, however, was not directly an issue in the consideration of Clapp, who was a career civil servant par excellence. Like Lilienthal, he testified in the hearings that he was an independent in politics. The Republicans had just come into control of the Senate and had not yet determined what policy they would follow with respect to Truman nominations. Although the appointments to the Atomic Energy Commission could not be held up indefinitely, some urged that the chairmanship of the TVA should be left vacant to be filled by a Republican President after the 1948 election. Although the vote in neither case followed strictly party lines, it is not to be doubted that partisan considerations greatly influenced the votes on both sides of the aisle. A number of Republicans who were disgusted at the charges against Clapp, and who believed he was well qualified, voted for him in spite of the opposition of their party.

One of the major issues in the Clapp nomination was the continuation of the policies and program of the TVA. Under the Congressional Reorganization Act of 1946, TVA legislation was assigned to the new Public Works Committee instead of to the Committee on Forestry and Agriculture. The composition of the Public Works Committee, to which Clapp's nomination was referred, was known to be hostile to the TVA and to pending proposals for other valley authorities. In passing upon the appointment of a chairman of the TVA, the Republican majority in the committee and in the Senate could hardly avoid its policy implications. The outstanding feature of the hearings before the Senate committee was not the spurious charges of Senator McKellar but the TVA program and operations, which Clapp ably defended.[46] Part of the opposition came from persons hostile to the TVA who wanted to see its program curtailed, and some of the support Clapp received may be attributed to support of the TVA. His defeat would have been an important step in changing the policy of the government concerning the TVA; it might have influenced the President to nominate a person acceptable to its opponents and thus pave the way for substantial curtailment of its program. The confirmation of his appointment was, in a sense, a vote of confidence and an approval of the policies and management of the TVA.

The Hearings

The testimony of Clapp before the Committee on Public Works occupied nine sessions, from January 21 through February 1, and filled 255 pages. In addition, toward the end of the hearings, Clapp was permitted to make a rebuttal statement, which filled 50 more pages of testimony. This is probably an all-time record in the length of testimony of a nominee under consideration by a Senate committee. Although the questions of Senator McKellar dealt for the most part with charges of Communism, the members of the committee inquired into every aspect of the work of the TVA. The various criticisms which had been voiced against the TVA were raised in the hearings, and Clapp was interrogated on its fertilizer program and the distribution of fertilizer to state agricultural extension services for experimental work; its financial operations; the division of costs of dams between electric-power and other programs; research and development activities, particularly quick freezing, strawberry-picking machines, ham-curing devices, portable threshers, and sweet-potato processing; information and publicity activities; contracts limiting the resale rates of TVA power; free rides in the TVA airplane; and similar matters. Clapp's testimony contains a full explanation of every phase of the TVA, including the legal authority, the policies followed, and the costs. Many questions were obviously antagonistic, often containing assumptions or implied accusations. Clapp's answers were always courteous and objective, and seldom if ever argumentative; nevertheless, he firmly stood his ground and never retreated in his defense of the TVA. Time and again he pointed out errors in the statements or assumptions of his questioners, but did so in so courteous and objective a fashion that no one could take offense. Senator McKellar's questions were, for the most part, charged with accusations, insinuations, and innuendoes; but not once did Clapp answer discourteously.

A significant feature of the hearings was the attempt on the part of a number of members of the committee to secure commitments from Clapp that he would favor modification or reconsideration of certain TVA policies to which they objected. It is seldom recognized how effectively skillful questions may be utilized in a confirmation hearing to elicit commitments from a nominee. Ordinarily, a nominee desires above all else to avoid antagonizing a member of the committee considering his nomination, and when quizzed on controversial policies, usually attempts to evade the issue or at least to qualify his answer if he is unable to express wholehearted agreement with his questioner. Many questions were asked of Clapp by members of the committee and by Senator McKellar, inquiring into his attitude on TVA policies. It would have been easy for him to have given qualified answers or to have stated that he was undecided, but Clapp took the opposite course of stating frankly and fully his support of the policies of the TVA, defending them against the implied criticism contained in the questions. For example, Senator Williams of Delaware interrogated him at length about the TVA fertilizer program, to which the senator was obviously opposed, but Clapp never hedged in his replies and never qualified them, nor did he suggest that the policies of the TVA in this field should be reconsidered. At one point in the hearings, Senator McClellan inquired of the nominee whether he had in mind any changes in the policies of the TVA. Clapp replied without equivocation that he favored continuation of the present policies without change.[47]

Senator McKellar based his attack on Clapp primarily on the charge that he was responsible for the alleged infiltration of the TVA by Communists and that Clapp personally was sympathetic and tolerant of Communists and Communism. He asserted that there were twenty-two present and former employees of the TVA who were "well-known Communists" and named them not once but repeatedly throughout the hearings. Reading from his list, McKellar inquired whether each of these persons was a Communist. Clapp replied in most instances that he could say from his own knowledge that they were not.[48]

Senator McKellar secured his list of alleged Communists employed, or formerly employed, by the TVA by taking the names of its employees who were mentioned in the hearings of the Dies committee, which had investigated Communist and subversive activities in labor unions in the Knoxville area in 1940, seven years earlier. Former Representative Joseph Starnes, who had served as chairman of the subcommittee which conducted these hearings, testified that it found little evidence of Communism in the area, and particularly little among the employees of the TVA. At the time of the investigation, out of sixteen thousand employees of the TVA it was found that three very minor employees had been members of the Communist party. One was discharged, another had left its employment, and the third—a young man, Henry C. Hart, who of his own accord had quit the party in disillusionment a year before the investigation—was retained after his case was fully reviewed. This handling of the cases apparently met with the satisfaction of the Dies committee. Starnes testified at the Clapp hearings that there was not "one iota of evidence" to show that the TVA board, the general manager, or anyone else in authority was in any way connected with the Communist party or sympathetic to it.[49] This statement had little if any effect on Senator McKellar, who continued to refer to TVA employees on his list as "well-known Communists" or as "Comrades."

One of the features of the hearing was a letter allegedly written by Henry C. Hart describing the activities of the Communist cell in the TVA. The letter was supposed to have been found in the files of the Communist party in Birmingham, but only a mimeographed copy could be produced; it was never substantiated as admissable evidence. Hart, a graduate student at the University of Wisconsin, on being brought before the committee, categorically denied that he had ever written such a letter.[50] The Dies committee had never used the letter as evidence, and no satisfactory proof was ever submitted that it was genuine. Nevertheless, Senator McKellar continually referred to it as if it were.

When asked by Senator McKellar whether he was a Communist, Clapp entered a categorical denial. Elsewhere in the hearings he stated that he had no patience with Communists and the Communistic line of thinking.[51] No witness at the hearings, not even former employees who had been discharged for cause, asserted that Clapp was a Communist or had any Communist sympathies. The charge that he had permitted Communists to be employed or retained by the TVA was disproved by reliable witnesses. The only testimony in support of McKellar's charges came from several former employees who had been discharged by the TVA for cause. These persons now attributed their discharges to a conspiracy of a Communist clique in the TVA, but they were unable to give any specific evidence to support their assertion. In his rebuttal statement, Clapp, citing the records of the TVA, pointed out glaring errors of fact in their statements.

Other Charges against the TVA

Although professing to be the friend of the TVA, Senator McKellar used the hearings to raise practically all the criticisms which had ever been voiced against the Authority. Before the hearings opened he submitted two letters of questions to Clapp.[52] The first question was: Under what authority had the TVA sent three engineers to Russia and also designed powerhouses for the Russian government? The answer stated that no engineers had been sent to Russia, but that TVA engineers had designed powerhouses for the Russian government under an arrangement made and paid for by the Lend-Lease Administration under authority of law. Other questions dealt with the authority of the TVA to set up its own system of personnel, to carry on flood control work and to retain its revenues; the alleged lobbying activities of the

TVA; the cost of its information and publicity section; the number of its employees and the total annual pay roll before the war and at present; its fertilizer program; its research activities; and similar matters. One question was whether Senator McKellar himself had ever recommended anyone for appointment, and if so, who was it? To this, Clapp replied that the files indicated that Senator McKellar had recommended several hundred persons, but that there was nothing improper in this, for it was the policy of the TVA under the initial act of Congress to accord to letters of recommendation from members of Congress no more and no less weight than it accorded to letters of recommendation from other responsible persons.[53]

Another charge by Senator McKellar, made at various times throughout the hearings, was that the TVA had opposed his reëlection by publishing unfriendly articles, which he maintained were "damnable lies."[54] Clapp explained that the publication referred to was the *Index of TVA News,* a mimeographed newssheet issued by the TVA to a number of its top employees to enable them to keep up with articles and editorials that appeared in the press about the TVA, and consisted entirely of excerpts and digests of such articles. Senator McKellar was indignant that condensations of editorials and articles unfriendly to him had been printed in this publication.

Witnesses Favoring the Nomination

The list of witnesses who favored the appointment of Clapp was impressive. It included Senators Hill and Sparkman of Alabama; Representatives Gore, Kefauver, Jennings, and Priest from Tennessee; and Jones and Raines from Alabama. It is significant that these members of Congress not only testified in support of Clapp but also attended most of the hearings on his nomination. This was indeed an extraordinary tribute to the nominee, probably unparalleled in the history of the Senate. Senators Hill and Sparkman took little or no part in the proceedings, however, except when they testified in behalf of Clapp. The presence of the Tennessee representatives obviously irritated Senator McKellar, who took them to task for supporting Clapp and for attending the meetings of the Senate committee.[55]

Senator Lister Hill stated in his testimony: "To reject this nomination, in my opinion, would be an act most harmful to the Tennessee Valley Authority.... I want to urge as strongly as I can a favorable report from this committee on the nomination."[56] Representative Kefauver stated that he had absolute confidence in Clapp, and that prior to the hearings he had never heard anyone question his patriotism or suggest that he was intimate with Communists or had Communistic leanings. "This attempt to blacken a good man's name because of a personal grudge," stated Kefauver, "goes against my grain."[57] Senator McKellar inquired whether he had not previously stated that he would testify for Clapp; Kefauver replied that he certainly had, "because I was very much shocked and I felt the attack upon him unjust and unfounded."[58]

Representative Gore stated that as a member of the Appropriations subcommittee before which the TVA came for funds he had found Clapp to be "forthright, conscientious, able, cooperative, and patriotic." "If you will permit me to say so, Mr. Chairman," said Gore, "much of this proceeding has appeared to me ludicrous, ridiculous, and preposterous." He went on to say that he thought that very great damage had been done to the agency.[59]

The testimony of the other members of Congress who appeared, as well as that of six members from Kentucky who submitted a joint letter of endorsement, was in a similar vein. In addition, a number of leading citizens of the Tennessee Valley, editors of newspapers, and persons speaking in behalf of chambers of commerce and other civic organizations appeared in behalf of Clapp, and many organizations sent in memorials of endorsement. Senator McKellar took obvious offense at their appearance; and at times attempted to belittle their testimony.

On February 28 the issue came to a vote in the Senate committee. The division did not follow a party line. Three Republicans—Revercomb, Watkins, and Cooper—and two Democrats—Chavez and Downey—voted in favor of Clapp; four Republicans—Cain, Martin, Malone, and Williams—and three Democrats—Overton, O'Daniel, and McClellan—voted against him. The vote thus stood 7 to 5 against confirmation. On the same day, President Truman reaffirmed his endorsement of Clapp, stating that he had contributed as much as anyone to the development of the TVA and was perfectly suited for the post to which he had been named.[60]

The Senate Debate

The nomination of Clapp did not come to a vote in the Senate until April 24, nearly two months after the committee reported it unfavorably. Consideration was postponed repeatedly, by unanimous agreement, in order that the vote on Lilienthal could be taken first. The debate was in great contrast to that on the confirmation of Lilienthal. Senator Revercomb of West Virginia presented the report of the committee and briefly reviewed the case, announcing that personally he would vote in favor of confirmation because he could not agree that any of the charges against the nominee had been sustained.[61] Senator Cooper of Kentucky also spoke briefly in support of confirmation on the following day, stating that he was not personally acquainted with Clapp, but that on the basis of the evidence brought before the committee, he saw no valid reason why Clapp should not be confirmed.[62]

No other speeches were made in his behalf, although in response to a question, Senator Hill stated that Clapp was "the best qualified man in the United States for the position," and that his appointment would be a wonderful example to the young men of America and encourage them to enter the public service.[63] The only speech of substantial length was made by Senator McKellar, who pleaded piteously with his colleagues to accord him the customary courtesy of taking his word about nominations to offices within his state.[64] In opening his remarks he complained that there were few members present and that he could not "very well convince members in their absence." Senator White rose to suggest the absence of a quorum, and although eighty members responded to roll call, few remained. Throughout his speech McKellar frequently deplored the absence of senators from the floor. Significantly he devoted most of his speech to a defense of his own action rather than to a discussion of the qualification of Clapp. Anticipating a second defeat at the hands of the Senate, McKellar plaintively declared that he was "hurt beyond expression" that many of his Democratic colleagues had forsaken him and voted for nominees whom he had opposed. He complained bitterly that the President had appointed Clapp "without saying beans to me." Concerning the nominee, Senator McKellar had little to say. At one point he declared that Clapp was a "very nice young man. He would make a splendid clerk in a grocery store or in a meat shop. He is a young man who means well, I have no doubt."[65] At another point, however, he stated that "Mr. Clapp is utterly incompetent and inefficient. I do not know of a Senator who, after examining him, would employ him as a clerk in his office."[66] He asserted that Clapp would be nothing more than a "stooge" to Lilienthal, who would continue to run the TVA.

No one rose to reply to the speech of Senator McKellar. Notwithstanding the unfavorable vote of the Committee on Public Works, the Senate voted 36 for confirmation and 31 against. Seven Democrats—Connally, George, Johnson of Colorado, McKellar, O'Daniel, Overton, and Stewart—voted against confirmation, and they were joined by 24 Republicans.

The contest over the confirmation of Gordon R. Clapp as chairman of the Tennessee Valley Authority is an outstanding example of the great length to which an individual member of the Senate may go in opposing a nominee. Senator McKellar's attack upon Clapp was obviously motivated by a personal, albeit a one-sided, feud against the management of the TVA. In this contest, as in that over the appointment of Lilienthal, he pressed unfounded charges against the nominee, and insisted that the committee conduct extended hearings; at these he virtually assumed the task of interrogating witnesses, although he was not a member of either committee. The callous manner in which the Tennessee senator smeared as Communists certain employees of the TVA who were not present and able to defend themselves showed a flagrant disregard for justice and fair play. Such proceedings lower the Senate in public esteem.

The Clapp case is of significance because it provided a full-dress review of the program of the TVA; it brought into the open the various charges and criticisms that had been raised and gave Clapp an opportunity to reply and to explain and defend the program. In some respects the hearing was comparable to a congressional investigation or to the question period in the British Parliament, though the committee was not under the necessity of making any findings of fact or reporting them to the Senate. Such a public hearing on charges and criticisms has certain merits both to Congress and to the agency concerned. The testimony of Clapp undoubtedly put at rest many rumors and stories which the TVA could not have otherwise answered so appropriately. But as a means of reviewing the program, policies, and administration of an agency, a confirmation hearing has definite shortcomings. The issues are brought into the hearing collaterally, and no decision on any of them is pending. They are raised in an attempt to discredit the nominee rather than to ascertain the facts, and are rarely pushed far enough to enable the committee to reach any definite conclusion. The final decision will always be a mixed one, being influenced by the personality of the individual and political considerations, as well as the administration of the agency.

The confirmation of the appointment of Gordon R. Clapp illustrates also how the process of confirming an appointment may be utilized to influence the policies of an agency. If one reads between the lines, he will recognize that many of the questions put to Clapp by committee members were designed to secure, as a condition of confirmation of his appointment, certain commitments concerning the policies of the TVA. Had he yielded to this pressure by individual members of the committee, who did not necessarily represent the majority will of the Senate, he might have secured their votes, but at the price of being committed to support policy changes that they desired. By taking a definite stand, however, he was assured of the active support of the friends of the TVA in the Senate, which was essential to his confirmation. In refusing to hedge or to qualify with respect to the policies of the TVA, although this might well have resulted in his rejection by the Senate, Clapp demonstrated a quality of courage seldom evidenced on such occasions.

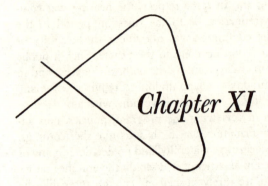

Chapter XI

THE REJECTION OF
LELAND OLDS

Courage is not implicit in the public service. It is very difficult to be a courageous public servant. The courageous ones are the ones who are decapitated; the ones who are amenable, the ones who go along, those are the ones who have no difficulty with their confirmations. That is why I think this confirmation is so very important, not only in connection with utility matters which are important in themselves, but in connection with the whole problem of public service. Anne K. Alpern, City Solicitor of Pittsburgh.[1]

THE CONFIRMATION of presidential nominations to independent regulatory commissions is always of especial importance, for members of these commissions are regarded as having a special relationship to Congress. The function of the Senate in passing upon the nominations is not limited to the technical qualifications of the nominee and his fitness for the office; it is appropriately concerned with his stand on broad policies and the effect his appointment may have upon the functioning of the commission. Often the character and attitude of the officers who head an agency have as much to do with its policies as the legislation under which it operates. The Senate must therefore consider whether a nominee to a regulatory commission is in sympathy with the objectives of the laws which he will be called upon to administer, and whether he will support policies which are agreeable to the majority of the Senate. Legislative battles over governmental policies may arise not only when new legislation is under consideration but equally well when appointments or appropriations are being considered; contests won at one stage are often lost at another. The contest over the confirmation of Leland

Olds, nominated for a third term to the Federal Power Commission in 1949 and rejected by a vote of 53 to 13, affords a striking illustration of the forces that may influence the Senate in passing upon nominations to independent regulatory bodies, as well as the close relation between appointments and legislative policies.

The Contestants and the Issues

Early in June, 1949, President Truman submitted the nomination of Leland Olds for a third term as member of the Federal Power Commission. He did not propose it until near the end of Olds's term of office, because another nomination to the commission—that of Thomas Buchanan—had been held up in the Senate for about a year and the President desired to have it acted upon before submitting that of Olds. Both men were known for their support of effective public regulation of utilities and were opposed by the public-utility, oil, and natural gas interests which were regulated by the commission.

Leland Olds had served for ten years on the Federal Power Commission, had for several years been its chairman, and was widely recognized as one of its most able and effective members. His professional standing in the field of public-utility regulation was attested to in the hearings by Professor James C. Bonbright of Columbia University, who said:

Leland Olds, in my opinion, is one of the country's most distinguished and most outstanding figures in the field of public-utility regulation. . . . In Leland Olds, the Federal Power Commission has enjoyed the services of a man who has devoted almost his entire professional life to becoming an expert in the exceedingly complex problems of utility regulation. Were it to lose these services, the Commission would lose a good part of the distinction that it now enjoys as a guardian of the public interest . . . in my opinion, millions of people in this country today are presently paying lower utility rates than they would be paying but for the presence of Leland Olds on the Federal Power Commission, and that has taken place along with not a deterioration but a positive improvement of the financial standing and soundness of the private-utility industry.[2]

During the ten years that he served as a member of the FPC, Olds took a leading part in the development of federal regulation of electric power, hydro-electric developments, and natural gas moving in interstate commerce. When his nomination came up for a second term, he was opposed by the electric-power group; but the charges against him were adequately answered. A number of state public-utility commissioners whose close relations with the industry were well known testified against him, alleging that he favored federal centralization of utility regulation at the expense of the state utility commissions; but public-utility commissioners from other states who favored effective regulation came to his defense, testifying that the FPC had been most helpful to the state commissions. In an attempt to charge him with Communist leanings, some references were made then to his earlier writings, which were to play so prominent a part in the 1949 contest; but neither the committee nor the Senate took any stock in such charges, and his appointment was readily confirmed.

Because of the prominent part which Olds had played in the development of federal regulation of the natural gas industry and his leadership in the opposition to the Kerr bill and earlier bills designed to cripple federal regulation, his reappointment in 1949 was vigorously opposed by the oil and natural gas interests. The electric-utility interests publicly took no part in the opposition, although it was generally assumed that they also opposed him. All the witnesses testifying against the appointment of Olds, as will appear below, were directly or indirectly connected with the oil and gas industry, and most of them came from the great natural-gas-producing area of the Southwest. The members of Congress from both houses who had spearheaded the drive to pass the Kerr bill or similar measures, now led the opposition to Leland Olds. Indeed, his principal opponent was Senator Kerr of Oklahoma, a wealthy oilman and the author of the bill which Olds had effectively opposed just before his nomination went to the Senate. Senator Kerr did not appear as a witness before the Senate committee and did not participate prominently in the Senate debate on the nomination, but he was generally credited with being the leading member of the group determined to block the reappointment. Senator Lyndon Johnson, chairman of the subcommittee which considered the nomination and leader of the fight against Olds in the Senate debate, was from Texas, the state producing the most oil and natural gas. Representative Lyle, also from Texas and the author of a bill in the Eightieth Congress to exempt the natural gas industry from effective federal supervision of prices, led the attack on Olds at the hearings and introduced the charge of Communism.

The opposition to Olds centered in the delegations from the oil- and gas-producing states of the Southwest; his support came principally from the states that are consumers of natural gas and hence are desirous of maintaining effective federal regulation of prices. The persons favoring his confirmation were principally representatives of consumer groups, public officials of cities in which gas rates had been lowered, and several distinguished authorities in the field of public utilities. "Clearly the battle over the confirmation of Leland Olds as a member of the Federal Power Commission," declared Morris L. Cooke at the hearing, "is a battle between the great body of people who are consumers, on the one side, and the monopolistic power and oil-gas interests on the other. It is a part of the battle which has been going on for years to bring these vital interests under some measure of public control. This battle must go on if democracy itself is to survive."[4]

The real issue in the Olds case was the Kerr bill. For several years the natural gas industry, joined by the oil industry, which produces natural gas as a by-product, had made a determined effort to amend the Natural Gas Act of 1938 so as to remove effective federal regulation of the price of gas moving in interstate commerce. In 1948 and again in 1949, measures of this kind had passed the House by large majorities but had been defeated in the Senate Committee on Interstate and Foreign Commerce by a divided vote. Olds, speaking as chairman of the Federal Power Commission, had been the outstanding opponent of these proposals before the committee. And despite the powerful backing of the Kerr bill, Olds courageously opposed it in the spring of 1949, just three months before his renomination came before this same committee. The supporters of the Kerr bill accordingly believed that the removal of Olds from the Federal Power Commission was essential to the passage of the measure.[5]

Background: The Drive to Amend the
Natural Gas Act of 1938

For an understanding of the Olds case, some knowledge of the background of the development of federal regulation of the natural gas industry, including the efforts of the industry to avoid federal price control, is essential. Under the Natural Gas Act of 1938, the Federal Power Commission was authorized to regulate the movement of natural gas in interstate commerce. This jurisdiction included the granting of certificates of convenience and necessity for the laying of new interstate pipe lines and the regulation of sales in interstate commerce. The production of natural gas and local distribution to consumers were specifically exempted from federal regulation, and both were subject to regulation under state laws. Local officials and state utility commissions, however, had found that they were unable to obtain rate reductions so long as the wholesale rates charged by interstate pipe companies to local distributing companies were unregulated; it was to correct this situation that the Natural Gas Act had been passed.

Acting on complaints lodged by local officials and state utility commissions, the Federal Power Commission, starting about 1940, undertook to regulate the prices charged local distributors by interstate pipe-line companies. In determining what rates were reasonable, the commission allowed the price paid for gas in the field, plus a reasonable charge for its transportation to the market. In 1940, however, the large interstate pipe-line companies were also large producers of natural gas, drawing 40 per cent of their gas from their own wells. The commission found it necessary to determine not only what were reasonable charges for transporting the gas but also the prices that these companies would be permitted to pay to themselves for gas at the well mouth; for if they had been free to fix the production price, regulation of transportation charges alone would have had virtually no effect in protecting the consumer.

By similar reasoning the FPC ruled that sales by subsidiary and affiliated companies to a parent pipe-line company were subject to federal regulation.

The field prices paid for natural gas by interstate pipe-line companies to so-called "independent" or nontransporting producers have not been regulated by the FPC.[6] Before the decision of the Supreme Court in *Interstate Natural Gas Company* v. *Federal Power Commission*[7] was handed down in 1947, it had been assumed that the provision of the Natural Gas Act exempting local production and the gathering of natural gas from federal regulation prohibited the FPC from regulating the field prices paid to independent producers. But in this case the Supreme Court held, in a unanimous decision, that all sales in interstate commerce were subject to federal regulation. At each step federal regulation has been contested in the courts; but in a series of decisions, the Supreme Court has upheld the authority of the commission.

Until recently the market for natural gas in the field was decidedly a buyer's market. The production greatly exceeded the available market, and small producers were virtually forced to sell at whatever price they could get from interstate pipe-line companies. However, during and after World War II, with the laying of great pipe lines to tap the urban and industrial markets of the East and Midwest, the situation changed rapidly. The demand by interstate pipe-line companies now exceeded available supplies, and the field prices steadily mounted. Although the FPC did not regulate field sales by independent producers, its regulation of the prices that interstate pipe lines might pay for gas from their own wells proved to be an effective bar against runaway prices.

The FPC has ordered reductions in the rates for natural gas totaling approximately $40,000,000 annually, and those reductions have been passed on to the consumer. Although field prices rose rapidly in the years following the war, they did not rise so rapidly as the prices of competing fuels—oil and coal. And although the industry has experienced great prosperity, including both high profits and a tremendous expansion with the opening up of new markets and the laying of giant pipe lines, it would reap far greater profits if the threat of federal regulation were removed.

Evidence submitted in the Senate hearings on the Kerr bill also indicates a high degree of concentration of gas production in the hands of a relatively few large producers. Three companies—Phillips Petroleum, Shamrock Oil and Gas, and Canadian River Gas—own one-half of the great Texas Panhandle field, which contains one-seventh of all known reserves in this country, and the thirty-three largest companies own 62.2 per cent of all known reserves. These large companies would receive tremendous profits if federal control were removed from the price of gas and prices rose. It has been estimated that an increase of five cents per thousand cubic feet in the field price of natural gas would increase the value of the holdings of the Phillips Petroleum Company alone in the Texas Panhandle and Hugoton fields by $389,000,000.

In view of these tremendous stakes, it is not surprising that the large natural gas companies strongly opposed the confirmation of the appointment of Lelands Olds. Failing in their fight to invalidate federal regulation in the courts, and unable to obtain the passage of legislation that would cripple or remove federal control over prices, they were anxious to secure a commission that would be more sympathetic to their position than the previous one. Two members of the commission had come round to the industry point of view. The appointment of a third member, Buchanan, who favored federal regulation, was held up by the Senate committee for a year, but was finally approved. If Olds could be rejected and a person sympathetic to the industry's point of view could be appointed, the way would be paved to secure the enactment of the desired amendments to the Natural Gas Act to remove federal regulation of the field price of gas.

The Hearings on the Nomination

On September 27, 1949, approximately four months after the nomination was submitted and three months after the term of Olds had expired, the subcommittee of the Senate Committee on Interstate and Foreign Commerce opened its hearings. Normally, Congress would have adjourned before this date, but the session dragged on. After a good many columnists and editorial writers had criticized the subcommittee for its evident intention of bottling up the nominations without any action, it was finally decided to hold hearings. Chairman Lyndon Johnson announced at the opening session that it was definitely planned to report the nomination to the Senate, even if the committee recommendation was unfavorable.

Other members of the subcommittee were McFarland, O'Conor, and Edwin Johnson (Democrats), and Bricker, Capehart, and Reed (Republicans). To persons familiar with their records, it was apparent that the committee when it began its hearings was unfriendly toward Olds and was opposed to the policies he advocated. Every member of the subcommittee—with the exception of Senator Reed of Kansas, who died in the autumn of 1949—voted for the Kerr bill when it came before the Senate the following year. The composition of the subcommittee of course greatly affected the trend of its hearings. Opposing witnesses were aided in their testimony and were asked leading questions, but witnesses favoring the nomination, though treated politely, usually were asked no questions. A quite different public impression would have been made had there been a single member of the subcommittee to ask searching questions of both sides. In attempting to refute the charges made against him, Olds always faced a hostile committee whose intention to reject his nomination was apparent.

A number of nationally prominent witnesses appeared in support of the nominee, including Professor James C. Bonbright of Columbia University and Morris L. Cooke, whose testimony has already been referred to, Adolph A. Berle, Ordway Tead, and Charles M. La Follette. They reviewed Olds's record in public-utility work in the state of New York and as a member of the Federal Power Commission and urged his confirmation because of his distinguished record, his devotion to the public interest, his technical qualifications in the public-utility field, and his courage as a public official. All stated that he was needed on the commission to carry out policies to protect the consumer.

Miss Anne K. Alpern, city solicitor of Pittsburgh and a past president of the National Institute of Municipal Law Officers, was one of a group of municipal officials who appeared in behalf of Olds. In her testimony before the subcommittee she declared that "consumers of this country have a very vital interest in men like Leland Olds, and in seeing that he is retained in the public service.... Democracy flourishes when men of this caliber are in high administrative positions and administer the law of our country so that capital may prosper and so that consumers can be protected." She also praised Olds for the courage he had displayed as a member of the commission in protecting the consumer by taking the leadership for effective public regulation of utilities.

Other groups whose representatives appeared in support of Olds included the C.I.O., several other labor organizations, the National Grange, Americans for Democratic Action, and associations of coöperatives. The same groups and the same witnesses had appeared earlier in the opposition to the Kerr bill, and their testimony was very similar at both hearings. They regarded the fight over the confirmation of the nomination of Leland Olds as a part of the struggle to end federal regulation of the price of natural gas, which they contended would increase the cost to the consumer by more than a hundred million dollars annually.

Those columnists and editorial writers who had earlier condemned the Kerr bill as a "gas grab" to benefit the oil and natural gas companies at the expense of the consumer now denounced the opposition to Olds as coming from the same interests. The members of the Senate subcommittee quite naturally smarted under the accusation that they were the willing tools of the public-utility, oil, and natural gas lobby, and that they were about to reject an able and courageous public servant to serve the ends of these selfish interests; their hostility to Leland Olds was due in part to the fact that they considered him responsible for this attack upon them.

The Communist Smear

The opposition to Olds was begun by Representative John E. Lyle of Corpus Christi, Texas, who based his attack on certain writings of Olds, prepared twenty-five years earlier when he was industrial editor of the Federated Press, a news service sold to the labor press and to labor unions. Selections from these writings in the 1920's were introduced to support the charge that Olds was either a Communist or a fellow traveler and that he had bitterly attacked various aspects of the American capitalistic system. The real reason for Representative Lyle's attack, however, as he made clear at the outset, was the fact that Olds had led the opposition to the Kerr and similar bills. At the opening of the Eighty-first Congress, Lyle had introduced such a bill (H.R. 79); and a similar bill introduced by Representative Harris (H.R. 1758) passed the House by a large majority. These bills had the active support of the oil and natural gas interests. Representative Lyle, who is from a district in which oil and natural gas are the leading industry and is a member of a law firm which reportedly represents large oil and gas companies, accused Olds of having presented "misleading statements, half truths, distorted statistics, and a multitude of devices designed and utilized to obscure the issue at hand." Olds, he declared, had "launched a bitter and vicious attack on these bills and those proposing them, inferentially characterizing the bills as an attempt to mulct ultimate consumers of millions of dollars."[8]

With respect to the articles Olds had written in the period from 1922 to 1929, Representative Lyle made twenty-four charges against him and submitted fifty-four photostatic copies of the articles to support these charges.

I am here to oppose Mr. Olds because he has—through a long and prolific career—attacked the church; he has attacked our schools; he has ridiculed the symbols of patriotism and loyalty such as the Fourth of July; he has advocated public ownership; he has reserved his applause for Lenin and Lenin's system, and he has found few words of praise for our American system; and, yes, gentlemen, he has seen fit to attack the men who serve as elected representatives in our Government—men such as you. He has characterized you as mere administrative clerks handling administrative details for "an immensely powerful ruling class."[9]

Throughout his testimony Representative Lyle tried to establish that Olds was a Communist, or at any event followed the Communist line. He labeled the Federated Press a "left-wing labor press service, closely identified with communist movements and groups." Most of the articles he placed in the record were taken from the *Daily Worker* or from *Industrial Solidarity,* Communist papers, though they also had appeared in about seventy-five other publications. The impression was created that Olds had been a writer for the *Daily Worker.* This he took pains to deny. In one of these articles Olds had advocated paid vacations for workers and praised the practice in Russia, widely commented on at the time, of setting aside large estates as rest and recreation centers for workers. In several other articles he had made favorable comments about certain developments in Soviet Russia, and Lyle cited them to show that Olds had favored the Communist system.[10]

The articles that Olds wrote for the Federated Press dealt with economic problems of the period of the 1920's. For the most part, they summarized and interpreted studies and reports of government and private research agencies, even including summaries of articles appearing in the *Wall Street Journal*. Those placed in the record by Representative Lyle were highly critical of economic policies and practices of the time. A number dealt with the sick coal industry and suggested, but did not actually advocate, some form of public ownership or nationalization. Others criticized the railroads for their anti-union policies and included some statements favorable to public ownership. On the basis of these articles, Representative Lyle accused Olds of advocating public ownership not only of railroads and coal mines but of all private industry.

In another article Olds had attacked the keynote speech of Senator Fess at the Republican national convention of 1928, a speech which cited, with approval, statistics to prove that industrial production had increased while labor costs had declined. Referring in the article to Andrew Mellon, Olds attacked the Republican party for its close association with big business and asserted that the policies of the government were being dictated by the "immensely powerful ruling group," while government officials merely carried out the administrative details. Representative Lyle charged Olds with attacking the government as being the servant of business, and with accusing the legislature—which Olds had not mentioned—of merely handling administrative details for an immensely powerful ruling group.

In another article Olds had maintained that the policies of certain endowed universities were dictated by wealthy donors and trustees; this was interpreted by Lyle as a blanket attack on all universities, and indeed on all education. Still another article concerning Bishop Cannon's reported speculations in the stock market criticized the church for passively accepting social and economic injustices and for not taking a more aggressive stand for economic reforms. On the basis of this, Olds, a deeply religious man, was accused of attacking all churches and all religion.

All the articles, written in the intellectual climate of the 1920's and dealing with financial, economic, and labor problems and abuses of the time, were made by Lyle to appear extremely radical. It should be borne in mind that they were written for a labor audience, to which they probably appeared entirely appropriate, and that similar criticisms of economic abuses were voiced by many prominent persons of the period, though not in so pungent a manner. Many of the articles written by Olds carried a punch sentence which, when taken out of context, appeared much more radical than the entire article. Only by the most flagrant distortion, by lifting sentences out of context and by actual misquotation, was Representative Lyle able to support his contentions that Leland Olds was a Communist at heart, that he was opposed to private ownership and to the entire capitalistic system, and that he had condemned the church, sneered at the flag, and looked with scorn upon government—particularly the legislative body—as the tool of big business.

Senator McFarland said that he was shocked by the charges and that they were the most serious he had ever heard in Congress. As Representative Lyle was testifying against Olds, Senator Reed broke in to say that here was a man whose writings showed him to be a "full-fledged, regular Communist."

Anticipating the attack that would be made upon him, Olds obtained permission to appear before the subcommittee and read a lengthy statement covering his entire career. In this statement he attempted to explain the philosophy which led him to produce what he admitted were "radical writings"; but it did not meet the charges and it did not deal directly with the real issue at stake—the Kerr bill and federal regulation of the price of gas. It included a brief review of the record of the Federal Power Commission during the preceding ten years, but for this account Olds was criticized by the chairman of the subcommittee on the ground that he claimed the credit for all the accomplishments of the commission.

During his testimony Olds was frequently interrogated by members of the subcommittee concerning his writings, and especially was asked to explain and defend key sentences that were objectionable. His favorable references to Russia came in for a good deal of comment and questioning, although Olds categorically denied that he had ever favored Communism. In fact, Olds denied each of the Lyle charges and asked the subcommittee to judge the articles in their entirety rather than on the basis of single sentences or parts of sentences lifted out of context. When asked whether he still held the same beliefs, he replied that the New Deal legislation had corrected many of the social and economic ills of the 1920's which he had described, and that on some subjects, particularly Russia, he had changed his mind.[11]

The charges of Communism and radicalism against Leland Olds were not new. Some of the same articles had been presented as evidence against him in 1944, but the charges then were not taken seriously. The chairman of the subcommittee that conducted the hearings on his nomination for a second term stated in reply to these charges: "I do not think that anyone believed that Mr. Olds was a Communist. I do not think that the Senator from Oklahoma believes that Mr. Olds is a Communist. I do not think anyone believed that."[12]

The Opposition of the Oil and Gas Interests

Of the fifteen opposing witnesses, all came from gas-producing areas and all were directly or indirectly connected with the gas industry. Seven represented gas-producing companies or associations of producers, and the connection of the other eight opposing witnesses with the gas interests was readily apparent though not always stated.[13] Most of the industry spokesmen represented small producers; representatives of the largest gas companies were significantly absent in the line-up of opposing witnesses.

The opposing witnesses offered the following three major arguments against confirmation of Leland Olds: (1) he stood for the regulatory policies that were harmful to the gas industry; (2) his writings indicated that he was a Communist and thus was unfit for office; and (3) the nominee was personally unfit for the office. "We believe that his confirmation would be against the best interests of the producers of gas and also of oil," said Russell B. Brown, general counsel of the Independent Petroleum Association of America.[14] "If Mr. Olds is reappointed," stated James A. Upham, president of the Ohio Oil and Gas Association, "we face but one destiny—full extinction.... So, our earnest prayer presented to you now is to give us some new Commissioner, not Mr. Olds, as we deeply feel the retention of Mr. Olds as a member of the FPC is a full threat to the free-enterprise system of this life in these United States."[15]

Most of the witnesses who appeared to oppose Olds repeated the charges of Representative Lyle that the nominee was a Communist, a radical, and unfit for office because of his opposition to the free-enterprise system. Several were unwilling to rest their opposition on these grounds and went on to abuse and vilify the nominee in language seldom heard in nomination hearings. One witness, who represented the Southern Minerals Association, declared: "Mr. Olds is boring from within; Mr. Olds is a termite; Mr. Olds is gnawing away the very foundations upon which this Government exists."[16]

Observations on the Hearings

From the outset it was apparent that the subcommittee was opposed to Olds. It is doubtful that the public hearings altered their opinions; but the Communist charges made by Representative Lyle, which were characterized by the Washington *Post* as "preposterous and despicable," undoubtedly influenced the vote of the Senate. Even though the charges were based upon gross misrepresentations of the writings of Olds, there was enough partial truth in them to cause some members to change their votes. They also afforded those who were opposed to Olds because of his record and his fight against the Kerr bill with other grounds on which to justify their votes. The Communist smear had nothing to do with the real issue—federal regulation of the price of natural gas—or with Leland Olds's qualifications and record for ten years as a commissioner.

In the hearings little or no attention was given to the record Olds had made as a member (for several years chairman) of the FPC during the preceding ten years, or to his stand on policies affecting federal regulation of the natural gas industry. The hearings were instead given over almost entirely to consideration of his writings of twenty years earlier. Under the circumstances, it would appear that these earlier writings were for the most part irrelevant, or at least of little importance, in comparison with Olds's long record as a member of the commission to which he was now renominated.[17] No question was raised by any member of the subcommittee concerning the relevance of these writings; on the contrary, they were cited by the committee to justify its vote against confirmation. There was little in Olds's record that the committee could openly attack. He was known for his able and courageous administration of the federal laws under the jurisdiction of the FPC, and he could not be criticized for defending policies that Congress had adopted by legislation and the Supreme Court had upheld in a unanimous decision.

The defense of Olds in the hearings was relatively weak and ineffective. The Communist smear, which was not unexpected, might have been answered more forcefully. Too much of the defense was carried on by Olds himself, in spite of the fact that others would have been better able to answer the unjust accusations made against him and might have forced the hearings back to the real issues involved. Apparently no attempt was made to line up favorable witnesses from the natural gas industry, who would have carried great weight. Before so hostile a committee, however, an effective defense undoubtedly would have been difficult.

President Truman's Intervention

Early in October, while the nomination was before the Committee on Interstate and Foreign Commerce, President Truman wrote to Chairman Edwin Johnson, urging the confirmation of Olds. "Mr. Olds," the President wrote, "is a nationally recognized champion of effective utility regulation; his record shows that he is also a champion of fair regulation.... The powerful corporations subject to regulation by the Commission have not been pleased with Mr. Olds. They now seek to prevent his confirmation for another term. It will be most unfortunate if they should succeed. We cannot allow great corporations to dominate the commissions which have been created to regulate them."[18]

Senator Johnson replied that the subcommittee "was shocked beyond description by the political and economic views expressed by Mr. Olds some years ago. We cannot believe that a person under our democratic capitalistic system holding such views is qualified to act in a quasi-judicial capacity in the regulation of industry."[19] In spite of the President's support, the subcommittee voted unanimously to reject the nomination; and the vote of the full committee was 2 for and 10 against confirmation.

After the full committee made its report to the Senate, President Truman, undaunted, took the extraordinary step of calling upon the Democratic party to support the nomination. On October 5, Chairman Boyle of the Democratic National Committee, acting on instructions from the President, sent a telegram to all state chairmen, requesting them to urge their senators to vote for the confirmation of Olds. His defeat, it was stated in the telegram, "would be a defeat for the millions of Americans who are entitled to fair power rates, and a victory for the power lobbyists and the Republican party."

At his press conference on the same date, the President defended his action in making a party issue of the appointment, on the ground that party discipline was essential to party responsibility.[20] Two days later, Senator Byrd placed the Boyle telegram in the *Congressional Record,* declaring that he was "shocked that the President of the United States would attempt to coerce the Members of the United States Senate in the exercise of their function in the confirmation of an appointment.... By implication, at least, Chairman Boyle threatens every Member of the United States Senate with the loss of patronage if the orders given in this telegram are not obeyed."[21]

Editorial comments for the most part were unfavorable to the Boyle telegram and to the attempt of the President to make a party issue of the appointment. The telegram, it may be noted, contained no threat or intimation that patronage would be withdrawn from senators who did not vote for confirmation. The final vote of the Senate, rejecting the nomination by 53 to 15, indicated that the President's appeal had little effect on the Democratic senators, though it may have contributed to the practically unanimous vote of Republican members against confirmation.

The Senate Debate

The renomination of Leland Olds came before the Senate on October 12, 1949. Senator Murray, who was unable to be present on that day, spoke in behalf of Olds on October 11. He maintained that the real issue was federal regulation of the price of natural gas and placed in the record a series of statistical tables taken from the reports of the FPC showing the huge profits of the natural gas industry since the end of World War II, the high degree of concentration of gas holdings in the hands of a few large companies, and estimates of the profits these companies would make if federal regulation were removed. He asserted that the value of the holdings of the large companies might well be enhanced by more than sixteen billion dollars if federal control over field prices were removed. The thesis that natural gas was a public utility and as such was subject to public regulation was sharply challenged by Senator Kerr, who inquired why the price of natural gas should be regulated if the prices of coal and of copper produced in Montana are not regulated.[22]

The Senate debate was opened on October 12 by Senator Johnson of Colorado, speaking in opposition to the appointment. He charged Olds with Communism and radicalism, as well as association with leading Communists when he was the industrial editor of the Federated Press. As a feature writer on the Federated Press, Olds had stooped to the vilest kind of rabble rousing, the senator said. He also stated that Olds was "slippery and evasive," and that he "hedged and quibbled, but...was not repentant." He went on to declare that, in his judgment, "Mr. Olds has not changed his offensive views regarding capital one iota, and...today, as when he was forty years of age, he believes capital should be confiscated and the profit system destroyed. A man having this kind of a warped mind is so far out of step with America that he is not qualified to sit in the seat of judgment and regulate our great utility industries."[23]

The most able statement in behalf of Olds was made by Senator Morse, who asserted that Olds and the two other members of the FPC who joined with him in policies were only attempting to carry out the provisions of the Natural Gas Act for the regulation of the sale of natural gas in interstate commerce. The authority of the commission, under the act, to do this, he pointed out, had been upheld by the Supreme Court in the Interstate case. "The oil and gas interests," said Senator Morse, "have tried unsuccessfully to have the law amended so that the Commission can not regulate their sales of gas to interstate pipe lines. They know that they can not get such legislation enacted, so I believe that they are now engaged in a last-ditch effort to accomplish the same purpose by opposing the reappointment of a Commissioner who refuses to interpret the act and circumscribe his powers and obligations to the public in accordance with the purposes of those interests."[24] The real test that should be applied in passing upon the renomination of Leland Olds, Senator Morse contended, was his record during two terms as a member of the Federal Power Commission. On this test, he declared, Olds ranked with the ablest public-utility commissioners in the country, and was regarded as one of the ablest by many businessmen who had appeared before the FPC when he was a member. His rejection, the senator concluded, "will discourage other men, devoted to the public interest, from running the risks of entering Government service."[25]

Also speaking in defense of the nominee, Senator Langer reviewed the debate that had taken place in 1944 when Olds's nomination had come before the Senate, and pointed out that the identical charges of radical and Communistic leanings then made by Senator Moore were dismissed as unfounded. "These 25-year-old charges," said Senator Langer, "...are now dug up and dusted off again in the attempt to discredit an honest, sincere and capable public servant who has given the best years of his life in attempting to bring about an equitable regulation of public-utility rates in the interest of the common people...." The senator also maintained that "the case against Leland Olds smells strongly of oil," and that "during the extensive hearings... not one iota of information was brought out which reflected on the record of this man as a public-power commissioner."[26]

Senator Humphrey placed in the record a number of editorials from newspapers throughout the country, many of them Republican, commenting on the case and supporting the confirmation of Olds. Practically all of these editorials pointed out that the real issue was the regulation of the price of gas. Senator Humphrey also defended Olds for his writings criticizing the economic conditions and practices that prevailed in the 1920's.[27]

The principal speech in opposition to Leland Olds was made by Senator Lyndon Johnson of Texas, chairman of the subcommittee that had considered the nomination. In his opening remarks Johnson declared that the reputation of Leland Olds was a myth, "a clever, appealing fiction, which is not supported by the record. It is a fiction which the man himself has labored skilfully and tirelessly through ten years in public office to impress on the public mind." Senator Johnson stated that he proposed to reveal the record of Olds, which he said was almost unnoticed and unknown, in order to disprove "the myth of Leland Olds, the knight in shining armor, doing tireless battle with the dragons of 'special privilege.'" The first myth to be exposed, said Senator Johnson, was that Olds was being opposed by the power lobby. He reported that not a single representative of the power interests had appeared in opposition to Olds, and that not one of the hundreds of letters and telegrams he had received opposing confirmation had come from a representative of an electric utility. What Senator Johnson did not point out was that the opposition to Olds had come from the oil and natural gas interests, and that the electric utilities, although not openly opposing him, had quietly but none the less effectively thrown their influence against him.

In spite of the fact that Leland Olds had had twenty years of experience in the public-utility field—ten years of it as a commissioner of the FPC—Senator Johnson asserted that he lacked practical experience and accused him of prejudice and bias against the utilities he regulated. In his words, "Leland Olds' record is an uninterrupted tale of bias, prejudice, and hostility, directed against the industry over which he now seeks to assume the powers of life and death. Never once in his long career has Leland Olds experienced, firsthand, the industries' side of the regulatory picture."[28]

Senator Johnson accused Olds of conducting an "insidious campaign of slander," of directing public criticism, of making "vile and snide remarks" to "undermine and discredit" the members of the commission who did not agree with him. This accusation was not supported by any evidence in the record. A similar accusation that Olds had also "forced the Commission staff into a goose-step march under the whip of his deliberate public abuse" appears equally unfounded. Finally, Senator Johnson charged Mr. Olds with building a political empire for his own insidious purposes. He then summed up his argument in the following words: "In the twenties he scoffed at private property as just another myth; in the thirties he said our democracy had been made a sham; in the forties he has intimidated his staff, discredited his fellow

Commissioners, fostered a smear on Congress, and taken the law into his own hands to substitute irresponsible confiscation for responsible regulation."[29]

The intemperateness of the attack on Olds in the Senate debate may for the most part be attributed to the fact that those who opposed him were smarting under the blistering criticism they had received at the hands of editorial writers and columnists. Olds's record was that of an able, intelligent, and scrupulously fair public official. His ability and effectiveness as a commissioner and his devotion to the public interest, rather than his radicalism, caused him to incur the bitter enmity of the natural gas and old industry.[30] In the Senate debate, as in the hearings, those who opposed Olds were not content only to smear him as a Communist and a radical but engaged also in personal abuse.

Conclusion

The contest over the nomination of Leland Olds for a third term as a member of the Federal Power Commission affords a striking illustration of the importance of the confirmation of appointments in the determination of governmental policies. He was rejected not because of his radical writings of some twenty-five years earlier, or because of the charge of Communism, although these caused the withdrawal of some newspaper support and made it easier for his opponents to bring about his defeat. The real issue was federal regulation of the price of natural gas, and his rejection was a victory for the gas and oil interests. Their opposition to Olds was due to the vigorous and effective role he had played in the development of federal regulation and to his determined opposition to the Moore-Rizley bill, the Kerr bill, and similar bills for which they had pressed in Congress.

The rejection of the nomination of Leland Olds was similar in many respects to the refusal of the Senate in 1834 to confirm the nomination of Roger Taney as Secretary of the Treasury. Both were bitterly opposed by a strong business group because of the policies the men had carried out. Taney had incurred the wrath of Nicholas Biddle when, acting under instructions from President Jackson, he had withdrawn federal deposits from the Bank; and his defeat was regarded by the Bank and its supporters as essential to the renewal of its charter. Similarly, the defeat of Olds was regarded by the oil and gas industry as essential in its fight for the removal of federal regulation of the price of natural gas. It is highly significant that after Olds was defeated for a third term, the oil and natural gas forces were able to push the Kerr bill through Congress the following year.

The opposition of the oil and gas interests to the reappointment of Olds is understandable, and senators identified with the industry doubtless had warned the President that he would be unable to secure Senate approval of Olds, and had recommended others for the position. His rejection by so overwhelming a vote of the Senate is not so readily explained, although the vote in favor of the Kerr bill the following year indicated that the policies he advocated were not agreeable to a majority of the Senate. Moreover, he was pictured in the Senate debate, as well as in private discussions, as a fanatical zealot with pronounced radical ideas. It is not surprising that he was unable to withstand the attack made on him in this period of nation-wide hysteria over Communism. The Senate vote also indicates that it is much easier for a determined and well-financed interest group to block the reappointment of an official who stands in its way than to secure a revision of federal law. As the city attorney of Pittsburgh declared in the hearings, the defeat of Olds serves as a warning to members of regulatory commissions not to incur the hostility of the interests they regulate, if they value their jobs.

An especially unfortunate aspect of the fight over Olds was that an able, intelligent, and courageous public servant, devoted in an extraordinary degree to the public interest, was forced to submit to public abuse and vilification of a kind that makes public service unattractive to men and women of the highest ability. In appraising the consequences, Senator Aiken in the Senate debate declared: "Certain public utilities of the country are out to destroy a man for performing his duty. I do not know of anything worse than that. I do not know of anything more detrimental to good government. I do not know of anything to make it more difficult to get men and women to perform the duties of public office."[31]

It is significant that after the Senate rejected Olds, President Truman nominated his own close personal friend, former Senator Mon C. Wallgren, and that Wallgren's appointment was promptly confirmed. Although Wallgren had a liberal record when a member of the Senate, no one expected him to become as great an authority in the field of public-utility regulation as Olds, or to provide leadership in the development of effective federal regulation. The commission soon took a stand more favorable to the gas and oil industry, Wallgren siding with the majority. Two years later it handed down a decision affecting the Phillips Petroleum Company in which it virtually abdicated its authority to regulate the field price of natural gas paid to nontransporting companies. Thus the purpose of the Kerr bill, which Truman had vetoed in 1950, was accomplished by administrative action.

Chapter XII

PRESIDENT TRUMAN'S FIGHTS
WITH THE SENATE

I think it would be most unfortunate if the Senate should ever take the position that when it comes to pass judgment ... upon lawyers who are recommended and nominated for judicial office, we should be influenced because of the position they took as legislators on what they considered to be the social and economic merits of given pieces of legislation. ... Lawyers, both liberal and conservative, if intellectually honest, will rise to the trust of impartial administration of justice when elevated to the bench. Senator Wayne Morse.[1]

WHEN TRUMAN became President in 1945 it was widely predicted that, as a former member of the Senate, he would not attempt to dictate to Congress but would bring about close and amicable relations between the White House and Capitol Hill. The honeymoon period did not last long. Truman's early deference to the wishes of Congress failed to produce effective teamwork in the passage of needed legislation. In the Eightieth Congress, when both houses were controlled by the Republican party, the break between the President and Congress reached a point seldom equaled in history.

President Truman incurred more contests over his nominations in the Senate than perhaps any other President. Instead of being deferential to the wishes of individual senators, at times he nominated persons known to be highly offensive to them, and occasionally he made nominations in the face of their almost certain defeat. For example, although Roosevelt had decided to find another post for Lilienthal rather than incur the wrath of McKellar by renominating him as chairman of the TVA, Truman promptly decided that since Lilienthal was the best man for the job, he would renominate him.[2] In many respects Truman's conflicts with the Senate over appointments were similar to those of Andrew Jackson. He did not hesitate to throw down the gauntlet to the Senate and was not afraid to take defeat when an important issue or the appointment of a trusted friend was at stake.

The Republican Eightieth Congress held up most of Truman's important nominations and subjected them to close scrutiny, and some Republican senators urged that it approve no long-term appointments to high positions. Curiously, none of Truman's nominations were actually rejected by this Congress, though 153 were withdrawn and on 11,692 the Senate took no action. In the 1948 session, when the Republicans were confident of victory at the forthcoming election, 11,122 nominations were returned to the President without any action by the Senate.[3] These, it is assumed, were principally nominations of postmasters and minor local officials. In major appointments after the 1946 election Truman sought to avoid controversies by nominating persons who were acceptable to the Republican Senate—in many instances career civil servants or persons who had never been active in politics. To positions having to do with the administration of foreign aid he appointed several prominent Republicans or businessmen whose nominations were unlikely to be opposed.[4] The most sensational confirmation contests in the Eightieth Congress, when the Republicans were in control of both houses, were over the nominations of Lilienthal and Clapp, both of whom were named just before the 1946 election.

Truman's contests with the Senate over nominations may be grouped into several categories. Early in his first term he was subjected to wide criticism for appointing to important posts close personal friends or "cronies" whose qualifications were meager. The nominations of Allen and Vardaman in 1946 and Wallgren in 1949 fall in this group. Another group—including Lilienthal, Biddle, Olds, Buchanan, Carson, and Murdock—were opposed because they were regarded as New Dealers. Although Truman was early criticized for his failure to appoint liberals to high federal offices, actually he faced more contests in the Senate over such appointments than did Roosevelt. Edwin W. Pauley's nomination to be Under Secretary of the Navy in 1946 was opposed not because he was regarded as a New Dealer, or because he was a close personal friend of Truman, but rather because of his oil connections and his solicitations of funds from the oil interests for the Democratic party. The nominations of Philip Perlman to be Solicitor General and James Boyd to be Director of the Bureau of Mines were opposed for reasons that had little or nothing to do with the stands taken by these men on social and economic issues or with their qualifications for office. Both nominations were approved after inexcusable delays. A final group whose nominations were contested consisted of nominees to local offices who had not been recommended by the

Democratic senators from the state in which the office was situated. On a single day in 1950 the Senate rejected three such nominations under the rule of senatorial courtesy.*

George E. Allen

One of the first appointments of President Truman to attract wide criticism for being a reward to a personal friend and crony was his nomination of George E. Allen to be a member of the Reconstruction Finance Corporation in 1946. Allen, a Mississippian and protégé of the late Senator Pat Harrison, was appointed by Roosevelt in 1933 as commissioner of the District of Columbia and served until 1938, when he went into business. He was active in political circles and for a time was secretary of the Democratic National Committee. He was a Truman supporter at the Democratic national convention in 1944 and made advance arrangements for Truman's political campaign in that year, forming a fast friendship with him. When Roosevelt died, Allen caught the next plane for Washington and went directly to the White House to place his services at the disposal of President Truman. He soon became one of the close advisers of the President, and was given various assignments, many requiring consultation with members of Congress. He was noted for his wit and his fund of anecdotes, and was known in Washington as the "court jester."

His appointment to the RFC came as no surprise. Since he occupied an office in the old State building adjoining the White House and frequently worked on top-level assignments, it was assumed that he would be rewarded with an important appointment. But his nomination to the RFC attracted widespread adverse comment. David Lawrence wrote in the *United States News* that the President had not looked beyond the circle of his own friends and party servants in choosing a member of the RFC.[5] The New York *Times* stated that "Washington critics remarked that the RFC, probably the world's largest and most complex business organization, does not need such special talents as Mr. Allen possesses, but does need others, more deeply rooted in corporate management."[6]

When he appeared before the Senate Banking and Currency Committee on February 7, Allen read a long list of companies of which he was a director and indicated that he would give up a position as director of public relations of an insurance company paying him a salary of $30,000 annually to accept the position on the RFC. It had been rumored that Truman planned to appoint him as chairman of the RFC, and in his testimony Allen brought chuckles from the committee and audience when he stated frankly that there had been a "thin hint" to that effect. According to *Time,* he showed "a great capacity to crack jokes about himself, a pleasant candor about his own ambitions and finances."[7] He conceded that he had no expert knowledge of insurance, chem-

---

* These cases are discussed in chap. xiii.

istry, or the other fields covered by the various companies of which he was a director, but said that he made available to them his legal knowledge and his advice on public relations.

The Senate Banking and Currency Committee voted 14 to 5 to recommend confirmation, 3 Republicans joining with 11 Democrats in voting in favor of Allen. When the nomination came before the Senate, Senator Taft, a member of the committee, led the opposition. He declared that this was one of three nominations, made "only because they are personal or political friends of the President," which "had excited the indignation of the people of this country." (The other two nominations were of Pauley and Vardaman.) "None of the nominees," asserted the Ohio Senator, "knows anything about the job to which he is appointed. . . . Mr. Allen knows nothing of banking which is the major function of the chairman of the Board of the Reconstruction Finance Corporation."[8] Continuing, he reviewed the great size and importance of the RFC and Allen's career chiefly as a greeter and public-relations man, quoting an editorial of the proadministration St. Louis *Post-Dispatch* that his appointment "elevates to a position of tremendous power and responsibility a man with almost no qualifications for the job. . . . Such appointments as these are a public affront, and cannot fail to provoke disquieting doubts of Mr. Truman's own competency."[9] Senator Taft also questioned the propriety of Allen's expressed intention of retaining some of the numerous directorships he held if they did not conflict with his duties.

Majority leader Barkley made the principal defense of the nominee, reviewing the long list of companies of which Allen was director and commending him as "an honorable man, a man of the highest integrity, a man of business honesty." If he was a good storyteller and had a sense of humor, said Barkley, so also was Lincoln.[10] After a motion to recommit the nomination to the committee was rejected by a vote of 43 to 27, in which Republicans Bridges, Capper, and Knowland joined with 40 Democrats voting against recommittal, the nomination was confirmed without a roll call.[11]

James K. Vardaman, Jr.

A nomination of President Truman in 1946 which attracted wide and adverse criticism was that of his old friend, political supporter, fellow reserve officer, and member of the White House inner circle, James K. Vardaman, to the Federal Reserve Board. When Truman became President he recalled Vardaman from Okinawa, where he was serving as a reserve officer in the Navy, and, in spite of the opposition of old-line Navy officers, made him his naval aide. Commodore Vardaman, son of rabble-rousing James Kimball Vardaman, once governor and later senator from Mississippi, had held junior banking positions in St. Louis and was head of the regional RFC office from 1933 until he became the president of the Tower Grove Bank and Trust

Company in 1937. In addition to being a close friend of President Truman, he was close to Secretary of the Treasury Snyder, and his duties were much more important than those usually assigned to the naval aide to the President.

The nomination of Vardaman was vigorously opposed by Senator Donnell of Missouri, who spent weeks collecting evidence to prove that Vardaman had not enough banking experience to qualify him for appointment to the Federal Reserve Board, and that he had been involved in charges of improper management and misappropriation of funds of the defunct Vardaman Shoe Company, which he had managed briefly before entering the service in 1941. These charges, which were based on rumor and hearsay, were not substantiated by reliable witnesses, and the members of the subcommittee criticized Senator Donnell for making allegations based on a lawsuit that had never been brought to trial.[12] A number of bankers were called before the committee, most of whom testified that Vardaman was not qualified for the appointment, though Emil Schram, head of the New York Stock Exchange and former head of the RFC, testified that he was well qualified. "The general feeling among bankers around St. Louis was that probably Vardaman had not enough experience for the position," testified W. L. Hemingway, a former president of the American Bankers' Association and president of the Mercantile-Commerce Bank of St. Louis.[13] Two other St. Louis bankers testified that Vardaman was not qualified, and a third that he believed him to be well qualified. It was reported that Marriner Eccles, then president of the Federal Reserve Board, had recommended the appointment.

At the conclusion of the lengthy hearings the subcommittee voted unanimously to recommend confirmation of the nomination, and only one member of the Banking and Currency Committee—Senator Tobey—voted against confirmation. In the Senate debate, which extended over three days, Senator Donnell spoke for thirteen hours in opposition to the appointment. Senator McFarland then stated that the hearings had not proved that Commodore Vardaman had done even one wrongful thing,[14] and Senator Millikin, also a member of the subcommittee, stated that Vardaman had been cleared of the charges and was "an honest man," and "above that minimum standard below which we must not go."[15] The appointment of Vardaman was confirmed by a vote of 66 to 9. It is significant that those who defended the nominee could only state that it had not been proved that he had done anything wrongful, and that he was an honest man. The Senate can hardly be said to have set for itself in this case a high standard of qualification for an appointment. If Eccles had recommended the appointment, as it was reported, he lived to regret it, for soon Vardaman was making speeches on banking and economic subjects which not only displayed his lack of qualifications but were at variance with the policies of the Federal Reserve Board.

Edwin W. Pauley

A nomination made by Truman early in his first term which resulted in much opposition in the Senate and attracted widespread public criticism was that of Edwin W. Pauley, nominated on January 18, 1946, to be Under Secretary of the Navy. It was generally understood that whoever was appointed to the position would become Secretary of the Navy when Forrestal resigned, as he had announced was his intention. The appointment of Pauley to a high federal office was expected. In the summer of 1945 he had been given the important assignment by the President, with the rank of ambassador at large, to negotiate reparations agreements with our allies with regard to both Germany and Japan. His conduct of the assignment had attracted generally favorable comment in the press, though after his nomination as Under Secretary, the well-informed Washington *Post* published a highly critical editorial.[16] President Roosevelt, who planned to appoint Pauley to the Navy post, had discussed the matter with Secretary Forrestal and had secured his agreement. Pauley was a prominent oilman from California and a regent of the state university, who had long been active in politics, serving for a time as treasurer of the Democratic National Committee.

The nomination was criticized on two grounds: first, it was regarded as a reward to Pauley for his political services to the party and for his support of Truman in 1944 for the vice-presidential nomination; and second, it was contended that an oilman should not be appointed Under Secretary of the Navy, especially with the expectation of becoming the Secretary. Because of its large oil reserves and its dependence on oil to operate its fleet, the Navy has a leading part in determining the oil policies of the government, particularly with regard to the preservation of oil reserves. It was expected that the Republican members of the Naval Affairs Committee would question the nominee about his position on oil matters and would challenge the appointment of an oilman to this post. Senators Willis and Brewster announced to the press their opposition to Pauley on this ground.[17]

When the hearings opened on January 31 Senator Tobey interrogated Pauley concerning his alleged efforts to get the federal government to drop its claim to offshore-oil rights, but Pauley denied that he had ever interceded with President Roosevelt, the Attorney General, or other federal officials on the subject. His statements were contradicted by Secretary of the Interior Ickes, who testified on the following day. Ickes, who at this session was a reluctant witness, threw a bombshell into the hearing when he related that Pauley had once stated to him that he could raise several hundred thousand dollars from the oil interests for the Democratic campaign fund if the government would agree to drop the suit testing the ownership of these reserves. The following day, the Washington *Post* came out in an editorial opposing the appointment, stating that Pauley had used his political position to advance his personal interest. Referring to the fact that Pauley owned a large interest in the Petrol Oil Corporation, which was tapping offshore oil under a lease from the State of California, the editorial stated that "his interest is in direct conflict with the interest of the United States Navy, which should jealously conserve this oil for the future defense of the nation."[18] The National Citizens' Political Action Committee, which had played an effective role in getting out the vote in 1944 for Roosevelt and Truman, telegraphed the President: "The country will not support you nor your administration if you continue to appoint men to high office who are lacking in ability or in a devotion to the public welfare."[19]

Ickes, the self-styled "curmudgeon," returned to the stand on February 5 and, reading from his diary, told of Pauley's activities in behalf of oil interests, particularly with regard to the government's suit to establish its claim to the offshore oil reserves. According to Ickes, Pauley had persuaded the President to postpone the suit for several years, but. Roosevelt, shortly before he died, had instructed the Attorney General to initiate a suit. Ickes declared that Pauley's proposition to secure $300,000 from the oil interests for the Democratic campaign fund (which Pauley vehemently denied) was the "rawest deal" ever made to him, and he had feared that it would lead to a major scandal. He testified that Pauley had approached him about the matter on the special train returning from the funeral of Roosevelt at Hyde Park, and he had recorded in his diary that this "more than ever confirmed my bad opinion of him."[20]

President Truman reaffirmed his confidence in Pauley at a press conference on February 7, stating that Ickes might well have been mistaken in his testimony. He repeated this position in the four subsequent press conferences before withdrawing the nomination on March 13. Truman stated that Pauley was an honest man and a capable administrator; after his press conference he called the Democratic members of the Senate Naval Affairs Committee to urge their support of Pauley. A poll of the committee made by the press at this time indicated that two Democrats and all seven Republican members would oppose the appointment, and nine Democrats would vote for it,[21] making a tie.

On February 13, Ickes, the last remaining member of Roosevelt's original Cabinet, resigned, giving the Pauley incident as the reason. "I have to spend the rest of my life with Harold L. Ickes," he declared, "and I could no longer, much as I regret it, retain my self-respect and stay in the Cabinet of President Truman."[22]

Although Ickes' resignation angered the Democratic members of the Senate, it was generally believed to have dealt a death blow to Pauley's fading chances of confirmation. Questioned again at his press conference, the President again defended his nomination, stating that Pauley had been recommended to him by Secretary Forrestal. This was subsequently confirmed by Forrestal when he testified before the Senate committee in support of Pauley, though he stated that the original suggestion had come from President Roosevelt.

When the hearings were resumed on February 19, Pauley categorically denied the various charges that had been made against him and placed in the record a number of letters from prominent persons endorsing him. Ickes later returned to the witness stand a third time, and stated that he would support Pauley for almost any other federal office except one dealing with oil.[23]

While the nomination was still before the Senate committee, pressure was placed on the President to withdraw Pauley's name. It was rumored that a number of Democratic senators had urged this course, and Senators Stewart and Pepper did so publicly. Senator Morse issued a statement calling on the President to withdraw the nomination that had "rocked the country." Early in the hearings, Senator Saltonstall inquired of Pauley whether he would be willing to ask the President to withdraw his name if the committee exonerated him of the charges against him.[24] After the hearings had dragged on for more than a month, Senator Tydings attempted to secure an agreement that the committee would affirm its confidence in Pauley's personal integrity on the understanding that his name would be withdrawn. Pauley advised the President that this solution would be agreeable to him but later announced that he wished to continue the fight in order to answer the charges.[25] Finally, on March 13, the President withdrew the nomination, the White House releasing at the same time the exchange of correspondence between Pauley and the President. In his letter requesting that his name be withdrawn, Pauley wrote to the President that the charges against him had been answered and had been shown to be false, but he felt that in the current hysteria he would be unable to render the service that the Navy and the country deserved. In his reply, President Truman wrote Pauley that his defense of his good name had been "valiant and conclusive," and that after the "vicious and unwarranted attacks" his integrity was unscathed, his ability unquestioned, and his honor unsullied.[26]

Arthur Krock pointed out in the New York *Times* that the action of Ickes as a member of the Cabinet in opposing a nomination of the President was unprecedented.[27] The press comment on the case generally stressed the "healthy public opinion" that after being aroused brought about the eventual withdrawal of the nomination. There was a great deal of opposition in the Senate and throughout the country to the appointment of an oilman to a top post in the Navy. The criticism of Pauley by the senators for his attempt to secure a governmental policy favorable to the oil interests in return for contributions to the Democratic party was somewhat hypocritical. This is a well-known practice which both political parties have followed for many years in raising campaign funds.[28]

Philip B. Perlman

The nomination in 1947 of Philip B. Perlman, a leading attorney of Baltimore, to be Solicitor General affords a striking example of delay by the Senate in acting on a nomination that had received the highest endorsements. The delay for a period of six months was due almost entirely to the opposition of one senator, Ferguson of Michigan, chairman of the subcommittee appointed to consider the nomination. The office, which had been vacant since October of the previous year, urgently needed to be filled in order that the incumbent might have time to prepare for the autumn session of the Supreme Court. After the nomination was made, three and a half months elapsed before the subcommittee opened hearings. Senator Ferguson denied that the delay was due to political considerations, explaining that the pressure of other duties, lack of an adequate staff, and his absence from Washington had prevented earlier consideration.[29] After the hearings had been continued for more than a month while the subcommittee inquired into the law practice of the nominee and his relationships with his law clients, the two Maryland senators talked to the Republican members of the committee urging that the nomination be reported out so that it could be acted on before Congress adjourned. A former chief justice of the Maryland court of appeals and a Republican, D. Lindley Sloan, wrote to Senator Wiley, chairman of the Judiciary Committee, urging prompt and favorable action: "These hearings were conducted in such a way as to make it clear that the subcommittee is not apparently interested in Mr. Perlman's undoubted qualifications so much as it is, for political or other reasons, or no reasons at all, in making an effort to delay and defeat the nomination, thus leaving the country without a Solicitor General and doing an irreparable injury to one of Maryland's outstanding citizens." He stated that the two Republican members of the committee had "apparently assumed two tacks—one tending to besmirch the character of Mr. Perlman, and the other to belittle him."[30]

The New York *Times* account of the delay in the case stated:

Mr. Perlman, a lawyer and adviser to many Governors and other officials of his home state, has waited just short of five months for confirmation. This has been true despite endorsement by the entire Maryland delegation in Congress, by unanimous resolutions of the Maryland Legislature and the Baltimore City Council, the Maryland State and Baltimore Bar Associations, and by many of the state's prominent jurists, Republicans among them.[31]

On July 8, Senator McGrath, the Democratic member of the subcommittee considering the Perlman nomination, bitterly attacked not only the delay but also the type of inquiry that was being conducted, saying that it was a "disgrace to the American way of doing things." He declared that the subcommittee had denied the constitutional rights of the nominee, had pried into the privacy of his own affairs and those of his clients, and had investigated matters which were none of the committee's business. "I have sat, Mr. President, in those committee hearings on the nomination of Mr. Perlman," said McGrath, "and have been ashamed of the questions which have been asked."[32] Several days later, Senator Tydings of Maryland offered a resolution to discharge the committee from further consideration of the nomination, stating that he was doing so as a precaution to ensure that the nomination would be reported to the Senate before adjournment.[33] On July 21, six months after the nomination was sent to the Senate, the Judiciary Committee voted 10 to 1 to report the nomination, the single dissenting vote being cast by Senator Ferguson.[34]

When the nomination was taken up by the Senate several days later, Senator Ferguson opposed confirmation, saying that the nominee had not been entirely candid in discussing certain cases and his relations with clients.[35] The reluctance of an attorney to discuss such matters in a public hearing is understandable. The appointment of Perlman was confirmed on the last day of the session by a vote of 58 to 21. Three years later President Truman wrote to Attorney General McGrath a letter of high commendation of Perlman, who had won thirty-two victories in thirty-six cases before the Supreme Court, stating that "his work brings great credit to himself, the Justice Department, and the United States Government; I honor him for it and want you to tell him so."[36]

Jed Johnson

The hearings on the nomination of Jed Johnson to the customs court in 1947 brought to light the extraordinary fact that two years earlier he had been nominated to the same post by President Roosevelt at the suggestion of Secretary of Interior Ickes in order to get him off the House Appropriations Committee. In testifying against the nomination in 1947 Ickes stated that he had urged the appointment of Johnson in 1945 for this purpose. He related that Johnson, once a minor employee of the Department of the Interior, had been elected to Congress from Oklahoma and as a member of the Appropriations subcommittee which passed on the budget of the Department had exerted improper pressures to secure favors for his relatives and constituents. One instance cited by Ickes was Johnson's insistence that the Department pay an exorbitant fee to his law partner for handling Indian litigation; another was his attempt to put his two brothers and a sister-in-law on the Department pay roll.

According to Ickes' testimony, he had admitted to President Roosevelt that Johnson was not qualified to serve on the customs court but had nevertheless urged his appointment on the ground that he would do "less harm" in that position than as a member of the House Appropriations Committee.[37] This admission that he had recommended the appointment of a man he regarded as unqualified was shocking to the members of the Senate subcommittee.

Roosevelt nominated Johnson for the job, but the Oklahoma Congressman declined the nomination. Two years later, however, after being defeated for reëlection, Johnson sought the position and was nominated by Truman. At the hearings, Johnson asserted that his feud with Ickes had arisen over his attempts to trim the budget of the Department of the Interior, which, he added, was filled with "pinks and reds." He categorically denied Ickes' charges and stated that he did not believe that Roosevelt had nominated him in 1945 to get him off the Appropriations Committee. John Collier, formerly Commissioner of Indian Affairs, however, corroborated Ickes' testimony.[38] After several members of the House and Senate testified in behalf of Johnson, the subcommittee voted unanimously to recommend confirmation, and he was subsequently approved by the Senate without opposition.

Doubtless there have been other instances of "kicking upstairs" a member of Congress who is troublesome to the administration, but this case was extraordinary in that the reason for Johnson's appointment was brought to light by the frank testimony of the doughty former Secretary of Interior. Despite Ickes' testimony, the veracity of which can scarcely be doubted, the nomination was approved.

Abe Murdock

After the passage of the Taft-Hartley Act in 1947 over the veto of President Truman, one of the persons appointed to the newly constituted National Labor Relations Board was former Senator Abe Murdock of Utah, a man with a strong prolabor record, who as a member of the House and later of the Senate had vigorously opposed similar amendments to the Wagner Labor Relations Act. On the ground that Murdock was unsympathetic with the major provisions of the law which he would be called upon to administer, his nomination was strongly opposed by Senator Watkins of Utah, who had defeated Murdock in the 1946 election, and by Senator Ball of Minnesota, one of the leading supporters of the Taft-Hartley Act. Perhaps in no other confirmation case has this issue been raised so clearly and so sharply. In Murdock's favor, however, were these facts: he was a former member of the Senate, he was well liked by his colleagues, and the Senate has a strong tradition in favor of the confirmation of former members.

In the hearings, Murdock was closely questioned by Senator Ball concerning his attitude toward the Taft-Hartley Act, and repeatedly stated that he recognized that it was the law of the land, and if his appointment was confirmed he would devote his energies to giving this law a fair and impartial administration. Senator Ball attempted to get the nominee to comment in detail on the provisions of the law, the President's statements in opposition to it, and his own earlier statement on similar proposed legislation; but Murdock evaded the questions, repeating that he was prepared to administer the law

honestly and impartially. He said: "I do not think the law needs sympathy
I think the law needs honest and impartial administration."[39] Senator Watkins
appeared in opposition, stating that he had nothing personally against the
nominee, but believed that as an ardent prolabor man he would be unable to
administer the law fairly.

By a vote of 9 to 3 the committee on July 25 recommended confirmation
But Senator Taft, the Republican leader, stated that he doubted whether it
would be possible for the Senate to act on the nomination before it adjourned
the following day. An amendment to the appropriations act, to provide that no
member of the board could be paid a salary until his appointment had been
confirmed by the Senate, was brought up on the following day by Senator
Ball; but it was rejected after Senators Barkley and Aiken spoke against it
Barkley opposed the amendment as directed at Murdock, who he said was a
"fair-minded, experienced, able and outstanding lawyer, who will be a very
creditable, acceptable and useful member of the board."[40] Congress adjourned
without taking action on the nomination, and President Truman gave the
nominee an interim appointment.

When Congress was reconvened in November, President Truman resubmitted the nomination of Murdock, and it came before the Senate for a vote
on December 16, 1947. Senator Watkins spoke against Murdock, reiterating
that there was nothing personal in his objection, but that he thought the
nominee was disqualified to act as a member of the board because of "his strong
pro-labor bias and the heavy obligation he was under to the labor union
leaders." Senator Ball, chairman of the joint congressional committee to watch
the operation of the Taft-Hartley Act, who had earlier opposed the nomination, now stated that on the basis of his observation of the administration of
the law he had become convinced that the nominee was doing a "fair and
impartial job" and was one of the ablest members of the board. Senator
Morse stated that the real test for a judicial position was not whether a man
was a conservative or a liberal, but rather whether he was intellectually
honest.[41] Murdock was then confirmed without a roll call.

James Boyd

The nomination of James Boyd to be Director of the Bureau of Mines, first
submitted in 1947, was not acted on by the Senate until two years later, because
of the opposition of John L. Lewis. As the head of the United Mine Workers of
America, Lewis doubtless felt that he should have been consulted about the
appointment, if not permitted to select the nominee. This contest illustrates
how a powerful organization can block an appointment in the Senate; but
when Lewis took the extraordinary step in 1949 of calling a nation-wide strike
in protest to the appointment, the Senate acted promptly and confirmed the
appointment. In opposing the appointment of Boyd, Lewis declared: "We

resent the fact that the Department of Interior plucked him out of obscurity without asking the men who are going to die in the mines if they are satisfied. The miners resent it from the bottoms of their hearts."[42] Lewis expected to be more than merely consulted; he regarded the position as one to which he should be permitted to name the nominee. His opposition was similar in this regard to the personal objection of a member of the Senate to an appointment in his own state about which he was not consulted. Lewis' action in calling a strike in March, 1949, to protest the appointment, however, forced the issue and virtually assured Boyd's prompt confirmation by a large majority.

Appearing at the hearings of the Public Lands Committee in 1947, Lewis declared that the appointment was a "political deal," and that Boyd, who was dean of the Colorado School of Mines, was not qualified, because he lacked "practical experience" in mining. "It is like employing a watchmaker to repair a steam shovel," declared Lewis. Citing statistics of the number of accidents and fatalities in mines, Lewis declared that Boyd was not qualified to be in charge of safety measures. "Mr. Boyd may be a good man," said Lewis, "good to his family, but we want someone who will be kind to the coal miners' families."[43]

A week later, after the Centralia disaster, when hearings were resumed, Lewis appeared again, charging that it had been due to the "criminal negligence" of Secretary of the Interior Krug, and protested that the "coal miners do not want to work in these mines with only the protection which would come from a man appointed by J. A. Krug to safeguard their safety."[44] After Congress adjourned without acting on the nominations, Truman gave Boyd a recess appointment, and subsequently gave him similar appointments in 1947 and 1948, though under the provisions of federal statutes Boyd received no pay—except for about four months in 1947—until his regular appointment was finally confirmed.

In the Senate debate on the nomination on March 16, 1949, Senator Martin of Pennsylvania maintained that the Senate should not be intimidated by John L. Lewis, and stated that he would vote for Boyd because of Lewis' action in calling a strike in protest against the appointment.[45] Senator Millikin of Colorado opposed the nomination on the ground that the miners did not have confidence in Boyd, and Neely of West Virginia objected that Boyd did not have "practical experience." Senator Watkins pointed out that the head of the inspection division in the Bureau of Mines was a man with twenty-five years' experience in coal mines and, as was well known, had been recommended for the position by the United Mine Workers. Every senator who spoke against Boyd came from a coal-mining state and justified his stand on the ground that the nomination was opposed by the miners of his state. In spite of the opposition, Boyd's nomination was approved by a vote of 50 to 11.[46]

Thomas C. Buchanan

One of Truman's nominations of liberals that was blocked in the Senate by the Republican Eightieth Congress was that of Thomas C. Buchanan, a former member of the Pennsylvania Public Service Commission, who was nominated to be a member of the Federal Power Commission on April 15, 1948. His nomination was supported by consumer groups and electric coöperatives but was opposed by the gas and electric-utility groups of Pennsylvania, whose spokesman in the hearing testified that Buchanan did not have a necessary "judicial temperament" for the job. After the hearing the subcommittee voted two to one against confirmation, but the Committee on Interstate and Foreign Commerce referred the nomination back to the subcommittee for further investigation. After Congress adjourned, President Truman gave Buchanan a recess appointment.[47] A year later the committee recommended confirmation by a vote of 9 to 1, and his nomination was subsequently confirmed without a roll call, Senator Martin of Pennsylvania making the only speech in opposition. Three years later, in 1952, when he was renominated, the same interests opposed the appointment, and the committee voted against confirmation, 9 to 4. After Congress had adjourned, President Truman gave Buchanan a recess appointment in 1952 as chairman of the commission.[48]

At the opening of the hearings in May, 1948, Senator Martin requested postponement in order that numerous persons who wished to testify could be heard. Stating that although the nominee was a man of "integrity and fine standing," Senator Martin declared that he "lacks judicial temperament and is incapable of a fair, unbiased, and unprejudiced approach to proceedings involving utilities and the public."[49] Senator Martin also raised a question about the nominee's sympathy for Communism, pointing out that in 1945 he had testified in support of the nomination of Leland Olds, who had been accused of association with Earl Browder and William Z. Foster. Although professing that he was not "questioning for one minute the Americanism of Mr. Buchanan," Senator Martin stated significantly: "We are in a position in America today where we must be on our guard constantly if we are to safeguard our free-enterprise system and our American way of life against a drift to a socialistic pattern of government."[50] He urged the committee to inquire into Buchanan's philosophy of government.

Although Senator Martin had stated that many persons, including a number of senators, wanted to testify against the nominee, actually few appeared, and these were subpoenaed. A former employee of the Pennsylvania Public Service Commission, who had left its employment to enter law school, was the leading opposing witness. Although he testified that he appeared on his own behalf, Senators Meyers and MacMahon regarded him as a witness for the power interests. His testimony, as well as that of several officials of gas and electric associations, was to the effect that Buchanan had favored electric coöperatives and was not impartial and judicious as a member of the commission.[51]

Testifying for Buchanan was Clyde Ellis, a former member of Congress and head of the National Rural Electric Cooperative Association, and Anne Alpern, city solicitor of Pittsburgh, who was later a leading witness in the 1949 hearings on the nomination of Leland Olds to the Federal Power Commission. Miss Alpern testified that Buchanan was eminently qualified and fair in his dealings with the utility interests. Their objection to Buchanan, she stated, stemmed "entirely from the fact that they feel that the consumers' interests will be adequately protected."[52]

When Congress convened in 1949, President Truman again submitted the nomination of Buchanan, then serving under a recess appointment. The Committee on Interstate and Foreign Commerce failed to take any action until May 26, when it submitted a report to the Senate recommending his confirmation. Reviewing the nominee's record, the report stated that Buchanan had "demonstrated an intense insistence upon adequate regulation of public utilities in the public interest," and that his testimony had indicated that he believed wholeheartedly in private enterprise in the public-utility field. The report quoted from the letters from the presiding judge of the Pennsylvania Superior Court, Chester H. Rhodes, who said that Buchanan was "a man of integrity and ability" and as a member of the Pennsylvania Public Service Commission had been "fair, just and impartial." A similar letter from Justice Jones of the Pennsylvania Supreme Court was quoted at length, as well as other briefer quotations from other prominent Pennsylvanians. The report closed with the statement that "justice and fair play" required that there be no further delay in the confirmation of Buchanan.[53]

John J. Carson

The nomination in 1949 of John J. Carson, Washington representative of the Cooperative League of the United States, to be a member of the Federal Trade Commission led to a conservative-liberal fight that had most of the aspects common to such contests. Carson had the active support of organized labor, the Cooperative League of the United States, the Farmers' Union, and consumer groups; but he was strongly opposed by the National Manufacturers' Association, the American Retail Federation, and certain other business organizations which come under the jurisdiction of the FTC. A story in the N.A.M. News called him a "fiery liberal" and stated that "he is regarded as a critic of many business practices, is energetic and would be expected to become very active as a member of the Federal Trade Commission in pushing investigations into business affairs."[54] One of the principal functions of the Federal Trade Commission, it may be noted, is to investigate unfair business practices and monopolies.

The opposition to Carson, however, was spearheaded by Fulton Lewis, Jr. a radio commentator, and by the National Tax Equality Association, an or ganization that had been conducting a widespread campaign against the priv ileged tax status of coöperatives. The past writings of Carson were combec for radical statements to be used in the campaign against him carried on by Lewis in his radio broadcasts, and these statements later became the basis o the inquiry into Carson's qualifications at the hearings. As usual in such con tests, sentences were taken out of context which when standing alone ap peared very left wing in tone, though the statements in their entirety gave nc such impression. One of the Carson quotations that Senator Brewster bitterly attacked turned out to be a paraphrase of a papal encyclical of Pope Pius XI the famous Quadragesimo Anno. When this fact was published in newspape: accounts it infuriated the senator.[55]

Not content with digging up the past writings of the nominee, which wer voluminous since Carson was formerly a newspaperman, his opponents pro duced at the hearings also a thirty-page mimeographed collection of excerpt taken from the book by Dr. James Warbasse, former president of the Coop erative League of the United States, *Cooperative Democracy*. These excerpt were intended to indicate that the Cooperative League was opposed to capi talism, and that anyone connected with the league was therefore disqualifiec to serve as a member of the Federal Trade Commission. Jerry Voorhis, Presi dent of the Cooperative League and a former member of Congress, testifiec that the utopian ideas contained in the book were those of the author, and tha he was not speaking for the league. Voorhis also made a plea for the right o coöperatives to exist in this country without harassment.[56] Upon interrogation Carson testified that he had never read the book by Dr. Warbasse that wa being quoted in opposition to his appointment.[57]

Several opposing witnesses asserted at the hearings that Carson was a cru sader and a zealot, and that he did not believe in the free-enterprise system In his testimony Carson denied repeatedly that he was opposed to privat enterprise and the capitalistic system, and attempted to explain the radica statements attributed to him as "campaign oratory" made in the midst of ; fight on coöperatives. When the hearings were concluded, the committe recommended the approval of the nomination by a straight party vote of 8 to 4

In the Senate debate Senator Bricker led the opposition. Prefacing his re marks by a statement that it was not the function of the Senate to interfer with executive responsibility and that he would vote against a nomination only if he determined that the nominee was "entirely unfit," he opposed the ap pointment of Carson to this post on the following grounds: first, that he wa not a Republican, though the position traditionally belonged to that party second, Carson had had no business experience; third, his writings indicatec that he was opposed to the capitalistic system, and moreover, he was a "dreame.

and fuzzy-minded."[58] Senator Magnuson, who made the principal speech in defense of the nominee, pointed out that the law did not require that the position be filled by a Republican, and that Carson was an independent. He discounted the allegations that Carson was opposed to the free-enterprise system, stating that the quotations used against him had been taken out of context, and he declared that no one had challenged the honesty and ability of the nominee. Carson was being opposed, he declared, because of his association with the Cooperative League of the United States. Closing the debate, Senator Humphrey stated that the issue was not merely whether a man should or should not be rejected because he was associated with the coöperative movement. "If the leadership of the minority party wants to line up with the National Tax Equality League...and the anticooperative movement in this country," he declared, the people of the country would know it by the vote on the nomination.[59] On the final vote, Carson's appointment was confirmed, 45 to 25.

Carl Ilgenfritz

The nomination of Carl Ilgenfritz to be chairman of the Munitions Board was rejected by the Senate on September 16, 1949, on the ground that it would be an undesirable precedent for a federal official to continue to receive a salary from a private corporation. Ilgenfritz, an official of the United States Steel Company, had been recommended to President Truman by former President Hoover as the best man in the country for the job. He had agreed to accept it for a period of one year on the condition that he would be permitted to continue to receive a salary of $70,000 annually from the United States Steel Company. In his testimony before the Senate Armed Services Committee, Ilgenfritz stated that he would not be able to meet his personal obligations on the government salary of $14,000 annually and was unwilling to forfeit his pension rights, which would be necessary if he resigned from the company.

The Committee on Armed Services by a divided vote recommended confirmation. In the Senate debate, which occurred on September 16, Senator Tydings, chairman of the committee, defended the nomination as an emergency matter and stated that the appointment was similar to that of dollar-a-year men during the recent war. The opposition was led by Senator Byrd, who contended that it would be an unwise precedent. This position was strongly supported by Senator Morse, whose statement Senator Byrd placed in the record, and by a number of other senators of both political parties. Byrd pointed out that it was common practice for the Senate in confirming persons for high federal office to insist that they give up their private income and sever their connections, and cited a number of such instances. All participants in the debate conceded that Ilgenfritz was unusually well qualified for the post and

212] THE ADVICE AND CONSENT OF THE SENATE

spoke of him only in terms of high praise. The vote did not follow party lines; 16 Democrats and 12 Republicans voted for confirmation; 22 Democrats and 18 Republicans voted against it.[60]

Mon C. Wallgren

On February 3, 1949, President Truman nominated his close personal friend and former colleague in the Senate, Mon C. Wallgren, who had been defeated for reëlection as governor of the state of Washington in 1948, as chairman of the National Security Resources Board. The nomination attracted considerable opposition in the Senate and out on the ground that Wallgren was not qualified to head the agency charged with planning the industrial mobilization of the country for national defense. As a former member of Congress, Wallgren generally voted for New Deal measures, but was regarded as a political lightweight. He was elected to the Senate in 1940 and served with Truman on the Special (Senate) Committee Investigating the National Defense Program; in 1944 he was elected governor of Washington. Before entering politics in 1932, Wallgren operated a small-town retail jewelry and optical store and had won the regional billiard championship.

"The best thing that can be said about Mon Wallgren," stated the New York *Herald Tribune,* "is that he enjoys the friendship and confidence of the President.... An impartial observer would hardly pick him on the demonstrated record as the planning genius and economic mobilizer envisaged under the National Security Act to keep tabs on America's resources against all emergencies.... Mr. Wallgren, an old crony out of a job, likes Washington life, and the President is taking care of him."[61] Quoting the Hoover Commission report that "we cannot entrust the government of today to second rate men and women," the Washington *Post* said that the Wallgren nomination was "a revival of 'government by crony' which we thought went out of fashion with Warren G. Harding."[62] The Chicago *Daily News* stated that Wallgren was "unquestionably an amiable gentleman, a good fishing companion, graduate of an optometry school, a skillful golfer, and a champion billiard player," but not qualified for "an assignment of staggering importance."[63]

When the hearings opened on February 17, Republican Senator Cain of Washington appeared in opposition to Wallgren. Stressing the importance of the office and the high qualifications that should be possessed by the person filling it, Cain asserted that Wallgren was not qualified and charged him with having appointed Communists and fellow travelers to his administration as governor of Washington. Senator Cain also attacked the nominee on his record as governor and aired the various charges of political spoils and graft that had been made against his administration. Although Cain disclaimed any personal animus against the nominee, it quickly became apparent that most of his charges were personal, and they were discounted accordingly. The numerous reports, newspaper accounts, and miscellaneous materials that Senator Cain had placed in the record of the hearings were later used in his six-hour speech on the floor of the Senate opposing the appointment.[64] This speech was made in the midst of a filibuster by a group of Southern senators against taking up a civil rights bill; hence it was referred to in the press as a filibuster within a filibuster. For the aid he gave the Southern senators in their filibuster, it was rumored, Cain was promised assistance in his fight on Wallgren.

Wallgren's administration as governor of Washington had been marked by many charges of spoils politics, patronage appointments, the sale of liquor licenses to clubs, improper use of a state yacht, and other matters. When questioned in the hearings about these charges, Wallgren replied that they were merely "politics," explaining that such charges had been made against him by the Republican press of Washington throughout his political career. When Senator Saltonstall inquired about the alleged sale of liquor licenses, Wallgren said that "it is a long story." The Massachusetts senator then interjected: "You say it is a long story. I think it is fair for us to know because if there is any criticism of those things then you are not a proper man to hold this very important job."[65]

The most illuminating part of the hearings was the interrogation of the nominee by Senator Saltonstall, who, seeking to ascertain what his qualifications were for the chairmanship of the National Security Resources Board, asked Wallgren if he had ever made any study of such subjects as the steel business, coal supply and distribution, shipping, copper, the textile industry, food supply, and similar matters. In his reply Wallgren referred to his experience as a member of the Truman committee and as governor of Washington, stating that it would be difficult to find a man who was well versed in the various industries mentioned. "The President," he continued lamely, "seems to have this confidence in me, and seems to feel that my experience would carry me through on the job."[66]

At the conclusion of the hearings the committee voted 7 to 6 against confirmation. Except for Senator Byrd, who voted with the Republicans, the vote followed party lines. By a unanimous vote it adopted a resolution stating that it believed Wallgren was a "loyal and patriotic citizen," and that the committee had "found no evidence to support any allegations that he was lacking in integrity."[67] In an individual statement issued to the press, explaining his vote, Senator Byrd stated that he took no stock in the "unsupported charges" against Wallgren and did not believe that he had any sympathy with Communism. In spite of the strenuous efforts of the administration to get the committee to reverse its action and to report the nomination to the Senate, or to secure enough votes in the Senate to discharge the committee, the nomination remained bottled up in committee until two months later, when it was withdrawn. After the President withdrew the nomination, Senator Byrd made a statement on the floor of the Senate explaining his vote, saying that he had given the "utmost consideration" to the qualifications of Wallgren for this position, and had made his decision "entirely without political or personal bias" for what he regarded as the best interests of the country. "After the most careful consideration of all factors involved, I reached the definite conclusion, as did a majority of the committee, that former Governor Wallgren was not competent to perform in a satisfactory manner the duties of the Chairman of the National Security Resources Board."[68]

In the following October, Truman nominated Wallgren to the Federal Power Commission in place of Leland Olds, who had been rejected by the Senate, and the nomination was promptly confirmed by a vote of 47 to 12. Senator Cain's request for hearings on the nomination was refused by the Senate Interstate and Foreign Commerce Committee, and the committee unanimously recommended confirmation of Wallgren.[69] In the Senate debate, Cain again opposed Wallgren, but this time he spoke only briefly.[70] Senator Byrd was the only Democrat to vote against confirmation. The courtesy of the Senate held. If the President expected Wallgren to fill the role of Leland Olds on the FPC, he was mistaken in his man. No one expected that Wallgren would ever become a leading authority in the field of public-utility regulations, as Olds was, but it was assumed that he would support the President's program, particularly in the regulation of the price of natural gas. This assumption proved to be unfounded, for Wallgren frequently sided with the group of commissioners that were sympathetic to the point of view of the natural gas industry, and two years later he voted with the majority not to extend federal regulation to the field price of natural gas, when a test case involving the Phillips Petroleum Company came before the commission.[71] Through this decision the commission carried into effect precisely the policy contained in the Kerr bill, which Truman had vetoed in 1950 and Congress had failed to pass over his veto.

Chapter XIII

THE COURTESY OF
THE SENATE

"Senatorial courtesy" is a necessary development in the perfecting of an extra-constitutional party practice in our federal system. It is as essential to the proper functioning of party government under our federal plan as any other extra-constitutional function, such as, for example, our national convention system.... It would be dangerous, as it has been dangerous, both to the constitutional and extra-constitutional position of the presidency for the President to act without the advice of senators. This I know has been done; great offense has been given. It has always brought about party dissension and it will always destroy party unity. A Senator of the United States has as much right to expect respect for his position as a representative of a sovereign state as has a President to expect respect for his. Senator Elbert D. Thomas.[1]*

Get rid of this "courtesy of the Senate." The Senate has a right to pass upon appointments. The Constitution secures it that right ... The reason for the opposition to a man's appointment to public office to aid the Executive in executing the laws ought to be a public reason, that is, a reason founded upon the character of the appointee, his fitness or his unfitness morally, mentally, or physically, but it ought not to flow out of the personal feeling of a Senator. Senator John Sharp Williams.[2]

THE CONTROVERSY in 1951 between Senator Paul Douglas of Illinois and President Truman over the appointment of two federal judges in that state, which attracted nation-wide attention, provides a recent illustration of the unwritten rule of senatorial courtesy. Following the customary practice, Senator Douglas conferred with party leaders and members of the Illinois bar, and in January recommended to Attorney General Mc-

Grath the appointment of William H. King, Jr., and Judge Benjamin F. Epstein. Six months later, in July, President Truman sent in the nominations of two other persons for these judgeships—Municipal Judge Joseph P. Drucker and Cornelius J. Harrington. Several days later, Douglas took the unusual step of asking the Chicago Bar Association to conduct a poll of its members in order to ascertain whether they preferred his choices or those of the President. The results were overwhelmingly in favor of the persons whom Douglas had picked. Armed with this corroboration of the desirability of his candidates, Douglas appealed to the courtesy of the Senate in opposing the nominations of the President. He was sustained unanimously by the Judiciary Committee, and the Senate rejected the President's nominations without a roll call.

Following the precedent of two similar cases which arose in 1950, Douglas did not make the customary assertion that the President's nominees were "personally obnoxious" to him. To the contrary, he stated that they were "worthy" men, but that he regarded his own choices as better qualified and based his objection to the nominations on the method by which they were made—that is, the President had not nominated the men Douglas had recommended. The controversy over the Illinois judgeships was exceptional also in other regards. The senator had exercised unusual care and had selected two persons of outstanding qualifications for appointment to the federal bench, whereas the President's nominees were not so well qualified.*

Typically, contests between the President and members of the Senate over appointments arise when the President declines to nominate the candidate proposed by a senator of his party, ordinarily on the ground that the senator's nominee has not the proper qualifications for the office to be filled. At times the President has cut off the customary patronage of senators of his party who have opposed his legislative program. The fact that Senator Douglas recommended well-qualified persons for the Illinois judgeships should not obscure the fact that the custom of permitting the senators of the party in office to select the persons for federal appointment in their own states results in patronage appointments. The actual selections frequently are made by the party leaders rather than by the senators, and these federal offices are commonly used to reward party workers or the supporters of the senators. In the past, unqualified persons have often received the necessary political sponsorship and have been appointed.

The contest over the Illinois judgeships is the most recent of a long line of cases in which the President has been rebuffed by the Senate when he rejected recommendations of senators of his own party for appointments in their own states. George Washington suffered a similar rebuff several months after the first session of the Senate opened, when his nomination of one Benjamin Fishbourn to the post of naval officer of the Port of Savannah was rejected, not

* This contest is reviewed in detail in chap. xvii, below.

because the nominee lacked qualifications but because the two Georgia senators had a candidate of their own. The next day, Washington nominated their
candidate, but at the same time, he wrote a sharp letter to the Senate requesting it thereafter, before rejecting a nomination, to ascertain his reasons for
making it.* The custom of permitting the senators of the party in power
to select the person for appointment to federal offices within their states, however, did not become firmly established until many years later. Washington
insisted that under the Constitution the nominating power rested with the
President alone, and followed the practice of consulting not only members of
the Senate but members of the House and other prominent citizens.† In the
course of time, the practice of consulting members of the Senate about appointments in their states was transformed into the custom of permitting them
to name the person to be appointed, with the President retaining only a veto
over their recommendations.³ In states represented in the Senate by members
of the opposite party, the President turns to the party leaders in the state for
their recommendations, though in this case he is freer to reject their
nominations.

The Grounds for Personal Objections

The custom of senatorial courtesy is the sanction by which a majority of the
Senate may require the President to nominate the candidate proposed by the
senator or senators from the state in which the office is situated, provided they
belong to the same party as that of the President. Under the custom, any member of the Senate may block the confirmation of a nomination by stating that
the nominee is "personally obnoxious" or offensive to him. In the past it has
not been necessary for the senator to do more than merely indicate his opposition to a nomination, and repeat the customary formula. An objection to a
nomination does not mean that the nominee is actually "personally obnoxious"
to the objecting senator; it frequently involves no animus whatever but merely
indicates that the senator has another candidate. Formerly it was not necessary
or even expected that the objecting senator give any reasons to support his
objections. He needed merely to rise in his seat and announce that the nominee
was "personally obnoxious" to him, and if he notified the chairman of the
committee to which the nomination had been referred of his objection, the
nomination would not be reported to the Senate.

The application of the unwritten rule of courtesy was the subject of an
extended debate in the Senate in 1932 when the nomination of Charles A.
Jonas, a former Republican Congressman from North Carolina, to be a federal district attorney in that state was being considered. Senator Bailey of
North Carolina, recently elected to the Senate, entered a personal objection,
but asserted paradoxically that there was nothing personal in his objection.

* See pp. 40–41.
† See p. 37.

Bailey objected to a statement that Jonas had given to the press after his defeat for reëlection in 1930, which charged that election frauds were prevalent in the state and stated that they could not be cleaned out by attempts at criminal prosecution of the offenders. Although Bailey had once made much more severe allegations of election frauds in the state, he declared that the appointment was personally obnoxious to him because Jonas had brought the Commonwealth of North Carolina "into obloquy," had impeached its good name, and had asserted that justice could not be had in its courts in election cases.[4]

The principal issue in the debate was whether the senator from North Carolina had brought himself under the rule of courtesy. Several leading Republican senators stated that they would honor the objection and vote against the nomination only if Senator Bailey would state unequivocally that the nominee was "personally obnoxious" to him. The Senate voted to reject the nomination, but a few days later Senator Hastings moved to reconsider, stating that he was convinced that the North Carolina senator had not come within the rule of "personal obnoxiousness," because he had stated that his objection was not personal. Senator Bailey declared again that his objection was not personal, and that he would not take advantage of his worst enemy by reason of any supposed privilege resting in him because of his position. Referring to the code of sportsmanship, he stated that he had been "bred to believe that a man should not shoot a bird on the ground, or a rabbit in the brush, or a duck in the water," and that he did not propose to "take advantages like those." Senator Johnson of California stated that an objection was not tenable "except it be of a personal character," but Senator Reed of Pennsylvania stated that the senator from North Carolina was making his path very hard. If he would simply state that the nominee was personally objectionable, Senator Reed said, he would vote against confirmation, but if the matter were left to his own judgment, he would have to vote the other way. When Senator Bailey replied that he had stated that the nominee was personally obnoxious to him and had given his reasons, Senator Reed exclaimed:

Ah! but then why does the Senator use the words "personally obnoxious" at all? If he has reasons against the confirmation, all well and good; let us weigh the reasons; but the fact of the nominee being personally obnoxious to him or not does not seem to me to enter into the case at all. If he puts it on the ground of a disqualification of this nominee because of what he has done, that is one thing. If he puts it on the ground of his being personally obnoxious to him, that is something totally different, so far as I am concerned.

... In other words, it depends on where the responsibility lies. If the Senator from North Carolina will assume the responsibility of saying this nominee is personally obnoxious, then I vote with him; but if he puts on me the responsibility of saying whether this man's newspaper interview is a sufficient reason for rejecting him, I should be forced in all honesty to say "no," I do not think it is a sufficient reason.[5]

Although formerly a senator who entered a personal objection was not required to give any facts to support his position, since 1930 the objecting senator has been expected to state his reasons so that the Senate can judge whether they are adequate. When Senator Schall appeared before a Judiciary subcommittee in 1931 opposing the confirmation of Gunnar Nordbye to be a district judge in Minnesota, Senator Blaine maintained that mere political opposition was not sufficient grounds for voting against an appointment, and that an objection should be based upon a statement of facts which justified the opposition. Senator Schall responded by filing the signed statements of several persons testifying that the nominee had made disparaging remarks about him.[6] The question whether an objecting senator is required to give his reasons also arose in 1934 when the nomination of Daniel D. Moore to be collector of internal revenue in Louisiana was being considered. Senator Long entered a personal objection. Several scheduled hearings on the nomination were postponed by the Finance Committee at Long's request, and when they were finally held, the Louisiana senator appeared briefly, standing on his right to enter a personal objection without stating his reasons. The committee refused to accept this objection, and reported the nomination to the Senate with a recommendation for approval. Senator Long, it may be noted, was not only at "outs" with the administration but was not in the good graces of his colleagues in the Senate.

In the Senate debate on March 23, 1934, Senator Long opposed the nomination on the ground that the nominee was "personally obnoxious" to him and stoutly maintained that under the custom of the Senate such an objection required no explanation or justification.[7] Senator Wheeler defended the right of Senator Long to enter a personal objection without giving his reasons, saying that to his knowledge this had never been required.

The Senator from Louisiana [Wheeler stated] under the rules of the Senate, had a perfect right . . . to feel, when he filed a statement saying that the nominee was personally objectionable to him, that it would not be necessary for him to go before the committee and disclose all the facts and circumstances as to why he objected to him. The Senator from Kentucky has been in politics long enough to know that many times a man may be absolutely objectionable to him for many reasons and yet he would dislike to stand on the floor of the Senate and go into details as to why the man was personally objectionable to him.[8]

Senator Barkley said that although formerly no explanation was required, in recent years the practice had been for a senator who entered a personal objection to an appointment to give his reasons for it, so that the Senate might pass upon them. Otherwise, he declared, the arbitrary exercise of personal objections "would make it impossible for an Executive to appoint anybody who could be confirmed."[9]

In the hearing on the nomination of William S. Boyle to be district attorney in Nevada in 1939, to which Senator McCarran objected, Senator Norris, a member of the subcommittee, insisted that the Nevada senator state the grounds for his objection, saying that "common honesty compels that course."[10] Senator McCarran complied with the request of Senator Norris and stated his reason, which was essentially the same as that of the two Georgia senators who opposed Washington's nomination of Benjamin Fishbourn in 1789: the senator had another candidate whom the President had not accepted. This has indeed been the usual ground for an objection, though the formula and the allegations have varied. McCarran had proposed the reappointment of W. P. Carrville, and regarded the appointment of Boyle, a prominent Nevada attorney and former Democratic national committeeman, as a "slap" at him by the President. McCarran, who was a candidate for reëlection in 1938, interpreted the President's withdrawal of his customary patronage as intended to indicate to the voters of Nevada that he did not have the support of the administration. This McCarran considered an affront, comparable to but more subtle than the President's announced opposition to several other Democratic senators who were up for election that year. "Mr. Boyle," he said, "is personally offensive to me because he has lent himself to a conspiracy to take from me my standing as a Member of the Senate of the United States and has lent himself to defeat the will, or rather the words, of the Constitution of the United States, which says that the Senators of the United States shall affirm, recommend, and advise."[11]

The reasons Senator Glass gave for his objection to the appointment of Judge Floyd H. Roberts to a district judgeship in Virginia in 1939 were similar. The two Virginia senators had recommended two persons to the Attorney General for the appointment, but the President sent in the name of Judge Roberts, who had the backing of Representative Flannagan, a consistent supporter of the administration's legislative program and a member of the anti-Byrd faction in Virginia politics. Judge Roberts had a distinguished record as a state judge, and it was conceded by the two Virginia senators that he was well qualified. In response to the customary inquiry sent to them by the chairman of the Judiciary Committee concerning the nomination, Senators Glass and Byrd replied: "This nomination is utterly and personally offensive to the Virginia Senators, whose suggestions were invited by the Department of Justice only to be ignored."[12]

Many other instances could be cited of objections that were due to the fact that the senator had another candidate. In 1906, when a federal judgeship appointment in New York was under consideration, Theodore Roosevelt refused to accept the recommendation of Senator Platt, one of the Republican leaders of the Senate, and proposed instead another person whom he believed to be better qualified. Senator Platt wrote to the President that it should be sufficient for him to state which man he preferred, but Roosevelt refused to accept this contention and insisted on appointing the man whom he regarded as best qualified.* Senator Platt did not enter an objection to the nominee. In Wilson's administration Senators O'Gorman, Martine, and Reed entered objections to nominees about whom they "had not been consulted," an expression commonly used to indicate that the President did not nominate the senator's candidate. The nomination of Charles H. Naut in 1921 to be collector of internal revenue in Ohio was opposed by Senator Willis, who had another candidate. In an editorial commenting on the case, the New York *Times* on June 15, 1921, stated: "The overshadowing, the supreme question is, does the President or the Senator have the power of appointment to Federal offices in the Senator's State?"

In a similar case in 1950 the Senate rejected the nomination of M. Neil Andrews to be district judge in Georgia on the objection of the two Georgia senators, who had recommended another person. Their position was exactly the same as that of the two Georgia senators who objected in 1789 to the nomination of Benjamin Fishbourn. "When the senators of the same political party as the President have been requested to make a recommendation," declared Senator Russell, "they have a right to believe that if the man they recommend is qualified the recommendation will be followed. Otherwise the constitutional power of the Senate to advise and consent to a nomination means nothing; it has no significance." He went on to state that he considered the "action taken to be in derogation of the rights of individual senators and of the dignity of the Senate as a coordinate branch of the Government. It is contrary to custom, and in defiance of the constitutional powers of the Senate."[13] No defense was made of the nomination, and it was rejected without a roll call.

On the same day, the Senate rejected the nomination of Carroll O. Switzer to be a district judge in Iowa, on the objection of Senator Gillette of that state, who stated that he regarded the nomination as a "personal affront." He complained that the Department of Justice had not come to him to ask for his suggestions; after he went to the Department, however, he was invited to make recommendation. Thereafter he went to a great deal of trouble to inquire into the qualifications of candidates, asked the local bar associations to hold a secret ballot on the persons under consideration, and submitted the name of the person who received the largest number of votes. The President's nominee, a former Democratic candidate for governor, was at the bottom of the poll. Senator Gillette denounced the nomination as a "political machination," and the Senate rejected it without a roll call.[14]

In the contest over the Illinois judgeships in 1951, Senator Douglas entered an objection, not to the persons nominated by the President, but to the method by which the nomination was made—that is, to the failure of the President to

---

* See chap. vi, above.

accept his recommendations. The effect of this new variation is to free the objecting senator from the unpleasant task of attacking the qualifications or fitness of the person nominated by the President. The formula is new, but the effect is identical with the old rule under which members of the Senate rose and merely stated that the nominee was "personally obnoxious" to them.

It has been said on the floor of the Senate that when a senator enters a personal objection to a nominee it is to be presumed that he has good reasons for taking such action and the objection can be taken as an indication that the nominee is not suitable for the appointment.[15] The evidence, however, is to the contrary. Typically, a personal objection is entered when the objecting senator concedes that the nominee is fully qualified, which may or may not be openly stated. In opposing the President's nominations to the Illinois judgeships in 1951, for example, Senator Douglas stated that the nominees were "worthy" or "eminent" men, and Senators Glass and Byrd admitted that Judge Roberts of Virginia, whom they had opposed in 1939, was fully qualified. In the Senate debate on the Jonas appointment in 1932, Senator Walsh, who supported the objection of Senator Bailey, stated: "There seems to be no serious question about the ability of Mr. Jonas as a lawyer nor as to his general character."[16] Similarly, Senator Reed said that the nominee was "perfectly competent," and that the President was justified in making the appointment.

These cases are typical of many others in which the Senate rejected nominees who were recognized as being fully qualified, for reasons that had nothing whatever to do with their qualifications. In some instances, however, an objecting senator has attacked the nominee, asserting that he lacked the necessary qualifications or was an unfit person; but such attacks have usually been transparently political in nature, revealing the animus of the senator rather than verified evidence unfavorable to the nominee.[17] As a general rule, when the President turns down the recommendation of a senator of his party for an appointment in the senator's state, he anticipates the opposition of the senator and therefore is particularly careful to choose a person of outstanding qualifications. This, however, was not true in the contest over the Illinois judgeships in 1951.

Often, personal objections are due to the fact that the nominee is a political opponent of the senator voicing the objection. Thus Senators Byrd and Robertson of Virginia opposed the nomination of Martin A. Hutchinson of that state to be a member of the Federal Trade Commission in 1950. Hutchinson had formerly been a prominent member of the Byrd organization, and Byrd, when governor, had appointed him to some of the highest and most influential offices in the state. He had since become a leader of the anti-Byrd faction and had run against Senator Byrd in the Democratic primary of 1946. Although the Virginia senators did not use the words "personally obnoxious," and they alleged that Hutchinson did not have the requisite qualifications for the office, it was quite clear that their objections were political.[18] Prominent citizens of the state, many associated with the Byrd organization, sent in letters and telegrams speaking of the nominee in the highest terms. Douglas Southall Freeman, editor of the Richmond *New Leader* and a celebrated author, wrote that Hutchinson was a distinguished lawer who "measures up to every require-ment, professional and personal, for the important office," and that his rejec-tion because of mere factional Virginia politics would be "intolerable" and "contrary to the best traditions of American democracy.... Were the nomi-nation of Mr. Hutchinson to be rejected, another would be added to the un-happy list of men denied opportunities for reasons that will not stand the light of day."[19]

In the Senate debate Senator Byrd discoursed at length on senatorial cour-tesy and the importance of the functions of the FTC, and advanced the propo-sition that the senators from each state should be the ones to decide whether a citizen of their state should be confirmed for a national office. "Quite nat-urally," he said, "the Senators from Virginia are in the best position of any Senators to advise on the fitness and qualifications of Mr. Hutchinson or any other Virginian who may be proposed for an important public office." The Senate voted 59 to 14 to reject the nomination, sustaining the objection, though the objecting senators had carefully avoided using the customary formula.[20]

In the contest over the Nordbye appointment in 1931, Senator Schall as-serted that the nominee was his bitter enemy, and Senator McCarran made the same assertion in opposing the appointment of William S. Boyle in 1939. Boyle, however, testified that he had always supported the senator in Nevada politics, and this statement was never refuted. In 1915 the Democratic Senate honored the personal objection of Senator Gallinger, a Republican, to George Rublee's nomination to the Federal Trade Commission. Rublee had managed the campaign of the fusion candidate who opposed Gallinger in the 1914 election, which the New Hampshire senator asserted had been conducted in an offensive manner. This, however, was disputed by Senator La Follette, who stated that Rublee had always been courteous to Senator Gallinger. After the Senate failed to act on the nomination, Wilson gave Rublee a recess ap-pointment, but in 1916 he was rejected* in spite of the fact that he was a person of the highest character and qualifications.[21] In the famous controversy between President Garfield and Senator Conkling over the appointment of W. H. Robertson as collector of the Port of New York, Conkling's objection, which led him to resign his seat in the Senate when he was unable to block confirma-tion, was due to the fact that Robertson was the leader of the opposing faction of the New York Democratic organization. In 1943 Senator O'Daniel blocked the appointment of Judge Allred, who had run against him for the Senate the preceding year. And Senator McKellar's bitter fight against the appoint-

---

* See chap. vi, above.

ment of David Lilienthal as chairman of the Atomic Energy Commission in 1947 was due to his belief that Lilienthal was his political opponent.

A senator of the minority party may enter a personal objection to a nominee, and in numerous instances the Senate has sustained such objections. Since members of the minority party cannot expect to control the federal patronage in their states, however, they have little incentive to oppose nominations made by the President, and if they enter a personal objection, they are expected to indicate that the nominee is, in fact, personally objectionable to them. An objection by a minority senator is supposed to be based only on personal grounds, but in practice it is frequently difficult to distinguish between personal and political objections. Senator Bailey of North Carolina asserted his objection to the nomination of Charles A. Jonas in 1931 on the novel ground that the nominee had offended the commonwealth of North Carolina; but the press of North Carolina regarded the objection as political, as it apparently was. Senator Gallinger's objection to George Rublee in 1916 apparently was political, though the senator asserted that it was personal. Senator Long of Louisiana, who invoked the rule of courtesy on several occasions when he was a minority senator, succeeded in blocking the appointment of Ernest A. Burguieres as commissioner of the Port of New Orleans in 1931, in spite of the fact that the objection was obviously political. The two senators from Georgia, in 1927 and again in 1928, were able to prevent the confirmation of William J. Tilson, who was nominated by President Coolidge to a district judgeship in that state, despite the fact that Tilson was endorsed by a practically unanimous bar and the Democratic Atlanta *Constitution* stated that he was an "able, fair, and impartial judge."[22] Their stated objection to the nominee, who was a brother of Representative John Q. Tilson of Connecticut, Republican leader of the House, was that he was not a resident of the district. He was later appointed to the customs court and his appointment was confirmed without objection.[23]

Although a personal objection of a senator to a nomination ordinarily does not indicate any unfriendly relations between the senator and the nominee, in a few instances there has actually been personal animosity. Curiously enough, in the two most notable cases involving actual and justifiable animus the Senate declined to honor the objection. In both, however, the objections were raised by senators who were not held in high esteem by their colleagues. In 1938 the Senate confirmed the appointment of F. Roy Yoke to be collector of internal revenue of West Virginia over the bitter opposition of Senator Holt of that state, who stated objections that were highly personal. At the hearing and again in the Senate, Holt related that in a school assembly as a youth he had heard the nominee, who was then the principal of a high school, say about his father: "Old Doc Holt ought to be lined up against a white wall and shot until his blood stained the wall." He went on to relate the bitter feud that had long existed between his family and that of the nominee, and that Yoke had also made highly uncomplimentary remarks about his mother. The assertions of the senator, which were not disproved, constituted the strongest possible grounds for entering a personal objection to a nominee. In the debate, Senator Bailey, who presented the report of the committee recommending against confirmation, stated that if these grounds were not sufficient, "Let us throw the rule of personal obnoxiousness out of the window, and never let it come back here again."[24]

Senator Neely, who sponsored the appointment of Yoke, defended his nominee against the objection, saying that these statements had been made during the first World War, when feeling in the state ran very high against Senator Holt's father, who had been the Socialist candidate for governor and had opposed the war. Because Senator Holt had on numerous occasions shown marked discourtesy to his colleagues, they declined to extend the rule of courtesy to him and voted 46 to 15 to approve the appointment.

A similar case was that of Edwin R. Holmes, who was confirmed for a judge-ship on the circuit court of appeals in spite of the bitter objection of Senator Bilbo of Mississippi. The contest was one between the two senators from that state, with the President taking no part. The real reason for Bilbo's objection to Judge Holmes, who had served for a number of years as a federal district judge, was that Harrison had urged the appointment on the President and the Attorney General without conferring with him. Senator Bilbo declared that he had been "double crossed" and that he was "in the market for a col-league who will have some respect for me."[25] He did not rest his objection, however, on this ground alone. Since the judicial circuit included five or six states, a senator from any one of the states could not claim the right to name the person to be appointed. He based his objection on the ground that thirteen years earlier, when he was a candidate for governor of Mississippi, Judge Holmes had found him in contempt of court and sentenced him to serve thirty days in prison and pay a fine of $1,000. This sentence, Bilbo declared, was in-tended to label him a "jailbird" and to ruin his political career.[26]

In a long and bitter tirade, which took four hours and filled thirty-eight pages of the *Congressional Record*,[27] Bilbo attacked Judge Holmes, charging him with "judicial incompetency and abuse unparalleled in the court of this country." On a later date Senator Bilbo again addressed the Senate, attacking Judge Holmes for "unlawfully sentencing hundreds of people of Mississippi to the federal penitentiary for violations of the prohibition act."[28] Not content with attacking the nominee, Bilbo dragged before the Judiciary Committee at the hearings and before the Senate in the debate the fact that Senator Harrison had gone through bankruptcy as the result of unfortunate real estate ventures during the depression, connecting Judges Holmes with the case. This attack on Senator Harrison, who had long served in the Senate and was highly re-garded by his colleagues, doubtless disgusted and offended other senators.

The Judiciary Committee reported the nomination of Holmes to the Senate with a unanimous recommendation for confirmation. In the debate, Senators Burke (Democrat) and Austin (Republican) termed Bilbo's charges against Holmes "frivolous"[29] and stated that the sentence for contempt imposed on Bilbo by Judge Holmes was merited by the facts. By a vote of 59 to 4 the Senate rejected the personal objection of Senator Bilbo and voted for confirmation of the appointment. The Senate, in this case, had looked behind the charges and examined the facts, and had found insufficient cause for rejection. It should be noted, however, that the fight was not between the President and a senator but rather between the two senators, one an old and highly respected member of the Senate, the other a junior member who was not favorably regarded by his colleagues. A personal objection of a senator against the nominee of the President is one thing, but against the nominee of another senator it is a quite different matter.

Senators from the South have at various times objected personally to the appointment of a Negro to an office within their states. In 1903, when the senate was in recess, President Theodore Roosevelt gave an interim appointment to W. D. Crum, a Negro, to be collector of the Port of Charleston, South Carolina, fully aware that the appointment would provoke the objection of the senators from that state. When the Senate failed to act on the nomination at the following session, Roosevelt gave Crum another interim appointment, and when he was subsequently rejected by the Senate, appointed him to a position in the District of Columbia. This appointment was confirmed.[30] A similar case was that of Walter L. Cohen, a Negro, nominated to be comptroller of the customs for the Port of New Orleans. The Senate, on March 2, 1923, at the end of the session, rejected the nomination because of the objections of Senators Ransdell and Broussard of Louisiana. After Congress adjourned, President Harding gave Cohen a recess appointment, and the following autumn President Coolidge sent his name to the Senate again, only to have it rejected a second time, on February 18, 1924, by a vote of 37 to 35. After a conference with Republican leaders, President Coolidge intimated that he would not submit another nomination but upon adjournment of Congress would give Cohen another recess appointment.[31] A month later the Senate reversed itself and by a vote of 39 to 38 confirmed Cohen to the office which he had filled for a year without pay.

Appointments to Which an Objection
May Be Made

The rule of courtesy is ordinarily invoked only against appointments to offices situated within the state of the objecting senator, such as those of judge, district attorney, marshal, and collector of internal revenue. It has also been invoked at times against nominations of national officers, whose offices are not situated in one of the states, by a senator from the state of residence of the nominee, but this usage is uncommon. Although in recent years it has repeatedly been stated on the floor of the Senate that the rule does not apply to national officers, the Senate in 1950 rejected the nomination of Martin A. Hutchinson of Virginia as a member of the Federal Trade Commission because of the opposition of Senator Byrd. The personal objection of Senator Hill of New York to the appointment of Messrs. Hornblower and Peckham to the Supreme Court in 1894, which prevented their approval, and the objection of Senator Gallinger to George Rublee, nominated by Wilson to the Federal Trade Commission in 1915, are other examples of the application of the rule to national officers. On several occasions the Senate in recent years has declined to honor a personal objection to an appointment to a national office. Thus the objection of Senators McKellar and Stewart to the reappointment of David Lilienthal to the board of the TVA in 1945 was not sustained. In 1947 McKellar was unable to block the appointments of Lilienthal and Clapp, though he stated specifically that they were "personally obnoxious" and objectionable to him. In 1930 Senator Brookhart of Iowa bitterly opposed the appointment of Hanford MacNider of Iowa to be United States minister to Canada and stated to the Committee on Foreign Relations that MacNider was "personally obnoxious" to him. The committee, nevertheless, reported the nomination favorably to the Senate, stating that it was the prerogative of the Senate to decide whether such an objection should apply to the appointment of a foreign minister. The Iowa senator had often departed from the Republican ranks in the Senate, and his objection was not sustained.[32]

Senator La Follette of Wisconsin invoked the rule of senatorial courtesy against the appointment of former Representative John J. Esch of Wisconsin in 1921 to the Interstate Commerce Commission, but the Senate confirmed his appointment by a vote of 52 to 3. La Follette's objection to the appointment was due to the part Esch had played in the passage of the railway act that bore his name. In an editorial commenting on the case, the New York *Times* stated that doubtless a senator who stood higher in the favor of the party would have been able to block the appointment.[33]

In passing upon a personal objection of senators to a nomination, the Senate takes into account the standing of the senator, as well as the grounds of his objection, and whether the office is one situated within the state of the senator or is a national office. When the Senate declines to honor an objection, its reason for doing so is usually that the objecting senator is not in good standing with his colleagues. Thus the Senate at various times rejected the objections of Senators Holt, Long, Bilbo, Brookhart, and the elder La Follette when he had broken with the leadership of his party. A senator who has not shown the usual courtesies to his colleagues may be denied the courtesy of the Senate.

Defense and Criticisms of the Rule of Courtesy

In the extended discussion of the rule of senatorial courtesy in the Senate debate on the Jonas appointment in 1931, Senator Watson, the Republican leader, stated the rule as he saw it, saying that he had followed "the policy of voting against the confirmation of any man appointed to a federal position if and when a Senator from the State in which he lived rose in his place on the floor of the Senate and stated that the appointment was personally obnoxious and personally offensive to him."[34] In the debate in 1932 over the nomination of Ernest A. Burguieres, to which Senator Long objected, Senator Bingham of Connecticut stated: "I believe that when a Senator from a sovereign state stands up on the floor of the Senate and states that a nominee is not fit to hold a certain office, is personally obnoxious to him, that it is my duty, believing as I do, to vote with him, no matter how many of my friends may feel differently about the matter."[35] At the hearings on the nomination of Judge Floyd H. Roberts in 1939, Senator King of Utah declared that under no circumstances would he vote for "any nominee against the protest of the Senators from that state, where they state that the nominee is personally objectionable to them."[36] And in the debate on the nomination of Daniel D. Moore in 1934, Senator Wheeler of Montana stated that if a senator of either party entered a personal objection against a nominee, he would vote against his confirmation and he would expect other senators to do the same for him.[37]

Senator McCarran entered a plea to his colleagues to sustain his objection in the debate over the Boyle nomination in 1939, saying: "When will the hour come when one of you will stand as I stand here, and what will be your request on that occasion?"[38] A similar plea was voiced by Senator Neely in the debate on the Yoke nomination in 1938. With engaging frankness, Senator Neely defended his position, saying that in all the years he was a minority senator he had never entered an objection to the patronage appointments of his Republican colleague from West Virginia. "Throughout those years it was my opinion, and it is my opinion still, that the duly recognized dispenser of federal patronage in his State should, in the absence of manifest inefficiency or glaring disability on the part of the appointee, be unhampered in the matter of choosing those of his constituents upon whom Federal appointment should be conferred."[39]

In the debate on the Jonas appointment in 1932 the rule of senatorial courtesy was defended by Senator Dill, who stated: "I attach a good deal of weight to the fact that the Senators from Mr. Jonas' State look upon him as personally objectionable. I believe that that is an objection that ought to have great weight with Senators, and it does have great weight with me."[40] He thought it unlikely that any member of the Senate would declare that a nominee was personally objectionable to him without having "reasons which would justify any fairminded man in considering him personally objectionable."

A recent defense of the custom under which senators of the party in power are permitted to select the judges to be appointed in their states, and hence of the sanction of senatorial courtesy, was made by Senator Douglas when the two contested Illinois judicial appointments came before the Senate in 1951. Contending that the provision in the Constitution requiring the advice and consent of the Senate to appointments was not intended to be "lightly construed," he declared that "the Senate was expected to play an active part in selecting federal judges." He stated also that the President "cannot, in the nature of things, in the vast majority of instances, know the qualifications of lawyers and local judges within a given State as well as do the Senators from that State."[41] This position, to be sure, was advanced by members of the Constitutional Convention who favored giving the appointing power to the legislative body. It was stated at the turn of the century by Henry Cabot Lodge in the following words:

Nothing therefore is more inept than to criticize a President because he consults the Senators from a State in regard to an appointment in or from that State. The Senators are his constitutional advisers. In some way he must consult them, and it is impossible that any President should be able to know enough about the men in forty-five states to enable him to appoint intelligently unless he could avail himself of the knowledge of those who represent the several states. The consultation of the Senators by the President, therefore, is nothing more than carrying out the intent of the Constitution in the manner which practice has shown to be a convenient one.[42]

One of the strongest defenses of the custom was made by Senator Adams in the debate on the McKellar rider in 1938 to extend senatorial confirmation to all employees outside the civil service who received salaries of $5,000 or more. Adams said that his experience with the members of the Senate had led him to have the highest regard for their integrity and public spirit. "In the few places and at the few times I have had a chance to make appointments," he said, "I challenge comparison of the efficiency and integrity of the appointees with the efficiency and integrity of men who have been appointed by administrative boards and bodies. . . . The other members of the Senate and I are responsible to the people."[43] Senator Norris retorted that this speech could have been made by "the leader of any political machine in the United States— a machine kept alive solely by patronage." Continuing, he said: "When the Senator from Colorado or any other senator says he fixed up his appointments all right, and that the appointees were all good men when he got through with them, I desire to respond that if he should do that in all cases, and go to the extreme to which he ought to go in order to find out whether they are good men or bad men, he would not have any time . . . to do anything else in the Senate; he would be an office boy."[44] Senator Norris declared that the system of patronage appointments of postmasters "smells to high heaven." Senator

McCarran inquired what the distinction was between the appointments of postmasters and those of district attorneys, to which Norris replied "both of them smell to high heaven."[45]

In the debate on the Jonas appointment in 1932 Senator Borah also condemned the rule of courtesy, saying he had become "convinced it was unsound and not in the public interest.... The public is interested in just one proposition and that is whether the nominee is one who would be a fit public servant. Is he able, is he a man of integrity? The public is not interested in whether I like him or dislike him, or whether he is personally obnoxious to a Senator, or whether he is not. In my opinion, there is only one safe rule the Senate can apply, and that is whether the nominee is a fit man to fill the place, not whether he is objectionable to someone."[46] And in the debate on the same appointment Senator Hastings expressed grave doubts about the wisdom of the rule, saying that he did not "believe the people of this country are going to permit the personal pique of an individual Senator to defeat the nominee of a President for any office."[47]

In 1938 Senator Borah introduced a resolution calling for the discontinuance of the custom of senatorial courtesy on the ground that it was contrary to public policy.

WHEREAS, it has been the practice of the Senate to refuse to confirm a nominee of the President upon a statement by a Senator from the State affected that such nominee is personally objectionable; and whereas the matter of confirmation should be determined by the qualifications and fitness of the nominee, and not by the personal feelings, likes or dislikes of a Senator; and whereas such practice transfers the power of rejection or confirmation from the Senate as a whole to a single Senator, in violation of the spirit, if not the letter, of the Constitution; therefore be it

Resolved, That the Senate discontinues and disapproves of such practice and will hereafter not respect or give effect to objections based upon the fact that said nominee may be declared personally offensive or personally objectionable to a Senator."[48]

Senator Borah might have added in his resolution that senatorial courtesy also, in effect, transfers the function of nomination from the President to the senators of the individual states, provided they are of the same party as the President. His resolution was referred to the Rules Committee and was never reported back to the Senate.

In 1942 Senator La Follette said in the debate on a postmaster appointment in Wisconsin: "I have never since I have been a member of the body, raised the question of personal privilege and declared that a nominee is personally obnoxious to me, because I have never believed in that so-called unwritten rule of the Senate."[49] The following year, Senator Hatch, in opposing the McKellar bill (S. 575) to extend senatorial confirmation to all employees receiving at least $4,500, stated that when appointments have to be confirmed by the Senate, senators from the states affected actually make them, leaving

he President with only a veto power. "The right to reject, which the Constitu-
ion vests in the Senate, has become the right to select."[50] Even stronger oppo-
ition to the rule of courtesy was expressed by John Sharp Williams in 1921,
vhen he declared in the Senate that he would resign his seat before he would
·ent his private spleen or voice his private enmity to defeat a nomination,
'without being able and willing to give a public reason for his defeat."[51]

The Constitutional Issue

Discussions of the rule of the courtesy of the Senate have usually turned, not
•n its practical effects—whether the custom is in the public interest and how
t affects appointments—but rather on whether it is authorized and is in ac-
:ordance with the spirit and intention of the Constitution. The leading de-
'ense of senatorial courtesy made by Senator Elbert Thomas of Utah in 1939
n connection with the Roberts case, as well as the statement of Senator
Douglas in 1951, stressed the constitutional issues. The leading attack on the
:ustom, which was made by President Roosevelt in his letter to Judge Roberts
n 1939, was likewise based on interpretation of the Constitution. In the Rob-
:rts case the constitutional issues were sharply drawn, though the contest was
strictly a partisan fight between the President and the Virginia senators.

In the spring of 1938 the two senators from Virginia, on invitation of the
Department of Justice, submitted the names of two persons whom they
·ecommended for appointment to a new judgeship in western Virginia. The
persons whom they recommended were both prominent members of the Byrd
organization in Representative Flannagan's district and had opposed him in
:he preceding election. Flannagan, who belonged to the anti-Byrd faction in
Virginia politics and supported the New Deal, urged the appointment of
Judge Floyd H. Roberts. Both persons recommended by the senators, as well
as Judge Roberts, were conceded on all sides to be eminently qualified.

Newspaper reports had been published in Virginia that spring to the effect
that the President planned to turn over the federal patronage in the state to
the anti-Byrd faction of the Democratic party, and that Governor Price would
control it. When Senator Glass heard this report he wrote to the President
asking if it were true; but Roosevelt declined to confirm or to deny it. He
invited Glass to submit his recommendations as usual but maintained that the
President had the right to consult with anyone whom he chose, including
"Nancy Astor, the Duchess of Windsor, the WPA, a Virginia moonshiner,
Governor Price, or Charlie McCarthy."[52] When the interim appointment of
Roberts was announced in the summer of 1938 the Virginia press termed it
a "declaration of war" on the two Virginia senators. Before the appointment
Roosevelt wrote to the two senators to inform them of his decision, justifying
it on the ground that Roberts was the best-qualified man; Glass immediately
telegraphed that he would enter a personal objection if the appointment of

Roberts came before the Senate. The President had a difficult choice to make. He had been asked to choose between the candidate proposed by the only member of the Virginia delegation who supported the New Deal program, Representative Flannagan, and two persons recommended by the Virginia senators, who had consistently voted against the administration. Moreover, the two Virginia senators had recommended two prominent attorneys who resided in Flannagan's district and had opposed him.

At the hearing on the nomination, Senators Byrd and Glass entered a personal objection to Roberts, charging that the President had turned over the federal patronage in Virginia to Governor Price, an anti-Byrd man. Senator Byrd testified that the nomination had been made for the "purpose of being offensive to the Virginia Senators."[53] Appearing in support of Judge Roberts was Governor Price, who stated that he had neither been consulted about the nomination nor had been given control over the federal patronage in Virginia. Two former governors and a large delegation favorable to Judge Roberts were on hand, but only the governors and Judge Roberts were permitted to testify in his favor.

The Judiciary Committee voted 15 to 3 against confirmation. Senators Van Nuys and King, before any witnesses were heard, stated that under no circumstances would they vote in favor of a nomination against which a personal objection of the two senators of the state had been raised. The nomination was rejected by the Senate without debate, by a vote of 72 to 9, which was said to be the largest vote ever recorded against a presidential nomination.

The controversy over the case did not end with the Senate's rejection of Roberts. Two days later the President wrote a long letter to Judge Roberts, reviewing the case and commenting particularly on the constitutional issues. Senators Glass and Byrd promptly issued replies to Roosevelt's letter, and editors and columnists joined in the public debate over the merits of the case. Stressing the point that no criticism whatever had been raised against Judge Roberts, President Roosevelt wrote him that he was the "unfortunate victim" of the unwritten rule of senatorial courtesy. Under this rule, which Roosevelt stated was not a part of the Constitution, the Senate "on somewhat rare occasions has rejected nominees on the ground of their being personally obnoxious to their Senators, thus vesting in individual Senators what amounts in effect to the power of nomination." In the present case, he went on to say: "The Senators from Virginia have in effect said to the President—"We have nominated two candidates acceptable to us; you are hereby directed to nominate one of our candidates, and if you do not we will reject the nomination of anybody else selected by you, however fit he may be."

The constitutional procedure, Roosevelt wrote, is for the President to receive "advice, i.e., recommendations from Senators," but also to receive recommendations and advice from any other source he sees fit, and to make the nomination on the basis of his best judgment. Referring to the "time-hallowed courtesy" that permits senators and others to make recommendations for nomination, he went on to state that "every President has sought information from any other source deemed advisable." Although Presidents have usually followed the recommendations of senators in making nominations, the letter continued, in many cases they have not. The power of confirming or rejecting nominations rests not with individual senators but with the Senate as a whole, and it was the intention of the Constitution, the President contended, that this power should be exercised "solely on the ground of the fitness of the nominee." The rule of senatorial courtesy, he declared, amounts to a delegation of the confirmation power of the whole Senate to individual members, and has resulted in the rejection of men of outstanding ability, not because they were unfitted for office, but "on the sole ground that they were personally obnoxious to the Senator or Senators from the State from which they came." In closing his letter to Judge Roberts, President Roosevelt expressed the hope that the case might "create a greater interest in the Constitution of our country, a greater interest in its preservation in accordance with the intention of the gentlemen who wrote it."[54]

Senator Glass issued a blistering reply in which he termed the President's letter "unprecedented," "most extraordinary," and "inaccurate." What the Virginia senators objected to, stated Senator Glass, was "the delegated power of the President's political vice regent in Virginia to veto Senatorial nominations." The courtesy of consulting the senators of a state concerning nominations to federal offices in their state had existed for years, he declared, "and a reading of the debates shows that the writers of the Constitution intended it to be perpetual."

Senator Glass vehemently denied that the two Virginia senators had in effect said to the President that they would oppose any nominee other than those whom they had recommended. "We were prepared to accept any capable man," he declared, "who was not deliberately intended to be offensive to us by himself completely ignoring us and willingly making himself the beneficiary of an attempt to dishonor us in our State and among our colleagues." Senator Byrd stated in his reply that the failure of the administration to accept the person recommended by the two Virginia senators was due to the fact that they had not "accepted orders from the White House," and that the nomination of Judge Roberts was a political maneuver to chastise and disparage them. He deplored the use of judicial appointments for partisan purposes and declared that the power of appointment of district judges was divided equally between the President and the Senate, and neither should seek to exercise virtually the sole power in such appointments.[55]

On February 9 Senator Thomas of Utah challenged the assertion of President Roosevelt that the power of nomination under the Constitution rested exclusively with the President and that he was free to consult with whomever he wished. Conceding that the phrase "advice and consent" historically meant simply an "affirmative vote," Senator Thomas maintained that in American constitutional practice it had come to mean that the President must secure the advice of the Senate before he submits a nomination. "In regard to appointments," he said, "it [advice and consent] has generally been interpreted as a dual action and the Executive has taken advice. He, of course, cannot take the advice of 96 Senators about appointments to office in 48 States; therefore, he must of necessity, take the advice of those who are close to the problem." The President, he contended, has a "constitutional duty" to seek the advice of the senators of his party concerning appointments in their states, and "where possible" to accept it. He asserted that senatorial courtesy, although indefinable, is a "necessary development in the perfecting of an extra-Constitutional party practice in our federal system."* Although the function of the executive in some appointments had become at times "merely a perfuctory one," Senator Thomas stated, this had never been true of the Senate, and he warned that Presidents will continue to be made and unmade by the actions of the Senate. With characteristic senatorial myopia, he declared that the Senate is "the only creature of the government which has remained continually in existence," and "will remain that body around which Government will revolve."[56]

The contention of Senator Thomas that the President has a "constitutional duty" to seek the advice—that is, the nominations—of senators of his party for appointments in their states, and "where possible" to follow them, has several obvious flaws. The wording of the Constitution is: "The President ... shall nominate, and by and with the advice and consent of the Senate, shall appoint ..." The provision for the advice and consent of the Senate thus relates not to the power to nominate, which is vested exclusively in the President, but is required before an appointment can be made. The phrase "advice and consent" historically has meant a simple action of approval or disapproval, and the debates of the Constitutional Convention indicate that it was so regarded when the section was adopted. That the power to nominate was vested solely in the President was maintained by Washington and has been so interpreted by Presidents since that time, as well as by members of the Senate on various occasions. "It will be the office of the President to NOMINATE," wrote Hamilton in *The Federalist*, "and, with the advice and consent of the Senate, to APPOINT. There will, of course, be no exertion of choice on the part of the Senate. They may defeat one choice of the Executive, and oblige him to make another; but they cannot themselves CHOOSE—they can only ratify or reject the choice of the President."[57] History has proved that Hamilton was in error in thinking that there would be no disposition on the part of members of the Senate to urge appointments on the President, but his statement may be taken as a correct interpretation of the intention of the framers of the Constitution.

* See the quotation at the beginning of this chapter.

The distinction between the nominating power and the power of appointment was well stated by Senator Norris in the debate on the nomination of William S. Boyle in 1939, as follows:

He [the President] is not required to get the consent of the Senate to nominate. There is no constitutional provision which requires the President to consult with Senators. He may consult with all the Senators, with no Senators, with anyone he pleases to consult, so far as his power to make a nomination goes. When he comes to make an appointment, then he must have the consent of the Senate, and he does not make an appointment until he gets that consent. That is what we are to pass on now. If we approve, not the appointment, but if we approve the nomination, then the President is empowered, although he could not be compelled, to make the appointment when we have approved the nomination.

We ought to bear these two powers distinctly in mind. The Senate has nothing to do with nominations under the Constitution. It is up to the President to nominate and he is absolutely supreme. He can discuss a nomination with a thousand people, if he so desires, and he can make the nomination without discussion with anyone.[58]

Another weakness in the contention that the Constitution requires the President to consult with the senators of each state about appointments within their states, and to nominate their candidates "wherever possible," is that the "advice and consent" requirement applies not to individual senators but to the Senate as a body. If this provision should be interpreted as requiring the President to seek and follow the advice of individual senators about appointments within their states, the President would have to consult with senators of the opposite party as well as those of his own party—something that no one has ever contended should be done. To bring the Constitution in line with Senator Thomas' interpretation of it—an interpretation often advanced by other members of the Senate—it would need to be amended to read as follows:

The Senators of the same party as the President shall nominate persons to be appointed to offices within their respective states, and the President shall forward such nominations to the Senate, unless he finds that the nominee is unqualified, in which case he may nominate another person. In passing on nominations to such offices the Senate shall ascertain the wishes of the Senators of the State in which the office is situated, provided they belong to the same party as the President, and if either object, it shall reject the nomination.

The practice of the President to consult with senators of his own party about appointments in their states is based on custom and party tradition, not on the Constitution. The custom leaves him some discretion and room for negotiation and accommodation. To hold that the President has little or no discretion, but has a constitutional duty to nominate the person recommended by the individual senator or senators from the state in which the office is situated would, in effect, turn the nominating power over to the individual senators and make the function of the President truly perfunctory. It would destroy any semblance of responsibility for appointments—the prime consideration of the framers of the Constitution in vesting the appointing power in the President.

The objections to the rule of senatorial courtesy are weighty. This unwritten rule is the sanction by which members of the Senate of the party in power are able to dictate appointments to federal offices within their own states. In effect, it transfers the nominating function for these offices from the President to the individual senators of his party, leaving the President with only a veto on the choices of the senators. It is the means by which patronage appointments are retained for subordinate federal officers, who should be placed under the regular career service and should be selected by the departmental officers to whom they are responsible.

Under the rule of courtesy the Senate delegates its constitutional function of passing upon nominations to the individual senator or senators from a particular state and rejects nominees without regard to their qualifications or fitness for office. Although the Constitution does not require the Senate in acting on Presidential nominations to consider the qualifications of the persons nominated, unquestionably this was the intention of those who framed it. If the Senate were to delegate its legislative function in particular cases to an individual member and act without regard to the merits of proposed legislation, it would merit severe condemnation. Yet this is exactly what it does with regard to its executive function of passing upon nominations when it accepts a personal objection of an individual senator and votes in disregard of the qualifications of the nominee.

With respect to field offices situated within a single state, senatorial courtesy, in effect, transfers both the nominating power of the President and the confirming power of the Senate to the senators from that state, provided they belong to the party in office. In both regards it is contrary to the letter and the spirit of the Constitution. The framers of the Constitution did not trust the President to exercise the appointing power without some check by another body, yet under senatorial courtesy the same senators who select the persons to be nominated by the President later pass upon their own choices. Through the custom of courtesy the Senate is deprived of any effective voice in passing upon nominations to these offices.

The effects of political selection of the heads of federal field offices in the Treasury, Justice, and Post Office departments, which is based on senatorial courtesy, have been serious, as the current scandals in the Bureau of Internal Revenue abundantly indicate. These scandals have brought to light conditions of graft, political influence, bribery, and maladministration that have existed for years and were partially revealed by earlier investigations. In most instances these conditions are directly traceable to the patronage selection of the local collectors and their chief assistants, though the latter were placed under civil service ten years ago. These shocking revelations of political spoils are proof enough that political appointments are bad appointments regardless of whether the patronage is dispensed by the President, by the senator, or by the local political leaders.

Chapter XIV

PROCEDURE

The secret executive session is one of the relics of antiquity that still remains in the United States Congress....

But ... certainly there is no argument in this day and time of our advanced political thought for the consideration of nominations for public office behind closed doors. The people have a right to know the character of men that are being thrust upon them in high official positions.... Why, ... for a long time the opinion has prevailed among the people that [when] we close these doors, we exclude from this Chamber everybody but Senators and three or four trusted and confidential employees, and that we traffic here through senatorial courtesy to confirm political nominees.... We should so conduct ourselves as to elicit their confidence. It can not be done when secrecy shrouds our actions. Senator Pat Harrison.[1]

Nominations Made by the President

CIVILIAN APPOINTMENTS, with which this study is primarily concerned, may be divided into two categories: (1) departmental positions in which the President looks to the department to initiate the nominations and handle all the preliminary conversations and investigations; and (2) major offices for which the White House itself initiates the nominations. Postmasters, collectors of internal revenue, customs officers, district attorneys, marshals, and judges of lower courts clearly fall into the first category, and Cabinet officers and members of boards and commissions fall into the second. When a vacancy occurs in an existing commission the President usually confers with the chairman of the commission or other members to secure their recommendations, and often members of Congress who are especially interested in the work of the particular commission make recommendations. Businesses and industries regulated by federal commissions are understandably eager to secure the appointment of commissioners sympathetic to their point of view, and often they exert strong pressure, usually through intermediaries, to secure the appointment of persons whom they regard as satisfactory.

Nomination to certain higher positions, such as the assistant secretaries of executive departments, chiefs of important bureaus, members of administrative boards or courts, and the like, may be initiated either by the department concerned or by the White House. In such appointments the national chairman of the party usually wields considerable influence, and members of the Senate often seek such appointments for their followers.

The vast majority of nominations are made on the recommendations of the responsible department officers to fill vacancies within their departments, and for these appointments the President's action is almost entirely a formality. It is unlikely that the President has any firsthand knowledge or information concerning 99 per cent of the nominations he sends to the Senate. Even so, an undue amount of his time is taken in passing upon the one nomination out of every hundred to which he gives personal attention. Most Presidents have complained about the drain on their time and energy in appointing minor officers and employees.[2] It appears that before 1913 the President himself handled a large part of the distribution of patronage, interviewing office seekers, party leaders, and members of Congress seeking jobs for their constituents; but when Wilson became President he announced that all departmental appointments would be handled by the departments concerned, and that he would see only applicants whom he had invited.*

The departments in which large numbers of the offices are filled by presidential appointment—notably Treasury, Post Office, and Justice—have established procedures for receiving recommendations from members of Congress and party organizations, and for investigating the character of persons under consideration. A different procedure is used by the Army and Navy in handling the thousands of promotions of regular officers which require senatorial confirmation. Similarly, the appointments and promotions of members of the Foreign Service, the United States Public Health Service, and the Coast and Geodetic Survey, all of which also require senatorial confirmation, are handled under quite different procedures.

Presidential nominations initiated by the executive departments, except promotions from the existing staff, are usually preceded by an investigation of the persons under consideration. The FBI conducts such investigations for the Justice Department, the Treasury Department utilizes one of its five investigative units, and the Post Office Department has a special unit to investigate candidates for postmasterships. The investigations thus made, with some exceptions, are generally limited to questions affecting the character and

* See above, chap. vi.

reputation of persons under consideration. Ordinarily these special investigative staffs are not qualified to evaluate the administrative, professional, or
technical qualifications of candidates. The FBI, however, looks into the professional standing of attorneys who are being considered for federal appointment
to the bench or as district attorneys. For the higher administrative positions,
judges, and some other offices, the departments conduct also another type of
inquiry touching upon the qualifications, competence, political support, and
suitability of the candidate. Each department follows its own practice in this
regard; often an administrative assistant to the secretary is given the
assignment.

The standards which the several departments apply in passing upon persons under consideration for a presidential appointment vary widely. The
offices of postmaster, marshal, collector of internal revenue, collector of customs, and so forth, which operate within the several states, are regarded as the
political patronage of members of Congress or the party organization; hence
the departments make little attempt to require more than that the person
selected have a satisfactory reputation in the community and have no criminal
record. As indicated in a subsequent chapter, this method of appointing officers
who head large federal field agencies produces unfortunate results, for little or
no attention is given to the administrative and professional qualifications of
the persons thus selected. Not infrequently the candidates who secure the party
endorsement are found to have questionable records. The party organizations
or members of Congress on whose recommendation they are chosen may have
little appreciation of the qualifications needed; in any event they have no
responsibility for administrative results. It is only by accident and good fortune
that in some instances well-qualified persons are appointed to these offices.*

Nominations of persons to fill the highest offices—to be members of the
Cabinet, heads of independent agencies, and members of independent commissions—are made on the personal selection of the President, who often
confers with leaders of his party and others about such choices.

Presidential nominations are submitted to the Senate by written communications. Washington thought that it would be disagreeable and embarrassing
both to the President and to the Senate if nominations were made in person
and the President were present when they were discussed by the Senate.† It
has always been the practice for the President or the departments concerned,
on request, to supply to the Senate or to its committees information concerning the qualifications of nominees. For some offices it is customary for the
departments to supply a brief biographical statement about the nominee, which
is transmitted to the Senate with the nomination. Unless there is some question
about the propriety of a nomination, ordinarily no request is made for addi-

---

* This point is discussed more fully in chap. xviii.

† See chap. iii, above.

tional information. If an objection is raised, however, the subcommittee considering the nomination usually calls upon the department to supply detailed information. In the early history of the country several committees of the Senate sought to confer with the President concerning his nominations. Both John Adams and James Madison strongly objected to this practice, and Madison sent a message to the Senate maintaining that it was contrary to the Constitution. Thereafter no further attempt was made by a Senate committee to confer formally with the President about a nomination, though informal consultations between the President and members of Congress are common and it has never been contended that they are in any way improper.

Requests for information about nominees are usually made to the departments concerned, and ordinarily such information is supplied. Presidents, however, have consistently asserted the right to withhold confidential information. The right of Congress to have access to confidential records of the departments has frequently been the subject of controversy. As early as 1803 Jefferson warned his Secretary of the Treasury not to show letters of recommendation "even to our friends," for prominent citizens would not write frankly about the qualifications of candidates unless they were assured that their letters would be treated in confidence. He stated that Washington had always resisted very strongly attempts to have him produce such letters.*

The right of the President to refuse to inform Congress concerning his instructions to departments or what transpired at a Cabinet meeting was vigorously stated by Jackson in response to a Senate resolution in 1833, introduced by Clay, calling upon him to transmit a document that he was alleged to have read to his Cabinet concerning the withdrawal of federal funds from the United States Bank. "The Executive is a co-ordinate and independent branch of the Government equally with the Senate," wrote Jackson, "and I have yet to learn under what constitutional authority that branch of the legislature has a right to require of me an account of any communication, either verbal or in writing, made to the Departments acting as a Cabinet council."[3] When the Senate attempted in 1886 to inquire into the reasons for removals, Cleveland directed the departments to reply that it was not in the public interest to supply the information requested. After the Senate had passed a resolution censuring the Attorney General, Cleveland sent a message to the Senate asserting the right of the President to withhold the information requested.†

In the past ten years the same issue has been raised several times, notably in connection with the McCarthy charges against the personnel of the State Department and in the investigations conducted by the House Committee on Un-American Activities. In 1941 Chairman Vinson of the House Naval Affairs Committee requested the Attorney General to supply that committee

* See chap. iii, above.
† See chap. vi, above.

with all FBI reports of investigations arising out of strikes and subversive activities since 1939, and all future reports. Attorney General Jackson declined,
stating that these were confidential documents of the executive department to
aid the President in the enforcement of the laws, and that it would not be in
the public interest to make them available to Congress or to the public. In his
letter Attorney General Jackson gave the following reasons why these confidential reports should not be supplied: (1) the effectiveness of the FBI would
be seriously injured by making public information which it had secured in
confidence, thus revealing its sources; (2) disclosure would prejudice the
national defense, as well as our international relations; (3) the files contain
much hearsay and unverified information and accusations, which if made
public would injure innocent persons.[4]

In 1943 the War and Navy departments, acting on instructions from the
President, declined to reveal certain information to a House committee investigating the Federal Communications Commission, on the ground that it
would be contrary to the public interest. Again, in 1944, J. Edgar Hoover,
head of the FBI, refused to testify before the same committee, and was supported in his refusal by Attorney General Biddle. A similar refusal occurred
in 1948 when the Secretary of Commerce, under orders from President Truman, refused to supply the confidential file of the loyalty investigation of Dr.
Edward U. Condon, who had been charged by the House Un-American
Activities Committee with being the "weakest link in our atomic security."[5]
On March 15, 1948, the President issued an executive order forbidding all
executive departments and agencies to furnish information concerning the
loyalty investigations of their employees to any court or committee of Congress, except on his express approval.[6]

The issue came up in 1947 when the nomination of David Lilienthal to be
chairman of the Atomic Energy Commission was being considered. After
Senator McKellar had charged Lilienthal with appointing Communists to the
staff of the commission, Senator Bricker proposed that the Senate subcommittee employ its own staff to investigate the loyalty of the employees of the commission. When this proposal was rejected by the subcommittee, Bricker next
proposed that the personnel records of all employees be secured and placed in
the record before the Senate. This proposal was also rejected. Senator Hickenlooper, chairman of the subcommittee, subsequently wrote to the President
requesting that he make available to the committee "such information and
reports" on the nominees to the commission "as may be possessed by you" or
might be in the possession of the FBI or other investigative agencies of the
government. To this request the President replied that the files of all the investigating agencies had been checked again and had been found to contain
no derogatory information about any of the nominees; he declined, however,
to forward the reports.

It has long been the established policy that all such investigative reports are condential documents of the executive department of the Government and that conressional or public access to them would not be in the public interest. I believe that would be unwise to change this established policy and to set a precedent that ould seriously prejudice the future usefulness of these investigating agencies.[7]

The personnel files of the commission were examined at the direction of ie President to ascertain whether they contained any information or allegaons that any of the employees of the commission had been charged with Communist leanings or affiliations. In five cases, charges of this kind were ound in the files, and a confidential memorandum summarizing this informaon was prepared for the Senate committee. In spite of the fact that the aformation was based on rumor, hearsay, and unverified charges, and in pite of the preponderance of the evidence submitted to the committee that one of the employees were guilty of such accusations, Senator Bricker proceeded to put the memorandum in the *Congressional Record*.[8] No better illusation could be given of the precise reason that files of investigative agencies hould not be made public or supplied to committees of Congress.

In the Senate debate on the Lilienthal nomination in 1947, Senator Wherry nquired why the committee had not subpoenaed the files of the FBI, declaring hat "the membership of the committee, passing on the qualifications of these ominees, should have in its possession every record it desires. . . . Certainly, a enator who is called upon to advise and consent to a nomination should have very right that any employee of the FBI has to look over these records. . . . I annot understand why any tradition or custom should prevail that would eny the committee the right to see the entire FBI reports on these men."[9] enator Hickenlooper cited the opinions of the Attorney General to the effect nat the confidential files of the FBI could not be subpoenaed by Congress, ecause of their secret nature, and stated that the only exception to the rule vas in connection with the nomination of judges. He also added that there vere no FBI investigations of the appointees to the commission.

In the special investigation of the McCarthy charges against the State Deartment in 1950, Senator Tydings, chairman of the subcommittee conducting he investigation, requested the President to supply the confidential reports oncerning the persons named by Senator McCarthy as either Communists or Communist sympathizers. In a lengthy letter of March 28, 1950, the President eclined to do so, explaining in considerable detail why it would be contrary o public policy to permit the subcommittee to have access to the confidential les of the FBI.[10] The members of the subcommittee and its staff were pernitted, however, to see summaries of the information in the FBI files conerning these persons.

The issue arose again in 1953 when Senator McCarthy led an attack on the omination of Charles E. Bohlen to be ambassador to the Soviet Union, assert-

ing that the confidential FBI file contained derogatory information about th
nominee. Senator McCarran declared that the Senate should not act on th
nomination until every member of the Senate had an opportunity to examin
the file. But Senator Taft, Republican leader, strongly opposed opening u
the FBI files to all members of the Senate, or even to the members of th
Foreign Relations Committee, saying that such a procedure would wreck th
FBI. Senators Taft and Sparkman were designated to examine the file. Afte
they examined a lengthy summary of the contents of the file—but not th
file itself—and reported their findings to the Senate, the nomination wa
confirmed.*

An exception to the general rule has been made in respect to persons nom:
nated to be federal judges. About 1940 the Senate Judiciary Committee refuse
to act on certain nominations to the bench until it was supplied with the re
sults of the FBI investigations. An arrangement was worked out by which th
results of the FBI investigations of judicial nominees would be made availabl
to the Judiciary subcommittees in the following manner: a member of th
FBI staff would bring the investigative file to a closed session of the sub
committee and, reading from it, would summarize the information which i
contained and would answer questions.[11] This practice, which still prevails, ha
made a great difference in the action of the Judiciary Committee in passin;
upon persons nominated to be federal judges. It has made it possible for th
committee to maintain higher standards and to reject nominees with question
able records who formerly would have been approved. As a result, individua
senators exercise greater care in recommending persons for judicial appoint
ment, knowing that they will have to pass the muster of this investigation
the Justice Department and the President are also mindful of the fact tha
judicial nominees will not be approved if significant derogatory informatio
has been discovered in the investigation. Although the FBI investigation i
valuable as a means of avoiding the appointment of persons with questionabl
records, it does not safeguard against the appointment of persons with poo
qualifications but with spotless records.

The Rules and Procedures of the Senate

The rules of the Senate provide that all nominations, unless otherwise ordered
shall be referred to the appropriate committee.[12] In the early years of the Senat
it was customary to act on nominations without referring them to committee
for consideration, and in 1822 a motion to refer all nominations to committee
was tabled.[13] In acting on nominations, the Senate relied on the statements o
members from the state in which the office was situated, and occasionally othe:
senators would give their opinions.† Describing the early procedure of th

---

* An account of the Bohlen case is given in chap. xvi, below.
† See chap. iii, above.

Senate in passing on nominations, Kerr states: "Ordinarily only when the person nominated was unknown or charges were made against him, or in case of nomination of one who had charge of disbursements of money, was the nomination referred to a committee. Sometimes the nominations of ministers were referred to the committee on foreign affairs to inquire into the expediency of the appointment."[14] It was not until 1868 that the Senate rules were amended to require the referral of all nominations, unless otherwise ordered, to the appropriate committee. At that time it was also provided that nominations should not be considered on the same day they are reported by a committee, except by unanimous consent.[15]

It is the customary procedure of the Senate committees upon receiving a nomination to notify the senators from the state in which the office is situated; for national offices not situated within a particular state, the senators from the state in which the nominee resides are notified. If no reply is received within a week, it is ordinarily assumed that the senators have no objection, and the nomination is acted on. If there is no objection, ordinarily nominations are routinely reported to the Senate with a favorable recommendation.

The customary procedure was described on the floor of the Senate in 1922 by Senator McCumber as follows:

... The moment any nomination is sent to the committee, the chairman hands that nomination to some Senator and asks him to consult with both the Senators from the State of the nominee to ascertain whether the nomination is satisfactory to them.

That is ... the step which always has been taken, whether the Democratic Party or the Republican Party has been in control. If the nomination is satisfactory and it is so reported to the committee, the committee act upon it. If, however, any extraneous matters have come to the attention of the committee to indicate that there will be opposition to the nomination, ... the nomination is always held in abeyance until such opposition may be heard.[16]

If there is objection, ordinarily a subcommittee is appointed by the chairman of the committee to consider the nomination, and it has become customary in recent years for subcommittees to be utilized for certain nominations even if there is no objection. In considering a nomination, subcommittees may or may not conduct hearings, and if hearings are held, they may be open or closed. The usual practice in recent years, however, is to conduct hearings in open session, and to invite the nominee and other interested persons to appear. It is unusual, however, for nominees to the Supreme Court to be invited to appear before the Judiciary Committee.[17] When Felix Frankfurter was nominated to the Supreme Court in 1939, Senator Neely, chairman of the subcommittee, invited him to testify, but he declined, stating that he did not like to leave his law classes at Harvard for even a single day. Later, however, he did appear when the subcommittee asked him to do so, but prefaced his statement by saying that he did not wish to testify in support of his own nomination.

Frankfurter pointed out to the subcommittee that, "except only in one instance, involving a charge against a nominee concerning his official act as Attorney General, the entire history of this committee does not disclose that a nominee to the Supreme Court has appeared and testified before the Judiciary Committee." He went on to state that although the nominee's record should be carefully scrutinized, he thought the personal participation of the nominee would not be of assistance to the committee or in the best interests of the Court, and declined to express his personal views on any controversial political issues affecting the Court.*

Ten years later when President Truman nominated Judge Sherman Minton, a former senator from Indiana, to the Supreme Court, the Judiciary Committee voted 5 to 4 to invite Minton to testify. The invitation apparently was inspired by Senator Ferguson, who wished to question the nominee concerning his support of President Roosevelt's proposal to increase the number of members of the Supreme Court in 1937. In his reply Judge Minton questioned the propriety of his appearance before the committee, quoting from the statement of Justice Frankfurter. Concerning his support of the Court "packing" plan, Judge Minton stated that as a member of the Senate and as assistant majority whip he had taken a strongly partisan attitude, but that after his appointment to the circuit court of appeals, no one could charge that partisanship had affected his decisions.[18] After receipt of Judge Minton's letter, the committee reversed its action inviting the nominee to testify and voted 9 to 2 to report the nomination to the Senate favorably. The issue whether the nominee should be required to appear and testify was raised in the Senate debate on a motion to recommit the nomination, which was voted down, 45 to 21.[19]

Nominees to lower courts ordinarily do not testify before Senate committees considering their nominations, for reasons similar to those that apply to nominees to the Supreme Court, but will be heard if they wish to reply to any charges made against them. It is generally felt that the personal appearance of judicial nominees is not desirable, unless there are special circumstances requiring them to testify. Although the same reasoning does not apply to persons nominated to administrative positions, it is questionable, as a rule, whether the committee is aided by the personal appearance of the nominee. If there are opposing witnesses the hearing may take the form of a trial of the nominee, which is undesirable from every point of view. The appearance of the nominee gives the impression that he is a candidate for the office, which is unfortunate even if true. The nominee may be interrogated at the hearing concerning his views on policies that may come before him as a federal officer, and thus may be led to make commitments that are not in the public interest. A nominee is strongly impelled to give answers that are acceptable to the members of the committee interrogating him, and thus may express views that are not based

* For a review of this case, see chap. xvii, below.

on full consideration of all the relevant facts and considerations.²⁰ It is generally preferable for the Senate committees to pass upon nominees on the basis of their past records rather than to solicit their opinions in the course of the hearings.

On the assumption that before a nomination is made the department concerned and the President have conducted appropriate investigations and have satisfied themselves that the nominee possesses the necessary qualifications and is a suitable person for the office, committee hearings are scheduled ordinarily only if a protest has been made. They are utilized to afford the protestants an opportunity to state their objections to the nomination, and the nominee and the administration an opportunity to answer. Only in the highly exceptional cases are any objections raised, and these are often motivated by a special interest or political considerations. It is doubtless true that some of the worst nominations have been uncontested, and some of the best ones have been bitterly opposed. Formal hearings as a device for inquiring into the facts have obvious limitations. They afford the opponents of a nominee—often cranks and persons with no valid claim for consideration—an opportunity to smear the nominee with irresponsible and sometimes vicious charges. Senate committees should utilize more staff work in preparation for hearings, they should normally require witnesses to submit written statements ahead of time, and should permit only those in possession of firsthand knowledge and verifiable facts to testify. The investigations of a competent professional staff will ordinarily constitute a better basis for judgment on the suitability of nominees than will testimony at formal hearings.

The hearings on the nomination of Felix Frankfurter to the Supreme Court in 1939 afford an excellent illustration of opposition by cranks and extremists and the airing of vicious and unsupported charges. Of the ten opposing witnesses who appeared, several admitted that their opposition was based in part on the fact that Frankfurter was a Jew. Senator Borah strongly protested against such testimony, and at one point threatened to leave the room if the witness based his objections on racial or religious grounds. One witness was opposed to Frankfurter because he was not born in this country. Several witnesses claimed to be officers of organizations with high-sounding titles, such as "Constitutional Crusaders of America," "League for Constitutional Government," "American Federation Against Communism," and "American Indian Federation," but upon inquiry, several of these organizations proved to be entirely or mostly fictitious. Their loose assertions that the nominee was sympathetic to socialism and Communism, and was a left-winger were not supported by the evidence. Mrs. Elizabeth Dilling, author of *The Red Network,* testified that the nominee was a dangerous radical, but she also placed Senators Borah and Norris of the subcommittee, as well as other prominent members of the Senate, in the same category. After one witness had finished his testimony, Chairman Neely observed that he had not given the committee a "scintilla" of evidence concerning Frankfurter's qualifications.* The New York *Times* account of the second day of the hearings reported that "the type of evidence offered by the three witnesses turned a projected serious inquiry into a near farce."[21]

After the public hearings, if any have been held, the subcommittee meets in a closed executive session to vote on its recommendation to the full committee. The nomination may be held up at this stage and not reported to the committee, or it may be reported with a favorable or an unfavorable vote or even without any recommendation. When the recommendation is brought before the full committee, a vote is taken, at which time the committee may take up any aspect of the case in its consideration. If the committee vote is favorable, the nomination is reported to the Senate and placed on the executive calendar. Ordinarily, if the action of the committee is unfavorable, or if the committee fails to act, the nomination is held in committee. Most rejections are due to the action or inaction of the committee; very few nominations are rejected by a vote of the Senate. In the twenty-year period from 1929 through 1948, only 84 nominations were thus rejected—an average of only 4 per year. Within the same period a total of 15,263 nominations, or an average of 763 annually, were not acted on. It should be noted, however, that the major part of these nominations on which the Senate failed to act were made during the sessions of 1932–1933, after the Republicans had been defeated in the election of 1932, and in 1947–1948, when the Republicans controlled the Senate and the Democrats controlled the administration.[22] In 1950, which may be taken as a typical year in which the same party controlled both the administration and Congress, 25,699 nominations were submitted by the President, 25,590 were confirmed, 6 were withdrawn, 4 were rejected, and the Senate failed to act on 99.[23]

Under the rules of the Senate, at the end of each session, or when it recesses for a period of more than thirty days, all nominations on which it has failed to act are returned to the President and will not be considered again unless the President submits the nomination anew when the Senate reconvenes.[24] The favorite way to block a nomination is to hold it in the committee to which it is referred. If either the chairman of the committee or the chairman of the subcommittee appointed to consider the nomination is opposed to it, the nomination may never be considered at all. It is not uncommon for nominations to which an objection has been entered by a member of the Senate to be held up in committee for months, and then considered only if sufficient pressure is exerted on the committee.

Usually nominations are reported to the Senate with a simple recommendation that the Senate give or not give its "advice and consent"; in hotly contested cases the committee may submit a written report stating the reasons for its

* See review of this case in chap. xvii, below.

action, and there may be a majority and a minority report.* Nominations are placed on the executive calendar, which may be called up for consideration at any time. A motion to take up executive business is not debatable. Ordinarily such motions are made by the majority leader, or by the senator acting in his place, and are usually made near the end of a legislative day. When the Senate takes up the executive calendar, nominations are considered in the order in which they are filed, subject to the rule that twenty-four hours must have elapsed since the nomination was reported by the committee.

The great majority of nominations are acted upon without debate and without a formal vote. The nominations of military and naval officers for promotions, postmasterships, and certain other nominations are usually voted en bloc by unanimous consent. When a nomination is debated on the floor of the Senate, the chairman of the committee or the subcommittee to which it has been assigned customarily makes the opening speech presenting the recommendations of the committee. The debate that follows may be brief, or it may continue for days. Unless the Senate by majority vote in closed session decides otherwise, the debate is conducted in an open executive session. Before 1929 the rules of the Senate provided that nominations be considered in closed executive session. An account of the movement which led to the revision of the rules to provide for open executive sessions follows.

Open or Closed Sessions?

From 1789 to 1793 the Senate transacted all its business in closed sessions, though from the very beginning there was a demand that the doors be opened. Several motions to this effect were made in the first two sessions but failed of adoption.[25] On February 11, 1793, the Senate opened its doors for the first time, while considering the seating of Albert Gallatin from Pennsylvania. And on February 24, 1793, the Senate adopted a resolution to open the doors during the consideration of legislative business, beginning with the next session, and provided for the construction of a gallery. In contrast to the House of Representatives, which has always met in open session, the Senate continued to use closed sessions to transact part of its business. Nominations were considered in closed executive sessions until 1929, though in a few instances the rule was set aside and open executive sessions were held.[26]

In 1800 the Senate adopted a rule that confidential documents from the President and all treaties laid before the Senate should be kept secret until the injunction of secrecy was removed,[27] and in 1820 a similar rule was adopted concerning nominations.[28] In 1844, the rules were amended to provide that any officer or member of the Senate convicted of disclosing for publication any written or printed matter directed by the Senate to be held in confidence should

---

* In the famous Brandeis case there were not only majority and minority reports, but four of the five members of the subcommittee filed individual reports. See chap. vii, above.

be liable to dismissal if an officer, or to explusion if a member. The rules were further amended in 1868 to provide: "Any Senator or officer of the Senate who shall disclose the secret or confidential business or proceedings of the Senate shall be liable, if a Senator, to suffer expulsion from the Body, or if an officer, to dismissal from the service of the Senate, and to punishment for contempt."[29]

In 1841 Senator Allen of Ohio made a motion to amend the rules to provide for open executive sessions for the consideration of nominations, which he renewed in four consecutive sessions, but to no avail. Salmon P. Chase made a similar motion in 1853 and secured the support of Sumner and Douglas, but the motion received only 14 favorable votes.[30]

After the contest between Cleveland and the Senate in 1886 over the right of the Senate to inquire into the reasons for the President's removal of executive officers, the demand was again voiced that the Senate open its doors during the consideration of nominations. Early in the session, Senator Platt of Connecticut introduced a resolution to accomplish this purpose, and on April 13, 1886, he made a speech in the Senate in defense of his motion, citing previous attempts to change the rule. He contended that secret sessions aroused suspicion of the public about what went on behind closed doors and reduced confidence in the Senate. "Every senator knows," he said, "that very largely through the country the idea is that we bargain with each other about confirmations,... or that through some idea of Senatorial courtesy we fail to oppose men whom we ought to oppose or favor men whom we ought not to favor."[31]

Senator Platt contended that open sessions would lead to better appointments and reduce the evils of political patronage. "Bad men will not be presented here for discussion," he declared, "if it be understood that their characters and qualifications are open for public discussion and are to receive public consideration." He pointed to the three to four thousand civilian officers outside the civil service whose appointments were confirmed by the Senate. Each of these, he contended, exerted far greater political influence than the minor clerks who had been placed under civil service, and he declared: "It is a farce and a mockery and a delusion to talk about civil service reform as an accomplished fact while this goes on."[32] He viewed the reform of Senate procedure in considering nominations as a part of the larger issue of civil service reform and strongly criticized the solicitation by members of Congress of appointments for their constituents, which he said took half or more of the Senate's time. "Go stand on the steps of the White House," he said, "and see who goes there." Later in the debate, Senator Platt condemned senatorial patronage even more strongly: "I have found it the general if not the universal custom of Senators to solicit nominations at the hands of the President, and then come here and act on those nominations in secret session. If there be a more monstrous impropriety than that I do not know what it is."[33] Public sentiment, he stated, which had compelled the opening of the doors of the Senate for legislative business demanded open executive sessions of the Senate.

Senator Logan argued for open sessions, saying that honest men would welcome an open investigation, and men with bad records should not be nominated for public office. "Let the doors of this chamber be open when men's names come before the Senate, and confirmation through the mysterious agency of 'Senatorial courtesy' will give place to the honest man whose fair record boldly courts public inspection."[34] Senator Gibson declared that the "secret inquisition" into "baseless charges" against nominees was repulsive and "the most disgusting work ever committed to gentlemen." Open sessions, he maintained, would put an end to charges springing from such motives.[35]

In defense of secret sessions Senator Hoar maintained that the consideration of nominations was an executive function and as such should be conducted in closed meetings. "The advocates of this new rule," he stated, "can not point to a spot on the face of this earth, with one possible exception, where either of these two functions, assenting to treaties or selecting officers for public appointment, is performed by a deliberative assembly whose discussions are public."[36] The contention that senators regarded public offices as their patronage, he maintained, was a myth, which belonged to a time that had passed, never to return. Senator Morrill maintained that closed sessions were necessary because the consideration by the Senate related to personal matters and required "careful examination as to the character fitness and qualifications of the nominee," which the Senate performed "impartially and conscientiously." The general public, he contended, takes little interest in "these personal matters." "What do the people of Iowa," he inquired, "care about who is postmaster of Louisville, Kentucky?"[37] With equal logic he might have asked: "Why should the senators from Iowa be required to pass upon the appointments of postmasters in other states?"

Dorman B. Eaton, who had served for twelve years as United States Civil Service Commissioner, and whose duties in Washington gave him ample opportunity to observe the practices of the Senate in passing upon appointments, strongly criticized secret sessions as "one of the most prolific sources of partisanship and corruption in our politics."[38] He condemned the "vicious continuation of Senatorial usurpation under the tenure of office acts," and the unwillingness of members of the Senate to surrender their patronage.[39] Instead of the careful and impartial examination of nominees, which Senator Morrill maintained the Senate conducted, Eaton described the "corrupt influences, the bartering of votes in the Senate," and the fraud and venality in local politics, which he maintained were due to the use of local federal offices as political spoils.[40] After repeated postponements, Senator Platt's resolution finally came to a vote on December 15, 1866; it was defeated 33 to 21.

In 1915 Senator Kenyon endeavored without success to amend the rules to discontinue the practice of considering nominations in secret session, and in 1921 Senator Harrison of Mississippi, with the support of Senator Borah, made another unsuccessful attempt.[41] In defense of his motion, which provided for consideration of nominations in open session unless a closed session was ordered by a two-thirds vote, he characterized the secret session as one of the "relics of antiquity."*

Senator Harrison pointed out that what transpired in closed sessions usually "trickled out" to the press, but frequently in an inaccurate form. He advanced this as another excellent reason for lifting the ban of secrecy, and concluded with a plea that "secrecy and seclusion" be abolished and the "searchlight of publicity" be thrown on Senate proceedings. Senator Borah contended that the people had as much right to know about the qualifications of nominees for federal offices as about candidates who ran for public office, and he maintained that unfit nominees to the federal bench who were confirmed behind closed doors would not be approved in open session.

The amendment was opposed by Senator John Sharp Williams of Mississippi, who maintained that consideration of the qualifications of a man for office should be held in closed sessions so that the members could speak frankly without incurring the danger of needlessly injuring the reputation of the nominee. The Harrison amendment was lost by a vote of 47 to 27.[42]

In 1925 Senator Heflin secured the floor and began a speech dealing with a newspaper attack on him for opposing the confirmation of Harlan Stone for the Supreme Court. When a point of order was raised, Senator Heflin contended that he had a right to answer the charges, as a personal privilege, but the chair ruled that he was out of order.[43] Two days later, Senator Cummins, who was again in the chair, announced that his ruling had been in error, and on the following day Senator Heflin spoke for an hour against the confirmation of Stone. Whereupon Senator Sterling, chairman of the Judiciary subcommittee to which the nomination had been referred, rose to defend Stone. Senator Reed of Pennsylvania and Senator Reed of Missouri objected to the debate as contrary to the Senate rules. Senator Dill asserted that everything which was said on the floor of the Senate had already appeared in the press and maintained that the rule of closed sessions was silly. "The truth of the matter," declared Senator Dill, "is that this whole question is public business and ought to be discussed in public." When the nomination of Stone was taken up on February 5, 1925, a motion was adopted to consider it in open session.[44]

A week later, Senator Dill introduced a resolution to amend the rules to provide for open sessions unless two-thirds of the members voted for a closed session. He pointed out that before the doors were opened to consider the nomination of Attorney General Stone, many rumors and charges were

---

* See quotation at the beginning of this chapter.

bandied about, which disappeared after an open session. "Practically everything done in executive session," said Dill, "has been printed regularly in the newspapers. The trouble is that the facts are more or less garbled, and often the attitude of Senators who make addresses is entirely misrepresented."[45]

A year later the issue arose again over the nomination of Thomas F. Woodlock to be a member of the Interstate Commerce Commission. After the nomination had been confirmed in executive session a vain effort was made to have a roll call published.[46] Senator Pittman subsequently introduced a resolution to permit individual senators to disclose how they voted on a nomination and to authorize publication of the Senate vote if the nomination was approved by a majority.[47] The motion was supported by Senator Robinson, who favored publishing all votes on confirmations, though he did not favor publication of the debate. Senator Neely introduced an amendment to require open sessions for the consideration of nominations, and Senator Norris moved to publish all votes on confirmation actions. Senator Bingham of Connecticut, however, favored tightening up the secrecy provision by providing that the vote on nominations be by secret ballot so that none of the senators themselves would know how the others voted.[48] Although Senator Curtis, Republican leader and chairman of the Rules Committee, announced that his committee would proceed at once to consider the resolution, no action was taken.

In January, 1929, the ire of the leaders of the Senate was aroused when the vote of the Senate in closed executive session on the confirmation of Roy O. West as Secretary of the Interior was published in full by the United Press. Senator Curtis intimated that the correspondent who had given out the detailed vote would be denied the right to appear on the Senate floor, and threatened to deprive all press association representatives of this right. Senator Dill again opposed the rule of secrecy, saying: "Why men holding the high office of Senator want to keep their votes secret is beyond my imagination and a violation of the spirit of democracy."[49] Senator Norris issued a statement attacking the rule of secrecy, saying that "public business should be transacted in public."[50]

Later in the same session, Paul Mallon, a United Press correspondent, published the vote in executive session on the nomination of former Senator Lenroot of Wisconsin to be judge of the customs court of appeals. This created a furor in the Senate and led finally to the revision of the rules to provide for open executive session. The nomination was bitterly opposed by the Progessives in the Senate, with whom Lenroot had parted company. They accused him of association with Albert Fall, who had been forced out of the Cabinet under a cloud.

On May 21, 1929, Senator Blaine of Wisconsin started to read into the *Congressional Record* the roll-call vote on the Lenroot nomination, which had been published in the Washington *News*. Senator Reed of Pennsylvania objected and made a point of order but was overruled by the chair. Senator Blaine then secured unanimous consent to have the article inserted in the record. The rule of secrecy was severely criticized by several senators, and it was pointed out that many members no longer observed it.

The following day, Senator Reed reported a resolution from the Rules Committee severely condemning the breach of the rules which had resulted in the publication of the Lenroot vote as a "willful disregard of the obligation of duty and honor resting upon everyone admitted to an executive session, tending to bring contempt upon the Senate." He announced that the Rules Committee had unanimously passed a resolution to exclude the United Press Association representatives from the floor, and stated that the committee would summon witnesses to a hearing on the following Monday in an effort to determine who was responsible for giving out the vote.

Senators La Follette and Johnson maintained that the Rules Committee had no right to extend or to curtail the privileges of the floor and demanded that the Senate rules, which had never extended these privileges to any news-papermen, be enforced. Vice-President Curtis sustained them and announced that in the future the rule would be carried out. The Rules Committee planned a closed session to investigate the disclosure of the Lenroot vote, but Mallon declined to attend unless it were open and unless he could be represented by counsel. An open session was then held, at which Mallon flatly declined to reveal the source of his information. Senator Moses reported to the Senate that "the meeting was public and I think all present will agree that is was fruitless."[51]

Senator Connally thereupon introduced a resolution providing for open executive sessions, and the Rules Committee immediately secured unanimous consent that all such resolutions be referred to it for consideration. Senator La Follette procured an agreement that it should report back such a resolution within a week. The issue came to a vote in the Senate on June 18 when the Rules Committee reported out an amendment to the rules to permit open sessions when ordered by a majority of members. The proposed rule also significantly provided that the vote on nominations in closed sessions should be published in the *Record*. Senator Robinson of Arkansas offered a substitute amendment to provide that sessions should be open unless ordered closed by a majority vote. His amendment did not provide for the publication of the vote if taken in closed session but instead authorized individual senators to make public their own votes.

By this time the issue had attracted nation-wide attention, and it was a foregone conclusion that the Senate would at last amend its rules to provide for open sessions. In opposing the Robinson motion Senator Moses declared that every senator present could recall at least four recent instances in which "irreparable damage" would have been done to the reputation of the nominee, and "unnecessary anguish caused many innocent people" if the nomination had been considered in open session.[52] Senator Fess maintained that "in secret sessions we would be freer to go into all of the items of interest in cases of appointments and of treaties."[53] The only statement at length in support of closed sessions was made by Senator Smith of South Carolina, who argued than an open discussion of the qualifications of nominees would result in injury to their reputations. "At present," he declared, "any man can stand on this floor, and in the discussion of a man for an office, can damn him forever, without recourse on the part of the individual, who perhaps not by his own choice is brought here as a nominee. The President may send down some name ... and then that man is the victim of whoever sees fit even to suggest a charge against him."[54] Senator Smith suggested that if the doors were opened, the immunity of members against libel and slander suits should be removed.

The debate was concerned principally with an amendment offered by Senator Norris that the vote on nominations in executive session be published. In defense of his amendment Senator Norris said that "a roll call of the Senate, whether taken in secret or in public, is a part of the official record of public business." He contended also that a secret vote was contrary to the provision in the Constitution that one-fifth of the members present could require the taking of the yeas and nays, thus establishing a record of the vote.[55] Senator Robinson opposed the amendment of Senator Norris on the ground that it would be unfair to make public the vote taken in a closed session without giving members the right to explain the reasons for their votes.[56] In supporting the Norris amendment, Senator La Follette pointed out that in many cases the vote on the confirmation of a nomination was more important than votes on legislative measures, and in any case the vote in closed session would leak out and be published in the press, often in garbled form. On the roll call the Norris amendment lost by a narrow vote; the Robinson amendment was then adopted by a vote of 69 to 5. After 140 years the Senate finally opened its doors and provided for open executive sessions when considering nominations.[57]

Recess Appointments

Anticipating that vacancies would arise while the Senate was not in session, Article II, section 2 (3), of the Constitution provides that: "The President shall have the power to fill up all vacancies that may happen during the recess of the Senate, by granting commissions which shall expire at the end of their next session." The power of the President, under this section, to make recess appointments has been used extensively throughout the history of the country. In 1804, John Quincy Adams, then a member of the Senate from Massachusetts, wrote to his father: "In all possible cases provisional appointments are made during the recess so that when the Senate meet, the candidates proposed to their consideration are already in possession of the office to which they are to be appointed."[58]

The ambiguity of the word *happen* has led to differences of interpretation and to repeated controversies concerning the power of the President to make recess appointments. If it is held to mean *happen to exist,* then the President is authorized to fill any vacancy from whatever cause; but if it is interpreted to mean *happen to occur,* the President may make recess appointments only to fill offices which became vacant after the Senate had adjourned. Washington evidently assumed that the latter interpretation was correct, and on one occasion requested and secured legislative permission to make recess appointments to some military offices created by an act passed near the end of the session.[59] Soon, however, the first interpretation came to be followed. In 1813 when the Senate was in recess, Madison appointed a commission of three persons to negotiate a peace treaty with England, giving the commissioners the rank of envoy plenipotentiary.* When the nomination of the envoys came before the Senate for its approval, Senator Gore introduced a resolution that their appointment during the recess of the Senate and without its advice and consent was not authorized by the Constitution. He contended that vacancies did not *happen* during the recess of the Senate, because the offices had not previously been filled.[60] His resolution did not come to a vote. By confirming the appointments, the Senate indirectly sanctioned the appointments but did not thereby end the controversy over the meaning of the section.† Both Madison and John Quincy Adams subsequently defended the right of the President to institute new missions to foreign countries and to appoint ministers when the Senate was in recess.[61]

Whether the President may make a recess appointment to fill a vacancy that existed when the Senate was in session has also been the subject of several controversies. The power of the President to make recess appointments has been discussed in a number of reports of Senate committees and has been the subject of numerous opinions of the Attorney General. In spite of earlier disagreement, it is now well established that the President may fill a vacancy however it may arise, even though the office was vacant when the Senate was in session.[62] The federal statutes, however, now forbid the payment of the salary of any person appointed in the recess of the Senate to an existing office that was vacant when the Senate was in session, until the appointment has been confirmed by the Senate. This prohibition, however, does not apply if the vacancy occurred within the last thirty days of the session of the Senate, or if the Senate failed to act on the nomination.[63]

May the President give a recess appointment to a person previously rejected by the Senate for the same office, or on whose nomination the Senate failed to act? When the nomination of Charles Beecher Warren for Attorney General was being considered by the Senate in 1925, President Coolidge announced

* See chap. iii, above.
† For other aspects of the contest over these nominations, see chap. xvi, below.

that if the Senate failed to confirm the nomination, he would give Warren a recess appointment after the adjournment of the Senate. The legality of this proposed course was challenged by Senator Walsh, but Senator Butler placed in the *Congressional Record* a lengthy memorandum citing many instances of renomination and recess appointment of persons who had been rejected by the Senate.[64] The list included a number of instances of persons once rejected whose appointments were subsequently confirmed. Although the propriety of such an appointment may be questioned, its legality is well established.

Senate Reconsideration of Nominations

A vote on a nomination may be reconsidered on the same day the vote is taken, or within the next two days of actual executive sessions of the Senate. Rule 38 of the Senate provides that a nomination which has been approved shall not be forwarded to the President until the time for motions to reconsider has elapsed; but it is the usual practice to waive the rule and transmit the nomination as soon as it is approved. If the nomination has been returned to the President, a motion to reconsider must be accompanied by a motion to request the President to return the nomination to the Senate. In the past, Presidents have complied with such requests as a matter of comity with the Senate, unless the appointment was already made and a commission issued before the President received the request from the Senate.[65]

Chapter XV

CABINET OFFICERS
AND HEADS
OF INDEPENDENT AGENCIES

An insidious whisper has been whispered around this Chamber. It is that the Senate has no responsibility; that we should say to the President: "This is your office. Do with it as you please. Handle it as you might your own private property, and then in the end we will hold you responsible." Mr. President, a falser doctrine was never promulgated. It is false in fact, false in theory, false in logic, and infamous to a degree that can scarcely be portrayed. Senator James Reed of Missouri.[1]

I do not believe that there is any greater burden that can be laid upon human shoulders than the Presidency of the United States.... He is charged with full responsibility for the executive department. If there is any right upon which he should jealously insist, if there is any right that we should zealously see that he retains, it is the right to name those with whom he is to work in that department, and particularly the official family, who are close to him, and his nearest advisers. I cannot conceive, Mr. President, how we as Senators can in justice to the Chief Executive, deprive the President of that right. There is not a Senator in the Chamber who would not insist on such a right were he President of the United States....

One of the last men on earth I would want in my Cabinet is Harry Hopkins. However, the President wants him. He is entitled to him. I think it is absolutely unjust for persons like myself, who harbor resentments, to deprive the President of his right. I shall vote for the confirmation of Harry Hopkins. Senator Guy M. Gillette of Iowa.[2]

THE FOLLOWING four chapters consist of an analysis and evaluation of the operation and effects of senatorial confirmation for each of the major types of federal officers for which Senate approval is required. A different kind of review is conducted by the Senate for nominations in each of these major groups of officers. Its customs, traditions, and practices in considering nominations to the Cabinet, for example, are quite different from those it follows in passing on nominations to the courts or of postmasters. Nominations of judges and independent regulatory commissioners are scrutinized frequently with unusual care and are often contested, whereas nominations of officers of the armed forces and postmasters are usually routinely approved en bloc without individual consideration.

Cabinet Officers

By well-established custom, the Senate accords the President wide latitude in the selection of the members of his Cabinet, who are regarded as his chief assistants and advisers. It is recognized that unless he is given a free hand in the choice of his Cabinet he cannot be held responsible for the administration of the executive branch. In the last hundred years only two nominations to the Cabinet have been rejected—Henry Stanbery in 1867 and Charles B. Warren in 1925. Both were nominated to be Attorney General. In the history of the country only seven Cabinet nominations have been rejected. Four occurred in 1843 and 1844 after Tyler had broken with the Whigs and had become a President without a party following in Congress. His nominations to the Cabinet were rejected not for any lack of qualifications but rather because senators of both parties desired to embarrass him.*

The other three rejections of Cabinet nominations similarly occurred under somewhat unusual circumstances. Roger Taney, nominated in 1834 by Jackson to be Secretary of the Treasury, was rejected because he had carried out the President's instructions to withdraw federal funds from the Bank of the United States, the charter of which was soon due to expire. In the autumn of 1833 Secretary of the Treasury Duane refused to comply with the President's instructions and was removed from office, and Taney, who was then serving as Attorney General, was given a recess appointment in his place. After Taney began to withdraw federal funds, Nicholas Biddle, head of the Bank, struck back by calling loans and creating a money panic throughout the country, hoping thereby to create public pressure on the government to recharter the Bank. When Congress met in the following January the Bank issue was rocking the country. After debating for three months the Senate passed a resolution condemning the withdrawal of federal funds, but it failed to pass the House. Knowing the strong opposition which the nomination of Taney would meet in the Senate, Jackson delayed sending it in until the final week of the session. Impatient at this deliberate delay, the Bank senators and representatives had already attacked Taney, charging that he was the "pliant tool" of the President; but his supporters replied that, to the contrary, Taney had

---

* These cases are reviewed in chap. v, above.

urged upon the President the withdrawal of federal funds from the Bank. The Bank forces regarded the defeat of Taney's nomination as essential in their fight for a new charter. The Senate vote followed the usual alignment on Bank issues, resulting in his rejection by 28 to 18. The following year, Jackson nominated Taney to the Supreme Court, and again he was rejected, though subsequently he was nominated to be Chief Justice and the nomination was confirmed.*

Henry Stanbery, who was rejected as Attorney General in 1867, had previously held the office, resigning to serve as one of the counsel of President Johnson during his impeachment trial. When he was subsequently renominated to the office, a majority of the Senate, smarting under its failure to convict the President, rejected Stanbery. This action, which occurred in a period of intense bitterness and hostility between the President and a majority of the Senate, cannot be regarded as a valid precedent.

The most significant rejection of a Cabinet nomination occurred in 1925 when the Senate rejected that of Charles B. Warren to be Attorney General. After the serious scandals in the Harding administration, which had involved several members of the Cabinet, including Attorney General Daugherty, who was forced to resign, the Senate was in a mood to examine with care any nominations to that office. Warren was a man of national prominence who had earlier served as our ambassador to Japan and subsequently to Mexico and was a former national committeeman and influential member of the Republican party. He was the head of a leading law firm of Detroit and the president of the Michigan Sugar Refining Company, which was closely associated with and partly owned by the American Sugar Refining Company (the Sugar Trust). On the floor of the Senate he was vigorously attacked because of his association with the Sugar Trust, which, it was asserted, disqualified him for the office of Attorney General, in which he would be responsible for the prosecution of antitrust actions.

When the Senate by an unexpected vote rejected Warren, President Coolidge promptly renominated him, issuing a statement in which he expressed the hope "that the unbroken practice of three generations of permitting the President to choose his own cabinet will not now be changed, and that the opposition to Mr. Warren, upon further consideration, will be withdrawn in order that the country may have the benefit of his excellent qualities and the President may be unhampered in choosing his own method of executing the laws."[3] But his plea was of no avail; in spite of the fact that the press generally praised the nomination, the Senate rejected Warren a second time.†

Recent contests over the appointments of Harry Hopkins and Wallace to the Cabinet have been recounted in an earlier chapter. A notable contest arose in 1953 over the appointment of Charles E. Wilson, who resigned as president

* See chap. iv, above, for a more detailed account.
† See chap. viii, above.

of General Motors Corporation to become Secretary of Defense; the nomination was held up for a number of days until Wilson finally agreed to dispose of his common-stock holdings in that company, which were valued at about $2,500,000. With contracts totaling about $5,000,000,000 at the end of 1952, General Motors was the largest contractor to the Department of Defense. In addition to the common stock he held, Wilson was due to receive future bonuses of common stock, as well as other bonus payments and a pension, and his wife owned about 10,000 shares of common stock in the company.

When the advance announcement was made of the nomination of Wilson, Senator Byrd of Virginia, a well-wisher of the new administration, informed the associates of the President-elect of a provision in the United States Code that prohibits any officer or employee of the government from conducting business dealings with a private firm in which he has any direct or indirect pecuniary interest.[4] As head of the Department of Defense, Wilson would necessarily be responsible for contracts entered into with General Motors, irrespective of whether he personally took any part in their negotiation. When Wilson appeared before the Armed Services Committee of the Senate on January 15, 1953—actually before his nomination was sent to the Senate—he was questioned closely about whether he planned to retain his interest in General Motors and whether his retention of his holding of stock would not conflict with the statute. At this time Wilson saw no impropriety in retaining his General Motors stock and serving at the same time as head of the Department of Defense. That he had not already secured expert legal advice on the subject occasioned considerable surprise, but his insensitivity to the ethical issues involved was even more disturbing to some members of the committee.[5] And he made the unfortunate statement, which was widely quoted, that "What's good for General Motors is good for the country."

Wilson's reluctance to dispose of his stock in General Motors was understandable; such a transaction would require him to pay about a half million dollars in income taxes. However, numerous other persons in accepting appointment to the Cabinet had severed their business connections and had disposed of their stock in companies doing business with the departments they headed. Secretary of the Treasury Humphrey, a leading industrialist and a wealthy man, without waiting for the issue to be raised, secured competent legal advice and disposed of his holdings of stock in companies doing business with the Treasury Department. Various means were explored whereby Wilson might be permitted to retain his stock in General Motors. It was suggested that an act exempting him from application of the law might be passed, or that a special exemption might permit him to avoid payment of the income taxes on the sale of the stock; but sentiment mounted in the Senate against making any exception to the rule or approving the appointment unless he disposed of his stock. Eisenhower delayed sending Wilson's nomination to the Senate until the issue was resolved; he was advised by members of the Senate Armed Services Committee that there was only one solution—for Wilson to dispose of his stock. Finally, Wilson agreed to this course, and the President sent his nomination to the Senate on January 22.

On January 23 Wilson appeared again before the Senate Armed Services Committee, and agreed to dispose of his stock by April 1. He stated that he planned to make a gift of not to exceed 20 per cent of it to his children and grandchildren. Upon this assurance, the committee voted to recommend confirmation of the appointment. The nomination came before the Senate on January 26, and after a debate of several hours, it was confirmed by a vote of 77 to 6, five Democrats and Independent Morse voting against confirmation. The leading speech in opposition to the appointment was made by Senator Morse, who stated that he was more concerned about Wilson's lack of sensitivity to the ethical principle behind the law than with his failure to meet the technical requirement of the law. He also said that he did not believe it would be possible for Wilson to divorce himself from a feeling of affinity with or a bias in favor of General Motors, and contended that it is bad public policy for the head of a company that had such large contracts with the Department of Defense to be appointed Secretary of the Department. He also referred to the fact that Wilson had large holdings in oil and natural gas companies that also did business with the government. Senator Lehman opposed the nomination on the ground that Wilson had an indirect, if not a direct, interest in the prosperity of General Motors since his wife still held a block of 10,000 shares and other members of his family were heavy stockholders. He stated that the appointment would be most "unfortunate" and would lessen public confidence in the armed services. Senator Smith of North Carolina, a former president of the American Bar Association, spoke against the appointment on the ground that Wilson could not relieve himself of the responsibility for the dealings of the Department of Defense with General Motors, and contended that his appointment, in spite of his agreement to dispose of his stock, would still be contrary to the meaning and provisions of the statute. All those who spoke against the nomination affirmed their full confidence in the ability, integrity, and loyalty of Wilson.

The defense made of the appointment was brief. Senator Saltonstall reviewed the hearings and Wilson's agreement to dispose of his stock, and spoke of the nominee as a man of known ability as an executive, and of his recognized character and integrity. Senator Byrd spoke at some length about his own misgivings but stated that he was satisfied after Wilson had agreed to dispose of his holdings in General Motors. Several senators issued veiled warning that they would not vote to approve other nominations in similar circumstances until the nominees had sold any stock they had in companies doing business with the departments to which they were appointed.[6]

The Senate had several precedents for its action. Two days after A. T. Stewart, whom Grant had nominated to be Secretary of the Treasury, was unanimously confirmed by the Senate, it was discovered that he was not eligible under the act of 1789 creating the Treasury Department, for as the head of a large department store he undoubtedly was "directly or indirectly concerned or interested in carrying on the business of trade or commerce." Grant asked Congress to pass a joint resolution exempting Stewart from the operation of the law, but when passage of such a resolution encountered the opposition of Sumner, withdrew his request and nominated G. S. Boutwell to "fill a vacancy" in the office. Similarly, the question was raised repeatedly whether Andrew S. Mellon was not disqualified for the same office; but the objection was voiced after he had served in the office for several years, and the issue never came to a vote in the Senate. The nomination of Edwin W. Pauley to be Under Secretary of the Navy in 1946 raised similar questions; his nomination was rejected because the Senate considered that it would be unsound public policy to place a man identified with the oil interests in a position in which he would have to make policy decisions affecting that industry, if not his own company.* There have been other instances, not publicized, in which committees of the Senate have insisted that nominees dispose of holdings that might lead to a conflict of interest. The issue also arose in 1953 in connection with the nominations of Roger M. Kyes, a General Motors executive, to be Under Secretary of Defense, Harold E. Talbott to be Secretary of the Air Force, and Robert T. Stevens to be Secretary of the Army. After the Wilson appointment was approved, all agreed to dispose of their holdings, and their nominations were confirmed.

Cabinet nominations formerly were approved without referral to committees. When a group in the Senate attempted to block the nominations President Hayes had submitted for his Cabinet in 1877, and had them referred to committees, public protest was so loud that the Senate approved them all within three days. Since 1900 it has been customary to refer to committees all Cabinet nominations except those of members or former members of the Senate; these, as a courtesy, are usually approved without referral.

The custom of the Senate in passing on Cabinet nominations has been discussed several times in the debates on contested nominations since 1929, when the Senate opened its doors for the consideration of nominations. It was discussed at length in the debate on the Warren nomination in 1925, which by a special rule was conducted in open session, and to a lesser extent in the debates over the nominations of Hopkins in 1939 and Wallace in 1945. Senators who have opposed Cabinet nominations have usually conceded that the President should be permitted wide discretion in the choice of members of his Cabinet, and that nominees should not be rejected merely because they hold

* See chap. xii, above.

views that are not agreeable to a majority of the Senate. In justifying their opposition they have contended that the Senate has a constitutional function to perform in passing on all nominations, which was never intended to be perfunctory. Thus Senator Reed of Kansas, who led the opposition to Hopkins when he was nominated to be Secretary of Commerce in 1939, prefaced his remarks by stating that the President should be allowed the "maximum latitude in choosing his own advisers," and Senator Vandenberg used that same expression in announcing his opposition to Hopkins. In the debate on the Warren nomination in 1925, however, Senator Reed of Missouri maintained that the nominations of Cabinet officers should be treated exactly as nominations to other offices and declared that legally there was no such body as the President's Cabinet. He asserted that the Attorney General was not the assistant or adviser of the President but was responsible to the law and to Congress. This extreme position, which virtually denied the existence of an executive power, is contrary to the well-established custom of the Senate and has found little support from other members, though it may be noted that Senator Taft in opposing the nomination of Wallace as Secretary of Commerce in 1945 advanced the position that the Senate is free to reject a Cabinet nomination for any reason it deems appropriate.*

The reasons for according the President a free hand in the choice of members of his Cabinet, provided his nominees are persons whose character and integrity are not seriously challenged and are not for any reason disqualified for office, has been stated many times.† In the debate on the nomination of Harry Hopkins to be Secretary of Commerce in 1939, Senator Walsh of Massachusetts, though criticizing the presence of politics in the administration of the WPA under Hopkins, stated that the President's nominations to his Cabinet should not be rejected "except for grave and unmistakable disqualification." In asking to be excused from voting on the nomination, Senator Glass said that he disapproved of practically everything Hopkins had said or done, but that the President should have the "widest possible latitude" in the choice of his Cabinet, and "if he wants men of the Hopkins type to advise him, I think he ought to be allowed to select them." During the controversy over the nomination of Wallace to be Secretary of Commerce in 1945, Walter Lippmann wrote that for the Senate to attempt to control the President's selections of his Cabinet, and to reject a man because a majority of the Senate did not like him or did not approve his ideas, would be contrary to well-established constitutional usage, a "usurpation" by the Senate of an executive function, and "incompatible with our form of government." In the Senate debate Senator Taft declared that this argument was "nonsensical," and that any college boy knows more about the Constitution than Lippmann had exhibited in this

---

* For an account of the Hopkins and Wallace cases, see chap. ix, above. See the quotation from Senator Reed at the beginning of this chapter.

† See, for example, the quotation from Senator Gillette at the beginning of this chapter.

article. Lippmann tartly replied that "what Senator Taft does not know on this subject, as on a good many others, is most of what there is to be known about it."[9]

What precisely is the effect of the custom of the Senate to accord the President "wide latitude" in the choice of members of his Cabinet? The custom did not prevent a practically solid line-up of Democratic senators in 1925 against Warren, and of Republican senators in 1939 against Hopkins, and in 1945 against Wallace. Apparently it affects chiefly the senators of the majority party, whom it tends to hold in line in support of the President's nominations to his Cabinet. In each of these contests a few senators of the majority party voted against the President's nominee, but most of these were senators who had broken with the administration or who were pronounced independents. The vote in contests over Cabinet appointments usually follows party lines. Senators of the party in office may criticize the nominee, but they usually vote for him, justifying their vote on the ground that the President should be permitted to choose his own Cabinet. Senators of the opposite party usually concede this point but nevertheless find sufficient reasons to justify a vote against the nomination.

The special custom of the Senate with regard to nominations to the Cabinet unquestionably gives the President greater discretion in his choices than he has in making appointments to other high federal offices. For example, Wallace would probably not have been approved for any high office outside the Cabinet in 1945, and Hopkins would have faced a much stiffer fight in securing Senate approval had he been nominated for an office not in the Cabinet. The effect of the custom has been for the Senate usually to limit its consideration of Cabinet nominations to questions touching on the fitness and qualifications of the nominee and to reject Cabinet nominees only for positive disqualification.

There are other reasons why nominations to the Cabinet are rarely rejected. Most Cabinet nominations are made by the incoming President in the "honeymoon" period at the outset of his term, just after he has been elected to office and enjoys the good wishes of the country for a successful administration. To obstruct a new President in getting his administration under way, or to attack his choices of members of his own Cabinet is considered bad form and poor politics. In choosing the members of his Cabinet, the President necessarily must give foremost consideration to their ability to work with Congress, and it is uncommon for him to name persons who do not command the confidence and respect of many members of the Senate.

Assistant and Under Secretaries

It is somewhat paradoxical that although the President is accorded wide discretion in the choice of the heads of executive departments, who are his advisers on policy issues and his chief assistants in putting his policies into effect, his nominations of lesser officers who have much less to do with policy determination are scrutinized with greater care by the Senate. If the purpose of senatorial confirmation is to enable the Senate to have a veto on the appointment of policy-determining officers, as has often been stated, it would seem that the Senate should exercise the greatest care in the approval of Cabinet officers, who are the major policy-determining officers, and give less attention to nominations to subordinate posts. Experience, however, has amply demonstrated the wisdom of permitting the President to choose the members of his own Cabinet; it is essential that he choose them if he is to be held responsible for the administration of the executive departments. The same reasoning, however, applies with equal force to lesser officers. Heads of executive departments and agencies cannot be held responsible for the administration of their departments unless they are permitted to name their own chief assistants.[10]

There have been relatively few contests over the nominations of under secretaries and assistant secretaries of executive departments. Until recently the number of such positions was far fewer than it is today. The only contests that have attracted widespread attention in recent years were those over the nomination of Tugwell to be Under Secretary of Agriculture in 1934, the nominations of the six Assistant Secretaries of State under Stettinius in 1945, and the nomination of Pauley to be Under Secretary of the Navy in 1946. The Tugwell contest was marked by the familiar pattern of conservative opposition to a nominee whose writings were cited to prove that he had radical leanings; the opposition came chiefly from Republicans. Tugwell was confirmed by a large majority at a time when Roosevelt's popularity was at its height. The opposition to the persons nominated as Assistant Secretaries of State when Stettinius became Secretary came from the opposite quarter—from liberal Democrats who opposed the appointment of persons whom they identified with great wealth. The majorities which the administration nominees received in both cases would indicate that the rule which applies to Cabinet nominations is generally followed in nominations to the "little cabinet."*

The contest over the nomination of Pauley in 1946 affords a striking parallel to that over Warren in 1925. Both were men of great wealth and prominence; both had held high offices within the party; both had previously served in important diplomatic assignments. Despite their ability and demonstrated competence, both were, in effect, held to be disqualified for the particular office to which they were nominated. The opposition to Pauley arose over the fact that he was a wealthy oilman and had been nominated to an office which had much to do with determining the oil-conservation policies of the government. The Pauley and Warren cases indicate that the Senate will reject a Cabinet nomination if it considers the person disqualified for the particular position or regards his appointment as contrary to sound policy, irrespective of his standing, prominence, and general qualifications.

---

* These cases have been reviewed in earlier chapters.

The Heads of Independent Commissions and Agencies

Outside the regular executive departments there are numerous boards, commissions, offices, and agencies whose heads or members are also appointed by the President and confirmed by the Senate. The statutes creating these agencies invariably provide for this method of appointment, and it is required for the heads and assistant heads of new agencies created by the President under reorganization plans, unless appointment is under the classified civil service.[11] There are nearly two hundred officers in charge of such agencies who are appointed by the President, subject to the confirmation of the Senate.* A number of commissions and other agencies that formerly were independent have been placed under one of the executive departments, though they still enjoy varying degrees of semiautonomous status.

These independent (or semi-independent) boards, commissions, offices, or agencies carry on a wide variety of functions and exercise important powers. From the point of view of this study, the most important group consists of the independent regulatory commissions, including the commissions on Interstate Commerce, Federal Trade, Securities and Exchange, Federal Power, Federal Communications, and others. These exercise broad regulatory powers over certain industries or segments of the economy. A second group includes the temporary agencies created for the present military emergency, such as the Office of Defense Mobilization and the Office of Price Stabilization. Other independent agencies exercise certain incidental regulatory functions in the conduct of activities which are predominantly administrative in character. The United States Maritime Commission (now in the Department of Commerce), the Railroad Retirement Board, the Civil Service Commission, and the Director of Selective Service fall within this group. Several commissions, including the Atomic Energy Commission, the Tennessee Valley Authority, and the Reconstruction Finance Corporation, administer large-scale operations that involve important policy decisions. Another group, including the General Services Administrator, the Public Printer, and the Director of Central Intelligence, carry on administrative functions of a nonregulatory character. The Council of Economic Advisers and the National Security Resources Planning Board, both in the Executive Office of the President, have planning and research functions. There are several commissions which are wholly advisory; and several independent officers, including the Comptroller General and the Librarian of Congress, carry on activities primarily for the Congress itself. A final group consists of a number of judicial bodies, such as the War Claims Commission and the Motor Claims Commission.

These independent agencies and commissions vary widely not only in their

* See list in Appendix, below.

powers and functions but also in their relations to the President and to Congress. The General Services Administrator and the Administrator of Veterans' Affairs are directly responsible to the President. The Comptroller General, however, is regarded as the agent of Congress, who would be appointed by the Congress itself if that were possible under the Constitution. He is given a long term of office and is specifically exempted from the removal power of the President in order that he may have the independence which his office requires. The independent regulatory commissions are also often referred to as the "arms" of the Congress and usually are not considered a part of the executive branch. They have been created to carry on regulatory activities in important areas of the economy which have become too complex for the Congress to regulate by means of ordinary legislation, and exercise highly important rule-making as well as judicial and administrative functions. It may be questioned whether these independent regulatory commissions may be validly regarded as the "arms" of Congress and therefore as independent of the President. Like strictly executive agencies, they have been created to execute the laws and derive their powers from acts of Congress. Nevertheless, because of the nature of their functions, it is generally recognized that they should enjoy a substantial degree of independence from executive control.

In this section the main subject of discussion will be the practices of the Senate in passing upon appointments to the independent regulatory commissions and to other important commissions, such as the Atomic Energy Commission, the TVA, and the RFC. The President's appointments of single administrators to head independent agencies are treated very much like Cabinet appointments, and the Senate rarely contests the President's nominations to the Civil Service Commission or other agencies which serve in a staff capacity to him. The various advisory commissions are not regarded as of great importance, and nominations to them are rarely contested.

"It is of paramount importance," stated the Senate committee recommending the legislation creating the Federal Trade Commission, "that men of the first order of ability should be attracted to these positions."[12] The success or failure of these independent commissions will in large part be determined by the qualifications and character of the commissioners who direct their work. "If the vastly important tasks assigned to our regulatory commissions," writes Professor Cushman, "are ever handled on a level of maximum efficiency and statesmanship, it will be because we have found the formula for manning the commissions with men of outstanding ability and unquestioned integrity."[13] In establishing these commissions Congress was actuated by the belief that better-qualified persons could be secured than would be available if the functions were performed by the regular executive departments. Yet this expectation has not been realized. Professor Cushman in his excellent study of *The Independent Regulatory Commissions* has pointed out the great need for more commissioners of the caliber of the late Joseph B. Eastman and one or two of his colleagues on the Interstate Commerce Commission, and fewer commissioners whose appointments have been dictated by political considerations.[14]

The need for maintaining high standards of qualifications for these regulatory commissions was forcefully stated in 1930 by Paul Warburg, one of the original members of the Federal Reserve Board. "The scope of governmental regulation of business matters," he wrote, "all over the world will not decrease but rather increase in the next twenty-five years. Modern states can no longer succeed without it.... For us, the question is only, shall it be a non-partisan, expert regulation, or one changing with changes in party government." Warburg believed that businessmen should "feel toward these boards as lawyers do toward the Supreme Court," so that the government could call to them the ablest minds of the country in banking, industry, or trade.[15] The problem, as he saw it, was not only to ensure that the persons appointed to these commissions were highly qualified for the position, but also to safeguard against the control of the commissions either by "big business" or by politicians. The failure of President Harding to reappoint a chairman of the Federal Reserve Board, because of political pressure, and his appointment instead of persons without banking experience led Warburg to fear that service on the board in the future would be considered a "hazard rather than a high honor, and that this will exercise a disastrous influence in the years to come." After President Harding had made these political appointments, Warburg stated that "no banker, so far as I know sought appointment... nor was any particular banker urged for appointment by bankers' organizations."[16]

Herring points out in his study *Federal Commissioners* that very few persons from business are appointed to regulatory agencies.[17] The trend, which he noted in 1936, to draw persons rather from political life, most of whom have had some type of governmental experience, has apparently become even more pronounced today. The difficulties in the way of securing men of first-rate ability to accept appointment to these commissions are far greater than is generally recognized. The financial rewards which the government offers do not match in any way those offered by industry. Only by making these commissionerships posts of great prestige and honor, carrying real opportunities for public service, will they become attractive to persons whose abilities match the requirements of the positions.

The standards of qualification for membership on boards and commissions usually tend to deteriorate after those bodies have become established and as they grow older. This tendency is observable in state and local commissions as well as in those of the federal government. When boards and commissions are first established to deal with important governmental problems, they usually attract persons of high qualifications, and appointments at this stage are seldom dictated by narrow partisan or patronage considerations. Afterward, however, when their policies and procedures have become well established, their work becomes more routine and less challenging. Often the prestige of commissions suffers by reason of poor appointments, and narrow partisan considerations become controlling in subsequent appointments.

In selecting persons for appointment to federal commissions, the President is subject to serious limitations. These positions do not carry the same prestige as appointments to the federal bench, to diplomatic posts, or to the cabinet. To persons who are successful in their own walks of life, acceptance of an appointment to one of these commissions usually entails considerable financial sacrifice, as well as uncertainty of the future. The President is often impelled to use these appointments to strengthen the party and is always under strong pressures from influential members, in Congress and out, to appoint their candidates. Persons who have the most active and powerful political support are often those with the poorest qualifications. In many instances they are political hacks or lameduck congressmen who need jobs. Regional claims are often pressed on the President and sometimes become controlling.

The President and members of the Senate are also subject to strong pressures, direct and indirect, from business and labor groups interested in appointments to these commissions. The business or industry subject to regulation by a federal commission obviously desires to see persons appointed who are "safe and sound," and stands ready to oppose the appointment of persons it regards as unfriendly. Nominations to other federal offices, with few exceptions, are not of such direct concern to organized groups; hence they are much less likely to face active opposition. The business groups subject to regulation usually exert strong pressure on the President and the Senate to secure the appointment of persons they regard as favorable to them. Since it would be unseemly for them openly to support candidates, they usually work through their friends, particularly through members of Congress; but their influence is none the less extremely powerful. The support of industries is not infrequently solicited by active candidates who are prepared to make discreet assurances; usually it is given to those who have the necessary political sponsorship and who are regarded as friendly to the industry. Seldom do such candidates have any special qualifications for the appointment they seek, but this does not prevent them from securing political support and support from the industry concerned. It is invariably known to members of the Senate whether a nominee has the active support of the regulated business group or of labor, and such support usually aids the nominee in securing the approval of the Senate.[19]

Organized labor is similarly concerned with appointments to regulatory commissions and frequently lends its support to friendly candidates, sometimes with a unified front, sometimes divided. In addition to these pressures, the President must consider the general attitude and philosophy of persons under consideration, and whether they are in accord with the program and policies of the administration. Finally, personal factors often play an important role. The President may desire to appoint a friend to an important commission, irrespective of party, regional, or other pressures; or such an appointment may be pressed on him by close advisers. Mansfield points out that this factor has often been the controlling one and in some instances has resulted in the appointment of very good men, though often the reverse has been true.[19]

In selecting persons for appointment to regulatory commissions the President must necessarily consider whether they will meet with the approval or the opposition of the Senate, and what the effect of their nomination may be on his legislative program. The rejection of an important nomination lowers the prestige and influence of the President and may lead to strained relations with senators of his own party. He must give serious consideration to candidates pressed on him by members of Congress, particularly by the leaders whose support he needs to secure the adoption of his legislative program. It is well known that many commissioners owe their appointment to the intercession of a member of the Senate.[20] A person nominated to an important commission ordinarily must have a sponsor in the Senate who lines up the votes to assure his confirmation. Senators who press for appointments on regulatory commissions, it should be noted, are not held responsible for the policies or operation of these commissions; hence they are not likely to be greatly concerned about the qualifications of their candidates. They are influenced rather by other considerations and often seek these appointments as a reward for their followers. In some instances they are closely associated with interested business or labor groups and urge the appointment of persons who are backed by these groups.

Because of these various influences and pressures for appointments to federal commissions, which no President can escape or disregard, in many instances persons with inadequate qualifications are appointed. When selections are made to satisfy personal, partisan, and regional claims, or the pressures of interested groups, considerations of qualifications become distinctly secondary.

Presidential appointments to federal commissions have varied widely in quality. All Presidents have consistently chosen persons of higher caliber for some commissions than for others. Persons appointed to commissions with relatively high prestige, such as the Federal Reserve Board and the Interstate Commerce Commission, have been better qualified than those appointed to commissions with less prestige. All Presidents have at times yielded to political and other pressures and have made unsuitable appointments. In his scholarly study of the Interstate Commerce Commission, Professor Sharfman states that appointments to it have been, on the whole, creditable both to the President and to the Senate; yet he observed that there had been much unevenness in commission personnel and deplored the political deals which marked a number of appointments in the Coolidge administration.[21] Professor Mansfield, who was much more critical of the appointments to the ICC, stated in 1932 that only six or seven of the preceding twenty nominations to the commission had been made on the basis of merit.[22] Yet the ICC stands at the top of the regulatory commissions in prestige and has greatly benefited by the tradition of reappointment of incumbent commissioners, a practice which has not obtained to the same extent in other commissions.[23]

The personnel of most other federal commissions over the years has not, as a rule, been as good as that of the Federal Reserve Board and the ICC. The TVA, the Securities and Exchange Commission, and the Atomic Energy Commission have had able boards; but the Maritime Commission, Civil Service Commission, Federal Trade Commission, Tariff Board, and Reconstruction Finance Corporation have not been so fortunate. Federal commissions have usually had at least a nucleus of competent members who have to a large extent directed and set the tone of their work. Some political appointees have turned out to be useful and effective members, but most of them have been quite the opposite. In 1950 and 1951, two federal commissions were involved in serious charges of mismanagement, incompetence, and political favoritism, directly traceable to political appointments of members of these commissions. The Maritime Commission, which has had a long history of political administration, was investigated by several congressional committees and the Comptroller General over a period of several years after World War II; finally, in 1950, the entire commission was ousted as the result of the serious charges brought against it.[24]

The Reconstruction Finance Corporation was similarly involved in a series of sensational scandals, which were brought to light by the investigations of the Fulbright subcommittee of the Senate in 1951. As a result, the members of the commission were ousted and a single administrator was placed in charge of its operations.[25] It can hardly be doubted that the members of both commissions who were involved in these charges and scandals had been given their appointments because of political or personal influences. The members of the Maritime Commission had been approved by the Senate when their nominations came before it, and this was also true of two of the three members of the RFC who were involved in the scandals.[26] The scandals and charges of mismanagement of these two commissions afford striking evidence of the political influences which often dictate appointments of federal commissioners, and of the fact that appointment by the President and confirmation by the Senate do not constitute an adequate safeguard against bad appointments.

What tests has the Senate applied in considering nominations to regulatory commissions? The statutes creating these commissions provide that not more than a specified number of members shall belong to the same political party, thus requiring the commissions to be bipartisan in their membership.[27] Writers

n the subject have generally criticized the requirement as having little signi-
icance and tending to create bipartisan rather than nonpartisan commissions.
Professor Sharfman states that at no time have the political affiliations of
members of the ICC exerted any influence on their determinations, but the
bipartisan requirement has tended to increase the influence of patronage con-
iderations in appointments.[28] "From any other point of view than that of
patronage," Professor Mansfield wrote of the ICC, "the bipartisan provision
s obsolete and unnecessary. There is no longer need to fear that a dominant
party might use the Commission to oppress its rival. The Commission often
divides on rate and other decisions, but it has never divided along party lines
n any decision."[29] It may be assumed that the same has been generally, but not
nvariably, true of other commissions. It is of interest to note that the requirement of bipartisan membership of the ICC was strongly condemned in a
traffic journal editorial some years ago. "What has the political membership
of an appointee to do with his work on the commission? If this is a nonpartisan
nd quasi-judicial tribunal even to raise the question of partisan affiliation is
idiculous."[30]

Members of the Senate have usually commended the principle of bipartisan-
hip, and this is one requirement which Senate committees usually enforce.
Senator Norris, however, no partisan himself, strongly criticized the provision
n several occasions. In the debate on the executive reorganization bill in
938 he stated that "such boards should be nonpartisan rather than bipartisan"
nd related how, in Wilson's administration, he had opposed such a provision
n a law creating a farm loan board. "I considered that on any board of that
kind," he said, "it did not make any difference whether the members were all
Republicans or all Democrats, or whether any of them belonged to either party.
 think the best way to obtain a good board is to disregard partisan politics."
Continuing, he graphically described how this requirement had worked out
n this instance:

However, the provision to which I refer was put in the law; and to my astonishment when the subcommittee met in the committee room, it devoted nearly the
entire forenoon to discussing the politics of the men who had been nominated by
President Wilson to be members of the Board. The Democrats were not satisfied
with the three Democrats, and the Republicans were not satisfied with the two Republicans.... Nothing was said about their ability to perform the functions of their
ffice. That was admitted. There was no objection to them on that ground. They
were good men, able, and competent to carry out the work of the Board, but they
were not sufficiently strong politicians.

Before I went into the committee room I was lectured in the cloakroom by the
eader of the Republican side, who said he was dissatisfied with the Republican
ominees. He said: "There is only one question involved that you ought to con-
ider when you go to the subcommittee meeting. We do not care who the Demo-
rats are, but will the Republicans see to it that we get our share of the jobs? That
 the thing to be passed on."[31]

The requirement of bipartisanship has not provided any assurance that different points of view will be represented on the commission. Presidents have usually appointed members of the opposite party who were in general agreement with their own policies, and often have appointed persons who supported their candidacy in the preceding election. Indeed, it is not uncommon for the strongest supporters of the President's program to be commissioners of the opposite party. It is also significant that often the ablest members of the commissions have been independents and persons appointed to represent the opposite party.[32] In their selection the President has been under less political pressure and has not had to use these appointments to reward active partisans of his own party. Mansfield states that "the best thing that can be said for the bipartisan provision in the statute now is that it enables the President, if he so chooses, to disregard partisan consideration in the appointment of nearly half of the Commission."[33]

Nominees to independent commissions are usually questioned by the Senate committees concerning their party affiliation, and it is not uncommon for them to be opposed on the ground that they are not bona fide members of the party they are supposed to represent. Senators of both parties are often insistent that nominees be party "regulars" who are acceptable to the party organization. Candidates who have professed their party regularity have been looked upon with favor, whereas mugwumps, irregulars, and independents have often incurred opposition.[34] It may be noted, however, that party regularity has not always been required. Some of the ablest persons appointed to commissions have been independents or persons without political sponsorship. This has been notably true in promotions of members of the permanent staff to membership on the commission. David Lilienthal and Gordon Clapp both testified in 1947 that they were independent in politics.

Regional claims play an important part in appointments to regulatory commissions. There are not enough positions on any commission to satisfy the various regions and sections of the country, although some commissions have been increased in size to meet this demand and as a result have become too large for the most efficient operation. Senators who press for appointment of candidates usually advance the claims of their section for representation on the particular commission, and bills have frequently been introduced to require regional distribution of the membership of commissions. Fortunately, such provisions have not been adopted, except for the Federal Reserve Board, for which it is perhaps justified. The President necessarily must take regional factors into account, although he is not required by legislation to do so. A study of the appointments indicates that over a period of time a fair distribution of appointments from all sections of the country has been maintained.

The effect of regional claims was strikingly illustrated in several contests over appointments to the ICC in the period 1925 to 1928.[35] In 1925 President

Coolidge nominated Thomas F. Woodlock, a financial writer of the New York *Sun* and former editor of the *Wall Street Journal*, to the commission. Nominally a Democrat, Woodlock was very sympathetic to the claims of the railroads for increased revenues. His appointment was vigorously opposed by Senators Smith of South Carolina and Underwood of Alabama, both of whom asserted the right of the South to be represented on the ICC. In the preceding forty years only two Southerners had been appointed to the commission. Coolidge, after the Senate adjourned without acting on the nomination, it is reported, offered the post to a South Carolinian, and when he declined, gave Woodlock a recess appointment. When the lake cargo rate case came before the ICC several months later, Woodlock voted with the majority against the petition of the Pittsburgh coal interests for a rate reduction, thus incurring the opposition of the Pennsylvania senators. Faced also with the opposition of the Southern senators and the Progressives, who thought that Woodlock was too friendly to the railroads, his confirmation appeared unlikely. At this juncture, Commissioner McChord from Kentucky resigned, providing a vacancy on the commission, and to fill it Coolidge nominated R. V. Taylor of Alabama, who had the backing of Senator Underwood. Thereupon the Southern Democrats withdrew their opposition to Woodlock; but Senator Reed of Pennsylvania threatened to block every appointment to the commission until the claims of his state were recognized. Before the nomination of Woodlock came to a vote, Coolidge placated the Pennsylvania senators by assuring them that the next appointment would go to that state, and the White House announced that in future appointments the claims of Pennsylvania, the South, and the Southwest would be recognized. This agreement virtually assured the approval of Woodlock, whose appointment was confirmed after an acrimonious five-hour debate in which the charge of "deals" was freely made. Senator Reed saw nothing unethical in the understanding he had secured from the President, stating in the debate: "I have not opposed Mr. Woodlock for any reason except the non-recognition of Pennsylvania and her industries, and having won that point, I am glad to stand with the administration in the vote on Mr. Woodlock."[36]

In 1927, when the term of another commissioner of the ICC expired, President Coolidge nominated Cyrus E. Woods of Pennsylvania, who had the backing of the two senators from that state and Secretary of the Treasury Mellon. This nomination immediately aroused great opposition because of the lake cargo rate case which was pending before the commission in a rehearing. It was assumed that Woods, who had previously been the general counsel of the Pittsburgh Coal Company, would side with the several commissioners who had previously voted in favor of reduced rates for the Pittsburgh district. Senator Neely of West Virginia, whose coal-mining interests were vitally concerned by the rate case, led the opposition. It was charged that the commission was being stacked and that appointments were pawns in a patronage game. The New York *World* called the appointment the worst made by Coolidge since his nomination of Brossard and Warren. After a bitter fight, which lasted for a month, Woods was defeated by a vote of 48 to 31. Senator Reed next urged the appointment of Representative Temple of Pennsylvania; but Coolidge, evidently believing that he had lived up to his agreement, and unwilling to face a second fight over the same issue, gave the nomination to Ezra Brainerd, Jr., a resident of Oklahoma, another section which he had promised would be recognized.

A year later the regional fight between Pennsylvania and the other coal-mining states which competed for the Great Lakes market broke out again over the renomination of Commissioner John J. Esch. In the lengthy rehearing of the lake cargo rate cases, two commissioners, Aitchison and Esch, changed their votes, and Pittsburgh and some Ohio areas were granted preferential rates because of their shorter hauls. Senator Neely again led the fight on the nominee, freely admitting that his coal-operator constituents had told him that it was Esch's head or his own in the election which he faced that year. As it turned out, in was both, for Esch was rejected, and Neely was defeated in the Republican landslide of 1928.

In 1929, when the term of Taylor expired, President Hoover did not reappoint him but named instead a judge from Tennessee, R. M. Jones, a Republican who had the endorsement of the senators of Tennessee and Kentucky and other strong political support. Senator Underwood, the political sponsor of Taylor, was dead, and Hoover was doubtless strongly urged to recognized the claims of Republicans in the Southern states which he had carried in 1928. Senators Smith of South Carolina and Black of Alabama, who had succeeded Underwood, again demanded the appointment of a Southern Democrat, and when the nomination of Jones came up for a vote, it was referred back to the committee for hearings. Not wishing to undergo the grilling that Woods had earlier been subjected to, Jones asked that his name be withdrawn. To replace Jones the President nominated another Tennessean, Hugh M. Tate, a Knoxville attorney who had formerly held the same judgeship as Jones and who had the same backing. The nomination of Tate was opposed by the Southern Democrats, but it was confirmed by a vote of 48 to 18. "The really sound objection to Tate," states Professor Mansfield, "was not mentioned in the Senate debate. That was, that like so many other appointees he was fitted neither by training nor experience for his duties."[37]

Another appointment the following year also illustrated the strong influence of sectional claims. When Commissioner Campbell of Spokane, spokesman of the intermountain interests, retired in 1929 to return to private practice, his place was filled by William E. Lee, chief justice of the Idaho supreme court. Regional pressures are highly important factors in appointments to federal commissions. Professor Mansfield lists ten out of thirty-two appointments to the ICC in the period 1905 to 1931 in which geographical influences were clearly discernible.[38] There is, of course, a close relation between geographical claims and political influence.

There have been several recent instances in which members of regulatory commissions were actively opposed by the regulated industry because of their zeal in supporting effective regulation. In 1947 James M. Landis was not reappointed to the Civil Aeronautics Board, of which he had served as chairman, because of the opposition of the air lines. Although President Truman had assured Landis of his intention to reappoint him, the White House announced shortly before his term expired that he would not be reappointed. Landis stated to the press at the time that "there is no question that the airlines were against me. I am against monopolistic practices and a number of things that they have been doing."[39] James L. Fly resigned as chairman of the Federal Communications Commission at the end of 1944, to resume his law practice, after a bitter struggle with the largest radiobroadcasting companies.[40] Leland Olds, in 1949, and James Buchanan, in 1952, were rejected when renominated to the Federal Power Commission, because of opposition by the gas industry.[41]

The requirement of senatorial confirmation of appointments to independent regulatory commissions has not provided an effective safeguard against bad or unsuitable appointments. In many instances the President has nominated persons with political backing who were poorly qualified, yet few of such appointments have been rejected by the Senate. Most of the contests have turned rather on policy questions: whether the nominee favored vigorous public regulation or was sympathetic to the position of the regulated industry. Herring has pointed out that the Senate has not required that commissioners have a neutral attitude but has approved numerous appointments of persons known to have definite and pronounced biases on the subjects that come before the commissions to which they were appointed. For example, Robert L. O'Brien, who testified that he was a "Republican protectionist," was approved for the Tariff Commission in 1932, as was Commissioner Burgess, who before his appointment had for years been a lobbyist for high tariffs, and Commissioner Marvin, who previously had been the secretary of the Home Market Club of Boston.[42] It would be too much to expect commissioners with backgrounds such as these to maintain a judicial or scientific attitude on the problems of the tariff.

Except for the Federal Reserve Board, and possibly one or two other commissions, the Senate seldom makes an effort to inquire whether the nominee has special qualifications through training or experience for service on the particular commission. It is usually content if the person is a man of good reputation and standing and is not disqualified by statutory provisions. Yet the work of most of the regulatory commissions has become so technical and complex that commissioners can make little contribution until they have acquired a thorough background and understanding of the policies and procedures of the commission and also of the industrial, economic, and engineering problems with which it is concerned. Many commissioners when they are appointed are so old that it is unlikely that they will ever achieve the knowledge and proficiency that are needed. The criticism which the *Traffic World* made of the appointment of Claude R. Porter, a former Democratic Congressman from Iowa, to the ICC in 1928, that he was "well qualified in character and general attainments, but the usual objection lies that he has had no experience in the subjects with which he has to deal,"[43] would apply equally well to most initial appointments to federal commissions.

In several instances the Senate has approved nominees to independent commissions who were attacked on the ground that they lacked the necessary qualifications. Thus Truman's nominations of James K. Vardaman to the Federal Reserve Board and George E. Allen to the RFC in 1946 were attacked on this ground, but both were confirmed. The nomination of former Senator Mon C. Wallgren in 1949 as chairman of the National Resources Planning Board was blocked in the Armed Services Committee on the ground that he was not qualified for the heavy responsibilities of the post and did not have the necessary knowledge and experience to direct the planning of industrial mobilization for defense. Three years later, in January, 1952, for this post the Senate confirmed the nomination of Jack Gorrie, who had been an assistant to Wallgren when he was governor of Washington. If Wallgren lacked the necessary qualifications, it would appear that Gorrie was similarly handicapped. A few months after Wallgren was rejected in 1949, he was nominated and promptly confirmed to the position on the Federal Power Commission for which Leland Olds had been rejected, though Wallgren's qualifications for that post were little, if any, better than they were for the chairmanship of the National Resources Planning Board.*

The practice of the Senate in passing on nominations to nonregulatory commissions, such as the Atomic Energy Commission and the TVA, does not differ materially from its consideration of appointments to regulatory commissions. If the President has the support of a majority of the Senate, his nominations to such commissions are seldom contested. The widely publicized contests over the nominations of David Lilienthal to the Atomic Energy Commission and Gordon Clapp to the TVA board in 1947 may be attributed for the most part to the fact that the Republican party had captured control of the Senate in the 1946 election. When these nominations came before the Senate, the party was still undecided about the policy it would follow on nominations; some Republican senators (with the support of several Democrats) urged the rejection of all New Dealers and Fair Dealers who were

---

* The Wallgren case is reviewed in chap. xii, above.

nominated to important offices with long terms. It was generally conceded that
Lilienthal and Clapp were well qualified. When the charge that they were
sympathetic or tolerant of Communists was disproved, they were attacked as
New Dealers. The dominant motif of both contests was political. The Republican leaders were seeking a suitable issue for the 1948 campaign and were
maneuvering for position. In making his nominations, the President had
necessarily been faced with choices having significant political implications.
His choice of Lilienthal and Clapp to head these commissions indicated the
kind of policies and administration he would support. The opposition to them
by Senator Taft and certain other Republican leaders indicated support of a
different kind of policy. The decision of the Senate was just as important as
any legislation it might have passed on the subject.

The record of the Senate in passing upon appointments to independent
regulatory commissions, on the whole, appears to support the conclusion of
Professor Cushman:

> The results of the requirement of senatorial confirmation have been thoroughly
> bad in very many more cases than those in which the public interest has been pro-
> tected by it. The usual consequence of the requirement is to subject the appoint-
> ments to the customary tugging and hauling by which intersectional logrolling and
> partisan spoils are manipulated. It makes it much more difficult to establish a sound
> tradition for the appointment of able non-political officials or a tradition of re-
> appointment of able members whose services ought to be retained."

Yet there is little to indicate that appointment by the President alone, if this
were possible under the Constitution, would produce better results. What is
needed is the development of higher standards for appointment to these commissions, improved prestige of the commissions, larger compensation to its
members, and a tradition for the reappointment of commissioners who have
given good service. Since persons with backgrounds in regulated business or
industry are usually disqualified by statutory provisions, the government will
need increasingly to turn to the staffs of the commissions themselves for
persons with the kind of training and experience needed. Admission to the
bar, political experience, and a good reputation are not in themselves suitable
qualifications, though they have often been accepted as such.

DIPLOMATIC OFFICERS

The Senate has nothing whatever to do with the negotiation of treaties or the conduct of our foreign intercourse and relations save the exercise of the one constitutional function of advice and consent ... to the making of a treaty.... From the foundation of the Government it has been conceded in practice and in theory that the Constitution vests the power of negotiation and the various phases—and they are multifarious—of the conduct of our foreign relations exclusively in the President. And, Mr. President, he does not exercise that constitutional power, nor can he be made to do it, under the tutelage or guardianship of the Senate. Senator Spooner of Wisconsin.[1]

Mr. President, I think it is perfectly clear that under this proposed treaty [peace treaty with Germany] *no one can represent the United States and speak with authority as an officer of the United States on the Reparations Commission, or on any other commission, unless the office has been created by the Congress and the holder of the office has been confirmed by the Senate ... We cannot by statute or treaty take away the constitutional right of the President to authorize somebody to get information for him, but we can provide that the United States shall not be represented or committed or shall not participate in any proceeding under this treaty without the consent of Congress.* Senator Lodge.[2]

THE DOMINANT ROLE which the Senate plays in foreign relations is not due to its power of confirmation of diplomatic appointments; it is due rather to its power to approve or disapprove treaties, and to its power, in conjunction with the House, to vote funds and to enact legislation relating to our foreign policies. Although an early draft of the Constitution provided that ambassadors should be appointed by the Senate rather than by the President, they have always been regarded in a peculiar sense as the personal representatives of the President in his conduct of relations with foreign countries. Obviously they should be persons who enjoy the full confidence of the President; accordingly the Senate has seldom questioned a President's choice of diplomatic representatives. The growing practice within recent years to appoint career men to diplomatic posts has also tended to remove these nominations from the arena of controversy in the Senate. Under the custom which accords the President a free hand in the selection of members of his Cabinet, his choice of Secretary of State has rarely been seriously challenged in the Senate.* There have also been few contests over appointments of Assistant and Under Secretaries of State.

The present practice of according the President a relatively free hand in the choice of persons to assist him in the conduct of foreign relations has not always prevailed. In our earlier history, when the Senate passed on diplomatic appointments, it used the occasion to review the foreign affairs of the country, several nominations being debated for days. When Washington nominated ministers to Paris, London, and The Hague in 1791, the nominations were held up for several weeks while the Senate debated a resolution opposing the creation of such missions. Secretary of State Thomas Jefferson advised Washington that it was not within the powers of the Senate to pass upon the grade or destination of a diplomatic representative, but only upon the person named.† On January 17, 1792, Jefferson wrote to Thomas Pinckney, whose nomination as minister to England had been delayed: "Some members of the Senate, apprehending that they had a right of determining the *expediency* of foreign ministers, as well as the *persons* named, took that occasion of bringing forward the discussion of that question, by which the nominations were delayed two or three weeks."[3] In an opinion given to Washington on the powers of the Senate, Jefferson stated that "the transaction of business with foreign nations is *Executive altogether*. It belongs, then, to the head of that department, except as such portions of it as are especially submitted to the Senate. Exceptions are to be construed strictly."[4]

A motion was made in 1792 that in passing upon nominations of diplomatic representatives the Senate should not limit its consideration to the fitness of the nominee but should consider as well the need for the mission. Although the motion was defeated by a narrow majority, the Senate continued for a number of years to inquire into the expediency of establishing ministers at the foreign courts when initial nominations were submitted.[5] On this ground it unanimously rejected the nomination of William Short to be minister to Russia in 1809, at a time when our relations with both England and France were

---

* See, however, the account (in chap. iii, above) of Madison's inability to appoint Gallatin as Secretary of State because of the opposition of Senators Leib, Giles, and Smith, and the disastrous results when he acceded to their wishes and appointed a man in whom he had no confidence.

† See chap. iii, above.

strained, and Jefferson desired to exchange ministers with Russia. When Madison became President that year he nominated John Quincy Adams to the Russian court, and the Senate rejected him for the same reason by a vote of 17 to 15. Several months later, however, Adams was renominated and his nomination was confirmed.* In 1813 Madison's nomination of Jonathan Russell to be minister to Sweden was rejected on this ground, but six months later it was confirmed. Commenting on the rejection of John Quincy Adams as minister to Russia in 1809, Henry Adams later wrote:

Dislike of diplomacy was a relic of the old colonial status when America had been dependent on Europe,—a prejudice arising chiefly from an uneasy sense of social disadvantage. Whenever America should become strong and self-confident, these petty jealousies were bound to disappear, and her relations with other Powers would be controlled solely by her wants; but meanwhile the Senate in every emergency might be expected to embarrass the relations of the Executive with foreign governments, and to give untenable reasons for its conduct.[6]

At the outset of his term, Washington looked upon the Senate as a council to advise him in the conduct of foreign relations and sought to maintain close and consultative relations with it. He kept it informed on foreign affairs and, before entering into treaty negotiations with other powers, not only submitted nominations of commissioners to conduct the negotiations but accompanied his nominations with proposed instructions and other documents, often indicating the principal features of the treaty he proposed to negotiate. In this early period the Senate resolutions approving the appointment of commissioners to negotiate treaties commonly pledged the Senate to ratify the proposed treaty. In 1792, after the Senate had approved the appointment of William Carmichael and William Short to negotiate a treaty with Spain concerning the navigation of the Mississippi River, Spain expressed a desire to enter into a treaty dealing generally with commercial relations between the two countries. Jefferson advised Washington that it would be necessary to ask the Senate for its concurrence in the extension of the authority of the commissioners. The Senate agreed to the extension, pledging itself to ratify a treaty negotiated in conformity with the instructions.[7] Letters and other communications from other countries were at first often addressed to the President and the Congress, and frequently were forwarded to the Senate for its information, much to the perturbation of the British ambassador, who complained that they might be published in a "common newspaper."[8]

Washington's early conception of the Senate as an advisory council, particularly in foreign affairs, was in keeping with the prevailing ideas of members of the Constitutional Convention of 1787, in which it was frequently so referred.[9] It was a plausible assumption, based on the precedent of the gov-

* See chap. iii, above.

ernor's council in the colonies. It should be remembered, also, that initially the Senate consisted of only twenty-six members, not all of whom would ordinarily be in attendance. Jefferson, who was not a delegate to the Convention, took a different view of the relations between the President and the Senate in the conduct of foreign affairs and advised Washington that "the Senate is not supposed by the constitution to be acquainted with the concerns of the Executive department. It was not intended that these should be communicated to them."[10]

Washington's attempt to deal with the Senate as an advisory council ended in failure. In 1789 he attempted to consult personally with the Senate as a body concerning the negotiation of proposed Indian treaties and sent a note advising the Senate that he would call upon it for this purpose. The Senate, however, was unwilling to discuss the matter in his presence and referred it to a committee. Washington left the room in exasperation, saying that this "defeats the very purpose of my coming here."[11] Before the end of his second term Washington came to the conclusion that it was appropriate under the Constitution and expedient for the President to take the initiative in conducting treaty negotiations without submitting his plans and instructions in advance to the Senate for its approval. Because of the mounting tension between this country and England in 1794 over the seizure of American vessels and seamen, which threatened open war, four leading Federalist senators— Ellsworth, Cabot, Strong, and King—urged Washington to send a special envoy to London to attempt to secure an amicable settlement of the controversy. Hamilton was their first choice, but Washington, who accepted their plan, foresaw that Hamilton would be opposed in the Senate, and nominated their second choice—Chief Justice John Jay. On the advice of these senators, Washington did not submit his proposed instructions when he sent Jay's name to the Senate. It was generally recognized that the Senate would not be able to agree upon any particular instructions governing the negotiations.[12]

A minority of the Senate opposed the sending of a special envoy to England. Burr introduced a resolution that it was inexpedient and unnecessary because negotiations could be conducted by the minister to England at less expense, and the commissioning of Judges of the Supreme Court to such an office was mischievous, impolitic, contrary to the spirit of the Constitution, and tended to expose them to the influence of the executive. This resolution was voted down, and the following day another resolution calling on the President to "inform the Senate of the whole business with which the proposed envoy is to be charged" was also defeated. After a debate lasting three days, Jay was confirmed as special envoy, by a vote of 18 to 8.[13] Thereafter Washington followed the practice of informally conferring about treaty negotiations with Senate leaders who supported his administration rather than the Senate as a body. He discontinued the earlier procedure of submitting to the Senate for its information his proposed instructions to envoys nominated to negotiate treaties, but usually secured the Senate's approval of the appointment of envoys before opening treaty negotiations. In several instances Washington appointed special agents to negotiate treaties without submitting their names to the Senate. In October, 1789, he requested Gouverneur Morris, then in Paris, to go London as his private agent, "on the authority and credit" of Washington's letter, to "converse with His Britannic Majesty's Minister as to certain matters affecting the relations between the two countries." In 1792 he commissioned John Paul Jones to treat with Algiers, and in 1795 appointed David Humphreys commissioner plenipotentiary to negotiate a treaty of peace with Algiers.[14] The practice of prior consultation with the Senate about proposed treaties was discontinued, apparently with the approval of members of the Senate itself, who were reluctant to commit themselves in advance. The Senate, however, continued for a time to request the President to submit to it the instructions and other documents relating to treaty negotiations, and he supplied them on request.

The practice of submitting to the Senate the nominations of persons to conduct treaty negotiations with other countries continued until 1815. Thereafter regular diplomatic representatives or special agents, who were usually called commissioners, were used for this purpose.[15] The difficulties Presidents encountered in securing the approval of their nominees to negotiate treaties inclined them to follow this course. For example, in 1799, after the X Y Z affair, a group in the Senate opposed the appointment of William Vans Murray as special envoy to France to negotiate a treaty, and John Adams was able to secure approval of it only by adding the names of two others—Oliver Ellsworth and Patrick Henry—as a special mission.* A more celebrated case was the Senate refusal, in 1813, to approve the appointment of Albert Gallatin, Secretary of the Treasury, as a member of the mission to negotiate the Treaty of Ghent with England, until he had resigned from the Treasury.† The President's embarrassment over this, according to Quincy Wright, probably was the reason for discontinuing the practice of sending to the Senate the nominations of envoys.[16]

The practice of the President to appoint special agents to negotiate treaties, which has been followed since Washington's time, has been challenged several times in the Senate.[17] A notable debate occurred in 1831 over a treaty negotiated with Turkey by a special commission which Jackson had appointed without asking for Senate approval. Senator Tazewell, who led the opposition, conceded the right of the President to appoint special agents but contended that commissioners granted credentials to a foreign power and commissioned to negotiate a treaty were officers, hence confirmation by the Senate of such

* See chap. iii, above.
† See *ibid.*

ppointments was required by the Constitution. In defending the action of
he President, Senator Livingston maintained, to the contrary, that the treaty
ommissioners, although authorized to negotiate a treaty, were not officers but
vere instead the special agents of the President. He stressed the constitutional
ower of the President to use secret agents in the conduct of foreign relations,
s well as the well-established precedent of their use. By a narrow margin of
2 to 21, the Senate voted a contingent fund to the President to pay the com-
nissioners, but added a provision that this action should not be "construed as
anctioning or in any way approving the appointment of these persons by the
President alone, during the recess of the Senate, and without their advice and
consent, as commissioners to negotiate a treaty with the Ottoman Porte."[18]

The use of executive agents became an issue twice in Cleveland's administration. The issue first arose in 1888 when a treaty with Great Britain concerning
fishing rights in the North Atlantic, which had been negotiated by a special
commission including the Secretary of State, came before the Senate. The
majority report opposing the treaty attacked the appointment of such a commission without senatorial confirmation, stating that, "in evil times, when the
President of the United States may be under the influence of foreign and
adverse interests, such a course of procedure might result in great disaster to
the interests and even the safety of our Government and people."[19] Sherman,
who led the debate against the treaty, conceded that the appointment of such
a commission was within the power of the President. The minority, however,
did not let the objection go unanswered, and in its report submitted a table
showing that since 1792 the President had appointed 438 persons whose
nominations were not confirmed by the Senate, to negotiate treaties, and 32
with the advice and consent of the Senate, and that the Secretary of State had
appointed 3. Even more striking, the minority report pointed out that "an
interval of fifty-three years, between 1827 and 1880, occurred during which
the President did not ask the consent of the Senate to any such appointment."[20]

The appointment of James H. Blount by President Cleveland in 1893 as
special commissioner to Hawaii with "paramount" authority was similarly
challenged. Another notable debate over the power of the President to conduct
foreign relations through persons whose appointments were not confirmed
by the Senate arose in 1906 over Roosevelt's appointment of Ambassador
White and Minister Gummere as delegates to the Algeciras conference. The
President's earlier intervention in Panama in 1903 and the executive agreement he concluded with Santo Domingo in 1905 without securing the approval of the Senate had led to charges of executive usurpation. In defending
the President, Senator Spooner declared that "the Senate has nothing whatever to do with the negotiation of treaties or the conduct of our foreign intercourse and relations save the exercise of the one constitutional function of
advice and consent which the Constitution requires as a precedent condition

to the making of a treaty." Senator Spooner went on to state that the President negotiates treaties and may employ such agencies or persons as he sees fit for this purpose.[21]

The numerous debates in the Senate on the use by the President of executive agents without Senate confirmation have usually been partisan in character. Referring to such proposed resolutions denouncing the presidential use of executive agents, John Quincy Adams observed in his diary: "The parties in the Senate have always voted for or against these resolutions according as they supported or opposed the President."[22] When Woodrow Wilson sent Colonel House to Europe as his personal representative in 1913 and 1914, and John Lind to Mexico in 1914, there was great remonstrance that the Constitution had been violated, though neither man was given any rank or title. Later, when Wilson sent Elihu Root to Russia in 1917 at the head of a mission with the rank of ambassador, there was no similar objection.[23]

The well-established and almost invariable practice of the President to utilize regular members of the diplomatic corps or special agents without senatorial confirmation as negotiators of treaties has lessened the control that the Senate once exercised over his selections. In compensation, however, Congress has enacted legislation increasing its control over the President's conduct of foreign relations. Before 1855 the President was free to determine to which countries we should send diplomatic representatives and the grade that was appropriate under international law and treaties. Up to that time Congress had enacted no legislation restricting his discretion, and the appropriation acts did not limit the President in assigning diplomatic grades. In that year, however, an act of Congress specified the countries to which the United States would send diplomatic representatives with the rank of envoy extraordinary and minister plenipotentiary. Although Attorney General Cushing held the act contrary to the constitutional powers of the President and hence not mandatory, Congress has continued since to enact legislation of a similar character, specifying the countries to which this country will send representatives with the rank of ambassador.[24] Until March 4, 1913, the President had always had the unquestioned authority to send special missions to attend international conferences, and the missions were paid for out of his contingent fund or a subsequent appropriation; on that date Congress passed an act providing that thereafter the President should not accept or extend an invitation to participate in an international congress or conference without first having specific authority of law to do so.[25] Wriston points out that this provision, reversing an important legislative policy of many years' standing, was adopted at the last moment without any debate in either house and was passed in the Senate during a parliamentary wrangle over the order of business.[26] Presidents since have regarded the act as an unconstitutional encroachment of their power to conduct foreign relations, and at times—notably in the appointment of delegates to the Versailles Peace Conference—have ignored it.

Within recent years Congress has extended the requirement of senatorial confirmation also to appointments to international organizations and conferences, though such appointments formerly were filled by presidential appointment without the advice and consent of the Senate. One of the reservations adopted by the Senate in its debate on the Treaty of Versailles and the League of Nations in 1919–1920 originally provided that representatives of this country appointed as members of "said commission, committee, tribunal, court, councils, or conferences" should be approved by the Senate. Subsequently the amendment was changed to provide that the United States should be represented in the League of Nations or other agencies established by the treaty only in accordance with acts of the Congress providing for the appointment and defining the powers and duties of delegates.[27] The separate treaties of peace with Germany, Austria, and Hungary of 1921 contained similar provisions.[28] Senator Lodge, chairman of the Senate Foreign Relations Committee, stated that when this country took such an important step as participating in an international organization or commission—for example, the Reparations Commission—the representative should represent "the whole government of the United States and not simply the Executive." He thought it "undesirable that a person without the official character should be sent to take part or even merely as an observer to take part in a transaction of such importance."[29]

The issue arose again in 1945 when a bill was before Congress authorizing the participation of this country in the United Nations. The Senate bill as reported by the Committee on Foreign Relations required confirmation by the Senate of appointments of the United States representative and deputy representative to serve on the Security Council. Confirmation was also required of the appointments of representatives to the Economic and Social Council and the Trustee Council, except of members of Congress and officers whose previous appointment had been approved by the Senate. Confirmation was not required for delegates to the Assembly and representatives to various specialized agencies and committees under the United Nations. The report of the committee stated that it had given serious consideration to whether appointments of representatives to the Assembly should be confirmed by the Senate.[30]

In explaining the bill, Senator Connally, chairman of the committee, stated that it required Senate confirmation of the representatives of this country to the most important bodies of the United Nations, but that some members of the committee thought it would be "unseemly" to require confirmation of representatives to the Assembly, who in many instances might be members of the House. He pointed out that the President had always had the right to appoint representatives to international conferences without the approval of the Senate, and that representatives to the Assembly would serve for only temporary periods. He also stressed that representatives in the Assembly or other specialized agencies would have no authority to act for this country but would be under instructions from the government.[31]

Senator Millikin objected to the bill, saying that it would permit the appointment of any "political stumblebum," and offered a series of amendments to require senatorial confirmation of all representatives of this country, not only on the three major councils but also in the Assembly and all specialized agencies.[32] This amendment was supported by Senator Donnell, who said that the bill was a "clear abdication" by the Senate, and that it would make it "possible for individuals who have no capacity for service on these councils to be appointed without having the Senate of the United States have the power, even remotely, to object."[33] Senator O'Mahoney maintained that confirmation by the Senate would give our representatives added prestige and contended that "they would go into the Assembly clothed with the power of speaking both for the Executive and the Senate."[34] The Millikin amendments were voted down, not because they required Senate confirmation but because they established representatives to the Assembly as full-time officers, which would have precluded the appointment of members of Congress. The following day, Senator Connally brought in an amendment to require the approval of the Senate of representatives of this country not only to the three major councils but also to the Assembly, and of the principal representatives to any specialized agencies which may be created under the United Nations. This was agreed to without debate. Subsequently this provision was changed to require instead the confirmation of "the representative of the United States in any commission that may be formed by the United Nations . . . to which the United States is entitled to a representative."[35] The Economic Cooperation Act of 1948 similarly requires Senate confirmation of the appointments of the Administrator, Deputy Administrator, members of the Advisory Board, and the Special Representative in Europe.[36]

Although no contests occurred over nominations by President Truman of persons to have charge of the foreign aid programs, unquestionably his selections were influenced by the requirement of the advice and consent of the Senate. It is significant that before 1951 only one contest occurred over the nomination of American representatives to the United Nations and related international organizations. The nomination of Francis Biddle, former Attorney General and American member of the International Military Tribunal at Nuremberg in 1945 and 1946, as delegate to the United Nations Economic and Social Council in 1947 was held up in the Senate Foreign Relations Committee by Chairman Vandenberg. Five months later, Biddle, seeing no prospect of confirmation, asked that his name be withdrawn. Two reasons were offered explaining why his nomination had been blocked: first, he was regarded as an ardent New Dealer, which he admitted with pride; and second, a more cautious man was desired by Republican senators, who noted with apprehension the rapid expansion of specialized agencies under the Council. According to press accounts, Senator Vandenberg advised Under Secretary of State Acheson that he did not want another nomination contest between conservatives and New Dealers similar to that over Lilienthal, for he feared that it would hopelessly divide the Foreign Relations Committee.[37] After Biddle asked that his name be withdrawn, Willard Thorp, Assistant Secretary of State, was nominated and the nomination was promptly confirmed.*

In spite of the recent insistence by the Senate on its right to pass upon the appointments of United States representatives to international organizations and conferences, the President is accorded wide discretion in the selection of persons to aid him in the conduct of foreign relations. There have been fewer contests over diplomatic nominations than over nominations of any other group of federal officers except Cabinet members. In recent years, however, as the following accounts indicate, there has been an increasing tendency for diplomatic appointments to be contested. The opposition to the appointment of Edward J. Flynn in 1943 to be minister to Australia, which finally led to the withdrawal of his name, was said to be the first case in forty years in which a public hearing was held for a diplomatic nomination.

Edward J. Flynn

On January 8, 1943, Flynn announced to the press in New York his appointment as minister to Australia and also as personal representative of the President in the South Pacific, with the rank of ambassador. Since such announcements are invariably issued by the White House and are customarily released to the press in both countries, the announcement created an unfavorable public impression, which Flynn was never able to overcome. It was not until four days later that a White House announcement was issued. At the hearing Flynn explained that his premature announcement was due to a misunderstanding about the date on which the White House would issue a release.[38]

The nomination of Flynn, who was chairman of the Democratic National Committee and had been for many years Democratic boss of the Bronx in New York City, was greeted by unfavorable press comment and opposition by Republicans and antiadministration Democratic members of the Senate. Flynn had had no diplomatic experience and had no knowledge of Australia or the problems of the Pacific. In contrast, his predecessor, Nelson Johnson, who had been a career diplomat since 1907, was regarded as an authority on the Far East. In addition, Flynn had recently been under a grand jury investigation concerning the use of city-owned Belgian blocks in the construction of his country estate. The grand jury accepted Flynn's testimony that he knew nothing about it at the time the blocks were used, and that when he learned of it he paid for

---

* Thorp had been rejected by the Senate in 1934 as head of the Bureau of Foreign and Domestic Commerce because of the opposition of Senator Stephens of Mississippi. See chap. xviii, below.

the brick and the labor involved. Nevertheless, the case greatly injured his chances of approval by the Senate.

The opposition to Flynn was for the most part political opposition to the Roosevelt administration. Although he could not qualify as a person with diplomatic experience or as an expert on Australia and the Pacific area, he had had broad experience as a public official, as a national and local party executive, and as a practicing attorney. His qualifications, although in no sense outstanding, were equal to those of many earlier diplomats whose appointments had been uncontested. A successful lawyer in New York City, for ten years he had been secretary of state in New York and had then resigned to become United States Commissioner General to the World's Fair in New York in the late 1930's. The use of diplomatic posts to reward political supporters was nothing new, but the appointment of a New York City political boss who was also the national chairman of the party was particularly subject to attack. Wendell Willkie denounced the appointment as "vicious" and a "debauching" of the diplomatic service "revolting to all decent citizens."[39] In an editorial typical of the general comment of the press throughout the country, the Chicago *Daily News* opposed the appointment on the grounds that Flynn was not a diplomat, he had had no foreign or military experience, and had "no particular familiarity with Australia or Pacific problems."[40] The President of the Civil Service Reform League came out against the appointment as the payment of a political debt, and Bert Andrews of the New York *Herald Tribune* in reporting the hearings declared that Australia might be "puzzled as to whether America was trying to export Mr. Flynn as a diplomat or deport him as an undesirable."[41]

In the hearings Flynn came off better than might have been expected. The strong charges made against him by Senator Bridges failed to stand up on investigation. Senator La Follette stated afterward that although he had been somewhat prejudiced against Flynn at the outset, after following the testimony he had come to the "conclusion that the opposition had not presented a case against Mr. Flynn upon which I could conscientiously vote to reject a nomination."[42] Chairman Connally went further and declared that "the charges were in no particular sustained." In support of the nomination, he stated that "the widest latitude has always been accorded the President in the selection of his diplomatic representatives."[43]

The vote in the Foreign Relations Committee was 13 to 10 to recommend the confirmation of Flynn as minister to Australia. Twelve Democrats and one Progressive voted in favor of, and seven Republicans and three Democrats voted against, the nomination. The three Democrats who opposed Flynn— George of Georgia, Van Nuys of Indiana, and Gillette of Iowa—had all been opposed by Roosevelt in his 1938 attempted "purge" of antiadministration Democrats. It was evident that the nomination would be opposed in the

Senate not only by the Republicans but also by a group of antiadministration Democrats. Flynn's attempt to exercise control over federal patronage usually accorded to members of the Senate had made him unpopular with a number of Democratic senators. On January 31 he requested the President to withdraw his nomination, stating that he was "unwilling to permit my candidacy to be made the excuse for partisan political debate in the Senate."[44] According to press accounts, this was the first diplomatic nomination to be rejected since the Senate refused to confirm Benjamin Harrison's nomination of Murat Halstead, an Ohio journalist, as minister to Germany, because of a series of articles he had written denouncing the purchase of Senate seats.

Chester Bowles

The nomination of Chester Bowles, formerly governor of Connecticut and national Price Administrator at the end of World War II, to be ambassador to India was opposed in 1951 in a contest that followed party lines. At the hearings of the subcommittee in September only Bowles testified, there being no opposing witnesses; but when the subcommittee voted on his confirmation, the two Republican members—Brewster and Smith—voted against it. Senator Smith explained his vote on the ground that the Foreign Relations Committee had not been consulted by the President before he made the appointment. In the Senate debate on the nomination, Senator McMahon replied that this was a "very strange doctrine," and pointed out that no similar objection had been raised against the appointment of Walter Gifford, former head of the American Telephone and Telegraph Company and a prominent Republican, when he was nominated to be ambassador to Great Britain.[45]

The Republican opposition to Bowles in the Senate debate was based on the grounds that he had had no previous diplomatic experience and had never been in the Far East; hence he was not qualified to become our ambassador to India, "one of the danger spots of the world." Senator Taft declared that he could not think of anyone "who is less qualified to be Ambassador to India than Chester Bowles." He attacked the appointment also on the ground that Bowles's experience as an advertising man did not qualify him for the job, and stated: "The people of Connecticut did not think he made a very good governor, because they did not continue him as governor."[46] Democratic senators quickly replied by citing previous diplomatic appointments of defeated Republicans without any objection by the Senate.

Another ground of opposition was that Bowles had been given the appointment because of his contributions to the party. To this the Democrats replied by pointing to the recent appointment of several prominent Republicans to important diplomatic posts. Senator Aiken attacked the practice of using diplomatic appointments to reward large contributors to the party, but voted for Bowles. Another ground of opposition was that the appointment should have gone to a career diplomat. In a vote which closely followed party lines, the appointment of Bowles was confirmed, 43 to 33. Only one Democrat, Mc-Carran, voted against confirmation; five Republicans—Aiken, Langer, Lodge, Morse, and Margaret Chase Smith—voted for it. Bowles's record as ambassador subsequently attracted wide commendation.

Philip Jessup

One of the most sensational contests over a diplomatic appointment in recent years occurred in 1951 when Ambassador at Large Philip Jessup was named by the President, along with nine other persons, to serve as delegates and alternates to the autumn meeting of the General Assembly of the United Nations. Although Jessup had five times been confirmed to the highest offices by the Senate, three times as delegate to the General Assembly in the preceding years, his nomination was vehemently attacked by Senator McCarthy, who was joined by Harold Stassen, former governor of Minnesota and president of the University of Pennsylvania. Prior to committee consideration in September, 1951, Senator McCarran issued a statement urging the subcommittee to which Jessup's nomination had been referred to examine the files of his internal security subcommittee which, he asserted, would reveal "certain associations and activities of the nominee."[47] Before the Foreign Relations subcommittee opened its hearings, several witnesses testifying before the McCarran sub-committee were questioned about Jessup and were asked whether he had shown an "affinity for Communist causes," as Senator McCarthy had alleged in the preceding year. A retired brigadier general who had served as intelligence officer in the Far East testified that Jessup had told him in 1950 that recognition of Communist China was imminent, and a university professor accused Jessup, Lattimore, and other political scientists of following the Communist "line."[48] Stassen also testified before the McCarran subcommittee, alleging that Jessup had advocated a policy of softness toward the Chinese Communists. The fact that Jessup's nomination had been referred to another committee did not deter the McCarran subcommittee from inquiring into charges of his alleged association with Communists.

The hearings on the nomination of Jessup were opened with the testimony of Senator McCarthy, who testified for two full days. He accused Jessup of following the Communist line by opposing aid to Britain before Germany attacked Russia in 1941 and then changing his position. Although McCarthy could substantiate his charge that Jessup as a member of the America First movement had opposed aid to Britain in early 1941, he admitted, when pressed by the committee, that he had no evidence that Jessup had changed his position after Germany attacked Russia. Much of the testimony of McCarthy dealt with the Institute of Pacific Relations, with which Jessup had been actively associated and against which charges of Communist infiltration had subsequently been made. In one of the hearings Senator Ferguson of Michigan appeared to explain the fact that, although he also had been a member of the Institute, he had withdrawn his membership and was never active in the organization. Much of the testimony of Senator McCarthy dealt with Jessup's association with persons and organizations accused of being left wing or Communist-dominated. Mrs. Jessup, for instance, had once belonged to the China Aid Council. The fact that Jessup had earlier been a member of a number of organizations which also included among their membership other persons who were accused of being members of the Communist party or sympathetic to Communism was cited in an attempt to prove his "affinity" for Communist causes. McCarthy's testimony and exhibits were a striking example of an attempt to establish guilt by association. He asserted to reporters that Hiram Bingham, head of the Federal Loyalty Review Board, had told him that the board would have turned down Jessup as a bad risk if it had had the authority. Bingham, however, vigorously denied this, stating that he had never discussed the case with McCarthy. In the course of his testimony, McCarthy was accused of attempting to mislead the subcommittee by presenting excerpts from Jessup's testimony at the Hiss trial from which he had omitted significant sentences; and at the end of McCarthy's appearance Senator Fulbright declared, after numerous verbal exchanges with him: "I just want to say for the record that in all my experience in the Senate I have never seen a more arrogant or rude witness before any committee."[49]

The evidence of Senator McCarthy was rejected by all the members of the subcommittee except Senator Brewster. Senator Smith of New Jersey issued a public statement later when he joined with two other members of the subcommittee in voting against the confirmation of Jessup, in which he said: "I have known Philip Jessup for many years and I have absolute confidence in his integrity, ability, and loyalty to his country. I am convinced that he has not and has never had any connection with the Communist party."[50] Senator Gillette, who also voted against confirmation, issued a similar statement in which he condemned the "concerted campaign of unfair and unprincipled attacks" made on Jessup. Curiously, despite these statements, both Senators voted against Jessup on the ground that he had lost the confidence of the country. In addition, Senator Smith stated that Jessup had become "the symbol of a group attitude toward Asia which seems to have been proven completely unsound." Senator Gillette, however, stated to the contrary that there was only "the most meager evidence" that Jessup took any part in forming the China policy.[51]

The other principal witness to testify against Jessup was Harold Stassen, who had earlier testified before the McCarran subcommittee. The high light of his first statement was that he had been informed by the late Senator Vandenberg that at a conference at the White House in February, 1949, between the President and the congressional leaders, Jessup had advocated the withdrawal of military aid to Chiang Kai-shek. Evidence was subsequently introduced to prove conclusively that Jessup did not attend the conference in question, having been in New York City on that date. Stassen revised his testimony in a second appearance before the committee and accused Jessup of advocating a "soft" policy with respect to Communist China, asserting that Jessup "must have" consulted with Acheson about the China policy at the time. All of this Jessup later strenuously denied, accusing Stassen of using a "grasshopper technique of leaping from one unfounded allegation to another." Senator Sparkman attacked the Stassen testimony as "putting inference on inference" without any form of proof.[52] In his collaboration with Senator McCarthy, Stassen attracted much publicity but gained little, if any, credit.[53]

The final vote on Jessup in the subcommittee was 3 to 2 against confirmation, though two of those who voted against it—Smith and Gillette—stated publicly that they took no stock in the charges that had been made against him. On the last day of the session, on a motion introduced by Senator Sparkman, chairman of the subcommittee, the Senate by-passed the Foreign Relations Committee and confirmed the other nine delegates to the General Assembly, without taking any action on the nomination of Jessup. The motion was passed by unanimous consent; the objection of a single senator would have prevented any action. The opponents of Jessup were eager to bring his nomination to a vote, confident that they had enough votes to reject him; but this was prevented by the failure of the Foreign Relations Committee to act on the nomination.

Three days later, President Truman gave Jessup a recess appointment and issued a public statement that he was making the appointment because Jessup had "demonstrated by actual experience on numerous occasions that he is outstandingly well qualified for the position.... His service to this country has been faithful, conscientious, and highly effective." The President went on to state that the charges against him "were utterly without foundation, and some of the so-called documentation introduced in support of these charges bordered on fraud." He discounted the allegation that the American people had lost confidence in Jessup, saying that they make their judgments on the basis of fact and performance.[54]

Charles E. Bohlen

In 1953 a small group of senators, designated by the New York *Times* as "right-wing extremists" and "bitter-end isolationists," attacked the appointment of Charles E. Bohlen, a career Foreign Service officer, as ambassador to the Soviet Union, and succeeded in holding up Senate approval for a month during a critical period in our relations with Russia. The leading opponent of the nomination was Senator McCarthy of Wisconsin. Senators McCarran, Bridges,

Dirksen, Mundt, Welker, and others joined him, and the contest quickly became a test of strength between McCarthy and the Eisenhower administration. The State Department had been subjected to considerable public criticism for having yielded on previous occasions to McCarthy who, as chairman of the Senate Committee on Government Operations, was conducting an investigation of Communist influences in the Voice of America program. McCarthy's opposition to Bohlen was widely interpreted as an attack on the administration; no longer could it yield and maintain its standing in the Senate and the country. The significance of the contest was pointed out in a New York *Times* editorial:

> The attack on Mr. Bohlen is much more than attack on a career Foreign Service officer of great distinction. It is an attack on the integrity of the Executive Branch; and it is also another characteristic effort of a small but extremist group of Senators to humiliate the Administration and so to enlarge the scope of the legislative power that the Executive might be at the mercy of any ruthless demagogue on Capitol Hill.[55]

On February 27 President Eisenhower nominated Bohlen to be ambassador to Russia, a post which had been vacant for several months following the recall of Ambassador George Kennan. After the death of Stalin was announced on March 6, Under Secretary of State Smith urged prompt Senate action on the nomination in view of the critical situation. Secretary Dulles, testifying before the Foreign Relations Committee on March 18, declared that Bohlen was "uniquely qualified" for this particular assignment. He was a career Foreign Service officer who had entered the service in 1929 and had since served three tours of duty in Moscow, and spoke Russian fluently. In addition, he was recommended for the post by a special committee of distinguished retired Foreign Service officers, consisting of Hugh Gibson, Norman Armour, and Joseph Grew.

Many Republicans, however, disliked the appointment because Bohlen had been a participant in the conferences at Yalta and Potsdam and thus was associated with the previous administration. The nominee did not help matters when he testified before the Senate committee, for he refused to agree that the Yalta and Potsdam agreements had been "blunders." On March 13, Senator Bridges, president pro tem of the Senate, announced that there would be "formidable" opposition to the appointment, and Senators McCarthy and McCarran let it be known that they would oppose the appointment of Bohlen on the ground that he was a "poor security risk." The administration resisted the pressure put on it to withdraw the nomination, and on March 18 Secretary of State Dulles testified before the Foreign Relations Committee for three and a half hours in a closed session. According to the published newspaper accounts, the hearing dealt chiefly with the results of the FBI investigation of the nominee and the information contained in the FBI file on him. Already it had been rumored that the file contained derogatory information touching on the nominee's loyalty, associations, and personal life. Secretary Dulles took with him to the hearing a summary of the file and advised the committee in detail as to its contents. He stated that he personally had reviewed the file and that "it left no doubt of Bohlen's loyalty and security." In reply to a question, he stated that Bohlen had not been "cleared" by the security officer of the department, Robert W. McLeod, but that the "clearance" of the nominee had been referred to him and he took full responsibility for the decision.[56]

To counteract any reservations that members of the committee may have held concerning the appointment, Dulles assured them that the ambassador to Russia was not in a "policy-making position"; his function was to "report and interpret developments in the Soviet Union." He also pointed out that Bohlen then held a "very high level policy-making position" in the State Department. Following the testimony of Secretary Dulles, the committee voted 15 to 0 to recommend confirmation of the appointment, but the opponents were unmoved. Senator McCarthy stated to the press that it was a "bad" appointment that would antagonize the "Republican leaders" and intimated that he knew of the contents of the FBI file on Bohlen. He asserted that President Eisenhower would withdraw the nomination if he examined the Bohlen file.

The following day Senator McCarran, who was not a member of the Foreign Relations Committee, rose in the Senate and accused Dulles of having summarily overridden the decision of his security officer, Robert W. McLeod, who he said had refused to "clear" Bohlen. Furthermore, the Nevada senator asserted that according to reports of Dulles' statement to the committee, Dulles had misrepresented the facts and made it appear that McLeod had given his approval. This case, McCarran declared, provided the acid test of whether the administration would carry out its campaign pledges to "clean out" the State Department or whether it would follow the old policy of "cover up."[57] Dulles promptly replied in a statement to the press the following day, categorically denying McCarran's charges. He stated that there had been no difference between himself and McLeod over the clearance of Bohlen, but that McLeod had referred the decision to him, calling to his attention certain items of information that could be regarded as derogatory. The only "acid test" involved, declared Dulles, was whether the orderly processes of our government would survive or whether charges that lack even the substance of rumor would prevail against Foreign Service officers.[58]

The Senate debate, which opened on March 23, continued for three days. Senator McCarthy led the attack throughout. On the opening day he provoked a bitter controversy by accusing Dulles of misrepresenting the facts; he demanded that Dulles be recalled before the Foreign Relations Committee to testify under oath concerning whether he had overridden McLeod, and that McLeod also be summoned to testify.

Many of us [said McCarthy] have reason to believe that Mr. McLeod felt so strongly about that that he went directly to the White House, and spent 2½ hours there. I do not know that to be true, but that is the rumor prevalent on the Hill, and if it is true, ... that is in direct contradiction of what Mr. Dulles told the committee; and if Mr. Dulles' memory is bad on that point, then his memory must be extremely bad also as to what was in the files.[59]

Senator Taft sharply replied that this was a "ridiculous" suggestion, that Dulles' unsworn statement was just as good as his statement under oath, and he did not favor calling a subordinate official to testify on a matter on which his superior had elected to testify for the department.[60]

Taft pointed out that Dulles had not stated to the Foreign Relations Committee that McLeod had "cleared" Bohlen, but on the contrary had stated explicitly that the decision was his own. He proposed, however, since the contents of the FBI file had been questioned, that one or two members of the Senate Foreign Relations Committee be designated to examine the file. This was agreed to, and the following day Taft and Sparkman spent several hours reviewing a lengthy summary of the file. When the Senate resumed its consideration of the nomination on March 25, Taft reported that he had found nothing in the file to indicate that Bohlen was a bad security risk or was otherwise unfit, and that Bohlen's associations were such as anyone in his position would be expected to have. The sixteen pages of so-called derogatory information, reported the Ohio senator, consisted entirely of statements by persons who differed with Bohlen on foreign policy, all of whom stated that they had full confidence in his character, integrity, morality, and general reputation. "There was no suggestion anywhere by anyone reflecting on the loyalty of Mr. Bohlen in any way, or any association by him with communism or even tolerance of communism," said Taft.[61] This report was corroborated by Senator Sparkman.

Senator McCarthy, not wishing to attack the integrity and veracity of Senator Taft, abandoned his earlier charges that Bohlen was a poor security risk and now attacked the nominee on the ground that he had been associated with the previous administration, referring to the part he had played in the conferences at Yalta and Potsdam. Several opponents linked Bohlen's name with that of Alger Hiss, and the foreign policies of the previous administration came in for much excoriation. On the second day of the debate much was made of a statement by Hugh Gibson, one of the committee of three retired Foreign Service officers who had recommended Bohlen for the post, that he knew Bohlen only slightly and had not recommended him. Senator Knowland, floor leader in the absence of Senator Taft, replied that he had the letter in hand, which contained the signature of Gibson along with those of the other two members, recommending Bohlen for the post. Whereupon McCarthy demanded that Senator Dirksen be permitted to examine the letter, and Knowland replied in anger that this was the first time the veracity of his statement had been challenged on the floor of the Senate.[62] This contradiction was cleared up the following day when a further communication from Gibson was read into the record to the effect that he had indeed signed the letter recommending Bohlen for the post, though he knew him only slightly, but that the other two members of the committee were well acquainted with Bohlen and regarded him as well qualified for the assignment.

President Eisenhower made a statement to the press on March 26 giving unqualified support to the nominee. He declared that he had selected Bohlen because he regarded him as the best-qualified man in the country for the job, and he wanted to secure an ambassador who knew something of the Russian people and whose record had been that of dedication to this country. The President stated that he had known Bohlen and his charming family for years and had been a guest in their home.[63]

Another issue that arose in the Bohlen contest was the old question of whether members of the Senate are entitled to examine the confidential records of the FBI and other government investigating agencies. Senator McCarran, in his speech accusing Dulles of misrepresentation of the contents of the FBI files, stated that the appointment of Bohlen should not be acted on until every member of the Senate had an opportunity to examine "the full and complete file on this nominee." The Committee on Foreign Relations did not request permission to examine the file but accepted Secretary Dulles' summary of its contents. After the controversy arose over the accuracy of Dulles' report of the FBI file, Senator Taft proposed that two members of the Foreign Relations Committee be designated to examine the file, and this course was followed. Some senators advocated opening up all the confidential files to members of Congress, but Senator Taft stated that this would destroy the FBI. It was his view that the information should be available to Congress under proper safeguards.

The contest over the Bohlen appointment was almost entirely between two groups within the Republican party; but on the second day of the debate, Senator Lehman of New York spoke with great feeling against the type of attack which Senator McCarthy had made on the nominee. Pointing out that Bohlen was a career diplomat who had served his country for twenty-six years "with great ability and outstanding devotion," Lehman declared: "Mr. President, during all those years there has never been a blemish on his record. There has never been any reflection on his loyalty, his integrity, or his character; and yet, on the basis of flimsy rumor, this fine public servant has in recent days been pilloried and assailed; his character has been placed under suspicion, and his usefulness in the service of his country, of course, has been tremendously lessened."[64]

Senator Lehman deplored this type of "smear and attack," which he said followed the same pattern as that used against many other loyal, devoted, honest Americans, to create fear and "subvert the exercise of free speech, free assembly, and free association of men and women in law-abiding activities."

It is about time [said Senator Lehman] the American people called a halt to the unfounded, unfair, and vicious attacks on loyal and devoted men and women in this country, whether they be in public service or not—men and women who have been doing their full and unselfish duty toward their country and toward their fellow men.

Mr. President, all my life I have urged young people to go into the service of their Government. I did so because I thought there was no higher or more noble service one could render, save to defend his country on the field of battle, than to serve his country in peacetime.

. . . .

But . . . I am beginning to doubt whether I any longer have the right to encourage men to go into public service when all they can expect to receive is calumny and accusations of treason if their honest opinions sometime later prove to have been incorrect. And they can be subjected to attack and vilification if they do something which is a bit unorthodox or which does not meet the views or standards of a small group of men who would mold every one in their narrow and reactionary image. They must know that these days public servants are subject to sweeping accusations and charges by those who would like to stifle all freedom of speech and freedom of thought.[65]

On March 27 Bohlen's nomination was approved by a vote of 73 to 13; 39 Democrats and 34 Republicans voted for the nomination, and 11 Republicans and 2 Democrats voted against it. The next day, the New York *Times,* commenting on the confirmation, stated: "The delay has been entirely due to a destructive and wildly irresponsible attack on the integrity of the present Administration and of the constitutional system."

James B. Conant

President Eisenhower's appointment of James Bryant Conant, president of Harvard University, to be High Commissioner to Germany in 1953 also provoked opposition. The opposition was based on a statement attributed to Conant that indicated a prejudice against parochial schools, and on his alleged support of the harsh Morgenthau plan for Germany during World War II. At the hearings Conant denied both charges; but two senators continued to oppose his appointment on the ground that he had been too closely identified with the Truman administration[66] as an adviser to it.

Nominations of Secretaries of State

Nominations of the Secretary of State have rarely been opposed in the Senate. Above all else, the Secretary of State must be able to get along with the Senate, and the President must of necessity choose a person who commands the respect and friendship of the leading members of the Senate. This is well illustrated in recent appointments. Cordell Hull had a long and distinguished record in both houses of Congress and was held in highest esteem by his colleagues. This was also true of James Byrnes. Few men have ever commanded the respect that was accorded Marshall by members of Congress. Both Stettinius and Acheson before their appointments had held posts that involved close relations with the Senate, and both were unusually successful in these relationships. John Foster Dulles, a former senator, was held in high regard by members of the Senate.

The same considerations have applied to the nominations of Assistant Secretaries of State, which have seldom been opposed. In December, 1944, however, a contest arose over Roosevelt's six nominations of Assistant Secretaries. Only three days after Stettinius took office as Secretary of State succeeding Hull, the President sent to the Senate the nominations of Joseph Grew as Under Secretary, and William Clayton, Nelson Rockefeller, and Archibald MacLeish as Assistant Secretaries. Within a few days he submitted the names of James Dunn and Julius Holmes to fill two newly created posts as Assistant Secretaries. This represented an almost complete turnover of the top officials of the State Department; of those who had served with Hull, only Dean Acheson remained as Assistant Secretary. These nominations were opposed by a group of liberal senators, including Pepper, Guffey, Murray, and La Follette, who usually supported the administration. Objections were made to the nominations of Rockefeller, Clayton, and Holmes because of their connections with big business and financial interests, and it was asserted that the control of our foreign policy was being turned over to a "Wall Street" group. A number of senators from cotton states objected to the appointment of Clayton, whose brokerage firm did business throughout the world. In the hearing he was quizzed closely on his position with regard to cotton prices, government support, cartels, and international trade, and he was taken to task for his previous statements that this country would have to reduce the cost of production of cotton in order to compete with other countries. Senator Bankhead objected to Clayton's position that the price of cotton should be determined by the world market and that adjustments in cotton farming in this country should be made, particularly through mechanization, to enable it to compete in the world market. At one point he inquired of the nominee: "You believe that the American southerner should be required to sell his cotton at the same price as that the cheap Indian worker and the Egyptian worker get for their products"? Clayton denied this but stated that he did not "see that this has much to do with my duties as Assistant Secretary of State for foreign economic affairs." Bankhead retorted: "It has a good deal to do with your philosophy with reference to a great group of your fellow citizens. It has a lot to do with your filling that high place, from my standpoint."[107]

Archibald MacLeish was opposed on the ground that some of his earlier writings were critical of the capitalistic system. When he was called to testify a second time, Senator Clark of Missouri read to him excerpts from his earlier writings, which, taken out of context, appeared quite radical. When, at MacLeish's insistence, the entire paragraphs instead of single sentences were read, it was seen that instead of expressing his own views, MacLeish had stated and criticized positions taken by Communists and left-wingers. When Senator Clark read some selections from MacLeish's poems and asked him to explain their meaning, he replied that "one of the occupational hazards of writing poetry is that this sort of thing happens," and wondered "when John Hay came up for confirmation as Secretary of State, whether anybody read Little Britches and Pike County Ballads to him."[68]

Very few questions were asked of the other nominees after they had read their prepared statements. On December 14 the committee voted to recommend the confirmation of all six nominations; but the vote on MacLeish was a tie, which was broken by a telephone call from Senator Wagner.[69]

When the nominations came before the Senate, Senator Pepper moved to delay action until after the holidays, and the threat of a filibuster arose. Senator Bankhead opposed the nomination of Clayton because of the large foreign holdings of his company, which the senator said were "in competition with the American cotton farmer."[70] Three days later, Pepper stated in the Senate that President Roosevelt had assured him that if the nominations were put over, he would resubmit them after the recess, and Pepper announced that he was ready to vote. Senator Langer stated his opposition to having the State Department run by Wall Street and the House of Rockefeller and the House of Morgan, and in further objection to the nominations added that no one from North Dakota had been appointed.[71] Senator Johnson stated that he would vote against Grew because "I will not vote for turning the State Department over to the House of Morgan."[72] Senator Russell opposed Clayton because "his views on American agriculture . . . would be completely disastrous to the future of the cotton producers."[73] On the vote, the liberal wing of the Democratic members voted against the nominations; the Republicans, who usually voted against the administration on nominations, favored all six. All the nominations were approved by substantial majorities. The closest vote was on MacLeish, who was approved 43 to 25. Clayton was approved by a vote of 52 to 19. Commenting on the contest, the New York *Times* stated editorially two days later:

. . . The practice of requiring Senate approval of important nominations is a sound one; and when the nominations are made either for judicial office or for some post in which the appointee is to carry out the defined purposes of Congress, as in the Interstate Commerce Commission or the Federal Trade Commission, the Senate is justified in making an especially close scrutiny before it gives its consent. But when the nominees are appointed to purely administrative posts on the executive side of the Government—as was the case here—the presumption in favor of prompt approval is a strong one, provided they are men of personal integrity and honor.[74]

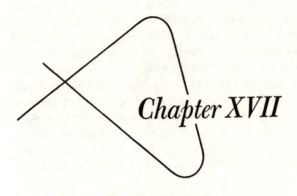

Chapter XVII

JUDGES

The "advice and consent" of the Senate required by the Constitution for such appointments was intended to be real and not nominal. A large proportion of the members of the Convention were fearful that if the judges owed their appointments solely to the President, the judiciary, even with life tenure, would then become dependent upon the executive and the powers of the latter would become overweening. By requiring joint action of the legislature and the executive, it was believed that the judiciary would be made more independent.

There was a second advantage which became more and more important as circuit and district courts were added to the federal judiciary. This was that a Senator from a given state would normally know the ability, capacities and integrity of the lawyers and judges within that state better than could a President. Senator Paul Douglas.[1]

After long experience and close observation I have reached the conclusion that senatorial meddling with judicial nominations is an unmixed evil. If the Senators from a state are to enjoy the prescriptive right to indicate to the President the man whom he is to nominate, the calibre of the nominee is apt to be determined by the quality of the Senators. If they are responsive to a corrupt local political organization or are themselves incapable of estimating judicial fitness, and if the President accepts their choice, he may inflict lasting injury upon the entire judicial system.... I know from experience what a glow of satisfaction a Senator feels when his judicial candidate is nominated and confirmed; but I also know how difficult it is to think straight and stand firm when one's own political fortunes may be involved in the choice. George Wharton Pepper.

Justices of the Supreme Court

OF THE 116 PERSONS nominated by Presidents to be Justices of the Supreme Court, 21, or nearly one-fifth, failed to receive the approval of the Senate. Nine were rejected when their nominations came to a vote; 10 were not acted on by the Senate, which is equivalent to a rejection; and 2 nominations were withdrawn by President Grant because of the public protest that was raised against them.[3] Two persons whom the Senate at first failed to approve—Roger Taney (in 1835) and Stanley Matthews (in 1881)—were subsequently renominated and confirmed.

It is striking that nearly one-fifth of the President's nominations to the Supreme Court were rejected, a proportion far higher than for any other federal office. It should be noted, however, that since 1894, a period of 58 years, there has been only one rejection out of a total of 35 nominations to the Court. In the preceding 105 years, 20 of the 81 nominees to the Court were rejected. Four of Tyler's nominees were rejected in the last two years of his term, and three of Fillmore's and three of Grant's nominations to the Court failed to secure Senate approval. The period from 1828 until Grant left office in 1877 was one of bitter partisanship, marked by the grosser forms of political patronage and spoils. Appointments were influenced greatly by political consideration, and the action of the Senate was fully as political as that of the President. Few of the rejections of Supreme Court nominations in this period can be ascribed to any lack of qualifications on the part of the nominees; for the most part they were due to political differences between the President and a majority of the Senate. Horace Greeley reflected the bitter partisanship of the period when he stated that he would oppose the confirmation of Jeremiah S. Black, nominated to the Court by Buchanan at the end of his term, even if Black possessed "all the virtues of Marshall and Story together."[4]

The record of the Senate since 1894, when it rejected two of Cleveland's nominations to the Court, indicates a decided trend away from the earlier partisanship in its consideration of Supreme Court appointments. The increasing role of the Supreme Court in passing upon social and economic measures has led to greater attention to the philosophy, record, and attitudes of nominees on such issues, and far less concern than formerly to their party regularity. Since 1900 only five nominations to the Supreme Court have faced serious opposition in the Senate: those of Brandeis (1916), Stone (1925), Hughes (1930), Parker (1930), and Black (1937). In every case the opposition was due to the philosophy and supposed stand of the nominee on social and economic issues rather than to partisan considerations.

In his scholarly review of the history of the Supreme Court, Charles Warren cites only four rejections in which charges of the lack of qualifications or unfitness of the nominee played an important part: those of John Rutledge (1795), Alexander Wollcott (1811), George H. Williams (1873), and Caleb Cushing (1874). (These cases have been reviewed in the preceding chapters.) He states that the other seventeen nominees were rejected by the Senate for political reasons. Several were outstanding in the legal profession.[5] Roger Taney, for example, who was rejected in 1835, was subsequently confirmed as

Chief Justice and became one of the greatest jurists in the history of the Court. Four of Tyler's nominations to the Supreme Court were rejected: those of John C. Spencer (1844), Reuben H. Walworth (1844), Edward King (1844), and John M. Read (1845). All four men were persons of high standing at the bar in their own states. Spencer, whom Warren characterized as "an eminently qualified lawyer," was rejected because he had accepted the post of Secretary of War and later that of Secretary of the Treasury at the hands of Tyler. Warren states that Walworth, who was chancellor of the state of New York, was "unquestionably of the highest legal ability" but was personally unpopular and was disliked by the Whigs of New York. And he describes Judge Edward King, who failed of confirmation, as a "distinguished lawyer of Philadelphia."[6] The evidence indicates that John Meredith Read of Philadelphia was also well qualified, but the Senate failed to act on the nomination.*

President Fillmore, as his term approached an end, also had difficulty in obtaining the approval of the Senate to his nominations. In August, 1852, he nominated Edward A. Bradford, who, Warren states, was a "leading lawyer of Louisiana"; but the Senate adjourned without acting on the nomination. He next nominated George E. Badger, a United States senator from North Carolina, who was reported to be the ablest lawyer practicing before the Court. But Badger was a conservative Whig, and the Democrats, who were in a majority, would not approve the nomination of an outgoing Whig President. For the same reason, the nomination of William C. Micou was rejected near the end of Fillmore's term.[7] All told, six of the nominations to the Supreme Court were rejected near the end of the term of a retiring President whose party had been defeated at the polls.[8] The Senate declined to act on these nominations, in order to permit the incoming President to make the appointments.

One of the ablest men rejected for the Supreme Court was Henry Stanbery, nominated by President Johnson in 1866. The Senate was determined to curb the President in every move, and countered by passing a bill to reduce the number of judges on the Court so that Johnson could make no appointments to it. Concerning Stanbery, who was Attorney General of the United States at the time of his nomination, the Philadelphia *Enquirer,* a leading Republican paper, said: "A most excellent appointment, and it is to be hoped that he will be promptly confirmed. His power of legal analysis, close reasoning, accuracy of statement, and concise, forcible expression have justly placed him at the head of the present Bar of the Supreme Court."[9]

Grant's nomination of his Attorney General, Ebenezer Rockwood Hoar, an able and distinguished attorney, to the Court in 1869 was greeted by the press as an admirable choice; but Hoar had offended many of the senators by his insistence upon the appointment of highly qualified persons to the circuit court

* These cases are reviewed in chap. v, above.

judgeships, and he was rejected.* Two of Cleveland's nominations, William B. Hornblower and Wheeler H. Peckham—both eminent New York attorneys—were rejected in 1894 when Senator Hill of that state invoked the rule of senatorial courtesy to oppose them.†

The most significant contests over nominations to the Supreme Court since 1900 have occurred over broad political issues, in contradistinction to partisan considerations. The most sensational confirmation contest in history occurred over President Wilson's nomination of Louis D. Brandeis in 1916. Although the opponents of Brandeis accused him of sharp legal practices and a lack of ethical standards appropriate to a member of the Court, the real reason for their opposition was that he was regarded as a dangerous radical. In the public hearings on the nomination, the charges against Brandeis were thoroughly discredited. Brandeis was recognized at that time as one of the ablest attorneys practicing before the Supreme Court, but his courageous fight against monopoly had incurred the bitter hostility of powerful groups in New England.‡

Opposition from exactly the opposite quarter confronted the nominations of Harlan F. Stone in 1925 and Charles E. Hughes in 1930. Hughes in particular was attacked by the Progressives in the Senate, led by Norris, who accused him of being closely identified with great wealth. Those who opposed Stone and Hughes lived to regret it, for both men proved to be great justices whose decisions reflected not only a high order of legal ability but also, in the main, a liberal outlook. Similarly, William Howard Taft later recanted his opposition to the appointment of Brandeis and came to regard him as an able and valuable member of the Court, though often they were on different sides. Judge John J. Parker was rejected when nominated to the Supreme Court in 1930, not because he was regarded as a conservative or identified with great wealth, as had been charged of Stone and Hughes, but because of the opposition of organized labor and the National Association for the Advancement of Colored People. The facts did not support the charges made against Judge Parker, and his record ever since has been that of an able, liberal judge. The clamor raised against him, however, and the assertion that the nomination had been made for political purposes resulted in his rejection.§

Contests over Court Appointments since 1933

Hugo M. Black.—In spite of the bitter fight that occurred in 1937 over his proposed "Court-packing" plan, Franklin D. Roosevelt had relatively little difficulty in securing Senate approval of his nominations to the Supreme Court. Only one of his eight nominees to the Court—Hugo M. Black—was seriously opposed, although several votes were recorded against Justices Frankfurter

---

* See chap. v, above.
† See above, chap. vi.
‡ The Brandeis case is recounted at length in chap. vii.
§ The Stone, Hughes, and Parker contests are recounted in chap. viii, above.

and Douglas. Soon after the Court fight of 1937 came to an abrupt end with the death of the Democratic floor leader, Senator Robinson, Justice Van Devanter took advantage of the recently enacted retirement law and retired on full pay in June of that year. Two months elapsed without a nomination to fill the vacancy, and speculation started that Roosevelt intended to wait until the Senate adjourned and then make a recess appointment. Since the vacancy existed while the Senate was in session, the question was raised whether the President legally could make a recess appointment. On August 2 the White House touched off a furor by announcing that Attorney General Cummings had advised the President that a recess appointment was within his power.* On the same day, Senator Vandenberg introduced a resolution in the Senate that it "was the sense of the Senate" that appointments to the Supreme Court should be made only while the Senate was in session. A hot debate over the propriety as well as the legality of a recess appointment took place. Senator Wheeler, who had led the opposition to Roosevelt's Court plan, declared that any self-respecting lawyer would not accept an appointment and sit on the bench until his nomination had been confirmed.[10]

The following day, at his press conference, Roosevelt hinted that a nomination would soon be sent to the Senate; but on the same day, Senator Borah contended in the Senate that there was no vacancy, arguing that Justice Van Devanter had not resigned and hence was still legally a member of the Court.

On August 12 President Roosevelt sent to the Senate the name of Hugo M. Black, one of the staunchest supporters of his legislative program, a senator who had strongly backed his Court proposal. The nomination came as a great surprise to the country and to all but two or three members of the Senate. As the New York *Times* said editorially the following day, it "dropped like salt into the political wounds already rubbed raw by the court issue." Black not only was an ardent New Dealer, more liberal in outlook than the Roosevelt administration, but as chairman of a Senate investigating committee he had ruthlessly exposed the shady practices of the utility lobby in Washington. The conservatives in both parties who had fought the Court proposal were horrified by the nomination. "As Minton, Schwellenbach, and La Follette rushed to congratulate Black," writes John P. Frank in his biography, *Mr. Justice Black*, "the stunned victors of the Court fight realized that F.D.R. was having his revenge."[11]

Senator Ashurst, chairman of the Judiciary Committee, moved immediately to take up the nomination in executive session without referral to committee, stating that it was an "immemorial rule" of the Senate to confirm one of its own members "without reference to a committee for the obvious reason that no amount of investigation or consideration by a committee could disclose

---

* This advice followed earlier opinions of the Attorney General. See chap. xiv for a discussion of the issue.

any new light on the character or attainments and ability of the nominee, because if we do not know him after long service with him, no one will ever know him." Subsequent events were to indicate in this case that the Senator was in error. Ashurst extolled Black in the highest terms as a "lawyer of transcendent ability, great, industrious, courageous in debate, young, vigorous, of splendid character and attainments ... I cannot conceive how the President could have made a wiser selection...."[12] His motion to approve the nomination without referral to a committee, as a courtesy of the Senate to one of its members, was blocked by Senators Burke and Johnson of California, and the nomination was referred to the Judiciary Committee. This was the first time in fifty years that the Senate had not extended the courtesy of immediate confirmation of the nomination of one of its members.[13] Within less than an hour Senator Ashurst announced to the press the membership of the subcommittee he had named to consider the appointment. All the Democrats on the subcommittee had supported the President's Court plan, and favorable action was assured.

Editorial comment in the press throughout the country on the following day was generally critical of the appointment. The New York *Herald Tribune* stated: "The naming of Senator Black to the Supreme Court ... is an affront to the Court and to the people.... The nomination is as menacing as it is unfit." "It is strictly a New Deal appointment," declared the Cleveland *Plain Dealer*. "With Black on the Court the administration will be assured of at least one vote in support of any Roosevelt measure whose constitutionality is assailed." The Chicago *Tribune* said the President had "picked the one who would be generally regarded as the worst he could find," and the New York *Times* deplored the nomination of Black, whom it regarded as "a bitter and uncompromising advocate of extreme New Deal measures." The Birmingham *Age-Herald* regretted the appointment, which it feared would stir up again the bitterness over the Court fight; it said, however, "we hold a faith in Hugo Black's fundamental sincerity and his broad mental caliber." And in support of the nomination the Louisville *Courier-Journal* said: "Black will carry to the Supreme Court the liberalism for which the President has fought—all the liberalism one man can carry." A week later, after Black had been confirmed, Herbert Hoover declared that the Court was already "one-ninth packed."[14]

The Judiciary Committee voted 13 to 4 in favor of confirmation. Those voting against it were Senators Burke and King, Democrats, and Austin and Steiwer, Republicans. Senator Norris, who was unable to attend because of illness, sent a letter to Senator Ashurst strongly supporting Black, stating: "He is a worthy representative of the common people. He understands their hopes and ambitions, and their liberties in his hands will be safe."[15]

When Black's nomination came before the Senate on August 16, Senator Bridges urged that it be recommitted to the Judiciary Committee for further inquiry and public hearings. This proposal was strongly opposed by Connally who declared that "hearings are for the information of the committee, not for the purpose of public amusement; not to have a legislative rodeo so that everybody may come in and have a good time."[16] In the debate on the following day, Senator Copeland attacked Black on the charge that he was or had been a member of the Ku Klux Klan and had been supported by the Klan in his race for the Senate in 1926. These charges had already appeared in the press.[1] Senator McGill of Kansas, speaking in defense of Black, asserted that the Ku Klux Klan charges made by Copeland, who was a candidate for mayor of New York City, were intended to appeal to Negro voters in the coming election.[18] Other senators who spoke against the nomination did not raise the Klan issue but based their opposition principally on the ground that Black was disqualified, though Johnson stated also that Black was not fitted by temperament and disposition for a judicial position. To the contention that Black had no judicial experience, except for a brief period as a police court judge, which was pointed to sarcastically by those opposing his confirmation, Connally pointed out that of the Justices then serving, Butler, Sutherland, Brandeis, Stone, and Roberts had had no previous judicial experience. "None of them ever sat on a bench," he exclaimed, "unless it was in the park."[19]

Senator Borah opposed the nomination on the legal ground that Black was not qualified because he had voted in favor of increasing the retirement pay of Supreme Court justices. He declared that although the committee had received hundreds of letters accusing Black of being a member of the Klan, there had never been an iota of evidence that he was a member. Borah stated that in private conversation before his nomination came up, Black had said he was not a member.

The final vote was 66 to 15 for confirmation. Six Democrats—Byrd, Burke, Glass, Copeland, Gerry, and King—and nine Republicans voted against it.

Less than a month had elapsed when the Black appointment broke into the headlines again. A series of articles by Ray Sprigle of the Pittsburgh *Post Dispatch* appeared in the press throughout the country exposing the fact that Black had once been a member of the Ku Klux Klan and that, although he resigned from the organization in 1925, he received Klan support when he ran for the Senate in 1926 and was given an honorary lifetime Klan "passport." The articles created a tremendous furor throughout the country. Many newspapers and prominent persons demanded that Black resign. Senator Norris came to the defense of Black, saying that he was "being subjected to all this criticism because he is a liberal...not because he is a Klansman."[20]

Justice Black, who was on a trip to Europe when these stories appeared, declined to make any statement. After his return to this country he made a brief radio address on the evening of October 1, which he prefaced by saying that, although under ordinary circumstances a Justice of the Supreme Court should not discuss a political maneuver, he felt justified in making a public statement because the situation was extraordinary. Admitting that he had once been a member of the Klan, he stated that he had resigned and had since had nothing to do with the organization. He said that his record in the Senate refuted any implication of racial or religious intolerance and that he had "consistently fought for civic, economic, and religious rights of all Americans without regard to race or creed." Negroes, Catholics, and Jews had been his close friends. In closing his short address, Black said, "When this statement is ended my discussion of the question is closed."[21]

The public furor over the appointment, which had already subsided, quickly ended. Two motions brought before the Supreme Court contesting Black's appointment were quickly disposed of, and he took his seat on the bench. His record on the Court has been the subject of wide differences of opinions. A strong defender of individual rights, a supporter of economic and social reform legislation, he remains anathema to conservatives and is accorded high praise by liberals. All agree, however, that he is able and thoroughly competent.

Felix Frankfurter.—The nomination of Felix Frankfurter, a distinguished professor of Harvard University Law School, to the Supreme Court on January 5, 1939, occasioned surprise, for it was expected that the appointment would go to the West, which was unrepresented on the Court. It was generally assumed, however, that Professor Frankfurter, a frequent adviser of the administration, whose students occupied many key positions in the federal government, sooner or later would be appointed to the Court. Although Frankfurter was known for his liberal views, his selection met with general approval, even from conservatives. Senator McNary, the Republican leader, stated to the press that Frankfurter was "learned and qualified," and, though he had hoped the appointment would go to a Westerner, he would support the nomination. Senator Norris, who had urged the appointment of Frankfurter, said that he was the logical successor to Cardozo, and his philosophy of the law was similar to that of Holmes, Cardozo, and Brandeis. Several senators of both parties who had actively opposed the President's Court plan likewise announced their support. But Representative J. Parnell Thomas, a Republican member of the House Committee on Un-American Activities, stated that the evidence taken by that committee indicated that Frankfurter belonged to a number of radical organizations and declared that he "could not conceive of a worse appointment." The President, he said, "might as well have appointed Earl Browder."[22]

At public hearings on the nomination the testimony of several witnesses who appeared in opposition to Frankfurter nearly turned the inquiry into a farce. The first witness, who identified himself as the national director of the "Constitutional Crusaders of America," claimed that he spoke for the unemployed, consumers, and old-age groups. When questioned, he admitted, however, that his organization consisted of one man. A later witness, who professed to speak for the "League for Constitutional Government," similarly admitted that this was his own "trade name." Several other witnesses who claimed to speak for organizations with similar titles appeared in opposition to the appointment. Throughout their testimony ran several common threads. They were opposed to Frankfurter because of his radicalism, his association with alleged left-wing organizations, and his foreign birth. Several witnesses made thinly veiled references to the fact that he was a Jew, and at one point Senator Borah threatened to leave the room if testimony concerning the nominee's religion were permitted.[23]

Professor Frankfurter was invited by Senator Neely, chairman of the subcommittee, to testify at the hearing on his nomination, but declined on the ground that he did not want to be absent from his classes. Through Dean Acheson, who acted as his representative, Frankfurter sent word that he would appear if the subcommittee so desired. When he appeared on the last day of the hearing, he said he thought it would be "improper for a nominee no less than a member of the Court to express his personal views on controversial issues before the Court." He expressed the view that a nominee's record should be thoroughly scrutinized by the committee, yet he doubted that much would be gained by the personal appearance of the nominee. He also pointed out that the records show only one instance in which a nominee to the Supreme Court personally testified before the Judiciary Committee. "My attitude and outlook on relevant matters," he said, "have been fully expressed over a period of years and are easily accessible."[24]

The members of the subcommittee questioned Frankfurter in some detail about his association with the American Civil Liberties Union. Senator Borah inquired what the position of the organization had been concerning Communism. Frankfurter replied that, so far as he knew, the organization had taken no position on Communism but had aided all alike—Communists, Republicans, Progressives, Democrats, and even Nazis and Klansmen—to secure their constitutional rights. A dramatic moment occurred when Senator McCarran asked the nominee whether he believed "in the doctrines of Karl Marx." Frankfurter replied:

"Senator, I do not believe that you have ever taken an oath to support the Constitution of the United States with fewer reservations than I have or would have now, nor do I believe that you are more attached to the theories and practices of Americanism than I am. I rest my answer on that statement." The audience broke into applause, which lasted two minutes.[25] A few minutes later, before the close of the hearing, Chairman Neely said that in view of the attempt on the part of a number of the witnesses to create the impression that Frankfurter was a Communist, he would ask him the direct questions: "Are you a Communist, or have you ever been one?" The witness replied: "I have never been one and am not now." Senator McCarran asked if he meant that he was not an enrolled member, and Frankfurter replied: "I mean much more than that. I mean that I have never been enrolled, that I have never been qualified to be enrolled, because that does not represent my view of life, nor my view of government."[26]

After the hearing, the Judiciary Committee voted unanimously to recommend the approval of Frankfurter, and when his nomination came before the Senate it was approved without dissent. The witnesses opposed to him had been so thoroughly discredited by their irrelevant, unsupported, and highly questionable testimony that the opposition collapsed. The case indicated the need of some provision for screening witnesses in confirmation hearings so that the time of Senate committees will not be wasted by persons who have no relevant facts to present and who wish to air malicious gossip or vicious charges that have no basis of fact.

Other Recent Nominations to the Court.—Of the other recent nominations to the Supreme Court, only those of Tom C. Clark and of Judge Sherman Minton, both in 1949, attracted any appreciable opposition. Senator Frazier of North Dakota attacked the nomination of William O. Douglas in 1939, but only three other senators joined with him in voting against his confirmation. Similarly, Senator Tydings launched a one-man attack on the nomination of Robert H. Jackson in 1941 on the ground that, as United States Attorney General, Jackson had failed to bring suit against a columnist who, the senator asserted, had made false accusations against him. When the vote was taken, only Tydings voted against the nomination.

The nomination of Clark was sent to the Senate on August 2, 1949, and a week later hearings were held by the Judiciary Committee. Clark was warmly supported by the two senators from Texas and by many judges of federal and state courts throughout the country, particularly from Texas. Four former presidents of the American Bar Association and numerous presidents of state and local bars sent commendatory telegrams.[27] Apparently an organized effort had been made to elicit these favorable comments. The press generally was lukewarm or critical. The Richmond *Times-Dispatch* characterized Clark as a "political partisan and a legal lightweight," who "would reflect no credit upon that tribunal."[28] The Washington *Post* stated that the selection did not meet the highest judicial standards and that Clark's name would not have appeared on any "list of distinguished jurists such as a conscientious President usually assembles before making an appointment to the Supreme Court."[29]

The opposition to Clark came principally from liberal and left-wing organizations who accused him of having failed, as Attorney General, to protect civil rights, and denounced him for the part he had played in loyalty investigations and his condonation of wire tapping by the FBI. Included in the list of opposing witnesses at the hearings were representatives speaking for the National Lawyers' Guild, Civil Rights Congress, Independent Progressive party, Communist party, and a number of individual labor unions. Thousands of telegrams and letters, evidently inspired by these organizations, were sent opposing the appointment of Clark.[30] Opposition from this quarter, needless to say, aided rather than injured the nominee's chances of confirmation. John L. Lewis and the United Mine Workers opposed the appointment because Clark had successfully prosecuted the union for its failure to observe the orders of lower federal courts directing the ending of strikes. The UMW official organ asserted that President Truman had "reached a new low in his selection of a successor for the late Supreme Court Justice Frank Murphy."[31]

The Judiciary Committee, after overriding attempts by Senators Ferguson and Donnell to have the nominee testify about the Justice Department prosecution of the 1946 election-fraud cases in Kansas City, voted 9 to 2 to recommend Clark's confirmation. In the Senate debate, which lasted three and one-half hours, Senator Ferguson led the opposition, making various charges against Clark's record as Attorney General. Senator Taft declared that it was "outrageous" that Clark had not been called to testify and said that this alone justified a negative vote. When the roll was called, only eight senators—all Republicans—voted against Clark.

After the death of Justice Rutledge in 1949, President Truman nominated Judge Sherman Minton, a former member of the Senate, to the Court. The nomination of Minton, who had served for eight years as a member of the circuit court of appeals, was greeted by mixed praise and criticism by the press but was commended by the bar. The opposition was due to his earlier record as a strong New Dealer when he was a member of the Senate, and especially to his support, twelve years earlier, of President Roosevelt's Court plan. The nomination received the unenthusiastic support of the two Republican senators from Indiana, Minton's home state; hence no concerted effort was made by the Republicans to block it. After a brief hearing, the Judiciary Committee voted 5 to 4 to invite Minton to testify. He declined to do so, however, on the ground that it would be improper for him to appear at the hearings, where he might be asked to testify on "highly controversial and litigious issues affecting the Court."* When his nomination came before the Senate, a determined effort was made to recommit it to the committee in order that Minton could be required to testify. After this motion was lost, the nomination was confirmed by a vote of 48 to 16.[32]

In making nominations to the Supreme Court, the President, as leader of his party, has necessarily taken political considerations into account, but they have been of a rather different type from those that are controlling in the appointment of judges to lower courts. Conservative Presidents have usually nominated conservatives to the Supreme Court, and liberal or progressive Presi-

* See chap. xiv, above.

dents have similarly chosen persons favorable to their programs.[33] There can be no valid criticism of this practice. The Senate, as well as the President, has given primary attention to the philosophy, outlook, attitude, and record of nominees to the Supreme Court with regard to social and economic problems of society. The contests that have taken place in the last fifty years over nominations to the Supreme Court have been concerned almost wholly with such issues, though not always openly so. Thus there was always strong opposition to Brandeis and Black because of their liberal views, although it was placed ostensibly on other grounds; the opposition to Stone, Parker, and Hughes was based on their reputation as conservatives. On the other hand, the nominations of Taft, a pronounced conservative, and Cardozo and Frankfurter, who were widely known for their liberal views, met with little opposition, because of the high public esteem in which these men were held.

The opposition to Hughes and Parker in 1930 because of their supposed conservatism was denounced as an attack on the sanctity of the Court itself. Senators Norris and La Follette replied that the Supreme Court has come to pass upon economic and social legislation and hence to decide upon governmental policies; the philosophy of persons nominated to the Court was therefore a pertinent consideration. In their study of *The Business of the Supreme Court,* Professors Frankfurter and Landis found that common law cases, which in 1875 amounted to 43 per cent, had dropped to 5 per cent by 1925. There were no cases under the "due process" clause in 1875, but in 1925 there were 20; in 1875 there were no cases under the commerce clause, but in 1925 there were 29.[34]

Writing in 1930, Frankfurter strongly defended the action of the Senate in considering the philosophy and outlook of a nominee to the Supreme Court. "The meaning of 'due process,'" he stated, "and the content of terms like 'liberty' are not revealed by the Constitution. It is the Justices who make the meaning. They read into the neutral language of the Constitution their own economic and social views.... Let us face the fact that five Justices of the Supreme Court *are* molders of policy, rather than the impersonal vehicles of revealed truth."[35] In an often quoted statement, Chief Justice Hughes, when he was governor of New York, once said: "We are under a Constitution, but the Constitution is what the judges say it is."

It is entirely appropriate for the Senate, as well as the President, to consider the social and economic philosophy of persons nominated to the Supreme Court. With the changed functions of the Court, considerations of this kind are more pertinent than the legal attainments and experience of nominees. In recent years few of the persons appointed to the Supreme Court have had experience as judges; for the most part they have been drawn from public life and have not been practicing attorneys at the time of their appointment.

The record of the Senate before 1900 in passing upon nominations to the Supreme Court was that of rejecting approximately one out of four, usually for partisan reasons; but in the last fifty years the Senate has rejected only one nomination to the Court, that of Parker in 1930. The rejection of Parker, an able judge who would have honored the Court, and the bitter fight over the nomination of Brandeis in 1916 do not add to the credit of the Senate, and this may also be said of the contests over the nominations of Hughes and Stone. On the whole, however, during the last half century the record of the Senate in passing on nominations to the Supreme Court has been creditable; the appointment of one outstanding Justice—Cardozo—has been attributed to the insistence of members of the Senate.

Judges of Lower Courts

The customs and traditions in the nomination and confirmation of judges of lower federal courts differ markedly from those that apply to the appointment of Justices of the Supreme Court. Indeed, the practices are rather different for each of the several types of lower court judges. The President has a much freer hand in the selection of judges of the circuit courts of appeal, whose districts cover several states, than of district judges, who serve within individual states. In the selection of judges of the tax court and customs court, as well as judges of the federal courts in the District of Columbia and the territorial courts, he likewise has a wider discretion, for members of the Senate may not claim the right to dictate these appointments though they often press for the appointment of their candidates. Primary attention will be given here to the appointment of district judges, the most numerous group.

By well-established custom, which has prevailed since about 1840, federal district judges are normally selected by the senators from the state in which the district is situated, provided they belong to the same party as the President. The senators, of course, consult with the party leaders in their states, who often make the actual selection. In states represented in the Senate by the opposite party, the President turns to the party organization for recommendations. Washington and other early Presidents consulted members of the House as well as the Senate about local appointments in their states, and also consulted other prominent citizens; they did not feel obligated to nominate the choice of the senators from the state in which the office was situated. Gradually, however, consultation developed into the custom of permitting the senators from the state or the party organization to make the actual choice, and by 1840 this was the well-established custom. It is not uncommon today for announcements of judicial appointments to be made by the sponsoring senator, and newspaper accounts feature the selection by the senators or by the party leaders—not the choice of the President and the Attorney General. In a recent session of Congress a Democratic representative from Pennsylvania arose to compliment Senator Myers of that state for his choice of a federal judge whose appointment had been recently confirmed. Twenty years earlier, at a hearing on a judicial nomination, Senator Reed indicated that he regarded the selection of district judges in his state to be his responsibility. Stating that he had "looked for a judge" from the Scranton–Wilkes-Barre region, Reed continued: "I thought for awhile that I had found a good man in Luzerne County, which is where Wilkes-Barre is, and then I thought I had found a man in Tunkhan-nock.... All of these men I considered. I wanted to get the best one.... So far as this being somebody else's choice, it is not. It is my choice. It is my free choice, uninfluenced by General Atterbury or anyone else."[36]

In his study *The Selection and Tenure of Judges,* Professor Evan Haynes of the University of California School of Law described the practice followed in the appointment of federal district judges, concluding with the observation: "The net result ... is that the Senate has expropriated the President's power of nomination so far as it concerns appointments of interest to senators of the party in power; and the President has virtually surrendered his power directly to local party politics as to appointments in states where senators are of the opposition."[37]

The practice of delegating the actual selection of federal district judges to individual members of the Senate, or to the party organization, which in-evitably results in political appointments, has often been criticized in the press and by eminent legal scholars. Writing in 1930, Dean Wigmore cited current instances of the actual selection of judges by senators instead of by the President and declared that the Constitution had been altered in practice to read: *"The individual Senator* from the State where an appointment is to be made shall *nominate."* Pointing out that the same practice applied to nomina-tions for administrative offices, which were regarded as the "personal game preserves" of senators, to be used in paying political debts, Dean Wigmore declared: "The time has come to abolish both of these unconstitutional practices. The Constitution never meant that the Senators should nominate."[38]

In a series of articles dealing with the federal judiciary, Professor Shartel stated that although presidential appointment and senatorial confirmation of Justices of the Supreme Court had been satisfactory, that system had not worked well for inferior judges and had resulted in political appointments. Describing the usual practice and its results, he stated:

But the fact that inferior judgeships are treated as "party pie" is not the worst of it. Worse is the fact that these judgeships have become local "party pie." District and circuit judgeships have come to be regarded as jobs to be handed out at the behest of the local party chiefs. The President has almost abdicated his power of selection.... Every vacancy results in a wild scramble and pulling of political wires which is only less hurtful to judicial independence and disinterestedness than is a popular primary or election.[39]

A defense of the custom which permits individual senators of the President's party or the party organization to select persons to be appointed to federal courts[40] has frequently been voiced by members of the Senate, who contend (1) that they are in a better position to pass upon persons for judicial appointments in their own states than the President or Attorney General, (2) that the Constitution intended that the senators should advise the President about nominations in their own states, and (3) that they are responsible to the people of their states for their selections.* Senator Norris, however, and some other members of the Senate have condemned the practice as resulting in patronage appointments. They have pointed out that in selecting persons for judicial appointment, the individual members of the Senate are necessarily influenced by considerations other than the qualifications and fitness of prospective appointees, and often the choice is dictated by the party organizations for strictly partisan purposes.[41]

Although the present practice of political appointment of federal judges has been severely condemned by writers on the subject, it should not be assumed that it uniformly results in poor appointments. Many senators maintain high standards in the choice of persons whom they recommend for judicial appointments—witness the selections of Senator Douglas of Illinois, which ranked far above the President's nominees in the referendum of the Illinois bar association.† Unfortunately, some members of the Senate have not maintained high standards, and state and local party organizations have often backed mediocre candidates, or worse. Some of the worst judicial appointments are made in states having senators who belong to the opposition party. It may be noted, however, that the President is freer to reject the recommendations of the party officers in these states than he is to turn down the candidate proposed by a senator of his own party.

The system is not satisfactory and needs to be altered to lessen partisan considerations and to bring about uniformly higher standards for judicial appointments. Partisan politics was probably the cause of the appointment of the nine judges against whom impeachment proceedings have been brought, and the larger number threatened with impeachment, a number of whom resigned under fire. The number of judges impeached, however, is not an accurate indication of the integrity and ability of the bench; there have been numerous judges who have been poorly qualified and even corrupt but who never committed acts that made them subject to impeachment. The federal judges who faced impeachment proceedings or who resigned while such proceedings were under contemplation had all, of course, been confirmed by the Senate. It does not appear that their nominations—with possibly one or two exceptions—were contested when they came before the Senate; this indi-

* These arguments are cited in chap. xiii, above.
† See *ibid.*

cates that the requirement of senatorial confirmation has not been as effective a safeguard against bad appointments as is often supposed.[42]

That the present system has resulted in political appointments to the federal bench is fully evidenced by the fact that Presidents of both parties generally appoint only members of their own party. Statistics compiled by Judge Evans A. Evans of federal judicial appointments from 1885 to 1941, from the first administration of Cleveland through the first two terms of Franklin Roosevelt, indicate that of the 545 appointments, 517, or 94.8 per cent, were of the same party as the President. Only 28 appointments of members of the opposite party were made in this period, of which 19 were under the Republican administrations of Taft, Coolidge, and Hoover and presumably were in the South, where the bar is preponderantly Democratic. According to this study, McKinley, Wilson, and Harding each made only one appointment to the bench from the opposite party; Cleveland and Franklin Roosevelt (up to 1941) made none.[43]

The practice of political appointments has resulted, after one party has been in office over an extended period, in a preponderance of judges who belong to that party. In 1933, at the end of President Hoover's term, of the federal judges with life appointments, 172, or 75 per cent, were Republicans; 57 were Democrats; and 2 of unknown party affiliation. By 1950 these proportions were reversed: 224 of the federal judges (72 per cent) were Democrats and 84 were Republicans.[44]

It is anomalous that the selection of the federal judiciary, which is expected to be above partisanship, should be turned over to the local party organizations. Various reforms have been advanced. It is usually assumed that the Senate would never consent to giving up its power of confirmation of judicial appointments; indeed, it would appear that the Constitution requires their approval by the Senate. Any reform must accordingly retain appointment by the President, by and with the advice and consent of the Senate.

The most notable attempt at reform of judicial appointments was made by President Hoover when he came to office in 1929. With the backing of the President, Attorney General Mitchell made a determined effort to elevate the standards for judicial appointments. The recommendations of senators and of the party were accepted if they came up to the standard, but it was hoped to reduce the influence of partisan considerations. In the first group of 11 judicial nominations sent to the Senate by Hoover in April, 1929, the White House made public the names of persons who had endorsed each nominee, a step that was praised by the press.[45] The Attorney General announced in a national broadcast the policy of the administration to appoint only judges of high qualifications and to make no appointments in reward for political activity.[46]

Hoover publicly announced that he would not accept the recommendations of several Republican state organizations in the South until they had cleaned house, and he publicly reprimanded them for proposing persons who were not qualified. In pursuing this course, however, the administration soon faced the bitter opposition of senators from Northern states who insisted on their customary patronage. On advice of the Attorney General, Hoover refused to nominate the candidate of Senator Schall to a judgeship in Minnesota. An unsuccessful attempt was then made to get the Minnesota senator to recommend another person whom the President and his Attorney General could approve, and finally Hoover sent in a nomination of his own choice, Gunnar Nordbye. Senator Schall blocked confirmation by entering a personal objection, and Hoover countered by giving Nordbye a recess appointment. The President subsequently accepted Schall's nominations for two other judgeships in Minnesota, and the Senator withdrew his objection to Nordbye.* For six months Attorney General Mitchell opposed the nomination of a judge proposed by Senators Capper and Allen of Kansas; but in October, 1929, after they had informed the President that they would support no one else, he withdrew his opposition, and Hoover sent the name of their candidate to the Senate. In commenting on the case, the New York *Times* stated in an editorial that "in the matter of federal appointments the President is to a large extent an agent, not a principal."[47]

A notable contest which arose in Pennsylvania soon after Attorney General Mitchell had announced the policy of the administration to insist on high qualifications for judicial appointments illustrates the difficulties that confronted the administration when it attempted to carry out such a policy. Senator Reed and the Pennsylvania Republican organization pressed for the appointment of Albert L. Watson, the judge of a Pennsylvania state court, to a federal district judgeship. The appointment, however, was opposed by the senior judge of the circuit court of appeals and many leading members of the bar on the ground that Judge Watson did not measure up to the standards of the federal bench; the evidence subsequently brought out at the hearings substantiated their position.[48] Attorney General Mitchell held up the nomination for several months until finally Senator Reed called at the White House and delivered an ultimatum that unless the President sent in the nomination of Watson he could expect no support from the Pennsylvania delegation in Congress.[49]

At the hearings on the nomination, General W. W. Atterbury, president of the Pennsylvania Railroad and Republican national committeeman from Pennsylvania, testified that he had recommended the appointment of Watson; but he made the amazing admission that he knew nothing of Watson's legal ability and had never met him until after he had recommended him for the appointment. While the nomination was pending before the Senate, Paul Y. Anderson of the St. Louis *Post-Dispatch* published two articles in which he stated that 147 of the 200 active members of the Scranton bar favored another candidate, whereas only 30 lawyers throughout the entire district favored

---

* See chap. xiii, above.

Watson; that Watson had appeared as counsel in only six cases in twenty-six years of practice; that most of his practice consisted of uncontested divorce cases; and that he had the active support of Atterbury, Joseph R. Grundy, and other leaders of the Republican organization but his nomination had been opposed by Attorney General Mitchell until Senator Reed forced a showdown.

When the hearings on the nomination were reopened in September, Senator Reed testified that he alone was responsible for the nomination and that the selection had not been made by General Atterbury. Attorney General Mitchell, in response to a request for a statement as to the qualifications of the nominee, declined to write a letter to the committee but appeared in an executive session. Governor Pinchot of Pennsylvania, who had appointed Watson to the state common pleas court, wired in opposition to the appointment.

When the nomination came before the Senate on December 16, 1929, it was strongly opposed by Senators Norris, Walsh, and La Follette. Senator Borah stated that he would vote against confirmation if the Attorney General would make a statement that he did not regard Watson as qualified for the position, and Senator Steiwer voiced a similar view. Pressed by members of the Senate for a statement, Attorney General Mitchell wrote a letter in which he stated that he considered Watson the best person "available" in Pennsylvania. Senator Reed defended the nomination, saying that he alone was responsible.[50]

Senator Walsh attacked Atterbury for the part he had played in the nomination, saying that as president of the Pennsylvania Railroad he ought not to be the national committeeman of a political party. "But at least," said Walsh, "he ought to keep his hands off the appointment of judges in States where his railroad runs." Senator Norris praised the President for the stand he had taken on judicial appointments and for his public denunciation of the Florida Republican organization for "peddling patronage for selfish reasons to incompetent aspirants," and expressed regret that he was unable to follow the same course with respect to the powerful Pennsylvania machine.[51]

Senator La Follette condemned the practice of permitting the individual senators or party organizations to dictate the appointment of judges in their own states, saying:

As I read the Constitution of the United States, it does not confer upon any single senator, or upon the political machine in any state, however powerful, the authority to dictate the selection of men who are to be placed for life on the Federal bench. Not even the President of the United States is vested with such power. The Constitution provides that the President shall submit nominations for these offices, and that the Senate—not a member of the Senate—shall advise and consent to the nomination before the President shall tender his nominee an appointment.[52]

When the vote was taken, the appointment of Watson as United States district judge was confirmed by a vote of 53 to 22.

After suffering these defeats at the hands of the Senate, President Hoover became more cautious in rejecting the nominees for judicial office who were sponsored by senators. The necessity for retaining the support of his party in the Senate must always greatly handicap the President in his attempts to enforce high standards for appointment, for he usually cannot afford the luxury of offending a powerful senator of his party. To the senator, the privilege of naming the most important federal offices within his state is a symbol of power on which his prestige with his followers depends. Consequently, when judicial appointments are at stake, members of the Senate are insistent that the appointments go to men of their choice, whose selection has usually already been announced in the press.

President Franklin D. Roosevelt was evidently less impressed with the importance of maintaining high standards for judicial appointments than his predecessor, and as a result, he had fewer conflicts with the Senate over nominations to the bench. He appointed a number of eminent attorneys to the circuit courts of appeals, in which he had a freer hand; but for district judgeships he ordinarily accepted the nominee with political backing without insisting on high standards of qualifications.[53] He followed a policy like that of Lincoln, who did not hestitate to appoint incompetent men to lesser posts when larger policies were at stake.*

The most significant contest between Roosevelt and the Senate over a judicial appointment to a lower court was that of Floyd H. Roberts of Virginia in 1939. There was never any question in this case concerning the qualifications of Roosevelt's nominee or those of the two persons proposed by the two Virginia senators. The contest was strictly political.†

In 1943, Senator O'Daniel, with the help of the Louisiana delegation, was able to block the confirmation of James V. Allred to the circuit court of appeals. Allred had resigned from the bench to run against O'Daniel for the Senate. After O'Daniel had retired from the Senate, Truman nominated Allred to be a district judge in Texas, and the nomination was approved without opposition. President Truman on several occasions disregarded the customary prerogatives of senators of the party in office by failing to nominate their candidates for local judgeships and naming persons of his own selection. As a consequence, he suffered several rebuffs at the hands of the Senate; on a single day in 1950 the Senate rejected three of his nominations, two of district judges on personal objection of the senators from Iowa and Georgia. In neither case does it appear that the nominee of the President was rejected because of any lack of qualification, though Senator Gillette contended on the floor of the Senate that his nominee was the choice of the bar of the district. It was never explained why the President had not followed the wishes of the senators in respect to these judgeships.‡

* See chap. v, above.
† This case is recounted in detail in chap. xiii, above.
‡ These cases are reviewed in chap. xiii.

Contest over Illinois Judgeships

In 1951 a contest which presented a number of unusual features occurred over the appointments to two new judgeships in the northern district of Illinois. Before invoking the custom of senatorial courtesy, Senator Douglas took the unusual step of asking the local bar associations to conduct a poll of their members to ascertain whether they preferred his choices or those of the President. The results by overwhelming majorities indicated that the selections of the senator were held in higher esteem by the bar than those of the President. This was the reverse of the usual situation. Senator Douglas recommended two persons of high qualifications whose selections were not dictated by political considerations, whereas the persons nominated by the President were evidently selected as the result of political deals and were not so well qualified. In another respect the case was unusual: Senator Douglas had generally supported the President's legislative program; hence the rejection of his nominees could not have been due to his voting record in the Senate.

In the autumn of 1950, Senator Douglas, following the customary practice, conferred with party leaders and prominent members of the bar to select the persons he would recommend for the new judgeships in Illinois. After the defeat of Senator Lucas in that year, Douglas was the sole Democratic senator from the state and according to established custom was entitled to name the persons to be appointed. On January 26, 1951, he recommended two persons to the Attorney General for appointment: Judge Benjamin Epstein, who for eighteen years had been a judge of the Illinois circuit court, and William King, Jr., a member of a leading law firm and former president of the Chicago Bar Association. Both men had the endorsement of Jacob M. Arvey, Democratic leader of Chicago.[54] The recommendation of Douglas for a third judgeship was accepted by the President and he was subsequently confirmed without opposition.

In spite of the backlog of cases piling up in the northern district of Illinois, the President took no action for a period of six months; then on July 13, he sent in the names of Municipal Judge Joseph J. Drucker, the nephew of Representative Sabath of Illinois, and Judge Cornelius Harrington. While the nominations were awaiting his decision, the President did not consult with Senator Douglas and did not advise him of his decision to nominate Drucker and Harrington instead of the two persons whom the senator had recommended. He did confer, however, with former Senator Lucas, who presumably urged him to nominate Harrington. The nomination of Drucker is another story. It was reported that President Roosevelt, before his death, had promised Representative Sabath, chairman of the House Rules Committee and a faithful supporter of the administration, to appoint Drucker "the next time," saying that he was then too young. When a vacancy did occur, however, President

Roosevelt appointed William J. Campbell, who was even younger than Drucker![55] Sabath bided his time, and when the bill creating the new judgeships in Illinois came before the House in 1950, he secured an understanding that Drucker would receive one of the appointments. In the hearing of the Judiciary Committee on the Drucker nomination, Sabath openly referred to this understanding in urging the approval of his nephew. Stating that he had been largely responsible for the passage of the bill in the House creating these judgeships, Sabath said: "At that time it was understood that one of these places would go to my nephew, of whom I am proud."[56] Similar agreements or deals have not been uncommon in the past in connection with legislation creating new judgeships, but never before have they been so openly admitted. The understanding was commonly known and was widely disapproved by the Chicago bar, which accounts in part for the adverse vote Drucker received in the polls. That Sabath saw nothing wrong in the understanding and regarded it as a valid reason for the approval of Drucker is in itself a significant commentary on the manner in which federal judges are appointed.

President Truman's rejection of the two persons recommended by Senator Douglas without consulting him, and his nomination of Drucker and Harrington, placed Douglas in an embarrassing position. As a supporter of the legislative program of the administration on most issues, he had no desire to engage in a public controversy with the President. He also did not wish to invoke the custom of senatorial courtesy and assert that the President's nominees were "personally obnoxious" to him. To the contrary, in a press release of July 17 he publicly stated that they were "worthy" men. But he considered the men he recommended better qualified and decided to oppose the President's nominations. His first step was to ask the Chicago and Cook County bar associations to conduct a secret poll of their members to ascertain whether they preferred his choices or those of the President.[57] In addition, Senator McCarran invited the Illinois Bar Association to poll its members in the northern judicial district, and on top of all this, the Chicago *Sun-Times* conducted its own poll of the 12,000 lawyers practicing in the city of Chicago. The results of all the polls indicated an overwhelming preference for the persons recommended by Senator Douglas. In the poll of the Chicago Bar Association, Judge Epstein, the choice of Douglas for the first judgeship, polled 3,656 votes; Judge Drucker, the President's nominee, polled only 553. For the second judgeship, the man recommended by Senator Douglas polled more than twice the number of votes received by the President's nominee. The other polls, though conducted somewhat differently, showed similar results. In the poll of the Illinois Bar Association, its members were asked also to indicate whether they regarded each person as qualified for the position of judge; on this poll, Drucker received only 594 "yes" against 1,948 "no" votes.[58]

With the backing of these polls, Douglas appeared at the committee hearings and opposed the President's nominations. In his testimony he reviewed the history of the cases, the failure of the President to consult with him, and the results of the poll, and defended the custom which accords to the senators of the party in office the privilege of selecting the persons to be appointed as judges in their own states.* Following the precedent in the Iowa and Georgia cases of the preceding year, he did not enter a plea that the President's nominees were personally obnoxious to him, but maintained that the manner of their nominations was obnoxious. In all his statements concerning the controversy Senator Douglas stressed that his concern was "to help get the best available judges for the federal bench." In the brief Senate debate on the nominations on October 9, before the vote in which the President's selections were unanimously rejected, Senator Douglas closed his statement with these words: "I must reluctantly raise my objection to the appointment of these candidates because of the manner and method of their selection, and because the result would, in my judgment, be antagonistic to the cause of good government and the maintenance of a strong, independent judiciary."[59]

Several pertinent observations may be made about the Truman-Douglas controversy over the Illinois judgeships. The evidence seems quite clear that Douglas exercised greater care in his selections than did the President. Yet it should not be assumed that Douglas had set about to select the best lawyers he could find. He was looking rather for the best "available" lawyers; this restricted his choice to Democrats, though probably most of the lawyers of the highest standing in the district were Republicans. Also he had to take into account racial and religious factors and find persons who were acceptable to the Democratic organization. In the hearings it was brought out that on one thing Truman and Douglas were agreed, namely, that one of the appointments should go to a Protestant, one to a Catholic, and one to a Jew. Within this frame of reference, Douglas undertook to find the best "available" persons for the appointment. Political considerations did not dominate the selections by the senator, but they were undoubtedly influential.

The fact that Senator Douglas recommended well-qualified persons for judicial appointment in Illinois should not obscure the fact that this method of selection typically results in political appointments, often of poorly qualified persons, and restricts appointments to members of the party in power. The results of the system are worst in states in which the party leaders rather than the senators dictate the actual selection. The more hardened the custom becomes of turning the selection over to the individual senators or to the party organizations, the worse the results will be. The development of a strong, independent judiciary does not require the maintenance of this system but rather its modification or abandonment.

It was not the intention of the framers of the Constitution that both the function of nomination and that of confirmation should be placed in the hands

---

* A part of the statement of Senator Douglas is quoted at the beginning of this chapter.

of the same individuals. They did not trust the President to appoint the principal officers of the government without some check on his appointing power. But they would have been less willing to place this power in the hands of individual members of the Senate, who are not responsible for the appointments they control. This result, however, has been achieved through the custom of senatorial courtesy, under which the Senate as a body has for the most part abdicated its function of confirmation of appointments.

The standards of qualifications for appointment to federal district courts are determined not by the President or the Senate—except for certain minimum requirements below which they will not go—but rather by the members of the Senate from the several states and the local party organizations. Some members of the Senate have insisted upon high standards and have recommended only fully qualified persons; other senators, however, have recommended persons for the federal bench who do not measure up to suitable qualification standards. Party organizations in most states regard federal judiciary appointments as patronage plums to be dispensed as a reward for party service, and it is not uncommon for nominations to be given to politician-lawyers of little standing at the bar, who have secured the necessary political support.

The political selection of federal judges has long been the subject of serious criticism, and various proposals have been made for its reform. The American Bar Association plan for judicial selections, approved by the House of Delegates in 1937, is worthy of serious consideration. This plan was proposed as a substitute for the popular election of judges, which is the rule in most of the states; but the same principles are applicable to the selection of federal judges. It provides a dual agency in the appointment of judges: (1) an official board or commission, consisting of lawyers elected by the bar itself and at least an equal number of laymen appointed by the governor, which would prepare a panel of persons recommended for judicial appointment; and (2) appointment by the governor, who would be restricted to persons named on this panel. Legislative confirmation of judicial appointments significantly was not favored, on the ground that it would "open the door to political deals and log-rolling."[60]

A council of judicial appointments, of the kind proposed by the American Bar Association and utilized in Missouri,[61] would probably have very great effect in elevating judicial standards. It is unlikely that Congress would enact legislation providing for such a plan; but the President could establish such a council or councils as advisory to him without legislative authorization, and could follow the practice of appointing only from the panel recommended by them. In a thoughtful editorial commenting on the controversy in 1950 between Senator Douglas and President Truman over the Illinois judgeships, the Washington *Post* condemned the present system of political appointment of federal judges and proposed that they be appointed from panels of outstanding lawyers selected by a committee representing the Attorney General, the federal bench, and the bar.[62]

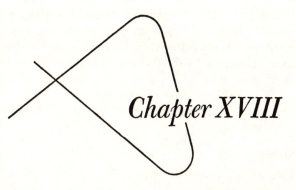

Chapter XVIII

ADMINISTRATIVE AND MILITARY OFFICERS

Under the President, the heads of departments must hold full responsibility for the conduct of their departments. There must be a clear line of authority reaching down through every step of the organization and no subordinate should have authority independent from that of his superior. The Commission on Organization of the Executive Branch of the Government (Hoover Commission).[1]

It is appropriate and desirable that major political offices in the Executive Branch of the Government be filled by persons who are appointed by the President by and with the advice and consent of the Senate.

On the other hand, the technical nature of much of the Government's work today makes it equally appropriate and desirable that positions of other types be in the professional career service. The administration of our internal revenue laws at the local level calls for positions in the latter category. President Truman, Message to Congress on the reorganization of the Internal Revenue Bureau, 1952.[2]

THE MAJOR CONTROVERSY over senatorial confirmation within recent years has arisen over proposals to extend the requirement to certain groups of subordinate administrative officers and employees. In the next chapter the history and debates over these proposals are reviewed. This chapter deals with the operation and effects of senatorial confirmation of the following classes of subordinate administrative and military officers: bureau chiefs, military and naval officers, officers of special career services, subordinate administrative officers in charge of field offices, and, finally, postmasters.

It is significant that three official commissions which studied the administration of the federal government—the Taft Commission on Economy and Effi-

326]   THE ADVICE AND CONSENT OF THE SENATE

ciency in 1912, the President's Committee on Administrative Management in 1937, and the Hoover Commission in 1949—each made the identical recommendation that administrative officers and employees below the level of assistant and under secretary of executive departments should be appointed by the department or agency head rather than by the President and the Senate and should normally be career civil servants. In the period from 1935 to 1943, however, there was a trend in the opposite direction, with the enactment of legislation extending senatorial confirmation to the appointment of various administrative officials and employees.

Bureau Chiefs

A major finding of the Hoover Commission in 1949 was that department heads do not have authority commensurate with their responsibility; it accordingly recommended that under the President they "must hold full responsibility for the conduct of their departments." The commission considered that the power of the department head to choose his subordinates, and to remove them if necessary, was essential to the development of internal loyalty and effective working relationships within the department. It found that the appointment of bureau chiefs by the President, by and with the advice and consent of the Senate, tends to remove the chiefs from responsibility to their department heads and to encourage them to work directly with the committees of Congress. This practice was criticized by the commission and its task force on departmental management as contrary to principles of sound organization and management. In order to assure a clear line of authority, it recommended that "as a rule" bureau chiefs should be appointed by the department heads rather than by the President, by and with the advice and consent of the Senate.[3] This recommendation was reiterated in its reports dealing with several departments, including Agriculture, Commerce, Interior, Post Office, and the proposed new department to administer education and social security.

Although it recognized that assistant and under secretaries of departments are political officers and therefore are appropriately appointed by the President, by and with the advice and consent of the Senate, the Hoover Commission recommended that administrative assistant secretaries also should be appointed by the head of the department, without senatorial confirmation. This recommendation was followed in legislation subsequently enacted to create the office of administrative assistant secretary.

The task force of the commission on departmental management reported that of the 73 bureau chiefs in the executive departments in 1948, 29 were appointed by the President, by and with the advice and consent of the Senate, and 31 were by statute placed under civil service. The remaining 13 were appointed by the department head, or by the President alone, and were not required by law to be appointed from the civil service. These statistics do not include the bureau chiefs of independent commissions and agencies, who probably exceed in numbers those in the executive departments. Bureaus in these agencies have been established by administrative action rather than by statute, and the bureau chiefs are not subject to senatorial confirmation. In the large majority of cases they are under the civil service.

The recommendations of the Hoover Commission paralleled the earlier recommendations of the President's Committee on Administrative Management in 1937, which was headed by Louis Brownlow. This committee recommended the extension upward of the merit system to include all positions in the government except the highest executive offices whose duties are policy determining in character, which should be "at the disposal of the newly elected President to enable him and his administration to control the service." The report of the committee stated that the number of policy-determining positions was relatively small, consisting of the heads of executive departments, under secretaries and assistant secretaries, members of regulatory commissions, the heads of a few large bureaus "engaged in activities with important policy implications," the chief diplomatic posts, and a limited number of other key positions.[4]

In the hearings of the Joint Committee on Government Organization in 1937 little attention was given to this recommendation, because of the preoccupation of the committee with other features of the President's recommendations. Senator Byrd inquired to what extent the provision would limit the power of the Senate to confirm appointments and requested a list of positions that would be affected, and Senator O'Mahoney expressed the opinion that for many of the bureau chiefs Senate confirmation should be required. Several other members expressed doubts of the wisdom of selecting bureau chiefs and other high administrative officials through civil service examinations, mistakenly assuming that this procedure would be required if these positions were placed under civil service. The brief discussion indicated an unwillingness on the part of the members of the joint committee to authorize the President to determine which positions were policy determining and to place all others under the civil service.[5]

The reorganization bill subsequently introduced by Senator Robinson, chairman of the joint committee and Democratic floor leader, provided for the extension rather than the curtailment of senatorial confirmation. Under it the heads of all bureaus, divisions, offices, or services which are directly responsible to and subject to control by the heads of departments, and all positions which the President found were policy determining in character, were thereafter to be appointed by the President and confirmed by the Senate.[6] Objections to this section were voiced by several of the department heads. Secretary Hull, long a member of the Senate, pointed out that under existing law the Secretary of State had the authority to "appoint chiefs of its bureaus, divisions and offices without the necessity of obtaining Presidential appointment or of submitting them to the Senate for confirmation," and stated that this authority was "essential to the efficient conduct of our foreign relations."[7]

Secretary Wallace of Agriculture made an even more vigorous objection. Agreeing that "policy-forming" officers must be appointed by the administration in power, he contended that such officers "would be seriously handicapped if they could not depend upon able and experienced men in administrative positions which are concerned, not with the formation of policies, but with giving properly determined policies full force and effect." He pointed out that although only one officer of the Department of Agriculture below the level of Assistant Secretary was then appointed by the President and confirmed by the Senate, the bill would increase the number to about twenty-five. "Through these twenty-five," he wrote, "the entire Department operates, and upon their ability, wisdom, and experienced acquaintance with Government operation, rests a very great responsibility." Continuing, he stressed the need for a career service which includes chiefs of bureaus.

Heads of bureaus and offices in this Department are the chief officers of scientific, regulatory, business, educational, and related units whose tenure in the past has not been affected by changes in the national administration. They are the top level of the career service. To place any of these officers within the realm of political appointments would seriously disturb from top to bottom the whole structure that has been erected without regard to political considerations.[8]

Most of the twenty-nine bureau chiefs appointed by the President and confirmed by the Senate are in two departments, the Treasury and the Navy. The bureau chiefs of the Navy are invariably appointed from the regular officers of the Navy, and their appointments, like those of other naval officers, are routinely approved by the Senate. It is perhaps due in part to historical accident that most of the bureau chiefs and the heads of major departmental units of the Treasury are subject to senatorial confirmation, whereas those of the State Department are not. Bureau chiefs in the other departments are usually appointed by the department head and are not subject to confirmation by the Senate. There appears to be little reason for the variation in practice.

It has been proposed at times that all bureau chiefs be appointed by the President and confirmed by the Senate.[9] In defense of such a provision it is contended that bureau chiefs are important officials, the heads of large organizations, and that they exercise important policy-determining functions. The trend fortunately has been in the direction of making the position of bureau chief nonpolitical, and appointments are normally made from the ranks of career civil servants. To throw the position into the arena of partisan politics would result in the appointment of persons without the necessary experience and qualifications to provide the leadership essential to efficient administration.

The bureau chiefships are key positions in the administrative structure and should be filled by persons of exceptional administrative and often professional qualifications. Political appointment would result in frequent turnover, weak administration, and great harm to the public service.

Although bureau chiefs have certain important policy functions, these relate to the preparation and execution rather than the determination of policies. Bureau chiefs are responsible for the preparation of programs and for recommendations to the departmental head and to Congress concerning proposed legislation, but they are not, in fact, *policy-determining* officers. When important policy decisions affecting the programs or operations of the bureau arise, they are decided by the department head or his chief assistants, and often require action by the Congress. There is a distinction, which is often overlooked, between the exercise of administrative discretion and the determination of policies.

There have been few contests in the Senate over appointments of bureau chiefs. In some departments, as for instance in the Navy, regular career employees are appointed as bureau chiefs; hence confirmation has become largely a formality. The contest over the appointment of James Boyd as Director of the Bureau of Mines in 1946, however, illustrates one of the undesirable effects of senatorial confirmation of bureau chiefs. The appointment of Boyd, who had been dean of the School of Mining of the University of Colorado, was opposed by John L. Lewis, ostensibly on the ground that he had had no practical experience in mining. The real reason appears to have been that Lewis, who as head of the United Mine Workers of America, expected to be consulted about the appointment, felt aggrieved that a person not of his choice had been named. For two years he was able to hold up the confirmation of Boyd, who continued to serve on recess appointments without compensation. Finally, in 1949, when it appeared that the Senate would act on the nomination, Lewis called a two weeks' nation-wide strike in protest. This action was greeted by vehement criticism in the press throughout the country, and the Senate moved promptly to approve the nomination. A number of senators of both parties from coal-mining states, however, voted against confirmation, doubtless because of the pressure of the organized miners in their own states.*

Another significant contest over the appointment of a bureau chief, which shows the Senate at its worst, occurred in 1934 when the Senate Commerce Committee rejected Dr. Willard Thorp as director of the Bureau of Foreign and Domestic Commerce. Thorp was an able economist and business analyst and had formerly been a professor of economics at Amherst College. As a member of the Social Science Research Council committee on statistics, he was called to Washington in 1933 to assist in the reorganization of the Bureau of Foreign and Domestic Commerce and was subsequently appointed director.

---

* The Boyd case is recounted in chap. xii, above.

At that time the staff of the bureau was being sharply reduced, but it was also subject to heavy pressure from Democratic office seekers. Thorp refused to employ political hacks in positions requiring expert qualifications, saying to one persistent applicant that the fact that a person was a "good Democrat" was not sufficient to qualify him for the position. The disappointed office seeker related to his congressman that Thorp had refused to give him a job "because he was a Democrat!"

When hearings were held on the nomination, Thorp was charged with having registered as a Republican, to which he replied that he was a technical man and not a partisan. Admitting that he had once registered as a Republican in Amherst, where that party was dominant, he stated that in New York he had registered as a Democrat and he would do the same if he lived in the South. Such political fickleness horrified the Southern Democrats on the committee.

The rejection of Thorp on May 9, 1934, by a vote of 11 to 5 of the Commerce Committee, was due mainly to the opposition of Senator Stephens of Mississippi, who was facing an election campaign with former Governor Bilbo as an opponent. Bilbo boasted to his friends that he had Senator Stephens "over a barrel" and would "give him hell" either way. If Stephens voted to confirm Thorp, he would attack him for putting a Republican into office, a high crime in the minds of Mississippi Democrats. But if he voted against Thorp, he would attack him for not backing the Roosevelt administration. Senator Stephens stated that the rejection of Thorp by the committee had nothing to do with his politics but was due to his lack of the necessary qualifications, a statement which Arthur Krock reported brought hoots of derision from informed persons in the Department of Commerce.

On the following day, Assistant Secretary of Commerce John Dickinson came out with a blast denouncing the "pecksniffian hypocrisy" in the Senate which had resulted in the rejection of Thorp, and threatening to resign unless a man of Thorp's caliber could be found to direct the Bureau of Foreign and Domestic Commerce. Dickinson stated that the opposition had been due to "fabricated and untruthful charges of a miserable, petty, partisan character," which had been circulated by a "very small clique of disappointed office seekers." Although he had no personal interest in Thorp's selection and did not know him personally at the time, Dickinson said that Thorp had "discharged his duties with admirable ability, fidelity and success" and had gained the respect and commendation of the business community and all who have had contact with his work.

In spite of his assurance that he would not withdraw the nomination, Roosevelt did so and designated Dickinson to act as director of the bureau until a suitable successor was found. Thorp subsequently served with distinction in several posts of the highest responsibility in the government, including those of Assistant Secretary of State and United States Representative at the United Nations and other international conferences, after being confirmed in these appointments without opposition.[10]

Military and Naval Officers

All regular appointments and promotions of officers of the armed services require the approval of the Senate. In 1951 the Senate confirmed 23,421 nominations of officers, rejected none, and failed to act on 16. These nominations are always confirmed en bloc, and except those of a few of the higher officers, are ordinarily not given individual attention. Senate confirmation of military and naval officers has become for all practical purposes an empty formality. Formerly it was not uncommon for members of the Senate to exert considerable influence on military and naval promotions, but this practice seems to have almost disappeared. Occasionally objection is raised by members of the Senate to the promotion of a particular officer, and as a result the list is withdrawn and the particular name dropped, but such cases are exceptional.[11] In quite exceptional cases, individual nominations of military or naval officers to the highest posts may become subjects of special inquiry, as, for example, the nomination of Admiral Sherman to be Chief of Naval Operations in 1949. In this instance there was no criticism of the nomination of Admiral Sherman, but the hearing furnished an occasion for an inquiry whether his predecessor had been removed for the part he had taken in the earlier controversy over the cancellation of the contract for building an extra large airplane carrier.

Senate approval of the many thousands of appointments and promotions of military and naval officers each year serves little purpose. In a single year, 1949, the Senate received and acted on 49,956 such nominations. Obviously it would be quite impossible for the Senate or for its Armed Services Committee to give individual attention to so large a number of personnel actions. If each nomination were considered for only one minute by the Senate committee, it would require 832 hours to pass upon the nominations submitted in 1949, or an average of more than 5 hours each day that the Senate is in session. If the Senate limited its consideration to a small number of the highest-ranking officers who are assigned to the chief military and naval posts and gave these appointments individual attention, confirmation by the Senate would become of greater significance. The routine approval of the many thousands of military and naval appointments and promotions deceptively gives the Senate the appearance of control over these positions, whereas it actually has little or none. Congress should concern itself not with these individual actions but rather with the personnel policies and practices of the armed services, conducting investigations from time to time when they are needed, and passing legislation on the subject. In defense of the present practice, it may be said that Senate confirmation for this group of officers has become so routine and so perfunctory that it does no harm, and it does provide the opportunity for objection to be raised in exceptional cases.

Officers of the Foreign Service, Coast Guard, Public Health Service, and the Coast and Geodetic Survey

Each of these services has its own special career system, into which persons enter as a result of examinations and are promoted under a merit system carefully prescribed by statutes and regulations. Officers in these services carry ranks comparable to members of the armed services. Indeed, the Coast Guard may be regarded as a part of the armed services, with a special status in time of peace. In 1951 the number of nominations acted on by the Senate in these several services was as follows: Foreign Service, 580; Coast Guard, 328; U. S. Public Health Service, 590; and Coast and Geodetic Survey, 36.[12] Senate confirmation of these nominations, like the confirmation of appointments of officers of the armed services, is a formality of little significance.

Subordinate Administrative Officers and Employees

Several hundred federal field officers, principally in the Treasury and Justice departments, are subject to senatorial confirmation. (Postmasters of the first three classes, totaling more than 21,000, who are also confirmed by the Senate, are treated in the next section.) These field officers include district attorneys, marshals, collectors of revenue and customs, and directors of federal mints. Until 1952 the 64 collectors of internal revenue were appointed by the President and confirmed by the Senate. Formerly, numerous other federal officers in the several states were subject to confirmation by the Senate. These included local port officers, surveyors, receivers and registers of land offices, Indian inspectors, pension agents, inspectors of steam vessels, and others.[13] With the passage of time most of these offices have been abolished and their duties assigned to others.

In recent years Congress has extended the requirement of senatorial confirmation to certain other classes of field officers who were not under civil service. For example, in 1935 it required Senate confirmation of state directors of the Work Projects Administration, the Public Works Administration, and the National Youth Administration, who received annual salaries of $5,000 or more. From 1935 to 1945, bills and riders were pressed at each session of Congress to extend the requirement of senatorial confirmation to subordinate administrative positions, but those that were enacted applied for the most part to temporary positions outside the civil service and were of limited or temporary effect. This effort to extend senatorial confirmation, which constituted the greatest threat to the civil service within recent years, is considered at length in the next chapter.

In its report on the Treasury Department, the Hoover Commission stated: "One of the chief handicaps to effective organization of the Department is the political appointment of Collectors of Internal Revenue and of Customs, and certain other officials. These appointments are regarded by some as sinecures. In any event, they form a bar to the orderly development of an experienced staff."[14] The same recommendation, but in even stronger terms, had been made by the House Committee on Appropriations in its report on the Treasury and Post Office departments appropriation bill in March, 1948, but without effect. Summarizing the results of an investigation which the committee had conducted, the report stated:

The most serious defect in the organization and operations of the Bureau is the fact that the men who are charged with the actual collection of the revenue, the collectors, are political appointees. The Commissioner, who administers the entire Bureau, does not have effective control over the collectors throughout the country. Whether collectors of internal revenue actively attend to the affairs of their offices or merely bask in their patronage appears to be largely a matter of their own volition.[15]

A similar finding and recommendation was also made by the special investigative staff of the House Appropriations Committee in 1947. "Collectors of internal revenue," this report stated, "are appointed under the patronage system, and the Bureau cannot exercise sufficient control over the collectors to insure a desirable operation in each of the 64 collection districts." Pointing out how the collectors were able to play politics by giving favored assignments to their friends and discharging other employees, the report recommended that "in the interest of economy and efficiency the patronage system should be eliminated."[16]

In spite of the mounting criticism of the Bureau of Internal Revenue little was done to reform it except to discharge employees found guilty of illegal practices and misconduct and turn them over to the Department of Justice for prosecution. The collectors in whose offices lax administration, irregularities, and worse were brought to light were permitted to remain in office. The fact that they had powerful political sponsors made it difficult for the bureau to remove them or to exercise effective control over them.

In 1951 the entire country was rocked by a series of sensational scandals which involved a number of the largest internal revenue offices. In February, Senator Williams of Delaware, who two years earlier had exposed the embezzlement of funds by the cashier of the internal revenue office at Wilmington, Delaware, exposed the corruption and incompetence which marked the administration of the collector of the third district, including most of metropolitan New York City. He read into the record names and crimes of ten former employees of this office who had been convicted of soliciting and accepting bribes and other crimes in the preceding five years. Quoting the report of the investigations conducted by the Bureau of Internal Revenue, he declared that the administration of this office had been bad for several years and had steadily become worse. In 1950 the collector was asked to resign, but he refused, defending himself on the ground that his office contained many political appointees who were incompetent and for whom he could not be held responsible. "How bad do conditions have to get before some action is taken?" exclaimed Senator Williams, who declared that "our system of tax collection is shot full of cheap, inexcusable, political manipulation."[17]

The special committee of the Senate to investigate organized crime, initially headed by Senator Kefauver, unearthed significant evidence of collusion between racketeers and others engaged in organized crime and officials of the Bureau of Internal Revenue, but the committee did not make any recommendation for taking the bureau personnel out of politics.[18]

A subcommittee of the House Ways and Means Committee, headed by Representative King of California, started a nation-wide investigation of the Bureau of Internal Revenue in 1951. The investigation revealed shocking instances of bribery, extortion, corruption, lax administration, and all sorts of questionable connections of a number of collectors and deputy collectors with business interests whose tax payments were under investigation. The collectors' offices in a number of the largest cities of the country—Boston, New York, Brooklyn, Chicago, St. Louis, Milwaukee, San Francisco, and others—were involved in these scandals. Before the end of the year, 166 Bureau of Internal Revenue employees, including 6 collectors, had been discharged on charges, and indictments were pending against many of these. "The disclosures," stated the New York *Times,* "have added up to this pattern of misdeeds: Bribery of officials to drop tax fraud cases; extortion of money from taxpayers under threat of prosecution; social and business connections between officials and men involved in tax frauds; the free use of 'names' of officials by questionable characters claiming 'influence'; pressures on tax officials from many sides, including Congress."[19] Although all 166 employees, except the 6 collectors, were under civil service, 40 per cent of them were political appointees who had been covered into the civil service by executive order after the passage of the Ramspeck Act of 1940.[20] Before this act was passed, deputy collectors were exempted from civil service and were appointed under the patronage system.

The commissioner of the bureau resigned in 1951 for reasons of health, and the assistant commissioner asked for a reassignment for the same reason. Neither was personally implicated in any wrongdoing, but each was held responsible for tolerating the conditions that were brought to light. The chief counsel of the bureau resigned, protesting that he had been unjustly accused, and T. Lamar Caudle, the Assistant Attorney General in charge of the prosecution of tax cases, was removed by President Truman. His testimony before the King subcommittee revealed highly questionable associations with business interests that were involved in tax litigation, and the acceptance of various favors and commissions from persons accused of "tax fixing."

Collector James P. Finnegan of St. Louis, who was subsequently convicted of accepting bribes to influence his decisions on tax matters, testified before the King subcommittee that he spent only two to four hours a day in the office and carried on his law practice on the side, from which he had received an income in excess of $100,000 for a three-year period. Much of this income was for representing business firms—several of which were in tax difficulties—in their dealings with the government. Finnegan's own tax returns were under investigation; his 1949 return showed deductions of $4,689 for entertainment, $3,093 for transportation, and $3,212 for hotel bills. After the facts of the case were exposed by the St. Louis *Post-Dispatch,* the first grand jury investigation failed to bring in an indictment. In St. Louis, as well as elsewhere, it was charged that the United States district attorney did not show any zeal in prosecuting such cases, and Judge George H. Moore warned that a real investigation was needed. The subsequent investigation and indictment of Finnegan was evidently due to the fact that Senator Williams secured confidential information on the case and revealed it on the floor of the Senate.

The facts concerning Collector Delaney of Boston, who was indicted and convicted of accepting bribes, were similar. Both men, as well as those in other cities who were dismissed, received their appointments through the backing of the party organizations and the Democratic senators from their states. Finnegan testified that he had been backed by Bennett Clark, who was then a senator from Missouri. Significantly, it was brought out in the hearings that there had been unfavorable reports in the Treasury investigations of Finnegan, Delaney, and James G. Smythe, a former collector in San Francisco, before their appointments; but apparently their political backing was strong enough to overcome this obstacle.

Commissioner Dunlap stated to the press in 1951 that fifteen of the sixty-four collectors of internal revenue were career employees who had been promoted from the ranks. None of these were involved in the scandals. The appointment of these career men, however, was not due necessarily to their competence and ability, but probably to the political backing they had secured. Twenty-five collectors, it was reported, were engaged in outside activities, which is now forbidden by the Bureau of Internal Revenue regulations.

After the Internal Revenue Bureau scandals broke, President Truman stated at a press conference that it was not planned to bring the collectors under the civil service, because if this were done it would be more difficult to get rid of them. However, the fact that several collectors refused to resign and remained in office for some time after their resignations had been demanded does not appear to support this contention. In October, Senator Kefauver came out in support of placing internal revenue collectors under civil service, and the following day the President took a similar stand, releasing a letter from Frank E. McKinney, recently installed as chairman of the Democratic National Committee, urging this course. In January, President Truman sent to the Congress a plan completely reorganizing the bureau. It abolished the sixty-four collectors and established in their place not to exceed twenty-five district commissioners, who would be career men appointed from the civil service. Several other top positions in the bureau that were formerly held by persons appointed by the President and confirmed by the Senate were also abolished, leaving only the office of commissioner and three others to be filled in that manner. These changes were stated by the President to be essential to strengthen the organization and to protect the government from "insidious influence peddlers and favor seekers." The President announced his determination to make the bureau "a blue ribbon civil service career organization."

In his message explaining his plan President Truman stated that the bureau should be manned "by persons who get their jobs and keep them solely because of their own integrity and competence." He referred to the greatly increased tax collections of the bureau, which had risen from five and a third billion dollars in 1940 to more than fifty billion in 1951, and from nineteen million tax returns in 1940 to eighty-two million in 1951. In the same period the number of employees had increased from twenty-two thousand to fifty-seven thousand. Truman declared that the existing organization of the bureau, as prescribed by law, was "archaic" and that efficient administration was greatly hampered by the fact that the collectors, who were politically appointed, were subject to local political situations and were not "fully responsive to the control of their superiors in the Treasury Department."[21]

It was freely predicted in the press that the President's plan would face stiff opposition in the Senate from members who were reluctant to give up their customary patronage of selecting the internal revenue collectors. A resolution was introduced in the House by Representative Hoffman to disapprove the plan, but it was voted down by a large majority after the members of the King subcommittee came out for the plan. Senator George of Georgia, chairman of the Finance Committee, introduced a similar resolution in the Senate, which was referred to the Committee on Government Operations (at that time called Committee on Expenditures in the Executive Departments) headed by McClellan of Arkansas. When hearings were conducted in February, most of the witnesses who appeared supported the plan; the opposition came chiefly from the members of the Senate. Former President Hoover issued a statement favoring the plan because it would take the Internal Revenue Bureau out of politics, a reform which the Hoover Commission had advocated three years earlier; the Citizens' Committee for the Hoover Report led the fight against the George resolution.

In the ten days of hearings it was apparent that a majority of the committee was opposed to the President's plan. Senator George contended that the fact that a number of internal revenue collectors were guilty of corruption was due not to the method of their appointment but rather to bad appointments, for which the President was to blame. To head off the President's plan its opponents urged that the bureau reorganization be done by legislation, and for this purpose Senator McClellan introduced a bill that included most of the features of the reorganization plan but left the collectors of internal revenue unchanged. "I don't believe the Civil Service Commission," he said, "has any more wisdom for selecting honest men than Senators have." Before the committee voted on the George resolution, President Truman made a last-minute appeal for it to sustain his plan; but this was unavailing. The committee voted 7 to 5 in favor of the George resolution.[22]

Before the plan came to a vote in the Senate, President Truman wrote a letter to Vice-President Barkley again urging its approval; in it he stated that the vote would indicate who was merely talking about corruption and who really wanted to do something about it. He declared that millions of taxpayers who were watching the action of the Senate would be able to tell "whether Senators are more interested in their political patronage than in good public service."[23] The letter infuriated opponents of the measure, and they denounced the President for impugning their motives, each declaring that he had no interest in political patronage.

The defense of the plan in the Senate debate was made by a group of junior senators, led by Humphrey, Moody, and Monroney, and including Benton, Aiken, Lehman, Dirksen, and Margaret Chase Smith. The central theme of their argument was voiced at the outset of the debate when Senator Monroney inquired of Senator McClellan if he would not agree that the "crux of the issue is whether collectors of internal revenue shall be removed from the patronage system and placed under the civil service system?" The Senator from Arkansas vehemently disagreed. In a brief statement Senator Smith of Maine said that she would vote for the plan because it would take the collectors of internal revenue out of politics, as had been earlier recommended by the Hoover Commission. She stated, moreover, that it gave members of the Senate a "chance to do more than just talk against corruption," it gave them an opportunity to vote against it.

All who spoke in favor of the President's plan denounced the system of patronage appointment of collectors of internal revenue. Senator Monroney referred to their selection by the "boys in the back room," and Senator Humphrey declared: "We are not babes in the woods in connection with politics ... The fact of the matter is that a political appointee knows how he got his appointment and to whom he owes his appointment. As the Commissioner of Internal Revenue pointed out, a political appointee owes his appointment not to the people, but to a Senator, a national committeeman, or some friend in the political structure."[24] Senator Benton declared that in a service which collects fifty billions of dollars of revenue annually, the country could no longer tolerate "the old-fashioned way of filling collectors' jobs by political patronage." He spoke also of the pressure of the self-interest of senators and their desire to "keep personal control of some patronage plums, regardless of how worm eaten those plums may be," and declared that those who failed to vote for the President's plan would have little right to criticize others for failure to fight corruption in government.[25]

In presenting the report of his committee in favor of the George resolution, Senator McClellan declared that the Senate should not be panicked into "voting in haste for a reorganization plan in name, without adequate consideration." He stated that under the plan, policy-determining officials "who would have control over the tax destiny of the American people" would be appointed under civil service. "Quasi-judicial power and authority with life and death powers over taxpayers," he asserted, "are reposed in individuals selected by the Civil Service Commission, with no remedy other than by appeal to the Tax Court." He attacked the plan also because it would result in no saving, and quoted from the testimony of Commissioner Dunlap, who had stated in the hearings that the plan was directed primarily at improving the efficiency of the service rather than safeguarding it against frauds and corruption. At the close of the debate Senator McClellan declared: "If we approve the plan we would be taking the political power away from ourselves, away from the control of this constitutional body ..."[26]

The opponents of the plan attacked the extension of civil service to collectors of internal revenue on the ground that senators were better able to select collectors than was the Civil Service Commission. This sentiment was voiced by Senator Hoey of North Carolina, who said: "I do not believe that civil service examinations will disclose the qualifications and fitness of a man to be a collector of internal revenue to the same degree or to the same extent that his qualifications can be explored by those who know him and know the State and know the situation and can make appropriate recommendations to the President." This argument was based on the erroneous assumption that appointments of collectors would be made on the basis of entrance examinations instead of by promotion from within the service.

Senator George raised a number of technical objections to the plan, asserting that it would take away the right of taxpayers to a jury trial in tax refund cases, and would "create a legal vacuum" by abolishing offices without creating new ones to replace them. Although the plan was publicly endorsed by former President Hoover, George asserted that it was contrary to the report of the Hoover Commission. He made much of the fact that under the plan about half the states would not have a district commissioner. "Arizona and Nevada," he declared, "would have to crawl over the mountains into California to adjust their tax matters." Pleading with the Senate to retain its constitutional powers, he said: "If the Senate yields to the pressure which comes from the press and from commentators, and columnists, without adequate information, and votes on this important question against its better judgment, irreparable damage will be done to the prestige of the United States Senate and to the legislative branch under the Constitution."[27]

Senator Millikin, chairman of the Senate Republican Conference, who had joined with Senator George in sponsoring the resolution disapproving the plan, asserted that President Truman had "grossly insulted" the Senate in his letter to Vice-President Barkley, and that the President was asking help in "diapering his badly soiled, unhousebroken political offspring."[28]

It was notable that none of the 34 senators who were up for reëlection in 1952 spoke against the plan, though 11 voted against it, all from safe states. In the final vote, 53 votes were cast in favor of the plan and 37 against it. Eighteen Democrats (14 from the South) joined with 19 Republicans in voting against the plan, and 30 Democrats and 23 Republicans voted in favor of it.

The Bureau of Internal Revenue has been taken out of politics. But the reform should not stop with the collectors of internal revenue; the collectors of customs, heads of local mints, and other field officers in the Treasury Department should be placed under civil service. The objections applicable to other patronage appointments apply also to these offices. But judging by the experience of the Bureau of Internal Revenue, it will take another series of scandals before these positions in the Treasury can be taken out of politics. President Truman's plans to place these officers under the civil service were rejected in 1952 by the Senate.

The appointment by the President, with the confirmation of the Senate, of district attorneys is subject to the same objections that apply to collectors of internal revenue. District attorneys exercise wide discretionary powers in determining whether persons charged with federal crimes shall be brought to trial, and their close association with political organizations has often led to charges of political influence and occasionally has resulted in serious scandals. The Wickersham Commission on Law Observance in 1931 pointed out that politically appointed prosecutors exercise "enormous powers of preventing prosecutions from getting to trial," and condemned the close relationship that frequently exists between corrupt political machines and organized crime. In its *Report on Prosecution,* the first recommendation called for the "elimination, so far as possible, in our system of government, of political considerations in the selection and appointment of federal district attorneys and prosecuting officers, and of appointments based on political activity or service." It likewise condemned "the claim of the Senate not merely to exercise a collective power of rejecting unfit nominations, but to dictate appointments as the patronage of the Senators."[29]

This report of the Wickersham Commission was hotly attacked by two members of the Senate. Senator Thomas J. Walsh (Democrat) retorted that politics is seldom absent in appointments made by the President, even to the Supreme Court. Senator Hiram Bingham (Republican) declared that "the Department of Justice is as likely to get good district attorneys by taking the advice of the Senators as by any other way," and asserted that the senators were responsible to the people of their states for their selections of persons to be appointed to federal offices.[30] This stock argument has often been advanced by the defenders of patronage appointments; but experience indicates that there is no effective responsibility for such appointments. Persons appointed as a reward for their services to the party or to an individual senator are seldom adequately qualified for the position, and in some instances they are persons of questionable reputation.

For somewhat different reasons, United States marshals, who are also subject to Senate confirmation, should be taken out of politics and placed under civil service. Their duties are purely ministerial; it is anomalous that they should remain outside the civil service. Little attempt is made by the Senate or by individual senators to maintain suitable standards for appointment. The position is invariably regarded as a patronage job to be awarded for service to the party or the senator, and at times persons with questionable reputations are appointed. A sensational case that occurred in San Francisco in 1951 illustrates the possibilities of blackmail and graft afforded by the position. The United States marshal for northern California—who had been appointed with the endorsement of the local party organization, the congressman from the district, and the United States senator—approached a wealthy prisoner in a local jail, threatening to have him removed to a distant federal prison with a reputation for harsh treatment of its inmates, unless he paid $2,000. The FBI was tipped off and, setting a trap, caught the marshal in the act of receiving the bribe. The FBI had held up the original appointment of this man for some time, because he had an earlier criminal record, but had eventually withdrawn its objection, presumably because of political pressure.[31]

In April, 1952, President Truman submitted a reorganization plan to Congress to place the ninety-four United States marshals under civil service, but the plan was rejected by the Senate on June 18 by a vote of 55 to 28. The Committee on Government Operations, to which the plan was referred, voted 9 to 3 against it. The grounds for the opposition, as given in the report of the committee to the Senate, were that (1) it was not a true reorganization plan since its only effect was to change the method of appointment of marshals, (2) it centered the power of appointment "behind an iron curtain in the Attorney General's office" and thus eliminated "the advice of the people's elected representatives upon the appointment of these important Federal officials in their respective judicial districts," (3) it removed the safeguard of senatorial confirmation, (4) it permitted transfers of marshals from district to district, (5) it would not accomplish economies, and (6) no evidence of fraud, inefficiency, or extravagance was presented that would justify adoption of the plan. The report stated: "The spokesman for the Department of Justice advised the committee that he knew of no single instance where mismanagement has recently existed in the marshal's offices, nor could he recall specific examples in the recent past."[32]

The minority report, signed by Senators Humphrey, Monroney, and O'Conor, supported the plan on the grounds (1) that the position of marshal is a nonpolicy one that should be placed under the civil service, allowing persons to be chosen on the basis of experience and qualifications; (2) that the plan would improve the service by permitting deputy marshals, already under civil service, to be promoted to the position of marshal on the basis of achievement; (3) that the plan would provide an improved structure of accountability in the Department of Justice by making marshals responsible to the head of the Department instead of to their political sponsors; and (4) that this reform had been recommended by each of the three national commissions that had surveyed the organization and administration of the federal government in the last forty years.

These arguments were restated by each side in the course of the Senate debate on the plan. Senator McCarran, chairman of the Judiciary Committee, which passes on patronage appointments under the existing law, led the attack. He characterized the plan as one that would result in "carpetbag" marshals—that the local people would have no voice in their selection—and asserted that under it persons from one section of the country might be appointed as marshals in other sections. He also stated that the plan would "demean" the office of marshal because it would no longer carry the prestige of senatorial confirmation. Senator Humphrey defended the extension of the merit system to marshals, saying that "the sooner we get law-enforcement activities completely divorced from the spoils system, the better off we shall be." In the final vote a large majority of senators of both parties voted to reject the plan, and those voting in its favor were equally divided between the two parties. The Democratic leadership opposed the plan, but the fight for it was led by three Democratic members.[33]

Postmasters

The largest group of civilian employees whose appointments are subject to confirmation by the Senate are postmasters of the first, second, and third classes; these in 1950 totaled 21,034.[34] This large group includes the postmasters of towns of less than 500 population in which the postmaster is the only regular full-time employee, as well as those of the largest cities with thousands of postal employees. Postmaster appointments have always been the largest and most important bloc of patronage under the control of members of Congress. Formerly postmasters were the key figures in the party organizations in most sections of the country, and each change of administration was accompanied by a clean sweep of postmasters throughout the country. Gradually, however, this has changed, and the grosser forms of political spoils have disappeared. Fourth-class postmasters were covered into the civil service by Presidents Theodore Roosevelt and Taft, and the Ramspeck-O'Mahoney Act of 1938 brought the first three classes under a form of civil service and gave them indefinite terms. Postmasters today are subject to the Hatch Act and can no longer actively participate in election campaigns.

In spite of these reforms, however, the practice of permitting members of the House of Representatives, if they belong to the party in office, to select the postmasters in their districts still continues, only slightly affected by the use of pseudo-civil-service examinations. In districts represented by members of the opposite party, the selection is made either by one of the senators from the state, if they belong to the party in office, or by the party organization. In any event, the party organizations are influential in the appointment of postmasters. Although the present practice is an improvement over the former custom, since postmasters are now appointed for indefinite terms and are debarred by law from engaging in politics, nevertheless it prevents the development of a true career postal service and results in the appointment of persons who have little qualifications and no knowledge or experience in postal operations. In spite of repeated recommendation by the Civil Service Commission, official commissions, and congressional committees that the Post Office be taken out of politics and that postmasterships be filled by career postal employees, the strongly entrenched system of political selection of postmasters continues.

Early History.—During the first fifty years of the federal government postmasters were appointed by the Postmaster General and were not subject to senatorial confirmation. Washington refused to interfere with the appointment of postmasters, of which in his time there were only seventy-five for the entire country.[35] In these early years it was the practice of the Postmaster General to consult members of Congress about the appointment of postmasters in their districts, but he also consulted other prominent citizens, and the postmasterships were not regarded as the patronage of the members of Congress. Commenting on some criticisms which had been made of certain postmaster appointments during his term, Jefferson wrote to Madison in 1814 that the President should be given greater control to prevent abuses, and that all appointments should be made by him or require his approval. He was, however, opposed to any "intervention" by the Senate, which he said would make matters worse.*

---

* Quoted in chap. iii, above.

Washington's practice of permitting the Postmaster General to have a free hand in selecting postmasters was followed until 1829, when Jackson became President. John Quincy Adams retained McLean in office as Postmaster General even though he was aware that McLean was appointing Jackson men to local postmasterships. Madison removed a Postmaster General who had appointed a personal friend as postmaster of Philadelphia over the protest of the members of Congress from that city.[36] After a squabble arose in the New York delegation over the appointment of the postmaster of Albany, President Monroe recommended to Congress in 1823 that "the appointment of postmasters, where the compensation exceeds a certain amount be made by nomination to the Senate, as other offices of the General Government are appointed."[37] Although bills were introduced earlier, it was not until 1836 that such a law was finally enacted. The act applied only to postmasters whose compensation exceeded $1,000 annually, and at the outset affected only 87 of the more than 11,000 post offices.[38]

By 1840 the practice was generally followed of permitting the representatives in Congress who belonged to the same party as the President to select the postmasters in their districts. If a district was represented by a member of the opposite party, a senator from the state, if he was of the same party as the President, was permitted to name the postmasters. This practice obtained not only for those postmasters subject to Senate confirmation but applied also to those appointed by the Postmaster General. In 1840 Postmaster General Niles complained that the calls of members of Congress about appointments took up half of each day, stating that he looked forward to "a little relief on the adjournment of Congress."[39] President Hayes undertook to curb the excesses of congressional control of local appointments, but the practice of consulting members of Congress about the appointments of postmasters continued. "The rule of the Department," wrote the Postmaster General in 1884, "is to regard the public wish in the selection of postmasters and, in order to arrive at this, the Member of Congress—if a Republican—or a Senator, if the Member is not a Republican, is generally relied upon to furnish trustworthy information."[40]

A bill was introduced in 1869 to make it unlawful for a member of Congress to solicit, recommend, or advise the President on the appointment of any person to office. A similar provision in the Pendleton Act of 1883 provided that no appointing officer of postmasters shall receive or consider recommendations from members of Congress.[41] This self-denying provision, however, included a loophole that permitted members of Congress to certify as to the character of candidates; hence it never had any effect in curbing the patronage appointments of postmasters. In 1890 a committee of the National Civil Service Reform League estimated that the appointment of postmasters took at least one-third of the time of members of Congress. The average member was reported to have 250 post offices in his district, and to receive 1,700 applications for appointment each term.[42]

Attempted Reforms.—In response to the widespread criticism of the system, Senator Henry Cabot Lodge in 1890 introduced a bill to establish competitive examinations for the office of fourth-class postmaster and to prohibit political influence in the appointment of postmasters of this class. But the bill, not winning the support of President Harrison, failed of passage. In defense of his bill, Senator Lodge declared that congressmen "are the true overlords of the fourth-class postmasters and the Post-Office Department is simply a great machine to record and execute their wishes. It is considered one of the inalienable rights of a Congressman to have a personal dependent in every minor post-office in his district."[43]

In 1902 Postmaster General Payne announced that fourth-class postmasters thereafter would not be removed, except, for cause, and President Roosevelt, near the close of his term, issued an executive order covering some 15,000 fourth-class postmasters into the civil service. The remaining fourth-class postmasters were placed under civil service by President Taft in 1912. A setback occurred when the Democratic party came into office in 1913; President Wilson issued an executive order requiring all postmasters of this class who received more than $180 annually to take a competitive examination and authorizing the Postmaster General to appoint any one of the three highest candidates who passed the examination. The effect of the order was that most of the Republicans who had previously been appointed fourth-class postmasters were replaced. Postmaster General Burleson announced that he would consult members of Congress (presumably only Democrats) concerning the character and fitness of the three eligibles for appointment in their districts. When the National Civil Service Reform League protested this practice, Burleson replied that he proposed to consult congressmen not as members of political parties but as representatives of the district![44]

President Taft repeatedly urged that postmasters of the first three classes—who are appointed by the President and confirmed by the Senate—be placed under civil service; but Congress took no action.* In 1917 President Wilson issued an executive order requiring that postmaster nominees pass a civil service examination and providing that only the name of the person who passed the examination with the highest rating should be certified to him for nomination to the Senate.[45] The order did not apply to the reappointment of incumbents who had given satisfactory service. Although Wilson was unable to cover postmasters of the first three classes into the civil service, the effect of the order was to establish bona fide competitive examinations for appointment. It was vigorously protested by Democratic members of Congress, many saying that it would wreck the political organizations in their districts. Some members of Congress asserted that not more than 10 per cent of the incumbent postmasters could pass a competitive examination—a most damaging admis-

* See chap. vi, above.

sion of the low standard of qualifications of politically appointed postmasters. The change, which was reported as "almost revolutionary in its effect on the political machines throughout the country," was commended editorially by the New York *Times* on the ground that the post offices should be taken out of politics and should be run as a business.[46]

Despite the protest of many Democratic members of Congress, Wilson refused to rescind the order. The evidence indicates that during the following four years it was fairly and honestly administered. An investigation of its operation conducted in 1921 by the National Civil Service Reform League indicated that of the 2,103 postmasters appointed under the order, 1,012 were Democrats, 907 were Republicans, and the remainder were independents or members of minor parties.[47]

When the Republican party came into office in 1921 one of the early acts of President Harding was to amend the Wilson order to provide for the rule of three instead of requiring the appointment of the person who stood first in the examination. This change resulted at once in the reintroduction of patronage appointments. When vacancies occurred in a district represented in Congress by a Republican, the Post Office Department gave a temporary appointment to the person recommended by the member of Congress. When examinations were given, months later, the acting postmaster thus appointed had little difficulty in passing the examination, which consisted principally of an oral interview and an investigation of the character and reputation of applicants. If the favored candidate did not rank among the top three, a new examination might be ordered. An investigation conducted by the National Civil Service Reform League two years after the order went into effect indicated that the examinations were in the main a sham, and that patronage appointments were the rule. Of the first ninety-two appointments investigated, ninety of the appointees were Republicans and only two were Democrats.[48] In 1922 the league issued a report stating that "postmasterships were meted out by Congressmen to their active political workers and were still regarded as political spoils to be filled with Republicans for partisan purposes."[49]

In spite of repeated recommendations of the Civil Service Commission that postmasters be brought under the classified civil service, the Harding order was continued by Presidents Coolidge, Hoover, and Roosevelt. In April, 1933, Postmaster General Farley announced that Republican postmasters would be permitted to serve out their terms if they were giving efficient service, and that in the filling of vacancies, "the department had no intention of abandoning the historic custom of inviting the advice of members of Congress with respect to the qualifications and fitness of eligible applicants in the various Congressional districts."[50] In July, 1933, however, President Roosevelt instructed Farley to prepare legislation placing all postmasters under civil service, and thereafter repeatedly urged the passage of such legislation.[51] In 1935 Senator

O'Mahoney introduced such a bill, and it was referred to the Committee on Post Offices and Post Roads, but because of the opposition of Senator McKellar, chairman of the committee, it was never considered by the committee.[52]

In 1936 President Roosevelt issued an executive order directing that only the name of the persons who received the highest score in the civil service examination for postmasterships should be certified to him for nomination to the Senate, thus returning to the practice followed during Wilson's second term.[53] The effect of the order was to put an end to the practice of permitting members of Congress to select from among the three candidates who stood highest, the one whom they wished to have appointed.

The Ramspeck-O'Mahoney Act of 1938.—In 1936 both major political parties adopted platform planks pledging the extension of civil service; and the following January, in transmitting to Congress the report of the Committee on Administrative Management, President Roosevelt called for the extension of the merit system "upward, outward, and downward" throughout the federal service to all but a relatively few policy-determining positions. Congress soon had an opportunity to vote on this recommendation as it applied to postmasters. Representative Ramspeck of Georgia, chairman of the House Committee on the Civil Service, introduced a bill (H.R. 1531) on the opening day of the session in January, 1937, to bring first-, second-, and third-class postmasters under civil service. It provided that in the future they should be appointed by the Postmaster General instead of by the President, and it repealed the requirement of confirmation by the Senate. Incumbent postmasters were permitted to serve out their terms, and could receive indefinite appointments under civil service upon passing a noncompetitive examination. The bill also authorized the filling of postmastership vacancies by promotions of postal employees or by competitive civil service examinations.

When the bill came before the House on January 28, 1937, it was opposed by two groups of members with opposite points of view: one group wanted to return to the patronage system, which had prevailed before President Roosevelt issued the executive order of the previous July; the other group objected because the bill did not go far enough in removing politics from postmaster appointments and permitted politically appointed postmasters to be covered into the civil service after passing a noncompetitive examination. This latter group foresaw that, with a return of the rule of three, members of Congress would again be permitted to make the actual selections and the examination would be virtually a sham. In response to a question, Ramspeck stated that he assumed that if the bill were enacted members of Congress would again be consulted about postmaster appointments. McClellan of Arkansas then stated: "We either ought to have a civil-service law that will take the whole responsibility and remove it from the Congressmen, and let the country know it, or we ought to have a law that places the responsibility with the Congressmen and hold them responsible."[54] Tobey of New Hampshire declared that the bill "pays tribute to civil service but it enthrones the spoils system." Representative Lucas of Illinois objected to the bill because it would leave the responsibility for the actual selection of postmasters with the members of Congress, and said that his only trouble in his last campaign came from disappointed candidates for postmasterships. Representative Hull opposed the bill on the ground that it meant a continuation of the spoils system and patronage indefinitely and would prevent a real civil service law from being enacted.[55]

In defense of the bill, Ramspeck declared that it would carry out the President's recommendation for the extension of civil service. But recognizing that this was not an argument that appealed to members who favored the old patronage system, he declared that the former patronage of postmaster appointments had already been taken away by the executive order of the preceding year, and to this group he held out the hope that under the bill they would again have a voice in the selection of postmasters in their districts.

When the bill was taken up in the committee of the whole, Representative Collins of Mississippi offered amendments which nullified its major provisions. "I do not know of any public officer in this country," declared Collins, "more capable of selecting a postmaster from that eligible list of three . . . than the Congressman who represents the particular district in which a vacancy exists . . . a Congressman is certainly more able to select a suitable one from an eligible list than some $2,500 clerk in the Civil Service Commission." An even more avowed defense of the spoils system was made by Representative Nichols of Oklahoma, who maintained that under the system the United States had become "the greatest Government under the sun," and asserted that he was "better qualified to select a man to be postmaster in any of my towns than any member of the Civil Service Commission."[56]

Although the Collins amendments were adopted by large majorities in the committee of the whole, where the votes of the members were not recorded, when the bill came before the House, Ramspeck moved to strike out these amendments and demanded a roll-call vote. The amendments were then voted down, 215 to 164. It was evident that a number of members who earlier had voted for the Collins amendments were unwilling to go on record as opposed to extension of the civil service to postmasterships.

In the Senate the bill was referred to the Committee on the Civil Service, and it remained buried in a subcommittee headed by Senator McKellar. Several months later, Senator O'Mahoney inquired in the Senate what progress the committee had made on the Ramspeck bill, and McKellar replied that two of the three members of the subcommittee were opposed to the bill, and that he had been able to find only four senators who favored it. Urging that the bill be reported out so that the Senate could act on it, O'Mahoney declared that the "confirmation of the appointments by the Senate for years without number has been a mere formal gesture." McKellar opposed the bill, saying that it would "take away the constitutional right of the Senate to pass upon first-, second-, and third-class postmaster appointments. I do not see how the author of the bill could ever have expected the Senate seriously to consider such a bill."[57]

Not content with holding the Ramspeck bill in committee, McKellar introduced his own bill, and it was referred to the Committee on Post Offices and Post Roads, which he headed. This bill (S. 3022) in effect repealed the President's order of July, 1936, and provided for a return to the method of appointment of postmasters that had previously prevailed. It was reported with a majority and a minority report in November, 1937. The majority report made a frank defense of spoils appointments of postmasters. It took the Civil Service Commission to task for its "determined effort . . . to obtain control of the appointment of first-, second-, and third-class postmasters."[58] The report stated: "A more imperfect method of securing an efficient, honest, and desirable postmaster could hardly be imagined. A more direct blow to democratic home rule would be difficult to devise. A more effective building of centralized bureaucracy here in Washington could scarcely be conceived." The majority report asserted that the patronage system of appointing postmasters was the ideal method, was in accordance with the Constitution, and had resulted in the finest post-office system in the world.[59]

The minority report, which was signed by Senators O'Mahoney, Logan, and La Follette, urged that the Ramspeck bill be substituted for the McKellar bill, and stated that these two bills presented a "clear-cut issue between the patronage system on the one hand and the merit system on the other." It voiced strong opposition to the McKellar bill, which it stated was "frankly based upon the theory that all postmasters drawing salaries of $1,100 or more should be selected by members of the House of Representatives." The minority report stated:

The theory that Members of Congress should be permitted to appoint postmasters is in violation of our constitutional system. The appointment of executive officers is an executive function and, when exercised by Members of Congress, through the acquiescence of the executive, tends to deprive the legislative branch of the legislative freedom it ought to enjoy and preserve.[60]

The minority report maintained that the assistant postmasters of first- and second-class post offices usually perform the duties of the postmaster, though they receive 40 per cent less salary, and urged the extension of the merit system to include all postmasters; this, it said, would improve the service, would increase efficiency, and would be an inspiration to every postal employee.[61] In a separate statement, Senator Bridges opposed the McKellar bill, which he said would perpetuate the spoils and patronage system, and favored legislation to place all postmasters under the classified civil service system, with vacancies filled by promotions from the ranks.[62]

On April 11, 1938, when the McKellar bill came before the Senate, Senator O'Mahoney offered the Ramspeck bill as a substitute, with the several important amendments described below. After a lengthy debate the O'Mahoney substitute bill was adopted by a vote of 49 to 20.

In the debate, Senator McKellar defended the old practice of the selection of postmasters by members of Congress, contending that congressmen were much better able to select postmasters than a civil service clerk in Washington. "I believe that the Representative," stated McKellar, "who is familiar with every post office and with every candidate for postmaster in his own district is the best man in the world to make the recommendation."[63] Senator Norris challenged this contention, pointing out that only congressmen of the party in power were permitted to select the postmasters in their districts, and that if McKellar really meant what he said, he would introduce a bill frankly giving the power of selection to members of Congress, irrespective of their party affiliation. The idea that members of Congress were personally acquainted with all people of prominence in their districts was also challenged by Norris. If the members really looked into the qualifications of competing candidates and made the kind of check that should be made, contended Norris, they would have little time for anything else. "We have enough to do," he said, "to attend to the business of the United States Government without selecting appointees to fill petty offices, the post offices of the country."[64] Citing illustrations to prove his point, he declared that patronage appointments by members was a liability rather than an asset when it came to their reëlection.

Senator McKellar defended the requirement of senatorial confirmation of postmasters as a "restraining influence ... of enormous value in securing the right kind of an officer to fill the place" and stated that its effect was to cause the President to "send in the very best men who can be found for the offices to be filled," but Senator Norris retorted that the system "smells to high heaven and everybody knows it." Senator Capper declared that "for a hundred years the post office has been the greatest 'feeding trough' in the country," and that the taxpayers had to "hold the bag for an annual postal deficit."[65]

In reply to a question, Senator O'Mahoney, who had formerly been the First Assistant Postmaster General, described the operation of the civil service examinations for postmasters, frankly admitting that they had been of little value.

The method in the past has been to send out a questionnaire to the candidate, and a few letters to the persons whose names the candidate furnishes as his endorsers. The candidate is requested to give the names of persons who have knowledge of his qualifications; and those names are then filed with the Commission, and letters go out to them. Sometimes inspectors have been sent out to go through the town and to interview businessmen with respect to the qualifications of the candidate; but the universal testimony of postal inspectors to me, and the information I received from the Civil Service Commission, was that in practically every case businessmen felt that it was just a form, that that sort of a civil-service examination meant nothing, and that the appointment was to be made for political reasons after all was said and done. So in the past, according to my way of thinking, these examinations have been worth very little."[66]

The O'Mahoney substitute amendment, which passed the Senate, contained several significant amendments to the Ramspeck bill. Under it postmasters of the first three classes continued to be appointed by the President and confirmed by the Senate; temporary appointments for a period of six months, or longer with the approval of the Civil Service Commission, were authorized; and residence in the delivery area served by the post office was made a requirement for appointment. Although these amendments to the Ramspeck bill attracted little attention at the time of the Senate debate, they were later greatly to affect the operation of the law. Senator O'Mahoney conceded in the debate that his bill made only two significant changes from the practice which then obtained with respect to postmaster appointments: (1) the President's order requiring the appointment of the person who stood highest on the eligible list was set aside, and (2) the terms of postmasters were made indefinite. The bill was subsequently amended by the Senate to provide terms of eight years. Senator Bankhead contended that the O'Mahoney bill differed in no material respect, except with regard to the term of office, from the McKellar bill.[67] Subsequently experience under the law has confirmed this contention. On a motion of Senator Glass the term of postmasters was changed to eight years.

After the bill passed the Senate, Robert L. Johnson, president of the National Civil Service Reform League, wrote to the members of the conference committee, stating that "the bill as finally passed by the Senate is of little practical value. It is a poor pretense of extension of the competitive merit system of selection of postmasters—a sham which is designed, we believe, to pull the wool over the eyes of the public and lull it into a false belief that postmasterships are actually being placed under the merit system."[68] An editorial in the New York *Times* also criticized the Senate bill and commended the provision of the House bill which abolished senatorial confirmation for postmaster appointments. The editorial observed that "such a diminution of its dignity that body could not bear." Referring to the senators who voted against the bill, defective as it was, the *Times* stated: "We may regret that fifty-five years after the passage of the Pendleton act there should still be twenty paleozoic politicians in the Senate who hanker or pretend to hanker for a return to the spoils system."[69]

When the bill went to conference, the Senate conferees insisted on retaining senatorial confirmation, and the House managers reluctantly agreed to this. The Senate members, on their part, agreed to the House provisions for indefinite terms for postmasters and for covering in incumbent postmasters after noncompetitive examination. The provision authorizing persons to serve with temporary appointments for six months or longer with the approval of the Civil Service Commission was also accepted by the House managers. In this form the bill was reported back to each house, and it passed with only brief debates in each. The Republican members of the House conference committee, Tobey and Rogers, refused to sign the report, on the ground that the bill was not a step in the direction of a real merit system, whereas Senator McKellar refused to sign on exactly the opposite ground.

Operation of the Ramspeck-O'Mahoney Act.—Political appointment of postmasters has continued under the act with little change from the practice that existed before 1936. When a vacancy occurs, the Post Office Department asks the representative from the district, if he belongs to the party in power, to name the person he desires to have appointed as acting postmaster. Six months or later, when a civil service examination is given for the job, the acting postmaster has little difficulty in ranking among the top three candidates. If he is not one of the top three, the examination is often thrown out and a new one conducted. When the results of the examination are announced, the congressman is again consulted and is permitted to choose from the three top candidates the one to be appointed. If the district is represented by a member of the opposite party, the senators from the state, if they belong to the party in power, are permitted to select the persons to be appointed as postmasters; otherwise the party organization makes the choice.

The civil service examinations for first-class postmasterships are unassembled; candidates are required to file a statement of their education and experience, and an investigator of the Civil Service Commission checks up on the qualifications of candidates by interviewing references and other citizens in the local community.[70] The final rating is determined by a board in the Civil Service Commission at Washington on the basis of this report. Education is given 20 points in the examination, and business and other experience, 80 points. Candidates for appointment as second- and third-class postmasters are given a written test, which consists of a general intelligence test, and are also rated on education and experience. Relatively little use has been made of the provision in the law permitting promotions from the ranks of postal employees, which was stressed by proponents of the legislation. In the first ten months of 1951, only 139 promotional appointments were made, whereas a total of 1,326 nominations were submitted to the Senate.[71] The requirement of local residence, as well as the custom of permitting the member of Congress to make the choice, have doubtless prevented greater use from being made of this provision.

An investigation conducted by the staff of the Senate Committee on Post Office and Civil Service in 1948 indicated that there were many questionable practices.[72] The Civil Service Commission has repeatedly recommended revision of the act to eliminate the requirement of Senate confirmation. "Genuine competition for these important posts," it stated in its report for 1945, "is not possible so long as the residents of the various communities of the country know that in most instances political considerations enter into the selection process." The Hoover Commission recommended that the Post Office be taken out of politics, that confirmation by the Senate be discontinued, and that the Postmaster General be given the power of appointment under merit standards fixed by the Civil Service Commission.[73] The report of its task force on the Post Office stressed the need not only to eliminate the political appointment of postmasters, but to fill vacancies normally by promotion from within the postal service, appointing outsiders only if suitable candidates were not available within the service.[74] The same recommendation had been made earlier by the President's Committee on Administrative Management in 1937, and by the Taft Commission on Efficiency and Economy in 1912.

In April, 1952, after approval of the reorganization plan placing field officers of the Bureau of Internal Revenue under civil service, President Truman submitted three additional plans to cover postmasters of the first three classes (totalling approximately 21,000 positions), collectors of customs, and marshals into the civil service. All three plans were approved by the House but were rejected by substantial majorities in the Senate. The President stated in his message defending the plans that these positions were nonpolicy-forming and should be placed under the merit system. He criticized the existing method of appointing postmasters in these words:

This procedure injects a hybrid mixture of political and merit considerations into appointments to offices which should be in the career service. It discourages many able persons from applying for these posts because they believe political preferment is the determining factor in appointment.

. . . .

I know, from personal experience in both the Congress and the Presidency, how much time and effort is lost and how we have been distracted from the consideration of issues of paramount national importance by the present method of appointing the officials covered by these reorganization plans. We must relieve ourselves of this burden of minor personnel actions in order to devote our efforts to the greater issues confronting our Government today.[75]

Plan number two permitted incumbent postmasters to continue in their jobs, but when vacancies occurred, the offices would be covered into the civil service, and postmasters thereafter would be appointed by the Postmaster General, under civil service rules. President Truman stated in his message that the plan would not become fully effective for a number of years. The Senate Committee on Government Operations, to which the plan was referred, voted 9 to 3 to recommend that it be set aside. The major argument advanced in the majority report was that it was not a reorganization plan, for the only change it provided was in the method of appointment of postmasters. The majority contended that if the method of appointing postmasters is to be changed, it should be done by legislation, and pointed out that Congress had rejected legislative proposals to accomplish this purpose. On the merits of the provision placing the appointing power in the hands of the Postmaster General, the report stated: "The plan ... will centralize absolute authority and control over the appointment of all postmasters in the Postmaster General, eliminating the existing check exercised by Congress upon the character, ability and suitability of applicants for the position of postmaster."

The majority contended, moreover, that the plan would not end politics in the appointment of postmasters but would transfer the political patronage from members of Congress to the Postmaster General, who would be free to consult with anyone he wished. "It is the considered opinion of the committee," stated the report, "that a Member of Congress, in whose district a vacancy exists, is far more qualified to determine whether or not a particular applicant is suitable for the position than is a civil service investigator...." This contention was based on the assumption that vacancies would be filled on the basis of examinations rather than by promotion from within the service, the normal procedure in the civil service.

Other arguments were advanced against the plan. It was pointed out that the Postmaster General had testified that the Department was operating "most efficiently" at the present time and the plan would not result in any economies. It was asserted that the plan would do away with the existing requirement that a postmaster must reside within the delivery area of his post office, though this was denied by those favoring the plan. The secretary of the National Letter Carriers' Association was quoted in opposition to the plan on the ground that it would lead to "vicious politics in the administrative branch of the government."[76] It is remarkable that the plan, which would have opened up promotional opportunities of career postal employees to include the 21,000 postmasterships, was opposed not only by the Letter Carriers' Association but also by a spokesman for the American Federation of Labor. This opposition doubtless affected the outcome.

The minority report submitted by Senators Humphrey, O'Conor, and Monroney defended the plan on the grounds that (1) efficient management of the postal service required placement of postmasters under the merit civil service system, (2) every postal employee should be able to aspire to and achieve appointment as postmaster of his community on the basis of demonstrated ability, (3) extension of the merit system to these nonpolicy positions would increase confidence in the civil service, and (4) appointment by the President and the Senate of hundreds of postmasters annually should be discontinued in order to free them to consider the greater issues of national policy. The report of the minority contended that the plan was within the authority of the Reorganization Act of 1949. In reply to the contention that the plan would vest too much power in the Postmaster General, it was pointed out that at present he has the power of appointing, subject to civil service procedures, several hundred thousand employees of the postal service other than postmasters, and all other department heads have this power. The minority contended also that under the plan the appointment of postmasters would conform to the standard practice followed in other civil service positions and would put an end to the use of these positions as political patronage.

The debate on the plan in the Senate on June 18 consisted chiefly of a restatement of the arguments advanced by each side in the majority and minority reports of the committee. Opening the debate, Senator McClellan of Arkansas, chairman of the committee, declared that the Post Office Department is recognized throughout the land "as being our most efficient department, and as being as free from corruption as any department in the Government." There is, he asserted, no need for a house cleaning. The real purpose of the plan, McClellan stated, is "to obviate senatorial confirmation, so that those in charge may consult whom they want to and disregard those whom they do not want to consult." Continuing, he advanced one of the leading arguments against the plan:

Mr. President, this plan would not eliminate politics from the matter. The politics in the post office appointments is exposed, revealed; we know where it is; we can put our finger on it; we can call it to account.... It is now proposed ... to put the matter behind an iron curtain of bureaucracy in a department where no one can know what goes on behind that iron curtain.

Senator McClellan asserted that approval of the plan would be an abdication of power to bureaucracy, would take the government farther away from the people and their elected representatives, and would "destroy the democratic process that keeps the Government close to the people."[77]

Senator Humphrey, speaking for the defenders of the plan, declared that political patronage is a "hangover" from the politics of the past and that Congress has vastly more important problems and policies to consider. "The essence of democracy," said Humphrey, "is to have the elected representatives of the people establish the public policy, and not to have them appoint every Tom, Dick, and Harry to every job that can be found."

Senator O'Conor condemned the present procedure for appointment of postmasters on the ground that it "cloaks, under the guise of civil service, what is, in fact, a patronage system." The essence of a true civil service system, he continued, is the provision of equal opportunity for all qualified persons, regardless of political affiliation, to compete for appointment on equal terms, and opportunity for all employees to be promoted on the basis of ability and experience. Neither of these essentials, said Senator O'Conor, is possible under the existing system, and the issue is between continuing the present patronage system or adopting a genuine merit system.

Senator Monroney declared that the present system of senatorial confirmation is "largely a hoax" and cited the fact that about one hundred appointments were approved by the Post Office and Civil Service Committee, on the preceding day, within less than thirty seconds. Senator Lehman summarized the case for adoption of the plan as follows:

There is nothing about these postmasterships which makes it necessary or desirable to have them filled by presidential appointment and Senate confirmation. Postmasters are the same kind of administrative field officials that are found in other departments. They should, according to sound administrative practice, be answerable to the Postmaster General. It is in him that both the President and the Congress should place responsibility and accountability for filling those places, and seeing that the postmasters do their jobs satisfactorily. It is the Postmaster General whom we should hold accountable for the recruitment of the best people available. His responsibility for these things should be clear, and uncomplicated by extraneous political considerations.[78]

When the vote was taken, 56 senators voted to set aside the plan and only 29 to sustain it. Twenty-eight Democrats and the same number of Republicans voted against the plan; of those voting to sustain it, 15 were Democrats and 14 Republicans. The vote on the plan, which foreshadowed similar votes on the plans to place customs collectors and marshals under civil service, showed once more that only under the pressure of strong public opinion, such as followed the exposures of corruption in the Bureau of Internal Revenue, is the Senate willing to give up its patronage.

The continued political appointment of postmasters of the first three classes has prevented the development of a true career service in the Post Office Department and will continue to have this effect as long as it exists. Because the rank and file of employees are effectively debarred from opportunity to advance through merit to the higher administrative posts, the postal service has been hampered in the recruitment of the most promising young men and women. It is equally hampered in making the most effective use of experienced employees who have acquired a high degree of expertness and have demonstrated administrative abilities. The efficiency of the postal service is greatly hampered by the practice of utilizing politically selected heads of field offices, ordinarily persons with no knowledge or experience in the administration of the service. The political appointment of postmasters is an anachronism that is not only harmful to the Department but requires much of the time of the President and members of Congress—time urgently needed for the consideration of problems of national interest.

Chapter XIX

RECENT PROPOSALS
TO EXTEND
SENATORIAL CONFIRMATION

The very fact that nominations have to come before the Senate for confirmation makes the appointing power exceedingly careful to select the right kind of men for appointment in the first place. It makes for good government; it makes for honest government; and ... I think that probably not half of that number would be submitted to the Senate because it would be found that a greater number was not necessary. Senator Kenneth McKellar.[1]

A few years of practical politics, or a few years in the Senate of the United States, would convince anyone when confirmations are had in the Senate, the Senators from the states affected actually make the appointments, leaving the President only a veto power. The right to reject, which the constitutional framers vested in the Senate, has become the right to select. Senator Carl A. Hatch.[2]

IN THE DECADE 1935 to 1945, at practically every session, bills or riders to appropriation acts were introduced in the Senate to extend the requirement of senatorial confirmation to specified groups of subordinate administrative officers and employees, and several such measures were enacted into law. Many of these bills or riders were introduced by Senator McKellar of Tennessee, the leading advocate of this type of legislation. The usual provision was that all employees of designated agencies who received a specified salary must be appointed by the President and confirmed by the Senate. The requirement usually applied retroactively to persons already employed, as well as to

[356

new appointments; most of these provisions applied only to employees in temporary, emergency, or wartime agencies, and hence are no longer operative.

These legislative proposals, which constituted one of the greatest threats to the merit system within recent years, were vigorously opposed by the National Civil Service League, the League of Women Voters, and other groups interested in the civil service. A number of these bills were directed primarily at the TVA in an attempt by Senator McKellar to secure control of the appointments to that agency. In 1943 and 1944, bills passed the Senate which would have required the confirmation of every employee, practically throughout the government service, whose annual salary was $5,000 or more ($4,500 or more in 1944).[3] These bills, which were generally denounced in the press as "patronage grabs," fortunately failed to pass the House.

Senate Confirmation of State Directors of the WPA and the PWA

One of the first measures of this type was the emergency relief appropriation act of 1935, which on the motion of Senator McCarran was amended in the Senate to require presidential appointment and Senate confirmation of any person exercising general supervision or any state or regional administrator who was paid a salary of $5,000 or more and was not already employed under another law. This provision was continued under subsequent relief appropriation acts until 1942 when the program was terminated. It passed in 1935 when both President Roosevelt and Relief Administrator Hopkins were away from Washington and hence were unable to oppose it. Hopkins accepted the provision, believing that he would be able to work with the Democratic members of the Senate, who, he recognized, would thereafter dictate the appointment of directors of the new work relief programs in their states.[4]

Before 1935 the relief program had been administered by the several states, with federal aid; hence the state directors were appointed by the governors of the states. Thereafter the program in each state was administered by a director appointed by the President and confirmed by the Senate. This required a change from state to federal administration, 'and from gubernatorial to senatorial politics in the appointment of the state directors. The position of Hopkins as Federal Relief Administrator was definitely weakened. Earlier he had been able to keep the administration remarkably free of politics by threatening to cut off federal aid if the state program was politically or incompetently administered. No longer did he have this potent sanction, and the actual selection of the directors thereafter was made by Democratic senators for their states. In fourteen states the incumbent state directors were continued under the new organization; but in other states new directors were appointed, and usually a new staff was recruited. Inevitably a large amount of confusion, duplication, friction, and administrative inefficiency resulted. In a number of states the new

WPA organizations were highly political, and appointments were treated as party patronage. It was impossible in these states to avoid partisanship in the administration of relief. Macmahon and his associates record their evaluations of the state directors of twenty-two states which they visited, as follows: of the twelve state directors with senatorial sponsorship, eight "seemed to have a poor understanding of what their job was about and to be more or less at a loss on details of WPA operations," and four were doing a good job. Of the ten states visited in which the administrators were not politically selected, seven were able and three were unqualified for the position.[5]

Within two years, widespread charges of politics and favoritism in the administration of the WPA led the Senate in 1938 to create a special committee—the Sheppard committee—to conduct an investigation. In its cautious report the committee stated that most of these charges were exaggeraed or were not sustained, but nevertheless it found "that there has been in several states and in many forms, unjustifiable political activity in connection with the work of the Works Progress Administration." It stated that in many instances funds appropriated for relief had been diverted to political ends.[6] Macmahon and his associates reported that the requirement of senatorial confirmation of the state directors "had a far-reaching and even crucial effect" on the administration of the program, but "ironically enough, the congressional investigations of politics in the works program carefully avoided any mention of it."[7]

The evidence indicated that in a number of states the federal relief program had become highly political and in some states it was marked by gross mismanagement and political favoritism. Hopkins utilized a special staff of investigators to unearth graft and corruption and was able to prevent the cruder forms of spoils; but he found it difficult, if not impossible, to avoid political and incompetent administration in certain states. In his testimony before the Senate Commerce Committee in 1939 concerning his nomination to be Secretary of Commerce, Hopkins defended the administration of the WPA, maintaining that in view of the magnitude of the job it had been kept relatively free of politics, though tacitly admitting that there were some states in which the administration had become political.[8]

The 1935 relief appropriation act also required senatorial confirmation of the state directors of the Public Works Administration, which was under the direction of Secretary of Commerce Ickes. In this case, however, it seems to have had little serious effect. The PWA program was continued on a grant-in-aid basis under which states and local governments were required to put up substantial amounts for the projects they sponsored. Ickes had already appointed state directors to assist the local authorities in submitting their plans and to make preliminary reviews. Usually they were engineers and had been selected for their special qualifications for the job; all their appointments were confirmed by the Senate when their names were submitted, and no change in personnel was made. Since all PWA grants required the approval of Ickes, there was no disposition by members of the Senate to force him to appoint state directors not of his own choosing.

In 1935 Senator Gore introduced an amendment to the NRA bill to require that all employees paid $4,000 or more, of this and any other agency of the government, be appointed by the President and the appointments confirmed by the Senate. Moreover, the amendment provided that recess appointees should not be paid a salary beyond sixty days after the opening of the next session of Congress unless their appointments were confirmed, and it contained the extraordinary provision that employees of the NRA and the AAA be reappointed and the appointments confirmed annually. The Senate adopted the Gore amendment by a vote of 43 to 28,[9] but on reconsideration, in spite of a one-man filibuster by Senator Long, reversed itself and defeated the amendment.[10] Similar amendments applicable to the civil service employees of the AAA, the Federal Alcohol Administration, and the Farmers' Home Corporation were also introduced by Senator Gore; these passed the Senate but were defeated in the House. In opposing one of these amendments, Senator O'Mahoney said: "When we undertake in this bill to provide that civil service employees must obtain confirmation by the Senate, then we are undermining the entire civil service system."[11]

The Social Security Rider.—In 1937 a rider was attached to the social security appropriation, and was finally adopted after being deadlocked in conference for several months, which required Senate confirmation of the appointments of all attorneys and experts of the Social Security Board not appointed under civil service and who received salaries of $5,000 or more. The Social Security Act of 1935 had authorized the board to appoint experts and attorneys outside civil service. In 1936 it carried on an extensive search throughout the country to recruit its top staff, and appointed more than two hundred persons in these categories. It should be noted that the Civil Service Commission at this time did not have a staff qualified to conduct the examinations for the several types of experts needed by the board to administer its program. The exemption of these positions from civil service had enabled the board to recruit able persons who would not otherwise have been available.

Before the enactment of the Social Security Act practically all the New Deal agencies set up to administer new programs were exempted from civil service, and a vast amount of political patronage was thus provided. By 1936, however, most of these appointments had been exhausted. The advance publicity concerning the social security program unfortunately indicated that a large number of employees would be required, without pointing out that most of them would be state rather than federal employees. The board consequently found itself under a great deal of pressure from members of Congress for patronage appointments. Believing that it was of the utmost importance to keep the administration out of politics, the board refused to yield to these pressures. Although a few appointments of qualified persons with congressional sponsorship were made to exempted positions, the board maintained a strict adherence to qualification standards. This policy resulted in a good deal of criticism and grumbling by members of Congress whose candidates were rejected.

In 1936 strained relations over a single appointment arose between the Social Security Board and Senator Glass of Virginia, chairman of the powerful Senate Appropriations Committee, which led the Senator eventually to insert a rider in the appropriation requiring Senate confirmation of all attorneys and experts not appointed under civil service whose annual salaries amounted to $5,000 or more. Senator Glass asked the board to appoint a woman who had once been employed by a local welfare agency in a minor clerical capacity. After investigating her qualifications the board found that she could not qualify as an expert, and since she was not on a civil service register, she could not be appointed to a clerical position. The board had entered into an arrangement with the Civil Service Commission that under the exemption provision it would make no appointments of experts and attorneys to positions paying less than $3,200 annually. All appointments to positions paying less than that amount were appointed from civil service registers. In addition, the board voluntarily agreed to submit to the Civil Service Commission for its review all proposed appointments of experts and attorneys to exempted positions, and it followed the policy of appointing only persons whom the commission found to be qualified for appointment at this grade.

When Senator Glass was informed that his nominee could not qualify as an expert, this arrangement with the Civil Service Commission was explained to him. Whereupon Glass insisted that the board submit the name of his candidate to the Civil Service Commission and let it decide whether she could qualify as an expert. Reluctantly the board agreed to this request, confident that the report would be unfavorable; but the Civil Service Commission staff, learning of the interest of the senator, ruled that his candidate would qualify as an expert. The board then faced an awkward dilemma: if it appointed a person without professional training or experience as an expert, it would be subjected to increased pressures to make similar appointments at the insistence of other members of Congress; but, if it refused to appoint the nominee of Senator Glass, the chairman of the Senate Appropriations Committee, the consequences might be even more serious. After much deliberation, the board finally decided to maintain its standards. To mollify the senator it was arranged for his nominee to be appointed to a position in the National Youth Administration. But Senator Glass by this time was thoroughly angry and offended and would not be placated.

Another event occurred which also angered the Virginia senator. The board found it necessary to delay the opening of some of the field offices it had planned, one of these being in Lynchburg, the home town of Senator Glass. When a news story appeared announcing this decision, Senator Glass, who believed that the board was acting under orders from the White House to discipline him, was highly indignant.

These were the events that led Senator Glass to insert a rider in the Independent Offices Appropriation bill of 1937 (H.R. 4046) to discipline the Social Security Board and its officers. In addition, the act reduced the salary of the executive director by $500 annually and made a cut of a million dollars in the item for administrative expenses of the board. No explanation of the retroactive requirement of senatorial confirmation of Social Security experts and attorneys was offered in the report of the Senate Appropriations Committee on the bill, and the rider was adopted by the Senate without debate. When the bill was sent to conference, however, the House conferees refused to accept the amendment, and the conference committee was deadlocked for weeks. The House agreed to an amendment proposed by its conferees requiring all experts and attorneys of the board to be placed under civil service; but this was also unacceptable to the Senate conferees. Finally, under the mounting pressure to pass the appropriation so that social security payments to the states would not be held up, the House conferees yielded, on the understanding that this bill would not become a precedent for the extension of senatorial confirmation to similar positions in other agencies. The rider was never debated in the Senate, the reasons for it being generally understood, but a notable debate occurred in the House before that body finally yielded.

In presenting the report of the conferees recommending that the House recede, Congressman Woodrum of Virginia said that "because of the great number of high salaried experts who have been appointed and because of the very widespread dissatisfaction over some of the appointments, some part of the Government should certainly have the right to review and pass upon the qualifications of those who have received these appointments."[12] Congressman McFarlane of Texas, speaking in support of the motion, stated that if these positions were confirmed, members of the House might be able to "get a few jobs for our constituents." He referred to the fact that the Texas members had a signed agreement with the senators of that state concerning the distribution of patronage. Woodrum replied that that was one way to look at the matter, but in his opinion it would be "a very unfortunate thing for the social security setup if it is ever plunged into partisan politics."[13]

In the House debate there was a good deal of criticism, mostly implied, of the appointments of experts and attorneys that the Social Security Board had made. Woodrum asserted that "there has been a great deal of complaint, some of it with merit, as to the manner in which the so-called experts of the Social Security Board have been appointed.... It has been stated that some of the people appointed as experts have not even been citizens of the United States.

It has also been stated that others were appointed at salaries which were very much above those to which they would be entitled."[14] In a similar vein, Democratic leader Rayburn said in closing the debate: "There is no question in my mind but what there is a condition in the Social Security Board that ought to be opened up and looked into."[15] One member of the House attacked the appointments of experts and attorneys made by the board, on the ground that they had been dictated by partisan politics.[16] Another asserted that hundreds of recent law school graduates had been appointed as attorneys for the board, and declared that this was one of the "wickedest wastes" in recent years.[17] The statement was a gross exaggeration. Approximately eighty attorneys had been appointed by the board. No one defended the appointments made by the board or pointed out that it had in fact made excellent selections and had maintained unusually high standards.

Several members of the House spoke in favor of the Glass rider. "I do not see where there is anything disgraceful," said Congressman Faddis, "in a legislator having any say in the appointment of minor officials of the Government. ...Politics and politicians are what made the United States of America, and made it the greatest nation in the world."[18] Robert Ramspeck, chairman of the House Committee on Civil Service, opposed the rider on the ground that the House was just as important as the Senate, and therefore it should not permit these jobs to come under the control of the latter. "I think we may well consider," said Ramspeck, "whether or not we are going to turn over to the body at the other end of the Capitol the right to run all the jobs in the Government service and have the key positions in the Government service throughout this land controlled by Members of that body. In this way they will control the promotions and appointments all the way down the line.[19] The same point was made by Congressman Maverick, who declared there was nothing in the Constitution which required that the Senate should confirm these employees.[20] Cochran of Missouri made one of the strongest speeches in opposition to the amendment, saying: "If there is one agency in the Government out of which politics should be kept it is the agency which is going to deal with the aged in this country. Put politics into the Social Security Board and it will ruin any administration.... This amendment ... is an assault on the merit system and means that the career man goes out of the picture as far as attorneys and experts are concerned."[21]

The National Civil Service Reform League urged the President to veto the bill, stating that the requirement of senatorial confirmation for these positions was "archaic," "unwarranted," and "would demoralize public service and make a career system ... impossible."[22] Roosevelt signed the bill, but sent a letter to the President of the Senate stating that he regretted the "unfortunate" provision requiring the confirmation of attorneys and experts of the Social Security Board, and expressing the hope that legislation would be enacted at an early date placing these positions under civil service. "I strongly recommend," he stated, "that all but policy-forming positions in the executive branch of the government be included within the merit system."[23]

On July 1, 1937, the President sent to the Senate nominations for the fifty-one positions in the Social Security Board for which confirmation was required by the Glass rider. Although these nominations would normally have gone to the Finance Committee, which had jurisdiction over social security legislation, they were referred to the Appropriations Committee. Four weeks later, on July 29, the first group of these nominations was reported to the Senate with a recommendation for approval. Senator La Follette objected to the delay, pointing out that the persons concerned had not been paid salaries since the first of the month. Senator Glass replied that the delay had not been caused by him, for he had sent out notices immediately to the senators of the states in which the nominees claimed residence, and the delay had been caused by their failure to reply.[24] On the following day when the nominations were taken up, Senator Byrnes, speaking for the Appropriations Committee, stated that the committee "knows nothing about individual cases" but had forwarded names from the list to the senators of the states listed as the residence of the persons nominated. He went on to state that the House conferees had objected to the requirement on the ground that the nominees would be unknown to their senators, which the events had proved to be the case.[25]

Senator Copeland stated that he assumed the persons on the list from New York were the patronage of his colleague, but said he had examined their personnel statements and had found them to be well qualified. He suggested that they be approved en bloc. Senator Wagner of New York, however, denied that he had anything to do with the nominations, stating that he was personally acquainted with only three of the persons on the list from New York, but declared that they were all eminently qualified. Senators Schwellenbach from Washington and Clark from Missouri objected that no appointments were made from their states. All the nominations reported by this date were approved without objection. Three days later, when a second group was confirmed, Senator Lewis of Illinois asked to have the name of Agnes Van Driel of his state returned to the committee for further investigation, stating that neither of the Illinois senators nor the member of the House from the district given as the residence of Miss Van Driel had ever heard of her, that he had not been honored by being asked to present her name to the Senate, and that she had been listed from Illinois because she once attended the University of Chicago. He indignantly declared that an investigation should be made to ascertain how "this lady came to be named and charged to the State of Illinois," and stated that "the official who is responsible for this kind of conduct" should "be brought before the committee for appropriate examination."[26] Miss Van Driel, a well-known social worker with extensive experience in Catholic welfare agencies, was in Europe when this occurred. Several days later, Senator Lewis, who evidently had heard from Illinois, asked that her appointment be confirmed. All nominations of the employees of the Social Security Board were thus finally approved.

Most of the senators to whom the names were referred evidently did little more than examine the personnel statement of the employees from their state; certain senators invited the employees on the list from their state to come in to see them, and questioned them about their residence within the state. In no instance does it appear that a senator conducted an investigation similar to those made by the board itself before making appointments, or attempted to pass upon the qualifications of these persons as experts. Since members of the Senate usually were uninformed concerning the duties of and necessary qualifications for the various expert positions on the staff of the board, they were obviously not in a position to pass upon the qualifications of the persons who were to fill them. The episode indicates the limitations under which the Senate must operate in passing upon persons for positions requiring special qualifications.

It is significant that every appointment on the list was confirmed, and indeed none was contested. If the Social Security Board had played politics and appointed incompetents to these positions, as had been asserted in the House debate, the investigation by the Senate failed to disclose it. The only remarks on the Senate floor concerning individual nominees were in terms of highest praise. Although there had been speculation whether Senator Glass would block the approval of the executive director of the board, Frank Bane, a resident of Virginia, whom he held primarily responsible for his differences with the board, he entered no objection, and Bane was confirmed without a contest. Apparently Glass was satisfied that he had sufficiently disciplined the board for its recalcitrance.

The Social Security Board thereafter entered into negotiations with the Civil Service Commission and within a few months arranged to place all the positions of experts and attorneys under civil service. A year later the Senate again inserted the requirement in the appropriation bill, though it now was of no practical effect, and when the House refused to yield, the matter was dropped.

Bills and Riders to Extend Senatorial Confirmation, 1937–1942

In 1937 several other appropriation riders and other bills were passed by the Senate to extend senatorial confirmation. Section 4(b) of the United States Housing Act of 1937 provided that appointments to positions paying in excess of $7,500 should be confirmed by the Senate. Macmahon states that the provision, which remained in effect until the reorganization of the housing agencies by executive order in 1942, applied to only four positions, and only seven different persons in all were confirmed by the Senate because of it.[27] As the bill passed the Senate, however, it required that the appointments of all employees of the Housing Authority paid in excess of $4,000 annually be confirmed. The House conferees strongly opposed such a provision, but a compromise require-ment of confirmation of all employees receiving in excess of $7,500 annually was accepted. The brief discussion of the subject in the Senate when the con-ferees reported on the final compromise is illuminating. Senator Connally stated that it was difficult for him "to understand why the House should oppose the Senate retaining the power of confirmation," to which Senator Walsh re-plied that the members of the House regarded the requirement as a move by the Senate "to control appointments, and would prevent the House members from recommending their personal or political friends." This position, how-ever, did not appear logical to the Texas senator, who said that the senators would "coöperate" with members of the House from their states, and that "Congress would really benefit by the Senate maintaining its right to confirm or reject. ... it inures to the benefit of the legislative branch."[28]

In 1938 Senator McKellar offered an amendment to the Independent Offices Appropriation bill to require senatorial confirmation of all attorneys and ex-perts in these agencies who were appointed outside civil service and who received salaries of $5,000 or more. In defense of his amendment, the Tennessee Senator declared: "I have never known the Senate to turn down a good man."[29] Senator Norris disagreed vehemently, stating that this provision would place "on the political pie counter" all appointments paying this salary. Commenting on the difficulties which it would cause the TVA, he pointed out that if the board wanted to appoint a special attorney, as it did in appointing John Lord O'Brian, one of the leading attorneys of the country, to represent it in the liti-gation testing the constitutionality of the TVA Act, it would be forced to get the President, "busy as he is," to make the appointment. The President, he said, would probably have to consult the senators, or risk having the nomination rejected. "This amendment," Norris declared, "would place the TVA ... right in the lap of the politicians, and the appointment of all officers receiving more than $5,000 would be put in the hands of the political job dispensers. If that were ever done, it would wreck or at least damage the agency almost beyond power of expression ... its adoption would be the worst blow the Tennessee Valley Authority has ever received."[30]

Senator McKellar retorted that if Norris' contention was true, then the Con-stitution, which required all officers to be confirmed by the Senate, was "en-tirely wrong." Throughout the debate McKellar and others supporting the amendment made little or no distinction between officers and employees—a crucial point in considering the constitutional aspects of the issue. Senator Glass defended the amendment, stating that there were "vastly more politicians" in the independent offices than in the Senate, and that they used politics in making appointments. Declaring that he hated and despised political patronage, Glass said that he and other senators were "just as capable of determining the efficiency of a man recommended for a $5,000 job as is any bureaucrat in Washington," and saw no reason why "the appointees of these miserable bureaucrats should not be reviewed by the Senate."[31]

Because of Senator Norris' criticisms of senatorial confirmation, Senator Adams of Colorado addressed the Senate in defense of the requirement, saying that he had always selected the best and most competent men for federal appointments in his state, and he was confident that other senators, who were also responsible to the people of their states, had exercised similar care in their selections. "I have never been able to understand," he declared, "why it is thought by some persons that the only individuals in the United States who are interested in inefficient government, the only corrupting influences in American public life, are those who derive their powers by election from the people of the several States . . ."[32]

Senator Norris responded that such a defense of political appointments could have been made by the leader of any political machine in the country which owed its strength to patronage, and that senators did not have the time to make the necessary investigations of candidates and attend to their legislative duties. "One cannot be a successful senator,..." he declared, "and take care of the public interests which are confided to him if all his time is taken up getting jobs for people, or seeing whether applicants are competent to fill positions." He went on to state that because of the limited time at their disposal members of the Senate were often mistaken about persons whom they recommended, and contended that political endorsements were of little value in selecting persons for technical and administration positions. "Suppose a chemist is to be selected," said Norris. "Can we find out whether he is a good chemist by inquiring whether he happens to be a good Republican or a good Democrat?"[33]

When the bill went to conference, the House managers refused to accept the McKellar amendment. In reporting the disagreement to the House, Representative Woodrum referred to the similar rider adopted in 1937 and stated that all the employees of the Social Security Board whose appointments were required to be confirmed by the Senate had been approved. "So the only possible net result of the procedure was that instead of having experts and attorneys in the Social Security Board who were more or less free of political pressure and influence, all of them had to secure congressional approval . . . they had to go and get the political endorsement."[34] Representative Dies inquired whether the Senate amendment would "in any wise change the present lack of power on the part of Members of the House to have anything to say about these appointments?" Woodrum replied that under some circumstances perhaps "an unusually active and enterprising Member might snag a job [applause], but with this provision in there I know he would not be able to do so." Representative

Cochran declared that the McKellar amendment was "about as vicious as any that could be added to an appropriation bill ... The President is responsible for the conduct of the executive branch of the Government, and if we are to continue to tie his hands by such amendments as this, how can we hold him to account for a proper stewardship?"[35]

Several members of the House attacked the McKellar amendment on the ground that it would enhance the power of the Senate and detract from that of the House. One member suggested that the approval of the House as well as that of the Senate should be required of appointments; but Dirksen of Illinois, who opposed the McKellar rider, stated that confirmation by the House would double the evil. By an overwhelming majority the House voted not to accept the amendments, and after four conference sessions, the Senate finally yielded.

In 1939 Congress authorized the use of not to exceed $100,000 of the appropriation to the Department of Commerce for the temporary employment of experts outside the civil service in the office of the Secretary, but the Senate attached a proviso that any person employed at a salary rate of $5,000 or more should be appointed by the President and confirmed by the Senate. Because of the objection of the House conferees, this figure was subsequently raised to $7,500.[36] The purpose of the request of Secretary Hopkins was to enable him to call in businessmen and economists from time to time for special assignments, without the necessity of recruiting them through the civil service. After Congress attached the requirement of senatorial confirmation, it appears that little, if any, use was made of the authorization, and after Hopkins left the Department the request was not renewed.

The appropriation act for the Department of Justice in 1939 similarly required Senate confirmation of all persons appointed at a salary of $7,500 or more in the antitrust division; this provision was continued from year to year until the 1948 appropriation act, when it was dropped. Macmahon states that up to the middle of 1943 no appointments were made by the Justice Department under the provisions of the rider.[37] The Selective Service Act of 1940 also provided that all persons "appointed, assigned, or detailed to a position the compensation of which is at a rate in excess of $5,000 per annum shall be appointed by and with the advice and consent of the Senate."[38]

In 1942 the Senate Appropriations Committee attached riders to the appropriation bills of the Office of Price Administration and the Office of Civilian Defense requiring confirmation of all employees receiving $4,500 or more a year, but the public protest was so great that both were defeated in the Senate. The National Civil Service Reform League protested that the "direct result of the imposition of senatorial confirmation would be the injection of partisan considerations into the appointment of all the higher paid positions and the discouragement of all applicants (no matter how well qualified) who do not wish to resort to outside influence." The New York *Herald Tribune* warned that "in such a crisis as at present there is no room for partisanship or personal influence," and the Washington *Post* called for the protection of OPA Administrator Leon Henderson "against the political appointees that would be foisted upon him if higher salaried positions were subject to senatorial confirmation." A similar rider applicable to the War Manpower Commission was adopted in 1942 over the strong protest of Chairman Paul V. McNutt, who stated that it would "unduly impede and delay the recruitment of the type of personnel we are trying to enlist in the Government service."[39] A year later Roosevelt urged the Congress to repeal this rider. With his message he sent a letter from the Director of the Bureau of the Budget, who stated that the operations of the War Manpower Commission were being seriously retarded by the requirement.[40] In a subsequent letter to the Speaker of the House and the President of the Senate, Roosevelt cited delays which had occurred in securing the Senate approval of persons nominated to field offices of the commission.[41] Chairman Paul McNutt testified before a Senate committee that in many instances the commission had been unable to get the best-qualified persons to accept appointment because "they simply did not feel that they wanted to subject themselves to what they called the possibility of embarrassment."[42] The rider continued in effect until the end of the fiscal year, but was dropped in the appropriation act for the following year.

The McKellar Bill of 1943

The most sweeping proposal for the extension of the requirement of senatorial confirmation to appointments of subordinate administrative employees was made by Senator McKellar in 1943.[43] The bill was approved by the Judiciary Committee and passed the Senate by a substantial majority but was never considered by the House. As introduced by Senator McKellar, it provided that "any person holding an office or position in or under the executive branch . . . and receiving compensation at a rate in excess of $4,500 a year for his services in such office or position shall be deemed to be an officer of the United States, to be appointed by the President, by and with the advice and consent of the Senate, and shall not be deemed to be an inferior officer who may be appointed by the President alone or by the head of a department."[44] It required not only that all appointments, but also all promotions, of persons receiving salaries in excess of $4,500 should be confirmed by the Senate, and provided that the terms of office of all persons previously appointed at salaries higher than this amount should be terminated on June 30, 1943, unless these persons were reappointed by the President and the appointments were confirmed by the Senate.

Before holding hearings on the bill, the subcommittee agreed upon a revised draft which lowered the specified salary to include all employees receiving $4,500, as well as those receiving salaries higher than this, but exempted employees serving in the armed forces on leave of absence from their civil service position and civil service employees who were appointed to their present positions before 1936.[45]

The principal witness at the single hearing on the bill was its sponsor, Senator McKellar, who declared that "every Tom, Dick and Harry" in the departments were appointing people and that more than 35,000 were receiving salaries of $4,500 or more. The Civil Service Commission, he stated, "cannot possibly have time to look into the qualifications of all these people." Presumably members of the Senate would have more time to consider their qualifications! Making no distinction between officers and employees, Senator McKellar contended that the Constitution required that the Senate confirm these employees and maintained that if nominations were sent to the Senate with a brief history of each person, "we won't have any Communists in our Government." He said he knew the people of his state far better than the Civil Service Commission, which he declared was "the greatest patronage institution in the world," and of the many people he had recommended for office during his official life, he said he recalled only three who failed to "measure up."[46]

In testifying against the bill, Chairman Mitchell of the Civil Service Commission stated that it would require Senate confirmation of many persons who had worked for thirty to forty years for the government, many with highly technical, scientific, or professional qualifications. The requirement of senatorial confirmation of persons after years of service, he declared, would greatly injure their morale, cause many to seek outside employment, and make it much more difficult to recruit able and ambitious young persons into the government service.[47] K. C. Vipond of the Civil Service Commission staff stated that he knew of many instances of career civil servants refusing promotions which involved appointment to a position requiring senatorial confirmation.[48]

On February 21, while the bill was still before the Senate committee, President Roosevelt wrote a letter to the Speaker of the House and the President of the Senate opposing the bill. In it he stated:

The proposal ... presupposed congressional responsibility for the operations of executive agencies. An agency head is responsible for the success or failure of his program. This accountability is dissipated if responsibility for the appointment of employees is divided.

Under our form of government the appointment of those officers who, in a fundamental sense, determine policy, has generally been subject to Senate confirmation. But the determination of policy is not synonymous with the exercise of administrative discretion. Neither does it include work performed by the vast numbers of technical and scientific personnel who occupy positions which fall above a salary figure of $4500 or any other arbitrary amount.[49]

Reviewing the recent legislation extending the civil service to practically all employees of the government, the President declared that "to turn the clock back by reversing this decision would be folly in peacetime. In war it would be little less than tragic." He pointed to the estimated 33,000 positions which would be added to the list of those appointed by the President and confirmed by the Senate and declared that he did not have the time personally to examine the qualifications of such a vast number of persons, and expressed the opinion that Senate confirmation would become a "rubber stamp process," or else would leave little time for the conduct of legislative business.

Senator McKellar promptly issued a statement to the press in reply, asserting that appointment by the President and confirmation by the Senate was the constitutional, the "American," way. He declared that his own bill would not interfere with civil service but would merely provide an "additional precaution," and stated that there was no politics in his bill. He charged that the President had ignored the Constitution by appointing, without confirmation by the Senate, at least ten high-ranking "policy determining officials," including James Byrnes, Director of Economic Stabilization; Harry Hopkins, Presidential Adviser; Nelson Rockefeller, Co-ordinator of Inter-American Affairs; E. R. Stettinius, Lend-Lease Administrator; and others.[50]

Several days later, Senator O'Mahoney announced that he would offer a substitute amendment to require senatorial confirmation, not of all employees receiving $4,500 annually, but rather of those who occupied policy-determining positions except employees with regular civil service status and assistants to the President. This proposal was attacked by Senator McKellar and others on the ground that administrative officers would determine which positions were "policy determining" and that such a provision would therefore have little effect in extending the number of positions for which Senate confirmation is required. The amendment which O'Mahoney subsequently offered did not use the phrase "policy determining," but enumerated the classes of positions which the author regarded as within this category, all of which were to be appointed by the President and confirmed by the Senate. These included the following: heads, assistant heads, and head attorneys of all departments and agencies; heads of bureaus, divisions, sections, and other subdivisions; all persons whose duties include the preparation or issuance of rules, regulations or orders; all persons whose duties include participation in conferences or discussions with persons from other departments or agencies, or with other bureaus, divisions, or sections in the same agency, for the purpose of determining policies or methods.

Although the O'Mahoney amendment omitted the objectionable requirement of Senate confirmation of all employees receiving an annual salary of $4,500, it was subject to many of the same objections as the McKellar bill. The heads of sections and subdivisions, whose appointments would be confirmed by the Senate, included thousands of first-line supervisors, many of whom at that time were receiving salaries much less than $4,500 annually. Many lower-grade employees participated in the preparation of rules, regulations, and orders, or took part in conferences with employees of other subdivisions on policies and methods; hence their appointments would require the approval of the Senate. One of the objections to the O'Mahoney substitute amendment was that it would be extremely difficult to determine which positions were included.

On March 3 the Judiciary Committee voted to accept the O'Mahoney substitute amendment in place of the subcommittee draft of the McKellar bill, but the committee then voted to add the key provision of the original bill—the requirement that all employees receiving salaries of $4,500 or more be appointed by the President and confirmed by the Senate. In this form the bill applied to many more positions than the original McKellar bill and hence was unacceptable to Senator O'Mahoney and other members of the committee opposed to the McKellar bill. It was approved by the committee by a vote of 9 to 5 and was reported to the Senate.[51]

When the bill came before the Senate it was accompanied by a minority as well as a majority report, the minority report being signed by Senators O'Mahoney, Ferguson, and Langer. Senator Hatch, who led the fight on the bill, submitted his views separately. The majority report contended that the bill extended senatorial confirmation only to positions that included policy making among their duties, glossing over the fact that it applied to many lower-grade jobs that were in no sense policy determining. Making no distinction between officers, inferior officers, and employees, it argued that the persons occupying these positions were officers and therefore, under the Constitution, should be appointed by the President and their appointments should be confirmed by the Senate. It stated that "it is essential that the fitness of federal *employees* be properly ascertained if a proper administration of the laws of the United States in relation to the several sovereign states is to obtain," and viewed with alarm "the astonishing growth of responsible Government positions which are today being filled without regard to these clear constitutional principles." The requirement of senatorial confirmation of persons appointed to these positions, it maintained, would strengthen and uphold the civil service, and "implement and insure the selection of competent persons of unquestioned ability to administer the laws of the United States.... In addition to this, it insures reasonable control and supervision by the people, through their representatives, of the Government itself and of its operations."[52]

This indiscriminate praise of the extension of the requirement of senatorial confirmation to an estimated 30,000 federal employees is in striking contrast to the comment on the bill by the New York *Times,* which termed the bill "a naked grab for senatorial patronage." Pointing out that no legislative body could possibly consider with any degree of care appointments to 30,000 positions and have any time left for other matters, the editorial continued: "If the

Senate attempts to exercise detailed controls that it is clearly unfit to exercise, it will soon find itself in effect deprived of the powers that it ought to exercise."[53]

Taking a position exactly opposite to that advanced in the majority report, the minority report attacked the bill on the ground that its provisions were contrary to the intent of the Constitution. "The Constitution," it stated, "does not deal with employees. It deals only with officers, and it does not even require the confirmation of the Senate of all officers." The minority report contended that the framers of the Constitution had never intended that employees, as contrasted with officers, would be passed upon by the Senate and that theretofore the practice had consistently followed this distinction. It asserted, moreover, that the bill reversed "the whole principle of the merit system, and places fully 30,000 inferior officers and employees within the political sphere. It is a step backward which the Congress should not take."[54]

In his individual views Senator Hatch attacked the bill even more vigorously, stating:

The extension of the powers of the Senate to advise and consent to the appointment of thousands and thousands of employed people who are not major officials of the government and who exercise no policy-making functions whatever, and in many instances who are skilled, trained, and scientific employees, might well amount to an actual invasion of the powers which are rightfully conferred on the Executive branch of the Government by the Constitution.[55]

Referring to the TVA, Senator Hatch stated that the bill would require the confirmation of 397 of its employees. Inasmuch as no criticisms had been made of the TVA appointments, he said he could not understand what good purpose would be served by the requirement; on the contrary, he foresaw that much harm would result.

It is not at all difficult to foresee vast danger to the whole Tennessee Valley Authority structure if these trained, skilled and scientific employees are required to go through the usual and customary channels which accompany officials required to be confirmed by the Senate. Surely it is unnecessary to discuss what those channels are. Every Senator knows full well how officials confirmed by the Senate are chosen. Everyone knows that in a great majority of instances partisan political endorsement must be had. This is not said critically; it is merely a statement of conditions as they actually exist. Mere statement of such conditions is, in the humble opinion of the writer, sufficient condemnation of the measure so far as it affects the Tennessee Valley Authority.[56]

In marked contrast to Senator Glass's earlier description of administrative officers of the federal government as "miserable bureaucrats," a letter written to the New York *Times* by Ordway Tead, a prominent author and editor and chairman of the regents of the university system of New York City, praised the devotion, competence, and loyalty of top career men in the federal government.

Such a bill if passed would be a disastrous blow to the effectiveness in office of these career men. It would prevent men of ambition and initiative from entering the federal service. It would nullify much of the merit system which our country has labored so long and arduously to build up. It would again lay important Federal positions wide open to political pull and pressures, directly and indirectly, to a degree of interference with administration by the legislative branch which could demoralize efficient operation.[57]

In the Senate debate Senator Lucas declared that the public regarded the bill as a "patronage grab" to place thousands of additional employees under the domination of the Senate. "It makes no difference how much one clothes the discussion with constitutional arguments," said Lucas, "when we get right down to brass tacks it is simply a question of wanting to control the appointments which are being made by the various bureaus."[58] He contended also that the bill would delay and frustrate the war effort because the war agencies would be told whom they could and could not appoint. Senator Lucas maintained that members of the Senate would not have the time to review the large number of appointments required to be confirmed.

I should like to have the Senators see the long row of files in my office ... containing the voluminous amount of correspondence which has accumulated with respect to practically every postmaster, and a similar amount of correspondence with respect to practically every rural mail carrier. These two outstanding examples of patronage alone demand more of a Senator's time than he should give to such a matter ... and that is especially true when Senators have so many weighty matters upon their minds dealing with Government as it affects the entire world.[59]

Senator McNary, the minority leader, inquired of Senator McKellar whether, with all his heavy duties as acting chairman of the Appropriations Committee, he had the time to pass upon the nomination of the thousands of employees who received salaries of $4,500 or more, adding that he personally did not have the time or inclination and thought that "something would be wrong with my head if I did have."[60] Senator McKellar replied that he would have the time and pointed out that military and naval nominations of approximately 100,000 officers were routinely confirmed by the Senate.[61]

Senator Hill offered an amendment to exempt the TVA, the personnel, accomplishments, and scientific work of which he praised highly. He stated that appointments in the TVA had been free from politics, and characterized the McKellar bill as one which "smacks of pie, pap, and patronage."[62] But the Hill amendment was lost by a vote of 15 to 58.

Senator O'Mahoney offered an amendment to strike out the provision that appointments of all employees who received $4,500 or more should be confirmed by the Senate. This motion and that of Senator Mead to refer the bill to the Civil Service Committee were voted down by a large majority. The bill carried by a vote of 42 to 29: 34 Democrats and 8 Republicans voted in the affirmative; 8 Democrats, 20 Republicans, and 1 Progressive voted in the negative.[63] In the House the bill was referred to the Civil Service Committee, whose chairman, Representative Ramspeck, a strong advocate of the merit system, stated that the bill "simply means turning over the entire government personnel to the Senators."[64] The bill was never reported by the House committee.

Not despairing, Senator McKellar the following year introduced a rider to the Independent Offices Appropriation bill requiring senatorial confirmation of all employees of the TVA receiving salaries of $4,500 or more. His amendment, which included also a requirement that all TVA revenues be paid into the Treasury and fourteen other crippling provisions applicable to the TVA, aroused a storm of protest and was dropped; but another amendment requiring senatorial confirmation of all employees receiving $4,500 annually in all government agencies was adopted.

After the passage of this amendment, the New York *Times* said: "The Senate voted itself one of the biggest patronage grabs in history, by requiring senatorial confirmation of all appointments to executive agencies carrying salaries of $4,500 or more." Observing that the House was being asked to "compromise" the measure in conference, the editorial stated: "There is no respectable compromise" on a measure "devised to dilute the personnel of the executive agencies by putting 'political hacks' ahead of qualified experts."[65] The House once more refused to agree to a rider of this type, and the Senate conferees finally yielded.

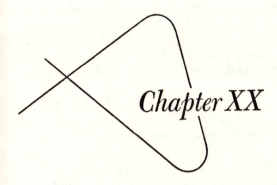

Chapter XX

EVALUATION: ISSUES AND
PROPOSED REFORMS

A ruler who appoints any Man to office when there is in his dominions another man who is better qualified for it sins against God and against the State. The Koran.

IN THIS CONCLUDING CHAPTER an attempt will be made to review and to evaluate broadly the operation and effects of senatorial confirmation of appointments in this country and to discuss the various trends, developments, and proposals for reform. The first part deals with the constitutional issues and the intentions of the framers of the Constitution. This is followed by an account of the practices, traditions and tests used by the Senate in passing on appointments. A third section reviews the effects of senatorial confirmation of minor administrative officers and employees and discusses various proposals for reform, and the concluding section consists of an over-all evalution.

The Constitutional Issues

The debates that have occurred in controversies between the President and the Senate over appointments have usually turned on constitutional issues, each side offering a different interpretation of the provision of the Constitution and the intention of its framers. The review of the debates on the subject in the Constitutional Convention of 1787 (in chapter ii) indicates that the final compromise, under which the President was given the power to nominate and, subject to the advice and consent of the Senate, to appoint, was intended to apply only to the principal offices and was never intended to be extended to minor officers and employees. Only two classes of officers were enumerated in

[375

the Constitution: Judges of the Supreme Court and diplomatic representatives abroad. Although the Constitution authorized Congress to establish inferior courts, the judges of such courts were not enumerated as officers whose appointments should be confirmed by the Senate. The extension of the requirement of senatorial confirmation to thousands of minor positions was not contemplated by the framers of the Constitution and is contrary to the spirit, if not to the provisions, of the Constitution.

The requirement of Senate approval of appointments by the President was intended as a safeguard against the danger that a future President might abuse the appointing power and use it to make himself a monarch. Writing a hundred years later Lord Bryce stated that this danger, if it ever existed, had passed. Civil service legislation has provided a far more effective protection against political appointments and abuses than is afforded by the requirement of senatorial confirmation which, indeed, has often had the opposite effect of introducing partisan politics into appointments.

It has been contended by some members of the Senate in recent years that the words "advice and consent" mean more than merely an act of approval or rejection, and that the President is required by the Constitution to consult with the Senate—actually with individual members—before making a nomination. Historical evidence does not support the contention. The section of the Constitution on appointments which reads, "The President ... shall nominate, and by and with the advice and consent of the Senate, shall appoint," indicates that the power to nominate was given to the President alone. The debates of the Convention indicate that "advice and consent" was regarded as simply to vote of approval or rejection. The phrase was used as synonymous with "approbation," "concurrence," and "approval," and the power of the Senate was spoken of as a "negative" on the appointment by the President. Hamilton stated in *The Federalist* (No. 66) that since the Senate could only approve or disapprove the President's selections, there would be no attempt on its part to exert a choice. It would be an extraordinary construction of the Constitution to hold that he must consult with the members of the Senate of his own party but not those of the opposing party.

If one principle in regard to appointments was prized above others by the framers of the Constitution, it was that of establishing definite responsibility. Time and again those who favored appointment by the President alone stated that since he would be responsible he would exercise care and appoint only fit persons. The irresponsibility of state legislatures in the exercise of the appointing power and their tendency to make unsuitable appointments through political intrigue was frequently mentioned in the debates. It was generally agreed that the lower house of Congress would be too large to exercise a voice in appointments, but it was thought that the Senate, being a smaller body, would exercise a salutary check on the appointing power of the

President. Some members of the Convention envisaged the Senate as a privy council to the President. (In the first session the House consisted of 65 members, the Senate of 26.) Those who favored the establishment of definite responsibility for appointments, and hence the vesting of the appointing power in a single executive, thought that they had achieved a victory in the final compromise, for they reasoned that the power to nominate was in no essential respect different from the power to appoint. History has proved that in this they were in error; for some positions the power to confirm has become virtually the power to appoint.

The long-established custom which requires the President to consult senators of his own party about nominations to federal offices in their states and, as a rule, to accept their choices, is based on party tradition rather than the Constitution and does not impose on the President a "constitutional duty." The custom, which is enforced by the unwritten rule of "senatorial courtesy," virtually transfers the nominating function for these offices from the President to the individual senators of his party. Most Presidents have yielded to the custom rather than jeopardize their legislative programs, but at times Presidents have asserted their power by refusing to nominate candidates proposed by senators who have opposed their legislative programs.

The Practices of the Senate in Passing on Nominations

The framers of the Constitution assumed that the Senate would act on the President's nominations primarily, if not solely, with regard to the qualifications and fitness of the nominees, and therefore believed that the requirement of Senate approval would constitute a salutary safeguard against bad appointments. It was expected that the role of the Senate would be mainly passive. The actual practice, however, has been quite otherwise. To Washington's discomfiture, the Senate held up a number of his nominations of diplomatic representatives to European capitals, to debate not the qualifications of the nominees but rather whether this country should send diplomats to these countries.

Most contests over the President's nominations have been grounded on political considerations rather than on the qualifications of the nominees. Many of the most dramatic political struggles in the history of the country have occurred over contested nominations. The rejection of the four Bank directors appointed by Jackson in 1833 and the rejection of Roger Taney's appointment as Secretary of the Treasury, for example, were not due to any lack of qualifications on the part of the nominees: they were crucial moves in the struggle between the Bank and anti-Bank forces. The rejection of Van Buren as minister to England in 1831 was brought about by Calhoun, Clay, and Webster, who regarded him as their principal opponent for the Presidency and believed that the rejection would end his political career. The contests between Senator Conkling of New York and Presidents Hayes and Garfield over appointments had little or nothing to do with qualifications; they were rather struggles over patronage. The fight over the nomination of Brandeis to the Supreme Court in 1916 was essentially a political struggle and may have been crucial to the outcome of the presidential election that year. It took all of the skill of the President, his Cabinet, and the Democratic leaders in the Senate to secure approval of the appointment of Brandeis after one of the greatest contests in the history of the Senate. The rejection of Charles Beecher Warren as Attorney General in 1926, immediately after Coolidge had been elected President by an overwhelming majority, greatly weakened the hands of the administration and the leadership of the President, as it was intended to do.

Senators of the opposition party often oppose nominations, even when they have little expectation of success, in order to embarrass the President and to discredit his administration. The qualifications of nominees have little to do with such contests, and those opposing a nomination are rarely at a loss to find reasons to justify their opposition. In the contest over the nomination of Lilienthal as chairman of the Atomic Energy Commission in 1947, Senator Taft advanced the extraordinary proposition that a senator was justified in voting against a nomination unless he regarded the nominee as the best-qualified man in the country for the job. Senators who belong to the President's party and support his program, however, usually vote for his nominations without too much regard to the qualifications of the nominee, and the vote in close contests usually follows party lines. It would appear that senators of the two parties apply quite different tests in passing on the fitness of nominees. The truth of the matter is that senators on both sides of the aisle recognize that contests over appointments are essentially political struggles or maneuvers for party advantage in which the qualifications and fitness of nominees are given only secondary consideration.

Not only do senators of the opposing party contest the President's nominations when they see a prospect of party advantage, but such contests provide senators of the President's party who oppose his program with an excellent opportunity to weaken his leadership. A faction opposing the President can usually count on support from members of the opposite party, and in crucial contests it is often able to defeat his nominations. Senatorial confirmation has thus facilitated the factionalism which has characterized political parties in this country.

The standards that the President and the Senate have maintained in federal appointments have varied widely. The Senate has not always insisted on high standards but on the contrary has approved many nominees with meager qualifications and some who proved to be persons lacking in integrity. The low standards that have often obtained are due to the system of patronage appointment rather than to the shortcomings of either the President or the members of the Senate. It is, of course, impossible for the Senate or its committees to examine carefully the qualifications of the several hundred important civilian appointments which it passes on annually, not to speak of the many thousands of appointments of military officers, postmasters, and other minor offices. Usually the Senate inquires into the qualifications of the nominee only when an objection has been entered, and the objection frequently has nothing to do with the nominee's qualifications. The usual practice is for the committee to which the nomination is assigned to notify the senators from the state in which the office is situated, or, if the office is a national one, the senators of the state in which the nominee resides; if they concur, and no objection is entered by others, the nomination is reported favorably without further investigation. One of the several forms of courtesy that senators extend to one another is not to inquire into or to interfere with patronage appointments. It is only with regard to certain offices, particularly the judiciary, that the Senate insists on standards of integrity and competence.

The tests applied by the Senate in considering nominations vary widely, depending in part on the character and importance of the office concerned and whether the nomination is one to which the Senate gives individual attention. Well-established custom accords the President wide latitude in the choice of members of his own Cabinet, who are regarded as his chief assistants and advisers. Only two Cabinet nominations have been rejected in the last hundred years, though a number were contested. The Senate's consideration of Cabinet nominations is by no means perfunctory, but the Senate does not attempt to dictate the President's selections. Today a Cabinet nomination will be rejected only if the nominee is definitely disqualified. The Senate does not require that Cabinet nominees hold views which are agreeable to a majority of senators, and it does not consider its approval as approval of the views of the nominee. In the debate on the nomination of Harry Hopkins to be Secretary of Commerce in 1939, for example, several Democratic senators stated that they did not approve of Hopkins' views but would vote to confirm him because he was the President's choice. Nor does the Senate attempt to substitute its judgment for that of the President concerning the qualifications of persons nominated to the Cabinet. When Cabinet nominations are closely contested, however, the vote usually follows party lines. Opposition senators, although they concede that the President should be given wide discretion in the choice of his Cabinet, have little difficulty in justifying a negative vote, and senators of the President's own party support his choice although they may express doubts about the wisdom of the nomination.

The tradition of the Senate to give the President a free hand in the choice of his own Cabinet recognizes that he must be permitted this discretion if he is to be held responsible for the conduct of the executive branch of the government. The fundamental division of powers between Congress and the President would be unworkable if the Senate attempted to dictate the appointments to the Cabinet. But this reasoning applies with equal force to department heads and to other officers in the choice of their principal assistants. A department head cannot be held responsible for the operation of his department if his principal assistants are not of his own choosing. In passing on the nominations of under and assistant secretaries, the Senate usually applies the rule it uses in considering Cabinet nominations. Nominees to these posts have rarely been rejected except for reasons thought to be disqualifying.

Nominations of judges to the lower courts, courts of appeal, and to the Supreme Court are scrutinized with unusual care. Hearings are now invariably held, reports of the FBI investigations are secured, and the comments of the bar associations are invited. A nominee with a questionable legal record, or one who is regarded as unqualified, would today be blocked by the Senate Judiciary Committee. Confirmation of judicial appointments by the Senate has operated, in many respects, much as the framers of the Constitution intended and has provided a safeguard against unfit appointments. Unfortunately, however, it has not resulted in uniformly high standards. The custom of senatorial courtesy, which the framers of the Constitution did not foresee, has in effect transferred from the President to the senators of his party the selection of district judges in their own states. This feature of judicial appointments has been strongly condemned by writers on judicial administration and by official commissions, but any fundamental reform appears unlikely. The fault of the system lies in the fact that judicial appointments of this grade are regarded as party patronage to be awarded to persons who have served the party or the individual senator and therefore are seldom given to persons who possess the highest qualifications. The standards, which are determined by the individual senators and the party organizations, vary greatly from state to state. Many members of the Senate have insisted on high qualifications, thereby incurring the displeasure of local political leaders. Others have maintained low standards. President Hoover and Attorney General Mitchell attempted to elevate the standards for judicial appointment under the present system, but with indifferent results. The basic reform needed is to curb the use of judicial appointments as party patronage and to provide for a more careful screening of prospective appointees before they are nominated. It has been suggested that a council on judicial appointments, selected by the President from the bench, bar, leading law schools and the public, might serve this purpose and eventually change the role of the Senate from that of selecting persons for judicial appointment to passing on the President's nominations, as contemplated by the framers of the Constitution.

Nominations of the members of regulatory commissions and the heads of other important boards and commissions, such as the Tennessee Valley Authority and the Atomic Energy Commission, are also scrutinized with care by the Senate. Congress looks upon the regulatory commissions as peculiarly its own agents, and the leading members of Congress of the President's party often influence appointments to these commissions. One of the significant features of appointments to regulatory commissions is the influence exerted by organized interest groups. These groups, which are directly affected by the policies and rulings of the commissions, understandably seek to secure the appointment of persons they regard as friendly to them, and they pull many wires, often through members of Congress, to accomplish this purpose. In a number of instances they have conducted extensive campaigns, sometimes openly, but usually behind the scenes, to block the appointment of persons whom they oppose. Commissioners who have displayed courage and zeal in supporting effective regulatory policies—as, for example, Leland Olds and Thomas Buchanan of the Federal Power Commission, James Landis of the Civil Aeronautics Board, and James Fly of the Federal Communications Commission—have found their reappointments blocked by industry opposition; whereas those who have "gone along" with the regulated industry have had little difficulty in their reappointments.

The qualifications of persons appointed to federal commissions have often left much to be desired. Generally speaking, new members at the outset of their terms rarely have any special qualifications. Although some of these persons have later become able commissioners, the practice of appointing persons with only general qualifications is not desirable. The first appointments to new federal commissions are usually of a high order; but with the passage of time, personnel standards usually deteriorate and appointments frequently come to be regarded as suitable rewards to deserving politicians, defeated members of Congress, and others with strong political sponsorship. Recently, two important commissions—the RFC and the Maritime Commission—were involved in serious scandals and charges of maladministration; both were reorganized and their administrations placed in the hands of a single administrator. It is hardly to be doubted that their troubles stemmed largely from political appointments. Too often in the past, appointments to these commissions were based on political or personal considerations or were due to sectional pressures, with only incidental attention to qualifications. Although the major responsibility for poor appointments rests with the President, who makes the nominations, it must be recognized that he is subject to strong political pressures, many of which emanate from the Senate itself.

The custom of the Senate in passing on diplomatic appointments has been similar to that which it follows for Cabinet nominations. Since the President is charged with the conduct of foreign relations, it has been felt that he should be permitted to choose persons to act as his agents. Throughout our history all Presidents have on occasion appointed persons to aid in the conduct of foreign relations without asking for Senate approval. After about 1815 it became the usual practice for the President alone to appoint persons to carry on treaty negotiations with other countries or to represent this country at international conferences or on international bodies. The charge has been made repeatedly in the Senate that this practice is contrary to the Constitution, but it is now well established that the President may utilize agents of his own choosing. In recent years, however, there has been an increasing tendency for Congress to require the approval of the Senate of appointments of our representatives to international bodies and conferences. Thus our delegates to the General Assembly, Security Council, and other commissions of the United Nations must be approved by the Senate. The appointments of representatives to the older international organizations, however, are not ordinarily submitted to the Senate for confirmation. In recent years also a number of contests have arisen over the appointments of diplomatic representatives, although formerly such contests were unusual. In 1951 the appointments of Philip Jessup as delegate to the United Nations General Assembly and Chester Bowles as ambassador to India were contested. The contests over these appointments were obviously political. It would be unfortunate if the Senate were to reverse its long-established practice of permitting the President wide discretion in the choice of the agents through whom he will conduct our foreign relations.

Nominations to federal field offices, such as those of district attorney, marshal, and collector of customs and internal revenue, are treated quite differently from nominations to other offices. The selection of these officers in each state is normally made by members of the Senate from that state, if they belong to the President's party; and the courtesy of the Senate requires other members to agree to the patronage selections of their colleagues. The Senate's action with respect to nominations to these offices usually consists in nothing more than ascertaining whether the nomination is agreeable to the senators from the state and, if they approve, routinely confirming it. Senators of the opposition party may object to nominations in their states, but they rarely do so, since they do not control such appointments. When, in somewhat rare instances, objections come from other quarters, the Senate committee to which the nomination is referred will consider the merits of the case. For local federal officers, the function of nominations has, in effect, been taken over by the senators from the state, if they are of the same party as the President; and the same senators who make the initial selection of the persons to be nominated later pass upon their confirmation. The custom of "senatorial courtesy" not only deprives the President of the nominating function, but it likewise deprives the Senate of its function of passing on such nominations.

The role of the Senate in passing on the nominations of postmasters, officers of the armed services and the Coast Guard, and the civilian officers of special career services, such as the Public Health Service, is almost wholly perfunctory.

The fact that these nominations must be approved by the Senate makes it possible for an objection to be raised against a particular promotion, but such objections are unusual. Little purpose is served today by the formality of presidential appointment and senatorial confirmation of these thousands of personnel actions.

In passing on the nominations, aside from those routinely approved en bloc, the Senate and its committees usually consider: (1) the character, reputation, and standing of the nominee; (2) his qualifications and experience with respect to the office to which he is nominated; and (3) his party affiliation, philosophy, stands on public issues, and attitudes and opinions on matters more or less related to the functions of the office to which he is nominated. Often the inquiry of the Senate committee is confined to the character and reputation of the nominee. This is necessarily true in many instances because members of the Senate do not have sufficient familiarity with the duties and responsibilities of officers whose nominations come before them to judge whether the nominee possesses the special qualifications required. Legislative bodies are prone to discount the need for special qualifications and to consider that good character and a moderately successful record in business, law, public office, or other walks of life qualify a person for most public offices. Today, at least, more is required. The officers in charge of the executive departments and independent agencies and the members of the important federal commissions need to be persons of high qualifications of a special kind. The administration of large enterprises such as the Atomic Energy Commission, the TVA, and the Social Security Administration, and the regulation of vast segments of our economy, such as banking, transportation, trade, gas and electric power, communications and aviation, have become highly complex, requiring persons with suitable experience and backgrounds. Neither the President nor the Senate has consistently maintained the necessary high standards for appointment to these commissions and other high federal offices, though it must be added that the salary and other rewards are not such as to attract persons with the highest qualifications.

Although the Senate has seldom required that nominees be specially qualified to perform the duties of the offices to which they were nominated, and has approved many persons with only general, and in many instances only mediocre, qualifications, it has occasionally rejected nominees because of some disqualification. A striking example is the 1953 appointment of Charles E. Wilson, former president of General Motors Corporation, to be Secretary of Defense. Because of a statute prohibiting any officer or employee of the government from representing the government in any transactions with business firms in which he has a direct or indirect pecuniary interest, Wilson's nomination was held up until he had agreed to dispose of his large holdings in General Motors. Under the same rule, several other members of Eisenhower's

Cabinet and their chief assistants were required to dispose of stocks in companies that did business with the department to which they were appointed. The Senate has insisted on observance of the conflict-of-interest statutes in approving appointments to high administrative positions. It was unwilling to approve the appointment of Edwin W. Pauley to be Under Secretary of the Navy in 1943, because of his large holdings in the oil industry. A similar case was that of Charles Beecher Warren, whose nomination as Attorney General was rejected in 1925 because of his previous association with the American Sugar Refining Company.

It has been contended at times that the Senate should consider only the character and qualifications of nominees and should not reject them because of their party affiliations, philosophies, attitudes, or views on public issues. The Senate has tended to follow this policy in considering nominations to the Cabinet but not to other offices. In voting on the nominations of members of independent commissions and judges the senators frequently have taken into consideration the philosophy of the nominee, and particularly his record or reputation as a conservative or as a liberal. The opposition of the Senate liberals to the appointments of Stone, Hughes, and Parker to the Supreme Court in the 1920's was denounced in the press at the time as an attack on the Court itself. It is appropriate for the Senate to consider the philosophy and general outlook of nominees to high federal offices, particularly to regulatory bodies and to the bench. These offices stand in a different position from that of the heads of executive departments for whose actions the President is responsible. Washington once stated that he would not knowingly appoint to an office of consequence a man "whose political tenets are adverse to the measures which the general government are pursuing," and all Presidents since have of necessity followed a similar policy, though some have been much more discerning than others in the selection of nominees who are sympathetic to their programs.

It is equally appropriate for the Senate to apply the same test and to reject nominees whose views are not acceptable to a majority. Governmental policies have often been influenced quite as much by the choice of the principal officers as by the legislation they administer. Those in charge of administrative agencies provide the leadership, prepare programs for the approval of the President and Congress, set the tone of the administration, and direct its operations. In passing on nominations, the Senate must consider the kind of leadership that may be expected from those who are nominated, and it is quite justified in rejecting a nominee who is not in sympathy with the legislative policies he would be required to administer and who presumably would not perform the duties of the office with vigor and zeal. It may be noted, however, that more often nominees have been opposed for exactly the opposite reason—because it was thought that they would administer the legislative policy with effectiveness and zeal. Those who are opposed to a legislative policy which Congress has adopted are able, often with great effect, to resume their opposition when appointments are made. A legislative policy may be greatly weakened or nullified if the officers in charge are lukewarm or opposed to it. Thus the battle over legislative policies is waged not only when legislation is under consideration but when appropriations are voted and when appointments are made.

The Senate is justified in considering a nominee's philosophy in regard to policies which he will be called upon to carry out if confirmed. But it should confine its consideration to subjects relevant to the duties of the office and should not inquire into general opinions or attitudes of nominees. All would agree that consideration or inquiry into the religious faith of the nominee is not appropriate. Similarly, discrimination against a person because of his race is equally unworthy and contrary to the spirit of our institutions. It is not without significance that several of the most sensational contests in the Senate have arisen over the nominations of Jews to high office.

One of the requirements commonly written into law with regard to federal commissions is that their membership shall be bipartisan. This is a requirement which the Senate has tended to enforce strictly; it is, of course, a simple test to apply. Other considerations touching on the qualifications of the nominee are much less tangible. Senate committees have tended to favor nominees who are regarded as party regulars and to look with less favor on political independents or irregulars. Nevertheless, the Senate has confirmed some persons who stated that they were independent in politics, and these persons have often been among the most able public officers.

There have been a number of instances in which nominees were opposed ostensibly because of some previous writings or statements. The attack by Clay, Webster, and other senators on Van Buren when he was nominated to be minister to England in 1831 was based on the letter of instructions which, as Secretary of State, he had given to the previous minister to that country, although the letter had been submitted earlier to the Senate and had then occasioned no criticism. John Rutledge, who had served on the Supreme Court, was rejected as Chief Justice in 1795 because of a speech he had made opposing the Jay Treaty with England; and Caleb Cushing, who had been a member of the Cabinet and a man of national prominence for years, was not confirmed when nominated to the Supreme Court in 1874, because of an innocent letter he had written to Jefferson Davis in behalf of a young man who was returning to the South. Leland Olds's writings more than twenty years earlier were dusted off and used effectively by his opponents to defeat his reappointment to the Federal Power Commission in 1949, even after he had served ten years on the commission. And the previous statements and writings of Tugwell, Hopkins, and Williams were similarly used to oppose their nominations. Perhaps the most extreme case was that of John Carson, whose appointment to the Federal Trade Commission in 1949 was opposed not only for his own writings but for those of another person—writings which the nominee stated at the hearings he had never read.

A nominee should be judged by his entire record and not by a few sentences—usually taken out of context—from his previous writings or statements. Those who oppose nominees often search through their entire records and writings for particular statements or episodes which they may utilize in their opposition. The effect usually is to center attention upon some statement or event of minor significance or relevance and thus to obscure the real issues and the reasons for the opposition.* The opponents of Brandeis in 1916, for example, did not place their opposition on their real reason—because they regarded him as a radical—but asserted that he had been guilty of sharp legal practice and unethical conduct, charges which were disproved in the hearings. There have been numerous instances of nominees who were openly opposed because they were regarded as radicals or as conservatives; but more often than not the real reasons for the opposition are concealed behind irrelevant charges and assertions. When the nomination of Thomas D. Jones to the Federal Reserve Board in 1914 was opposed because he was a member of the board of directors of International Harvester Company and a person of wealth, the opposition was denounced by Wilson as unworthy of the counsels of a great people.

One effect of the requirement of senatorial confirmation is that persons of strong convictions, who have taken sides on social and economic questions, are likely to face difficulty in being confirmed; but middle-of-the-road nominees, who have never become a part of such movements and have never expressed any strong convictions on controversial public issues usually face little difficulty. This is unfortunate. Although persons with strong biases should not be appointed to positions that call for judicial qualities, many offices call for persons with courage, vigor, and imagination, who feel strongly about the problems of society and have definite ideas, ideals, and convictions.

Public hearings on nominations, which today are generally used for the most important offices, are subject to serious limitations as a means of inquiring into the qualifications of nominees. In contested nominations, however, they are usually desirable and may be essential, but they should be supplemented by other forms of inquiry. On occasion, such hearings have afforded an opportunity for irresponsible persons of no standing to air malicious gossip and to launch unsupported attacks on the nominee. The hearings on the nominations of Justice Frankfurter in 1939 and Anna M. Rosenberg as Assistant Secretary of Defense in 1950 afford striking illustrations of this danger. Obviously, great pains should be taken to prevent the hearing from degenerating into an attempt to smear the nominee, or from taking on the appearance

---

* See James Reston's pungent article "Fourteen Simple Rules on How to Be Confirmed," quoted below, p. 437.

of a trial of charges against him. The government has undoubtedly been deprived of the services of many able and patriotic citizens who were unwilling to incur the risk of being exposed to attacks of this kind. Few persons would willingly undergo the ordeal Lilienthal and Clapp were subjected to in 1947. Some of these objections, however, could be avoided by a careful screening of witnesses, permitting only credible witnesses who have firsthand and pertinent information to testify. Others could be permitted to file statements, which, however, need not be published. When the nomination of Dean Acheson came before the Committee on Foreign Relations in 1949, Senator Connally announced that a public hearing would be held to hear "respectable" witnesses.

It appears that often undue emphasis is given in Senate committee hearings to testimony by the nominee in his own behalf. Testifying before the Judiciary Committee at its request in 1939, Felix Frankfurter, who had been nominated to the Supreme Court, expressed the view that it was of doubtful utility and propriety for the nominee to the Supreme Court to testify in a hearing on his own nomination. He pointed out that in only one case on record up to that time had a Court nominee been called to testify at such a hearing. He stated that it was proper for the committee to inquire into his views and philosophy but he believed that this could better be done by an examination of his previous writings and public statements, which were available to the committee, than by interrogation at a public hearing. He declined to discuss controversial public issues which might come before the Court, on the ground that it would be improper for him to do so. Ten years later, Judge Minton took the same position in a letter to the committee, declining to testify, and the committee withdrew its invitation. Nominees to the bench are not ordinarily invited to testify on their own nominations but are permitted to do so if they so request.

Although this reasoning does not apply equally to nonjudicial offices, it is doubtful whether, in the typical case, much is gained by inviting the nominee to testify in his own behalf. Nominees to the principal offices of the government are usually persons whose records are widely known and are readily available. Usually they are personally known to several members of the committee to which their nomination is referred. Their records, of course, should be scrutinized by the committee, with the assistance of its staff; but as a rule the nominee should not be required to appear to testify in his own nomination unless there are special circumstances that warrant his appearance. If he testifies, it is likely to give the impression that he is seeking the office, which is distasteful to men of standing and sensitiveness. Or the hearing may take on the appearance of a public trial, which is unfortunate. Occasionally the nominee is interrogated by members of the committee in a manner to invite him to make commitments on controversial policies which later he may be called upon to decide; this of course is not desirable.

The Extension of Senatorial Confirmation
to Subordinate Positions

Contrary to the evident intention of the framers of the Constitution, the appointing power of the President, by and with the advice and consent of the Senate, has been extended to thousands of minor offices and positions. The growth of the practice has been to a large degree hapazard and does not reflect a deliberate or considered policy. The number now totals approximately 124,000 positions, of which 98,000 are regular officers of the armed services. An examination of the list of positions subject to senatorial confirmation reveals many anomalies. Some minor and relatively unimportant positions, in which the duties are mostly routine and ministerial and call for the exercise of little discretion, are filled in this manner; but some of the more responsible positions, including headships of some large organizations, are not subject to senatorial confirmation. Many of these more responsible positions are under civil service; others are subject to appointment by agency or department heads.

The sheer number of positions now filled by presidential appointment and senatorial confirmation necessarily makes an empty formality of both appointment and confirmation in the vast majority of cases. The President cannot be expected to have any firsthand knowledge of the thousands of military and naval officers, for example, whose appointments and promotions cross his desk; this is even more true of members of the Senate, except for the casual or accidental acquaintance of senators with individual officers. Although the President and the Congress should exercise effective control over the policies that govern military and naval appointments and promotions, obviously the passing upon thousands of individual personnel actions is not a suitable means. The routine approval of thousands of such actions each year, about which neither the President nor the Senate has any information, provides the appearance but not the substance of control, and actually affords little protection against abuses and injudicious promotions. More effective control could be secured through suitable legislation establishing the policies and procedures that govern promotions in the armed services and through delegating the authority and undivided responsibility to the services themselves for individual actions. The President should appoint and the Senate should confirm only a small number of the top-ranking officers of each service. The number should be small enough to enable the President to give individual attention to each selection and to permit the Senate to examine the fitness of his nominees.

It may be inquired what purpose is served by requiring the President to appoint and the Senate to confirm the appointments of 21,000 postmasters throughout the country. Why should the President appoint and the Senate pass upon the appointment and promotion of physicians in the United States

Public Health Service? Or of engineers in the Coast and Geodetic Survey? Or of Foreign Service officers? Or of chief and assistant locomotive inspectors in the Interstate Commerce Commission? There is a need for reconsideration of the positions now filled by presidential appointment and senatorial confirmation, though realistically it may be doubted whether the Senate will agree to any substantial reduction in the number filled by this method.

For which offices should the President make appointments and the Senate confirm them? It has often been urged that only "policy-determining" offices should be filled in this manner. This was the recommendation by the President's Committee on Administrative Management in 1937, and it was restated by President Roosevelt in a number of messages to Congress urging the extension of the civil service and opposing legislative proposals to require senatorial confirmation of minor administrative employees. The same position has also been taken by a number of Senators in debates relating to senatorial confirmation. It may be questioned, however, whether the test of "policy determining" is a useful one in deciding which officers should be appointed by the President and confirmed by the Senate. There are wide differences of opinion concerning the meaning of the words "policy" and "determining."; consequently there is little agreement as to which offices are "policy determining." Members of the Senate have at times expressed the opinion that very subordinate employees often decide policies, and under this construction the application of the principle would result in a material expansion of the requirement of senatorial confirmation. When the Senate was debating the McKellar bill in 1943 President Roosevelt reminded it that "policy determining" was not to be confused with the exercise of administrative discretion.

The criterion of "policy determining" is valid and useful provided it is agreed that policy decisions are those relating to the major outlines of government programs and not those relating to the detailed administration. Also, emphasis should be given to the word *determining*. Only the major officers, the heads of departments or agencies and their principal assistants, determine policies, and the most important policies are determined not by any executive officer but by Congress itself. Many employees participate in the preparation of policies, and all employees of whatever rank assist in the execution of policies; but only political officers of the highest rank decide or determine what the policies shall be. The heads of bureaus, it may be noted, do not ordinarily determine policies; when new and controversial issues arise or new policies and programs are under consideration, bureau chiefs and other subordinate administrative officers collect information, make recommendations, and prepare policies, but the actual determination is made by the department head or his assistants. If the policy is highly important, if it impinges on other departments, or if it has significant political implications, the department head will probably feel obligated to submit it to the President for his determination.

And in most instances it will have to be passed upon by Congress when the necessary legislation is considered and when funds are voted to carry it out.

The President should appoint and the Senate should confirm only the major officers of the government. These may be classified broadly into the following groups: (1) political officers who assist the President in deciding upon major policies and who share with him the responsibility for his administration, including the heads of executive departments, assistant and under secretaries, the heads of independent agencies, and a small number of officers at lower levels in charge of programs of a political or controversial character; (2) judges; (3) members of independent boards and commissions; (4) diplomatic representatives to other countries and to international bodies; and (5) the highest-ranking military and naval officers.

There are several important reasons why the President should not appoint subordinate officers below these levels. In the first place, the heads of departments, bureaus, or other agencies can be held responsible only if they have the selection of their immediate assistants. It is essential that this principle be followed from top to bottom of any organization. The power to appoint and to remove is basic to executive control. Certain limitations and restrictions on the appointing power are necessary under a civil service system, but these restrictions apply principally to original appointments at lower grades and should not be permitted to interfere materially with the filling of the higher positions by selection from among the career employees. When administrative positions at the higher levels are filled by political appointment and the selection is made by persons other than those in charge, the results are invariably unsatisfactory. Not only are the key positions in the organization filled by incompetent appointees, but the persons in these positions owe their appointment and their loyalty to political sponsors rather than to administrative superiors. This was the situation in the Bureau of Internal Revenue which led congressional investigating staffs to report in 1948 that the commissioner did not have control of his own organization.

A second reason why the President should not appoint subordinate administrative officers is that he does not have the time to pass upon such appointments. The President has so many other duties to perform that he cannot take time to consider who would make a suitable postmaster of Devil's Lake, North Dakota; yet both Taft and Wilson had to spend a great deal of time over this one postmastership. Many Presidents throughout the history of the country have complained about the time-consuming burden of seeing office seekers and Congressmen about appointments. "I cannot exaggerate the waste of the President's time and the consumption of his nervous vitality," declared Taft, "involved in congressional intercession as to local appointments." The story is told that a friend of Lincoln once told him that he looked tired and worn and inquired if the news from the battle front was bad. Lincoln replied that it was not the war but a postmastership that was the cause of his weariness. Neither the President nor the Senate has the time to consider these thousands of appointments without neglecting matters vastly more important.

A third reason why the President's appointing power should be restricted to the top political and policy-making positions is that he is under great pressures to make political appointments and to award federal offices to persons who have served the party. No President can resist these pressures. Presidential appointment of minor administrative officers necessarily results in patronage appointments. This, of course, is not true of the officers of the armed services and those in the civilian career services, such as the Foreign Service, in which appointments are invariably from within the service. The retention of presidential appointment of postmasters prevents the office from becoming a part of the career service, and this is true of other offices that are filled in this manner. The Hoover Commission in 1949, the President's Committee on Administrative Management in 1937, and the Taft Commission on Economy and Efficiency in 1912 made the identical recommendation—that positions below the level of assistant secretary of executive departments should not be filled by presidential appointment and senatorial confirmation but by the executive officers of the departments concerned and, as a rule, should be filled from the civil service. The career service should extend upward to include all but a few of the highest positions. The heads of departments and independent agencies of course must be at the command of the administration in office in order that it may direct and control the policies and operations of the government.

Generally speaking, most appointments of the President are subject to confirmation by the Senate. There are, however, a number of justifiable exceptions. In the Budget and Accounting Act of 1921, for example, it was purposely provided that the Director of the Bureau of the Budget should be appointed by the President alone and that his appointment should not be subject to the approval of the Senate. It was felt that the Director should be the "President's man" and that the Senate should have no voice in his selection. Similarly, the Hoover Commission recommended that the heads of all of the staff agencies in the executive office of the President be exempted from senatorial confirmation. This is probably wise in view of the intimate relationship between them and the President, and the fact that the President must have entire confidence in, and the undivided loyalty of, those who are his immediate assistants. The President has a right to choose his own advisers and chief assistants without the supervision of the Senate.

Proposals to extend the civil service to all positions in the government except a relatively small number of important policy-determining positions at the top, and hence to reduce the appointing power of the President, have at times been attacked on the ground that the President needs patronage to maintain the support of his party in Congress. The principal patronage positions filled by presidential appointment are those within the states; for example, those of judge, district attorney, marshal, collector, and postmaster. The patronage of these offices is traditionally a perquisite of the senators, except the selection of postmasters, which custom has assigned to members of the House. The offices are not at the free disposal of the President, and he is not likely to win over to his legislative program any members of the Senate by according them the patronage they regard as their own.

Patronage is an effective weapon to keep members of the party in line only when it can be granted or withheld as the occasion requires. With respect to appointments of local federal officers, the President's hands are tied because he must secure the approval of the Senate. If he withdraws the customary patronage of a senator of his party, he will usually find that his own nomination is blocked in the Senate. The control of patronage in their states is a symbol of power which is highly important to the senators. It is generally recognized that the senators, not the President or the head of the department, select the persons for federal appointments in their states. Candidates for office apply to their senators, party leaders and delegations wait on them, and newspapers carry stories concerning the probable choice of the senators for federal offices in the state. Senators bitterly resent any move on the part of the President to cut off their patronage, regardless of whether they have supported the President's program; they have often declared that such action was designed to discredit and degrade them in the eyes of the voters of their states.

The President consequently withdraws the patronage of a senator of his party only as a last resort after becoming convinced that the senator is an implacable foe. When this step is taken, the senator may be expected thereafter to become an embittered opponent of the President. The bitter enmity of several members of the Senate to Franklin Roosevelt after his first term may be attributed chiefly to the withdrawal of their patronage. Instead of creating party unity, as Senator Thomas maintained in his defense of senatorial courtesy in the Roberts case, the distribution of patronage often causes the relations between the President and senators of his party to become strained, and thus results in party disunity. Occasionally, bitter feuds arise between the two senators from the same state over the control of patronage, and the President finds it difficult to avoid incurring the enmity of one or both. When this occurs, federal appointments in the state may be held up for extended periods, for neither senator will agree to the nominee of the other.

Just as patronage is of questionable value to the President in the long run in his relations with members of the Senate, for somewhat the same reasons it is doubtful whether it is of much real value to the senators themselves. Senators must of necessity consult with prominent political leaders about such appointments and often are subjected to great pressures from competing candidates and their sponsors. It is a common saying that every patronage appointment results in one ingrate and ten enemies. The distribution of patronage is a time-consuming task which brings to the senator much grief and little satisfaction. Minority senators, who have little or no patronage to distribute, are as successful in maintaining their political strength as senators who have control over the federal patronage in their states. As long as the present system obtains, however, senators of the party in power are virtually forced to play the game and to insist on the customary patronage. If they were freed of the responsibility for these local federal appointments, they would escape a thankless task, one that often leads to criticisms and enmity. Although some senators have favored placing minor positions under civil service, the majority have opposed such legislation. As a result of nation-wide scandals, President Truman was able in 1952 to secure Senate approval of his reorganization plan to abolish the office of collector of internal revenue and to place all field positions of the Bureau of Internal Revenue under civil service. Similar plans applying to postmasters, marshals, and collectors of customs, however, were rejected by the Senate.

In defending their prerogative to name the persons to be appointed to federal offices within their states—provided they belong to the party in control of the administration—members of the Senate have often contended that they maintain high standards of qualifications and, knowing the people of their states, are better able than the Civil Service Commission to make the selection. This contention overlooks the obvious fact that under a true career system, the persons selected for executive positions are employees with years of experience in the service, whose work has been under close observation of their superiors over a long period of time. They have a background of knowledge and experience which cannot be matched by an outsider, and, as a rule, they have demonstrated the necessary administrative qualifications.

Moreover, the factors that influence a member of the Senate in selecting persons to be appointed as the heads of regional offices are quite different from those that govern the choice of the responsible executive officers. The responsible administrator must accept the blame if the unit he heads is badly administered or if an officer whom he appoints is incompetent or corrupt; consequently he is under strong compulsion to select subordinates with care and to insist that they have the necessary experience and qualifications. A senator, however, is not subject to the same considerations. He is not responsible for the administration of the federal offices in his state. If they are incompetently administered or corrupt, it is the head of the agency, not the senator, who is blamed. Witness the scandals in the Bureau of Internal Revenue in 1951 which forced out of office the top officials of the bureau, though the local collectors under fire were not persons of their choosing. Senators must be re-elected; hence they must maintain the support of powerful political leaders and their own followers. If they have the selection of federal officers or employees, they must consider the effects of each appointment on their following and on the party strength and are likely to choose the person who has the strongest backing or who has conducted the most active campaign for the appointment. "In the matter of obtaining office," former President Taft once declared, "frequently it is leg muscle and lack of modesty which win, rather than fitness and character."

Even if a senator has every desire to select the best-qualified person, irrespective of party considerations, it is quite unlikely that he is sufficiently acquainted with the precise duties of the office to judge the qualifications of available candidates. As John Stuart Mill pointed out: "One of the great faults of legislative participation in the appointing process is that members of the legislative body, unfamiliar with the duties of a particular office and the qualifications and experience which are necessary, ordinarily consider any person of good reputation and some business or other experience as adequately qualified."

This observation is illustrated by the practice followed heretofore in the appointment of collectors of internal revenue. Although the Treasury Department has for years investigated the candidates proposed by senators or the party organizations, it has not been able to require that nominees have any knowledge or experience in the business of collecting revenue, which has become a highly involved and complex activity. Nor has the Department been able to insist that nominees shall have demonstrated administrative experience and ability in other lines of work which would qualify them to head a large organization. It has been able to insist only that nominees have a good reputation, and it has not always been able to insist even on that. Several of the collectors who were discharged in 1951 and against whom indictments were brought had questionable records before they were first appointed; some had been involved in difficulties over their own tax returns! The experience in appointing postmasters has been similar. The investigative staffs inquire into the reputation and standing of the politically sponsored candidates but make little or no attempt to inquire into their qualifications for the job. The damaging effect on the administration of a large enterprise, such as the collection of internal revenue or the postal service, in which the heads of the largest field offices have had no previous qualifying experience and no knowledge of the particular service, is at once apparent. The reform greatly needed—one that was finally effected in the Internal Revenue Service after sensational scandals had rocked the country—is to place these top field positions in the civil service so that they may be filled by the promotion of competent, experienced career personnel.

Evaluation

The experience of this country with the requirement of senatorial confirmation of the appointments of the President has been quite different from that contemplated by the framers of the Constitution. Intended as a safeguard against unfit appointments and expected to apply only to the major officers of the government, the requirement has been extended to more than a hundred thousand officers and employees, the vast majority of whom hold quite subordinate positions. And though the framers of the Constitution expected that the Senate would exert no choice of its own but merely pass upon the nominations of the President on the basis of their qualifications, this expectation has not been realized. Custom and tradition have decreed that the actual selections in many instances shall be made by individual members of the Senate, the President's role being merely to exercise a veto power. The Senate has seldom attempted—even in its early history when the number of appointments it passed upon were few—to give careful consideration to the qualifications possessed by the President's nominees.

On the whole, the requirement of senatorial confirmation has not elevated the standards of appointment to federal offices. Members of the Senate have frequently contended that it causes the President and his advisers to exercise great care in selecting persons for appointment for they know that his nominees must pass muster before the Senate; but the actual effect has often been otherwise. In selecting persons for appointment, the President may be more concerned with the nominee's likelihood of being confirmed than with his qualifications. The President's nominations are usually opposed for political reasons rather than for the nominee's lack of qualifications, though lack of qualifications is usually asserted to be the reason. The requirement of senatorial confirmation materially restricts the President's choice; persons of the highest qualifications are frequently passed over because they do not have the necessary political sponsorship, or because of the possibility that their nominations would be contested. The nominations of many able men have been opposed for reasons that have little bearing on the qualifications of the nominees—their politics or lack of politics, the section of the country from which they come, a previous stand on some subject which has little relevance to the duties of the office to which they are nominated, or, indeed, because the opposing senator has another candidate.

All Presidents are understandably reluctant to incur the risks of contests over their nominations, for such contests in the past have often impaired their public support and injured their prestige and leadership. Leading citizens are reluctant to permit their names to be sent to the Senate for a federal appointment if they have reason to believe that a contest will ensue. A nominee is never able effectively to answer irresponsible charges which may be made against him in committee hearings or on the floor of the Senate, and many able and patriotic citizens have declined appointments that required senatorial confirmation. However, many persons of mediocre qualifications but with strong political sponsorship have been nominated and their nominations have been confirmed without opposition.

Offices for which senatorial confirmation of appointments is required are generally regarded as political and therefore to be awarded as party patronage. (This, to be sure, is not true of officers of the armed services or of civilian commissioned services with their own career systems.) The effect of the requirement is to increase the pressures on the President and the department for patronage appointments to these offices. This has been notably true in appointments of local federal officers for which senatorial confirmation is necessary. These officers—including judges, district attorneys, United States marshals, collectors of internal revenue and customs, postmasters, and a few others—have always been regarded as party patronage to be awarded by the members of Congress who belong to the party in office, or by the local party organizations. Finally, in 1952, after a series of scandals, President Truman submitted reorganization plans to bring most of these offices under the civil service, thus carrying out the recommendations of three official commissions which had studied the organization and administration of the national government; but only the order applying to collectors of internal revenue was approved by the Senate.

The pressures for patronage appointments to offices subject to confirmation by the Senate are not limited to field positions but apply also to members of federal commissions, Cabinet and subcabinet posts, and other national offices. It is appropriate for the President, in selecting persons to fill the chief policymaking posts in his administration, to take into account political considerations and to appoint only persons who are in general agreement with his program and in whom he has confidence. However, a distinction must be made between appointments dictated by this type of broad, national consideration and appointments dictated by narrow partisanship and local patronage considerations. The patronage appointee whose appointment is to reward him for his services to the local party organization or to a member of Congress is not only likely to be poorly qualified but often is not in sympathy with the program of the administration. Appointments to important posts in the government which are dictated by patronage or narrow partisan reasons have not strengthened the party system but have weakened and at times have discredited the administration. Senatorial confirmation has increased rather than lessened the pressures on the President to make partisan and patronage appointments, even to major policy positions. No President who is mindful of the necessity for retaining congressional support of his legislative program can afford to disregard such pressures.

If the President had the exclusive power of appointment of the major policy-determining officers of his administration, and did not have to secure the approval of the Senate, partisan considerations would in all probability be less influential in his choices, and more persons of first-rate ability would be appointed. To be sure, there would be a danger that he would utilize these appointments to build up a personal political machine; but the undivided responsibility that would thus be placed on the President for his appointments would probably afford a greater safeguard against bad appointments than the requirement of the approval of the Senate.

Historical evidence indicates that the requirement of senatorial confirmation of the President's appointments has not provided the salutary safeguard against unfit appointments that Hamilton expected, but has rather confirmed the judgments of Madison and John Adams, who expressed doubts concerning the wisdom of the provision. There have been few unfit appointments rejected by the Senate, but appointments of many able men have been denied confirmation for political reasons which would not stand the light of day. The principal effects of senatorial confirmation of appointments has not been to subject the President's nominees to a careful scrutiny of their qualifications, as the framers of the Constitution intended, but has served rather (1) to perpetuate patronage appointments to many offices and positions which should be placed in the career service, and (2) to afford the opposition party and insurgents within the ranks of the President's party an opportunity to attack his administration by contesting his nominations. Most contests over nominations represent little more than a struggle for power, the maneuvering of party leaders for issues in the next election. The opposition party usually opposes the President's nominations whenever it sees an opportunity to secure political advantage, ordinarily with little regard to the qualifications or fitness of the nominee.

Although there are undoubtedly some merits in providing a ready means whereby the opponents of the administration may attack it not only for its policies but also for the persons it selects for public office, on the whole the disadvantages outweigh the advantages. The possibility of contests over nominations makes it more difficult for the administration in office to secure the services of able men. The major disadvantage, however, is that it weakens the responsibility of the President and the party in office for the policies and the conduct of the government. Definite responsibility can be maintained only if the President and the heads of departments and agencies are given a free hand in the selection of their principal assistants.

It should be recognized also that members of the Senate are subject to little criticism or clear-cut responsibility for their votes on the President's nominations. This is in great contrast to their responsibility for votes on legislative proposals. Formerly the votes on nominations were taken in secret sessions, but even today, when the votes are taken in open session, it is extremely uncommon for a senator to be attacked for his vote on a nomination. Opinions differ widely on the qualifications and fitness of persons for public office, and something may always be said for or against a nominee, regardless of his qualifications.

In spite of its shortcomings, the requirement of senatorial confirmation of the President's appointments to the major political offices of the government is a basic part of the Constitution and plays an important part in our system of executive-legislative relationships. There is no prospect that it will be repealed. If limited to those offices enumerated in the Constitution, and to other major offices of the government—the heads of departments and agencies and their principal assistants—it serves a useful purpose in assuring that these chief policy-determining officers will be agreeable to a majority of the Senate. The number of officers thus appointed should be relatively few, so that both the President and the Senate may be able to give these appointments their personal attention; otherwise the process degenerates into an empty formality.

A drastic reduction in the number of appointments made by the President and confirmed by the Senate would result in a number of significant improvements in the federal service. It would lead to the extension of the career system to many positions now filled by political appointees and would thus make the federal service more attractive to persons of ability. It would enable the government to utilize better the expertness and experience of its qualified, regular employees by advancing them to higher administrative positions now filled by political appointment. It would establish greater internal responsibility for the operation of executive departments and agencies, for subordinate officials would owe undivided loyalty to their administrative superiors. It would give the President and his department heads a freer hand in the selection of their principal assistants, which is essential if they are to be held responsible for the conduct of the government. Instead of weakening, it would strengthen the role of the President as the leader of his party and would lessen the disputes over patronage, which in the past have often marred his relations with the Senate. It would also strengthen the role of the Senate in passing upon the President's selections for the chief policy-determining offices of the government. Nothing is gained by the routine and purely formal approval by the Senate of thousands of appointments of subordinate officials and employees. The Senate has far greater matters which require its attention.

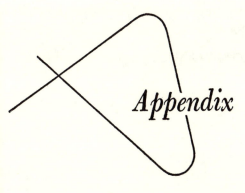

Appendix

POSITIONS SUBJECT TO CONFIRMATION
BY THE SENATE

1. *Statistical Summary*

Executive departments	682
Boards and commissions	130
Administrative agencies (with single heads)	68
Advisory bodies	48
Representatives to international organizations	57

Total		985
Judges	336	
Postmasters, first, second and third classes	21,034	
Special career services		
Foreign Service	1,675	
Public Health Service	2,276	
Coast and Geodetic Survey	168	
Total, civilian		26,474
Military officers (of all ranks of the regular establishments)		
Army	26,000	
Navy	41,000	
Air Force	22,000	
Marine Corps	6,000	
Coast Guard	3,000	
Total, military		98,000
		124,474

2. *List of Positions*

This list has been compiled from the following sources: U. S. Civil Service Commission, *Positions Not under the Civil Service*, 83d Cong., 1st sess., S. Doc. 18, 1953; Clerk of the Senate, *Civilian Nominations* (published annually); a list supplied the author by the United States Civil Service Commission, with statutory citations; the *Government Manual,* 1950–1951. The list is believed to be substantially complete as of February, 1952; but since changes are made from year to year, it is possible that a few positions have not been included.

EXECUTIVE DEPARTMENTS

Agriculture
  Secretary
  Under Secretary
  Assistant Secretary
  Rural Electrification Administrator
  Farm Credit Administration
    Governor
    Cooperative Bank Commissioner
    Land Bank Commissioner
    Production Credit Commissioner
    Intermediate Credit Commissioner
  Farmers' Home Administrator
  Commodity Credit Corporation Advisory Board (5)
    Number of positions in the Department of Agriculture   15

Commerce
  Secretary
  Under Secretary
  Under Secretary for Transportation
  Assistant Secretary (2)
  Solicitor
  Administrator for Civil Aeronautics
  Director, National Bureau of Standards
  Patent Office
    Commissioner
    Assistants (3)
    Commanders (7)
    Examiners (9)
  Chief, Weather Bureau
  Coast and Geodetic Survey
    Director
    Assistant
  Civil Aeronautics Board (5)
  Director of the Census
  Federal Maritime Board (3)
    Number of positions in the Department of Commerce   40

Defense
The secretaries, deputy secretaries, assistant secretaries and undersecretaries of the three military departments are civilians. All other offices are filled by military personnel whose appointment to the particular post is made by the President and confirmed by the Senate. However, one exception is the chairman of the Military Liaison Committee to the Atomic Energy Commission; he must be a civilian.

  Secretary of Defense
  Deputy Secretary of Defense
  Under Secretary
  Assistant Secretaries of Defense (3)
  Chairman, Military Liaison Committee to the Atomic Energy Commission
  Military Liaison Committee to the Atomic Energy Commission (6)

Chairman, Joint Chiefs of Staff
Chairman, Joint Technical Planning Committee
Chairman, Research and Development Board
Director of the Staff, Personnel Policy Board
Chairman, Munitions Board
Executive Director, European Coordinating Committee
Chief of Staff, Supreme Headquarters Allied Powers in Europe
Deputy Director, Mutual Defense Assistance
Representative to Standing Group, North Atlantic Treaty Organization
    Number of civilian positions in the Department of Defense 23

ARMY

Secretary
Under Secretary
Assistant Secretaries (2)
Army Chief of Staff
Vice Chief of Staff
Director, Joint U. S. Military Advisory and Planning Group in Greece
Chief of Engineers
Assistant Chief of Engineers
Quartermaster General
Assistant Quartermaster General
Inspector General
Adjutant General
Assistant Adjutant General
Judge Advocate General
Commander in Chief and Military Governor of Germany
Deputy Commander in Chief, U.S. Zone, Germany
Representative, Military Staff Committee to the United Nations
Chief of Finance
Continental Army Commanders (7)
Territorial Army Commanders (4)
Overseas Army Commanders (4)
Director, Personnel and Administration
Director of Logistics
Chief of Ordnance
Chief of Chemical Corps
Chief Signal Officer
Chief, National Guard Bureau
Chief Chemical Officer
Deputy Chief of Staff, G-3
Deputy Chief of Staff, Operations and Administration
Assistant Chief of Staff, G-1
Surgeon General
Assistant Surgeon General
Commandant, Armed Forces Staff College
    Number of positions held by military personnel 47

NAVY

Secretary
Under Secretary
Assistant Secretary
Assistant Secretary for Air
Chiefs of Bureaus (Aeronautics, Medicine and Surgery, Naval Personnel, Ordnance, Ships,
    Supplies and Accounts, Yards and Docks) (7)
Chief of Naval Operations

Vice Chief of Naval Operations
Inspector General
Deputy Chiefs of Naval Operations (5)
Judge Advocate General
Chief of Naval Research
Chief of Naval Material
Chief of Information
Director of Budget and Reports
Commander in Chief, Atlantic and U.S. Atlantic Fleets
Task Fleet Commanders (2)
Commander, Military Sea Transportation Service
Commander, Western Sea Frontier
Commander, Air Force, U.S. Pacific Fleet
Member, Military and Naval Staff Committee of the United Nations
    Number of positions held by naval personnel 31

MARINE CORPS

Commandant of the Marine Corps
Assistant to the Commandant
Commandant at Quantico
Commanding General, Fleet Marine Force, Atlantic
Quartermaster General
    Number of positions held by Marine Corps personnel 5

AIR FORCE

Secretary
Under Secretary
Assistant Secretaries (2)
Chief of Staff
Vice Chief of Staff
Special Assistant to the Chief of Staff
Deputy Chiefs of Staff (Operations, Material, Comptroller, Personnel) (4)
Judge Advocate General
Inspector General
Commanding General, Air Research and Development Command
Commanding Generals (Material Command, Defense Command, Training Command,
    Military Air Transport, Strategic Air Command) (5)
Member, Military and Naval Staff Committee of the United Nations
Commandant, Air University
Overseas Air Commanders (4)
    Number of positions held by Air Force personnel 25

Interior

Secretary
Under Secretary
Assistant Secretaries (3)
Commissioner of Indian Affairs
Director, Geological Survey
Director of the Bureau of Mines
Solicitor
Governors of Alaska, Guam, Hawaii, Virgin Islands, Puerto Rico (5)
Secretary of the Territory of Alaska
    Number of positions in the Department of the Interior 15

Justice

Attorney General
Deputy Attorney General

Assistant Attorneys General (8)
Solicitor General
Assistant Solicitor General
Commissioner of Immigration and Naturalization
Board of Parole (8)
U. S. Attorneys (93)
U. S. Marshals (93)
    Number of positions in the Department of Justice 207

Labor

Secretary
Under Secretary
Assistant Secretaries (3)
Solicitor
Commissioners of Labor Statistics
Wage and Hour Administrator
Director of Women's Bureau
    Number of positions in the Department of Labor 9

Post Office

Postmaster General
Deputy Postmaster General
Assistant Postmasters General (4)
Purchasing Agent for the Post Office Department
Comptroller
Advisory Board for the Post Office Department (7)
    Number of positions in the Post Office Department 15

State

Secretary
Under Secretary
Assistant Secretaries (10)
Counselor
Legal Adviser
Director of Foreign Military Assistance
Technical Cooperation Administrator
    Deputy
Chairman, International Development Advisory Board
Director for International Security Affairs
Ambassadors and Ministers (69)
    Number of positions in the Department of State 88

Treasury

Secretary
Under Secretary
Assistant Secretaries (2)
Treasurer of the U. S.
Assistant Treasurer of the U. S.
General Counsel
Assistant General Counsel for Bureau of Internal Revenue
Director of the Mint
Superintendents of the Mint (3)
Commissioner of Internal Revenue
Assistant Commissioners of Internal Revenue (2)
Special Deputy Commissioner
Comptroller of the Currency

Register of the Treasury
Assistant Register of the Treasury
Collectors of Internal Revenue* (64)
Officers of the U. S. Mints and Assay Offices (23)
Commissioner of the Bureau of Narcotics
Collectors of Customs (44)
Engraver of the Mint
Superintendents of U. S. Assay Office (2)
Surveyor of Customs (1)
Comptrollers of Customs (6)
Appraiser of Merchandise
    Number of positions in the Department of the Treasury 162
        Total in Executive Departments 682

JUDICIAL BRANCH

Supreme Court
  Chief Justice
  Associate Justices (8)
Circuit Courts of Appeal (65)
District Courts (215)
U. S. Court of Claims
  Chief Justice
  Associate Justices (4)
U. S. Court of Customs and Patent Appeals
  Chief Judge
  Associate Judges (4)
U. S. Customs Court (9)
Territorial Courts
  Alaska (4)
  Hawaii (2)
  Puerto Rico, Virgin Islands, Canal Zone (1 each)
Court of Military Appeals (3)
Tax Court of the U. S.
  Presiding Judge
  Judges (15)
    Number of positions in the Judicial Branch 336

BOARDS AND COMMISSIONS

Atomic Energy Commission
  Members (5)
  General Manager
California Debris Commission (4)
Civil Service Commission (3)
Commodity Credit Corporation (6) (Agriculture Department)
Council of Economic Advisers (3)
Court of Military Appeals (3)
Displaced Persons Commission (3)
District of Columbia Commission
  Commissioners (2)
  District of Columbia Redevelopment Land Agency (5)
  Recorder of Deeds
Export-Import Bank of Washington (4)
Federal Coal Mine Safety Board (3)
Federal Communications Commission (7)

* Placed under civil service by Reorganization Plan No. 1, 1952.

Federal Deposit Insurance Corporation (2)
Federal Power Commission (5)
Federal Reserve System (7)
Federal Trade Commission (5)
Indian Claims Commission (3)
Interstate Commerce Commission
    Commissioners (11)
    Director of Locomotive Inspection
    Assistant Directors of Locomotive Inspection (2)
Mississippi River Commission (4)
Motor Carrier Claims Commission (3)
National Labor Relations Board (Labor Dept.)
    Members of Board (5)
    General Counsel
National Mediation Board (3)
National Security Training Commission (5)
Philippine War Damage Commission (3)
Railroad Retirement Board (3)
Renegotiation Board (5)
Securities and Exchange Commission (5)
Subversive Activities Control Board (5)
Tennessee Valley Authority (3)
War Claims Commission (3)
U. S. Tariff Commission (6)
    Number of positions in boards and commissions 130

ADMINISTRATIVE AGENCIES (with a single head)

Central Intelligence Director
Federal Civil Defense Administrator
    Deputy
Defense Materials Procurement Administrator
Defense Mobilization Administrator
Defense Production Administrator
Economic Cooperation Administration
    Administrator
    Deputy
Economic Stabilization Agency
    Administrator
Director of Price Stabilization
Members Wage Stabilization Board (22)
Federal Defense Administration
    Director
    Deputy
Federal Mediation and Conciliation Service
Federal Security Agency
    Administrator
    Chief of Children's Bureau
    Commissioner of Education
Federal Works Administrator
General Accounting Office
    Comptroller General
    Assistant
General Services Administrator
Government Printing Office: Public Printer
Housing Expediter

Housing and Home Finance Agency
  Administrator
  Public Housing Administrator
  Federal Housing Administrator
Home Loan Bank Board (3)
Library of Congress
Mutual Security Agency
  Director
  Deputy
  Assistants (2)
National Archives
National Security Resources Board
  Chairman
  Vice Chairman
Office of Price Stabilization
Panama Canal
Reconstruction Finance Corporation
  Administrator
  Deputy
Selective Service Director
Small Defense Plants Administrator
U. S. Commissioner to the International Exposition,
  Republic of Haiti
U. S. High Commissioner for Germany
Veterans Administrator
War Assets Administration
  Number of positions in administrative agencies 68

ADVISORY BODIES

Public Advisory Board for MSA (13)
U. S. Advisory Commission on Educational Exchange (5)
National Science Foundation
  Director
  Members of Board (24)
U. S. Advisory Commission on Information (5)
  Number of positions in advisory bodies 48

REPRESENTATIVES TO UNITED NATIONS AND RELATED ORGANIZATIONS

Advisory Commission of the UN Relief and Works
  Agency for Palestine Refugees in the Near East
Advisory Commission to the Agent General of the
UN Korean Reconstruction Agency
Commission on the Status of Women
Conciliation Commission for Palestine (3)
Economic Commission for Asia and the Far East (2)
Economic Commission for Europe (2)
Economic Commission for Latin America
Economic and Employment Commission
Economic, Employment and Development Commission
Fiscal Commission
General Assembly
  U. S. representatives (3)
  Alternates (3)
Good Offices Committee of the Security Council on Indonesia

Human Rights Commission
Kashmir Commission
North Atlantic Council
  U. S. representative
  Deputy
Population Commission
Security Council
  U. S. representative
  Deputy
Social Commission
Special Balkan Commission (2)
Statistical Commission
Transport and Communications Commission
Truce Commission for Palestine
UN Advisory Council for Libya
UN Commission for Indonesia
UN Educational Scientific and Cultural Organization
  U. S. representatives (5)
  Deputies (5)
    Number of positions in United Nations and related organizations 46

OTHER INTERNATIONAL BODIES

International Claims Commission (3)
International Bank for Reconstruction and Development
  U. S. Governor
  Alternate
  U. S. Executive Director
  Alternate
International Monetary Fund
  U. S. Governor
  Alternate
  U. S. Executive Director
  Alternate
    Number of positions in other international bodies 11

MISCELLANEOUS

Postmasters, first, second, and third class   21,034
Special career services
  Foreign Service (1,675)
  Public Health Service (2,276)
  Coast and Geodetic Survey (168)
Military officers (of all ranks of the regular establishments)
  Army 26,000
  Navy 41,000
  Air Force 22,000
  Marine Corps 6,000
  Coast Guard 3,000
                                      ————
                                     98,000

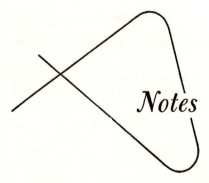

CHAPTER I

INTRODUCTION

[1] James Bryce, *The American Commonwealth*, New York, Macmillan Co., 1922, I, 111.
[2] Lindsay Rogers, *The American Senate*, New York, Crofts Co., 1931, p. 28. The quotation is used by permission of Appleton-Century-Crofts, Inc.
[3] The statistics cited here are from an annual publication of the Clerk of the Senate, *Civilian Nominations*, Washington, Government Printing Office.
[4] The most thorough published study of the subject is in George H. Haynes, *The Senate of the United States*, Boston, Houghton Mifflin Co., 1938, chap. xiii. See also Rogers, *op. cit.*, pp. 22–31; Herbert W. Horwill, *The Usages of the American Constitution*, London, Oxford University Press, 1925, chap. vii; Arthur W. Macmahon, "Senatorial Confirmation," *Public Administration Review*, III (1943), 281–296; Dorothy G. Fowler, "Congressional Dictation of Local Appointments," *The Journal of Politics*, VII (1945), 25–57; Charles S. Hyneman, *Bureaucracy in a Democracy*, New York, Harper & Bros., 1950, chap. 10; and Felix Nigro, *Public Administration Readings and Documents*, New York, Rinehart & Co., 1951, pp. 443–459. Lucy M. Salmon, *History of the Appointing Power of the President* (Papers of the American Historical Association, Vol. I, No. 5), New York, G. P. Putnam's Sons, 1886, and Carl Russell Fish, *The Civil Service and the Patronage*, Cambridge, Harvard University Press, 1920, are very useful. My "The Senatorial Rejection of Leland Olds: A Case Study," *American Political Science Review*, XLV (1950), 674–692, and "The Courtesy of the Senate," *Political Science Quarterly*, LXVII (1951), 36–63, in slightly expanded form are included in this volume. An unpublished doctoral dissertation by Felix Nigro, "Senate Confirmation," University of Wisconsin, 1948, has been very helpful to me.
[5] Appointments to the following advisory bodies require senatorial confirmation: U. S. Advisory Commission on Educational Exchange, U. S. Advisory Commission on Information, and the National Science Foundation.
[6] Robert Luce, *Legislative Problems*, Boston, Houghton Mifflin Co., 1935, pp. 117–123.
[7] Charles Warren, *Congress, the Constitution and the Supreme Court*, Boston, Little, Brown & Co., 1935, p. 29. In Connecticut, Delaware, Georgia, New Jersey, North Carolina, South Carolina, and Virginia judges were appointed by the state legislatures; in four states—Massachusetts, Maryland, New Hampshire, and Pennsylvania—they were appointed by the governor, by and with the advice and consent of the upper chamber.
[8] Sidney George Fisher, *The Evolution of the Constitution of the United States*, Philadelphia, J. B. Lippincott Co., 1897, pp. 171–173. Provision for an executive council was made in New York (1777), Maryland (1776), Massachusetts (1780), Vermont (1777), Pennsylvania (1776), Delaware (1776), New Jersey (1776), and Virginia (1776); the powers of the council, however, were not the same in all states.

[9] See Fish, *op. cit.*, pp. 87 ff.
[10] Gilbert Mazur, "Senatorial Confirmation in the States," unpublished M.A. thesis, Berkeley, University of California, 1951.
[11] See Harold A. Stone, Don K. Price, and Kathryn Stone, *City Manager Government in the United States,* Chicago, Public Administration Service, 1940, pp. 94–106.
[12] John Stuart Mill, *On Liberty and Considerations on Representative Government,* Oxford, Basil Blackwell, 1946, pp. 166–167.
[13] Bryce, *op. cit.,* pp. 61–62.
[14] D. W. Brogan, *Government of the People,* New York, Harper & Bros., 1933, p. 382; Harold D. Laski, *Studies in Law and Politics,* New Haven, Yale University Press, 1932, p. 174; Herman Finer, *The Theory and Practice of Modern Government,* New York, Dial Press, 1932, I, 716–718. See also Horwill, *op. cit.,* chap. vii.
[15] Woodrow Wilson, *Congressional Government,* 15th ed., Boston, Houghton Mifflin Co., 1900, pp. 235–237.
[16] Henry J. Ford, "Usurpation by the Senate," *New Republic,* I (Jan. 9, 1915), 17. Later, the nomination of Professor Ford by his friend Woodrow Wilson to be a member of the Federal Trade Commission, failed to receive Senate confirmation.
[17] Dorman B. Eaton, *The Term and Tenure of Office,* New York, G. P. Putnam's Sons, 1882, pp. 20–21, and *Secret Sessions of the Senate,* New York, 1886, pp. 5–9; William Dudley Foulke, *Fighting the Spoilsmen,* New York, G. P. Putnam's Sons, 1919, p. 58.
[18] Haynes, *op. cit.,* II, 760.
[19] Luce, *op. cit.,* p. 128.
[20] W. F. Willoughby, *Principles of Legislative Organization and Administration,* Washington, The Brookings Institution, 1934, pp. 104–105.
[21] Hyneman, *op. cit.,* p. 179.
[22] *Ibid.,* p. 183.
[23] *Ibid.,* p. 191.
[24] *Ibid.,* p. 192.
[25] William Howard Taft, *Our Chief Magistrate,* New York, Columbia University Press, 1916, p. 63.
[26] The leading case is *United States* v. *Germaine* (1878), 11 U.S. 508. See also Charles E. Morganston, *The Appointing and Removal Power of the President,* 70th Cong., 2d sess., S. Doc. 172 (1929), citing cases.

CHAPTER II

DEBATES ON THE APPOINTING POWER IN THE
CONSTITUTIONAL CONVENTION

[1] Gaillard Hunt and James Scott Brown, eds., *The Debates of the Federal Convention of 1787,* reported by James Madison, New York, Oxford University Press, 1920, p. 55.
[2] *Ibid.,* p. 519.
[3] Art. II, sec. 2, provides: "The President . . . shall nominate, and by and with the Advice and Consent of the Senate, shall appoint Ambassadors, other public Ministers and Consuls, Judges of the Supreme Court, and all other officers of the United States, whose appointments are not herein otherwise provided for, and which shall be established by Law: but the Congress may by Law vest the Appointment of such inferior officers, as they think proper, in the President alone, in the Courts of Law, or in the Heads of Departments."
[4] Hunt and Brown, eds., *op. cit.,* p. 54.
[5] *The Federalist,* ed. Edward Gaylord Bourne, New York, Tudor Publishing Co., 1937, No. 76.
[6] Hunt and Brown, eds., *op. cit.,* pp. 39–40.
[7] Charles Warren, *The Making of the Constitution,* New York, Little, Brown & Co., 1929, p. 179. On the appointing power in the state constitutions and colonial charters, see Sidney George Fisher, *The Evolution of the Constitution of the United States,* pp. 171–173.
[8] Warren, *op. cit.,* p. 327.

[9] Lucy Salmon, *History of the Appointing Power of the President*, chap. 2.

[10] For a summary of the debate on this issue, see Leonard D. White, *The Federalists*, New York, Macmillan Co., 1948, chap. 2.

[11] *The Federalist*, No. 70.

[12] Hunt and Brown, eds., *op. cit.*, p. 25.

[13] June 1, 1787. *Ibid.*, p. 38.

[14] *Ibid.*, p. 39.

[15] *Ibid.*, p. 56.

[16] *Ibid.*, p. 57.

[17] Max Farrand, ed., *The Records of the Federal Convention of 1787*, New Haven, Yale University Press, 1911, I, 128.

[18] *Ibid.*, p. 100.

[19] *Ibid.*, I, 292; Hamilton's plan in full, which was not presented to the Convention, is reproduced in Vol. III, pp. 617–630.

[20] *Ibid.*, II, 136.

[21] For the debate on this date, see Hunt and Brown, eds., *op. cit.*, pp. 274–277.

[22] *Ibid.*, p. 275.

[23] *Ibid.*, p. 301.

[24] *Ibid.*, p. 415.

[25] *Ibid.*, pp. 562–563.

[26] *Ibid.*, pp. 464–465.

[27] *Ibid.*, p. 508.

[28] *Ibid.*, p. 529.

[29] *Ibid.*, p. 448.

[30] See the remarks of Gouverneur Morris, *ibid.*, p. 531.

[31] *Ibid.*, p. 529.

[32] *Ibid.*, p. 531.

[33] Paul L. Ford, *Pamphlets on the Constitution of the United States*, Brooklyn, 1888, p. 330. See also Farrand, ed., *op. cit.*, II, 638–639.

[34] Paul L. Ford, *Essays on the Constitution*, Brooklyn, 1892, p. 163.

[35] Robert Yates, *Secret Proceedings of the Federal Convention*, Richmond, 1839, p. 75.

[36] Ford, *Pamphlets*, p. 298.

[37] Jonathan Elliott, *The Debates in the Several State Conventions on the Adoption of the Federal Constitution*, Philadelphia, J. B. Lippincott Co., 1888, IV, 116–118.

[38] *Ibid.*, p. 134.

[39] *Ibid.*, p. 122.

[40] Farrand, ed., *op. cit.*, III, 79.

[41] Chief Justice Taft in delivering the opinion of the Supreme Court in *Myers* v. *United States*, 272 U.S. 119–120 (1926), stated that the power of advice and consent to appointments was granted to the Senate because of the objection of the smaller states to vesting the power in the President alone, who they assumed would come from the more populous states. The parts of the Constitutional debates he cited, however, do not support this interpretation. The same position is advanced by Felix A. Nigro, "Senate Confirmation" (unpub. doctoral dissertation), chap. 1.

[42] Elliott, *op. cit.*, II, 466–511. "It was expected by many," said Wilson, "that the cry would have been against the powers of the President as a monarchial power; indeed, the echo of such sound was heard sometime before the rise of the late Convention. There were men, at that time, determined to make an attack upon whatever system should be proposed; but they mistook the point of direction." Had the President been given the powers now being urged, Wilson continued, the opponents of the Constitution would have taken exactly the opposite line of attack.

[43] Nos. 66, 72, 76, and 77.

[44] *The Federalist*, No. 76.

[45] *Ibid.*

[46] *Ibid.*

[47] *Ibid.*

[48] *The Works of John Adams*, ed. Charles Francis Adams, Boston, Little, Brown & Co., 1852–1865, VIII, 464.

[49] The exchange of letters is found in Adams, *op. cit.*, VI, 427–442.
[50] *Ibid.*, p. 440.
[51] *Annals of Congress*, I, 385.
[52] *Ibid.*, p. 399.
[53] *Ibid.*, p. 614.
[54] These positions were summarized by Fisher Ames near the conclusion of the debate, *ibid.*, I, 559–564. See also Salmon, *op. cit.*, p. 18, and L. D. White, *op. cit.*, pp. 20–21.
[55] *Annals of Congress*, I, 480.
[56] *Ibid.*, p. 492. The same point was made by John Lawrence: "In the Constitution, the heads of departments are considered as the mere assistants of the President in the performance of his executive duties. He has the superintendence, the control, and the inspection of their conduct; he has an intimate connection with them; they must receive from him orders and directions; they must answer his inquiries in writing when he requires it." *Ibid.*, p. 504.
[57] *Ibid.*, pp. 604–605.
[58] *Ibid.*, p. 562.
[59] *Ibid.*, p. 578.
[60] *Ibid.*, p. 504.
[61] *Ibid.*, p. 518.
[62] Maclay wrote: ". . . whoever attends strictly to the Constitution of the United States, will readily observe that the part assigned to the Senate was an important one—no less than that of being the great check, the regulator and corrector, or, if I may so speak, the balance of this government. . . . The approbation of the Senate was certainly meant to guard against the mistakes of the President in his appointments to office. . . . The depriving power should be the same as the appointing power." *Journal of William Maclay, 1789–1791,* ed. Edgar S. Maclay, New York, Albert & Charles Boni, 1927, pp. 107–108.

CHAPTER III

EARLY HISTORY OF SENATORIAL CONFIRMATION OF APPOINTMENTS

[1] *The Writings of George Washington,* ed. John C. Fitzpatrick, Washington, Government Printing Office, 1931–1944, XXXVI, 504.
[2] *The Writings of Thomas Jefferson,* ed. A. E. Bergh, Washington, Thomas Jefferson Memorial Association, 1907, XV, 37.
[3] For an account of Washington's exercise of the appointing power, see James Hart, *The American Presidency in Action: 1789,* New York, Macmillan Co., 1948, chap. 4; Carl Russell Fish, *The Civil Service and the Patronage;* Leonard D. White, *The Federalists;* and Lucy Salmon, *History of the Appointing Power of the President.*
[4] *The Works of John Adams,* ed. Charles F. Adams, IX (1854), 561.
[5] Washington, *Writings,* XXX, 309 (May 5, 1789).
[6] *Ibid.,* XXXIII, 320–321 (April 9, 1794).
[7] *Ibid.,* XXXIV, 315.
[8] Quoted by Salmon, *op. cit.,* p. 27.
[9] *Senate Executive Journal,* I, 6–7.
[10] Edgar S. Maclay, ed., *Journal of William Maclay, 1789–1791,* p. 77.
[11] *Ibid.,* p. 78.
[12] Washington, *Writings,* XXX, 373–374.
[13] *Annals of Congress,* I, 66–67.
[14] The single exception: in 1921 President Harding went from his inauguration to the Senate chamber and presented the names of two senators in nomination for Cabinet positions. George H. Haynes, *The Senate of the United States,* p. 724.
[15] Jefferson, *Writings* (Bergh ed.), III, 15.
[16] *The Diaries of George Washington,* ed. John C. Fitzpatrick, New York, Houghton Mifflin Co., 1925, IV, 122.

[17] Maclay, *op. cit.*, p. 274.

[18] Griffith J. McRee, *Life and Correspondence of James Iredell*, New York, D. Appleton & Co., 1857, II, 278–280.

[19] Aug. 6, 1789. James D. Richardson, ed., *Messages and Papers of the Presidents*, Washington, Government Printing Office, 1899, I, 58–59.

[20] Maclay, *op. cit.*, p. 119.

[21] See Carl R. Fish, *op. cit., passim;* Leonard D. White, *op. cit., passim;* Gaillard Hunt, "Office Seeking during Washington's Administration," *American Historical Review*, I (1896), 270 ff.; Dorothy G. Fowler, "Congressional Dictation of Local Appointments," *Journal of Politics*, VII (1945), 27 ff.

[22] H. C. Lodge, *Life and Letters of George Cabot*, Boston, Little, Brown & Co., 1878, p. 94.

[23] Fish, *op. cit.*, p. 24, citing sources.

[24] James Parton, *Life of Aaron Burr*, Boston, Houghton Mifflin Co., 1892, pp. 196–197.

[25] The letter of Rutledge is quoted in full in Charles Warren, *The Supreme Court in United States History*, rev. ed., Boston, Little, Brown & Co., 1926, I, 127–128. For another account of the Rutledge case, see Richard Hayes Barry, *Mr. Rutledge of South Carolina*, New York, 1942, *passim.*

[26] Dec. 31, 1795. Jefferson, *Writings* (Bergh ed.), IX, 318.

[27] White, *op. cit.*, p. 276.

[28] Quoted by Salmon, *op. cit.*, p. 29.

[29] Oct. 4, 1800. Adams, *Works*, IX, 87.

[30] White, *op. cit.*, pp. 267–278.

[31] Apr. 22, 1799. Adams, *Works*, VIII, 636.

[32] Lodge, *op. cit.*, pp. 240–241. (Emphasis in original.)

[33] Adams' removals apparently did not exceed fifteen. Salmon, *op. cit.*, p. 31.

[34] Adams, *Works*, IX, 301–302.

[35] Mar. 25, 1789. Washington, *Writings*, XXXVII, 160–161.

[36] For an account of the episode, see John T. Morse, Jr., *John Adams*, New York, Houghton Mifflin Co., 1884, pp. 300–303.

[37] John A. Stevens, *Albert Gallatin*, New York, Houghton Mifflin Co., 1883, pp. 185–188.

[38] Fish, *op. cit.*, p. 47.

[39] See Charles E. Hill, *James Madison*, New York, Alfred A. Knopf, 1927, pp. 146–147; Lynton K. Caldwell, *The Administrative Theories of Hamilton and Jefferson*, University of Chicago Press, 1944, pp. 193–194.

[40] *The Writings of John Quincy Adams*, ed. Worthington C. Ford, New York, Macmillan Co., 1914, III, 83–84.

[41] Feb. 10, 1803. *The Writings of Thomas Jefferson*, ed. Paul L. Ford, New York, G. P. Putnam's Sons, 1892–1899, VIII, 210.

[42] *Ibid.*

[43] Mar. 10, 1814. *Ibid.*, IX, 460. See also quotations from Jefferson at beginning of this chapter.

[44] Henry Adams, *The Life of Albert Gallatin*, Philadelphia, J. B. Lippincott Co., 1880, p. 389.

[45] *Ibid.*, pp. 389–391.

[46] In his biography of Gallatin, John A. Stevens states: "Mr. Madison yielded to this dictation, and from this day forward was, as he deserves to be, perplexed and harassed by a petty oligarchy." Stevens, *op. cit.*, p. 305.

[47] John T. Morse, Jr., *John Quincy Adams*, New York, Houghton Mifflin Co., 1898, pp. 69–70.

[48] See Abbot E. Smith, *James Madison: Builder*, New York, Wilson-Erickson, 1937, p. 312, and Henry Adams, *op. cit.*, pp. 483–484, 501.

[49] Abbot E. Smith, in his biography of Madison, wrote: "With still more stupid factiousness . . . rejected Madison's nomination of Jonathan Russell as Minister Plenipotentiary to Sweden. In all Europe, the Baltic countries were the only ones showing the least symptom of regard for the United States, but the Senate was entirely concerned with its party strife." Smith, *op. cit.*, p. 312.

[50] *Senate Executive Journal*, II, 382 (1813).

[51] Charles R. King, ed., *Life and Correspondence of Rufus King*, New York, G. P. Putnam's Sons, 1894–1900, V, 313.

[52] Haynes, *op. cit.*, p. 732.

[53] Warren believed that Wollcott's rejection was due to political animosities and personal allegations rather than to the nominee's lack of legal ability. Warren, *op. cit.*, pp. 409–413.

[54] Ninian W. Edwards, *The Edwards Papers*, Chicago, Fergus Co., 1884, pp. 168–169.

[55] *Ibid.*, pp. 186–187.

[56] John Quincy Adams, *Memoirs*, Philadelphia, J. B. Lippincott, 1874–1877, VII, 424–425.

[57] Fish, *op. cit.*, pp. 65–70.

[58] Jefferson, *Writings* (Ford ed.), XV, 294–295.

[59] Quoted by John T. Morse, Jr., *John Quincy Adams*, p. 179.

CHAPTER IV

BATTLES BETWEEN ANDREW JACKSON AND THE SENATE

[1] Mar. 11, 1834. James D. Richardson, ed., *Messages and Papers of the Presidents*, Washington, 1899, III, 47.

[2] Marquis James, *The Life of Andrew Jackson*, New York, Garden City Publishing Co., 1940, p. 520.

[3] James Parton, *Life of Andrew Jackson*, Boston, Houghton Mifflin Co., 1859, III, 276.

[4] The account that follows is based chiefly on Claude G. Bowers, *Party Battles of the Jackson Period*, New York, Houghton Mifflin Co., 1928, pp. 80–87.

[5] *Ibid.*, p. 83.

[6] Amos Kendall wrote to Democratic leaders in New Hampshire that the President "has entire confidence in Mr. Hill and looks upon his rejection as a blow aimed at himself," and called upon the legislature to "wipe away the stigma cast upon this just and true man, by the unjust and cruel vote of the Senate." Quoted by Bowers, *ibid.*, p. 87. Marquis James states: "The senators also rejected Isaac Hill, and lived to regret it. Born in squalor, kicked and cuffed as a printer's ragged and oft-hungry apprentice, this frail, embittered cripple early in life had launched upon a career of revenge, opposing nearly everything the New England Brahmins held sacred. He refused to accept defeat now. Jackson stood by him and within a year the little lame Marat with a zealot's gleaming eyes returned to Washington, a senator from New Hampshire and a peer of those who had pronounced him unfit for a subordinate office in the Treasury." James, *loc. cit.*

[7] James, *op. cit.*, p. 500.

[8] *Ibid.*, pp. 567–580.

[9] Thomas Hart Benton, *Thirty Years' View*, New York, D. Appleton & Co., 1854, I, 219, gives an account of the debate, attributing to Calhoun this often quoted remark.

[10] *Congressional Debates*, VIII, Pt. I (Jan. 25, 1832), 1310–1311.

[11] *Ibid.*, p. 1320.

[12] *Ibid.*

[13] *Ibid.*, pp. 1325–1327.

[14] Benton, *op. cit.*, pp. 215–219.

[15] "All the speakers went through an excusatory formula, repeated with equal precision and gravity; abjuring all sinister motives; declaiming themselves to be wholly governed by a sense of public duty; describing the pain which they felt at arraigning a gentleman whose manners and deportment were so urbane; and protesting that nothing but a sense of duty to the country could force them to the reluctant performance of such a painful task." *Ibid.*

[16] Henry Wykoff, *Reminiscences of an Idler*, 1880, pp. 29–30, quoted by James, *op. cit.*, p. 595.

[17] John C. Fitzpatrick, ed., *Autobiography of Martin Van Buren*, Washington, Government Printing Office, 1920, II, 457–458.

[18] James, *op. cit.*, p. 595.

[19] For an account of the rejection of the Bank directors, see Benton, *op. cit.*, pp. 385–392.

[20] Quoted by Bowers, *op. cit.*, p. 324.

[21] Benton, *op. cit.*, p. 386.

[22] Richardson, ed., *op. cit.*, p. 42.

[23] Benton, *op. cit.*, p. 392.

[24] For an excellent account of the rejection of Taney, see Carl B. Swisher, *Roger B. Taney,* New York, Macmillan Co., 1935, pp. 190–288.

[25] *Ibid.,* p. 286.

[26] James, *op. cit.,* p. 588.

[27] *Ibid.,* p. 600.

[28] Richardson, ed., *op. cit.,* III, 576–591.

[29] For an account of the veto of the Bank bill, see James, *op. cit.,* pp. 600–602; Swisher, *op. cit.,* pp. 187–195.

[30] *Correspondence of Andrew Jackson,* J. S. Bassett, ed., Washington, Carnegie Institution, 1926–1935, V, 187.

[31] Swisher, *op. cit.,* p. 287.

[32] Jackson, *Correspondence,* V, 272; quoted in Swisher, *op. cit.,* p. 288.

[33] Charles Warren, *The Supreme Court in United States History,* I, 798.

[34] *Columbian Centinel,* Jan. 22, 1835; see also Washington *Globe,* Feb. 11, 1835; Boston *Courier,* Jan. 22, 1835; New York *Courier,* Jan. 19, 1835.

[35] Quoted by Warren, *op. cit.,* I, 801.

[36] *Ibid.,* p. 802.

[37] *Ibid.,* II, 10, 11, 14.

[38] *Congressional Record,* 38th Cong., 1st sess. (Mar. 31, 1864), p. 1363; quoted by Warren, *op. cit.,* II, 13–14.

[39] Quoted by Warren, *op. cit.,* II, 18.

[40] Quoted by Edward S. Stanwood, *History of the Presidency,* New York, Houghton Mifflin Co., 1928, I, 189.

CHAPTER V

EFFORTS OF THE SENATE TO CONTROL APPOINTMENTS

[1] James K. Polk, *The Diary of a President,* New York, Longmans, Green & Co., 1929, p. 318.

[2] *Congressional Record,* 53d Cong., spec. sess. (Apr. 7, 1893), p. 102.

[3] Carl Russell Fish, *The Civil Service and the Patronage,* pp. 169–172.

[4] Caleb Cushing as Secretary of the Treasury, 1843; David Henshaw as Secretary of the Navy, 1844; James M. Porter as Secretary of War, 1844; James S. Green as Secretary of the Treasury, 1844. George H. Haynes, *The Senate of the United States,* p. 761. Professor Fowler states that of Tyler's nominees the Senate also rejected 5 marshals, 1 attorney, 14 deputy postmasters, 31 custom officials, 4 receivers of public money, and 4 registers of land offices. Dorothy G. Fowler, "Congressional Dictation of Local Appointments," *Journal of Politics,* VII, 37.

[5] John C. Spencer, 1844; Edward King, 1844; Reuben Walworth, 1844; John Meredith Read, 1845.

[6] James Schouler, *History of the United States,* rev. ed., New York, Dodd, Mead & Co., 1894, IV, 431–433.

[7] Charles Warren, *The Supreme Court in United States History,* II, 117.

[8] Thomas H. Benton, *Thirty Years' View,* II, 629.

[9] Nathan Sargent, *Public Men and Events,* 1875, quoted by Warren, *op. cit.,* p. 110.

[10] Senator Crittenden, who had hoped for an appointment to the Supreme Court if Clay were elected President, wrote to Francis Granger: "His confirmation would have been a plain violation of all public political morality and would have made the Supreme Court an asylum for broken down, disgraced and guilty politicians." These quotations are given by Warren, *op. cit.,* pp. 112–113.

[11] *National Intelligencer,* April 26, 1844; quoted by Warren, *op. cit.,* p. 117. Warren declares that the statement was entirely unwarranted by the facts or by the eminent character of the nominees and that it illustrates the bitter hostility to the President.

[12] These quotations are given by Warren, *ibid.,* pp. 119–120.

[13] James K. Polk, *op. cit.,* p. 37.

416] NOTES

[14] *Ibid.*, pp. 46–49. Polk received reports that Buchanan, eager to be appointed to the Supreme Court himself, conspired with the six Democrats to bring about the rejection of Woodward. Relations between the two thereafter were strained, though Buchanan remained in the Cabinet and was later offered an appointment to the Court, which he eventually rejected.

[15] *Ibid.*, p. 72.

[16] *Ibid.*, p. 117.

[17] *Ibid.*, p. 116.

[18] *Ibid.*, p. 184.

[19] Warren, *op. cit.*, pp. 242–243.

[20] New York *Times*, Feb. 16, 1853, quoted by Warren, *op. cit.*, pp. 244–245.

[21] Fish, *op. cit.*, p. 170.

[22] Quoted by J. G. Randall, *Lincoln the President*, New York, Dodd, Mead & Co., 1945, I, 311.

[23] *Ibid.*

[24] Charles Fairman, *Mr. Justice Miller and the Supreme Court, 1862–1890*, Cambridge, Harvard University Press, 1939, p. 48.

[25] Fish, *loc. cit.*

[26] Charles A. Dana, Assistant Secretary of War, relates this story: When the admission of the state of Nevada was needed to ensure the adoption of the Fourteenth Amendment, Lincoln, believing that it would raise the morale of the federal armies in the field, stated: "It is easier to admit Nevada than to raise another million of soldiers." Expecting that the vote in the House would be extremely close, he asked Dana to see three Congressmen whose votes were in doubt. To Dana's question, "What will they be likely to want?" Lincoln replied: "I don't know. It makes no difference, though, what they want. Here is the alternative, that we carry this vote or be compelled to raise another million and fight no one knows how long. It is a question of three votes or new armies. . . . Whatever promise you make to them I will perform." Two of them wanted internal revenue collectors . . . the third an important appointment in the New York customhouse. They voted for the admission of Nevada, but Lincoln was assassinated before he could make good his promise, and Dana was unable to persuade Johnson to do so. C. A. Dana, "Reminiscences of Men and Events of the Civil War," *McClure's Magazine*, X (1898), 564–565.

[27] Harry J. Carman and Reinhard H. Luthin, *Lincoln and the Patronage*, New York, Columbia University Press, 1943, p. 336.

[28] *Congressional Globe*, 36th Cong., 2d sess. (Jan. 10, 1861), p. 309.

[29] Cited by George Wharton Pepper, *Family Quarrels: The President, the Senate, and the House*, New York, Baker, Voorhis & Co., 1931, p. 111.

[30] Fish, *op. cit.*, p. 187.

[31] *Cong. Globe*, 39th Cong., 1st sess. (1865), App. 338, quoted by Haynes, *op. cit.*, II, 800.

[32] For an account of this legislation, see Haynes, *op. cit.*, pp. 799–804; George Fort Milton, *The Age of Hate; Andrew Johnson and the Radicals*, New York, Coward-McCann, Inc., 1930.

[33] It was not until eighty years later that the Supreme Court passed upon the legal issue involved, holding that the power of removal was vested in the President, and the consent of the Senate could not be required. *Myers v. United States* (1926), 272 U.S. 52.

[34] Gideon Wells, *Diary*, Boston and New York, Houghton Mifflin Co., 3 vols., 1911, III, 375.

[35] *Cong. Globe*, 39th Cong., 1st sess. (July 10, 1866), p. 3701, and (July 18, 1866), p. 3909.

[36] Moorfield Storey and E. W. Emerson, *Ebenezer Rockwood Hoar*, New York, Houghton Mifflin Co., 1911, pp. 181–198.

[37] *Ibid.*, pp. 181–182.

[38] *Nation*, Dec. 2, 1869, Jan. 6, 1870; New York *Times*, Dec. 16, 1869; *Harper's Weekly*, Jan. 1, 1870. The quotations are given by Warren, *op. cit.*, II, 501–507.

[39] Storey and Emerson, *op. cit.*, pp. 193–194.

[40] *Ibid.*

[41] *Ibid.*, p. 197.

[42] Quoted by Warren, *op. cit.*, pp. 553–556.

[43] *Independent*, Dec. 11 and 25, 1875; quoted by Warren, *loc. cit.*

[44] Springfield *Republican*, Jan. 2, 1874.

[45] Warren, *op. cit.*, p. 557.

[46] Fish, *op. cit.*, pp. 209–221.

[47] George F. Boutwell, *Reminiscences of Sixty Years*, New York, McClure, Phillips & Co., 1902, pp. 282–284.

[48] George F. Hoar, *Autobiography of Seventy Years*, New York, Charles Scribner's Sons, 1903, I, 210–212.

[49] *Ibid.*, II, 46; W. E. Binkley, *The Powers of the President*, Garden City, Doubleday, Doran & Co., 1937, chap. vii.

[50] John W. Burgess, *The Administration of President Hayes*, New York, Charles Scribner's Sons, 1916, pp. 11–16.

CHAPTER VI

REASSERTION BY THE PRESIDENT OF HIS RIGHT TO NOMINATE

[1] *Diary and Letters of Rutherford B. Hayes*, ed. Charles R. Williams, Columbus, Ohio State Archaeological and Historical Society, 1924, III, 478–479.

[2] As quoted by Charles R. Williams, *Life of Rutherford Birchard Hayes*, Boston and New York, Houghton Mifflin Co., 1914, II, 87.

[3] C. R. Fish, *The Civil Service and the Patronage*, p. 204.

[4] *Ibid.*, p. 205. See also W. E. Binkley, *The Powers of the President*, pp. 125–182.

[5] Williams, *op. cit.*, II, 15–22.

[6] *Ibid.*, pp. 22–32. Professor Burgess later wrote of Hayes's Cabinet: "Taken all together, it was the strongest body of men, each best fitted for the place assigned to him, that ever sat around the council table of a President of the United States." John W. Burgess, *The Administration of President Hayes*, p. 65.

[7] Williams, *op. cit.*, p. 27.

[8] *Ibid.*, pp. 66–67.

[9] Of the many messages coming to the White House supporting the President in his fight with the Senate over his Cabinet, he prized most highly one in the handwriting of James Russell Lowell that said: "The course of the President is what we expected and heartily approve." It was signed by J. R. Lowell, Henry W. Longfellow, Charles W. Eliot, F. J. Childs, and C. E. Norton. Quoted by Williams, *op. cit.*, p. 29.

[10] Quoted by Williams, *op. cit.*, p. 106.

[11] *Ibid.*, p. 97.

[12] *Ibid.*, pp. 75–76.

[13] Hayes, *Diary and Letters* (Williams ed.), III, 473. See also Dorothy G. Fowler, "Congressional Dictation of Local Appointments," *Journal of Politics*, VII, 44.

[14] H. J. Eckenrode, *Rutherford B. Hayes*, New York, Dodd, Mead & Co., 1930, p. 268.

[15] *Ibid.*

[16] Williams, *op. cit.*, II, 86–87.

[17] Eckenrode, *op. cit.*, pp. 272–273.

[18] Williams, *loc. cit.*

[19] Eckenrode, *op. cit.*, p. 274.

[20] Quoted by Williams, *op. cit.*, p. 92.

[21] *Ibid.*, p. 94.

[22] Eckenrode, *op. cit.*, p. 277.

[23] The vote was 35 to 24 in favor of Merritt, and 31 to 18 in favor of Burt.

[24] Accounts of the episode are given by Donald B. Chidsey, *Roscoe Conkling*, New Haven, Yale University Press, 1935, pp. 279–341; T. C. Smith, *Life and Letters of James A. Garfield*, New Haven, Yale University Press, 1925, II, 1056–1058; G. H. Haynes, *The Senate of the United States*, pp. 745–747; Harold F. Gosnell, *Boss Platt*, Chicago, University of Chicago Press, 1924, pp. 25–29; T. C. Platt, *Autobiography*, New York, B. W. Dodge & Co., 1910, pp. 150–159.

[25] Quoted by Smith, *op. cit.*, pp. 1056–1057.

[26] See J. L. Connery, "Secret History of the Garfield-Conkling Tragedy," *Cosmopolitan*, XXIII (June, 1897), 150.

[27] Royal Cortissoz, *Life of Whitelaw Reid*, New York, Charles Scribner's Sons, 1921, II, 47.

[28] George F. Hoar, *Autobiography of Seventy Years*, II, 57.

[29] Cortissoz, *op. cit.*, p. 60.

[30] *Ibid.*, p. 61.

[31] Letter to Burke A. Hinsdale, Apr. 4, 1881; quoted by Smith, *op, cit.*, p. 1109.

[32] T. C. Smith, *loc. cit.*

[33] Garfield, *Works*, I, 499–515; quoted by Lucy Salmon, *History of the Appointing Power of the President*, p. 103.

[34] Platt, *op. cit.*, p. 152.

[35] *Ibid.*, p. 151.

[36] Haynes, *op. cit.*, II, 746.

[37] Grover Cleveland, *Presidential Problems*, New York, Century Co., 1904, pp. 45–46.

[38] *Ibid.*, p. 51.

[39] *Ibid.*

[40] *Ibid.*, p. 56.

[41] Quoted by Cleveland, *ibid.*, pp. 57–58.

[42] James D. Richardson, ed., *Messages and Papers of the Presidents*, VIII, 375–381.

[43] *Ibid.*, p. 377.

[44] *Ibid.*, p. 378.

[45] Binkley, *op. cit.*, p. 181.

[46] Hoar, *op. cit.*, II, 142. Commenting on the controversy between the President and the Senate, the *Nation* on March 11, 1886, stated: "There is not the smallest reason for believing that if the Senate won, it would use its victory in any way for the promotion of reform."

[47] *Congressional Record*, 49th Cong., 2d sess. (Dec. 14, 1886), pp. 113, 136–140; Fish, *op. cit.*, p. 207; Hoar, *op. cit.*, pp. 143–144; Binkley, *op. cit.*, pp. 181–182.

[48] Joseph B. Bishop, *Theodore Roosevelt and His Time*, New York, Charles Scribner's Sons, 1920, I, 235.

[49] *Ibid.*, II, 14–15.

[50] *Ibid.*, I, 248.

[51] *Ibid., I*, 443–444.

[52] Henry F. Pringle, *The Life and Times of William Howard Taft*, New York, Farrar & Rinehart, 1939, II, 608.

[53] *Ibid.*, p. 609.

[54] Most fourth-class postmasters had already been covered into the classified service by executive order, and in October, 1912, Taft issued an order covering the rest.

[55] Quoted by Pringle, *ibid.*, p. 610.

[56] *Ibid.;* William Howard Taft, *Our Chief Magistrate and His Powers*, New York, Columbia University Press, 1925, p. 65.

[57] Taft, *op. cit.*, pp. 65–66, 70–71.

[58] Woodrow Wilson, *Congressional Government*, p. 235.

[59] New York *Times*, Jan. 30, 1913.

[60] William G. McAdoo, *Crowded Years*, New York and Boston, Houghton Mifflin Co., 1931, pp. 188–189. Ray Stannard Baker wrote: "It was a shocking innovation. It quite overturned the firm political cosmos. . . . The Gridiron Club hit off the situation to perfection that spring when it staged a mournful quartet of office-seekers outside the White House, singing the plaintive refrain, 'It looks like snow.'" R. S. Baker, *Woodrow Wilson, Life and Letters*, Garden City, Doubleday, Doran & Co., 1931, IV, 26.

[61] Baker, *ibid.*, pp. 38–43, quotes the widely publicized letter of Bryan to Walter W. Vick, Receiver General of Customs of the Dominican Republic. See also W. D. Foulke, *Fighting the Spoilsmen*, pp. 229 ff.

[62] Baker, *op. cit.*, pp. 45–46.

[63] New York *Times*, Mar. 12, Apr. 16, 18, 22, 24, 25, 27, 30, May 8, June 6, 13, 25, 1913.

[64] *Ibid.*, Apr. 25, 1913.

[65] McAdoo records that the practice was abandoned because Republican senators "sometimes recommended the most incapable man on the list." McAdoo, *op. cit.*, p. 191.

[66] New York *Times*, Apr. 16, 18, 22, 27, 30, May 8, 1913.

[67] *Ibid.*, Jan. 20, 1914.

[68] *Ibid.*, Dec. 23, 1914; Jan. 10, Mar. 7, 1915.
[69] *Ibid.*, Dec. 19, 1914. Other articles about the appointment appeared on Dec. 21 and 22, 1914, and Jan. 5 and 7, 1915.
[70] *Ibid.*, Dec. 24, 1914.
[71] *Ibid.*, Jan. 15, 1915. Subsequently the appointment of Mrs. Bloom was confirmed.
[72] *Ibid.*, May 16, 1916.
[73] *Ibid.*, May 23, 1916.
[74] *Ibid.*, May 18, 1916.
[75] *Ibid.*, July 7, 8, Aug. 8, 11, 1914.
[76] *Ibid.*, Dec. 23, 1913; Jan. 14, Feb. 2, 1914.
[77] *Ibid.*, June 21, 1914.
[78] *Ibid.*, July 24, 1914. Baker, *op. cit.*, IV, 52–53, states that Jones was an old friend of Wilson from Princeton days and that Wilson had written to him on his own typewriter to ask if he would accept the appointment. The President said of Jones: "He is the one man of the whole number who was in a peculiar sense my personal choice."

CHAPTER VII

THE BRANDEIS CASE

[1] *Hearings on the Nomination of Louis D. Brandeis before the Subcommittee of the Senate Committee on the Judiciary*, 64th Cong., 1st sess., S. Doc. 409 (1916), I, 1226.
[2] *Ibid.*, II, 242.
[3] Quoted by Alpheus T. Mason, *Brandeis: A Free Man's Life*, New York, Viking Press, 1946, p. 484. Melvin O. Adams, a former U. S. district attorney in Boston and long a member of the bar, testified that the opposition came from "a group of men of high standing, like General Peabody, in the community who are in the network of State Street, which is our financial street, who state and think that Mr. Brandeis is not straightforward in his practice. . . . On the other hand, there is a large body of the bar, who, coinciding with what I have said as to his being a very able lawyer, a man of profound learning, also believe that he is actuated by lofty purposes, is honest and trustworthy." *Hearings on . . . Brandeis*, I, 766.
[4] This belief was confirmed by a series of articles which Brandeis wrote for *Harper's Weekly*, exposing unethical banking and financial practices. The series was later published as a book under the title *Other People's Money—and How the Bankers Use It*, New York, Frederick A. Stokes Co., 1914.
[5] For an account of Brandeis' part in the campaign, see Mason, *op. cit.*, chap. 24. The volume contains an excellent account of the fight over confirmation (chaps. 30, 31), as well as the earlier episodes in Brandeis' career concerning which charges were made in the hearings. In the pages that follow, I have drawn heavily on this scholarly work.
[6] *Ibid.*, p. 386. Elbert Hubbard wrote: "He works both ends against the middle. He gets them going and coming. . . . The Honorable Louis D. Brandeis of Boston, business baiter, stirrer-up of strife, litigious lurer on of hate and unrest, destroyer of confidence, killer of values, commercial coyote, spoiler of pay envelopes. . . . Brandeis is Gompers, Goldman, and Gyp the Blood rolled into one, and given a degree from Harvard. . . . Brandeis does not represent America." *Ibid.*, p. 387.
[7] This account of the consideration of Brandeis for the Cabinet post in 1912 is based chiefly on Mason, *op. cit.*, chap. 13.
[8] *Ibid.*, p. 389.
[9] *Ibid.*, p. 394.
[10] Alfred Lief, *Brandeis: The Personal History of an American Ideal*, New York, Stackpole Sons, 1936, pp. 345–357.
[11] These quotations are given in Mason, *op. cit.*, pp. 465–469, and in Lief, *op. cit.*, pp. 348–349.
[12] Lief, *op. cit.*, p. 350.
[13] *Ibid.*
[14] Quoted by Henry F. Pringle, *The Life and Times of William Howard Taft*, II, 952.
[15] Quoted by Mason, *op. cit.*, p. 468.

[16] *Hearings on ... Brandeis,* I, 8.

[17] Excerpts of the testimony of Brandeis are included in the *Hearings,* I, 5–62.

[18] *Ibid.,* II, 308.

[19] *Ibid.,* I, 65. Interstate Commerce Commissioner James S. Harlan testified that there had never been any thought on the part of the commission that Brandeis' statement was improper. "It was precisely the sort of view that we looked to counsel to express as a result of his study of the case ..." At another place he testified: "I do not understand that Mr. Brandeis was on either side. He was there in the public interest." *Ibid.,* II, 237–239.

[20] Quoted by Mason, *op. cit.,* pp. 472–473.

[21] *Hearings on ... Brandeis,* I, 123–124.

[22] *Ibid.,* p. 136.

[23] *Ibid.,* p. 271.

[24] *Ibid.,* p. 611.

[25] *Ibid.,* p. 751.

[26] *Ibid.,* p. 653.

[27] *Ibid.,* pp. 169–261, 713–747; see also Mason, *op. cit.,* chap. 14, and the majority and minority reports of the subcommittee.

[28] *Hearings on ... Brandeis,* I, 185–192.

[29] *Ibid.,* I, 453–460.

[30] *Ibid.,* II, 180–181.

[31] *Ibid.,* II, 252.

[32] Quoted by Mason, *op. cit.,* p. 180.

[33] According to the Philadelphia *Public Ledger* he said: "Some men buy diamonds and rare works of art, others delight in automobiles and yachts. My luxury is to invest my surplus effort, beyond that required for the proper support of my family, in the pleasure of taking up a problem and solving, or helping to solve it, for the people without receiving any compensation . . . I should lose much of the satisfaction if I were paid in connection with public service of this kind." Quoted by Mason, *op. cit.,* p. 329.

[34] Quoted by Mason, *ibid.,* p. 192. Brandeis' extraordinarily high standards of professional ethics are also shown by his refusal to take the business of the Ingersoll Watch Company. Appearing before a congressional committee in support of proposed legislation to permit price maintenance, which he favored to protect small merchants from cutthroat competition by chain stores, he met Mr. Ingersoll, who was also appearing in support of the bill. Ingersoll later offered Brandeis the law business of his company in Massachusetts, but Brandeis declined, explaining that he never took the law business of firms that were interested in legislation which he had supported as a citizen. Members of the subcommittee regarded this action as extraordinary, but the wisdom of it was all too apparent. *Hearings on ... Brandeis,* I, 976–983.

[35] *Ibid.,* II, 234.

[36] *Hearings on ... Brandeis,* I, 1226.

[37] Mason, *op. cit.,* p. 490. When Brandeis and Taft later served together on the Supreme Court their relations were quite friendly, though they differed widely in their outlook on social and economic questions and often were on opposite sides. Taft once said of Brandeis: "He brought to us all sorts of information as to economic conditions and other matters of the greatest value which we did not have before and never would have acquired otherwise." Quoted by Mason, *ibid.,* p. 629.

[38] *Hearings on ... Brandeis,* I, 770.

[39] Mason, *op. cit.,* p. 494. In his biography of Woodrow Wilson, William Allen White records that there was no truth in the notorious story about Mrs. Peck, and that he as well as many publishers had read the letters offered for publication. They were highly proper and contained not a line of amorous sentiments.

[40] *Hearings on ... Brandeis,* II, 240.

[41] An account of this meeting is given in Mason, *op. cit.,* pp. 503–504.

[42] *Ibid.,* p. 502.

[43] Quoted by Mason, *ibid.,* p. 467.

CHAPTER VIII

OPPOSITION BY SENATE LIBERALS TO THE APPOINTMENT OF CONSERVATIVES

[1] *Congressional Record,* 71st Cong., 2d sess. (Feb. 13, 1930), p. 3566.

[2] New York *Times,* Mar. 9, 1921.

[3] *Ibid.,* Apr. 19, 1929.

[4] *Ibid.,* Mar. 27, 1929. The states were South Carolina, Mississippi, and Georgia; the Republican organization in them was notoriously a small group of patronage-minded persons whose primary concern was to control federal offices within the state rather than to build up a strong party following. President Hoover, who had carried several Southern states in the 1928 election, desired to build up a strong and respectable Republican organization in all the Southern states.

[5] *Ibid.,* Oct. 22, 1929. The account reported that for some months the Florida party organization had been at loggerheads with the Republican national patronage committee.

[6] The charge was that he had accepted a fee for representing a client in a matter affecting the federal government, which was prohibited by statute. The defense was that Senator Wheeler had represented his client only before the state courts of Montana.

[7] Washington *Post,* Jan. 29, 1925. A similar editorial appeared in the New York *Times* on the same date.

[8] *Cong. Rec.,* 68th Cong., 2d sess. (Feb. 5, 1925), p. 3039.

[9] *Ibid.,* p. 3053.

[10] *Ibid.* Senator Norris later admitted that he had misjudged Stone. Richard L. Neuberger and Stephen B. Kahn, *Integrity; the Life of George W. Norris,* New York, Bobbs-Merrill Co., 1937, pp. 341–343.

[11] New York *Times,* Mar. 8, 1925.

[12] *Cong. Rec.,* 69th Cong., spec. sess. (Mar. 7, 1925), p. 18.

[13] *Ibid.,* p. 19.

[14] *Ibid.*

[15] *Ibid.,* p. 32.

[16] This point was contested by Senators Reed and Walsh, who contended that under earlier decisions such actions were illegal.

[17] *Cong. Rec.,* 69th Cong., spec. sess. (Mar. 10, 1925), p. 96.

[18] *Ibid.,* p. 94.

[19] *Ibid.*

[20] *Ibid.,* p. 100.

[21] New York *Times,* Mar. 12, 1925.

[22] Boston *Evening Transcript,* Mar. 11, 1925.

[23] New York *Times,* Mar. 16, 1925.

[24] *Cong. Rec.,* 69th Cong., spec. sess. (Mar. 14, 1925), p. 235.

[25] *Ibid.,* p. 244.

[26] *Cong. Rec.,* 71st Cong., 2d sess. (Feb. 11, 1930), p. 3450.

[27] Quoted by Neuberger and Kahn, *op. cit.,* pp. 343–345.

[28] *Cong. Rec.,* 71st Cong., 2d sess.. (Feb. 13, 1930), p. 3566.

[29] *Ibid.,* (Feb. 11), p. 3449.

[30] *Ibid.,* p. 3451.

[31] *Ibid.* (Feb. 12), pp. 3509–3513.

[32] *Ibid.* (Feb. 13), p. 3563.

[33] *Hearings before the Subcommittee of the Committee of the Judiciary, U. S. Senate, on the Confirmation of John J. Parker to Be an Associate Justice of the Supreme Court of the United States,* 71st Cong., 2d sess., 1930.

[34] *Ibid.,* pp. 2–3.

[35] *United Mine Workers of America* v. *Red Jacket Consolidated Coal and Coke Co.,* 18 Fed. 839 (1927).

[36] *Hearings . . . on the Confirmation of John J. Parker,* p. 27.

[37] *Hitchman Coal and Coke Company* v. *Mitchell*, 245 U.S. 229 (1917).
[38] Quoted in *Hearings . . . on the Confirmation of John J. Parker*, p. 43.
[39] *Ibid.*, pp. 61–70.
[40] *Ibid.*, p. 74.
[41] *Ibid.*, p. 75.
[42] *Ibid.*, pp. 77–78.
[43] *Cong. Rec.*, 71st Cong., 2d sess. (Apr. 28, 1930), p. 7793.
[44] *Ibid.*, pp. 7794–7795, 7808–7822.
[45] *Ibid.* (Apr. 29, 1930), p. 7930.
[46] *Ibid.*, p. 7938.
[47] *Ibid.* (May 2, 1930), p. 8192.
[48] *Ibid.* (Apr. 30, 1930), p. 8040.
[49] *Ibid.* (May 5, 1930), p. 8342.
[50] *Ibid.* (May 7, 1930), pp. 8475–8476.
[51] New York *Times*, May 8, 1930.

CHAPTER IX

OPPOSITION BY SENATE CONSERVATIVES TO THE APPOINTMENT OF LIBERALS

[1] *Congressional Record*, 76th Cong., 1st sess. (Jan. 19, 1939), p. 478.
[2] *Ibid.*, 79th Cong., 1st sess. (Mar. 22, 1945), p. 2605.
[3] *Ibid.*, 73d Cong., 2d sess. (June 8, 1934), p. 10836.
[4] *Hearings before the Committee on Agriculture and Forestry, U. S. Senate, on the Confirmation of Rexford G. Tugwell for Position of Under Secretary of Agriculture*, 73d Cong., 2d sess. (1934), p. 12.
[5] *Ibid.*, p. 124.
[6] *Ibid.*, p. 127.
[7] *Ibid.*, pp. 135, 139.
[8] New York *Times*, June 12 and June 13, 1934.
[9] *Cong. Rec.*, 73d Cong., 2d sess. (June 13, 1934), p. 11338.
[10] *Ibid.* (June 14), p. 11428.
[11] *Ibid.*, p. 11437.
[12] *Hearings before the Committee on Public Lands and Surveys, U. S. Senate, on the Nomination of Ebert K. Burlew to Be First Assistant Secretary of the Interior*, 75th Cong., 3d sess. (1938), p. 613.
[13] Senator O'Mahoney protested at Senator Pittman's questioning: "Let us be fair in the examination. There is no need in harassing the man." *Ibid.*, p. 231. When Burlew died several years later some of his close friends attributed his early death to the ordeal of the hearings.
[14] On Jan. 9, 1938, the New York *Times* noted that "Mr. Burlew's name was mentioned only once or twice today."
[15] *Hearings . . . on the Nomination of Ebert K. Burlew*, pp. 4, 9.
[16] *Ibid.*, pp. 8, 9.
[17] New York *Times*, Mar. 10, 1938.
[18] Thurman W. Arnold, *The Folklore of Capitalism*, New Haven, Yale University Press, 1937.
[19] *Hearings before a Subcommittee of the Committee on the Judiciary, U. S. Senate, on the Nomination of Thurman W. Arnold to Be Assistant Attorney General*, 76th Cong., 3d sess. (1938), p. 5.
[20] New York *Times*, Mar. 13, 1938.
[21] *Ibid.*, Dec. 23, 1938.
[22] *Ibid.*
[23] *Ibid.*, Jan. 4, 1939.
[24] *Hearings before the Commerce Committee, U. S. Senate, on the Nomination of Harry L. Hopkins to Be Secretary of Commerce*, 76th Cong., 1st sess. (1939), pp. 8–10.

[25] For an illuminating account of this subject, see Arthur W. Macmahon, John D. Millett, and Gladys Ogden, *The Administration of Federal Work Relief*, Chicago, Public Administration Service, 1949, chap. 12.

[26] *Hearings . . . on the Nomination of Harry L. Hopkins*, p. 13.

[27] *Ibid.*, pp. 20–21.

[28] *Ibid.*, pp. 93–95.

[29] *Cong. Rec.*, 76th Cong., 1st sess. (Jan. 18, 1939), p. 559.

[30] *Ibid.* (Jan. 23, 1939), p. 604.

[31] *Ibid.*, p. 600.

[32] *Hearings before a Subcommittee of the Committee on the Judiciary, U. S. Senate, Relative to the Nomination of Frank Murphy to Be Attorney General of the United States*, 76th Cong., 1st sess. (1939), pp. 3–4.

[33] *Cong. Rec.*, 76th Cong., 1st sess. (Jan. 17, 1939), p. 411.

[34] *Hearings before a Subcommittee of the Committee on Interstate Commerce, U. S. Senate, on the Nomination of Thomas R. Amlie to Be a Member of the Interstate Commerce Commission*, 76th Cong., 1st sess. (1939), p. 257.

[35] New York *Times*, Jan. 26, 1939.

[36] *Hearings . . . on the Nomination of Thomas R. Amlie*, p. 1.

[37] *Ibid.*, p. 2.

[38] *Ibid.*, p. 10.

[39] *Ibid.*, pp. 21, 23.

[40] *Ibid.*, p. 38.

[41] *Ibid.*, p. 45.

[42] *Ibid.*, p. 103.

[43] New York *Times*, Feb. 8, 9, 1939.

[44] Quoted in *Hearings . . . on the Nomination of Thomas R. Amlie*, p. 389.

[45] These letters are reprinted in the *Cong. Rec.*, 76th Cong., 1st sess., App., p. 1531.

[46] New York *Times*, Nov. 4, 27, 30, Dec. 21, 1944.

[47] Jonathan Daniels, *The Man from Independence*, Philadelphia, J. B. Lippincott Co., 1950, p. 243.

[48] New York *Times*, Jan. 22, 1945.

[49] *Hearings before the Committee on Commerce, U. S. Senate, on S. 375*, 79th Cong., 1st sess. (1945), pp. 13, 15.

[50] *Ibid.*, p. 26.

[51] *Ibid.*, p. 55.

[52] *Ibid.*, p. 71.

[53] Quoted by Russell Lord, *The Wallaces of Iowa*, Boston, Houghton Mifflin Co., 1947, pp. 546–547.

[54] *Hearings before the Committee on Agriculture and Forestry, U. S. Senate, on the Nomination of Aubrey W. Williams to Be Administrator, Rural Electrification Administration*, 79th Cong., 1st sess. (1945), p. 16.

[55] *Ibid.*, p. 44.

[56] *Ibid.*, p. 46.

[57] *Ibid.*, pp. 57–58.

[58] *Ibid.*, p. 76.

[59] *Ibid.*, p. 79.

[60] *Ibid.*, pp. 80–81.

[61] *Ibid.*, pp. 137–138.

[62] *Ibid.*, p. 168.

[63] New York *Times*, Feb. 21, 1945.

[64] *Hearings . . . on the Nomination of Aubrey W. Williams*, p. 312. Lucas declared that two of the men whose writings had been used extensively in the hearings by Williams' opponents, one a former member of the Dies committee staff, were persons of "very unsavory reputation, professional patrioteers who have made a very good thing of denouncing and slandering any and all—from President Roosevelt down—who happen to disagree with their own antediluvian ideas on social, economic and political questions."

[65] *Ibid.*, pp. 316–317.

[60] Washington *Post*, Mar. 12, 1945.
[67] New York *Times*, Feb. 25, 1945.
[68] *Cong. Rec.*, 79th Cong., 1st sess. (Mar. 13, 1945), pp. 2400–2402.
[69] *Ibid.*, p. 2468.
[70] *Ibid.*, p. 2400.
[71] *Ibid.*, p. 2606.
[72] *Ibid.*, p. 2605.
[73] *Ibid.*, p. 2652.
[74] New York *Times*, Mar. 24, 1945.
[75] St. Louis *Post Dispatch*, Mar. 24, 1945.
[76] *Nation*, Mar. 31, 1945, p. 349.

CHAPTER X

THE CONTESTS OVER THE APPOINTMENTS OF
DAVID E. LILIENTHAL AND GORDON R. CLAPP

[1] *Hearings before the Senate Section of the Joint Committee on Atomic Energy on the Confirmation of the Atomic Energy Commission and the General Manager*, 80th Cong., 1st sess. (1947), p. 131.
[2] As senator from Tennessee, where the TVA activities were centered, he could hardly have done otherwise.
[3] *Congressional Record*, 79th Cong., 1st sess. (May 21, 1945), p. 4806.
[4] *Ibid.*
[5] *Hearings . . . Atomic Energy Commission and the General Manager*, pp. 7–8.
[6] *Ibid.*, p. 15.
[7] One member of the committee insisted on his right to have any information he thought he needed, including the number of bombs manufactured, but after Senator Vandenberg stated that he was not sure that he wanted members of the joint committee of Congress to be given such information, the subject was dropped.
[8] When Lilienthal was called back to the stand on March 3, after a considerable interval, the following colloquy occurred: "The Chairman: Mr. Lilienthal, will you please step forward? I may say, Mr. Lilienthal, for the record, you are the same David E. Lilienthal who was on the stand heretofore.
"Mr. Lilienthal: Slightly worn down, but virtually the same.
"The Chairman: The committee may have some sympathy for that particular physical condition, as a result of its own experience. As Senator Vandenberg says, 'At least, we share it.'" *Hearings . . . Atomic Energy Commission and the General Manager*, p. 805.
[9] *Ibid.*, p. 121. The motive behind this question by Senator McKellar supposedly was to establish Lilienthal's foreign parentage and the fact that his parents were Jews.
[10] *Ibid.*, p. 130.
[11] *Ibid.*, p. 131.
[12] *Ibid.*, p. 132. The next day, Senator McKellar came to the hearing with a copy of Webster's definition of democracy, which he inserted in the record. The Tennessee senator compared this definition with the stirring statement by Lilienthal, saying: "I am unable to make any sense out of it, and I would like you to explain what it is. You said democracy is a belief in man's dignity. I want to know what you mean." *Ibid.*, p. 146.
[13] *Ibid.*, p. 288.
[14] New York *Times*, Feb. 11, 1947.
[15] *Ibid.*, Feb. 6, 1947.
[16] *Ibid.*, Feb. 13, 1947. See also United Press dispatch of Feb. 12, 1947.
[17] New York *Times*, Feb. 14, 1947.
[18] See newspaper stories in New York *Times*, Feb. 17, and San Francisco *Chronicle*, Feb. 15.
[19] New York *Times*, Feb. 14, 1947.
[20] *Ibid.*, Feb. 20, 23, 1947.

[21] *Ibid.*, Feb. 22, 1947.

[22] *Ibid.*

[23] *Cong. Rec.*, 80th Cong., 1st sess. (Mar. 24, 1947), p. 2450.

[24] *Ibid.*, p. 2451.

[25] *Ibid.*

[26] *Ibid.*, p. 2452.

[27] *Ibid.*, p. 2454.

[28] *Ibid.*, p. 2595.

[29] *Ibid.*, pp. 2859–2862.

[30] *Ibid.*, pp. 2850–2856.

[31] *Ibid.*, p. 2854.

[32] *Ibid.*, p. 2952.

[33] *Ibid.*, p. 2954.

[34] *Ibid.*, p. 2956.

[35] *Ibid.*, p. 3011.

[36] *Ibid.*, p. 3023.

[37] *Ibid.*, p. 3031.

[38] *Ibid.*, p. 3029.

[39] *Ibid.*, p. 3108.

[40] *Ibid.*, p. 3109.

[41] The New York *Times* story of the debate stated that Senator Barkley delivered his speech with "such fire that it left him gasping for breath." Apr. 4, 1947.

[42] *Cong. Rec.*, 80th Cong., 1st sess. (Apr. 3, 1947), p. 3116.

[43] *Ibid.*, p. 3241.

[44] Two years later, when he resigned to return to private life, Lilienthal replied to a reporter who had asked why he was retiring, "Don't you think I have had enough of the Senate?" Washington *Post*, Nov. 24, 1949.

[45] McKellar shuttled back and forth between the Clapp and Lilienthal hearings. Though not a member of either committee, he interrogated the nominees at greath length, as well as numerous witnesses called at his request.

[46] An editorial of the Chattanooga *Times* stated: "Many Washington stories about the hearing in the Senate Public Works Committee on the Clapp nomination have stupidly emphasized Mr. McKellar's charges of 'communism' and his attempt to link Mr. Clapp and various high officials of the TVA with communism. This is merely a red herring as people who know Clapp and the other officials readily recognize. The present attack is supported by the power lobby and the Fertilizer Trust." Printed in the *Hearings before the Senate Committee on Public Works on the Nomination of Gordon R. Clapp to Be a Member of the Board of Directors of the Tennessee Valley Authority,* 80th Cong., 1st sess., p. 500.

[47] *Hearings . . . on the Nomination of Gordon R. Clapp*, p. 202.

[48] The following is a sample of this interrogation:

"Mr. McKellar. The next man is ———. He is a well-known Communist employed by you in the TVA and who belonged to Branch No. 1, was he not?

"Mr. Clapp. I do not believe that ——— was a Communist, and I do not believe that anyone could prove that he was." *Ibid.*, p. 125.

[49] *Ibid.*, p. 220.

[50] Hart supported his denial by pointing out statements in the letter that he could not have made, and calling attention to the fact that the letter was signed "Henry C. Hart, Jr.," whereas his middle name was different from that of his father, and he had never signed his name in this way.

[51] *Hearings . . . on the Nomination of Gordon R. Clapp*, p. 33.

[52] The questions and answers are found in *ibid.*, pp. 81–89.

[53] One of the letters recommended to the TVA for its "best consideration" a person whom Senator McKellar later accused of being a Communist. *Ibid.*, p. 443.

[54] *Ibid.*, pp. 15–29, 497–502.

[55] *Ibid.*, pp. 401, 408, 414.

[56] *Ibid.*, p. 383.

[57] *Ibid.*, p. 406.

[58] *Ibid.*, p. 408.

[59] For the testimony of Gore, see *ibid.*, pp. 411–416.

[60] New York *Times*, Mar. 1, 1947.

[61] *Cong. Rec.*, 80th Cong., 1st sess. (Apr. 23, 1947), pp. 3847–3854.

[62] *Ibid.*, p. 3905.

[63] *Ibid.*, p. 3852.

[64] The TVA operates in a number of states; hence appointments to its board are not regarded as local or state in character.

[65] *Cong. Rec.*, 80th Cong., 1st sess. (Apr. 24, 1947), p. 3911.

[66] *Ibid.*, p. 3912.

CHAPTER XI

THE REJECTION OF LELAND OLDS

[1] *Hearings before a Subcommittee of the Committee on Interstate and Foreign Commerce, U. S. Senate, on Reappointment of Leland Olds to Federal Power Commission*, 81st Cong., 1st sess. (1949), p. 13.

[2] *Ibid.*, p. 13.

[3] *Hearings before a Subcommittee of the Committee on Interstate Commerce, U. S. Senate, on Leland Olds' Reappointment to the Federal Power Commission*, 78th Cong., 2d sess. (1944).

[4] *Hearings* (1949), p. 187. On September 9 while the nomination was still bottled up in the subcommittee, the Republican Kansas City *Times* commented editorially: "This looks like a drive to get at the Power Commission one way or the other. If its control can't be weakened by a new law, then the next best thing [for the big companies] is to block the man who has been carrying out the intention of the present law.... The real issue is the Kerr bill, which would remove the authority of the Commission from the producing end of the pipe lines. We believe that the bill will be very expensive to gas users, but if the natural gas Senators can win in an open fight, that's that."

[5] The following year, after the nomination of Olds was rejected, Congress passed the Kerr bill, but President Truman vetoed it. The Senate debate on the Kerr-Thomas bill in 1950 afforded a striking, if not intentional, tribute to Olds. Although he had not been a member of the FPC in the preceding year, both sides referred to him repeatedly in the course of the debate, and the opponents of the bill, led by Senator Douglas, followed closely the case he had earlier made for retention of federal regulation of natural gas prices. Douglas declared that if Olds had gone along with the gas industry in its move to secure exemption from federal price regulation, no objection would have been made to his nomination, and that when he opposed the Kerr bill, he did so with the knowledge that "his old writings of over 20 years back would be dug out and used against him, and that he would be at once smeared and probably defeated for confirmation." *Congressional Record*, 81st Cong., 2d sess. (Mar. 21, 1950), p. 3717. Senator Kerr also paid his respects to Olds, saying: "Mr. President, Leland Olds is gone. His dream of the socialization of a great industry died a-borning, but his memory lingers on in the efforts for unauthorized and unsound regulation. There are Senators who knowingly or unknowingly would resurrect his dream—his dream to confiscate through regulation, his dream to regulate without legislative authority." *Ibid.* (Mar. 24, 1950), p. 4021.

[6] The term "independent" refers to producers who do not own and operate interstate pipe lines; it has nothing to do with the size of the company or its affiliation with other companies. Some of the largest natural gas producers, with holdings worth hundreds of millions of dollars, are termed "independent" producers.

[7] 331 U.S. 682.

[8] *Ibid.*, p. 30.

[9] *Ibid.*, p. 29.

[10] One article, which appeared in the *Daily Worker* under Olds's name and to which Representative Lyle drew particular attention, gave an account of Communist classes which were starting and urged comrades to enroll. In his rebuttal testimony Olds categorically denied that he had ever written the article and offered the explanation that it was a case of a misplaced by-line.

[11] In the course of his testimony Olds was asked by Senator Lyndon Johnson whether he had ever addressed the Trade Union and Educational League, sharing the platform with Earl Browder. He replied that he remembered once speaking before this organization but could not recall where the meeting was held or who the other speakers were. Senator Johnson thereupon inserted in the record a copy of the *Daily Worker* of March 29, 1924, giving an account of the meeting, at which Browder and Olds were the principal speakers. The fact that twenty-five years earlier Olds had appeared on the same platform with Earl Browder was shocking to the senators. Lowell Mellett, in his syndicated column of October 1, pointed out that the senators might have been shocked even more had they examined Elizabeth Dilling's book, *The Roosevelt Red Record;* in it, Senator Taft, smiling, is pictured (on p. 59) with Earl Browder and two others just after they had addressed a National Youth Congress.

[12] *Cong. Rec.,* 78th Cong., 2d sess. (Sept. 12, 1944), p. 7692. The same charges of Communistic associations and leanings were also made on the floor of the Senate on May 27, 1943, by Senator Bridges, with quotations from some of the writings later used by Representative Lyle. At that time Senator Aiken stated: "I wish to say to the Members of the Senate today that of the Federal officials who have impressed me as being conscientious, honest, hard-working, and sincere, one of the foremost of them all is Leland Olds, Chairman of the Federal Power Commission. He did have work to do in my state. . . . I think he did it well in forcing down some of the outrageous write-ups in utility values which existed in Vermont and in other States. I know of one single instance where property valued at $50,000 for the purposes of assessment was written on the books of the utility company at a million and a quarter dollars; and that was not an isolated instance. . . . I believe him to be one of the most honest, courageous and hard-working public servants we have today." *Ibid.,* 78th Cong., 1st sess. (May 27, 1943), p. 4942.

[13] The opposing witnesses who were not directly connected with the gas and oil industry included a representative of the East Texas Chamber of Commerce, an attorney representing the association of county commissioners of Texas, three representatives from colleges in Texas and Arkansas, the chairman of the Arkansas Oil and Gas Commission, and two members of Congress from the Southwest.

[14] *Hearings* (1949) p. 262.

[15] *Ibid.,* p. 245. Guy I. Warren, president of the Texas Independent Producers and Royalty Owners Association, summarized the opposition of the industry as follows: "Mr. Leland Olds now proposes to take from the States the authority to regulate the production of natural gas. He proposes to subject every producer of natural gas, who sells his gas to an interstate pipe line, to the status of a utility. He would reduce the income of every producer of natural gas to what he deems would be a reasonable return on the investment of the producing property. He would leave nothing for reinvestment and the hazardous business of continuing to exploit and drill wildcat wells. . . . Gentlemen of the committee, this kind of regulation amounts to complete Federal dictatorship of business operations. No producer of natural gas could survive and continue to develop new reserves which are necessary to the future progress of this country." *Ibid.,* p. 255.

[16] *Ibid.,* p. 281. The most unbridled personal attack on Olds was made by an attorney from Houston, Texas, who asserted that Olds was "a traitor to our country, a crackpot and a jackass wholly unfit to make rules or regulations or to sit in judgment in any matter pertaining to privately owned property . . . *Ibid.,* pp. 259–261.

[17] In the Senate debate on Olds's renomination in 1944 Senator Hill declared that these old writings were "immaterial, incompetent, and irrelevant." *Cong. Rec.,* 78th Cong., 2d sess. (Sept. 12, 1944), p. 7693.

[18] Reprinted in *Cong. Rec.,* 81st Cong., 1st sess. (Oct. 4, 1949), p. 13759.

[19] *Ibid.,* p. 13760.

[20] An account of the President's press conference was given by Arthur Krock in the New York *Times* on Oct. 6; it was reprinted in the *Congressional Record* on Oct. 7.

[21] *Cong. Rec.,* 81st Cong., 1st sess. (Oct. 7, 1949), pp. 14121–14122.

[22] *Ibid.* (Oct. 11, 1949), pp. 14212–14226.

[23] *Ibid.* (Oct. 12, 1949), p. 14357.

[24] *Ibid.,* p. 14360.

[25] *Ibid.,* p. 14364. One of the most favorable testimonials for Olds which Senator Morse placed in the record was of more than usual interest, for it was from a prominent New York Attorney,

Roderick Stephens, who had represented interstate pipe-line companies before the FPC. *Ibid.*, p. 14361.

[26] *Ibid.*, p. 14368.
[27] *Ibid.*, pp. 14370–14375.
[28] *Ibid.*, pp. 14379–14380.
[29] *Ibid.*, 14384.
[30] During the debate in the Senate many testimonials of his fairness and ability as a commissioner were placed in the *Congressional Record*. A number of these were editorials of conservative newspapers; for example, Kansas City *Star* and *Times*, Milwaukee *Journal*, Portland *Oregonian*, and New York *Times*.
[31] *Cong. Rec.*, 81st Cong., 1st sess. (Oct. 12, 1949), p. 14377.

CHAPTER XII

PRESIDENT TRUMAN'S FIGHTS WITH THE SENATE

[1] *Congressional Record*, 80th Cong., 1st sess. (Dec. 16, 1947), p. 11449.
[2] Jonathan Daniels, *The Man from Independence*, pp. 291–292.
[3] The statistics are taken from a table in Floyd M. Riddick, *The United States Congress; Organization and Procedure*, Washington, National Capitol Publishers, 1949, p. 424.
[4] Examples of such appointments: Dwight Griswold, former Republican governor of Nebraska, to be head of the mission to Greece; Paul Hoffman, a prominent businessman and industrialist, to be head of the ECA; Averill Harriman, chief representative of the ECA in Europe.
[5] *United States News*, Feb. 15, 1946.
[6] New York *Times*, Feb. 4, 1946.
[7] *Time*, Feb. 18, 1946.
[8] *Cong. Rec.*, 79th Cong., 2d sess. (Feb. 18, 1946), p. 1396.
[9] *Ibid.*, p. 1403.
[10] *Ibid.*, pp. 1408–1409.
[11] *Ibid.*, p. 1413.
[12] New York *Times*, Feb. 20, 1946.
[13] *Ibid.*, Mar. 21, 1946.
[14] *Cong. Rec.*, 79th Cong., 2d sess. (Apr. 3, 1946), p. 3025.
[15] *Ibid.*, p. 3028.
[16] Washington *Post*, Jan. 19, 1946.
[17] New York *Times*, Jan. 20, 1946.
[18] Washington *Post*, Feb. 1, 1946.
[19] New York *Times*, Feb. 4, 1946.
[20] *Ibid.*, Feb. 6, 1946.
[21] *Ibid.*, Feb. 8, 1946.
[22] *Ibid.*, Feb. 14, 1946.
[23] *Ibid.*, Mar. 7, 1946.
[24] *Ibid.*, Feb. 27, 1946.
[25] *Ibid.*, Mar. 9, 1946.
[26] San Francisco *Chronicle*, Mar. 14, 1946.
[27] Timothy Pickering, Secretary of State under John Adams, went privately to a number of members of the Senate to oppose the appointment of Adams' son-in-law as Adjutant General. Leonard D. White, *The Federalists*, pp. 251, 278–280.
[28] This point was made by Chester Rowell in his column in the San Francisco *Chronicle*, Mar. 14, 1946.
[29] New York *Times*, May 15, 1947.
[30] *Ibid.*, June 27, 1947.
[31] *Ibid.*
[32] *Cong. Rec.*, 80th Cong., 1st sess. (July 8, 1947), p. 8399.
[33] *Ibid.* (July 14, 1947), p. 8830.

[34] New York *Times*, July 22, 1947.

[35] *Cong. Rec.*, 80th Cong., 1st sess. (July 26, 1947), pp. 10431–10435.

[36] New York *Times*, June 26, 1950.

[37] *Ibid.*, May 10, 1947.

[38] *Ibid.*, May 18, 1947.

[39] *Hearing before the Committee on Labor and Public Welfare, U. S. Senate, on the Confirmation of Nominees for the National Labor Relations Board*, 80th Cong., 1st sess. (1947), p. 59.

[40] *Cong. Rec.*, 80th Cong., 1st sess. (July 25, 1947), p. 10110.

[41] *Ibid.* (Dec. 16, 1947), pp. 11444, 11449.

[42] New York *Times*, Mar. 21, 1947.

[43] *Ibid.*, Mar. 21, 1947.

[44] *Ibid.*, Mar. 29, 1947.

[45] *Cong. Rec.*, 81st Cong., 1st sess., p. 2567. The same position was advanced by Kem of Missouri. *Ibid.* (Mar. 18, 1949), p. 2783.

[46] *Ibid.* (Mar. 22, 1949), pp. 2931–2936.

[47] New York *Times*, June 4, July 15, 1948.

[48] *Ibid.*, July 9, 1952.

[49] *Hearings before a Subcommittee of the Committee on Interstate and Foreign Commerce, U. S. Senate, on the Nomination of Thomas Chalmers Buchanan of Pennsylvania, to Be a Member of the Federal Power Commission for the Remainder of the Term Expiring June 22, 1952*, 80th Cong., 2d sess. (1948), p. 31.

[50] *Ibid.*, p. 32.

[51] After the nomination had been referred back to the subcommittee for further investigation, in June, 1948, Senator MacMahon stated on the floor of the Senate: "In the hearings which were held we discovered that the utilities of Pennsylvania had a front man named Dunlap, whom they sent here to testify against Buchanan, which he did not do very successfully. . . . If Buchanan's appointment is going to be blocked by the power interests, I think the people of the United States should know about it." *Cong. Rec.*, 80th Cong., 2d sess. (June 8, 1948), p. 7323.

[52] *Hearings . . . on the Nomination of Thomas Chalmers Buchanan*, p. 137.

[53] *S. Exec. Rep.* 6, 81st Cong., 1st sess. (May 26, 1949).

[54] Quoted in *Hearings before the Committee on Interstate and Foreign Commerce, U. S. Senate, on the Nomination of John J. Carson to Be a Member of the Federal Trade Commission*, 81st Cong., 1st sess. (1949), p. 88.

[55] *Ibid.*, pp. 85–90.

[56] *Ibid.*, pp. 212–232.

[57] *Ibid.*, p. 233.

[58] *Cong. Rec.*, 81st Cong., 1st sess. (Sept. 16, 1949), pp. 12972–12976.

[59] New York *Times*, Sept. 20, 1949.

[60] *Cong. Rec.*, 81st Cong., 1st sess. (Sept. 16, 1949), pp. 12943–12961.

[61] New York *Herald Tribune*, Feb. 17, 1949.

[62] Washington *Post*, Feb. 27, 1949.

[63] Chicago *Daily News*, Feb. 22, 1949.

[64] *Cong. Rec.*, 81st Cong., 1st sess. (Mar. 8, 1949), pp. 1988–2024.

[65] *Hearings before the Committee on Armed Services, U. S. Senate, on the Nomination of Mon C. Wallgren to be Chairman of the National Security Resources Board*, 81st Cong., 1st sess. (Feb. 17, 21, 24, 25, 1949), pp. 29–30.

[66] *Ibid.*, pp. 22–24. Senator Morse also asked Wallgren to submit a written statement of his qualifications, but apparently the statement was never submitted.

[67] New York *Times*, Mar. 16, 1949.

[68] *Cong. Rec.*, 81st Cong., 1st sess. (May 18, 1949), pp. 6406–6408.

[69] New York *Times*, Oct. 19, 1949.

[70] *Cong. Rec.*, 81st Cong., 1st sess. (Oct. 19, 1949), pp. 14989–14991.

[71] See the account by Drew Pearson in his syndicated newspaper column, July 19, 1951.

CHAPTER XIII

THE COURTESY OF THE SENATE

[1] *Congressional Record,* 76th Cong., 1st sess. (Feb. 9, 1939), p. 1284.

[2] *Ibid.,* 67th Cong., 1st sess. (May 14, 1921), p. 1454.

[3] This custom had evidently not become established by 1833. Joseph Story, in his famous *Commentaries on the Constitution,* stated then that the provision in the Constitution prescribing the method of appointment to office was "entitled to peculiar commendation," and discoursed at length on the superiority of the selection of persons for public offices by one man, who would be responsible and hence would exercise diligent care, instead of by a public body, "in which appointments will be materially influenced by party attachments and dislikes, by private animosities and antipathies, and partialities, and will be generally founded in compromises, having little to do with the merits of candidates, and will have much to do with selfish interests of individuals and cabals." In answer to the contention that the Senate might use this power to force the President to nominate their candidates, he stated that if this should "happen in a few rare instances," the President would have an effective countercheck.

The editor of the fifth edition (1891) commented on the original text: "It would be difficult to answer the reasoning of the text if the experience of the country had not refuted it; but we are driven to the confession that since these commentaries were first published it has gradually come to be understood that appointments to office, not regulated by the civil service law or other statute, are in the main practically in the control of members of Congress of the dominant party, to be given out upon party if not personal considerations.... When such considerations are suffered to have force, experience demonstrates that they are apt to supersede all others, to the degradation and injury of the public service." Joseph Story, *Commentaries on the Constitution of the United States,* ed. Melville M. Bigelow, Boston, Little, Brown & Co., 1891, II, 352–357.

[4] *Cong. Rec.,* 72d Cong., 1st sess. (Mar. 23, 1932), p. 6711.

[5] *Ibid.,* p. 7434.

[6] *Hearings before a Subcommittee of the Committee on the Judiciary, U. S. Senate, on the Confirmation of Hon. Gunnar H. Nordbye,* 71st Cong., 3d sess. (Feb. 26, 28, Mar. 2, 1931).

[7] *Cong. Rec.,* 73d Cong., 2d sess. (Mar. 3, 1934), p. 5235. "I have never held the duty to be imposed upon any member of the Senate to justify his reasons for stating that a nomination was personally obnoxious to him. I have held, as has been the majority of the thought in this body, that no member of the Senate was called upon to justify his statement that a nominee was personally objectionable to him, but that when a State sent its ambassadors to the Senate, under the great doctrine of State's Rights which my part of this country has held and upheld from the time the memory of man runneth not to the contrary, no Senator would have to present anything except his own objection and his own proposal that a nomination should not be confirmed by the Senate. I am not ... going to take the lead in destroying the prerogatives of the United States Senate."

[8] *Ibid.,* p. 5244.

[9] *Ibid.,* pp. 5244, 5251.

[10] *Hearings before a Subcommittee of the Committee on the Judiciary, U. S. Senate, on the Nomination of William S. Boyle to Be United States Attorney for the District of Nevada,* 76th Cong., 1st sess. (1939), p. 43.

[11] *Ibid.,* p. 42.

[12] *Hearings before the Committee on the Judiciary, U. S. Senate, on the Nomination of Floyd H. Roberts to Be United States District Judge for the Western District of Virginia,* 76th Cong., 1st sess. (1939), pp. 1–2, 44.

[13] *Cong. Rec.,* 81st Cong., 2d sess. (Aug. 9, 1950), p. 12105.

[14] *Ibid.,* p. 12106.

[15] See, for example, the statement of Senator Dill in the Jonas case, *Cong. Rec.,* 72d Cong., 1st sess. (Mar. 23, 1932), p. 6728.

[16] *Ibid.* (Mar. 23, 1932), p. 6711.

[17] For example, in 1931 Senator Long attacked the character of Ernest Burguieres, who had been nominated to be port commissioner of New Orleans, and in 1933 made similar charges against

Daniel Moore when he was nominated to be collector of internal revenue in Louisiana, though at the hearings leading citizens of the state testified that both nominees were men of excellent reputations. Senator Schall of Minnesota bitterly attacked Gunnar Nordbye, who was nominated in 1931 to be district judge in his state; but after President Hoover accepted his recommendations for other offices, Schall withdrew his objection to Nordbye. Senator Bilbo carried on a scurrilous attack on United States District Judge Edwin R. Holmes when he was nominated to the circuit court of appeals in 1935. The fight made by Senator O'Daniels of Texas on the nomination of James V. Allred to the circuit court of appeals in 1943 is perhaps the most striking example of an attack due to politics. Allred, a former governor of Texas, was subsequently appointed to a federal district judgeship, from which he resigned to run against O'Daniels for United States senator in 1942. Although his nomination was supported by the president of the Texas Bar Association and by many leading attorneys, it was not confirmed. After O'Daniels left the Senate, Truman nominated Allred for a district judgeship in 1949, and his nomination was confirmed without opposition.

[18] *Cong. Rec.*, 81st Cong., 2d sess. (Aug. 9, 1950), p. 12100.

[19] *Ibid.*, p. 12102.

[20] An illuminating account of the Hutchinson case is given by Stephen K. Bailey and Howard D. Samuel, *Congress at Work*, New York, Henry Holt & Co., 1952, pp. 137–146.

[21] New York *Times*, May 16, 18, 23, 1916.

[22] *Hearings before a Subcommittee of the Committee on the Judiciary of the U. S. Senate on the Nomination of William J. Tilson*, 69th Cong., 2d sess. (1927), p. 43.

[23] New York *Times*, July 8, 1926; Feb. 9, 1927; Feb. 7, 1928. After his rejection in 1927, Tilson was given a recess appointment by Coolidge.

[24] *Cong. Rec.*, 75th Cong., 3d sess. (daily ed., Jan. 11, 1938), p. 470.

[25] New York *Times*, Jan. 25, 1936. Other details were brought out in the *Hearings before a Subcommittee of the Committee on the Judiciary, U. S. Senate, on the Nomination of Judge Edwin R. Holmes*, 74th Cong., 2d sess. (1936).

[26] A suit for seduction was brought against the governor of the state by his secretary. Senator Bilbo, a close friend of the governor, at his request had attempted to settle the case out of court. The plaintiff and her attorneys regarded Bilbo as a key witness; but rather than testify against his friend, he dodged the service of a subpoena and, after he was subpoenaed, left the state to avoid appearing at the trial. When, after being postponed several times, the case was finally tried, Bilbo was still absent, and the plaintiff lost the case. Judge Holmes cited Bilbo for contempt and gave him a stiff sentence, which, however, was later reduced to ten days in prison. Bilbo conducted his campaign for governor from prison. Although the fact that he elected to go to prison rather than testify against a friend endeared him to many voters, he was defeated.

[27] *Cong. Rec.*, 74th Cong., 2d sess. (Mar. 19, 1936), pp. 3987–4024.

[28] *Ibid.*, pp. 10081–10084.

[29] *Ibid.*, pp. 4025–4030.

[30] George H. Haynes, *The Senate of the United States*, pp. 775–776.

[31] New York *Times*, Mar. 2, May 17, Dec. 11, 1923; Feb. 19, 26, 1924. See also Haynes, *op. cit.*, pp. 777–778.

[32] *Cong. Rec.*, 71st Cong., 2d sess. (June 20, 1930), pp. 11310–11313. See also New York *Times*, June 8, 12, 1930.

[33] New York *Times*, Mar. 21, 22, Apr. 17, 19, 23, 1921.

[34] *Cong. Rec.*, 72d Cong., 1st sess. (Mar. 23, 1932), p. 6727.

[35] *Ibid.*, p. 13487.

[36] *Hearings . . . on the Nomination of Floyd H. Roberts*, p. 2.

[37] *Cong. Rec.*, 73d Cong., 2d sess. (Mar. 3, 1934), p. 5244.

[38] *Ibid.*, 76th Cong., 1st sess. (June 29, 1939), p. 8227.

[39] *Ibid.*, 75th Cong., 3d sess. (Jan 11, 1938), p. 321.

[40] *Ibid.*, 72d Cong., 1st sess. (Mar. 23, 1932), p. 6728.

[41] *Ibid.*, 82d Cong., 1st sess. (daily ed., Oct. 9, 1941), p. 13101.

[42] Henry Cabot Lodge, *A Frontier Town and Other Essays*, New York, Charles Scribner's Sons, 1906, p. 75.

[43] *Cong. Rec.*, 75th Cong., 3d sess. (Feb. 25, 1938), p. 2430.

[44] *Ibid.*, pp. 2430–2431.

[45] *Ibid.* (April 11, 1938), p. 5207.

[46] *Ibid.*, 72d Cong., 1st sess. (Apr. 5, 1932), p. 7437.

[47] *Ibid.*, p. 7432.

[48] *Ibid.*, 75th Cong., 3d sess. (Jan. 12, 1938), p. 361.

[49] *Ibid.*, 77th Cong., 2d sess. (Sept. 14, 1942), p. 7128.

[50] *Ibid.*, 78th Cong., 1st sess. (June 13, 1943), p. 5822.

[51] *Ibid.*, 67th Cong., 1st sess. (May 14, 1921), p. 1454. "I can tell you how we can get along much better," Williams said. "Stop this infernal foolishness of senatorial courtesy. I met in the Senate one day a Democratic Senator just going out of the Chamber. He said, 'John, I should like to have you vote against the confirmation of a certain man whose name has been sent in for an office in my State.' I said, 'Why? Is he incompetent or dishonest?' He said, ' I do not know anything about him in that respect.' Then, remembering this absurdity of senatorial courtesy, I said, 'Is he personally *persona non grata* to you, personally obnoxious?' He said, 'I do not know anything about him. I never heard of him before in my life until his name was sent in by President Wilson, but I was not consulted about his appointment.' . . . Four days afterwards that Senator rose in his place in this Chamber and solemnly assured the Senate that 'the nominee was personally obnoxious' to him, and the nominee was defeated."

[52] This quotation was contained in Senator Glass's statement to the press, Washington *Post*, Feb. 9, 1939.

[53] *Hearings . . . on the Nomination of Floyd H. Roberts*, p. 45.

[54] The letter was published in full in the Washington *Star*, Feb. 8, 1939.

[55] Washington *Post*, Feb. 9, 10, 1939.

[56] *Cong. Rec.*, 76th Cong., 1st sess. (Feb. 9, 1939), pp. 1284–1285.

[57] *The Federalist*, No. 76. (Emphasis in the original.)

[58] *Cong. Rec.*, 76th Cong., 1st sess. (June 29, 1939), p. 8224.

CHAPTER XIV

PROCEDURE

[1] *Congressional Record*, 67th Cong., 1st sess. (May 14, 1921), pp. 1451, 1452.

[2] This was notably true of Polk, Lincoln, Hayes, Garfield, and Taft.

[3] James D. Richardson, ed., *Messages and Papers of the Presidents*, III, 136.

[4] *Opinion of the Attorney General*, April 30, 1941.

[5] These cases are reviewed by Edwin S. Corwin, *The President, Office and Powers*, New York, New York University Press, 1948, p. 141.

[6] New York *Times*, Mar. 5, 14, 16, 21; Apr. 8, 23, 1948.

[7] Printed in *Cong. Rec.*, 80th Cong., 1st sess. (Mar. 28, 1947), p. 2805.

[8] *Ibid.*, p. 2801.

[9] *Ibid.* (Apr. 1, 1947), p. 2938.

[10] New York *Times*, Mar. 29, 1950.

[11] For a period, the chairman of the subcommittee was permitted to read the file itself in the presence of the FBI representative, and at times the file was left with the chairman. The chairman of a subcommittee once took the FBI file to a public hearing; another member of the subcommittee picked it up and, reading from it, questioned the candidate about a divorce proceeding. The Attorney General threatened to discontinue the practice of supplying the results of the FBI investigations. The former practice of having the FBI representative appear and summarize the results of the investigations has been resumed. This account is based on information supplied by members of the staffs of the Attorney General and the Senate Judiciary Committee.

[12] Senate Rule 38, sec. 1.

[13] Clara H. Kerr, *United States Senate*, Ithaca, Andrus & Church, 1895, p. 106.

[14] *Ibid.*

[15] *Congressional Globe*, 40th Cong., 2d sess. (Mar. 3, 1868), p. 1630.

[16] *Cong. Rec.*, 67th Cong., 2d sess. (May 9, 1922), pp. 6555–6556.

[17] Apparently only three nominees to the Supreme Court have ever been called before the Senate committee to testify: Harlan Stone, 1925; Felix Frankfurter, 1939; and Robert H. Jackson, 1941.

[18] *Washington Post,* Oct. 4, 1949.

[19] *Ibid.,* Oct. 5, 1949. In an editorial on Oct. 6, the *Post* approved Judge Minton's refusal, stating that "no man nominated to such a position should be asked to testify in his own behalf."

[20] When Judge James P. McGranery testified before the Judiciary subcommittee conducting hearings on his nomination to be Attorney General in 1952, he was strongly pressed by several members to express his views on whether the President had the legal power to take over the steel industry, but he declined to do so. A case testing the constitutionality of the President's action was then pending before the Supreme Court. New York *Times,* May 7, 1952.

[21] *Ibid.,* Jan. 12, 1939.

[22] These statistics are computed from a table contained in Floyd M. Riddick, *The United States Congress; Organization and Procedure,* p. 424.

[23] *Cong. Rec.,* 81st Cong., 2d sess. (daily ed., Oct. 20, 1950), p. D1009.

[24] Senate Rule 38.

[25] Kerr, *op. cit.,* p. 40; Robert Luce, *Legislative Procedure,* Boston, Houghton Mifflin Co., 1922, pp. 334–335.

[26] The practice of conducting executive business in closed session has led to a loose usage of the phrase "executive session" as synonymous with "secret session." The Senate meets in executive session when it transacts executive business, regardless of whether the session is open or closed.

[27] *Annals of Congress,* II (Dec. 22, 1800), p. 769.

[28] *Senate Journal,* X, 66.

[29] *Ibid.,* LXII, 345–346. A review of the earlier rules of the Senate on the point is given in *Cong. Rec.,* 68th Cong., 2d sess. (Feb. 11, 1925), pp. 3480–3482.

[30] Albert B. Hart, *Salmon P. Chase,* Boston and New York, Houghton Mifflin Co., 1899, p. 116.

[31] *Cong. Rec.,* 49th Cong., 1st sess. (Apr. 13, 1886), p. 3427.

[32] *Ibid.,* pp. 3425, 3428.

[33] *Ibid.* (May 24, 1886), p. 4842.

[34] *Ibid.* (Apr. 15, 1886), p. 3507.

[35] *Ibid.* (May 24, 1886), p. 4841.

[36] *Ibid.* (June 30, 1886), p. 6312.

[37] *Ibid.* (June 30, 1886), p. 6309.

[38] Dorman B. Eaton, *Secret Sessions of the Senate,* New York, 1886, p. 5.

[39] *Ibid.,* p. 6.

[40] *Ibid.,* p. 9.

[41] *Cong. Rec.,* 67th Cong., 1st sess. (May 14, 1921), pp. 1450–1456.

[42] *Ibid.*

[43] *Ibid.,* 68th Cong., 2d sess. (Jan. 24, 1925), p. 2403.

[44] *Ibid.,* p. 3032.

[45] *Ibid.* (Feb. 11, 1925), pp. 3481–3482.

[46] One senator was reported as saying that "it would crucify me with my people if they knew I voted for Woodlock." New York *Times,* Mar. 27, 1926.

[47] *Cong. Rec.,* 69th Cong., 1st sess. (Apr. 2, 1926), pp. 6766–6778.

[48] New York *Times,* Apr. 3, 1926.

[49] *Ibid.,* Jan. 24, 1929.

[50] *Ibid.*

[51] *Cong. Rec.,* 71st Cong., 1st sess. (May 27, 1929), pp. 1955–1957.

[52] *Ibid.,* p. 3035.

[53] *Ibid.,* p. 3044.

[54] *Ibid.,* p. 3038.

[55] *Ibid.,* p. 3042.

[56] *Ibid.,* p. 3049.

[57] *Ibid.,* pp. 3053–3055. Senate Rule 38, sec. 2, provides that all sessions of the Senate shall be open unless a majority voting in closed session shall determine that a particular nomination shall be considered in closed executive session. The vote on nominations in closed sessions may be ordered published by a majority vote, and in any event any senator is authorized to make public his vote cast in a closed session.

[58] *The Writings of John Quincy Adams* (W. C. Ford, ed.) III, 83.

[59] G. H. Haynes, *The Senate of the United States*, p. 772.

[60] For a detailed account of the debate over the Gore resolution, see Henry M. Wriston, *Executive Agents in Foreign Relations*, Baltimore, Johns Hopkins Press, 1929, pp. 212–217.

[61] James Madison, *Letters and Writings*, Philadelphia, 1865, IV, 369; John Quincy Adams, *Memoirs*, VII, 96.

[62] One of the leading opinions of the Attorney General is that of Caleb Cushing in 1855 (*Opinions*, VII, 223): citing opinions of his predecessors, he stated that "howsoever a vacancy happens to exist, if it exists, it may be filled by temporary appointment of the President." Other opinions of Attorneys General are cited by Charles E. Morganston, *The Appointing and Removal Power of the President of the United States*, 70th Cong., 2d sess., S. Doc. 172 (1929), pp. 136–147.

[63] *U.S. Rev. Stat.* (1878), sec. 1761.

[64] *Cong. Rec.*, 69th Cong., 1st sess. (Mar. 14, 1925), p. 228.

[65] In *United States* v. *Smith* (1932), 286 U.S. 6, the Supreme Court held that the Senate could not recall for reconsideration a nomination after it had been forwarded to the President.

CHAPTER XV

CABINET OFFICERS AND HEADS OF INDEPENDENT AGENCIES

[1] *Congressional Record*, 69th Cong., spec. sess. (Mar. 7, 1925), p. 94.

[2] *Ibid.*, 76th Cong., 1st sess. (Jan. 20, 1939), p. 554.

[3] New York *Times*, Mar. 15, 1925.

[4] Sec. 434, title 18, *United States Code*, reads: "Whoever, being an officer, agent or member of, or directly or indirectly interested in the pecuniary profits or contracts of any corporations ... is employed or acts as an officer or agent of the United States for the transactions of business with such business entity, shall be fined not more than $2,000 or imprisoned not more than two years, or both."

[5] New York *Times*, Jan. 16, 1953, and daily thereafter until Jan. 27, 1953; see also Walter Lippmann, "Conflict of Interest," Washington *Post*, Jan. 26, 1953.

[6] *Cong. Rec.*, 83d Cong., 1st sess. (daily ed., Jan. 24, 1953), pp. 562–592.

[7] *Ibid.*, 76th Cong., 1st sess. (Jan. 20, 1939), p. 559.

[8] *Ibid.* (Jan. 23, 1939), p. 604.

[9] Washington *Post*, Feb. 13, 22, 1945; *Cong. Rec.*, 79th Cong., 1st sess. (Feb. 19, 1945), p. 1231.

[10] It is significant that Henry L. Stimson, wise in the ways of politics, would not accept the appointment as Secretary of War in 1940 until he was assured that he could name his principal assistant and thus be the undisputed head of the department. Henry L. Stimson and McGeorge Bundy, *On Active Service in Peace and War*, New York, Harper & Brothers, 1947, pp. 323–324, 341.

[11] 59 *U.S. Stat.* (1945), 613, sec. 4; 63 *U.S. Stat.* (1949), 205, sec. 4.

[12] 63d Cong., 2d sess., S. Rept. 597 (1914), p. 11; quoted by Pendleton Herring, *Federal Commissioners*, Cambridge, Harvard University Press, 1936, p. 6.

[13] Robert E. Cushman, *The Independent Regulatory Commissions*, New York, Oxford University Press, 1941, p. 759.

[14] *Ibid.*, p. 751.

[15] Paul M. Warburg, *The Federal Reserve System*, New York, Macmillan Co., 1930, II, 494.

[16] *Ibid.*, p. 838.

[17] Herring, *op. cit.*, chap. 3.

[18] In the hearing on the nomination of Wayne Coy to be chairman of the Federal Communications Commission in 1948, Senator Tobey, who was presiding, questioned him closely about rumors that he had the backing of officials of the National Broadcasting Company. Coy denied the rumors and stated that the officials of this company had backed another person and learned of his nomination when it was publicly announced. In answer to the question whether he was prepared to carry out the duties of the office in the public interest, Coy vigorously said that he was. Rarely are such questions asked of a nominee. *Hearings before the Committee on Interstate and Foreign Commerce*

of the U. S. Senate on the Nominations of Wayne Coy and George E. Sterling, 80th Cong., 2d sess. (1948), pp. 17-22.

[19] Harvey C. Mansfield, *The Lake Cargo Coal Controversy,* New York, Columbia University Press, 1932, p. 148. Of recent personal appointments, those by Truman of Mon C. Wallgren, first to the National Security Resources Board and later to the Federal Power Commission; James K. Vardaman, to the Federal Reserve Board; and George Allen, to the RFC, are examples.

[20] Herring, *op. cit.,* p. 84, gives several instances of commissioners who testified in the hearing that they owed their nomination to the influence of a member of the Senate.

[21] I. L. Sharfman, *The Interstate Commerce Commission,* New York, Commonwealth Fund, 1937, IV, 22–35.

[22] Mansfield, *op. cit.,* p. 148.

[23] Sharfman states that 25 of the 44 commissioners who had served before 1936 and were available had been reappointed; 11 had not. The 8 others had died, had resigned, or were serving their initial terms at the time of the study. Sharfman, *op. cit.,* pp. 38–41.

[24] See the report of the House Committee on Expenditures in the Executive Departments, *Further Inquiry into the Operations of the Maritime Commission,* 81st Cong., 2d sess. (May 18, 1950), H. Rept. 2104. Seldom has a public agency been subjected to such scathing criticism of its operations in an official report. The committee reported that the administration of the Marine Act had been and is "deficient," that the commission had operated on "unwarranted assumptions and error," in administering the subsidy program, and that there were many examples of "dilatory handling and procrastination," as well as "extreme administrative lassitude and indecisiveness." The report stated that many staff members occupying key positions showed a "marked lack of training and experience" and "incompetence," and it recommended that the Civil Service Commission reëxamine their qualifications.

[25] The press carried accounts almost daily of the RFC exposures in February and March, 1951.

[26] The Senate took no action on President Truman's nominations to the RFC in 1950, and after Congress adjourned, Truman gave the nominees recess appointments. He renominated them in 1951 after the scandals broke, and again the Senate did not act on the nominations. Two of the three members involved in the scandals had earlier been confirmed by the Senate on previous appointments.

[27] Bipartisan membership is required for the ICC, FTC, FPC, SEC, FCC, CAB, and the Maritime Board, but not for the Federal Reserve Board or the NLRB under the act of 1935. Cushman, *op. cit.,* table following p. 759.

[28] Sharfman, *op. cit.,* IV, 22–25.

[29] Mansfield, *op. cit.,* pp. 144–145.

[30] *Traffic World,* Feb. 15, 1930; quoted by Herring, *op. cit.,* p. 12.

[31] *Cong. Rec.,* 75th Cong., 3d sess. (Mar. 18, 1938), p. 3648.

[32] Although the administrations were Democratic from 1933 to 1953, the Republican members of the Civil Service Commission, for example, were persons of great ability and special qualifications. They included Professor Leonard D. White, Samuel Ordway, Arthur Flemming, and James Mitchell. In the earlier Republican administrations, the most able commissioners were usually Democrats.

[33] Mansfield, *op. cit.,* p. 144.

[34] When questioned about his party affiliation, Robert L. O'Brien, who was nominated to the Tariff Commission in 1932, declared that he was a "Republican protectionist" and had "voted for every Republican presidential candidate beginning with McKinley." In 1930, Commissioner Dennis declared that he was a "regular Democrat," and that no member of his family for three generations had been Republican. C. M. Jansky and Arthur Batcheller, nominated to the Federal Radio Commission in 1929 because of their special qualifications, were both rejected apparently because they were not party regulars and did not have political sponsorship. Herring, *op. cit.,* pp. 13–16.

[35] The following account of contests over appointments to the ICC is based on Mansfield, *op. cit.,* pp. 163–194. See also Sharfman, *op. cit.,* IV, 26–27, and New York *Times,* Dec. 24, 1925; Jan. 3, 25, Feb. 20, Mar. 6, 24, 27, 1926.

[36] Quoted by Mansfield, *op. cit.,* p. 170. See also New York *Times,* Mar. 24, 1926.

[37] Mansfield, *op. cit.,* p. 188.

[38] *Ibid.,* p. 149.

[39] New York *Times*, Dec. 31, 1947; Jan. 3, 4, 1948. Landis cited to the press instances of differences which he had had with Pan American World Airways and United Air Lines, two of the largest air transport companies.

[40] *Ibid.*, Nov. 3, 14, 1944; *Time*, Nov. 13, 1944.

[41] The renomination of Ray C. Wakefield to the FCC was withdrawn in 1947 because of industry opposition. New York *Times*, June 19, 28, July 11, 1947.

[42] Herring, *op. cit.*, pp. 13, 28–29, 74.

[43] Quoted by Mansfield, *op. cit.*, p. 184.

[44] Cushman, *op. cit.*, p. 758.

CHAPTER XVI

DIPLOMATIC OFFICERS

[1] *Congressional Record*, 59th Cong., 1st sess. (Jan. 23, 1906), p. 1418.

[2] *Ibid.*, 67th Cong., 1st sess. (Sept. 24, 1921), p. 5773.

[3] Thomas Jefferson, *Writings* (Bergh ed.), 1903, VIII, 285.

[4] *Ibid.*, III, 16. This statement of Jefferson was quoted with approval by Senator Spooner in a celebrated debate in the Senate in 1906 over the constitutional powers of the President to conduct our foreign relations. *Cong. Rec.*, 59th Cong., 1st sess. (1906), pp. 1417–1421; quoted in Edward S. Corwin, *The President's Control of Foreign Relations*, Princeton, Princeton University Press, 1917, chap. v.

[5] Joseph Story, *Commentaries on the Constitution of the United States*, II, 357.

[6] Henry Adams, *History of the United States*, New York, Charles Scribner's Sons, 1909, IV, 467.

[7] Ralston Hayden, *The Senate and Treaties: 1789–1817*, New York, Macmillan Co., 1920, pp. 54–57.

[8] Once when a letter and packet from the French government addressed to the President and Congress arrived, Washington forwarded it unopened to the Senate; whereupon Vice-President Adams returned them to the President, stating that it was the "opinion of the Senate that they might be opened with more propriety by the President of the United States." Henry M. Wriston, *Executive Agents in American Foreign Relations*, pp. 70, 102–103.

[9] For a discussion of the point, see Henry B. Learned, *The President's Cabinet*, New Haven, Yale University Press, 1912, p. 85.

[10] Jefferson, *op. cit.*, III, 17.

[11] This often repeated story was first recorded by Maclay in his famous *Journal*, pp. 128–133. John Quincy Adams recorded in his *Memoirs*, VI, 427, that Washington said "he would be damned if he ever went there again."

[12] Hayden, *op. cit.*, p. 71.

[13] This whole episode is treated at length in Hayden, *op. cit.*, chap. iv. See also Samuel F. Bemis, *Jay's Treaty*, New York, Macmillan Co., 1923, pp. 193 ff; and Wriston, *op. cit.*, *passim*.

[14] Quincy Wright, *The Control of Foreign Relations*, New York, Macmillan Co., 1922, pp. 328–331.

[15] *Ibid.*, p. 330.

[16] *Ibid.*, p. 249.

[17] The treatment of the subject presented here is based chiefly on Wriston's excellent study, *Executive Agents in American Foreign Relations*. See also Wright, *op. cit.*, p. 329, for a list of notable executive agents appointed by the Presidents, and their assignments.

[18] A full account of the debate is given by Wriston, *op. cit.*, pp. 237–258.

[19] Quoted by Wriston, *ibid.*, p. 285.

[20] Quoted by Wriston, *ibid.*, p. 287.

[21] *Cong. Rec.*, 59th Cong., 1st sess. (Jan. 23, 1906), p. 1418; quoted also in Corwin, *op. cit.*, pp. 170–171, and in Wriston, *op. cit.*, pp. 308–309.

[22] John Quincy Adams, *op. cit.*, IX, 131.

[23] Wriston, *op. cit.*, p. 205.

[24] Wright, *op. cit.*, pp. 326–327.

[25] 37 *U.S. Stat.* (1913), 913; *Comp. Stat.*, 7686.

[26] Wriston, *op. cit.*, pp. 129–130.

[27] Wright, *op. cit.*, p. 333.

[28] Wriston, *op. cit.*, pp. 152–153.

[29] *Cong. Rec.,* 67th Cong., 1st sess. (Sept. 24, 1921), p. 5772. President Harding desired to appoint a representative to serve on the Reparations Commission and the World War Debt Funding Commission, but Congress did not authorize membership on these commissions, and the President was represented by unofficial observers. Wriston, *loc. cit.*

[30] S. Rept. 717, to accompany S. 1580, 79th Cong., 1st sess., Nov. 8, 1945.

[31] *Cong. Rec.,* 79th Cong., 1st sess. (Nov. 26, 1945), pp. 10969-10970.

[32] *Ibid.* (Nov. 30, Dec. 3, 1945), pp. 11246, 11315–11319.

[33] *Ibid.* (Nov. 30, 1945), p. 11245.

[34] *Ibid.* (Dec. 3, 1945), p. 11318.

[35] Public Law No. 264, 79th Cong., 1st sess., 59 *U.S. Stat.* (1945), 620.

[36] 62 *U.S. Stat.* (1948), 137.

[37] Accounts of the Biddle contest are given in the New York *Times,* May 13, 1947.

[38] *Hearings before the Committee on Foreign Relations, U. S. Senate, on the Nomination of Edward J. Flynn to Be Minister to Australia,* 78th Cong., 1st sess. (1943), p. 24.

[39] *Time,* Jan. 18, 1945; New York *Times,* Jan. 15, 1943.

[40] As reported in *Time,* Jan. 25, 1943.

[41] *Ibid.,* Feb. 1, 1943.

[42] New York *Times,* Jan. 28, 1943.

[43] *Ibid.*

[44] *Ibid.,* Feb. 1, 1943.

[45] *Cong. Rec.,* 82d Cong., 1st sess. (daily ed., Oct. 9, 1951), p. 13108.

[46] *Ibid.,* p. 13109.

[47] New York *Times,* Sept. 21, 1952.

[48] *Ibid.,* Sept. 21, 26, 1951.

[49] *Hearings before a Subcommittee of the Committee on Foreign Relations, U. S. Senate, on the Nomination of Philip C. Jessup to Be U. S. Representative to the Sixth General Assembly of the United Nations,* 82d Cong., 1st sess. (1951), p. 142.

[50] New York *Times,* Oct. 19, 1951.

[51] *Ibid.,* Oct. 18.

[52] *Ibid.,* Oct. 16.

[53] During the contests over Jessup and Bowles, James Reston, Washington correspondent of the New York *Times,* published (Oct. 19) "Fourteen Simple Rules on How to Be Confirmed." These were:

"1. Be sure you are for the things that are going to be popular six or seven years from now.

"2. Don't join anything, ever.

"3. Don't let your wife join anything, either.

"4. Don't get involved in foreign affairs questions at all if you can help it. If you can't help it, back the Monroe Doctrine and the Open Door Policy and be against Communism.

"5. If you must have political convictions about foreign policy questions (which is not recommended), make sure the President sends your nomination to Capitol Hill at a time when your convictions are popular.

"6. Be suspicious of the British. And if you know what they're up to today in northern Rhodesia, all the better.

"7. Don't write books.

"8. Master various cliches that are popular on Capitol Hill, including the following: (a) I am for adequate defense, but we must not spend ourselves into bankruptcy. (b) I am for helping other countries but they must first prove that they are helping themselves. (c) America cannot defend the whole world. (d) Communism is merely socialism in a hurry and I hate both from the depths of my soul. (e) I am not and have never been a Communist or a member of any Communist front organization.

"9. If possible, be Irish. This pleases Senator Pat McCarran, Democrat, of Nevada.

"10. Keep up with the Senate's favorites. A word of praise on your behalf by Bernard M. Baruch, for example, is worth maybe forty votes. Similarly, if you have any friends who are unpopular on Capitol Hill abandon them or, better, denounce them publicly.

"11. Glorify the days when we had no entangling alliances. This proves you are a 'sound fellow,' longing for the happy sunlit past.'

"12. Stay out of the Far East. If you go there, you will be expected to have views on it and somebody is bound to disagree with any views you have. Ignorance about it, however, is no disqualification.

"13. If possible have at least one reformed Communist testify on your behalf, preferably Louis Budenz, former editor of The Daily Worker.

"14. Never accept any invitation to any off-the-record meeting at the State Department without finding out first whether Harold Stassen is to be there."

[54] New York *Times*, Oct. 23, 1951.

[55] *Ibid.*, Mar. 25, 1953.

[56] *Ibid.*, Mar. 19, 1953. The Senate debates of Mar. 23–27 contain many references and quotations from the hearing.

[57] *Cong. Rec.*, 83d Cong., 1st sess. (daily ed., Mar. 20, 1953), pp. 2236–2238.

[58] New York *Times*, Mar. 21, 1953.

[59] *Cong. Rec.*, 83d Cong., 1st sess. (daily ed., Mar. 23, 1953), p. 2276.

[60] *Ibid.*, p. 2283. The debate as it appears in the *Congressional Record* contains the words "uncalled for" instead of "ridiculous," as reported in the New York *Times*.

[61] *Ibid.* (Mar. 25, 1953), p. 2363.

[62] *Ibid.*, p. 2382.

[63] New York *Times*, Mar. 27, 1953.

[64] *Cong. Rec.*, 83d Cong., 1st sess. (daily ed., Mar. 25, 1953), p. 2385.

[65] *Ibid.*, p. 2386.

[66] New York *Times*, Feb. 7, 1953.

[67] *Hearings before the Committee on Foreign Relations, U. S. Senate, on the Nomination of Joseph C. Grew to Be Under Secretary of State [and others for other offices]*, 78th Cong., 2d sess. (Dec. 12, 13, 1944), pp. 59–60.

[68] *Ibid.*, pp. 84–85.

[69] New York *Times*, Dec. 15, 1944.

[70] *Cong. Rec.*, 78th Cong., 2d sess. (Dec. 16, 1944), p. 9579.

[71] *Ibid.* (Dec. 19, 1944), pp. 9691–9694.

[72] *Ibid.*, p. 9716.

[73] *Ibid.*, p. 9717.

[74] New York *Times*, Dec. 21, 1944.

CHAPTER XVII

JUDGES

[1] Statement of Senator Paul Douglas before the Senate Judiciary Committee, Aug. 4, 1951 (mimeographed).

[2] George W. Pepper, *Family Quarrels: The President, the Senate, and the House*, pp. 89–91.

[3] Charles Warren, *The Supreme Court in United States History* (1928 ed.), II, 757–763, lists the nominations to the Court to 1925; I have added those since 1925. The nominees rejected by a vote of the Senate were: John Rutledge (Chief Justice), 1795; Alexander Wollcott, 1811; John C. Spencer, 1844; George W. Woodward, 1846; Jeremiah S. Black, 1861; Ebenezer R. Hoar (1869); William B. Hornblower, 1894; Wheeler H. Peckham, 1894; John J. Parker, 1930. The Senate voted to postpone action on John J. Crittenden, 1829; Roger B. Taney, 1835; Reuben H. Walworth, 1844; Edward King, 1844; George E. Badger, 1853. It failed to take any action on John M. Read, 1845; Edward A. Bradford, 1852; William C. Micou, 1853; Henry Stanbery, 1866; and Stanley Matthews, 1881. President Grant withdrew the nominations of George H. Williams and Caleb Cushing in 1874. Six persons whose nominations were confirmed declined to serve.

[4] William N. Brigance, *Jeremiah Sullivan Black*, 1934, p. 113; quoted by J. P. Frank, "The Appointment of Supreme Court Justices: Prestige, Principles and Politics," *Wis. Law Rev.* (1941), 172–210, 343–379.

[5] Charles Warren, *op. cit., passim.*

[6] See *ibid.*, II, 110–119.

[7] *Ibid.*, II, 242–245.

[8] Crittenden, Dec., 1828; Read, Feb., 1845; Badger, Jan. 1853; Micou, Feb., 1853; Black, Feb., 1861; Matthews, Jan., 1881.

[9] Quoted by Warren, *op. cit.*, II, 422.

[10] New York *Times*, Aug. 3, 1937.

[11] John P. Frank, *Mr. Justice Black*, New York, Alfred A. Knopf, 1949, p. 98.

[12] *Congressional Record*, 75th Cong., 1st sess. (Aug. 12, 1937), p. 8732.

[13] New York *Times*, Aug. 13, 1937. The last previous nomination of a senator referred to a committee was that of Justice Lamar, in 1888, who was not a member of the Senate at the time of his nomination, having resigned to accept a Cabinet post under Cleveland. Before that, however, nominations of senators or former senators had not infrequently been referred to committee.

[14] These quotations appear in the New York *Times*, Aug. 13, 18, 1937, and in J. P. Frank, *op. cit.*, pp. 99–100.

[15] Quoted by Frank, *Mr. Justice Black*, p. 100.

[16] *Cong. Rec.*, 75th Cong., 1st sess. (Aug. 16, 1937), p. 8964.

[17] Senator Copeland placed in the record a quotation from David Lawrence in the New York *Sun* of the previous day: "Senator Black is under charges widely made that he either was a member of the Ku Klux Klan or accepted its support for the election to the United States Senate in 1926. One of the obligations of the Klan at that time was discrimination against the Negro, against the Catholic, and against the Jew." *Ibid.*, p. 9069.

[18] *Ibid.*, p. 9077.

[19] New York *Times*, Aug. 18. The version in the *Congressional Record* does not include the reference to a park bench.

[20] Frank, *Mr. Justice Black*, p. 103.

[21] *Ibid.*, pp. 105–106.

[22] New York *Times*, Jan. 6, 1939.

[23] *Hearings before a Subcommittee of the Committee on the Judiciary, U. S. Senate, on the Nomination of Felix Frankfurter to Be an Associate Justice of the Supreme Court*, 76th Cong., 1st sess. (1939), *passim.*

[24] *Ibid.*, pp. 107–108.

[25] New York *Times*, Jan. 13, 1939.

[26] *Hearings . . . on the Nomination of Felix Frankfurter*, pp. 127–128.

[27] These telegrams are printed in *Hearings before the Committee on the Judiciary, U. S. Senate, on the Nomination of Tom C. Clark of Texas to Be an Associate Justice of the Supreme Court of the United States*, 81st Cong., 1st sess. (Aug. 9, 10, 11, 1949), pp. 2–29.

[28] Richmond *Times-Dispatch*, July 30, 1949; quoted in *Hearings . . . on the Nomination of Tom C. Clark*, p. 271.

[29] Quoted in *Hearings*, p. 73.

[30] These communications occupy 180 pages of fine print in the *Hearings*, pp. 180–359.

[31] *District 50 News*, Aug. 6; quoted in New York *Times*, Aug. 7.

[32] *Cong. Rec.*, 81st Cong., 1st sess. (Oct. 4, 1949), p. 13801.

[33] President Polk recorded in his *Diary* on Dec. 24, 1845, concerning an appointment to the Supreme Court: "I have never known an instance of a [former] Federalist . . . who was to be relied on in his constitutional opinions. All of them who have been appointed to the Supreme Court bench, after having secured a place for life became very soon broadly Federal and latitudinarian in all their decisions involving questions of Constitutional power. General Jackson had been most unfortunate in his appointments to the bench in this respect. I resolved to appoint no man who was not an original Democrat and a strict constructionist, and who would be less likely to relapse into the broad Federal doctrine of Judge Marshall or Judge Story." James K. Polk, *Diary*, p. 37. Pringle states that President Taft appointed men to the Supreme Court who would "preserve the fundamental structure of our government as our fathers gave it to us." Henry F. Pringle, *The Life and Times of William Howard Taft*, p. 536. And Professor Frank observed in his study of the appointment of Supreme Court justices that Taft knew how to pick conservatives. Frank, *loc. cit.* The record of the Court since 1940 indicates that Franklin D. Roosevelt was equally skillful in choosing persons who would uphold his program.

[34] Felix Frankfurter and James M. Landis, *The Business of the Supreme Court*, New York, Macmillan Co., 1927, p. 302.

[35] "The Supreme Court and the Public," 83 *Forum* 334 (June, 1930). (Emphasis in original.)

[36] *Hearings of a Subcommittee of the Committee on the Judiciary, U. S. Senate, on the Nomination of Albert L. Watson to Be United States District Judge, etc.*, 71st Cong., 1st sess. (1929), pp. 143–145.

[37] Evan Haynes, *The Selection and Tenure of Judges*, Newark, N. J., National Conference of Judicial Councils, 1944, p. 23.

[38] Editorial in 25 *Ill. Law Rev.* 929 (1930). Emphasis in original.

[39] Burke Shartel, "Federal Judges—Appointment, Supervision and Removal—Some Possibilities under the Constitution," 15 *J. Amer. Jud. Soc.* 22 (1931). For a similar statement, see Kenneth C. Sears, "The Appointment of Federal District Judges," 25 *Ill. Law Rev.* 54–55 (1930). See also Charles W. Smith, Jr., "President Roosevelt's Attitude toward the Courts," 31 *Ky. Law Jour.* 301–315 (1943).

[40] A qualified defense of senatorial influence on judicial appointments is made by Professor Kenneth C. Cole, "The Role of the Senate in the Confirmation of Judicial Nominations," *Political Science Review*, XXVIII (1934), 875–894; but his conclusions relate primarily to the appointment of Supreme Court justices rather than of judges of inferior courts.

[41] See George Wharton Pepper, *loc. cit.;* Robert Luce, *Legislative Problems*, pp. 128–129.

[42] Jacobus ten Broek, "Partisan Politics and Federal Judgeships Impeachment Proceedings since 1900," 23 *Minn. Law Rev.* 185, 204 (1939). See also Alexander Simpson, *A Treatise on Federal Impeachment*, Philadelphia, 1916.

[43] Evans A. Evans, "Political Influences in the Selection of Federal Judges," *Wis. Law Rev.* (1948), 330–351, 334–335. Attorney General Tom C. Clark stated in 1947 that of the 231 federal judges appointed from 1933 to 1947, 17 were Republicans, 9 of whom were appointed to U.S. courts, 6 to territorial courts, and 2 to lower courts in the District of Columbia. 23 *Amer. Bar Jour.* 110–112 (1947).

[44] Statement issued by the Justice Department, New York *Times*, Sept. 23, 1950.

[45] *Ibid.*, Apr. 29, 1929.

[46] Printed in *Cong. Rec.,* 71st Cong., 1st sess. (Dec. 17, 1929), p. 787.

[47] New York *Times*, Oct. 20, 1929.

[48] *Hearings . . . on the Nomination of Albert L. Watson*, p. 122.

[49] Washington *Post*, June 9, 1929.

[50] *Cong. Rec.,* 71st Cong., 2d sess. (Dec. 16, 1929), p. 728.

[51] *Ibid.*

[52] *Ibid.*, p. 786.

[53] On one occasion, when the Attorney General objected to a candidate because his legal education was poor, Roosevelt is reported to have observed: "You may think a lawyer ought to be a graduate of Harvard Law School to be appointed to the federal bench, but I do not."

[54] In the hearing of the Judiciary Committee on one of the nominations on Aug. 10, Senator Langer inquired of Senator Douglas whether he had conferred with Arvey about the selection; to which Douglas replied "certainly." Washington *Star*, Aug. 10, 1951.

[55] See Elmer Gertz, "Truman vs. Douglas," *Nation*, Aug. 4, 1951, p. 97.

[55] Chicago *Sun-Times*, Aug. 4, 1951; Chicago *Tribune*, Aug. 4, 1951.

[57] New York *Times*, July 18.

[58] *Cong. Rec.*, 82d Cong., 1st sess. (Oct. 9, 1951), p. 12840.

[59] *Ibid.*, p. 12839.

[60] American Bar Association, *The Improvement of the Administration of Justice*, Washington, 1949, p. 79.

[61] For an account of the operation of the Missouri plan, see Laurance M. Hyde, "Judges: Their Selection and Tenure," 30 *J. Amer. Jud. Soc.* 152 (1946); "Forty Lawyers Appraise Operation of California and Missouri Methods of Selecting Judges," *ibid.*, Vol. 31 (1948), p. 176.

[62] "The grave defect in the present system is that it leaves both the President and members of the Senate free to play politics with judicial appointments. . . . It is a reproach to our national intelligence that we permit politics to play so strong a part in the selection of the judges who determine our rights and safeguard our freedom. The answer certainly is not to turn over to members of the

Senate the full responsibility of choosing federal judges in their home states. Some senators base their recommendations on merit, as Senator Douglas did, but others make more flagrant use of judgeships for political purposes than does the President. The best arrangement might be to have each judicial appointment made from a panel of outstanding lawyers selected by a committee on which the Attorney General, the judicial council of the circuit concerned, and the practicing bar would be represented. Such a restraint upon the President and the members of the Senate would ... cost them something in terms of political power. At the same time it would immeasurably increase the prestige of any President and add to the confidence of the people in the judicial system." Washington *Post*, quoted in 35 *J. Amer. Jud. Soc.* 99 (1951).

CHAPTER XVIII

ADMINISTRATIVE AND MILITARY OFFICERS

[1] Commission on Organization of the Executive Branch of the Government, *General Management of the Executive Branch*, Washington, 1949, p. 34.

[2] New York *Times*, Jan. 15, 1952.

[3] Commission on Organization, *op. cit.*, p. 38.

[4] Committee on Administrative Management, *Administrative Management in the Government of the United States*, Washington, 1937, pp. 8–9.

[5] *Hearings before the Joint Committee on Government Organization*, 75th Cong., 1st sess. (1937), pp. 103–109.

[6] S. 2700, sec. 203, 75th Cong., 1st sess. (1937).

[7] *Hearings before the Select Committee on Government Organization, U. S. Senate, on S. 2700*, 75th Cong., 1st sess. (1937), p. 444.

[8] *Ibid.*, p. 364.

[9] The O'Mahoney amendment to the McKellar bill of 1943, which the Senate adopted, so provided, but it extended senatorial confirmation far below the level of bureau chiefs in the administrative hierarchy.

[10] This account is based on interviews and on the New York *Times*, May 10, 11, 12, 1934.

[11] In 1947 there was objection to the promotion of Lt. Col. James A. Killion to a full colonelcy in the regular army, because of his previous conviction of permitting cruel and unusual punishment in the disciplinary barracks at Litchfield, England. The explanation offered by the White House was that his name had been included on the list of promotions only because the statutes required that promotions be based strictly on seniority. After objection was voiced by members of the Senate, Killion's name was stricken off. Killion unsuccessfully brought suit to force the inclusion of his name on the promotion list. New York *Times*, Apr. 1, July 4, 23, 31, 1947.

[12] Computed from *Civilian Nominations*, United States Senate, 1951.

[13] For a list of such officers formerly subject to confirmation, see *Congressional Record*, 49th Cong., 1st sess. (Apr. 13, 1886), p. 3428.

[14] Commission on Organization of the Executive Branch of the Government, *Report on the Treasury Department*, p. 17.

[15] 80th Cong., 2d sess., H. Rept. 1532 (1948), p. 10.

[16] *Preliminary Hearings before the Subcommittee of the Committee on Appropriations, House of Representatives, on the Treasury Department Appropriation Bill for 1949*, 80th Cong., 1st sess. Pt. 2 (1947), p. 51.

[17] *Cong. Rec.*, 82d Cong., 1st sess. (Feb. 5, 1951), p. 950.

[18] Special Committee of the United States Senate to Investigate Organized Crime in Interstate Commerce, *Second Interim Report*, Feb. 28, 1951, p. 26; *Final Report*, Aug. 31, 1951, pp. 9–10. The committee commended the establishment of a racket squad in the Justice Department and a special fraud squad in the Bureau of Internal Revenue.

[19] New York *Times*, Dec. 23, 1951.

[20] Executive Order No. 8743 (Apr. 23, 1941).

[21] New York *Times*, Jan. 15, 1952.

[22] *Ibid.*, Mar. 6, 1952.

[23] *Cong. Rec.*, 82d Cong., 2d sess. (daily ed., Mar. 13, 1952), p. 2278.

[24] *Ibid.*, p. 2203.

[25] *Ibid.*, p. 2205.

[26] *Ibid.*, pp. 2174–2177, 2303.

[27] *Ibid.*, pp. 2191–2198.

[28] New York *Times*, Mar. 14, 1952. This quotation does not appear in the *Congressional Record.*

[29] Commission on Law Observance, *Report on Prosecution*, Washington, Government Printing Office, 1931, p. 9.

[30] New York *Times*, June 9, 1931.

[31] San Francisco *Chronicle*, Apr. 13, 1951.

[32] *Reorganization Plan No. 4 of 1952, Providing for Reorganizations in the Department of Justice*, 82d Cong., 2d sess., S. Rept. 1749, pp. 2–5.

[33] *Cong. Rec.*, 82d Cong., 2d sess. (daily ed., June 18, 1952), pp. 7622–7629.

[34] Postmaster General, *Annual Report*, 1950–1951, p. 26. The classification of post offices is based on their annual gross receipts: Class 1, $40,000 and over; class 2, $8,000–$40,000; class 3, $1,500–$8,000; class 4, under $1,500. *Postal Laws and Regulations*, 1948, title xiv, sec. 137.30.

[35] Dorothy C. Fowler, "Congressional Dictation of Local Appointments," *Journal of Politics*, VII, 27. I have drawn heavily from this scholarly study in the section that follows.

[36] Fowler, *ibid.*, p. 32.

[37] James Monroe, *Writings*, VI, 336; quoted by Fowler, *ibid.*, p. 33.

[38] Fowler, *ibid.*, p. 36.

[39] Welles Papers (Library of Congress), June 2, July 25, 1840; quoted by Fowler, *ibid.*, p. 36.

[40] Gresham Papers (Library of Congress), Feb. 13, 1844, to F. N. Stevens; quoted by Fowler, *ibid.*, p. 46.

[41] "That no recommendation of any person who shall apply for office or place under the provisions of this act which may be given by any Senator or Member of the House of Representatives, except as to the character or residence of the applicant, shall be received or considered by any person concerned in making any examination or appointment." 22 *U.S. Stat.* 403 (1883), sec. 10.

[42] *Nation*, Apr. 17, 1890.

[43] *Ibid.*, Apr. 6, 1893; quoted by Fowler, *op. cit.*, p. 48.

[44] Fowler, *op. cit.*, p. 52.

[45] Executive Order No. 2569A (Mar. 31, 1917).

[46] New York *Times*, Mar. 7, 8, 9, 1917.

[47] These statistics are cited in *Good Government*, LIV (Nov., 1937), p. 70.

[48] *Ibid.*, p. 71.

[49] New York *Times*, May 15, 1922.

[50] *Ibid.*, Apr. 17, 1933.

[51] *Ibid.*, July 13, 1933.

[52] Farley announced his support of the O'Mahoney bill soon after it was introduced (New York *Times*, Feb. 7, 1935); the next year, President Roosevelt again strongly endorsed legislation placing the first three classes of postmasters under civil service (New York *Times*, Feb. 22, 23, 1936), but no action was taken in Congress until the following year.

[53] Executive Order No. 7421 (July 20, 1936).

[54] *Cong. Rec.*, 75th Cong., 1st sess. (Jan. 28, 1937), p. 517.

[55] *Ibid.*, pp. 519, 525, 527.

[56] *Ibid.*, pp. 528, 529.

[57] *Ibid.* (Aug. 3, 1937), p. 8114.

[58] 75th Cong., 2d sess., S. Rept. 1296 (Nov. 16, 1937), p. 3.

[59] *Ibid.*, p. 8.

[60] *Ibid.*, p. 10.

[61] *Ibid.*, pp. 10–11.

[62] *Ibid.*, p. 14.

[63] *Cong. Rec.*, 75th Cong., 3d sess. (Apr. 11, 1938), p. 5193.

[64] *Ibid.*, p. 5211.

[65] *Ibid.*, pp. 5192, 5196, 5207, 5216.

[66] *Ibid.*, p. 5203.

[67] *Ibid.*, p. 5197.
[68] *Good Government*, LV (May, 1938), 27.
[69] New York *Times*, Apr. 13, 1938.
[70] The detailed regulations and procedure are described in a publication of the U. S. Civil Service Commission, *Information Regarding Postmaster Positions Filled through Nomination by the President for Confirmation by the Senate*, 1951.
[71] *Cong. Rec.*, 82d Cong., 1st sess. (daily ed., Nov. 14, 1951), and letter to the author from Commissioner James M. Mitchell.
[72] *Postmaster Appointments under Civil Service*, 80th Cong., 2d sess., S. Rept. 1777 (1948).
[73] Commission on the Organization of the Executive Branch of the Government, *Report on the Post Office*, pp. 9–10.
[74] Commission on the Organization of the Executive Branch of the Government, *Task Force Report on the Post Office*, p. 44.
[75] 82d Cong., 2d sess. (1952), H.R. Doc. 424, p. 3.
[76] 82d Cong., 2d sess., S. Rept. 1747 (1952), p. 13.
[77] *Cong. Rec.*, 82d Cong., 2d sess. (daily ed., June 18, 1952), pp. 7599–7600.
[78] *Ibid.*, p. 7620. The debate is reported on pp. 7594–7621.

CHAPTER XIX

RECENT PROPOSALS TO EXTEND SENATORIAL CONFIRMATION

[1] *Congressional Record*, 78th Cong., 1st sess. (June 3, 1943), p. 5364.
[2] *Ibid.* (June 13, 1943), p. 5822.
[3] In the following account of these several legislative proposals to extend senatorial confirmation, I have drawn heavily on the notable article of Arthur W. Macmahon, "Senatorial Confirmation," *Public Administration Review*, III (1943), 281–296.
[4] The following account of the practical operation of the requirement of senatorial confirmation of state directors of the federal relief works program has been taken for the most part from Arthur W. Macmahon, John D. Millett, and Gladys Ogden, *The Administration of Federal Work Relief*, chap. 12.
[5] *Ibid.*, p. 274.
[6] 76th Cong., 1st sess. (1939), S. Rept. 1, Pt. I, p. 39.
[7] Macmahon *et al., op. cit.*, p. 269.
[8] *Hearings before the Commerce Committee, United States Senate, on the Nomination of Harry L. Hopkins to Be Secretary of Commerce*, 76th Cong., 1st sess. (1939), pp. 8–10.
[9] *Cong. Rec.*, 74th Cong., 1st sess. (June 11, 1935), p. 9038.
[10] New York *Times*, June 12, 13, 14, 1935.
[11] An account of these amendments, including the above quotation, is given in *Good Government*, LII (Jan.–Mar., 1935), 1–8.
[12] *Cong. Rec.*, 75th Cong., 1st sess. (June 18, 1937), pp. 5987–5988.
[13] *Ibid.*, p. 5988.
[14] *Ibid.*, p. 5987.
[15] *Ibid.*, p. 5996.
[16] *Ibid.*, p. 5988.
[17] *Ibid.*, p. 5996.
[18] *Ibid.*, p. 5994.
[19] *Ibid.*, p. 5994.
[20] *Ibid.*, p. 5995.
[21] *Ibid.*, p. 5992.
[22] *Good Government*, LIV (July–Aug., 1937), 50.
[23] *Cong. Rec.*, 75th Cong., 1st sess. (June 29, 1937), p. 6492.
[24] *Ibid.*, p. 7814.
[25] *Ibid.* (July 30. 1937), p. 7902.
[26] *Ibid.* (Aug. 4, 1937), p. 8203.

[27] Macmahon, *op. cit.*, p. 285.

[28] *Cong. Rec.*, 75th Cong., 1st sess. (Aug. 21, 1937), pp. 9584–9585.

[29] *Ibid.*, 75th Cong., 3d sess. (Feb. 25, 1938), p. 2426.

[30] *Ibid.*, pp. 2426–2427.

[31] *Ibid.*, p. 2427.

[32] *Ibid.*, p. 2430.

[33] *Ibid.*, p. 2431.

[34] *Ibid.*, p. 3862.

[35] *Ibid.*

[36] 53 *U.S. Stat.* (1939), 907.

[37] Macmahon, *op. cit.*, p. 286.

[38] 54 *U.S. Stat.* (1940), 897.

[39] For an account of the controversy over these proposed riders, including the above quotations, see *Good Government*, LIX (July–Aug., 1942), 25–27.

[40] 78th Cong., 1st sess., H. Doc. 60 (Feb. 1, 1943).

[41] *Cong. Rec.*, 78th Cong., 1st sess. (Feb. 22, 1943), p. 1175.

[42] Senate Committee on Military Affairs, 78th Cong., 1st sess., *Hearings on Civilian Nominations in the War Manpower Commission*, p. 43.

[43] S. 575.

[44] *Hearings before a Subcommittee of the Committee on the Judiciary, U. S. Senate, on S. 575*, 78th Cong., 1st sess. (Feb. 11, 1943), p. 1.

[45] *Ibid.*, pp. 2–4. Senator McKellar urged that the bill apply to all employees receiving $3,800 or more annually.

[46] *Ibid.*, pp. 3–23.

[47] *Ibid.*, pp. 40–44. In a letter to Senator Van Nuys, chairman of the Judiciary Committee, Mitchell said that it "puts all the well trained and most competent personnel of the Federal Government on notice that their tenure of office or employment is to be uncertain after June 30, 1943." *Ibid.*, p. 72.

[48] *Ibid.*, p. 45.

[49] New York *Times*, Feb. 21, 1943.

[50] *Ibid.*

[51] New York *Times*, Mar. 4, 1943.

[52] *Senate Confirmation of Officers and Employees of the United States*, 78th Cong., 1st sess., S. Rept. 180 (1943), pt. 1, pp. 4–7. (Emphasis supplied.) It is of interest that the title of the report includes the word *employees*, though the power of the Senate to confirm applies only to officers.

[53] New York *Times*, Feb. 26, 1943. Similar editorials appeared in the *Times* on April 6, 7, June 8, 16, and 20.

[54] S. Rept. 180, pt. 2, p. 2.

[55] *Ibid.*, pt. 3, p. 2.

[56] *Ibid.*, p. 9.

[57] New York *Times*, Feb. 20.

[58] *Cong. Rec.*, 78th Cong., 1st sess. (June 3, 1943), pp. 5279, 5281.

[59] *Ibid.*, p. 5280.

[60] *Ibid.*, p. 5363.

[61] At the President's press conference on Feb. 16, Irving Brant of the Chicago *Sun* stated that he had estimated that if only one in a hundred of these nominations required by the bill were contested, and the Senate allowed only ten minutes debate to each, it would require an average of forty-five minutes for each day it was in session. The New York senators, at the rate of ten minutes per appointment, would have to devote four and a half hours a day to the task. When asked to comment on these estimates, the President replied, "Thou hast said it." New York *Times*, Feb. 17, 1943.

[62] *Cong. Rec.*, 78th Cong., 1st sess. (June 14, 1943), p. 5805.

[63] New York *Times*, June 15.

[64] *Ibid.*, June 16.

[65] *Ibid.*, Mar. 29, 1944.

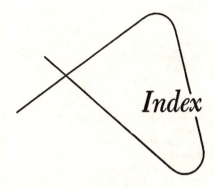

Index

Cooper, John S., on Clapp, 175
Cooperative League of America, 210
Council, executive (on appointments): Hamilton on, 6, 28; debated in Constitutional Convention, 24–25; Adams on, 29
Courtesy of the Senate. *See* Senatorial courtesy
Coy, Wayne, 434 n. 18
Crittenden, John J., on Spencer, 415 n. 10
Crum, W. D., 226
Cummins, Albert B., on Warren, 121
Curtis, George William, 77
Cushing, Caleb: nomination for Secretary of Treasury rejected, 67; nomination as Chief Justice withdrawn, 76, 385; opinion on recess appointments cited, 434 n. 62
Cushman, Robert, on appointments to independent regulatory commissions, 268–269, 279

Dana, Charles A., on Lincoln's use of patronage, 416 n. 26
Davie, William R., 26
Davies, Joseph E., 97
Departments, procedure in submitting recommendations of nominees to the President, 239
Dickinson, John (1732–1808), in Constitutional Convention, 23–24
Dickinson, John (Assistant Secretary of Commerce, 1933–1935), 330
Dill, Clarence: on senatorial courtesy, 228; favors open sessions on nominations, 252–253
Dilling, Elizabeth, 247
Diplomatic officers, confirmation of, by Senate: role of the Senate, 39–40, 381; Henry Cabot Lodge on, 280; Henry Adams on, 282; under Washington, 282–283; use of special agents, 284–286; representatives to international organizations, 287–288; Secretaries of State, 299–300; Assistant and Under Secretaries of State, 300–301; contested appointments: Francis Biddle, 288, Willard Thorp, 289, Edward J. Flynn, 289–291, Chester Bowles, 291–292, Philip Jessup, 292–294, Charles Bohlen, 294–299, James B. Conant, 299
District attorneys, appointment of, 339–340
Dixon, Joseph M., 131
Donnell, Forrest C.: on Vardaman, 199; on appointments to UN, 288
Douglas, Paul: controversy with Truman over appointments of two Illinois judges, 215–216, 221–222, 321–323; on appointment of judges, 229, 302; on Olds, 426 n. 5

Drucker, Joseph J., 216, 321–323
Duane, William J., 59, 61
Dulles, John Foster, testifies for Bohlen, 295–296
Duskin, George M., 88–89

Eaton, Dorman B.: on senatorial confirmation, 9; on secret sessions of the Senate in considering nominations, 251
Edwards, Ninian, and Monroe, 51
Eisenhower, Dwight, urges approval of Bohlen, 298
Eliot, Charles W., on Brandeis, 99, 112
Ellsworth, Oliver: in Constitutional Convention, 22, 25, 26; on balloting on nominations, 38
Esch, John J., rejected for ICC, 276
Evans, Evans A., cited, 317
Executive council. *See* Council

Farley, James A., and postmaster appointments, 345
Federalist, The, quoted, 6, 18, 27, 234, 376
Federal Bureau of Investigation: investigations of prospective nominees, 239–240; files confidential, 242–244, 297, 298; investigation of judicial nominees, 244, 432 n. 11
Ferguson, Homer: on Lilienthal, 165; opposes appointments of Perlman, 203–204, and of Clark, 312
Fess, Simeon D., on secret session on nominations, 255
Field officers. *See* Officers, administrative
Filene, E. A., 109
Fillmore, Millard: and the Senate, 70–71; nominations to Supreme Court, 304
Finer, Herman, on senatorial confirmation, 8–9
Finnegan, James P., 335
Fish, Carl Russell: on appointments under Washington, 42; on appointments of John Quincy Adams, 52; on Lincoln's appointments, 72; on control by Congress over appointments, 73, 79
Fishbourn, Benjamin, rejected as naval officer, 27, 40–41, 216–217
Flannagan, John W., Jr., 231
Fly, James L., 277
Flynn, Edward J., nomination as minister to Australia contested, 289–291
Ford, Henry J., on senatorial confirmation, 9
Forrestal, James, 201–202
Foulke, William Dudley, on senatorial confirmation, 9
Four Years Act (1820), 51